Neural Bases of Speech, Hearing, and Language

Neural Bases of Speech, Hearing, and Language

Edited by

❏ **David P. Kuehn, Ph.D.**

Associate Professor, Department of Speech and Hearing Science,
University of Illinois at Urbana-Champaign,
Urbana, Illinois

❏ **Margaret L. Lemme, Ph.D.**

Associate Professor of Communication Science,
Department of Speech Communication,
University of Denver,
Denver, Colorado

❏ **John M. Baumgartner, Ph.D.**

Assistant Professor,
Department of Communicative Disorders and Sciences,
Rush University; Speech-Language Pathologist,
Rush-Presbyterian-St. Luke's Medical Center,
Chicago, Illinois

Foreword by
Ronald W. Netsell, Ph.D.

Professor, Department of Otolaryngology and Human Communication,
Creighton University School of Medicine;
Director, Center for Speech and Language Disorders,
Boys Town National Institute for Communication Disorders in Children,
Omaha, Nebraska

A College-Hill Publication
Little, Brown and Company
Boston/Toronto/London

College-Hill Press
A Division of
Little, Brown and Company (Inc.)
34 Beacon Street
Boston, Massachusetts 02108

Library of Congress Cataloging in Publication Data
Main entry under title:

Neural bases of speech, hearing, and language / [edited by] David P.
  Kuehn, Margaret L. Lemme, John M. Baumgartner.
     p.   cm.
  "A College-Hill publication."
  Bibliography: p.
  Includes index.
  ISBN 0-316-50491-2
  1. Neurolinguistics. 2. Speech. 3. Hearing. 4. Neurophysiology.
5. Neuroanatomy. I. Kuehn, David P. II. Lemme, Margaret L.
III. Baumgartner, John M.
QP399.N45   1989
153.6—dc19   89-2825
                                   CIP

ISBN 0-316-50491-2
Printed in the United States of America
MV-NY

CONTENTS

FOREWORD

Neural Bases of Speech, Hearing, and Language brings together contemporary information on the neuroanatomy and neurophysiology of human communication. This text is timely and will prove valuable to a wide range of readers.

Several advances in the past twenty-five years make *Neural Bases of Speech, Hearing, and Language* an important text. Our knowledge of normal neural mechanisms and neuropathologies in human communication is increasing at a rapid rate. As a result, and in contrast to even ten years ago, many more individuals with neural disorders of speech production or language are receiving treatment and improving their communication skills. Clinicians who are not familiar with the contents of *Neural Bases of Speech, Hearing, and Language* may better serve these individuals with handicaps after reading this book.

Brain imaging techniques now provide data on the sites of neuropathology (using computerized tomography or magnetic resonance imaging) and the focused or distributed nature of their influences on the "working brain" (as estimated by positron emission tomography). Studies that combine these imaging techniques are only beginning. However, even the early results have provided important confirmations or challenges to various axioms on the neurology of speech and language.

Now, more than ever, the study of human communication and its disorders is truly an interdisciplinary effort. *Neural Bases of Speech, Hearing, and Language* should provide students of other brain and behavioral sciences a clear understanding of what is known and not known about the neural mechanisms of speech, hearing, and language.

Ronald W. Netsell, Ph.D.

PREFACE

Most students of communication sciences and disorders are required to follow courses in the biology and, more specifically, the neural bases of speech, hearing, and language. Students often find the human nervous system to be a marvel of complexity and the underpinnings of neuropathologies to be very difficult to comprehend. Students who have little educational background in biology most likely will experience difficulty in understanding new terminology and may be confused by basic aspects of neuroanatomy and neurophysiology. To complicate matters, there are few comprehensive up-to-date textbooks available that deal exclusively with the neural bases of speech, hearing, and language. Professors usually use a series of neurology textbooks or journal articles and adapt them to the needs of students in communication sciences and disorders. Thus, *Neural Bases of Speech, Hearing, and Language* is designed to meet the needs of students who seek detailed information about the neuroanatomy and neurophysiology of speech, hearing, and language. We hope that upper-level undergraduates and graduate students will find that this volume offers understandable coverage of neurologic correlates of communication behaviors and that it will serve as a stimulus to further understanding and reading in this broad area of study.

Because we believe that an edited book provides a greater variety of views and is more representative of current expertise, we have invited established authors to prepare accessible and yet critical accounts of the state-of-the-art in their disciplines. The contributors share a fascination with the nature of human communication and the means whereby we use it, and each has made fundamental contributions in his or her specialty. We owe them a profound debt of gratitude for providing a far more authoritative and up-to-date account than we could have achieved on our own. We hope that the reader will agree that they have expressed very complicated information in accessible language without sacrificing attention to detail.

The organization of the book is an outgrowth of our experience in trying to lead students systematically through the broad and complex topics within the neural bases of speech, hearing, and language. We begin with an introductory chapter on studying the nervous system from a speech science perspective. In the second chapter, John Baumgartner and William Bentley provide an overview of basic neuroanatomy. Charles Larson's chapter follows with an examination of basic neurophysiology. Basic foundation concepts are completed with a consideration of developmental neuroanatomy and neurophysiology presented by Paul Bunger. The neuroanatomy of speech, human's unique behavior, is dealt with by Jesse Kennedy and David Kuehn, and the neurophysiology of speech is addressed by Steven Barlow and Glenn Farley. Robert Harrison and Ivan Hunter-Duvar review the subtleties of the neuroanatomy of hearing, and Ben Clopton reviews the complexities of the neurophysiology of hearing. In the language area, Catherine Mateer begins the coverage with a comprehensive review of neural correlates of language function. David Caplan and Howard Chertkow complete the volume with information from neurolinguistics, the study of brain mechanisms subserving language.

We have already expressed our thanks to our authors. Our very special thanks also go to Lynne Herndon, Editor in Chief and Publisher, Medical Division, Little, Brown and Company, who has worked with and supported us from the early ideas about this book through the final editing of this volume. We also wish to thank our many students who have enriched our professional experiences and who are responsible for the initial impetus for this book. Our hope for this book is that it will ultimately have positive impact on the lives of persons with neurogenic communication disorders.

D. P. K.
M. L. L.
J. M. B.

CONTRIBUTING AUTHORS

Steven M. Barlow, Ph.D.
Scientist and Coordinator, Speech-Orofacial Physiology Laboratory, Boys Town National Institute for Communication Disorders in Children, Omaha, Nebraska

John M. Baumgartner, Ph.D.
Assistant Professor, Department of Communicative Disorders and Sciences, Rush University; Speech-Language Pathologist, Rush-Presbyterian-St. Luke's Medical Center, Chicago, Illinois

William H. Bentley, M.D.
Chief of Neurology, Aurora Presbyterian Hospital, Aurora, Colorado

Paul C. Bunger, Ph.D.
Associate Professor, Department of Anatomy, University of South Dakota, School of Medicine, Vermillion

David Caplan, M.D., Ph.D.
Associate Professor of Neurology, Harvard Medical School; Director, Higher Cortical Function Unit, Massachusetts General Hospital, Boston

Howard Chertkow, M.D., F.R.C.P.
Assistant Professor, Department of Neurology and Neurosurgery, McGill University, Montreal, Canada

Ben M. Clopton, Ph.D.
Associate Professor, Department of Otolaryngology, University of Michigan, Ann Arbor

Glenn R. Farley, Ph.D.
Laboratory Coordinator, Motor Physiology Center for Speech and Language Disorders, Boys Town National Institute for Communication Disorders in Children, Omaha, Nebraska

Robert V. Harrison, Ph.D.
Director of Otological Research, Department of Otolaryngology, The Hospital for Sick Children, Toronto, Canada

Ivan M. Hunter-Duvar, Ph.D.
Formerly Professor, Department of Otolaryngology, The Hospital for Sick Children, Toronto, Canada

Jesse G. Kennedy III, Ph.D.
Associate Professor, Department of Communication Sciences and Disorders, University of Montana, Missoula

David P. Kuehn, Ph.D.
Associate Professor, Department of Speech and Hearing Science, University of Illinois at Urbana-Champaign, Urbana, Illinois

Charles R. Larson, Ph.D.
Associate Professor of Speech and Language Pathology, Northwestern University, Evanston, Illinois

Margaret L. Lemme, Ph.D.
Associate Professor of Communication Science, Department of Speech Communication, University of Denver, Denver, Colorado

Catherine A. Mateer, Ph.D.
Associate Professor, Department of Speech and Hearing Sciences, University of Washington, Seattle

Neural Bases of Speech, Hearing, and Language

CHAPTER 1

Studying the Nervous System:
Communication Science Perspective

Margaret L. Lemme • David P. Kuehn • John M. Baumgartner

❏ Normal Communication and
the Nervous System

❏ General Survey of
Communication Disorders
and Neuropathologies

❏ Need for Studying the
Nervous System

❏ Methods of Investigating the
Nervous System

NORMAL COMMUNICATION AND THE NERVOUS SYSTEM

Human communication is a multidimensional and exceptionally complex phenomenon. To develop communication normally and to continue to use it normally thereafter, a number of processes must occur. For comprehension, one must be able to receive stimuli through a number of sensory modalities. The stimuli, or signals, that make up the message to be understood must be identified against a background of other stimuli. It requires that the person be at least minimally alert and attentive to the signal being sent. The signal must then be processed and meaning derived through identification of specific meaningful patterns of the signal and reference to one's previous knowledge and experience. Such processing implies the ability to access previously stored information and to draw associations between this information, or pieces of it, and the signal or message just received. For production, one must formulate the content to be sent and code it based on principles of the language system involved (e.g., phonologic, semantic, grammatical, pragmatic). One must then produce the message using one or more output modalities (e.g., verbal, gestural). Regardless of the modality chosen, the final event consists of the contraction of many muscles, which in turn move structures. To be normal these movements must be carried out within definite temporal and sequential restraints. Optimum accuracy and efficiency are related to speed, range, and precision of the sequences of movements. This bare-bones sketch of communication seems to apply regardless of the model one might use to further divide and subdivide each of these processes.

This text does not discuss the neural bases of all aspects of human communication. Such an undertaking would require coverage of multiple sensory systems, multiple symbol systems, and the generation and execution of movement utilizing any of multiple output systems. Instead, it discusses the neural bases of speech, hearing, and language. Speech is the most studied output and hearing the most studied input modalities of human communication. Language is viewed as the central mediating process that allows one to make sense of the linguistically meaningful information that is heard and to formulate the content of the message one wishes to send.

Speech is the acoustic result of respiratory, phonatory, and articulatory processes; normal speech, however, is more than the result of structural and muscular integrity. It involves also the programming of muscle movements, and this programming occurs in the central nervous system (CNS). It involves conduction and refinement of impulses from the cortex to peripheral nerve nuclei, and so it involves connections among tracts in the CNS and nerves in the peripheral nervous system (PNS). It involves conduction of impulses along peripheral nerves and the transmission across synaptic junctions at the end of those nerves. Then muscles become involved, which also function according to certain neural principles. Finally, there are speech structures, some of which undergo considerable movement during speech, for example, the velum and others that do not move nearly as much.

The basic neuromotor program for speech therefore involves conduction and refinement along specific neural tracts, transmission across synapses, conduction along peripheral nerves, myoneuronal transmission, degrees of muscle contraction—all relative to resting tone—and structural movement. It is these areas to which the neuroanatomic and neurophysiologic bases of speech pertain. One can approach these topics by starting with CNS programming and then proceed peripherally. Such an approach might then address specific corticobulbar tracts, cranial or spinal nerves, and the muscles they innervate. Just as valid is an approach that starts with a speech process (e.g., respiration, phonation, articulation) and identifies the muscles involved, working centrally toward brainstem structures and upward. There are some aspects of the neural control of speech that are well understood and others that are not. Chapters 2, 3, 4, 5, and 6 discuss speech in various ways.

Hearing refers to the behavior of the auditory system. When one thinks about hearing and communication, concepts at first appear deceptively simple. It is often said that people learn language and speech primarily by hearing it. It seems certain that acquisition of speech and speaking in a particular language are normally integrally linked to hearing that language, but it is in no way an explanation of *how* one hears and how the CNS handles the input it receives from the peripheral auditory mechanism. How is it that the vibrations of the bones in the middle ear lead to the conduction of neural impulses along the vestibulocochlear (VIII) cranial nerve? How are various parameters of the signal handled by the auditory system? How are signals relayed up through the brainstem, and are they just relayed or is there significant processing of those signals as they are relayed? How long does it take for signals to be relayed and processed on the way up? How can it be measured? Can these measures be used as an indication of neuropathology? What subcortical structures are involved, and to what extent do they seem to be involved in processing or acquisition of meaning? How are signals dealt with at the cortex, and what kinds of connection are there between primary auditory areas of the cortex and association areas such that what we hear evokes the range of cognitive and emotional responses that it does? Throughout it all, what is the effect of the ear through which the signal was received and the side(s) of the brain responding to that signal? The answers to these and many other more specific questions form the substance on which the neural bases of hearing are made. Chapters 2, 3, 4, 7, and 8 deal in various ways with questions about the neural bases of hearing and the auditory system.

Issues pertaining to the neural bases of language are addressed in this text in terms of how the brain responds to language input and how it works to formulate language output. Language is an area we know less about than either speech or hearing. At a simplistic level one is tempted to think of individual parts of the brain or, more generally, one side of the brain carrying out tasks such as recognition, perception, comprehension, association, intersensory integration, formulation, and programming. Certainly these processes do occur, and just as certainly they can be impaired or language in some way can be impaired when the brain is injured. However, it does not come close to explaining how the intact brain functions with respect to the complex events that make up language. Study of the neural bases of language is a mul-

tidisciplinary activity and requires at least a working knowledge of neuroanatomy, neurophysiology, linguistics, and methods of study in neurology.

Recognizing what is known, what is not known, and where one might look next requires a sensitivity to the important balance between the interests of laboratory researchers and clinicians as well as the balance between advancing science and respecting the needs of patients with brain damage. All of these factors make the assimilation of what is known in this area difficult. It is nonetheless an exciting and rewarding enterprise, for humans use more complex language systems than any other species. The capacity to do so and the manner in which language is used are characteristics that make each of us unique individuals. It is for these same reasons that impairment in an individual's language function can be devastating to all those involved. Chapters 2, 3, 4, 9, and 10 address, in various ways, issues related to the neural underpinnings of language.

To summarize, communicative functioning deals with complex interactions between incoming information (sensory input), comprehension and formulation of messages ("central" processes of language), and the sending of messages (motor output). The sensory input relevant to language is multimodal and the output can and does include a variety of forms. In this text we have chosen to focus on spoken language and hence the neural bases of the input modality of hearing, the comprehension of speech and formulation of what is to be said, and the output modality of speech. Comprehending, formulating, and sending spoken messages occurs against a background of ongoing neurologic activity having to do with level of alertness, awareness of but not overstimulation by endogenous and exogenous stimulation (selective attention), and motivation. The next section provides an overview of communication disorders that can occur when the neural bases of speech, hearing, or language are impaired.

GENERAL SURVEY OF COMMUNICATION DISORDERS AND NEUROPATHOLOGIES

For human communication to occur normally an entire sequence of sensorineuromuscular events must occur properly. A developmental malformation, a disease, an injury, or a degeneration that disrupts this sequence may produce a communication disorder. The site and extent of the abnormality determines the nature, severity, and permanence of the disorder that results.

This section is a general survey of communication disorders, emphasizing neurogenic impairments, rather than a comprehensive source of the disorders of speech, hearing, and language. It preserves the framework established in the former section and thus presents disorders of the (1) auditory receptor, (2) central processor or language system, and (3) speech effector segment.

DISORDERS OF AUDITORY RECEPTION

The receptor system, when one considers spoken language, consists of the ear and its associated central auditory tracts to the cerebral cortex. The major communication processes that are conducted within this system are signal transmission and prelinguistic neural coding. Dysfunctions that occur may produce loss in auditory sensitivity and reduced speech discrimination.

Hearing loss is one of the most common health-handicapping conditions among children and adults. A major problem for these individuals is not the hearing loss per se but the fact that the hearing sense is the foundation on which the unique human communication system is built. Normal hearing is prerequisite to normal speech and language acquisition and to subsequent monitoring. The effects of hearing loss on communication abilities depend on various factors: (1) age of onset and identification; (2) type, degree, configuration, and stabil-

ity of hearing loss; and (3) age and amount and type of habilitation/rehabilitation (Northern and Lemme, 1986; Quigley and Kretschmer, 1982).

Degree of impairment refers to the severity of the hearing loss and is an important consideration. Common descriptive terms used to identify degree of hearing loss include mild (26 to 40 dB), moderate (41 to 55 dB), moderate to severe (56 to 70dB), severe (71 to 90/95 dB), and profound hearing loss (96 dB or above) (Bess and McConnell, 1981). The impairment caused by a hearing loss is also a function of (1) whether it is unilateral or bilateral and (2) the slope of the loss (i.e., flat, gradually falling, or sharply falling audiometric curve).

Hearing losses are generally identified as *conductive* or *sensorineural*. When a combination of the two types of loss occurs, it is called a *mixed hearing loss*. When an individual displays auditory dysfunction, although the peripheral hearing mechanisms are functioning within normal limits, the loss is called a *central auditory defect*.

CONDUCTIVE HEARING LOSS

Conductive hearing loss occurs when there is interference of any sort in the transmission of sound from the external auditory canal to the inner ear and rarely exceeds a hearing threshold level of 60 dB (American National Standards Institute, 1969). Its primary effect is a loss of hearing sensitivity, not of speech discrimination abilities. Causes of conductive loss include obstruction in the ear canal; problems associated with tympanic membrane movement; otitis media; and congenital abnormalities of the external ear, ear canal, or middle ear. A common conductive impairment found in children age 12 years and younger is otitis media, an inflammation of the middle ear space. Children who have recurrent episodes of otitis media beginning before age 2 are likely to have delayed speech and language development (Kaplan, Fleishman, Bender, Baum, and Clark, 1973). Most conductive hearing losses can be corrected by medical treatment or surgery.

SENSORINEURAL HEARING LOSS

Sensorineural hearing loss occurs when there is damage to the hair cells of the cochlea or the auditory nerve fibers. The loss can range from mild to profound. Unlike conductive loss, there is typically reduced ability to discriminate speech as well as loss of hearing sensitivity.

Common causes include a congenital abnormality, viral and bacterial infections, drug toxicity, head trauma, noise exposure, and aging. Unfortunately, most hearing losses of sensorineural origin are not responsive to medical intervention.

There are numerous etiologies of prelinguistic sensorineural hearing loss in both genetic and nongenetic categories. Approximately 50 percent of childhood hearing loss is attributed to heredity (Bess and McConnell, 1981). Hearing loss alone or as a part of a syndrome that includes other impairments (e.g, neurologic, cognitive, or visual deficits) can be inherited genetically. Hereditary syndromes that are characterized by hearing loss include Usher's syndrome (retinitis pigmentosa with sensorineural hearing loss), Pierre Robin sequence (craniofacial skeletal disorder, cleft palate, occasional mental retardation, conductive and/or sensorineural hearing loss), and Waardenburg's syndrome (white forelock, lateral displacement of medial canthi, and sensorineural hearing loss). Congenital factors, those associated with pregnancy and birth, are also frequent causes of sensorineural hearing loss in children. They may involve disorders of embryologic development, maternal infections, Rh incompatibility, toxic factors, anoxia, and occasionally trauma to the inner ear. Note that many of these conditions are also causes of congenital brain damage.

Hearing-impaired children demonstrate the same innate abilities to acquire speech and language as their hearing peers if they are not multihandicapped by other serious conditions such as visual defects, emotional or behavioral problems, cognitive deficits, and perceptual-motor defects. However, if moderately to severely impaired, they cannot acquire language primarily through audition and must depend on vision as their language-learning modality. This dependency frequently results in an overall delay of speech and language development.

During childhood and later, acquired lesions of the inner ear structures may result from bacterial and viral infections (e.g., mumps, meningitis, viral pneumonia), drug toxicity, excessive noise exposure, head trauma, or growing older. Only in adults is sudden unilateral hearing loss caused by Ménière's disease, thought to be a result of excessive fluid pressure in the cochlear duct (Sataloff, 1966). The most common adult disorder is presbycusis, the bilateral sensorineural hearing loss associated with the aging process. Presbycusis is a poorly understood disease process, and its exact etiology remains unknown. The effects of aging on the auditory system probably begin during adolescence, but it is later in life that the progressive hearing loss becomes significant enough to interfere with communication.

Disorders of the auditory nerve are less common than disorders of the inner ear. One such disorder is the acoustic nerve tumor, or acoustic neuroma, a benign tumor that typically arises from the vestibular portion of the vestibulocochlear (VIII) nerve. Pressure is put on the nerve fibers located in the internal auditory canal, including the facial (VII) nerve, inferior and superior vestibular nerves, and auditory nerve, as the tumor grows. This pressure can create specific symptoms, for example, hearing loss, vertigo, tinnitus, and facial weakness, that assist the physician in accurately diagnosing the tumor (Weaver and Northern, 1976).

Disorders of the central auditory nervous system (CANS), consisting of the auditory pathways from the cochlear nucleus to the auditory cortex, are much more difficult to diagnose because usually there is no loss in hearing sensitivity. Furthermore, unlike peripheral disorders, lesions of the CANS may manifest as abnormal auditory function on the side, or ear, opposite the etiologic site of the disorder.

DISORDERS OF CENTRAL PROCESSING

The central language processor consists of the cortical and subcortical complexes that lie between the auditory receptor and the speech effector segments. The communication processes that occur in this segment allow the individual to perceive consciously, derive meaning from a spoken message, establish representations, and formulate a linguistic message. Although the neuroanatomy of this complex system is beginning to be understood, there is still much speculation as to how these neurologic structures process linguistic information. Malfunctions and damage that occur within the central processor disrupt or inhibit language function or linguistic comprehension, integration, and formulation.

There are two common ways to classify the various communication disorders that result from malfunction and damage within the central processor. One is to distinguish the problems of children from those of adults. The second separates communication disorders based on their primary symptomatology (i.e., language comprehension, integration, or formulation disorder). Childhood and adult language disorders are reviewed in this chapter. Language disorders in relation to functional anatomy are discussed in Chapter 9.

LANGUAGE DISORDERS IN CHILDREN

Developmental Language Disorders

The inability to understand and express meaning effectively through the use of verbal symbols—developmental language disorders—is the most prevalent group of childhood language disorders. There are two major approaches to the study of language disorders in children: etiologic-categoric and descriptive-developmental. There are advantages and limitations to both approaches; however, the traditional approach involves the classification of disorders by their etiologies and is thus more consistent with the contents of this text.

McCormick and Schiefelbusch (1984) classified language disorders in children into five etiologic categories.

1. Language and communication disorders associated with sensory deficits. Included are children who have hearing and visual impairments.
2. Language and communication disorders associated with severe emotional-social dysfunctions. Included are children who are classified as psychotic, schizophrenic, or autistic.
3. Language and communication disorders associated with cognitive problems, that is, mental retardation.
4. Language and communication disorders associated with CNS damage, mild to severe. Included are children who are classified as learning-disabled when the damage is mild or as having developmental aphasia when the damage is severe.
5. Language and communication disorders associated with motor disorders. Included are children who have motor deficits (e.g., cerebral palsy) or damage to the nervous system, (e.g., spina bifida).

Autism

The autistic population includes a broad range of children who evidence language, communicative, cognitive, behavioral, and social learning problems. Specific perspectives relating to the cause of autism, that is, psychological-psychoanalytic (Bettelhiem, 1967), neurologic (Ornitz and Ritvo, 1968), or central language disorder (Churchill, 1978), have been proposed but not proved. A central problem related to this disorder is an inability to integrate communicative function with other aspects of language, a schism between function and form (Tager-Flusberg, 1981). Phonological and syntactic skills develop relatively intactly, whereas semantic and pragmatic skills are deficient.

Mental Retardation

The American Association on Mental Deficiency defined mental retardation as a significantly subaverage general intellectual functioning existing concurrently with deficits in adaptive behavior and manifesting during the developmental period (Grossman, 1983). There is a high incidence of neurologic disorders in this population, especially those individuals who are severely to profoundly affected. The overall development in mental retardation is one of delay, which is also reflected in the delayed speech and language development.

Language-Learning Disability

Kirk (1963) was one of the first to propose the term *learning disability,* a discrepancy between a child's achievement and the apparent capacity to learn. The National Joint Committee on Learning Disabilities presented the following definition (Hammill, Leigh, McNutt, and Larsen, 1981).

Learning disability is a generic term that refers to a heterogeneous group of disorders manifested by significant difficulties in acquisition and use of listening, reading, writing, reasoning, or mathematical abilities. These disorders are intrinsic to the individual and are presumed to be due to central nervous system dysfunction. Even though a learning disability may occur concomitantly with other handicapping conditions or environmental influences, it is not the direct result of those conditions or influences.

The term is descriptive rather than diagnostic and does not denote a specific cluster of characteristics or a specific etiology. Many researchers currently believe that language deficits are implicated in most learning disabilities, including dyslexia (Mattingly, 1972; Shankweiler, Liberman, Mark, Fowler, and Fisher, 1979; Vellutino, 1977). The reader is referred to Wallach and Butler (1984) and Wiig and Semel (1984) for a comprehensive review of language-learning disabilities and other related topics.

Developmental Aphasia

The term *aphasia* has been used to refer to certain relatively uncommon language disorders in children. They have been defined as congenital or developmental disorders caused by brain damage (Eisenson, 1972) or without evidence of neuropathology (Stark, 1980). One can be more confident that a childhood aphasia is similar to adult aphasia after the preschool years when at least most language development has been completed normally.

Developmental Apraxia of Speech

Although language disorder or a developmental aphasia may accompany and complicate a diagnosis (Eisenson, 1972; Rosenbek and Wertz, 1972), children with developmental apraxia, an articulation disorder that is resistant to treatment, do understand language. Use of the term *apraxia*, which emphasizes a motor planning disorder, differentiates these children from those with a central language impairment. Investigations designed to delineate diagnostic characteristics of developmental apraxia are reported in the literature (Aram and Horowitz, 1983; Rosenbek and Wertz, 1972; Williams, Ingham, and Rosenthal, 1981; Yoss and Darley, 1974), although its diagnosis remains controversial (Love and Fitzgerald, 1984).

ADULT LANGUAGE DISORDERS

Disorders of the central communication processes that occur in adults are usually the result of acquired brain damage ranging from accidental head injury to cerebrovascular accidents. Diffuse CNS disease, metabolic disease, and toxicity can also result in neurogenic communication disorders. The outstanding symptoms are a reduction or loss of language functions that were previously well established (i.e., listening, reading, speaking, writing). These disorders range from disturbances that disrupt the entire communication process to deficits of only relatively specific speech-language skills.

Adult Aphasia

A unitary view of adult aphasia (Darley, 1969, 1982) suggests that it is a multimodality reduction in capacity to interpret and formulate meaningful linguistic elements due to brain damage. In this view, impairment of language-specific functions (i.e., listening, reading, speaking, writing) is disproportionate to impairment of other sensory, intellectual, and motor functions. This unitary view of aphasia exists in the literature with positions that stress classification (Benson, 1979; Goodglass and Kaplan, 1972, 1983; Kertesz, 1979). Most aphasic adults show some degree of expressive involvement in conversational speech, which has led to a widely used dichotomous classification: nonfluent or fluent. Nonfluent aphasia is usually associated with anterior lesions and fluent aphasia with posterior lesions of the cerebral hemisphere dominant for language processing (Benson, 1967)—the left hemisphere in most people.

Although aphasia classification systems are numerous and sometimes confusing, the Boston Classification System (Goodglass and Kaplan, 1983), which reflects the Wernicke model interpreted by Geschwind, is the most widely used current clinical classification system: Broca's aphasia, Wernicke's aphasia, conduction aphasia, global aphasia, anomic aphasia, and various transcortical aphasias. This system (see Table 9-1) and other aspects of adult aphasia are discussed further in Chapter 9. In addition, there are numerous excellent texts that can provide the interested reader with more complete information on adult aphasia (Brookshire, 1986; Chapey, 1986; Darley, 1982; Davis, 1983; Goodglass and Blumstein, 1973; Holland, 1984; Lesser, 1978; Sarno, 1981; Schuell, Jenkins, and Jiménez-Pabón, 1965).

Related Disorders

Several disorders of input and output processing are related to aphasia because they are caused by damage to the nervous system and may interfere with communication. They may accompany aphasia and may be confused with it. At a high level of input processing, focal brain damage may result in an uncommon disorder known as *agnosia* in which sensation is experienced but without recognition or knowing. This disorder is sensory-modality-specific for auditory stimuli (auditory agnosia), visual stimuli (visual agnosia), or tactile stimuli (tactile agnosia). Cases of auditory agnosia for speech, also called pure word deafness, without deficits in other language modalities are rare. Modality-specific acquired reading disturbance due to brain injury is called pure word blindness, pure alexia, or alexia without agraphia.

Modality-specific impairments of motor functions used for communication can also occur with acquired brain injury. At a high level of motor function, volitional control of movements for the purpose of speaking can be disrupted without muscle weakness, slowness, or incoordination. This articulation disorder, characterized by decreased capacity to select and sequence muscle movements for volitional phoneme production, is called *apraxia of speech* (Darley, 1969). It sometimes accompanies aphasia because the area of the brain that is responsible for speech programming is located near the areas responsible for language functions. The interested reader may choose to read more about apraxia of speech from several sources (Darley, Aronson, and Brown, 1975; Perkins, 1983; Rosenbek, 1985; Rosenbek, McNeil, and Aronson, 1984; Wertz, LaPointe, and Rosenbek, 1984). A disturbance in the volitional movements of the tongue, lips, and jaw for nonspeaking purposes, called oral apraxia or buccofacial apraxia, may or may not coexist with apraxia of speech.

Dementia

Interest in adult language disorders formerly focused primarily on aphasia and its related disorders. Currently, however, consideration has broadened to include adult communication disorders subsequent to dementia, right hemisphere impairment, and closed head injury.

Dementia is a brain disease of adult and geriatric populations that affects intellect, memory, personality, and communicative function. Its cardinal feature is deterioration of cognitive functions due to diffuse bilateral brain damage. It is commonly associated with Alzheimer's disease (accounting for approximately one-half of the cases), vascular dementia caused by many small infarctions, and coexistence of these conditions (Tomlinson, 1977). Other causes include, among others, Parkinson's disease, Pick's disease, Huntington's disease, and

Korsakoff's disease. Language impairment is present in all stages of dementia (Bayles, 1982, 1984; Obler and Albert, 1981), although the language changes are subtle in the early period. Research has demonstrated that semantic knowledge is more reliant on cognition than phonologic and syntactic knowledge (Bayles, 1982; Obler, 1983). Articulation is usually spared in dementing diseases not associated with movement disorders such as Parkinson's disease. Some communication investigators have chosen to refer to these disorders as the language of general intellectual impairment (Darley, 1969; Halpern, Darley, and Brown, 1973; Wertz, 1985).

Right Hemisphere Communication Deficits

A dramatic clinical observation is the difference between left-hemisphere-damaged patients and right-hemisphere-damaged patients; the former have obvious language disturbances after medical stabilization, and the latter typically do not. Right-hemisphere patients may have essentially intact linguistic processes (phonology, syntax, and semantics), but they are communicatively deficient in their verbal output, which has been described as "bizarre and inappropriate" (Collins, 1976; Myers, 1978). At the core of this problem is a disturbance of the attentional and perceptual mechanisms underlying nonsymbolic, experiential processing, which appears to disrupt reception and expression of complex contextually based communicative events (Myers, 1986). Nonlinguistic disorders include effects of impaired attention and perception, whereas extralinguistic disorders (i.e., affective, prosodic, and pragmatic disturbances) are a cardinal feature of this communication deficit.

Closed Head Injury Communication Disorders

Closed head injury, in which the primary mechanism of injury is a blunt blow to the head associated with acceleration/deceleration forces (Levin, Benson, and Grossman, 1982), has been labeled the great silent epidemic of our time (Adamovich, Henderson, and Auerbach, 1985). Head injury leaves many survivors with physical, cognitive, behavioral, and communicative impairments. Symptoms reflect commonly occurring anterior frontolimbic lesions related to impairment of self-direction, self-monitoring, and self-initiation, as well as inhibition, judgment, and problem-solving. Bilateral anterior temporal lobe lesions are related to memory impairments and emotional reactivity. Diffuse lesions are related to disorders of attention, concentration, and efficiency of information processing (Adamovich et al., 1985; Pang, 1985). Additionally, verbal impairments typically are associated with closed head injury. Observed language disorders may include "confused language" (Halpern et al., 1973), "subclinical" aphasic deficits (Sarno, 1984), and "cognitive-language" impairments including disorganized discourse, weak verbal learning, and inadequate use of language for reasoning and problem-solving (Szekeres, Ylvisaker, and Holland, 1985).

DISORDERS OF THE SPEECH EFFECTOR

The effector segment of the human communication system involves the motor area of the cortex, the precentral gyrus, and includes the descending tracts, feedback loops, subcortical linkages, cranial nerves, and muscles requisite for neuromotor control of speech. Damage within this segment, which may occur at any point along the pathway from cerebrum to speech musculature, is caused by numerous disorders, each producing distinctive motor speech disturbances.

DYSARTHRIA

Dysarthria refers to a group of related speech disorders resulting from disturbances in muscular control of the speech mechanism due to central or peripheral nervous system damage (Darley et al., 1975). Some degree of weakness, slowness, incoordination, or altered muscle tone characterizes the activity of any combination of the basic speech processes of respiration, phonation, and articulation. Some authors also use dysarthria to classify isolated single-process motor speech impairments, such as an isolated articulation problem due to hypoglossal (XII) nerve involvement, isolated palatopharyngeal incompetence of neurogenic origin, or isolated dysphonia due to unilateral vocal fold paralysis.

The dysarthrias can be classified according to the subject's age at the time of onset, etiology, disease entity, neuroanatomic area of impairment, cranial nerve involvement, or speech process involved. A useful clinical classification system reflecting neuromuscular condition and

probable neuroanatomic origin emerged from the Mayo Clinic study reported by Darley and associates (1969a,b; 1975). These authors also described distinctive speech patterns for the various types of dysarthria resulting from lesions in different regions of the nervous system. In the Mayo classification system, flaccid and spastic dysarthria, caused by flaccid paralysis and spasticity of the peripheral speech musculature, respectively, are self-explanatory. In ataxic dysarthria muscular incoordination is a cardinal feature. Hypokinetic dysarthria in parkinsonism appears to be caused by a lesion in the basal ganglia and is reflected in rigidity of the speech musculature. Lesions in the basal ganglia can also cause types of hyperkinetic dysarthria, for example, a type associated with chorea characterized by quick, spontaneous, uncontrolled movements, and a type associated with dystonia, consisting of slow, continuous, uncontrolled movements. Mixed dysarthrias are common in: (1) the degenerative disease amyotrophic lateral sclerosis, sometimes referred to as Lou Gehrig's disease; (2) Wilson's disease, an inherited disorder of copper metabolism; and (3) multiple sclerosis, an inflammatory disease resulting in areas of demyelination in the nervous system. Several reports of adult dysarthria are available (Darley, Aronson, and Brown, 1975; McNeil, Rosenbek, and Aronson, 1984; Netsell, 1986; Perkins, 1983; Rosenbek and LaPointe, 1985).

DEVELOPMENTAL DYSARTHRIA: CEREBRAL PALSY

Developmental dysarthria is common in the cerebral palsy population, with 75 to 85 percent of the children demonstrating obvious speech problems. Cerebral palsy refers to a full range of disease complexes that reflect nonprogressive damage of multiple causation to cortical and subcortical areas of the brain and have their inception during the period from conception to approximately 2 to 3 years of age (Mysak, 1971). It is complicated by mental retardation, hearing loss, or perceptual and behavioral disorders in some children. Problems in the development and production of speech and language frequently accompany the more common forms of cerebral palsy (i.e., spasticity, athetosis, ataxia, and mixed). Because cerebral palsy is a microcosm of the spectrum of neurologic disabilities, it reflects a wide range, variety, and combination of communication disorders of respiration, phonation, articulation, hearing, and language.

Oral musculature impairment and swallowing problems of cerebral palsied individuals (Sloan, 1977) vary widely from one patient to the next. Inappropriate reflexive behaviors, disorganized lingual movements, delayed swallowing reflex, and reduced pharyngeal peristalsis may be present.

SWALLOWING DISORDERS

Swallowing is a function that requires fine neuromotor control. Involved in this control are the cortex and the corticobulbar and corticospinal tracts as well as six cranial nerves: trigeminal (V), facial (VII), glossopharyngeal (IX), vagus (X), spinal accessory (XI), and hypoglossal (XII). Various neurologic conditions may result in swallowing disorders, commonly called dysphagia (Groher, 1984; Logemann, 1983). Dysphagia occurs among all age groups, from newborns to the elderly, and may result from a variety of medical conditions. In adults, many patients demonstrate swallowing disturbances after brainstem or anterior cortical strokes (Donner, 1974; Kilman and Goyal, 1976). Many of the degenerative neuromuscular diseases (e.g., Parkinson's disease, amyotrophic lateral sclerosis, multiple sclerosis) are characterized by dysphagia that worsens over the course of the disease.

NEED FOR STUDYING THE NERVOUS SYSTEM

With such a large array of neuropathologies that lead to disorders of speech, hearing, language, and related processes, it is obvious that a thorough understanding of the structure and function of the nervous system is necessary to effectively manage such disorders. Basic information is needed with regard to normal as well as abnormal neuroanatomy and neurophysiology.

As discussed in the next section, there is frequently an interaction among diagnostic, prognostic, treatment, and investigative approaches wherein a given procedure or instrumental device is used to provide information across all

four categories. Thus diagnostic information obtained from computed tomography (CT) concerning site of lesion in many patients may eventually provide useful research data. Chapter 9 includes specific examples.

METHODS OF INVESTIGATING THE NERVOUS SYSTEM

The nervous system is amply protected within the human body. Although it is an obvious advantage for the well-being of the individual, it renders investigation of the nervous system difficult. However, great strides are being made in improving technology for studying the nervous system, particularly in the area of imaging techniques. There is a wide spectrum of methods that have been used to study the nervous system, and many of these techniques are still being developed.

Investigating the nervous system involves an evolutionary process. Scientists study abnormal physical or psychological behavior in relation to abnormal neuroanatomy and neurophysiology. Such relations generate testable hypotheses leading to various treatment regimens that may be applied to a large number of people. Although a treatment typically has been tested thoroughly in animals, humans become the experimental population when they are exposed to it. Unfortunately, the treatment may not always work or may have unacceptable side effects. Such negative information, however, can be helpful for generating new hypotheses and testing new treatment options.

Ideally, it would be best to obtain a full understanding of the normal nervous system before treating the abnormal. One could then determine how a disordered system differs from normal. Unfortunately, because of the invasive nature of many investigative techniques, it is not justifiable to subject normal humans to certain procedures. If a person's life depends on an accurate diagnosis, however, the invasive nature of a technique must be accepted for that patient.

Many of the techniques described in this section are used for diagnostic purposes. Although the emphasis in this book is on the *normal* nervous system, it should be kept in mind that often a greater understanding of what is wrong with a mechanism provides valuable information about how it might function normally. Much of the basic information presented in later chapters has been derived from the clinical as well as the nonclinical techniques discussed below.

GROSS AND MICROSCOPIC OBSERVATIONS

GROSS TECHNIQUES

The most obvious and technically easiest method of examining a structure is simply to view it as a whole in relation to other, similar structures. For example, as casual observers we recognize a normal range of facial features after having viewed many faces over our life-spans. We are able to detect a nose that is excessively large, eyes that are too widely spaced, or a jaw that is too far forward without actually making measurements. If measurements are obtained, more definitive statements can be made about whether specific facial characteristics are close to the mean.

The nervous system can be examined in such a manner. With regard to the human nervous system, gross observations obviously cannot be made routinely in vivo because nervous system structures cannot easily be accessed without damaging overlying tissues. It is possible, and sometimes necessary, to expose portions of the nervous system during surgery, but information about the anatomy of the whole system certainly would be limited using this approach. Larger portions of the nervous system can be exposed and removed during autopsy or gross dissection in the anatomy laboratory.

Autopsy is a postmortem examination of the body that typically is conducted shortly after death. The tissue specimens being examined are "fresh" and, as such, are pliable and easy to manipulate. Pathologies of the nervous system, such as atrophy (shrinking of tissue), accumulation of blood, and space-occupying lesions, can be detected at autopsy. This method was used over a century ago by the French surgeon Pierre-Paul Broca when he discovered a cystic cavity in the third frontal convolution of a man who had an expressive language disorder prior to his death.

The nervous system can be examined in the anatomy laboratory after the body has been embalmed, preserving the tissues. The situation lends itself more readily to careful measurements than does autopsy, which typically is limited by time constraints. Also, specimens are usually more readily available in the anatomy laboratory.

Geschwind (1979) and his colleagues measured the upper surface of the temporal lobe of 100 human brains after appropriate dissection and found that the left side in that region generally is larger than the corresponding region on the right side. Asymmetry was noted in the same region in human fetal brains as well, and Geschwind therefore concluded that there is an anatomic propensity for language dominance in the left hemisphere. Other portions of the nervous system could be dissected, measured, and compared in a similar fashion.

Lesions in circumscribed regions within the nervous system have been induced experimentally in laboratory animals. For example, Larson, Byrd, Garthwaite, and Luschei (1980) lesioned specific areas of the brain of monkeys using a suction method. They found that following recovery from surgery, tongue, jaw, and facial muscle coordination was impaired as a consequence of the brain lesioning. It should be noted, however, that lesion studies, whether postmortem in humans or experimentally induced in animals, must be interpreted with caution. The alteration or obliteration of a specific area of the brain leading to a behavioral change does not necessarily indicate that the sole or even primary function of that region is to effect the behavior observed. Instead, the modification of a certain anatomic component may adversely affect a whole constellation of interactive networks, the negative outcome being the change in behavior observed.

MICROSCOPIC TECHNIQUES

Gross observations typically provide information about the topography of the nervous system and give general information about structural size and shape. Microscopic techniques must be used if detailed information at the cellular level is desired. Standard light microscopes are capable of magnifying objects several hundredfold. Electron microscopes can provide magnification in the thousands.

Typically, tissue samples to be viewed using a light microscope are embedded in a medium such as paraffin, sliced thinly (e.g., 6 micrometers) to allow light to pass through, placed on glass slides, and finally stained. Special stains are necessary for differentiating nerve tissue from surrounding structures. At the beginning of this century, the Spanish neuroanatomist Santiago Ramón y Cajal used a stain discovered previously by Camillo Golgi to show that the nervous system consists not of a continuous uninterrupted network but of discrete cells that communicate with each other at synapses. Today various stains are used depending on the specific structure of the nervous system to be viewed. For example, a Nissl stain colors cell body nuclei and Nissl bodies but leaves cytoplasm clear.

Chemicals may be used to "label" structures that later can be identified microscopically. A common technique is to inject a substance called horseradish peroxidase (HRP) into a region or, more directly, into a muscle or nerve within a live animal. The HRP is transported through the entire length of the nerve cell, and the animal is then killed. The suspected destination of the nerve fibers can be verified microscopically by examining that region for HRP-labeled cells, which appear darkly stained.

Another example of chemical labeling involves injecting a radioactive substance (e.g., deoxyglucose) into the bloodstream. The rate of uptake in the neurons is directly related to the metabolic activity of those neural cells. The accumulation of radioactive deoxyglucose can be measured by placing thin sections of frozen nerve tissue on radiation-sensitive film that will display the labeled cells when the film is developed. It is a powerful method of studying regional brain activity in relation to various stimuli. A relatively noninvasive imaging technique involving the same concept but using radiation-sensitive cameras instead of anatomic sections can be used with humans and is discussed later.

Whereas whole cells can be viewed using light microscopy, the *details* of cells can be viewed using electron microscopy. With light microscopy, an image is formed due to differential absorption of light that passes through a specimen mounted on a glass slide. A series of objective magnification lenses then direct the

light image to the viewer's eye. With transmission electron microscopy, instead of a light source an electron beam is electromagnetically focused on the specimen. The electrons that impinge on the specimen are differentially scattered, thereby forming an image. The electron image formed then is magnified by electromagnetic lenses. The magnified electron image strikes a fluorescent screen making the image visible to the human eye.

A special type of electron microscope called a scanning electron microscope (SEM) allows detailed investigation of the surface structure of minute particles. With this technique, the electron source is demagnified, forming a finely focused electron spot. The electron spot, or probe, scans the surface to be viewed much like that of a television camera. The theoretical resolution of SEM is the size of the electron probe, about 2 to 5 nm. A detector is placed near the scanned surface to receive radiation that results from bombardment of the electrons. That signal in the form of a reflected image is then amplified and used to illuminate a television monitor or cathode ray tube. Examples of SEM photomicrographs of portions of the inner ear are shown in Chapter 7.

A combination of scanning and transmission techniques, referred to as STEM (scanning transmission electron microscopy), allows the operator to choose which electrons emerging through the object are used to form the image. This system enables imaging of single atoms (Crewe, Wall, and Langmore, 1970).

ELECTRICAL RECORDING

ELECTROENCEPHALOGRAPHY AND EVOKED POTENTIALS

Electroencephalography (EEG) is a technique by which electrical activity generated in the brain is recorded via surface electrodes attached noninvasively to the scalp. Brain wave frequencies may vary from a maximum of around 50 Hz (Hertz = cycles per second) to as slow as 1 Hz, but frequencies tend to cluster at certain rhythms. Four main frequency intervals are recognized: alpha (8 to 13 Hz), beta (more than 13 Hz), theta (4 to 7 Hz), and delta (less than 4 Hz).

Alpha activity is recorded in the posterior quadrants of the head and is typical of the normal, relaxed, waking state with eyes closed.

Eye opening and attention decreases the voltage amplitude of the alpha rhythmic activity. Beta activity is a normal rapid rhythm that is recorded over the anterior quadrants of the head. Theta activity typically is observed in normal adults in a drowsy state and in normal awake children. Theta activity is abnormal in a fully awake adult. Delta activity is observed in normal infants and sleeping adults but is abnormal for other conditions (Daube, Sandok, Reagan, and Westmoreland, 1978).

The EEG has proved to be useful clinically for diagnosing major conditions such as epilepsy, drug overdose, and brain death. However, the relation between the EEG and electrical activity of specific neural structures is complex because the structures are not "hard-wired" to the scalp electrodes. Instead, electrical *fields* are involved that interact with each other and are attenuated variously as they pass through layers of the head (Nunez, 1981). This problem can be circumvented to some degree by inserting electrodes on or in nerve tissue (discussed below).

Another limitation of EEG is that it is usually not linked to specific activities but, rather, to general levels of arousal. This limitation is addressed by a technique referred to as the recording of "evoked potentials," which represents the response to various stimuli. Three stimulus modalities commonly are used to elicit evoked responses: auditory, visual, and somatosensory (Owen and Davis, 1985). Auditory and visual stimuli are delivered to the ears and eyes, respectively. Somatosensory stimulation involves delivery of electrical pulses typically to the median nerve at the wrist or to the tibial nerve at the ankle.

As for EEG recordings, evoked potential recordings make use of noninvasive scalp electrodes. However, the evoked activity is so small that the stimulus usually is repeated many times, and the scalp recorded response is averaged by computer to extract it from background electrical noise.

The recording of auditory evoked potentials has had a large impact on the field of audiology and has been the subject of numerous clinical studies. The obvious application of the technique is to test the integrity of the auditory pathways, particularly in subjects who do not, or cannot, cooperate in traditional behavioral audiometry. The technique also has been used as a more general neurologic test, such as for diagnosing multiple sclerosis.

Attempts have been made to equate peaks in the evoked waveform with specific sites along the auditory pathway. For example, the first peak (wave I) has been assigned to the auditory nerve. However, it appears that such a one-to-one mapping may be too simplistic and that individual peaks may represent simultaneous activity in different parts of the pathway (Moller, Janetta, and Bennett, 1981).

NERVE RECORDING AND STIMULATION

If there is appropriate access, any portion of the nervous system can receive an electrode for recording neural activity in response to a stimulus; or an electrode can be used to stimulate a nerve, thereby effecting some physiologic behavior. The technique of somatosensory evoked potentials mentioned in the previous section is an example of such an approach. That is, a nerve such as the median nerve is stimulated transcutaneously via a surface electrode, and an electrical event is recorded at the scalp.

The stimulating and recording electrodes need not be remote from each other anatomically. Thus in nerve conduction studies the stimulating electrode may be placed below the elbow, for example, and the recording electrode on the hand. Conduction velocity is determined by dividing the distance traveled along the nerve (between the two electrodes) by the time interval between the stimulation artifact and the recorded action potential. This test, which can be done noninvasively using surface electrodes for both stimulation and recording, is a routine diagnostic procedure in neurology clinics.

The direction of nerve conduction measured may be from a peripheral site to a central site (i.e., toward the core of the nervous system), in which case sensory nerve conduction is measured and the subject feels a slight shock. The reverse also can be carried out; that is, nerve conduction along a motor nerve from a more central site to a peripheral site can be determined. The electrical event in response to motor nerve stimulation can be recorded with an electrode receiving impulses either from the more distal parts of the peripheral motor nerve or from a muscle innervated by that nerve.

Neural stimulation and recording can be done separately. An example of neural stimulation without recording is that used for controlling pain. Surface electrodes have been used to suppress pain in circumscribed body regions (Abram, 1985). Electrodes have been implanted in the spinal cord to relieve back pain (Maiman, Larson, and Sances, 1985) and into the substance of the brain to suppress remote pain (Groth, 1985). The neural mechanisms involved in such analgesic effects of nerve stimulation remain controversial. Another application of nerve stimulation is that of "electrotherapy" (McNeal and Bowman, 1985). Surface electrodes are used to stimulate motor nerves, thereby aiding in restoring functional movements or in exerting increased muscle force therapeutically.

Recording can be done without imposed electrical stimulation. Indeed many studies have been conducted in which electrodes were positioned at various sites along the auditory pathway and neural activity was recorded in relation to acoustic signals. This line of investigation is explored in Chapter 8. With regard to speech production, many studies have used the technique of electromyography. With this procedure, electrodes are placed in or near muscles, and electrical activity is recorded in relation to body structure movements. Several studies of this type are discussed in Chapter 6.

As mentioned previously, electrical activity travels through body tissues in the form of field potentials, thereby spreading activity to surrounding structures. Therefore with transcutaneous stimulation the electrical signal may reach the target nerve but possibly other nerves as well. With surface recording, electrical events from the target nerve or muscle may reach the electrode, but activity from other nerves or muscles also may be recorded. To increase the precision of both stimulation and recording, subcutaneous techniques can be utilized. Using fine needles to record or to transport small wires into muscles, it is possible to obtain intramuscular recordings with minimal subject discomfort. However, if muscles or nerves must be exposed to gain access, obviously this approach is not suitable for routine investigation in normal humans. Thus animals or humans undergoing surgery have been used as subjects when nerve or muscle exposure is necessary.

The degree of precision for stimulation and recording depends on the method of interfacing the nerve or muscle to the equipment. The degree of anatomic exposure and the size of the stimulating and recording electrodes are impor-

tant considerations. The classic studies of Penfield and colleagues (Penfield and Roberts, 1959) made use primarily of surface stimulation of surgically exposed cerebral cortex in awake human patients. The purpose of such stimulation is to avoid excision of critical areas when treating patients exhibiting epileptic seizures. The speech areas of the cerebral cortex are "mapped" by stimulating focal points while the patient talks. Induced dysarthria, dysphasia, speech arrest, or vocalization suggests critical areas for speech control.

More recent investigation of brain functioning has made use of the technique of intracortical microstimulation (Abbs and Welt, 1985). With this technique, fine stimulating electrodes are inserted into the cerebral cortex, eliciting general body movements and even contraction of individual muscles.

Nishio and his colleagues (Nishio, Matsuya, Ibuki, and Miyazaki, 1976; Nishio, Matsuya, Machida, and Miyazaki, 1976) isolated several cranial nerves in rhesus monkeys, stimulated those nerves electrically, and measured induced action potentials in muscles of the upper pharynx. Their study corroborated the hypothesized innervation to those muscles from the nerves stimulated. In effect, this technique is a physiologic analogue of the anatomic method involving transport of horseradish peroxidase (or other anatomic markers) in that both methods trace specific neural pathways to their destinations.

IMAGING

CONVENTIONAL RADIOGRAPHY

X-ray techniques have been used for many years to observe the nervous system. Their obvious advantage is that the nervous system can be imaged in the living subject without the need for surgical exposure. Standard x-ray films (radiography or roentgenography) are useful for detecting traumatic or other aberrations involving the covering (i.e., the skull or spine) of the nervous system. However, if only internal abnormalities are involved, the similarity in density of nerve tissue versus adjacent soft tissue structures and body fluids necessitates the use of contrast procedures to differentiate the structures.

The low density of air makes it a convenient natural contrast medium in some x-ray studies. *Pneumoencephalography* involves withdrawing a small amount of cerebrospinal fluid (CSF) and replacing it with an injection of air. The exchange is made via a lumbar puncture in the lower regions of the spine, and the air eventually travels through the subarachnoid space that invests the CNS. Space-occupying lesions are observed if they displace the brain ventricles that contain CSF or if they prevent filling of the subarachnoid space with the air contrast. An examination that is limited to the spinal region (not the brain) is referred to as *myelography* and may involve injection of either air or a liquid paste contrast material.

If the ventricular system cannot be outlined by contrast material because of blockage of the subarachnoid space, it is possible to gain access by drilling a small hole in the skull and injecting the contrast material directly into the ventricles through a hypodermic needle. Either air or a suitable liquid contrast material may be injected. This procedure is referred to as *ventriculography*.

A useful technique for diagnosing neuropathology is *angiography*, which involves injecting contrast material into the arterial system of the brain. Space-occupying lesions may be identified by their displacement of large vessels. An aneurysm (dilated arterial wall) is apparent as a localized accumulation of contrast material, and arterial blockage is observed as an abrupt termination of contrast material.

Enhanced photographic and computerized technology have improved conventional radiographic techniques. An example is *digital subtraction angiography* (Nudelman and Roehrig, 1985). With this technique a video camera receives the x-ray image of the brain before and after injection of a radiopaque dye. The images are digitized and stored in the computer, allowing "subtraction" of the first image from the second. Because the radiopaque dye within the cerebral arteries in the second picture is the only major difference between the two images, the vessels remain and other structures are subtracted from the enhanced picture. The vessels are thereby clearly visualized.

The techniques described thus far in this section have been useful for studying the nervous system. A major limitation, however, with respect to imaging techniques is that they provide only a two-dimensional perspective. The imaging techniques described below have greater potential for three-dimensional investigation of the nervous system and some already have had limited application in that capacity. The technology is changing rapidly, and exciting new developments continue to emerge.

COMPUTED TOMOGRAPHY

Computed, or computerized, tomography (CT), also referred to as computerized axial tomography or computer-assisted tomography (CAT), is a specialized x-ray technique that has had a substantial impact on health care. CT is far superior to conventional x-ray techniques for differentiating among tissues of similar density such as gray versus white matter of the brain or a brain tumor and surrounding tissue. Thus although costly, CT has become a common diagnostic instrument.

Instead of a large x-ray beam, as in conventional radiography, that may encompass the head, CT makes use of a small beam, less than 1 cm wide, that passes through a single plane of the head or body. X-ray detectors are positioned on the opposite side of the body to receive the rays that pass through and are attenuated by the body. The x-ray detectors either rotate in concert with the x-ray tube or are stationary, forming a circle around the patient. Reconstructing the image of a particular body plane makes use of the mathematical concept that structures can be outlined from the infinite set of all their variably attenuated projections. In practice, a large number of projections are used, requiring approximately 2 seconds of irradiation and data acquisition time per slice and another 15 to 30 seconds for computer processing to reconstruct the image. A typical brain scan consists of "slices" 8 to 10 mm thick at intervals of about 8 to 10 mm.

CT has been used for a variety of applications. A number of investigators have studied the site and size of brain lesions in relation to type and severity of aphasia syndromes (Naeser, 1983). (Chapter 9 deals with this specific application.) Three-dimensional reconstruction using CT scans has been utilized in craniofacial surgery (Vannier, Marsh, and Warren, 1983). Although still in a developmental stage, it appears that dynamic CT reconstruction can provide motion studies of various parts of the body (Robb, 1985).

NUCLEAR IMAGING

Conventional Brain Scanning

The early methods of nuclear imaging are called radioisotopic encephalography or, simply, brain scanning. The technique involves injecting a radioactive substance into the body. The injected substance emits gamma rays, a form of electromagnetic energy, that are received by a special camera called a gamma camera placed near the patient. The gamma ray energy (photons) emerging from the patient strike a "scintillation" crystal within the gamma camera, producing flashes of light that are arranged according to the pattern of the source within the patient. The pattern of light flashes (scintillations) is converted to an image that reflects a concentration of gamma energy in the patient.

Normally, substances consisting of large molecules, such as the radioactive pharmaceuticals used for brain scanning, cannot reach the parenchymal substance of the brain because of the blood–brain barrier. This barrier is a natural filtration system associated with the capillary network supplying the brain with blood. Thus in a healthy brain the intravenously injected radiopharmaceutical is prevented from reaching brain tissue and is deposited with the normal flow of blood in brain "receptacles" such as the sagittal and transverse venous sinuses. However, if there is a brain lesion, it may disrupt the normal blood–brain barrier, allowing the radioactive substance to leak into the brain at the site of the lesion. The accumulation of radioactive material emits a relatively high-level gamma discharge, signaling the site of the brain lesion.

It takes approximately 1 hour for the radioactive substance to accumulate in the brain. Lack of cerebral flow following injection of the substance is strong evidence of brain death (Mettler and Guiberteau, 1986).

Radioisotopic nuclear imaging of the sort described above shares a limitation with conventional radiography: They both result in two-dimensional images of three-dimensional objects and are difficult at times to interpret. Tomographic techniques, as the name "tomography" implies, provide information about *planes* (in reality, sections) of the body, thereby facilitating interpretations about visual images. CT, described above, is one such technique that uti-

lizes x-rays passing through a patient to yield tomographic images. The principles of nuclear energy also can be used to produce tomographic images. These techniques are discussed below.

Positron Emission Tomography

In a fashion similar to conventional nuclear imaging, positron emission tomography (PET) uses injection of a radioactive substance into a patient. However, with PET, the radioactive material attaches to metabolically active compounds in the brain. Such attachment gives rise to a "positron" wave that travels only a short distance before colliding with and "annihilating" a neighboring electron. This annihilation reaction produces a burst of energy in the form of two gamma photon rays that are emitted in exactly opposite directions. Crystal gamma-ray detectors positioned around the patient receive the gamma rays emitted from the patient. Two photons that are registered simultaneously but are 180 degrees apart indicate that a positron–electron annihilation has occurred. The source points of the annihilations are determined, and an image is reconstructed. The mathematic principle of computer reconstruction is similar to that of CT reconstructions.

Because PET images reflect differences in brain glucose metabolic rate, the technique provides information about brain *function*, which is a major advantage compared to all the other imaging techniques discussed so far in this chapter. However, a major limitation of PET is its great cost due in part to the necessity of having a cyclotron in the immediate vicinity. The cyclotron produces the positron-emitting radioactive material, which is effective only a short time and therefore cannot be stored or transported over long distances.

Single Photon Emission Computed Tomography (SPECT)

SPECT is a technique that shares some features with the other nuclear imaging techniques discussed thus far. It involves injection of a radioactive substance and uses a gamma scintillation camera to receive emitted gamma rays from the patient. Similar to PET, the image obtained is a tomographic image that is related to metabolic activity in the brain and therefore provides some information about brain function. The method of image reconstruction is similar to that of CT and PET scanning. Both PET and SPECT differ from CT imaging in that the latter involves transmission of radiation *through* the patient from an external source, whereas the former two involve emission of radiation from *within* the patient by an internally injected source. SPECT is less costly and more convenient than PET because the former uses a more standard gamma camera and commercially available radioisotopes instead of those produced in a cyclotron. Currently, however, PET is more commonly used because of its better spatial resolution, which provides more clearly discernible images.

Regional Cerebral Blood Flow

Halsey, Blauenstein, Wilson, and Wills (1980; see also Lassen, Ingvar, and Skinhøj, 1978) have pointed out that regional blood flow increases in an area of the brain carrying out a specific task. Presumably, it is due to local generation of carbon dioxide from the oxidative metabolism of glucose. Thus depletion of oxygen would require increased blood flow to meet the metabolic need. The technique to measure regional cerebral blood flow (rCBF) takes advantage of this biologic behavior by measuring changes of blood flow in the brain and thus, by inference, changes in metabolic activity levels.

The technique is similar, in principle, to other nuclear imaging techniques discussed thus far. A radioactive substance, usually xenon 133, is injected into the internal carotid artery or inhaled. The inhalation method is less invasive and has the added advantage that the two cerebral hemispheres can be assessed simultaneously, thereby studying brain asymmetry. This assessment is especially important in language studies when questions of hemispheric dominance are being addressed.

Radiation uptake and clearance from the brain are monitored by various types of scintillation detector probes. Typically, the probes are either flat blocks placed on either side of the patient's head and containing rows of detectors or a helmet containing detectors arranged as radial spokes. The output intensity of the crystal detectors is proportional to the energy absorbed and therefore to the level of radiation emitted from a circumscribed region within the patient's brain. Blood flow levels are portrayed as different colors on the computer screen in relation to calibrated flow rates or as percentage change in flow rates relative to the resting state.

The measurement of blood flow has been applied to a wide range of clinical problems, such as headache, seizures, and strokes (see Horner and Chacko, 1984, for review). Lassen and Roland (1983) have shown that blood flow increases in brain regions that would be expected to be active in relation to various sensory stimuli. Thus blood flow increased in the temporal, parietal, and occipital lobes in response to auditory, tactile, and visual stimulation, respectively.

Wood (1980) has compared various techniques of assessing brain activity in relation to corresponding behaviors. He pointed out that the rCBF measurement is attractive to neuropsychologists because of its particular level of spatial and temporal resolution, which is neither too fine nor too gross. The spatial resolution of the rCBF technique is a compromise between the fineness of single electrode recordings and the more global technique of electroencephalography. The information provided by rCBF pertains to limited regions of the brain perhaps responsible for task-specific activities. Temporally, the rCBF technique is a compromise between the fast response of electrical recording techniques and the slow response of PET. Whereas PET may require as long as an hour for the uptake of radioactive material to stabilize, rCBF requires only about 2 to 3 minutes. Thus a sustained, repetitive task that involves some degree of cognitive integration might be ideally assessed by the rCBF method.

ULTRASONOGRAPHY

Ultrasonography, or more simply sonography, is perhaps best known for its application in fetal imaging, in which case it has become rather routine. If used specifically for imaging brain structures, the technique is sometimes referred to as echoencephalography. Ultrasonography appears to be safe, and compared to most other techniques discussed in this chapter it is easy to use and less costly.

The technique involves placing an ultrasound transducer against the body part of interest. The high-frequency signal sets up a vibrational wave that passes through the adjacent tissue structures. As tissue discontinuities (e.g., bone versus soft tissue versus air) are encountered, an echo is produced, sending a vibrational wave back to the transducer, which also serves as a receiver. The transit time between the issued signal and the returned signal is measured and converted to a spatial image that is displayed on a computer's monitor. Echoencephalograms can provide information about shifts in the position of midline brain structures, thereby indicating the presence of a space-occupying lesion.

The speed of propagation of the ultrasonic wave far exceeds the movement speed of body structures. Therefore dynamic images of moving structures, such as the heart, can be obtained using ultrasonographic scans.

A more recent application of ultrasonography involves its ability to detect changes in frequency of a moving object as the object approaches or retreats from a certain location. This parameter is demonstrated by the change in pitch associated with a train as it passes a street crossing. The phenomenon is known as the Doppler effect. Using the Doppler principle, it is possible to locate the position of changes in the flow of blood as the blood is accelerated through a constriction. Major constrictions can eventually lead to a stroke. Ultrasonography is a safe method of detecting arterial blockages that subsequently might be removed surgically.

MAGNETIC RESONANCE IMAGING

Magnetic resonance imaging (MRI), or nuclear magnetic resonance (NMR), as it also is called, probably has the greatest potential of all the imaging techniques available for providing a better understanding of the nervous system and other structures of the body. As with ultrasonography, MRI has no known biologically hazardous side effects; and compared to CT, MRI provides more clearly delineated images of internal body structures. MRI technology is being developed and improved rapidly; and although expensive, the number of its applications in medicine and industry have proliferated. Motion studies ("cine MRI") are now possible and should be especially useful for imaging the heart.

MRI involves placing a subject in a strong electromagnetic field—so powerful that the subject cannot have certain metal objects inside the body (e.g., surgical clips). The magnetic field has the effect of positioning the protons of hydrogen atoms along the lines of the magnet's force. Hydrogen atoms are abundant in the soft tissues and fluids of the body. After alignment, the protons continue to vibrate somewhat at a certain frequency depending on the strength of the magnetic force applied to the body. A radiofrequency (RF) pulse, tuned to the frequency of the vibrating protons, is delivered to the body and momentarily tips the protons from their alignment. Quickly, however, the protons spin back to the original alignment when the RF signal is turned off. This "spinning back" produces a signal that is detected by receivers placed adjacent to the body.

The intensity of the signal received, which eventually leads to the production of an image, depends on the density and distributional pattern of hydrogen atoms in various structures of the body. Bone is "transparent" to MRI because of its general lack of hydrogen molecules. However, bony structures are outlined by the images of overlying and underlying soft tissue.

Compartments called "voxels" (volume elements) are located by establishing a magnetic gradient in three planes within the body. The z-plane is head-to-foot, the y-plane is front-to-back, and the x-plane is left-to-right. The stronger the magnetic force, the greater is the frequency of the vibrating protons mentioned above. By gradually varying the magnetic field strength along a continuum in each plane and by "striking" protons with different tuned RF pulses, it is possible to locate specific points (i.e., voxels) within a subject.

As with other sophisticated imaging systems, a computer is necessary to compile the enormous amount of data for reconstructing the image. Although the MRI image is inherently three-dimensional because of the tri-plane magnetic gradients, the images portrayed are typically in layers (thus tomographic sections) and 7 mm thick and sequenced at about 10-mm intervals. The mathematic principles of reconstruction are similar to those used for CT. MRI is capable of producing remarkably detailed images that approach the quality of photographs of actual anatomic sections.

NEUROPHARMACOLOGY

The nervous system normally works as a multifaceted series of connections and reciprocal connections between individual neurons, muscles, and glands. It is not so much that structures relate to function as it is that cellular constituents make up those structures. A whole new area of neuroscience has developed since it was shown that interactions between neurons, other neurons, muscles, and glands (adrenal glands, pituitary gland) involve a chemical process that is carried out through the synthesis, presynaptic release, and then postsynaptic receptor binding of specific chemicals called *neurotransmitters*. The use of drugs to selectively alter neurotransmitter activity has become one of the principal methods for studying the nervous system. Use of pharmacologic agents to study the nervous system may take many forms, including application of chemicals to cells in the laboratory, injection of chemicals into selected sites in the nervous system of experimental animals to study behavioral changes, or use of pharmacologic agents to treat diseases of the nervous system. A given transmitter may be present at a number of locations throughout the nervous system but not present at other locations. Conversely, a given location in the nervous system contains one or more specific transmitters but not others.

NEUROTRANSMITTERS

This section provides an introduction to a number of known neurotransmitters and locations in which they are active. Each is part of a system that consists of those substances that interact to synthesize the transmitter and those that work to break it down in some way after its release into the synapse. Information related to the identification of newly discovered neurotransmitters and their roles in the nervous system has been accumulating rapidly. Coverage of this material could constitute an entire textbook, and the interested reader is encouraged to pursue this information in any of the excellent reviews available (Bevan and Thompson, 1983; Gilman, Goodman, Rau, and Murad, 1985; Katzung, 1987; Spiegel and Aebi, 1981). Although full coverage cannot be given to the topic of neurotransmitters, it is important at this point to introduce, on a superficial level, a number of those neurotransmitters that are well known and to briefly indicate their relevance to communication disorders. These transmitters and others are discussed in more specific ways in later chapters.

One major transmitter system that has been

the topic of serious study for an extended period of time is the cholinergic system. In this system acetylcholine is the neurotransmitter. It is active at a number of sites throughout the human CNS. In addition, acetylcholine is a known transmitter in the peripheral nervous system (PNS) at the neuromuscular junction, autonomic ganglia in both divisions (sympathetic and parasympathetic) of the autonomic nervous system (ANS), and at the postganglionic synapse in the parasympathetic division of the ANS. Acetylcholine is deactivated in the synapse by acetylcholinesterase (AChE), and thus its action can be enhanced or reduced indirectly by stimulating AChE (which would reduce the effectiveness of acetylcholine) or inhibiting AChE (which would enhance the effectiveness of acetylcholine).

A second well-studied transmitter system is the catecholaminergic system (known as catecholamines) in which dopamine is one transmitter. Functions directly related to the action of dopamine are said to be dopaminergic. Dopamine is active at CNS locations including the basal ganglia, the limbic system, and others. Within the basal ganglia, a complex balance of dopamine and acetylcholine is necessary for normal function. Another division of the catecholaminergic system is the noradrenergic system, in which norepinephrine is the transmitter. Norepinephrine is active in the PNS at the sympathetic, postganglionic synapse and in a number of other locations throughout the CNS.

There are several other neurotransmitters that appear to be related to speech, hearing, and language, but specific mechanisms are unclear. Brief coverage of these neurotransmitters follows. As is true throughout later chapters, the interested reader is encouraged to investigate the literature.

Serotonin (5-hydroxytryptamine, 5-HT) is a substance that, in addition to its effects in the periphery, has been shown to function as a neurotransmitter at synapses in several regions of the CNS. The specific locations at which this substance works, the mechanisms of action, and the types of behavior related specifically to serotonin are not well understood. It has been hypothesized that neurons containing serotonin may be either directly or indirectly involved in such complex behavior patterns as sleep, hallucinations, depression, and memory. The role of serotonin in these patterns of behavior has been demonstrated only indirectly by the finding that changes in the previously mentioned activities occur when drugs that act selectively on serotonin are used.

γ-Aminobutyric acid (GABA), an amino acid, is another, less well understood neurotransmitter. A review of published material on what is known about GABA indicates that progress in elucidation of the site and mechanisms of action for this transmitter has been hampered by the lack of drugs and procedures that allow those drugs to act selectively as either GABA agonists or antagonists. GABA is present in many locations throughout the CNS, and it seems that its role is primarily inhibitory. Glycine, another amino acid (like GABA), is frequently said to be a neurotransmitter, although its specific functions, mechanisms of action, and distribution are less well understood than those of the neurotransmitters already mentioned. There seems to be a consensus, however, that glycine is primarily an inhibitory transmitter.

Histamine is another chemical whose effects in the periphery have been studied seriously for many years; moreover, reviews of central neurotransmitters always mention histamine. Specifics of how and where it works are not known. There are other putative or suspected transmitter substances under investigation and, as mentioned previously, this area is rapidly expanding.

PHARMACOLOGIC AGENTS

Pharmacologic agents whose mechanisms of action relate to changes in specific neurotransmitters are important for managing a number of neurologic and psychiatric diseases. Following are several examples that touch on the importance of neuropharmacology as a treatment as well as an investigative technique. The types of patients one sees and the context in which one works determine in large part the drugs encountered and the depth of knowledge needed.

Psychopharmacology and *pharmacokinetics* are terms that refer to studies of the relation between neurochemistry, pharmacology, drug interactions, and behavior. The behaviors of interest may range from those necessary for survival, such as appetitive behavior, to those of a more advanced and multidimensional nature, such as attention, learning, memory, or other dimensions of cognition, and motor performance on complex tasks including speech.

In cases in which a pharmacologic agent is available that will alter a specific neurochemical balance and if that balance is thought to play an etiologic role in a particular clinical problem, the effect of administering the drug can be used to either support or seriously question the considered diagnosis. Similarly, drugs with predictable neurochemical effects can be used to treat clinical problems that are known to have neurochemical imbalances or deficiencies as their etiology. Following are some examples that specialists in communication disorders (especially speech) are likely to encounter with some frequency. Clinical research in this area sometimes requires a delicate balance between the need to administer pharmacologic agents for the purpose of gaining information and the need of the patient.

With respect to differential diagnostic decisions, a classic example of the application of neuropharmacology involves the disease myasthenia gravis. In this disease there is an inefficient use of acetylcholine once it is present at the neuromuscular junction such that skeletal muscles rapidly become impaired with sustained activity because of reduced function (in contrast to availability) of acetylcholine. To demonstrate that it is indeed the patient's problem, edrophonium chloride (Tensilon) is injected. Tensilon prolongs the action of acetylcholine because it retards the activity of AChE, which in myasthenia should yield a dramatic, rapid improvement in skeletal muscle function. Unfortunately, the effect of Tensilon, although rapid in onset, is of short duration. A positive Tensilon test is strongly suggestive of myasthenia. To the extent that the disease involves the neuromuscular junction between motor cranial nerves and skeletal muscle, the injection of Tensilon should produce a dramatic reduction of the flaccid dysarthria associated with myasthenia. The medications used to treat myasthenia follow the same general theme; that is, they target AChE and thereby the effectiveness of available acetylcholine. Much remains to be learned in this area, but the relation between neurochemistry and both diagnosis and treatment is apparent.

Another example of etiologic and treatment implications for a disease that affects communication is Parkinson's disease (PD). It is well known that in PD the substantia nigra (a group of nuclei in the brainstem) do not produce enough dopamine for normal function of the basal ganglia and create characteristics of hypokinesia (see later chapters). Medical treatment has revolved around the use of agents that selectively facilitate dopamine. The drawback to this focus is that the delicate balance between dopamine and acetylcholine in the basal ganglia may be offset in the opposite direction and create a situation in which dopamine is functionally dominant over acetylcholine (the reverse of PD). The result of this unfortunate situation is excessive and unwanted movements, called hyperkinesias, rather than the restricted movement and resting tremor so prevalent in PD. Both the hypokinetic characteristics of PD and the hyperkinetic characteristics related to possible side effects of treatment (a relative dominance of dopamine over acetylcholine) are reflected in speech. Cognitive function also may worsen in PD, but the neurochemical basis for this defect is not well understood.

Another clear example of neuropharmacology and communication is the situation in which patients with psychiatric diagnoses are treated with a class of drugs that includes the major tranquilizers, more accurately called neuroleptics. Although the psychiatric symptoms may improve, unwanted and uncontrollable movement disorders may develop. Such disorders may include hypokinetic symptoms because the drugs that improve day-to-day psychiatric function unfortunately block or reduce the effectiveness of dopamine. Thus the acetylcholine in the basal ganglia becomes relatively dominant over the dopamine, and hypokinesia ensues. On the other hand, prolonged use of these drugs may lead to supersensitivity of the postsynaptic membrane to dopamine, which leads to a relative overabundance of dopaminergic motor effects called tardive dyskinesia. The complex chemical balance needed for normal basal ganglia function and the effects of drugs are discussed elsewhere (Bevan and Thompson, 1983, especially those chapters concerning neuroleptic drugs and antiparkinsonian drugs; Noback and Demarest, 1981; Weiner and Goetz, 1981).

There are other examples of neuropharmacologic agents and various aspects of communication: medications that lower thyroid function; medications that damage the vestibulocochlear (VIII) nerve or central auditory sites; medications that affect timing and coordination of complex movements such as speech (e.g., muscle relaxants, anticonvulsants); medications that re-

duce alertness; and medications that, when present at toxic blood levels, produce a poorly defined kind of mania or agitation (corticosteroids, Dilantin, amphetamines, or other CNS stimulants). Note that pharmacologic agents that produce nervous system changes can and do impair, or improve, communication.

SUMMARY

This chapter presents the nervous system from a communication science perspective by introducing the relation between normal aural-oral communication and the nervous system, briefly surveying neurogenic communication disorders, and identifying methods for investigating the nervous system. It presents the nervous system as the source of all communication behavior, from the reception of meaningful stimuli to the production of intelligible utterances.

Because the brain is broadly organized into transmissive and integrative systems, the neurologic substrates involved in both normal and abnormal speech, hearing, and language behaviors are classified as receptive functions (hearing), central integrative functions (language), and effector functions (speech production). The remainder of the text is organized in conformity with this classification, addressing the neuroanatomy and neurophysiology of speech, hearing, and language. Clinicians and researchers who study this book will have a much improved comprehension of the neural mechanisms that are disrupted in speech-, hearing-, and language-impaired patients and thus a greater understanding of the neurogenic disorders of speech, hearing, and language.

Ancient Greeks thought the function of the brain was to cool the blood. In today's world its function has been compared to that of a giant computer. Animal models and neurologic studies of humans with acquired brain lesions contributed to the knowledge of neuroanatomy and neurophysiology. Anatomy, the first method used to study the nervous system, progressed from phrenology to more systematic techniques. New and continuing advances and experiments have led to increased knowledge of the functions of the nervous system and will undoubtedly play a significant role in both understanding and treating communication disorders.

REFERENCES

Abbs, J. H., and Welt, C. Structure and function of the lateral precentral cortex: significance for speech motor control. In R. G. Daniloff (ed.), *Speech Science: Recent Advances*. San Diego: College-Hill Press, 1985.

Abram, S. E. Transcutaneous electrical nerve stimulation. In J. B. Myklebust, J. F. Cusick, A. Sances, and S. J. Larson (eds.), *Neural Stimulation* (Vol. 2). Boca Raton: CRC Press, 1985.

Adamovich, B. B., Henderson, J. A., and Auerbach, S. *Cognitive Rehabilitation of Closed Head Injured Patients: A Dynamic Approach*. San Diego: College-Hill Press, 1985.

Aram, D. M., and Horowitz, S. J. Sequential and non-speech praxic abilities in developmental verbal apraxia. *Dev. Med. Child. Neurol.* 25:197, 1983.

Bayles, K. A. Language function in senile dementia. *Brain Lang.* 16:265, 1982.

Bayles, K. A. Language and dementia. In A. L. Holland (ed.), *Language Disorders in Adults*. San Diego: College-Hill Press, 1984.

Benson, D. F. Fluency in aphasia: correlation with radioactive scan localization. *Cortex* 3:373, 1967.

Benson, D. F. *Aphasia, Alexia, and Agraphia*. New York: Churchill Livingstone, 1979.

Bess, F. H., and McConnell, F. E. *Audiology, Education and the Hearing Impaired Child*. St. Louis: Mosby, 1981.

Bettelheim, B. *The Empty Fortress—Infantile Autism and the Birth of the Self*. New York: Free Press, 1967.

Bevan, J. A., and Thompson, J. H. (eds.), *Essentials of Pharmacology*, (3rd ed.). Philadelphia: Harper & Row, 1983.

Brookshire, R. H. *An Introduction to Aphasia* (3rd ed.). Minneapolis: BRK Publishers, 1986.

Chapey, R. *Language Intervention Strategies in Adult Aphasia*. Baltimore: Williams & Wilkins, 1986.

Churchill, D. *Language of Autistic Children*. New York: Wiley, 1978.

Collins, M. The minor hemisphere. In R. H. Brookshire (ed.), *Clinical Aphasiology Conference Proceedings*. Minneapolis: BRK Publishers, 1976.

Crewe, A. V., Wall, J., and Langmore, J. Visibility of single atoms. *Science* 178:1338, 1970.

Darley, F. L. Aphasia: input and output disturbances in speech and language processing. Presented at dual session on aphasia to the American Speech and Hearing Association, Chicago, 1969.

Darley, F. L., Aronson, A. E., and Brown, J. R. Differential diagnostic patterns of dysarthria. *J. Speech Hear. Res.* 12:246, 1969a.

Darley, F. L., Aronson, A. E., and Brown, J. R. Clusters of deviant speech dimensions in the dysarthrias. *J. Speech Hear. Res.* 12:462, 1969b.

Darley, F. L., Aronson, A. E., and Brown, J. R. *Motor Speech Disorders*. Philadelphia: Saunders, 1975.

Darley, F. L. *Adult Aphasia*. Philadelphia: Saunders, 1982.

Daube, J. R., Sandok, B. A., Reagan, T. J., and Westmoreland, B. F. *Medical Neurosciences: An Approach to Anatomy, Pathology, and Physiology by Systems and Levels*. Boston: Little, Brown, 1978.

Davis, G. A. *A Survey of Adult Aphasia*. New York: Prentice-Hall, 1983.

Donner, M. Swallowing mechanisms and neuromuscular disorders. *Semin. Roentgenol.* 9:273, 1974.

Eisenson, J. *Aphasia in Children*. New York: Harper & Row, 1972.

Geschwind, N. Specializations of the human brain. *Sci. Am.* 241:180, 1979.

Gilman, A. G., Goodman, L. S., Rau, T. W., and Murad, F. (eds.), *The Pharmacological Basis of Therapeutics* (7th ed.). New York: Macmillan, 1985.

Goodglass, H., and Kaplan, E. *The Assessment of Aphasia and Related Disorders*. Philadelphia: Lea & Febiger, 1972.

Goodglass, H., and Blumstein, S. *Psycholinguistic Investigations of Aphasia*. Baltimore: Johns Hopkins University Press, 1973.

Goodglass, H., and Kaplan, E. *The Assessment of Aphasia and Related Disorders* (2nd ed.). Philadelphia: Lea & Febiger, 1983.

Groher, M. E. *Dysphagia: Diagnosis and Management*. Boston: Butterworth, 1984.

Grossman, H. *Classification in Mental Retardation*. Washington, D.C.: American Association on Mental Deficiency, 1983.

Groth, K. Deep brain stimulation. In J. B. Myklebust, J. F. Cusick, A. Sances, and S. J. Larson (eds.), *Neural Stimulation* (Vol. 2). Boca Raton: CRC Press, 1985.

Halpern, H., Darley, F. L., and Brown, J. R. Differential language and neurologic characteristics in cerebral involvement. *J. Speech Hear. Disord.* 38:162, 1973.

Halsey, J. H., Blauenstein, V. W., Wilson, E. M., and Wills, E. L. Brain activation in the presence of brain damage. *Brain Lang.* 9:47, 1980.

Hammill, D. D., Leigh, J. E., McNutt, N. G., and Larsen, S. C. A new definition of learning disabilities. *Learning Disability Quarterly.* 4:336, 1981.

Holland, A. L. *Adult Language Disorders: Recent Advances*. San Diego: College-Hill Press, 1984.

Horner, J., and Chacko, R. Cerebral blood flow. In R. H. Brookshire (ed.), *Clinical Aphasiology: Proceedings of the Conference*. Minneapolis: BRK Publishers, 1984.

Kaplan, G. K., Fleishman, J. K., Bender, T. R., Baum, T., and Clark, P. Long-term effects of otitis media: a 10 year cohort study of Alaskan Eskimo children. *Pediatrics* 52:577, 1973.

Katzung, B. G. (ed.), *Basic and Clinical Pharmacology* (3rd. ed.). Norwalk, CT: Appleton & Lang, 1987.

Kertesz, A. *Aphasia and Associated Disorders: Taxonomy, Localization, and Recovery*. Orlando: Grune & Stratton, 1979.

Kilman, W., and Goyal, R. Disorders of pharyngeal and upper esophageal sphincter motor function. *Arch. Intern. Med.* 136:592, 1976.

Kirk, S. A. Behavioral diagnosis and remediation of learning disabilities. Conference on Exploration into the Problems of the Perceptually Handicapped Child, Evanston, Fund for Perceptually Handicapped Children, 1963.

Larson, C. R., Byrd, K. E., Garthwaite, C. R., and Luschei, E. S. Alterations in the pattern of mastication after ablations of the lateral precentral cortex in rhesus macaques. *Exp. Neurol.* 70:638, 1980.

Lassen, N. A., Ingvar, D. H., and Skinhøj, E. Brain function and blood flow. *Sci. Am.* 239:62, 1978.

Lassen, N. A., and Roland, P. E. Localization of cognitive function with cerebral blood flow. In A. Kertesz (ed.), *Localization in Neuropsychology*. New York: Academic Press, 1983.

Lesser, R. *Linguistic Investigations of Aphasia*. New York: Elsevier, 1978.

Levin, A. S., Benton, A. L., and Grossman, R. G. *Neurobehavioral Consequences of Closed Head Injury*. New York: Oxford University Press, 1982.

Logemann, J. *Evaluation and Treatment of Swallowing Disorders*. San Diego: College-Hill Press, 1983.

Love, R. J., and Fitzgerald, M. Is the diagnosis of developmental apraxia of speech valid? *Aust. J. Hum. Commun. Disord.* 12:71, 1984.

Mattingly, J. G. Reading, the linguistic process, and linguistic awareness. In J. F. Kavanaugh and J. G. Mattingly (eds.), *Language by Ear and by Eye*. Cambridge: MIT Press, 1972.

McCormick, L., and Schiefelbusch, R. L. *Early Language Intervention*. Columbus: Charles E. Merrill, 1984.

McNeal, D. R., and Bowman, B. R. Peripheral neuromuscular stimulation. In J. B. Myklebust, J. F. Cusick, A. Sances, and S. J. Larson (eds.), *Neural Stimulation* (Vol. 2). Boca Raton: CRC Press, 1985.

McNeil, M. R., Rosenbek, J. C., and Aronson, A. E. *The Dysarthrias: Physiology, Acoustics, Perception, Management*. San Diego: College-Hill Press, 1984.

Maiman, D. J., Larson, S. J., and Sances, A. Spinal cord stimulation for pain. In J. B. Myklebust, J. F. Cusick, A. Sances, and S. J. Larson (eds.), *Neural Stimulation* (Vol. 2). Boca Raton: CRC Press, 1985.

Mettler, F. A., and Guiberteau, M. J. *Essentials of Nuclear Medicine Imaging* (2nd ed.). Orlando: Grune & Stratton, 1986.

Moller, A. R., Janetta, P., and Bennett, M. Intracranically recorded responses from the human auditory nerve: new insights into the origin of brainstem evoked potentials (BSEPs). *Electroencephalogr. Clin. Neurophysiol.* 52:18, 1981.

Myers, P. S. Analysis of right hemisphere communication deficits: implications for speech pathology. In R. H. Brookshire (ed.), *Clinical Aphasiology Conference Proceedings*. Minneapolis: BRK Publishers, 1978.

Myers, P. S. Right hemisphere communication impairment. In R. Chapey (ed.), *Language Intervention Strategies in Adult Aphasia*. Baltimore: Williams & Wilkins, 1986.

Mysak, E. D. Cerebral palsy speech syndromes. In L. E. Travis (ed.), *Handbook of Speech Pathology and Audiology*. New York: Appleton-Century-Crofts, 1971.

Naeser, M. A. CT scan lesion size and lesion locus in cortical and subcortical aphasias. In A. Kertesz (ed.), *Localization in Neuropsychology*. New York: Academic Press, 1983.

Netsell, R. *A Neurobiologic View of Speech Production and the Dysarthrias*. San Diego: College-Hill, 1986.

Nishio, J., Matsuya, T., Ibuki, K., and Miyazaki, T. Roles of the facial, glossopharyngeal and vagus nerves in velopharyngeal movement. *Cleft Palate J.* 13:201, 1976.

Nishio, J., Matsuya, T., Machida, J., and Miyazaki, T. The motor nerve supply of the velopharyngeal muscles. *Cleft Palate J.* 13:20, 1976.

Noback, C. R., and Demarest, R. J. The somatic nervous systems and the basal ganglia. In C. R. Noback and R. J. Demarest (eds.), *The Human Nervous System: Basic Principles of Neurobiology*. New York: McGraw-Hill, 1981.

Northern, J. L., Lemme, M. L. Hearing and auditory disorders. In G. H. Shames and E. H. Wiig (eds.), *Human Communication Disorders: An Introduction*. Columbus: Charles E. Merrill, 1986.

Nudelman, S., and Roehrig, H. Photoelectronic-digital imaging for diagnostic radiology. In R. A. Robb (ed.), *Three-Dimensional Biomedical Imaging* (Vol. 1). Boca Raton: CRC Press, 1985.

Nunez, P. L. *Electric Fields of the Brain: The Neurophysics of EEG*. New York: Oxford University Press, 1981.

Obler, L. K., and Albert, M. L. Language and aging: a neurobehavioral analysis. In D. S. Beasley and G. A. Davis (eds.), *Aging: Communication Processes and Disorders*. Orlando: Grune & Stratton, 1981.

Obler, L. K. Language and brain dysfunction in dementia. In S. Segalowitz (ed.), *Language Functions and Brain Organization*. New York: Academic Press, 1983.

Ornitz, E., and Ritvo, E. Perceptual inconstancy in early infant autism: the syndrome of early infant autism and its variants including certain cases of childhood schizophrenia. *Arch. Gen. Psychiatry* 18:76, 1968.

Owen, J. H., and Davis, H. *Evoked Potential Testing: Clinical Applications*. Orlando: Grune & Stratton, 1985.

Pang, D. Pathophysiologic correlates of neurobehavioral syndromes following closed head injury. In M. Ylviasaker (ed.), *Head Injury Rehabilitation: Children and Adolescents*. San Diego: College-Hill Press, 1985.

Penfield, W., and Roberts, L. *Speech and Brain—Mechanisms*. New York: Atheneum, 1959.

Perkins, W. H. *Dysarthria and Apraxia*. New York: Thieme-Stratton, 1983.

Quigley, S. P., and Kretschmer, R. E. *The Education of Deaf Children*. Baltimore: University Park Press, 1982.

Robb, R. A. X-ray computed tomography: advanced systems and applications in biomedical research and diagnosis. In R. A. Robb (ed.), *Three-Dimensional Biomedical Imaging* (Vol. 1). Boca Raton: CRC Press, 1985.

Rosenbek, J. C., and Wertz, R. T. A review of 50 cases of developmental apraxia of speech. *Lang. Speech Hear. Services Schools* 3:23, 1972.

Rosenbek, J. C., McNeil, M. R., and Aronson, A. E. *Apraxia of Speech: Acoustics, Linguistics, Management*. San Diego: College-Hill Press, 1984.

Rosenbek, J. C. Treating apraxia of speech. In D. F. Johns (ed.), *Clinical Management of Neurogenic Communicative Disorders*. Boston: Little, Brown, 1985.

Rosenbek, J. C., and LaPointe, L. L. The dysarthrias: description, diagnosis, and treatment. In D. F. Johns (ed.), *Clinical Management of Neurogenic Communicative Disorders*. Boston: Little, Brown, 1985.

Sarno, M. T. *Acquired Aphasia*. New York: Academic Press, 1981.

Sarno, M. T. Verbal impairment after closed head injury: report of a replication study. *J. Nerv. Ment. Disord.* 172:475, 1984.

Sataloff, J. *Hearing Loss*. Philadelphia: Lippincott, 1966.

Schuell, H., Jenkins, J. J., and Jiménez-Pabón, E. *Aphasia in Adults*. Philadelphia: Harper & Row, 1965.

Shankweiler, D., Liberman, I. Y., Mark, L., Fowler, C. A., and Fisher, F. W. The speech code and learning to read. *J. Exp. Psychol.* 5:531, 1979.

Sloan, R. The cinefluorographic study of cerebral palsy deglutition patterns. *J. Osaka Dent. Univ.* 11:58, 1977.

Spiegel, R., and Aebi, H. J. *Psychopharmacology: An Introduction*. New York: Wiley, 1981.

Stark, J. Aphasia in children. In R. W. Rieber (ed.), *Language Development and Aphasia in Children*. New York: Academic Press, 1980.

Szekeres, S. R., Ylvisaker, M., and Holland, A. L. Cognitive rehabilitation therapy: a framework for intervention. In M. Ylvisaker (ed.), *Head Injury Rehabilitation: Children and Adolescents*. San Diego: College-Hill Press, 1985.

Tager-Flusberg, H. On the nature of linguistic functioning in early infantile autism. *J. Autism Dev. Disord.* 11:45, 1981.

Tomlinson, B. E. The pathology of dementia. In C. E. Wells (ed.), *Dementia*. Philadelphia: Davis, 1977.

Vannier, M. W., Marsh, J. L., and Warren, J. O. Three dimensional computer graphics for craniofacial surgical planning and evaluation. *Comput. Graphics* 17:263, 1983.

Vellutino, F. R. Alternative conceptualizations of dyslexia: evidence in support of a verbal-deficit hypothesis. *Harvard Educ. Rev.* 47:334, 1977.

Wallach, G. P., and Butler, K. G. *Language Learning Disabilities in School-Age Children*. Baltimore: Williams & Wilkins, 1984.

Weaver, M., and Northern, J. L. The acoustic tumor. In J. L. Northern (ed.), *Hearing Disorders*. Boston: Little, Brown, 1976.

Weiner, W. J., and Goetz, C. G. (eds.), *Neurology for the Non-Neurologist*. Philadelphia: Harper & Row, 1981.

Wertz, R. T., LaPointe, L. L., and Rosenbek, J. C. *Apraxia of Speech in Adults: The Disorder and Its Management*. New York: Harcourt Brace Jovanovich, 1984.

Wertz, R. T. Neuropathologies of speech and language: an introduction to patient management. In D. F. Johns (ed.), *Clinical Management of Neurogenic Communicative Disorders*. Boston: Little, Brown, 1985.

Wiig, E. H., and Semel, E. M. *Language Assessment and Intervention for the Learning Disabled* (2nd ed.). Columbus: Charles E. Merrill, 1984.

Williams, R., Ingham, R. J., and Rosenthal, J. A. A further analysis for developmental apraxia of speech in children with defective articulation. *J. Speech Hear. Res.* 24:496, 1981.

Wood, F. Theoretical, methodological, and statistical implications of the inhalation rCBF technique for the study of brain-behavior relationships. *Brain Lang.* 9:1, 1980.

Yoss, K. A., and Darley, F. L. Developmental apraxia of speech in children with defective articulation. *J. Speech Hear. Res.* 17:399, 1974.

CHAPTER 2

Basic Neuroanatomy

John M. Baumgartner • William H. Bentley

❑ Basic Neuroanatomic
  Terminology

❑ Microscopic Neuroanatomy

❑ Gross Anatomy of the Brain

❑ Gross Anatomy of the
  Spinal Cord

❑ Basic Anatomy of the
  Peripheral Nervous System

❑ Motor and Sensory Systems

BASIC NEUROANATOMIC TERMINOLOGY

This chapter reviews basic neuroanatomic terminology, divisions, and subdivisions. This information provides the necessary frame of reference or structure around which to organize detailed discussions of issues in neuroanatomy. Neuroanatomy at first may seem like an insurmountable tangle of terms, structures, and relative planes of reference. As one delves further into a specific topic, however, as the authors of each of the following chapters have done, confusion can easily overcome clarity. Confusion can be avoided if, when considering a particular aspect of neuroanatomy, one asks: Which nervous system is involved, what level in that system is involved, and what type of structure is involved? If one strives consistently to identify the system, the level, and the type of structure, the fine details fall into place more readily than if a less systematic approach is used.

PLANES OF REFERENCE

Much of neuroanatomy is learned by studying photographs, drawings, or other images. To properly conceptualize what one is looking at, one must first recognize the view or plane of reference from which one is looking. There are three major axes or planes of reference: (1) sagittal, (2) frontal or coronal, and (3) transverse. The sagittal plane divides the structure into left and right parts with a midsagittal plane doing so at the midline. The frontal or coronal plane divides the structure into front and back parts. The transverse plane is perpendicular to the long axis of a part. The same structure looks different when viewed from each of these perspectives; and just as important, the position of structures relative to each other can be demonstrated in alternative ways by varying the plane or axis of reference.

DIRECTIONAL OR COMPARATIVE TERMINOLOGY

This paragraph defines terms that pertain to the human brain. Ventral or anterior means toward the front of the brain, whereas dorsal or posterior means toward the back. Rostral, cranial, or superior means toward the top, whereas caudal or inferior means toward the bottom. Medial means relatively closer to the midline, whereas lateral means relatively farther from the midline. Proximal means relatively closer to a given reference point, whereas distal means relatively farther from the point. It is important to remember that these terms are relative, not absolute.

NERVOUS SYSTEMS

Although it is common to speak of the human nervous system as if there were only one, in anatomic terms there are a number of systems. These divisions form the basis for categorizing not only normal neuroanatomy but also relative locations or types of neuropathology. The central nervous system (CNS) refers to the brain and spinal cord. The brain is further divided into various components, as is the spinal cord. Because each of these various components is located in the brain or spinal cord, each is said to be central. The CNS communicates with the rest of the body through the peripheral nervous system (PNS), which refers to all neural tissue outside the CNS. Just as the broadest anatomic divisions of the CNS are the brain and spinal cord, the broadest anatomic divisions of the PNS are the cranial nerves and spinal nerves. There are direct connections between the brain (central) and the cranial nerves (peripheral), just as there are direct connections between the spinal cord (central) and the spinal nerves (peripheral).

The PNS is fairly straightforward if it is thought of in strictly anatomic terms. There are 12 pairs of cranial nerves, and each pair has specific functions. Similarly, there are 31 pairs of spinal nerves, and each pair carries information to and from a specific part of the body. It is important, especially in a text dealing with speech and hearing, to think of the PNS anatomically. There is, however, another way in which the PNS has been categorized. Instead of thinking in terms of whether a part of the PNS exits or enters the brain versus the spinal cord, one can categorize the PNS in terms of the peripheral structure(s) innervated. When categorized in this way, the PNS consists of the somatic nervous system (SNS) and the autonomic nervous system (ANS). The SNS is that part of the PNS that innervates skeletal (or striated) muscles, and the ANS is that portion of the PNS that innervates smooth muscles, cardiac muscle, and glands. The ANS also can be subdivided into sympathetic and parasympathetic divisions based on the manner in which smooth muscle, cardiac muscle, and glands are affected. The sympathetic system is primarily concerned with activating the body during emergency and stress situations, whereas the parasympathetic system is primarily concerned with conservation and restoration of body resources.

One should use the organizational structure for classifying the PNS that best fits the purpose at hand. What is essential is the concept that parts of the brain and spinal cord are parts of the CNS and are referred to as central. Pathology in these structures is *central pathology.* Similarly, cranial nerves, spinal nerves, the somatic system including skeletal muscles, and the ANS are peripheral. Pathology in these structures is said to be *peripheral pathology.*

MICROSCOPIC NEUROANATOMY

NEURONS AND RELATED TERMS

The basic structural and functional unit of the nervous system is the nerve cell, called a *neuron.* This specialized cell has unique properties that allow it to be stimulated by other neurons (the stimulation can be inhibitory or excitatory), summate that stimulation, reach a threshold of excitability, and fire an electrical or spike potential down its length toward other neurons, muscles, or glands. Each neuron is composed of three major components known as dendrites, a cell body or soma, and a single axon. Each neuron has many dendrites, and these structures receive stimulation (inhibitory or excitatory) and convey it to the cell body. The cell body contains the nucleus and a number of other

specialized structures including mitochondria, Nissl substance, and Golgi apparatus. The dendrites and cell body constitute what is often referred to as the *receptor zone,* and the response of this zone is graded and decremental.

The response of the receptor zone is graded in that there is a small response to each bit of stimulation. These small, step-by-step responses are called *excitatory* or *inhibitory postsynaptic potentials* (EPSPs and IPSPs). The response is decremental in that the amplitude of each small response diminishes with time and distance. Thus the stimulation must add up, or summate, over a finite period of time for the neuron to excede the threshold of excitability necessary to fire a spike potential. In contrast to the receptor zone, the axon (conducting zone) responds to an adequate accumulation of stimulation in an all-or-none and nondecremental way. The spike is conducted along the length of the axon, and there is no loss of amplitude over time or distance. The entire process of nerve conduction is electrochemical in nature, having to do with the movement of molecules across the membrane that surrounds the neuron.

In much of the central and peripheral nervous systems the axons are surrounded by an insulating material known as *myelin.* In myelinated axons the movement of molecules across the membrane occurs only at specific locations where there is a break in the myelin sheath. These interruptions in the myelin are known as *nodes of Ranvier,* and conduction in these neurons "hops" from node to node. It is known as *saltatory conduction* and is much faster than conduction in unmyelinated neurons.

Neurons require specialized cells around them for physiologic support. In the CNS support cells are known as glial cells and are collectively referred to as *neuroglia.* In the PNS support cells are called Schwann cells and are collectively referred to as *neurolemma.* Conduction of neural impulses is complex and is explained in detail in Chapter 3.

One can be misled into thinking that neuron, nerve, and tract are interchangeable terms, but they are not. *Neuron* refers to an individual nerve cell. A *nerve* is a bundle of neuron fibers traveling in the PNS. *Tract* refers to neuron fibers traveling in the CNS. Thus a collection of neuron fibers in the PNS is called a nerve, and the same arrangement in the CNS is called a tract. Each is composed at its most basic level of individual neurons. The term nerve root refers to a group of PNS neurons at the specific point where they connect directly with the CNS.

There are several other terms that are worth discussing. *Ganglion* (plural is ganglia) is a term that refers to groups of cell bodies that lie in the PNS and form a kind of nerve center, or point of intercommunication. *Nucleus* refers to the same sort of collection of cell bodies in the CNS. There is a major exception to the distinction between ganglion and nucleus, and that is the *basal ganglion*. This term refers to a specialized group of nuclei located in the CNS. The basal ganglion receives more attention at a number of locations later in this text.

In neuroanatomy it is common to refer to gray matter and white matter. *Gray matter* refers to those parts of the nervous system that actually look gray on inspection and are composed primarily of dendrites, cell bodies, and neuroglia. *White matter* refers to the processes of neurons that project from one point to another, and so white matter is composed primarily of axons. The exception to this white–gray dichotomy is the diffuse combination of gray and white matter found throughout the brainstem, called the *reticular formation*.

TRANSMISSION AND MUSCLE ACTION

In addition to neurons and neural conduction, two other major areas related to microscopic neuroanatomy should be introduced: neural transmission and muscle action. Neural transmission refers to structures and functions that allow transmission of a neural impulse across a synapse. Synapses occur between neurons (axoaxonic, axosomatic, or axodendritic), between an axon and a muscle, and between an axon and glandular cells. Transmission across a synapse is either inhibitory or excitatory depending on the specific transmitter substance involved. The response of the nervous system to sensory stimulation begins with the activity of the peripheral receptor system and proceeds into the CNS and up toward the cortex. Once the receptor(s) for a given sensation have stimulated adequately· the involved peripheral nerve, the other synapses involve connections between neurons at various levels of the nervous system. Reflexes sometimes are triggered

as the stimulation moves up through the system.

Motor control proceeds from the CNS out to peripheral muscles. Refer to Chapter 3 for further discussion of neural transmission. Mechanisms of muscle action are detailed in Chapters 3 and 5. Generation of a spike potential, conduction down the axon, transmission across synapses, and muscle contraction are the major mechanisms through which the nervous system works. Each of these areas is an important branch of neuroscience. Pathologies in these processes represent distinct types of neurologic disease.

GROSS ANATOMY OF THE BRAIN

MENINGES

The meninges are layers of tissue that surround the brain and spinal cord. There are three meninges: pia mater, arachnoid, and dura mater. The dura mater adheres to the inner surface of the skull and as such is the outermost of the three meninges. The dura mater is a tough, fibrous lining that forms folds and partitions that separate the two cerebral hemispheres and the superior surface of the cerebellum from the inferior occipital lobes. The dura is actually a two-layered membrane within which in certain regions venous drainage accumulates in channels called *sinuses*. The superior sagittal sinus is an example. The space between the skull or spinal cord and the dura is known as the epidural space. The space deep to the dura is known as the subdural space. Bleeding that is potentially damaging to the tissue can occur in these spaces (epidural or subdural hematoma) as a result of trauma resulting in compression of the underlying brain tissue.

The middle meningeal layer, the arachnoid, lies in the fluid-filled space deep to the dura. It is more delicate that the dura and does not contain blood vessels. The innermost of the meninges, the pia mater, is a thin membrane that adheres closely to the surface of the brain and spinal cord. The space between the arachnoid and pia mater, known as the subarachnoid space, contains cerebrospinal fluid (CSF).

SUBDIVISIONS OF THE BRAIN AND CLASSIFICATION SYSTEMS

In most discussions the brain is divided into the telencephalon, diencephalon, mesencephalon, metencephalon, and myelencephalon. Each is a horizontal level and is subdivided as specific structures at that level. The embryologic development of specific structures from each of these major subdivisions is discussed in Chapter 4. The following brief description is intended only to mention major brain structures and the subdivisions in which they are located, providing the

Fig. 2-1. Supratentorial level of the brain. (From Daube, J. R., and Sandok, B. A. *Medical Neurosciences.* Boston: Little, Brown, 1978. With permission.)

student with an organizational scheme on which to place more detailed information at a later time.

The *telencephalon* includes the paired cerebral hemispheres, including both cortex and white matter immediately deep to the cortex. In addition, the telencephalon includes the deep structures collectively known as the basal ganglia. The central portion of the olfactory (I) nerve also passes through the telencephalon and is known at this level as the olfactory tract. The *diencephalon* is the major subdivision located deep to the telencephalon. The diencephalon is composed primarily of deep midline structures as well as structures located at the base of the brain as it is viewed from below. Important diencephalic structures include the thalamus, hypothalamus, hypophysis or pituitary gland, and the central portions of the optic (II) nerve known at this level as the optic tract. The diencephalon is continuous at its caudal end with the *mesencephalon*, or midbrain. Below this level is the *metencephalon*, which includes the cerebellum, pons, and a number of cranial nerve nuclei. Finally, the *myelencephalon* consists

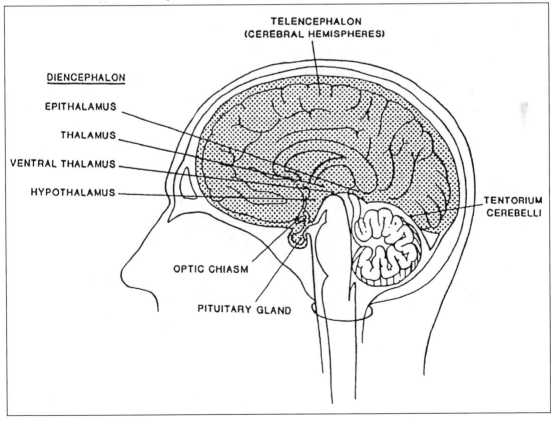

consists of the medulla oblongata and numerous cranial nerve nuclei. The medulla is bordered inferiorly by the spinal cord.

Brainstem is a term that usually refers collectively to the midbrain, pons, and medulla. It does not include the cerebellum. Some authors include the diencephalon in the brainstem. Bulbar is a term used to refer in general to the brainstem rather than specific components of it. Thus corticobulbar refers to a system connecting the cortex and brainstem. The term pseudobulbar is often used with respect to clinical symptomatology and refers to the site of a lesion above the brainstem, but it is not specific beyond this description.

There is another organizational scheme used to localize the general level of the nervous system involved in disease or injury and, in turn, the specific structures involved. This system refers to the *neuraxis* and the structures located within each level. The levels of the neuraxis include the supratentorial, posterior fossa, spinal,

and peripheral levels. The supratentorial level includes the cerebral hemispheres and the olfactory and ophthalmic tracts. The posterior fossa includes the brainstem, cerebellum, and cranial nerve nuclei. The spinal level includes the spinal cord and spinal nerve roots that attach directly to the spinal cord. The peripheral level includes cranial nerves, spinal nerves, and the specific structures they innervate.

The preceding discussion makes it clear that there are a number of classification systems used to help organize basic neuroanatomy. No one system is better than another, and the reader is encouraged to become familiar with the terminology in each system. Figures 2-1 and 2-2 display structures located at the supratentorial and posterior fossa levels of the neuraxis.

Fig. 2-2. Posterior fossa level of the brain. (From Daube, J. R., and Sandok, B. A. *Medical Neurosciences.* Boston: Little, Brown, 1978. With permission.)

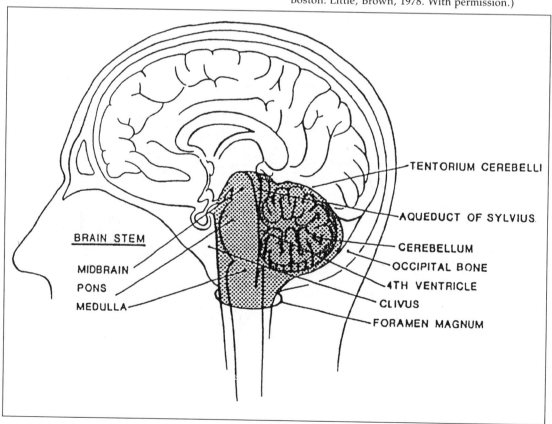

SURFACE VIEW OF CEREBRAL CORTEX

The paired cerebral hemispheres are joined by the large corpus callosum. The surface of each hemisphere is called the cortex and consists of a combination of grooves called sulci or fissures and ridges or convolutions called gyri. A number of these sulci and gyri serve as major landmarks, dividing the hemispheres into the frontal, parietal, temporal, and occipital lobes.

Many areas of the cortex have been numbered based on the Brodmann classification system (see Chapter 3), so a given area may have both a name and a Brodmann number. Figure 2-3 demonstrates many of these cortical landmarks. In the following section Brodmann's numbers appear in parentheses following the name of the area to which they refer.

The frontal lobe extends from the front or anterior aspect of the brain posteriorly to the central sulcus or fissure of Rolando. Immediately anterior to the central sulcus is the precentral gyrus or primary motor area (Brodmann No. 4). Anterior to this structure is the supplementary

Fig. 2-3. Cortical landmarks. (From McKeough, M. *The Coloring Review of Neuroscience.* Boston: Little, Brown, 1982. With permission.)

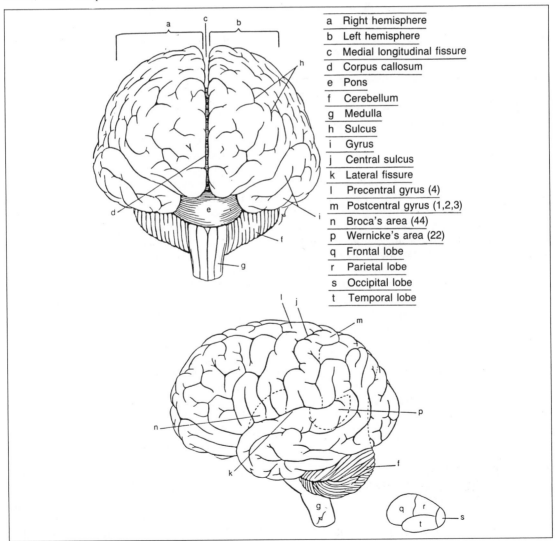

a	Right hemisphere
b	Left hemisphere
c	Medial longitudinal fissure
d	Corpus callosum
e	Pons
f	Cerebellum
g	Medulla
h	Sulcus
i	Gyrus
j	Central sulcus
k	Lateral fissure
l	Precentral gyrus (4)
m	Postcentral gyrus (1,2,3)
n	Broca's area (44)
p	Wernicke's area (22)
q	Frontal lobe
r	Parietal lobe
s	Occipital lobe
t	Temporal lobe

motor cortex (6). Inferior and slightly anterior to these areas of the frontal lobe is Broca's area (44). The parietal lobe extends from the central sulcus posteriorly to the occipital lobe. The inferior boundary of the parietal lobe is the sylvian fissure or lateral sulcus. Immediately posterior to the central sulcus (or anteriormost in the parietal lobe) is the area known variously as the postcentral gyrus, primary sensory cortex, somesthetic cortex, or somatosensory cortex (1, 2, 3). The temporal lobe lies on the lateral and inferior portion of each hemisphere and is bordered superiorly by the sylvian fissure and posteriorly by the boundary of the parietal and occipital lobes. Heschl's gyrus or primary auditory cortex (41) and auditory association cortex (42) are located on the superior temporal gyrus. Located posterior to Heschl's gyrus is Wernicke's area (22). Other landmarks located in the temporal-parietal-occipital boundary area are the angular gyrus (39) and supramarginal gyrus (40). The occipital lobe is the posteriormost lobe that can be visualized on the surface of the cortex. The primary visual cortex (17) is located at the posterior pole of the occipital lobe. The insula is another prominent part of the cortex and is located deep in the sylvian fissure. It can be seen on the lateral view when the temporal lobe is moved slightly downward away from the sylvian fissure.

It is important to remember that, although specific areas of the cortex are frequently referred to as if they were a single unit, the cortex is actually made up of six layers of cells. The layers are named, in order: molecular (outermost layer), external granular, external pyramidal, internal granular, internal pyramidal, and polymorphic (innermost layer). Granular layers contain cells that are primarily sensory in function, whereas pyramidal layers contain cells that are primarily motor in function. Thus localization of cortical function depends not only on the specific area of the cortex but on the relative distribution of cells in each layer of the part of the cortex.

DEEP TELENCEPHALIC STRUCTURES: LIMBIC SYSTEM AND BASAL GANGLIA

There are a number of structures located deep in the cerebral hemispheres and on the medial surface of the brain that function in a complex, integrative way in the regulation of both memory and emotion. Although many of these structures have been identified individually, it is their integrative function that leads to the concept of the limbic system. Although an individual may suffer neurologic damage that can be localized to a relatively specific area, the behavioral result is not specific but, rather, a disruption of one or more processes of memory or emotion. Similarly, disordered emotional behavior has long been linked to limbic system dysfunction, although specific correlations between neuroanatomic sites and specific components of emotional behavior constitute a topic that is much debated. The relation between the brain and emotional behavior has implications not only for basic neuroscience but also for clinical management of a variety of disorders. Data on the relation between brain lesions and both memory and the expression of emotion are discussed in Chapter 9.

Structures that compose the limbic system are best seen on medial or midsagittal sections of the brain. Major components of this system include the hippocampus (a medial extension of the temporal lobe), the fornix (which originates in the hippocampus), and the cingulate gyrus (seen as the gyrus immediately above the readily identifiable corpus callosum). Other structures include the amygdaloid complex, septal area, uncus, and parahippocampal gyrus (Fig. 2-4). The role that each of these structures plays in neuroanatomic and neurochemical pathways is significant in understanding how the limbic system mediates behavior.

The basal ganglia consists of a number of masses of gray matter that play a significant role in motor control. Although there are several telencephalic structures that are always included in the basal ganglia, there are structures at other levels that may or may not be described as part of the basal ganglia. The telencephalic structures that comprise the basal ganglia are collectively called the corpus striatum. The corpus striatum can be further subdivided into the striatum and the globus pallidus. The striatum comprises the putamen and the caudate nucleus. These structures are best seen on a coronal view such as that of Figure 2-5. On such a view it can be seen that the globus pallidus and putamen are lateral to the large collection of white fibers known as the internal capsule. The caudate is medial to the internal capsule but im-

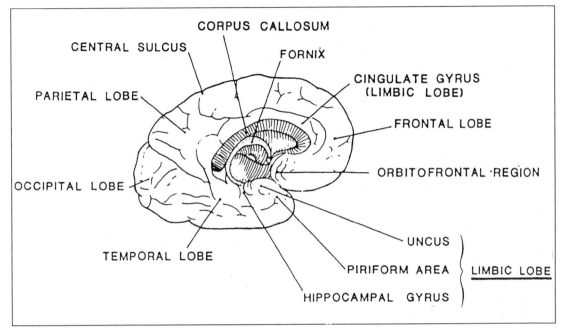

Fig. 2-4. Medial or midsagittal view of limbic structures. (From Daube, J. R., and Sandok, B. A. *Medical Neurosciences*. Boston: Little, Brown, 1978. With permission.)

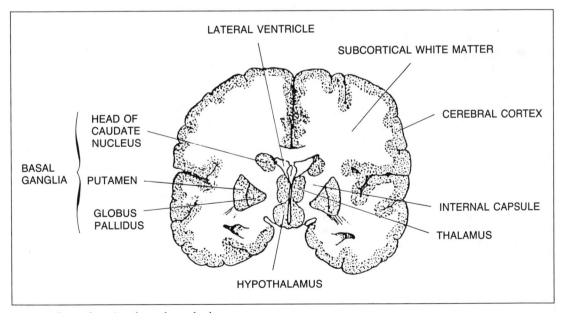

Fig. 2-5. Coronal section through cerebral hemispheres showing deep telencephalic and diencephalic areas. (From Daube, J. R., and Sandok, B. A. *Medical Neurosciences*. Boston: Little, Brown, 1978. With permission.)

mediately lateral to the lateral ventricle. The caudate nucleus is a complicated structure with an anteriorly located head, a body that stretches in a superior and posterior direction, and an inferiorly directed tail. Thus as one makes coronal cuts at various levels, the portion of the caudate that is visible is not always in the same horizontal location. The amygdaloid body or nucleus is attached to the tail of the caudate and is sometimes included as part of the basal ganglia, although other authors include it in the limbic system. The claustrum is a thin band of gray matter that is also frequently included in the basal ganglia.

The previously described structures constitute telencephalic components of the basal ganglia, but understanding the role of the basal ganglia in motor control requires inclusion of other structures, especially the substantia nigra (located in the midbrain) and the cerebellum, which has connections to the basal ganglia. The purpose of this chapter is to assist the student in placing various structures at the appropriate level in the nervous system, and so discussion of the function of this complex motor system is not included here. Refer to the brief overview of motor systems later in this chapter and to the more detailed information in Chapters 3, 4, 5, and 6.

DIENCEPHALON

The diencephalon is the part of the brain that forms the transition between the multiple structures of the telencephalon and the brainstem. Some authors include it in the brainstem. It consists of the medially located third ventricle and the structures that surround it. Neuroanatomy texts differ in regard to the specific structures included under the heading "diencephalon." We believe that it is important by way of introduction and orientation to include at least the thalamus, hypothalamus, optic tracts including the optic chiasm, and the hypophysis or pituitary gland, which is attached to the base of the hypothalamus.

The thalamus is by far the largest division of the diencephalon and is the major integrative collection of nuclei between multiple subcortical structures and the cortex. The thalamus is involved in four major functions: sensation, motor control, regulation of rhythmic cortical

activity, and higher-order processes such as language and emotion. The role of specific thalamic nuclei is a complicated topic and is not dealt with here. The thalamus plays an important role in speech motor control, hearing, and language, and its function for each of these is discussed in the chapters dealing with the respective speech, hearing, and language systems.

The hypothalamus is located at the base of the diencephalon and makes up much of the floor and lateral walls of the third ventricle. The hypothalamus plays an integral role in regulating the ANS and in such functions as body temperature, emotional expression, and endocrinologic function. The latter role is achieved through its connection with the pituitary gland, the central regulatory gland in the endocrine system.

MESENCEPHALON OR MIDBRAIN

If one does not include the diencephalon as part of the brainstem, the midbrain can be said to be the superiormost part of the brainstem. Basic anatomy of the midbrain can be organized around the cerebral aqueduct, which passes down through the midbrain, connecting the third ventricle with the fourth ventricle. The cerebral peduncles are located anterior to the cerebral aqueduct, and the tectum, or roof, of the midbrain is dorsal to the cerebral aqueduct. The peduncles can be divided further into the anterior crus cerebri and the more posterior tegmentum. The substantia nigra runs the vertical length of the midbrain between these two divisions of the peduncles. The tegmentum contains a number of nuclei, including the red nucleus and the nuclei for the oculomotor (III) and trochlear (IV) nerves. The tectum, or roof, contains the corpora quadrigemina, or paired superior and inferior colliculi.

PONS

The pons is located immediately inferior to the midbrain and anterior to the fourth ventricle. Like the midbrain, the basic anatomy of the pons can be organized into ventral (anterior) and dorsal (posterior) divisions. The ventral aspect of the pons contains large numbers of descending motor fibers and pontine nuclei, which make connections between the cortex and the cerebellum. Dorsal to this part of the pons are the paired medial lemnisci, carrying sensory information. The dorsal part of the pons includes the medial longitudinal fasciculi and the tegmentum, which is continuous with the tegmentum of the midbrain. The trigeminal (V) nerve attaches to the lateral aspect of the pons, and the nuclei of the abducens (VI) and facial (VII) nerves are also located in the pons. At the junction of the pons and medulla are a number of important nuclei, including the trapezoid body, portions of the olivary complex, cochlear nuclei, and vestibular nuclei.

MYELENCEPHALON OR MEDULLA OBLONGATA

The inferiormost portion of the brainstem is the medulla. The superior border of the medulla is the pons, and the inferior border merges with the spinal cord at roughly the level of the foramen magnum. The ventral medulla contains the paired pyramids, and the pyramidal decussation is located inferiorly. Portions of the olivary complex are located in the upper and lateral medulla. Multiple nuclei in this area help form connections between ascending sensory information, descending motor information, and the cerebellum. In the posterior medulla the paired fasciculi gracilis and cuneatus terminate on their respective nuclei gracilis and cuneatus. These structures are important links in the system carrying sensation from the trunk and limbs. The vestibulocochlear (VIII) nerve attaches roughly at the pons–medulla junction, and the glossopharyngeal (IX), vagus (X), spinal accessory (XI), and hypoglossal (XII) nerves attach to the brainstem at various locations along the medulla.

CEREBELLUM

The cerebellum is located dorsal to the brainstem and to the fourth ventricle. It is connected to the brainstem through three major bundles of fibers known as the superior, middle, and inferior cerebellar peduncles. The anatomy of the cerebellum is complex but basically consists of right and left cerebellar hemispheres connected by the midline vermis. Each hemisphere has an outer gray cortex, and an inner white area composed of fibers, that surround a number of deep nuclei (gray matter). There are additional comments regarding the cerebellum and motor control later in this chapter and in Chapters 3, 5, and 6.

VENTRICULAR SYSTEM

The ventricles are useful landmarks around which various parts of the brain can be grouped. At this point their usefulness as anatomic landmarks and functions in the brain make a brief review worthwhile. The ventricles are located deep in the brain and are derived embryologically from the central canal (see Chapter 4). CSF, formed within the ventricles by the choroid plexus, circulates through the system and then into the subarachnoid space before it is removed by the venous system. There is a lateral ventricle located in each of the cerebral hemispheres. The lateral is the largest of the ventricles and is anatomically divided into an anterior horn (in the frontal lobe), a body (in the parietal lobe), a posterior horn (occipital lobe), and an inferior horn (temporal lobe). The left and right foramina of Monro allow communication between the lateral ventricles down to the third ventricle, which is located medially in the diencephalon. The aqueduct of Sylvius, or cerebral aqueduct, courses from the third ventricle down through the length of the midbrain and connects with the fourth ventricle, which is dorsal to the pons and medulla but ventral to the cerebellum. The CSF then exits the fourth ventricle via the foramina of Luschka and Magendie and enters the subarachnoid space.

Knowledge of basic anatomy of the ventricular system is a prerequisite to understanding a number of diagnostic procedures and pathologic conditions. Compression, dilation, or displacement of a ventricle can be seen radiographically and is helpful for locating the site and type of lesion. If CSF circulation or absorption is impaired, the relative amount of CSF increases and causes dilation of the ventricles (hydrocephalus). Nearby brain structures are compressed by this dilation. Space-occupying lesions may displace a ventricle and thus be more readily visualized. An intracranial hem-

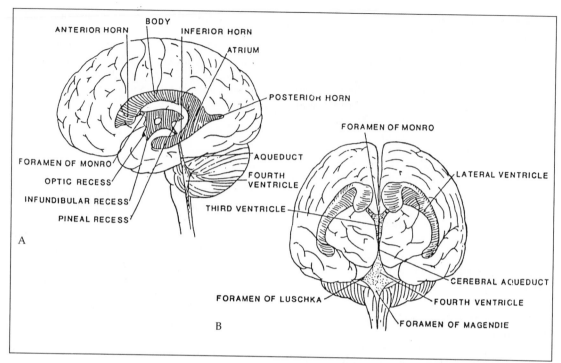

Fig. 2-6. Ventricular system. A. Lateral view. B. Frontal view. (From Daube, J. R., and Sandok, B. A. *Medical Neurosciences*. Boston: Little, Brown, 1978. With permission.)

orrhage and accumulation of fluid may be observed radiographically or in the contents of the CSF. Meningitis (bacterial and viral) can be identified by studying the CSF. Clearly in clinical situations where the pathology includes the ventricular system, knowledge of the relation between various parts of the system and of specific neuroanatomy is likely to be helpful for understanding the resulting impaired behavior. The ventricular system is illustrated in Figure 2-6.

CEREBRAL BLOOD SUPPLY

Arterial blood supply to the brain can be divided basically into the anterior and posterior systems. The anterior system begins with the paired internal carotid arteries, each of which is a branch of the common carotid artery. They ascend in the neck and enter the base of the brain just lateral to the optic chiasm. Here the internal carotid arteries bifurcate into the anterior and middle cerebral arteries. The anterior cerebral artery supplies mostly medial structures in each hemisphere, and there is communication be-

tween the right and left anterior cerebral arteries via the anterior communicating artery. Each middle cerebral artery sends off multiple branches to supply most of the lateral surface of each hemisphere. The posterior system begins with the paired vertebral arteries, each of which is a branch of the subclavian artery. The vertebral arteries ascend through the cervical vertebrae and enter the brain through the foramen magnum. Each vertebral artery (left and right) ascends along the ventrolateral side of the medulla. At the pons–medulla junction the two vertebral arteries merge to form the basilar artery. The basilar artery continues to ascend to the level of the midbrain, where it bifurcates into the left and right posterior cerebral arteries. Each posterior cerebral artery gives off numerous branches, which collectively supply the brainstem, parts of the diencephalon, posterior parts of the cerebral hemispheres, and the cerebellum.

When the blood vessels at the base of the brain are viewed from below, one can see what is called the circle of Willis. It includes the

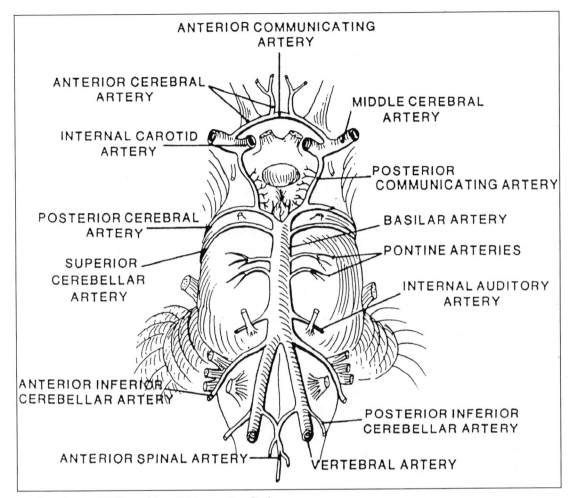

ANTERIOR COMMUNICATING ARTERY

ANTERIOR CEREBRAL ARTERY

MIDDLE CEREBRAL ARTERY

INTERNAL CAROTID ARTERY

POSTERIOR COMMUNICATING ARTERY

POSTERIOR CEREBRAL ARTERY

BASILAR ARTERY

SUPERIOR CEREBELLAR ARTERY

PONTINE ARTERIES

INTERNAL AUDITORY ARTERY

ANTERIOR INFERIOR CEREBELLAR ARTERY

POSTERIOR INFERIOR CEREBELLAR ARTERY

ANTERIOR SPINAL ARTERY

VERTEBRAL ARTERY

Fig. 2-7. Circle of Willis and branching arteries. Circle of Willis surrounds the optic chiasm and pituitary gland. (From Daube, J. R., and Sandok, B. A. *Medical Neurosciences.* Boston: Little, Brown, 1978. With permission.)

portions of the posterior cerebral arteries at this level, the posterior communicating arteries (which extend from each posterior cerebral artery to the ipsilateral internal carotid artery), part of the internal carotid arteries, the anterior cerebral arteries, and the anterior communicating artery between the two anterior cerebral arteries. Although this "circle" appears symmetric in drawings, in reality it frequently is not. There are many branches off this circle that supply diencephalic structures, the basal ganglia, the internal capsule, and other structures in the area. The branches of each cerebral artery are too numerous to describe here. Figure 2-7

shows the circle of Willis and a number of branching arteries. It is worth restating that, in general, the anterior blood supply goes to primarily supratentorial structures, including deep and lateral portions of the cerebral hemispheres, whereas structures in the posterior fossa (e.g., the cerebellum and brainstem) are supplied by the posterior blood supply.

GROSS ANATOMY OF THE SPINAL CORD

The spinal cord is the portion of the CNS that is surrounded by the vertebral column. This column consists of a series of bony vertebrae including, in descending order, seven cervical, twelve thoracic, five lumbar, and five fused vertebrae known as the sacrum and, last, the coccyx. The spinal cord travels within the spinal canal, which is formed by the shape of the vertebrae. The body of each vertebra lies anterior to the spinal canal, with lateral bony arches projecting posteriorly. There are openings known as intervertebral foramina between each pair of bony arches, and the 31 pairs of spinal nerve roots extend from the cord to the periphery through these foramina.

The spinal cord itself is cylindrical and extends from the base of the medulla to approximately the level of the second lumbar vertebra. The termination is cone-shaped and called the conus medullaris. Extending below the conus is the cauda equina, which is composed of roots of the lower lumbar, sacral, and coccygeal nerves. The cauda equina derives its name from the fact that it resembles a horse's tail. The cord and cauda equina are surrounded by the meninges. The subarachnoid space containing CSF continues down to the level of the second sacral vertebra.

Like the brain, the cord is composed of major divisions characterized by white and gray matter. When seen in cross section there is a characteristic H-shaped central gray area surrounded by white matter. This central gray matter is arranged into dorsal or posterior horns on each side, an intermediate zone, and an anterior or ventral horn on each side. The amount or shape of the gray (relative to white) matter changes at various levels of the cord as a function of the complexity of neural innervation needed at that level of the body. Thus at cervical and lower lumbar levels, where there is input and output to and from the extremities, the H or gray matter is enlarged relative to its size in the thoracic region. The white matter of the cord is composed of ascending and descending long fiber pathways.

FUNCTIONAL ORGANIZATION

The gray matter of the cord consists primarily of cell bodies. The dorsal horns (right and left) are a central continuation of the dorsal roots and contain cell bodies mainly related to incoming sensory stimulation. The ventral horns com-

prise the central component that leads to the ventral roots of spinal nerves. The ventral roots are neurons with cell bodies in the CNS, and they provide innervation to both skeletal muscles and the autonomic nervous system. The white matter in each half of the cord is arranged in three funiculi (columns): posterior, lateral, and anterior. The funiculi are further divided into tracts, or fasciculi. The posterior fasciculi are primarily sensory and include the fasciculi cuneatus (from upper limbs) and gracilis (from lower limbs), which synapse in the medulla as mentioned previously. The fasciculus gracilis contains some of the longest neurons of the body, extending uninterrupted from the foot to the brainstem. The fasciculi located in the anterior white matter are composed primarily of descending motor fibers, and the lateral white matter contains a mix of ascending and descending fasciculi.

The organization of the cord helps explain one of the most basic components of neurologic function, the *reflex arc*. In the most basic reflex, sensory stimulation of a specific kind enters the spinal cord via the dorsal root at one level of the cord. It travels from the dorsal root to the ventral horn on the same side via a small interneuron. It then triggers a motor reflex or response to the stimulation, which exits at the same level in the cord via the ventral horn, through the ventral root, and out to the appropriate muscle(s). This basic dorsal-to-ventral arc is the foundation on which more complicated reflexes are based. Patterns of reflexes become more complicated as a function of increasingly diverse input to the spinal cord and the activity of neurons that travel vertically in gray matter. Such activity may link several levels of the cord, which in turn leads to output at a level that may be different from the original input.

BASIC ANATOMY OF THE PERIPHERAL NERVOUS SYSTEM

The peripheral nervous system (PNS) links the brain and spinal cord with the periphery. Anatomically, this linkage is accomplished through the 12 paired cranial nerves and the 31 pairs of spinal nerves. The functions carried out by the PNS include innervation of the skeletal musculature of the body, smooth muscles lining the viscera, cardiac muscle, and glands. Skeletal muscle function is said to be somatic, whereas the latter types of function are said to be autonomic (the ANS). Thus thorough coverage of the PNS would include a discussion of the somatic and autonomic functions of cranial and spinal nerves. Furthermore, one would need to describe both sensory and motor components of somatic and autonomic functions, and coverage of the ANS would need to be subdivided into its sympathetic and parasympathetic divisions. Such coverage is beyond the scope of this text. The following section is designed to provide only an overview of the anatomic organization of the cranial and spinal nerves. Refer to later chapters for material on the involvement of specific components of the PNS in speech (Chapters 4, 5, and 6) and hearing (Chapters 4, 7, and 8).

CRANIAL NERVES

There are 12 pairs of cranial nerves (CNs). In addition to their names, these nerves are numbered using Roman numerals. The numbering is in descending order with respect to the level at which they enter or exit the brain, so that CN I is the superiormost and CN XII the inferiormost. The cranial nerves can be classified into those whose functions are sensory only, motor only, or have both sensory and motor components. A *sensory cranial nerve* is a collection of individual neurons whose cell bodies lie in the periphery and whose axons are conducting toward the brain. These cranial nerves enter the brain at a certain level and synapse onto the next part of the sensory system to which they belong. The collective synapses within the CNS of a given sensory cranial nerve would comprise a nucleus within that sensory system. A *motor cranial nerve* is comprised of a collection of neurons whose cell bodies lie in the brain and whose axons exit the brain at a certain level and conduct out into the periphery toward the muscle(s) innervated by that nerve or branches of that nerve. The collections of cell bodies in the brain are the nuclei for these nerves. The cranial

nerves that are both sensory and motor are comprised of a mixture of neurons, some conducting toward the brain and others away from it.

The concept of the nucleus of the cranial nerve in contrast to its peripheral portion is important for understanding both normal and pathologic function. The clinical picture created by a peripheral pathology may be that of sensory or motor function that is rather selectively impaired; motor impairment, for example, reflects reduced or absent innervation to muscles. If the pathology is central (in the case of cranial nerves it would mean in the brain), there may be less focal impairment and the type of motor impairment is different from that seen with peripheral lesions. This concept is mentioned again later in this chapter when the basic anatomy of vertical sensory and motor systems is introduced.

Table 2-1 presents the names, numbers, level of exit or entrance into the brain, and general function of each cranial nerve. Throughout this text, the convention of naming the cranial nerve and identifying its number in parentheses, for example, facial (VII) nerve, is used. Note that the oculomotor (III) through the hypoglossal (XII) nerves enter or exit the brainstem and only the olfactory (I) and optic (II) nerves enter above this level. Following are some general comments about each of the cranial nerves and combinations of them that subserve certain functions.

The olfactory (I) nerve is sensory, and its cell bodies are located in the mucosa of the nasal cavity. The axons project directly back and enter the brain at the level of the telencephalon, after which the olfactory system is comprised of the olfactory bulb and the olfactory tract. The optic (II) nerve is sensory for vision, and the equivalent of cell bodies is located in the retina of each eye. The nerve travels posteriorly to the optic chiasm, located just above the pituitary gland in the diencephalon. Some of the fibers cross to the contralateral side here, but others do not. The optic system then proceeds centrally, with involvement of nuclei in the thalamus, the superior colliculi of the midbrain, and the occipital lobe. The optic system is an important indication of CNS status as the area or field of vision impaired can be used with relative specificity to determine site of lesion. The optic system is also a useful indicant of intracranial pressure in that increased intracranial pressure may be reflected

TABLE 2-1. OVERVIEW OF CRANIAL NERVES

Nerve	Name	CNS level	General function
I	Olfactory	Telencephalon	Sensory: smell
II	Optic	Diencephalon	Sensory: vision
III	Oculomotor	Midbrain	Motor: eye movements, pupillary constriction
IV	Trochlear	Midbrain	Motor: eye movements
V	Trigeminal	Mid pons	Sensory: ophthalmic and maxillary areas of face Motor: mandibular musculature
VI	Abducens	Inferior pons	Motor: eye movement
VII	Facial	Pons–medulla junction	Sensory: taste Motor: facial expression, stapedial reflex, elevation of hyoid bone Other efferent: lacrimation, salivation
VIII	Vestibulocochlear	Pons–medulla junction	Sensory: balance and hearing
IX	Glossopharyngeal	Medulla, n. ambiguus	Sensory: tongue, pharynx, tonsils Motor: pharyngeal musculature
X	Vagus	Medulla, n. ambiguus	Sensory: viscera of neck, thorax, abdomen Motor: larynx, pharynx, soft palate
XI	Spinal accessory	Medulla, n. ambiguus	Motor: strap muscles of neck
XII	Hypoglossal	Medulla	Motor: tongue

by changes in the appearance of optic discs (papilledema).

The oculomotor (III), trochlear (IV), and abducens (VI) nerves are all motor in function and collectively regulate eye movement and autonomic functions of the eye (e.g., pupillary constriction. The nuclei of the oculomotor and trochlear nerves are located in the midbrain, with the nucleus of the oculomotor nerve just superior to the trochlear nerve. The location of the nucleus of the abducens nerve is generally said to be in the lower pons, but the nerve exits the brainstem at the pons–medulla junction. Careful analysis of eye movements can be of considerable localizing value, as there are predictable patterns of dysfunction associated with either central or peripheral lesions affecting each of these nerves.

The trigeminal (V) nerve has both sensory and motor components. Sensations of various kinds from the superficial and deep regions of the face are conducted to the brainstem via this nerve. The motor component is directed primarily to the muscles of chewing (mastication). The collective fibers of the trigeminal (V) nerve contact the brainstem at the level of the midpons. The name "trigeminal" derives from the fact that, peripherally, the nerve divides into three branches: the ophthalmic, maxillary, and mandibular nerves. The names of these divisions correspond well with the regions of the face with which they are involved. The motor component of the trigeminal (V) nerve is primarily part of the mandibular division.

The facial (VII) nerve, like the trigeminal (V) nerve, has both sensory and motor components. The facial (VII) nerve makes contact with the brainstem at approximately the pons–medulla junction. Because it passes through the cerebellopontine angle and the internal auditory meatus, pathology involving these areas may disrupt function of this nerve. The motor fibers of the facial (VII) nerve supply the many muscles of facial expression, the stapedius muscle in the middle ear, and the suprahyoid musculature. Motor aspects of autonomic function mediated by the facial (VII) nerve include salivation and lacrimation. Sensory fibers of the facial (VII) nerve include those for taste on part of the tongue and general sensation from the external auditory meatus. With respect to facial expression, it is significant to remember that volitional and reflex or automatic movements are not controlled in exactly the same way, such that a lesion may have a more significant impact on volitional movements (e.g., smiling on command) than on reflexive movements utilizing the same muscles. It is also significant to note that the facial (VII) nerve neurons innervating muscles of the lower half of the face originate from the nucleus on the contralateral side of the brainstem, whereas there are neurons from both the right and left facial (VII) nerve nuclei innervating muscles in the upper half of the face. This arrangement explains why a central lesion damaging input to the nucleus of the facial (VII) nerve on only one side affects only the lower half of the face and on the opposite side of the lesion.

The vestibulocochlear (VIII) nerve is actually two sensory nerves: the cochlear or auditory nerve for hearing and the vestibular nerve for balance. The functions of this nerve are detailed in Chapters 7 and 8. The vestibular and cochlear portions of the nerve attach to the brainstem at the pons–medulla junction. On the way, they travel near the cerebellopontine angle and pass through the internal auditory meatus; therefore, like the facial (VII) nerve, they can be affected by pathology involving these areas. Note that the vestibulocochlear (VIII) nerve travels within the temporal bone, and pathologic processes involving this bone are a threat to both hearing and balance.

The glossopharyneal (IX), vagus (X), and spinal accessory (XI) nerves can be grouped because the origin of motor neurons in these nerves is a collection of nuclei in the medulla known as the nucleus ambiguus. The glossopharyngeal (IX) nerve is both sensory and motor in function. Sensory components of this nerve have their receptors in a variety of locations including the tongue, external ear, external auditory meatus, membranes in the middle ear, faucial pillars, tonsils, and upper pharynx. Motor innervation is supplied to the stylopharyngeus muscle and in some degree (presumably through the pharyngeal plexus) to the soft palate.

The vagus (X) nerve is both sensory and motor in function and is the most complex of the cranial nerves. Sensory receptors are located in a variety of locations, including the external ear, pharynx, larynx, thorax, and autonomic components of the abdominal cavity, heart, and lungs. The vagus (X) plays a role in such sensations as hunger, abdominal fullness, and nausea, as well as cardiovascular and respiratory function. Motor control exerted by the vagus (X) includes innervation of palatal muscles (but not the tensor veli palatini), pharyngeal muscles, and all intrinsic laryngeal musculature. There are two large divisions of each vagus (X) nerve known as the superior laryngeal nerve and the recurrent, or inferior, laryngeal nerve. The superior nerve takes a fairly direct course

and innervates the cricothyroid muscle of the larynx. The recurrent branch, however, has multiple divisions, some of which travel down into the thorax and below to subserve a variety of functions. All intrinsic laryngeal musculature other than the cricothyroid is innervated by the recurrent laryngeal nerve on each side. The left recurrent nerve has a longer course than the right. The role of the vagus (X) nerve in speech and especially vocalization is referred to in more detail in Chapters 5 and 6.

The spinal accessory (XI) nerve is motor in function and has both a cranial, or bulbar, division and a spinal division. The distribution of the bulbar division is anatomically similar to that of the recurrent laryngeal nerve, whereas the spinal division courses in a more inferior direction and innervates the sternocleidomastoid and trapezius muscles of the neck.

The hypoglossal (XII) nerve is motor in function and innervates intrinsic musculature of the tongue as well as a number of extrinsic muscles of the tongue. Clearly this cranial nerve is important for speech production as well as such vegetative functions as chewing and swallowing. More specific discussion of the hypoglossal (XII) nerve is in Chapters 4, 5, and 6.

SPINAL NERVES

There are 31 pairs of spinal nerves. Each serves both sensory and motor functions in connecting the spinal cord and specific segments of the body. These specific segments are known as *dermatomes,* although they are not truly distinct, as there is overlap between contiguous dermatomes. In the periphery the sensory and motor components are joined and travel as a spinal nerve, but as the nerve gets close to the spinal cord it is divided into a dorsal and a ventral root. Sensory fibers enter the dorsal root, which includes a dorsal root ganglion consisting of collections of cell bodies. The dorsal horn gray matter of the spinal cord is a continuation of the dorsal root of the spinal nerve. Sensory information can be distributed up to higher levels in the CNS via connections from the dorsal horn to funiculi ascending in the white matter. Reflexes can be mediated by immediate connections from dorsal roots to ventral roots. The motor or ventral root consists of fibers whose cell bodies are located in the ventral horn gray matter of the spinal cord. These fibers are also responsive to input from descending motor fibers traveling in the white matter (funiculi) of the spinal cord.

This brief coverage of spinal nerves points out a number of important general characteristics. All spinal nerves have both sensory and motor components. This is different from cranial nerves in that some are motor, others are sensory, and the remaining are mixed. The sensory input always enters the spinal cord (and therefore the CNS) via the dorsal root, and the motor output always exits via the ventral root. The gray matter of the spinal cord contains interneurons that allow the functions of relaying sensory information to higher CNS levels, mediating reflexes, and connecting neurons in descending motor tracts with motor neurons that exit ventrally.

MOTOR AND SENSORY SYSTEMS

Up to this point parts of the nervous system have been discussed individually and in a superior-to-inferior progression. Such a piece-by-piece approach is necessary if one is to understand where a given structure is located and what other structures are located at that same horizontal level. Knowing where structures are and the names of their components is not useful, though, if one does not also grasp how various parts of the nervous system connect with each other so as to work in an integrated way to carry out specific functions or respond to specific stimulation. Therefore this chapter concludes with basic consideration of the vertically oriented systems responsible for skeletal muscle movement and the response of the nervous system to sensory stimulation.

DIRECT MOTOR SYSTEM

The direct motor system is vertically organized and consists of neurons whose cell bodies lie in the cortex on each side and whose axons project down to mediate the initiation and con-

trol of skilled voluntary movement. It was once thought that these cells originated in the precentral gyrus of each hemisphere, but this idea has been shown to be inaccurate (see Chapters 3 and 6 for more details). This system is usually referred to as the *pyramidal system,* and because the fibers originate from each hemisphere there is a right pyramidal tract and a left pyramidal tract. The pyramidal system can be further subdivided into the corticobulbar and corticospinal tracts. The *corticobulbar tract* consists of individual neurons, each descending from the cortex to the nuclei of one of the motor cranial nerves. These nuclei lie in the brainstem, and so the corticobulbar system does not extend beyond the inferior boundary of the medulla. The *corticospinal tract* consists of individual neurons that descend from the cortex in each cerebral hemisphere to the ventral horn gray matter of the spinal cord, where they innervate specific spinal nerves. Thus it can be seen that the superiormost parts of the system contain the fibers descending toward all the motor cranial nerves plus the motor neurons descending to all the spinal nerves. As the system descends, fibers exit at successive levels to synapse with their intended "target." These descending neurons are frequently referred to as upper motor neurons (UMNs) so that the terms pyramidal, corticospinal, corticobulbar, and UMN all refer in some way to this direct motor system.

The basic anatomy of the system is as follows. Each pyramidal tract arises from cells in the cortex of one hemisphere—hence there is a right and a left tract—and descend through the corona radiata in the telencephalon into the internal capsule in the diencephalon. The corona radiata consists of large masses of white matter composed of collections of motor fibers descending from the cortex and sensory fibers about to enter it from below. The internal capsule is similar to the corona radiata but is immediately inferior to it, and its fibers are concentrated in a smaller area. The pyramidal tract then enters the brainstem and descends through the cerebral peduncles of the midbrain, the ventral pons, and the pyramids of the medulla. As the left and right tracts pass through the brainstem, fibers exit from each side and synapse onto the nuclei of motor cranial nerves: oculomotor (III) and trochlear (IV) in the midbrain; abducens (VI) and facial (VII) in the pons; vagus (X), spinal accessory (XI), and hypoglossal (XII) in the medulla. At the caudal medulla all of the corticobulbar fibers have already exited and most of the corticospinal fibers on each side cross (decussate) to the other side. The crossed fibers descend in the lateral funiculi of the spinal cord and comprise the lateral corticospinal tract. The uncrossed fibers descend in the anterior funiculi and comprise the anterior corticospinal tract. The fact that most corticospinal fibers start on one side and then cross to the other side in the inferior medulla explains the primarily contralateral relation between limb movement and brain control.

INDIRECT MOTOR SYSTEM

Traditionally, the indirect motor control system has been referred to as the "extrapyramidal" system because the components of the system do not pass through the pyramids of the medulla. However, it is apparent that it is not a single system but, rather, a complex collection of connections between the cortex and other structures. Rather than initiate and generally guide skilled voluntary movement, as does the pyramidal system, the various components of the indirect system refine the accuracy of complex movements and inhibit unwanted movements. Lesions in this system thus yield deficits involving the accuracy or timing of an intended movement or the inability to control involuntary movement. To review all of the indirect pathways that are involved in movement is beyond the scope of a text directed at speech, hearing, and language. Therefore in this chapter the basic anatomic pathways involving the basal ganglia and the cerebellum in the control of movement are outlined. It should be stressed that pathways from the red nucleus, reticular formation, and vestibular nuclei extend down to spinal nerves (rubrospinal, reticulospinal, and vestibulospinal tracts, respectively), but, as important as they are, they have been omitted from this chapter.

The basal ganglia, as was noted previously, consist of the striatum (caudate nucleus and putamen) and the globus pallidus. When one considers the basal ganglia from the standpoint of motor control, the substantia nigra in the midbrain also must be included. The striatum receives input from the cerebral cortex and the substantia nigra, as well as from a number of thalamic nuclei. The major motor output from the basal ganglia is via the globus pallidus, and its major input is from the striatum. The globus pallidus sends motor output to a number of locations, including motor thalamic nuclei and several brainstem nuclei. The motor input to the thalamus is relayed up to the cortex, with reciprocal connections from the cortex back down to the striatum and then to the globus pallidus. One can see that it is a complex system of motor circuitry involving multiple levels of the brain (telencephalon, diencephalon, brainstem). It is made even more complicated by the fact that function of these circuits is based on a delicate balance among several neurotransmitters, including dopamine, acetylcholine and γ-aminobutyric acid (GABA). The net effect of the system is modulation of the output of the direct system. Lesions yield patterns of deficits characterized by reduced mobility (hypokinesia) or excess or involuntary mobility (hyperkinesia). This system and its role in movement is discussed in more detail in Chapters 3, 5, and 6. Aspects of indirect motor pathways and vestibular and auditory reflexes are considered in Chapters 7 and 8.

The cerebellum is an important structure in that it plays a major role in the coordination of groups of muscles during phasic movement, especially skilled phasic movement (speech is an excellent example). In brief, the cerebellum is able to receive sensory input (proprioceptive, somatic, vestibular) because of the cerebellar peduncles connecting it to the nuclei located in the brainstem. The cerebellum responds to this input by sending motor output back to brainstem nuclei (from which further connections can be made) and to the motor cortex. The pathway to the cortex includes a synapse in the ventrolateral nucleus of the thalamus. Hence motor fibers from the basal ganglia and the cerebellum synapse in the thalamus. The cerebellum and its role in motor function are discussed in more detail in Chapters 3, 5, and 6. Figure 2-8 illustrates the indirect motor system.

BASIC SENSORY NEUROANATOMY

There are numerous types of sensation, and each type involves a complex series of struc-

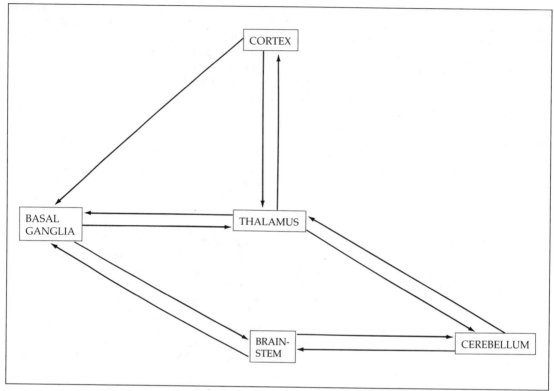

Fig. 2-8. Major components of the indirect motor system.

tures and connections. There is, however, a basic pattern to the way in which any type of sensation is dealt with in the nervous system, and it is this general pattern that is presented here.

The basic pattern consists essentially of a three-neuron chain. The first neuron includes sensory receptors that detect stimulation and translate it into a neural response. The neural response is conducted along either a spinal sensory or cranial sensory nerve (depending on the type and site of stimulation) toward the CNS. These sensory, or afferent, neurons then synapse onto nuclei of the second part in the chain. The second-order neural response is conducted up the spinal cord if it came in a spinal nerve or directly into the brainstem if arrival was via a cranial nerve. All second-order neural responses eventually course through the brainstem, primarily traveling in the medial and lateral lemnisci and into the diencephalon, where there is a synapse with sensory nuclei in the

thalamus. The only sensation that does not involve a synapse in the thalamus is smell via the olfactory (I) nerve. The third part of the chain is the thalamocortical connection. Fibers travel from the thalamus up through the internal capsule, then the corona radiata, and finally to the appropriate primary sensory area in the cortex.

It must be emphasized that this three-part chain is the minimal organizational structure for transmitting sensation. As afferent fibers travel up they may make additional connections in the brainstem, and these connections, in turn, allow input to the cerebellum and reciprocal descending activity via tracts such as the rubrospinal, tectospinal, reticulospinal, and others. Similarly, it must be emphasized that sensation is not merely being relayed up to the brain. There is considerable processing, gating, and intersensory integration going on at subcortical levels. Concepts regarding sensation are presented in more detail in Chapters 3, 7, and 8.

CONCLUSION

An attempt has been made to familiarize the reader who is new to neuroanatomy with concepts regarding the names of structures and where they are located. A systematic approach that groups structures on horizontal axes helps one remember where structures are relative to each other and relative to major landmarks. Organizing neuroanatomic structures along vertical axes allows one to appreciate complicated sensory systems and all the reactions a sensation may bring about as it travels through the nervous system. Such organizational concepts also allow one to better appreciate complicated motor systems and why movement can be lost, increased, or reduced in accuracy and coordination depending on the level of the lesion. Once armed with the concepts of horizontal levels, vertical levels, the names of major structures, and the basic components of the various nervous systems, one can proceed to studying specific types of function in detail.

BIBLIOGRAPHY

Chusid, J. G. *Correlative Neuroanatomy and Functional Neurology* (19th ed.). Los Altos, CA: Lange, 1985.

Curtis, B. A., Jacobson, S., and Marcus, E. M. *An Introduction to the Neurosciences*. Philadelphia: Saunders, 1972.

Daube, J. R., and Sandok, B. A. *Medical Neurosciences*. Boston: Little, Brown, 1978.

Gardner, E. *Fundamentals of Neurology* (6th ed.). Philadelphia: Saunders, 1975.

Liebman, M. *Neuroanatomy Made Easy and Understandable* (2nd ed.). Baltimore: University Park Press, 1983.

McKeough, M. *The Coloring Review of Neuroscience*. Boston: Little, Brown, 1982.

Netter, F. H. *The CIBA Collection of Medical Illustrations, Vol. I: Nervous System; Part I: Anatomy and Physiology*. West Caldwell, NJ: Ciba Pharmaceutical Co., 1983.

Noback, C. R. *The Human Nervous System*. New York: McGraw-Hill, 1967.

Noback, C. R., and Demarest, R. J. *The Human Nervous System: Basic Principles of Neurobiology* (3rd ed.). New York: McGraw-Hill, 1981.

Patton, H. D., Sundsten, J. W., Crill, W. E., and Swanson, P. D. *Introduction to Basic Neurology*. Philadelphia: Saunders, 1976.

Weiner, W. J., and Goetz, C. G. (eds.). *Neurology for the Non-Neurologist*. Philadelphia: Harper & Row, 1981.

CHAPTER 3

Basic Neurophysiology

Charles R. Larson

❏ Membranes

❏ Synapses

❏ Muscle

❏ Sensory Mechanisms

❏ Higher Functions

To understand neurologic disorders affecting complex behaviors such as speech and language, it is essential to understand basic neurophysiologic mechanisms, including neuron membrane properties, synaptic function, and reflex mechanisms. This chapter begins with the molecular structure of nerve membranes and current understanding of the functions of these molecules. It then progresses through a discussion of how individual nerve cells function and how cells interact at the synapse. The chapter then treats mechanisms of muscular contraction and the neural control thereof. Some sensory structures thought to be important in control of muscle contraction and the general issue of motor coordination are presented, but many other types of sensory receptors are ignored. The chapter concludes with discussions of the roles of major divisions of the central nervous system in motor coordination.

MEMBRANES

STRUCTURE

Membranes of all living cells share some common functions, the most obvious being to maintain the integrity of the intracellular constituents (cytoplasm). Hand in hand with this function is that of prohibiting, or at least reducing, the ability of external substances from entering the cell. Membranes of cells are described as being "semipermeable" because some particles can pass through them whereas others cannot. Membranes are also found within the cells, surrounding the cell nucleus and other parts of the cell such as mitochondria.

Two major types of molecule compose cell membranes, the first being phospholipid molecules. These molecules are composed of a fat (lipid) portion and a phosphate group. Together, these components take a form resembling a clothespin with an enlarged head region and two smaller strands extending like legs from the head. One end of this molecule has an affinity for water (hydrophilic) and the other end for oil (hydrophobic). In a water solution containing such molecules, the molecules would have a natural tendency to align themselves as two thin sheets (bilayer) such that the hydrophobic ends would face each other toward the middle of the membrane, and the hydrophilic ends would face outward toward the water interface found outside and inside the cell (Fig. 3-1). In this way the phospholipid molecules form much of the membrane wall of cells (Stein, 1980).

In the most primitive type of cell, the membrane may serve only the function of enclosing the cell contents, which is accomplished by the phospholipid molecules. Most cells, however, must interact with the environment. For this purpose the second major type of molecule comprising cell membranes has evolved: the complex protein molecules. For the purpose of this discussion, protein molecules are organized into four groups.

The first group, *structural proteins*, may have no other function than to help maintain the integrity of the membrane. The phospholipid molecules themselves exist in a fluid state, and the structural protein molecules help to hold them together. The remaining types of protein molecules are more important as far as nerve cells are concerned.

Pump proteins, the second major type of protein molecule, are important in maintaining the correct balance of ions (electrically charged particles) on either side of the membrane wall. These molecules are adenosine triphosphate (ATP) pumps, meaning they utilize energy stored in phosphate bonds and "actively" transport ions from inside to outside the cell, or vice versa. The structure of pump proteins is unknown, but their functions have been deduced from electrophysiologic experiments. The most important pump protein molecule to be discussed is the sodium (Na)-potassium (K) exchange pump, which helps maintain the correct balance of Na and K ions on either side of the membrane.

The third important type of protein molecule found in nerve cells is called a *channel protein*. Channel proteins extend from the inner surface of the membrane to the outer surface, and a pore through the center of the channel forms a means of communication between the inside and the outside of the cell (Fig. 3-1). The details of the structure of the wall of the pore through the channel are unknown, but through genetic cloning experiments and by the application of

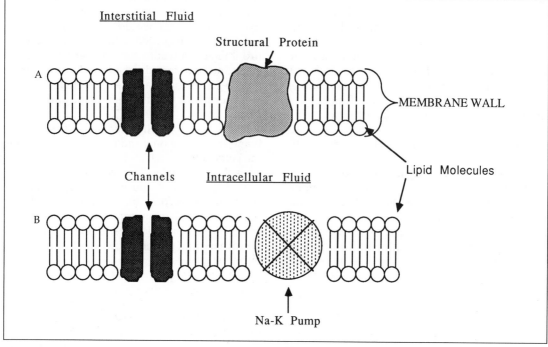

Fig. 3-1. Some of the main types of molecule found in nerve cell membranes. For details see text.

pharmacologic agents it is known that the pores must consist of hydrophilic amino acid chains and are filled with water. An important property of channel proteins is their "gating" ability. *Gating* refers to the property of either increasing or decreasing the ability of certain ions to pass through the channel, much like a swinging door. Unfortunately, the precise mechanisms and structure of the gates are unknown, although several models have been proposed (Hille, 1984).

Channels are named after the type of ion for which they are most selective. An Na channel is most selective for Na ions; in the open state, they mainly allow Na ions to pass through and inhibit the passage of other types of ions. In many instances, channels are not totally selective, and hence some ions "leak" through. Channels are also sensitive to some types of energy, which cause them to change their state. Most channel proteins to be discussed are sensitive to an electrical potential (voltage) and readily gate, or change, their state (from closed to open) when a suitable voltage change occurs. An important feature of channel proteins is that the conformational change triggered by the

voltage is not dependent on energy metabolism. One may think, therefore, of a channel opening and closing much like the operation of a transistor, which changes states in response to voltages. Although present research suggests that there are not too many types of Na channels in vertebrates, there appear to be scores of K and chloride (Cl) channels (Hille, 1984).

The last type of protein to be discussed is the *receptor*. In some ways receptors act much like channel proteins, and in some cases it appears they may be an integral part of a larger complex of channel proteins. The distinguishing characteristic of receptor proteins is that their state is altered (from closed to open) by the attachment of a specific molecule. The most widely studied receptor molecule is the acetylcholine receptor found at the vertebrate nerve–muscle junction. Here a neurotransmitter substance (acetylcholine) acts as the agent to bind with the receptor and causes a conformational change in the receptor protein. The channel then allows passage of certain types of ions.

MEMBRANE POTENTIALS

RESTING POTENTIAL

Fluids contained inside (intracellular) and outside (interstitial) cells contain charged particles called *ions*. Ions in fact comprise all matter. Ions have an electrically positive or negative charge depending on the relative balance of protons ($+$) and electrons ($-$) comprising them. Normally, substances such as Na, K, or Cl always have a positive or negative charge. Thus Na is usually written as Na^+, K as K^+, and Cl as Cl^-. Calcium (Ca) has two positive charges and is written as Ca^{2+}. If equal numbers of positive and negative ions coexist in a medium, that medium has a neutral charge; but if positive ions predominate, the medium is positively charged. In living cells, different types of ions are found in greater or lesser concentrations on either side of cell membranes. K^+ ions are in greater concentrations inside cells, and Cl^- and Na^+ ions are in greater concentrations outside cells. Inside cells there are also found high concentrations of large negatively charged ions called anions (A^-). Because of the relative concentrations of the various ion types, intracellular fluid is normally negatively charged with respect to interstitial fluid. For nerve and muscle cells, the electrical potential (voltage) measured inside with respect to outside the cell is in the range of -60 to -90 millivolts (mV). This voltage is termed the *resting membrane potential* (Em). Because the membrane potential is dependent on the relative concentrations of intracellular and extracellular ions, it is possible to express the Em mathematically. The Nernst equation describes the *equilibrium potential* (Ek) for a single ionic species based on the relative concentrations of intracellular and extracellular ions. Ek is that potential wherein the net forces acting to drive the ions across the membrane equal each other; it is described next.

In terms of neural membranes, the two paramount forces acting to drive ions across the membrane are those resulting from concentration gradients (diffusion) and those from electrostatic forces. Regarding a single ion species, if a concentration gradient exists across a membrane, ions tend to flow from the area of high concentration to low concentration. Thus given sufficient time and lack of opposing forces, ions diffuse across the membrane (assuming it is permeable to that ion), and eventually concentrations of that ion equilibrate across the membrane. The electrostatic force results from the physical attraction of plus and minus charges. Conversely, charges of like polarity repel each other. Considering an ion species such as K^+, a high concentration of intracellular ions tend to force them out, whereas the negative charge inside the cell tends to hold K^+ charges inside and attract K^+ charges from outside the cell. Starting from an initial time (zero) with high internal K^+ concentrations, K^+ ions diffuse out of the cell. Concurrently, the negative intracellular charge tends to hold K^+ charges inside the cell. With the departure of K^+ ions from the cell, the net force of diffusion diminishes as the electrostatic force increases (the loss of positive charges creates a more negative charge). Eventually, the two forces equal each other, there is no additional net movement of K^+ ions, and K^+ is said to be in a state of equilibrium. The Ek of an ion species exists when diffusion forces equal electrostatic forces.

By measuring the Ek for Na^+, it has been found that Na^+ ions are far from equilibrium with respect to the resting membrane potential. That is, the inside concentrations of Na^+ ions are low and yet the concentration gradient and electrostatic forces should force Na^+ ions inside the membrane. The most widely accepted reason for this imbalance is the Na^+ pump or the Na^+-K^+ exchange pump. The pump carries about three Na^+ ions outside the cell for every two K^+ ions carried inside. It may seem pointless for the pump to exchange Na^+ and K^+ ions across the membrane, but this mechanism actually helps to establish the resting membrane potential. Consider that a pump that extrudes Na^+ also carries K^+ ions into the cell. Because membranes are about 50 times more permeable to K^+ than to Na^+, K^+ ions are continually diffusing out through the membrane even though the pump carries them inward. As K^+ leaves the cell by its own diffusion, the loss of positive charges creates a negative charge inside the cell. Thus it is important to realize that the pump does not separate charges, but the charge separation results from the outward diffusion of K^+ ions. As will become evident later, the pump also maintains low internal concentrations of Na^+. There is thus a steep concentration gradient for Na^+ ions, and the negative internal electrical charge creates a strong force acting to attract Na⁺ ions inside the cell (Ruch and Patton, 1965; Stein, 1980). Figure 3-2A illustrates the relative concentrations of different types of ions both inside and outside a cell. The size of the symbols denotes the relative concentrations of the ions.

ACTION POTENTIALS

Nerve and muscle·cells act similarly to other cells insofar as maintenance of the resting membrane potential is concerned. The uniqueness of nerve and muscle cells with respect to other types of cells is that they are excitable and capable of transmitting impulses along the length of the cell. When a nerve or muscle cell is excited, the transmembrane voltage changes from the resting state to an active state momentarily.

The change to the active state, known as the *action potential*, is a result of the gating of excitable ion channels and movement of ions across the membrane, which are driven by electrostatic and diffusion forces. To understand action potentials, it is first necessary to understand the passive electrical properties of membranes. For this discussion, nerve membranes are consid-

Fig. 3-2. A. Concentrations of ions found inside and outside cells. The relative size of the symbol denotes its concentration. Large symbols indicate large concentrations of a particular type of ion. The large arrow indicates that Na⁺ ions are not in a state of equilibrium and are driven by both concentration gradients and electrostatic forces into the cell. B. The charge along a membrane varies as a function of time and distance. Each of the curves (t = 1, 2, 3, and 4) shows how the charge at any point on the membrane increases as a function of time. Similarly, the distance along the membrane increases as a function of time.

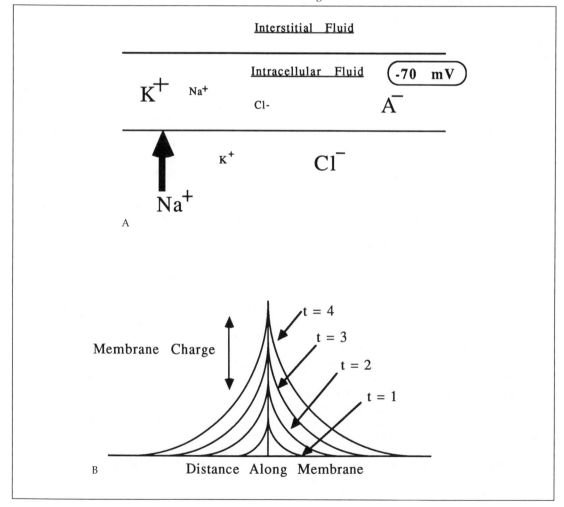

ered to act like a piece of copper wire or cable, thus exhibiting "cable properties."

The mixture of ions and fluid inside and outside cells acts as an electrical conductor. This same mixture also has some resistance to the flow of electrical current. Electrical current flow can be described as the movement of ions through a medium. Ordinarily, a single ion does not travel far before it collides with another ion, thus propelling the second one into motion. In the process, the first ion loses some energy in the form of heat. All conductors have some electrical resistance, and materials differ in their relative amounts of resistance. Nerve cell membranes offer considerably more resistance to current flow than do the surrounding fluids. Also, because the membrane separates charges, it may be described as a capacitor. (A capacitor is an electrical device that separates charges.) If a microelectrode is placed inside a nerve fiber and is connected to an electrical source such that current flows through the electrode, most current flows along the length of the fiber rather than across the membrane. As current flows along the fiber, energy is gradually lost as a result of the internal resistance of the fiber, and such loss is a function of the length of the fiber and its diameter. Large-diameter fibers, like large copper wires, have low internal resistance, and hence an electrical current travels farther than a similar current source in a small fiber.

At the same time that ions travel longitudinally along the fiber, some are attracted to oppositely charged ions across the membrane wall. Thus ions tend to collect along the wall of the membrane. Positively charged ions on the inside of the membrane are attracted to negatively charged ions outside the membrane. Positively charged ions outside the membrane are repelled from the membrane, and so there is movement of positive ions away from the outside of the membrane wall. This movement is called *capacitive current flow* because ions do not travel through the membrane but merely release like charges on the opposite side of the membrane. The collection of positive charges on the inside of the membrane is called *charging* the membrane, which is necessary before an action potential (AP) can be generated.

As described above, the introduction of an electrical stimulus inside a fiber causes internal longitudinal current flow and capacitive current flow across the membrane. The distance along the membrane that current flows and the time required to "charge" a unit of membrane are known, respectively, as the "time" and "space" constants of the membrane. Figure 3-2B illustrates the relation between the amount of charge along the membrane as a function of time and distance. With greater time, more charge builds up at any one point along the membrane and spreads a farther distance along the membrane. It is important to understand that these "cable" properties are determined by the size of the fiber, which determines the longitudinal resistance to current flow. For a given amount of time, current flows farther and charges a greater area of membrane in a large fiber than the same current source in a small fiber.

The "charging" of the membrane changes the voltage potential across the membrane. Given an initial resting membrane potential of -70 mV (internal negative), an electrical stimulus causes the membrane to depolarize, or move toward 0 mV. When the voltage reaches a value of approximately -55 mV, threshold is reached and the AP is generated. *Threshold* is a term referring to the level of depolarization at which an AP is generated. The threshold level of various types of nerve and muscle cells varies somewhat. At threshold, the initiation of the AP can be clearly understood only by an analysis of the ion channels in the membrane wall. Hodgkin and Huxley (1952) provided the first comprehensive description of the events involved in generation and propagation of the AP. Since then, some refinements and changes have been made in the theory, but for the purposes of this chapter the original Hodgkin and Huxley model suffices to explain the AP.

As previously mentioned, ion channels increase their permeability to a particular ion type (gating) in the presence of a change in voltage. In the case of nerve cells, when threshold is reached Na^+ channels suddenly open and Na^+ ions are allowed to pass easily through. Recall that there is a large concentration of Na^+ ions outside the membrane; and because they are positively charged and the inside of the membrane is negatively charged, the Na^+ ions are driven through the channels into the cell. Figure 3-3A illustrates the flow of Na^+ ions toward and through the membrane at the point of the AP. At that point, the large concentration of Na^+ ions makes that region of the membrane positively charged. Figure 3-3B provides a tem-

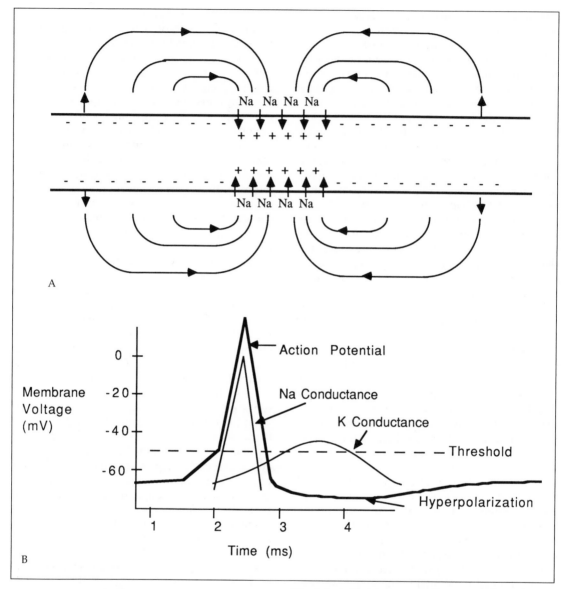

A

B

Membrane
Voltage
(mV)

Action Potential

Na Conductance

K Conductance

Threshold

Hyperpolarization

Time (ms)

Fig. 3-3. A. Na⁺ ion current flow across the membrane wall creates a positively charged area at the point of the action potential. Na⁺ ions are drawn to the membrane by current paths and are driven through the membrane by a concentration gradient and electrostatic charge. B. Action potential, Na conductance, and K conductance curves as a function of time. Dashed line indicates the relative magnitude of threshold voltage, or that level of depolarization at which an action potential is triggered. The curves for Na and K conductance are not drawn to scale on the ordinate, but merely reflect the relative timing of their changes.

poral description of the AP, and Na⁺ and K⁺ conductance changes through the membrane. As Na⁺ ions pass through the membrane, the inside of the fiber becomes more positive, causing more Na⁺ channels to open, thus allowing more Na⁺ ions to pass through. This regenerative process is known as the Hodgkin cycle. Hodgkin and Huxley originally described the opening of Na⁺ channels in terms of three events (presumably three mechanisms of the Na⁺ channels), but it has since been disputed. As can be seen in Figure 3-3, while the Na⁺

permeability is increasing, the membrane potential becomes more positive and eventually reaches a value of approximately $+20$ mV. Thus the Na^+ ions are being driven toward their equilibrium potential of $+60$ mV. The latter potential is not reached, however, which may be explained by the following processes.

At about the time that the membrane potential reaches its peak (approximately $+20$ mV), Na^+ permeability suddenly decreases and falls to 0. This decrease in Na^+ permeability is known as *inactivation* and is controlled by mechanisms of the Na^+ channels. It is important to realize that inactivation is not merely closing of the open channels; it is a separate process. During the period of inactivation, the Na^+ channels cannot reopen, and this time is called the "absolute refractory period." The inactivation of Na^+ channels and the drop in Na^+ permeability is in part responsible for the drop in the curve representing the AP of Figure 3-3B. The mechanisms of channel gating and inactivation are currently unknown.

Referring again to Figure 3-3, note that the curve representing K^+ conductance rises more slowly than that of Na^+ and has a much longer time course. These different temporal properties imply that the mechanisms of Na^+ and K^+ gating must be vastly different. Because K^+ is found in high concentrations inside the cell, and at the time of K^+ channel opening the membrane is at least partly depolarized, it becomes evident that K^+ ions pass through their channels out of the cell driven by diffusion and electrostatic forces. This efflux of K^+ is partly responsible for the rapid repolarization of the membrane on the tailing edge of the action potential. It is also known that the elevated K^+ conductance following the AP causes the membrane potential to become more negative or hyperpolarized. During this lengthy period of hyperpolarization, known as the "relative refractory period," another AP may be generated but only by a stronger stimulus than that required with the membrane at the normal resting membrane potential.

At the beginning of this discussion of the mechanisms involved in the generation of APs, it was imagined that a stimulus was introduced with a microelectrode inside the cell. Because this artificial event occurs only in the laboratory, it is necessary to consider normal mechanisms. To understand the generation of APs requires a discussion of synaptic and receptor events,

which appears later in this chapter, but for now think of an existing AP at an instant in time on a nerve fiber. This AP acts as a stimulus itself for adjacent regions of the membrane. Indeed, the AP sets up a flow of current along the length of the membrane and so charges adjacent regions of the membrane capacitively. That is, charges of opposite polarity build up on either side of the membrane. When the potential in adjacent regions reaches threshold, Na^+ channels open, and the AP is generated. This process repeats itself for every segment of the fiber. In this way, the AP is propagated along the entire length of the fiber.

Before proceeding with a discussion of AP conduction velocity in fibers, it is appropriate to review some of the implications of the above discussion. First, when an axon is depolarized and an AP is generated, the AP always causes complete depolarization of the membrane. Because the magnitude of APs does not vary, even though the stimulus initiating them may change in strength, AP amplitude does not convey information; it is only the frequency of APs that carries information in the nervous system. Second, the absolute and relative refractory periods during and following an AP prohibit APs from being conducted backward along a fiber (unless artificially stimulated in the laboratory). Third, the generation of APs relies on relatively simple, passive physical factors (gating of channels and flow of ions through channels) rather than on the utilization of metabolic energy, thereby reducing the energy requirements of the organism enormously.

ACTION POTENTIAL CONDUCTION

Recall from the discussion of cable properties that for a large-diameter fiber current flows farther and charges units of membrane more rapidly than in a small-diameter fiber. Therefore in the large fiber adjacent regions are charged sooner than in small fibers. Consequently, APs are propagated more rapidly in large fibers than in small fibers. In fact, in unmyelinated fibers AP conduction velocity increases with the square root of the diameter of the fiber. In other words, one fiber conducts an AP twice as fast as a fiber one-fourth as large.

Unmyelinated fibers are rather rare in higher forms of animal life, and it appears that myelinated fibers have evolved to increase AP conduction velocity without greatly enlarging the

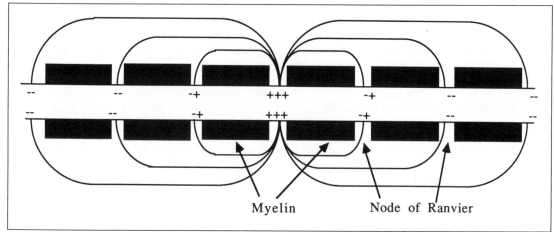

Myelin   Node of Ranvier

Fig. 3-4. Saltatory conduction. At the center of the fiber there is an action potential with a concentration of positively charged ions. Current flows from this node to other nodes to charge them. When adjacent nodes are charged, the channels open and an action potential is generated there.

diameter of fibers. Myelin is a fatty substance wrapped tightly around fibers, thereby insulating them from interstitial fluid. In the internodal regions of the membrane (that part covered with myelin) the membrane acts as a poor capacitor, and hence it is difficult to charge a membrane at these locations. Interspersed along the membrane are breaks in the myelin known as the nodes of Ranvier. There is a much higher concentration of channels at the nodes than in the internodal regions, and the membrane is a much better capacitor at the nodes. When a stimulus (or an AP) is applied to a fiber, current paths follow the length of the membrane, and ions build up only along the membrane wall at the nodes where oppositely charged ions lie across the membrane (Fig. 3-4). Thus charging occurs only at the nodes, where the channels are also located. A stimulus therefore triggers an AP at a node, and an AP at a node depolarizes (charges) only adjacent nodes. When threshold is reached at adjacent nodes, ion channels open, and the AP is generated. The AP may then be said to "hop" from one node to another, a process called saltatory conduction. Because the internodal regions are not charged, more ions build up at the nodes, and time is not spent charging the internodal regions. Thus APs, by hopping from node to node, travel at a much higher velocity than in unmyelinated fibers. The speed of conduction in myelinated fibers is directly proportional to fiber diameter.

As discussed above, the separation of charged particles across membranes creates a potential across the membranes, and the voltage-sensitive channels then selectively allow certain ions to pass through the membrane and create the AP, which is then propagated along the length of the fiber. It is important to keep in mind that voltage changes would not spread far in fibers were it not for the AP. The AP is regenerated at each node, and this process can be likened to an amplifier that recurrently boosts the strength of a signal. When the AP reaches the end of a fiber, an entirely different mechanism is responsible for transmitting the signal to adjacent cells.

SYNAPSES

NEUROMUSCULAR JUNCTION

When an AP reaches the axon terminals or synapse, it triggers the release of a chemical substance, known as a *neurotransmitter,* which flows across a space (synaptic cleft) and then either excites or inhibits the next cell (postsynaptic cell). This process is called *synaptic transmission.* Synapses are exceedingly important in the nervous system because they are the only mechanism for communication between neurons. Synapses are also important because they can modulate the flow of impulses; they can either cause an increase in the number of APs or reduce the number of APs generated in the postsynaptic cell. Many neurologic diseases have their etiology in excessive or deficient quantities of one or more neurotransmitters, and many drugs have an effect by modulating synaptic activity. Because synaptic transmission is an integral part of both normal and disordered neurologic function and because of its importance in understanding pharmacologic effects, it has considerable relevance to neurogenic communicative disorders and is therefore discussed in some detail in the following section.

The most widely studied and best understood synapse is the vertebrate neuromuscular junction. This model is used for discussing synapses in general. The synapse includes the enlarged region of the axon terminal, the endfoot or endplate, the membrane of the adjacent postsynaptic cell, and the synaptic cleft separating the two cell membranes. The transmitter substance at neuromuscular junctions is acetylcholine (ACh). Both the presynaptic and postsynaptic membranes of the synapse are specialized for their essential roles. Figure 3-5 illustrates the primary structural features of synapses and the chain of events that occur during synaptic transmission. The presynaptic endplate has within it tiny spherical structures known as vesicles and a densely staining region known as the active region. The postsynaptic membrane contains many receptors or receptor proteins, as described above. Because of the specialized pre- and postsynaptic membranes, synaptic transmission is unidirectional.

When an AP arrives at the endplate, a series of events occur that lead to synaptic transmission. The first event is the opening of Ca channels, which allows Ca^{2+} ions to enter the cell. The exact role of Ca^{2+} in synaptic transmission is unknown, but it may facilitate attachment of vesicles to the presynaptic membrane. If Ca^{2+} is not present, synaptic function is reduced or eliminated. It is generally believed that ACh is stored in the vesicles; and when Ca^{2+} enters the endplate, vesicles move toward the active zone where they attach themselves to the presynaptic membrane. Once attached, the vesicles open up into the synaptic cleft, and the ACh is released (exocytosis) into the cleft. Following

exocytosis, the vesicles move away from the membrane wall (endocytosis) and form spherical vesicles again. In the process of endocytosis, it is believed that the vesicles may take up loose molecules of ACh remaining close to the presynaptic membrane.

The synaptic cleft is a space of about 20 nanometers wide, which the ACh molecules traverse in about 100 microseconds and then attach to a receptor. When two ACh molecules attach to a receptor, they cause increased permeability for Na^+ and K^+ ions that results in depolarization of the postsynaptic membrane. When an AP initiates synaptic action, several vesicles undergo exocytosis and thereby excite most if not all of the receptors. The combined depolarization produced by all active receptors is called a miniature endplate potential (MEPP). A single MEPP is insufficient to generate a muscle AP, but there are usually several MEPPs produced in each muscle fiber.

A motoneuron (MN) is a neuron found within the brainstem or spinal cord and sends its axon out to a group of muscle fibers within a muscle. Each MN axon divides into many smaller branches (fascicles), each ending in an endplate. An AP in an MN axon travels to each endplate simultaneously and synaptically produces MEPPs at each synapse. Since a MEPP is a small, localized depolarization in the postsynaptic cell, the spread of depolarizing current is dictated by the cable properties of the postsynaptic cell. If several MEPPs occur near the same place on the membrane, the depolarizing current summates and depolarizes a region of the muscle cell sufficiently to generate a muscle AP. The muscle AP, like an axonal AP, is a regenerative process that is propagated along the full length of the muscle cell (or fiber).

Another important aspect of synaptic function is the elimination of excessive ACh from the synaptic area. Not all ACh attaches to receptor sites, and those excess molecules could reexcite receptors that had already been excited by an AP. In such a situation, a single MN AP could cause repetitive, and uncontrolled, muscle contractions. Excessive ACh is eliminated by diffusion into the extracellular space; there is some reuptake of ACh by the presynaptic membrane; and another chemical, acetylcholinesterase (AChE), recaptures choline for further synthesis into ACh by the presynaptic cell. Some drugs (e.g., Prostigmin) block the action of AChE and allow ACh to remain at the synapse

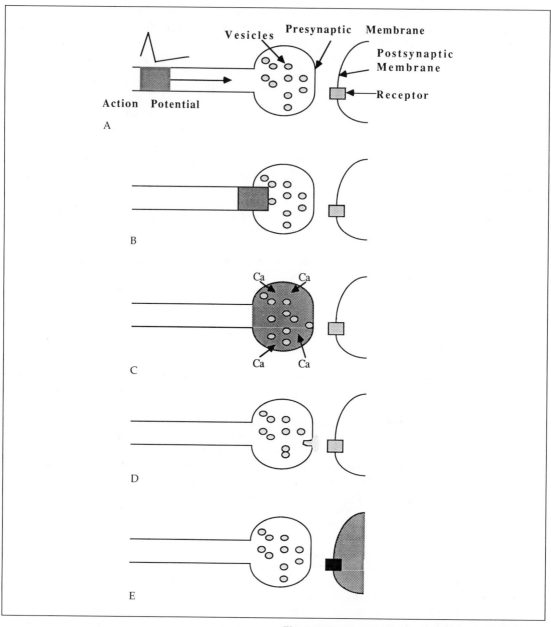

Fig. 3-5. Sequence of events during normal synaptic transmission. Depolarized membranes are indicated by shading. A. Action potential approaches the axon terminal. B. Action potential arrives at end plate. C. Entry of calcium ions causes vesicles to attach to presynaptic membrane. D. Exocytosis. Neurotransmitter enters synaptic cleft. E. Neurotransmitter binds with receptor. Depolarization of postsynaptic membrane.

longer, which leads to greater endplate potential and hence greater muscle strength (Kandel and Schwartz, 1985). Drugs such as curare compete with ACh for receptor sites and can thereby block neuromuscular transmission and cause paralysis. Myasthenia gravis is a disease of the neuromuscular junction in which antibodies react with the ACh receptors and reduce the number of available receptor sites. When ACh is released by the presynaptic membrane, there are fewer receptor sites available, the postsynaptic endplate potential is reduced in amplitude, fewer muscle action potentials are generated, and there is a reduction in muscle strength.

CENTRAL NERVOUS SYSTEM SYNAPSES

In many ways central nervous system (CNS) synapses are similar to the neuromuscular junction (NMJ), but there are some important differences as well. With CNS synapses, a neurotransmitter traverses the synaptic cleft to bind with receptors on the postsynaptic membrane, as with the NMJ. However, there are many transmitter substances other than ACh in the CNS, but each cell produces only one type; this property is known as Dale's law. Also, CNS synapses may be either excitatory or inhibitory, whereas the NMJ is always excitatory. Excitatory synapses produce excitatory postsynaptic potentials (EPSPs), and inhibitory synapses produce inhibitory postsynaptic potentials (IPSPs). Like MEPPs, EPSPs and IPSPs are small, localized, nonpropagated potentials and may be understood on the basis of receptor proteins and the flow of ions across the membrane (Kandel and Schwartz, 1985).

In an excitatory CNS synapse, an EPSP causes depolarization in the postsynaptic cell by simultaneously opening channels for both Na^+ and K^+ ions. Na^+ and K^+ ions then flow toward their equilibrium potentials, the algebraic sum of which is close to -20 mV. Like MEPPs (which are found only in muscle cells), each EPSP is small (2 to 3 mV) and lasts a few milliseconds. Therefore in most cases a single EPSP does not depolarize a cell to threshold. It requires many EPSPs occurring in close temporal and spatial proximity to depolarize a membrane to threshold. The addition of EPSPs in time is known as temporal summation; spatial summation refers to their summation over an area of the membrane.

The mechanisms of IPSPs are different from EPSPs. One way in which IPSPs function is that they cause an increase in permeability of both K^+ and Cl^-. Because the equilibrium potential of each ion species is near the resting membrane potential, the summation does not drastically alter the membrane potential. This action does, however, cause stabilization of the membrane near the equilibrium potential. The explanation of stabilization (or shunting) goes as follows. If many channels in a given area of membrane open, the electrical resistance across that area is reduced. According to Ohm's law ($E = I R$), if resistance (R) is reduced, a given synaptic input current (I) produces less membrane depolarization (E). Another way in which IPSPs function is by opening channels that allow increased permeability of just K^+. In this case, the membrane is hyperpolarized, and it becomes more difficult to generate an AP.

Another form of inhibition is known as presynaptic inhibition. To understand this mechanism, it is necessary to know that the amount of transmitter substance released at a synapse is proportional to the absolute size of the AP. (Although the peak voltage of an AP remains roughly constant, the *absolute size* may vary depending on whether the membrane was partially depolarized or hyperpolarized before the onset of the AP.) A small AP causes release of lesser amounts of transmitter substance. It also should be realized that synapses often occur between an axon of one cell and an axon of a second cell near the latter's endplate. Excitation at such a synapse causes partial depolarization of the second cell's axon and endplate. If an AP arrives at the second cell's endplate while it is partially depolarized, the amount of transmitter substance released by that cell is less than normal. With reduced amounts of transmitter substance released, the postsynaptic cell is depolarized less, thereby reducing its chances of triggering an AP in the postsynaptic cell.

When considering the interactions of cells through synapses, it is important to keep in mind that a given cell may receive synaptic input from thousands of other cells, a property called *convergence*. Also, an axon from a single cell may branch and form synapses with many other cells, a property called *divergence*. It should also be kept in mind that a cell receives IPSPs and EPSPs from different sources. Many of the IPSPs and EPSPs are active simultaneously. If many more EPSPs are active, the cell will likely depolarize to threshold and produce an AP. If many IPSPs are active, chances of triggering an AP are reduced. Thus one can think of a cell as an "integrator" that constantly summates excitatory and inhibitory inputs; and whenever the excitatory inputs reach threshold, an AP is generated.

MUSCLE

STRUCTURE

Skeletel, or striated, muscles are important in that they provide the energy to move our limbs, enable us to breathe, phonate, and move our articulators. Other muscles of the blood vessels and gut (smooth muscle) are less important for the purposes of this book and are not discussed. The morphology of muscles may be understood by considering a large muscle, its components, and how the groups of molecules work together to produce movement or force. Figure 3-6 shows a large skeletal muscle composed of small bundles called fascicles. Each fascicle in turn is comprised of individual muscle fibers, or cells, composed of myofibrils. A myofibril is arranged in such a way that when viewed under a microscope it has a striated appearance. The light and dark bands are due to the regular arrangement of thin and thick filaments that make up the myofibrils. The filaments in turn are comprised of protein molecules. Figure 3-7 shows that the dark striations (A bands) are due to the arrangement of the thick filaments. The light bands (I bands) are due to the arrangement of thin filaments. In the middle of the I band is a narrow line called the Z line, which is thought to be a point of attachment of the actin filaments. The distance from one Z line to another is called a sarcomere and is the basic unit of muscle length. When a muscle changes its length, the sarcomeres also change their length.

To understand the mechanism of muscular contraction, it is necessary to know how the thick and thin filaments fit together. The thick filaments are made up of proteins called myosin. As can be seen in Figure 3-6, each myosin molecule is a long stand with a "head" region that is bent laterally. In a thick filament, there are many myosin molecules, each lined up with the tail in one direction and the head in the other. Furthermore, each head, or cross bridge, is at a staggered distance from adjacent molecules and is rotated at an angle of 60 degrees from the adjacent molecule. The thin filaments are made up of three molecules: actin, troponin, and tropomyosin. As seen in Figure 3-6, the combination of the molecules resembles a twisted double strand of beads. When viewed

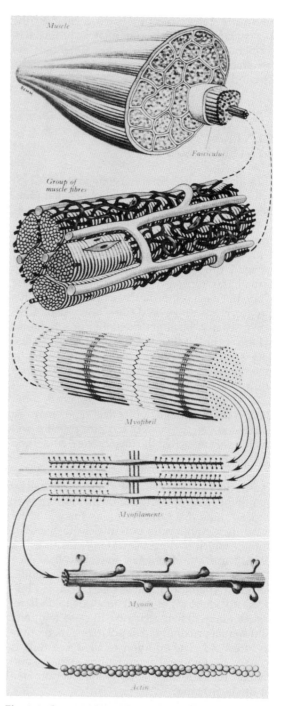

Fig. 3-6. Components of muscles. Proceeding from the top down, a muscle is composed of fasciculi, which are composed of groups of muscle fibers surrounded by networks of sarcoplasmic reticulum. Each muscle fiber is composed of numerous myofibrils composed of myofilaments (actin and myosin molecules). (From Warwick, R., and Williams, P. L. *Gray's Anatomy*, 35th British Edition. Edinburgh: Churchill-Livingstone, 1973. With permission.)

from the end (Fig. 3-7A), it may be seen that the thin and thick filaments form a hexagonal array. Each myosin molecule has cross bridges branching out in six directions and is surrounded by six thin filaments (Fig. 3-7A,B). Each thin filament is surrounded by three thick filaments. In the resting state it is believed the cross bridges are actually attached to the actin molecules.

SLIDING FILAMENT THEORY

The mechanisms of muscular contraction are now discussed in terms of the molecular events. The most widely accepted theory on muscle contraction is called the sliding filament theory. Returning again to the longitudinal view (Fig. 3-7), it can be seen that there is some overlap between the thin and thick filaments. Furthermore, cross bridges form a bond between the two filaments. According to this theory, when muscle contracts, the cross bridges release their bond with the actin molecules, rotate away from the tail end of the myosin molecule, rebond with another actin molecule, rotate toward the tail end, and release; and then the process repeats itself. Each time the cross bridge reattaches to an actin molecule and rotates, it pulls the actin molecule in one direction and the myosin molecule moves in the opposite direction. This process has been likened to a person pulling himself along a length of rope by grabbing it with his hands, releasing one hand, pulling with the other, regrasping, pulling, and so on. Another analogy is a rowing scull in which oars are pulled out of the water, rotated backward, dipped into the water, rotated forward, and then pulled out of the water again. The oars pull in one direction and the boat moves in the other. Because the thin filaments are attached to the Z lines, they are pulled toward each other and the sarcomere is shortened. In a muscle there are many sarcomeres situated end to end, and the shortening of each one results in the total length of the muscle becoming shorter by the combined length changes of all sarcomeres.

The process described above is the mechanical result of biochemical events resulting from a muscle AP. To fully understand muscle contraction, it is necessary to learn how nerve impulses become translated into muscle contraction. As discussed previously, an AP in a motoneuron arrives at the endplates of the axon filaments.

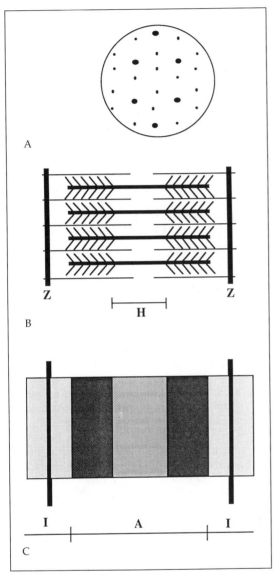

Fig. 3-7. A. Organization of actin and myosin molecules as seen from the end of a myofibril. Large dots represent myosin, and small dots represent actin molecules. B. Longitudinal representation of the arrangement of actin (thin lines) and myosin (thick lines) molecules in striated muscle. Diagonal lines between actin and myosin molecules represent cross bridges. C. Striations seen in a longitudinal view of striated muscle. This drawing is oriented with respect to the molecular arrangement seen in B to illustrate how the arrangement of molecules contributes to the striations. Z = line forming the point of attachment of actin molecules. The distance from one Z line to the next is a sarcomere. I band = region of actin molecules without cross bridges or overlap of myosin molecules. H band = center region of sarcomere where only myosin molecules may be seen. A band = region of sarcomere containing myosin molecules and overlap with actin molecules.

ACh is released at the neuromuscular junction; and it then travels across the synaptic cleft, binds with receptors, and leads to endplate potentials, which then summate and generate a muscle AP. In most skeletal muscle the endplates are located near the center of the length of muscle fibers. From here the muscle AP travels in each direction toward the end of the muscle fiber. As with nerve fibers, the characteristics of the membrane are important in the propagation of APs, for it is here that the voltage-sensitive channels are located. Muscle fiber membranes are unique in the sense that the surface is not smooth but has many invaginations. These invaginations result in tunnels, or tubules, that go right through the center of the fiber and are known as the transverse tubules, or T tubules. Inside the fiber, additional tubules branch off and link adjacent tubules, forming the sarcoplasmic reticulum (Fig. 3-6). It is thought that APs may be conducted at least part way through the T tubules, which if true would lead to APs being present inside the muscle fibers as well as on the outside surface.

Contained within the sarcoplasmic reticulum is a high concentration of Ca^{2+} ions. When a muscle AP is generated, Ca^{2+} ions from the sarcoplasmic reticulum move into the region of the myofibrils containing the actin and myosin molecules. The presence of Ca^{2+} ions initiates the muscle contraction process. Active metabolic energy then causes rotation of the cross bridges. As long as Ca^{2+} is present, this process continues. Each time a muscle receives an AP, it has been estimated that the cross bridges go through the series of rotations about 16 times, resulting in shortening of the sarcomere and a muscle twitch. After the AP has passed, Ca^{2+} returns to the sarcoplasmic reticulum, and muscle contraction ceases. The muscle then may return to its former length because of its internal elastic properties.

An important prediction made by the sliding filament theory is that strength of muscle contraction should be related to the number of active cross bridges. Because individual cross bridges are too small to be seen and their individual contributions to muscle strength cannot be measured, the length of the sarcomere has been measured and correlated with muscle strength. Figure 3-8 illustrates the results of an experiment done on frog muscle and shows the relation between sarcomere length and muscle tension. The inset of Fig. 3-8 illustrates the proposed arrangement of the thin and thick filaments that would account for the amount of overlap, numbers of active cross bridges, and the tension development. As can be seen, at long muscle lengths there is little overlap, and relatively few cross bridges are active. As the muscle gets shorter, there is greater overlap and more active cross bridges, and the muscle produces more tension. At very short muscle lengths, muscle tension falls off again, presumably because of some nonlinearity in the sliding filaments and the number of active cross bridges. One suggestion for this nonlinearity is that at shorter lengths the thin and perhaps the thick filaments extend into the next sarcomere, thus interfering with cross bridge formation.

MOTOR UNIT

Before explaining how single twitches relate to muscle contraction in general terms, it is necessary to introduce new concepts. The basic unit of muscle function is the *motor unit*. A motor unit (MU) is comprised of a single motoneuron (MN), its axon, and all the muscle fibers it innervates. Most skeletal muscles contain thousands of muscle fibers but many fewer MUs. A single MU may have a few hundred muscle fibers, as in the case of muscles of the thigh, back, trunk, or other muscles for which fine control is not crucial. On the other hand, muscles controlling the fingers, eyeball, and larynx may have as few as ten muscle fibers per MU. In the latter types of muscle, movement can be controlled very finely. Thus there is a relation between the size of an MU (expressed as the number of muscle fibers per axon) and the amount of control over a muscle. This relation has been expressed as the innervation ratio. Properly defined, the *innervation ratio* refers to the number of muscle fibers in a muscle divided by the number of axons in the motor nerve to that muscle. The result is the average number of muscle fibers innervated by a single axon. The innervation ratio has not been determined for all muscles of the body. For example, it is not known how many muscle fibers are innervated by a single axon in facial or lingual muscles.

To understand how the amount of muscular contraction is controlled and graded, it is helpful to consider a hypothetical experiment in

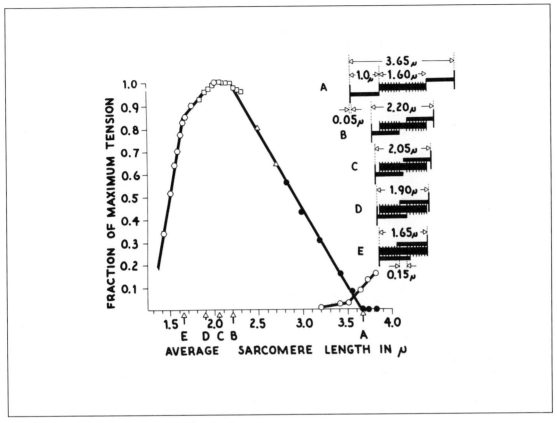

Fig. 3-8. Results of an experiment illustrating how the sliding filament theory of muscle contraction would account for the force produced in a muscle as a function of its length. At each length, indicated on the abscissa of the graph as sarcomere length, the tension of a few muscle fibers was measured. The inset at right shows the proposed actin and myosin molecules. A. There is no overlap, and no cross bridges are attached, resulting in no active force production. B. There is maximal overlap, and tension is maximal. C. There is complete overlap, with myosin molecules extending into the center region of the H band. D. There is double overlap of myosin molecules and force declines. E. The myosin molecules meet Z lines, and tension is further reduced. The curve to the left was produced by stimulating the muscle fibers to maximal tetanic contraction. The curve represented by open symbols is the passive tension produced from the same muscle fibers as those indicated by closed circles. (From Ruch, T. C., and Patton, H. D. *Physiology and Biophysics*. Philadelphia: Saunders, 1965. With permission.)

which a single axon from an MN is stimulated, and the tension developed by the MU is measured. Figure 3-9A illustrates the experimental setup and the results. As stated above, a single AP results in a brief period of muscle contraction known as a twitch. In Figure 3-9B, it is seen that a twitch builds to a peak tension and then drops off again. Note that the time to reach peak tension is much longer than an AP. Note also that the peak tension is rather low. If an axon is stimulated repetitively, a series of twitches is observed (a, in Fig. 3-9C). If the frequency of stimuli is increased, the frequency of the twitches increases and eventually a frequency is reached at which the tension from one twitch builds upon that of the previous one. Such a condition is called unfused tetanus. If the frequency of stimulation is further increased, the twitches come closer upon one another and the amount of tension developed is greatly increased over that of a single twitch (b and c, in Fig. 3-9C). At a certain high frequency, the twitches come so close together that there is

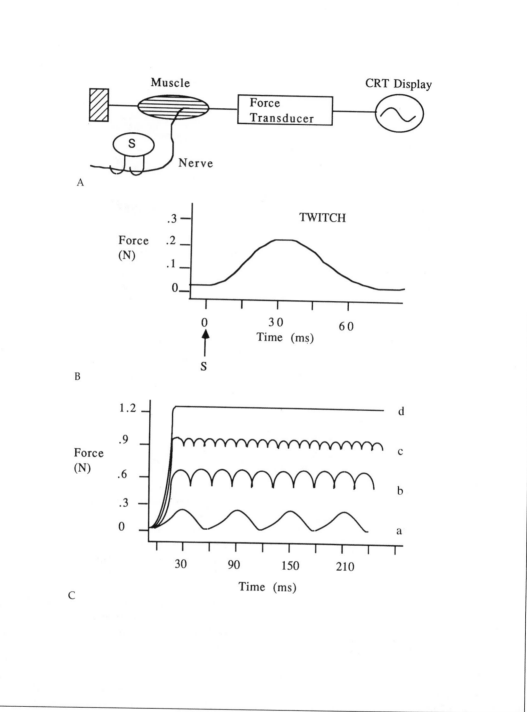

Fig. 3-9. A. Hypothetical experimental setup designed to measure strength of muscle contraction. A muscle is stimulated by electrodes (S) on its nerve trunk. The force produced by the muscle is measured with a force transducer and displayed on the face of an oscilloscope (CRT). B. Muscle twitch. At time 0 a stimulus is delivered to the nerve and the muscle responds with a brief "twitch." C. Force produced by a motor unit when it is stimulated at increasing frequencies (a to d). At low frequencies, individual twitches are observed. At increasing frequencies, individual twitches summate and produce greater amounts of force. At d, high frequency of stimulation produces a maximal amount of force without any ripple; it is known as "fused tetanus."

no observable "ripple" on the tension record; this condition is called fused tetanus (d, in Fig. 3-9C) and is the maximal amount of force that those muscle fibers may generate.

The above example illustrates how the amount of muscle contraction may be graded for a single MU. However, it should be noted that the maximal amount of force generated is rather low, and in unfused tetanus the contraction may exhibit considerable "ripple," or tremor. To get around this problem, several MUs may be activated simultaneously. Then even though one MU may be firing at a low rate and would be producing unfused tetanus if measured in isolation, by adding several MUs, each firing out of synchrony with each other, the resultant force produced by all MUs would be rather smooth. Moreover, the force produced by several active MUs is greater than that produced by a single MU. Thus there are two ways in which the force of muscular contraction may be graded and controlled: One way is to vary the rate of discharge of a single MU, and the other is to recruit additional MUs into activity. Although the nerve stimulation example is an artificial situation, muscles are normally controlled in a similar fashion.

Another important mechanism involved in normal muscle contraction relates to the size of different MUs. The size of an MU refers to the size of the cell body, the diameter of the axon, and the number of muscle fibers it innervates. Within a population of MN cell bodies in the spinal cord or brainstem there is a continual gradation from small to large sizes. Small MNs have smaller axons and fewer muscle fibers in their MUs than large MNs. It has been demonstrated in many animals and muscles that the size of an MU relates to strength of contraction. Small MUs produce small amounts of tension, and large MUs produce large amounts of tension. Therefore by activating large MUs, greater muscle force may be produced.

In 1965, Henneman, Somjen, and Carpenter proposed the above described relation, and it has since been called the *size principle*. There are additional features of the size principle that make it important in motor control. Recall from the above discussion of "cable properties" of neurons that the size of a neuron determines its internal electrical resistance. Small neurons have greater resistance than large neurons. Also recall that because of this size difference, large axons conduct APs at a higher velocity than

small axons. A feature of the size principle makes it relevant to the recruitment process described in this section: Consider a large MN and a small MN cell body. From microscopic examination it has been found that the cell bodies and dendrites of MNs are densely covered with synapses. Equal-sized patches of membrane on the large and small MN would have an equal number of synapses. If all the synapses in a given patch were excitatory and active at the same time, there would be an equal amount of synaptic current flowing through the membrane patches of each MN. However, the MNs differ in their internal resistance. Using Ohm's law, $E = IR$ (E = membrane depolarization, I = synaptic current, and R = internal resistance), it may be seen how the amount of depolarization would differ in the two MNs even though the numbers of active synapses in the patches of membrane are the same. With the two MNs, the synaptic current (I) is equal, but the internal resistance (R) of the large cell is less than that of the small cell. Therefore simple mathematics shows that the amount of depolarization in the small cell would be greater than in the large cell. For example, suppose the internal resistances of large and small MNs are 1 and 3 megohms, respectively. If the synaptic current were equal to 6.7×10^{-9} amperes, the large cell would depolarize by 10 mV and the small cell by 20 mV, enough in the latter case to reach threshold for an AP. If the number of active synapses increases, the large MNs are depolarized more and would likely generate APs.

In terms of normal muscle contraction, weak muscle tensions are produced by activating a few excitatory synapses in an MN pool, which excites only the small MNs. They fire at a low rate and produce little tension. If the number of excitatory synapses is increased, the small MNs fire at a higher frequency, and greater muscle strength is produced. As the number of excitatory synapses is increased further, large MNs begin to be recruited, which produce greater tension, and their force is added to that of the small MUs, producing greater overall strength of contraction. In this process, muscle force may be graded over a considerable range. Recall also that in muscles such as those controlling the fingers and some speech muscles, because there are few muscle fibers per MN, the amount of force gradation is fine. That is, it is possible to make small adjustments in the strength of contraction. On the other hand, in large muscles of the trunk, with many more muscle fibers per MN, as each MN is recruited the level of force output jumps considerably, and the ability to grade force is limited.

SENSORY MECHANISMS

RECEPTORS

Sensory systems provide a means for individuals to be made aware of the world around them. They are constantly exposed to a variety of stimuli such as sights, sounds, smells, tastes, temperature, and mechanical events, e.g., touch or pressure. Accordingly, individuals are equipped with specialized nerve endings, called *receptors,* that are sensitive to one or more of these stimuli. Each receptor sends action potentials to the CNS along its own sensory afferent fiber. Within the CNS these sensory fibers synapse with second-order sensory cells that transmit impulses to other parts of the CNS. Farther along additional synapses are made, and ultimately through this process sensory stimuli are perceived and interpreted.

Most of this section deals with peripheral aspects of sensory systems, in part because much more is understood about it. Traditionally, sensory receptors have been classified into three groups. *Exteroceptors* are those that receive stimuli from the external world such as vision and audition. Exteroceptors also include contact receptors (mechanoreceptors), which are sensitive to touch and pressure of the skin and mucous membranes. *Proprioceptors* provide sensation relating to body position and awareness. *Interoceptors* provide sensation about internal bodily events such as blood pressure (Carpenter and Sutin, 1983).

Regardless of which type of sensory receptor one is studying, there are certain basic phenomena that are the same or similar. Thus by studying one receptor, it is possible to learn something about all receptors. All receptors perform the same basic function of *sensory transduction—* the process of converting some type of stimulus to APs. The process of interpreting the APs (*sensory perception*) is done by the CNS. Most receptors are sensitive to different stimuli, but each responds best to a particular stimulus,

known as the *adequate stimulus.* For example, receptors in the retina of the eye are most sensitive to light, but pressure against the side of the eyeball can result in the perception of visual images. The concept of the adequate stimulus relates to the first process in sensory reception— energy transformation.

Energy transformation is a process that is usually not done by the receptor itself but by other morphologic structures. The auditory system is an excellent example. The pinna, middle ear, and inner ear have various components that transform aerodynamic energy into mechanical energy, which is then transformed into APs by the neural receptors in the inner ear. Sensory receptors in the skin and muscles do not have such complex structures to transform energy and in some cases may respond directly to a stimulus, e.g., temperature.

Once energy has been transformed to a form that is suitable for a particular receptor, the receptor accomplishes the transduction process. Energy transduction is done in a manner similar to that for the generation of APs by other neural elements. The stimulus causes an increase in Na^+ and K^+ permeability at the site of the receptor. The time constants of the receptor membranes are much different from those of membranes discussed previously. As a consequence, the depolarization resulting from these permeability changes may last a long time. The depolarizing potential in the sensory receptor is called the "generator potential" (GP) and is restricted to the area of the receptor itself; i.e., it is a nonpropagated potential. Furthermore, the magnitude of the GP is related to the intensity of the stimulus and in some receptors lasts for the duration of the stimulus. In some receptors the relation between the magnitude of the GP and the stimulus is logarithmic, and in others it is linear.

The GP derives its name from the fact that it generates APs. The actual generation of the APs is usually not done in the receptor itself, however. It appears that APs are generated near the point where the axon leaves the receptor, sometimes called the axon hillock. The depolarizing potential of the GP invades the axon for a short distance where voltage-sensitive ion channels are located (Fig. 3-10A). These channels respond to the depolarizing potential in the same way as described earlier in this chapter by the transitory opening and closing of Na^+ and K^+ channels. These actions result in the generation

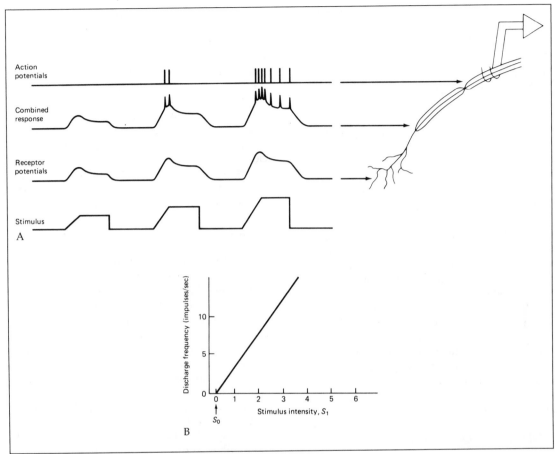

Fig. 3-10. A. Results from an experiment recording impulses from a sensory afferent fiber at three locations. The top trace illustrates action potentials recorded from a distal portion of the axon. The second trace shows the interaction of the nonpropagated generator potential (GP) with action potentials (APs) near where the APs are triggered. The third trace shows the GP recorded at the receptor region itself. The fourth trace shows the stimulus. B. The firing frequency of afferent fiber APs is plotted as a function of stimulus intensity. (From Kandel, E., and Schwartz, J. *Principles of Neural Science,* 2nd ed. New York: Elsevier, 1985. With permission.)

of APs, which are then propagated centrally. It has been demonstrated in several types of receptor that the frequency of APs generated by a receptor is directly related to the magnitude of the GP (Fig. 3-10B). Because the intensity of a stimulus is coded by the firing frequency of action potentials, the CNS is able to perceive different intensities of stimulation by monitoring the frequency of AP discharge in a single neu-

ron. However, in real life, many receptors respond to a stimulus simultaneously.

As mentioned above, the GP may last the duration of the stimulus, and in other cases it does not. In some types of receptor the GP may last only a brief time, whereas the applied stimulus may last much longer. As a result of the differing durations of the GPs, the length of the train of APs generated by a receptor varies. Receptors that develop GPs lasting a long time are called slowly adapting receptors. Receptors generating only short-duration GPs are called rapidly adapting receptors. Slowly adapting receptors provide sensory awareness of stimuli for as long as the stimulus lasts. Rapidly adapting receptors provide sensory awareness about the onset and offset of stimuli. By having populations of receptors, some coding onset and offset of stimuli, some coding duration of a stimuli, and most coding intensity of a stimulus, it may be seen how various aspects of stimuli are transduced and the information sent to the CNS.

SENSORY RECEPTORS INVOLVED IN SPEECH

There are several types of sensory receptors involved in speech. Perhaps the most obvious form of sensation used for speech control is audition. However, there are other types of receptors important for speech control as well. Various types of mechanoreceptors and proprioceptors provide the brain with information concerning the mechanical properties of tissues as well as the positions and movements of articulators during speech. This type of information is thought to be important when learning how to speak, making adjustments for articulatory inaccuracies, and planning sequential movement patterns of the articulators during speech. For example, if a given articulator such as the tongue is to be moved to a new position within the oral cavity, the brain needs to know the present position to plan the move. If such sensation is deprived through anesthetics, articulatory inaccuracies develop and speech becomes dysarthric.

GOLGI TENDON ORGANS

Golgi tendon organs (GTOs) are a type of proprioceptor found within the tendons situated between muscles and bones or cartilages. Although they are widely found in muscles innervated by spinal nerves, they have not been found in as great abundance in muscles innervated by cranial nerves. Their comparative lack in muscles of the cranial nervous system may be partly related to less intensive anatomic investigations of these muscles. Within a given tendon, there are numerous GTOs, each lying "in series" with 10 to 20 muscle fibers. Each GTO is innervated by a sensory fiber called a Ib afferent fiber. The Ib afferent fibers travel to the spinal cord, where they make a synapse with an interneuron, which in turn forms an inhibitory synapse with MNs of the same muscle (homonymous) attached to the GTO. Thus when a muscle contracts, it excites GTOs within its tendon; APs travel to the spinal cord and, through the interneuron, synaptically cause inhibition of the homonymous muscle.

Functionally, it was originally thought that the inhibitory action of GTOs on homonymous muscles served a protective function. That is, if a muscle was stretched or contracted so forcefully as to damage the limb, the GTOs would inhibit the muscle contraction and prevent damage. Houk and Henneman (1967) showed by recording from individual GTOs that the above description was incorrect; that is, because each GTO is attached to only a few muscle fibers, each is sensitive to small amounts of muscle contraction. If the information conveyed centrally by GTOs is passed to higher cortical centers, it may underlie the ability to appreciate the strength of muscle contraction.

MUSCLE SPINDLES

Muscle spindles have been studied more extensively than GTOs, and their functions are better understood (for a review see Matthews, 1972). One reason for their more intensive investigation relates to their morphology (Fig. 3-11). Muscle spindles are the only receptors of the somatic motor system that have their own independent motor innervation. The MNs innervating muscle spindles are called gamma or fusimotor neurons, and their axons are called gamma static, gamma dynamic, and beta fibers. In addition to these three types of motor fiber, muscle spindles have two types of sensory afferent fiber, termed Ia and II, or primary and secondary afferent fibers. Inside the capsule forming the spindle are two types of small muscle fiber (intrafusal fibers), termed nuclear chain and nuclear bag fibers. Nuclear bag fibers have been further categorized as bag 1 and bag 2 fibers. Most spindles have at least one bag and chain fiber. The names of the intrafusal fibers derive from the arrangement of the nuclei found within the central (equatorial) region of the fibers. In bag fibers the nuclei are arranged as a clump in the enlarged equatorial region of the fiber. In chain fibers the nuclei are arranged as a single line within the fiber.

The fusimotor fibers enter the capsule of the spindle and terminate as endplates on the intrafusal fibers. Gamma D (dynamic) fibers terminate on a restricted region near the end (polar region) of bag 1 fibers only and cause nonpropagated APs in them. Gamma S (static) fibers terminate closer to the equatorial region of bag 2 and chain fibers and propagate APs. Beta fibers terminate on both bag 1 fibers and extrafusal fibers found outside muscle spindles. The

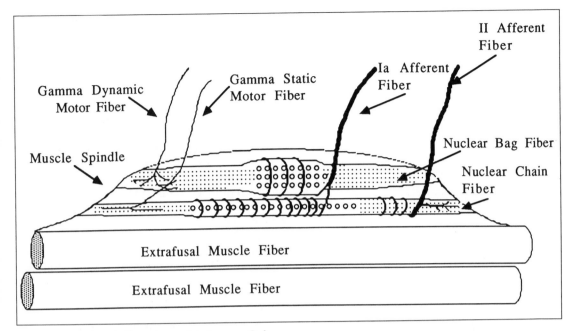

Gamma Dynamic
Motor Fiber

Gamma Static
Motor Fiber

Ia Afferent
Fiber

II Afferent
Fiber

Muscle Spindle

Nuclear Bag Fiber

Nuclear Chain
Fiber

Extrafusal Muscle Fiber

Extrafusal Muscle Fiber

Fig. 3-11. Muscle spindle and associated axons. Only a single nuclear bag and chain fiber are shown along with two extrafusal fibers, to which the spindle is attached. For details see text.

primary (Ia) fibers originate from annulospiral receptors located in the equatorial region of bag and chain fibers. The axons of these receptors are the largest in mammalian nerves, with diameters of 12 to 20 micrometers. Secondary (II) fibers arise from flower-spray receptors located just outside the equatorial region of chain fibers primarily. Each Ia and II axon arises from several receptors of the same spindle. Thus an AP in one of these fibers is a result of actions at different receptor sites. Primary afferent fibers make monosynaptic excitatory connections with homonymous MNs in the spinal cord. They also make disynaptic inhibitory connections with MNs of antagonist MNs. Secondary afferent fibers make disynaptic excitatory connections with homonymous MNs also. Each type of afferent fiber also travels to higher levels of the nervous system.

Muscle spindles are found within the bellies of muscles and are attached at each end to extrafusal muscle fibers. This arrangement is termed *in parallel*, and it implies that as the length of extrafusal muscle fibers changes the spindle length changes also. Physiologic studies have shown that spindles are sensitive to

muscle length changes. The details of the response of spindles to muscle length changes have been elucidated by controlled experiments on anesthetized animals. Figure 3-12 illustrates the response of Ia and II endings to "ramp"-shaped changes of muscle length with and without gamma motor activation. As can be seen, Ia endings respond vigorously to the ramp portion of the stretch, and then the rate of discharge declines somewhat as the new length change is maintained. By presenting ramps of different velocities, it has been found that Ia endings are sensitive to velocity of muscle stretch and somewhat less sensitive to steady position, i.e., the length change after the ramp portion of the stimulus. Secondary endings, in contrast, do not respond as well to the velocity component of the ramp; instead, their firing rate is largely determined by the overall steady position change. These response patterns are seen in the absence of action by the fusimotor system and are described as "passive" properties of the spindles. The responses are probably similar to what one would observe if one were relaxed and someone else or some other force suddenly stretched a limb. When the gamma fibers are stimulated, the responses of the Ia and II endings change, as may be seen in Figure 3-12.

The results of the experiments on muscle

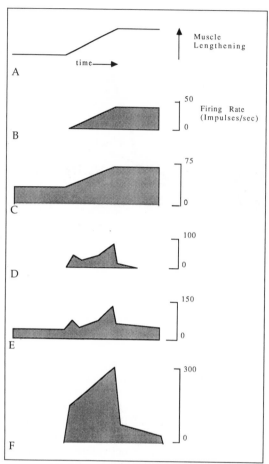

Fig. 3-12. Responses of muscle spindle afferent endings to a ramp stretch stimulus with and without activation of fusimotor fibers. A. "Ramp-shaped" stretch stimulus applied to a muscle. B. Response of a secondary ending to the stimulus. C. Response of a secondary ending to the same stimulus but when the gamma static fibers have been activated. D. Response of a primary afferent ending to a ramp stretch. E. Response of a primary afferent ending with added gamma static stimulation. F. Response of a primary ending with added gamma dynamic stimulation.

that was trained to raise and lower his jaw. The top trace illustrates vertical jaw movement, the second trace is the discharge of a secondary afferent fiber, and the third trace is the firing frequency of the fiber. It may be seen that as the jaw moves down the firing frequency of the fiber increases. If the third trace were inverted, its pattern of firing rate changes would closely match that of actual jaw position. It is clear from Figure 3-13 that secondary endings can transduce jaw position accurately. From such results it is suggested that similar receptors in the speech muscles of humans would be helpful for monitoring the movements and positions of articulators.

In addition to providing awareness of articulator movements and positions, spindles (and possibly other receptors) have been implicated in certain automatic, or reflex, responses to length changes. It is generally agreed that muscle spindles are responsible for the well known "knee jerk" reflex. Figure 3-14 illustrates how this reflex operates and provides information on how spindles could reflexively control the positions of other limbs or articulators. When the patellar tendon of the knee is struck by a hammer, the tendon is stretched, as is, in turn, the quadriceps muscle of the thigh. This stretch also stretches the muscle spindles, which respond with a burst of impulses sent to the spinal cord. There, Ia endings monosynaptically excite homonymous MNs, and they send a burst of APs back to the quadriceps muscle, causing it to shorten and thus kick the lower leg forward. In the more general sense, this reflex is called a stretch reflex because the stimulus stretched the muscle.

In normal situations the role of muscle spindles in muscles of the limb is to help maintain posture. Consider again the quadriceps muscle: As a person is standing gravity attempts to pull him down. During this attempt the quadriceps muscle would be stretched by the bending of the knee joint. As the joint is bent, the muscle is stretched, and the spindles reflexively excite the quadriceps muscle to prevent lengthening of the muscle and bending of the knee. Thus the stretch reflex helps to maintain posture automatically. The stretch reflex in jaw muscles helps to prevent the jaw from oscillating up and down as one is walking or running. Stretch reflexes in other muscles would likely have different functions. For example, in the tongue, muscle spindles may be used to control the length

spindles have led to the idea that the primary and secondary endings are sensitive to velocity and length of muscle, respectively. Those experiments were done on anesthetized animals. Since then, experiments have been done on humans and awake animals, and the results have been largely corroborated. Figure 3-13 shows the response of a secondary ending to changes in jaw movement made by an awake monkey

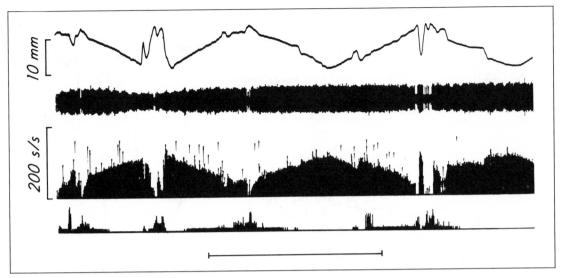

Fig. 3-13. Responses of a secondary muscle spindle ending to stretch of jaw-closing muscle. Top trace shows jaw position (upward jaw movement is indicated by the upward deflection of the trace); second trace shows firing frequency of a secondary afferent fiber; and third trace shows electrical activity from the jaw-closing muscle. The muscle spindle ending responds with the greatest firing rates when the jaw is lowest and the muscles are longest. Time bar is 1 second. (From Larson, C. R., Finocchio, D. V., Smith, A., and Luschei, E. S. Jaw muscle afferent firing during an isotonic jaw-positioning task in the monkey. *J. Neurophysiol.* 50:61, 1983. With permission.)

of certain fibers and, thereby, the position of the tongue. Muscle spindles in laryngeal muscles may help regulate length or stiffness of muscles and, thereby, the fundamental frequency of the voice.

MECHANORECEPTORS

Mechanoreceptors found in other tissues may be important for speech production as well. For example, there are apparently no muscle spindles or GTOs in the lips, and yet the lips comprise one of the most highly innervated areas of the body and one that is important for speech. Information on sensory receptors in human labial tissue is scarce, although considerably more is known about sensory receptors in monkey labial tissue. Monkey lips are endowed with a variety of mechanoreceptors, such as free nerve endings, corpuscular type endings, Meissner corpuscles, Merkel discs, and Ruffini endings

(Halata and Munger, 1983; Munger and Halata, 1983). Mechanoreceptors of similar types also have been found in the epithelium of the tongue, palate, and laryngeal tissues (Byers and Yeh, 1984; Marlow, Winkelmann, and Gibilisco, 1965; Wyke and Kirchner, 1976). Some of these endings are sensitive to light touch, some to temperature, some to movement of the skin, and some to vibratory stimuli. The variety of sensory receptors in human labial tissue is not known, nor has their physiology been widely studied, but it is likely that humans possess many of the same types of mechanoreceptors in their labial tissue as do monkeys. These receptors, which are capable of transducing various types of mechanical stimuli, probably also respond to stimulation resulting from contraction of labial muscles, stretching and deformation of the labial tissue, and contact between the lips and other structures such as the teeth, tongue, and the opposing lip. In the tongue, palate, and larynx, the mechanoreceptors would also be sensitive to tissue deformation, contact with other structures, and movement. Therefore these mechanoreceptors are likely important in many of the reflexes associated with the speech mechanism as well as for motor control of these structures during speech.

In this section, proprioceptors and their possible roles in sensory awareness of position and movement of muscles have been discussed. It should be stressed that other types of receptor also participate in reflexes, including the stretch

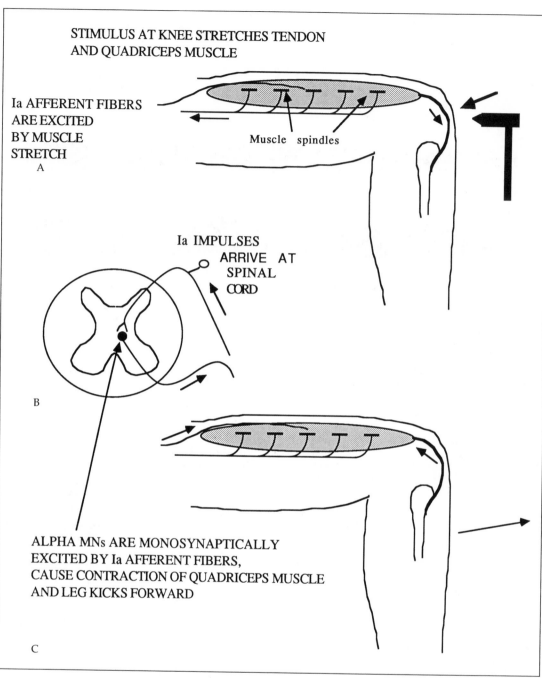

STIMULUS AT KNEE STRETCHES TENDON AND QUADRICEPS MUSCLE

Ia AFFERENT FIBERS ARE EXCITED BY MUSCLE STRETCH

A

Muscle spindles

Ia IMPULSES ARRIVE AT SPINAL CORD

B

ALPHA MNs ARE MONOSYNAPTICALLY EXCITED BY Ia AFFERENT FIBERS, CAUSE CONTRACTION OF QUADRICEPS MUSCLE AND LEG KICKS FORWARD

C

Fig. 3-14. Mechanisms of the monosynaptic "knee jerk" reflex. A. A hammer delivers a blow to the knee, stretches the tendon attached to the quadriceps muscle, and thereby stretches the muscle and excites muscle spindle afferent endings (Ia). B. Impulses from muscle spindle afferent endings (Ia) arrive at the spinal cord, make a monosynaptic connection with the motoneuron, and the motoneuron sends an impulse out its axon toward muscle. C. Action potential from the motoneuron arrives at the muscle; it causes the muscle to contract and kick the leg forward.

reflex. It is probable that in most reflexes no single receptor type is exclusively involved at the expense of other receptors. Indeed, in normal motor control, populations of different types of receptor constantly send impulses to the CNS conveying information about all states of structures. From the standpoint of physiologic investigations, it is advantageous to study a single receptor type at one time, but one should not forget the contributions of the others.

SENSORY SYSTEMS IN THE CNS

Sensory afferent fibers from the spinal nervous system enter the spinal cord through the dorsal root. The cell bodies of these neurons are located in the dorsal root ganglion adjacent to the spinal cord. In the cranial nervous system, many afferent fibers also have their cell bodies located in ganglia outside the skull. The only known exception are some types of periodontal receptors and muscle spindle afferent fibers from the jaw. After entering the CNS, fibers travel to a nucleus where they make synaptic connections with the second order sensory cells. For the spinal system, the second-order cells are located in the cuneate and gracile nucleus. There are several such nuclei for the cranial system. The second-order sensory cells then project either to the ventral posterior lateral or ventral posterior medial nucleus of the thalamus. Synaptic connections are made there with third-order sensory fibers that project to the cerebral cortex. Afferent fibers from proprioceptors such as muscle spindles, after entering the spinal cord, also ascend in a fiber tract known as the column of Clarke to the midbrain region and enter the cerebellum by way of the anterior medullary velum (House and Pansky, 1967). Information about length of muscles, positions of the limbs, and articulators from proprioceptors are used by the cerebellum to assist in posture control and in the coordination of movements during locomotion and speech.

Although the sensory relay nuclei for the second- and third-order neurons are generally termed "relay" nuclei, a term that implies that information is merely transferred from one cell to the other, it is a misleading concept. Wherever there is a nucleus in the CNS or a group of cell bodies, there are synapses between cells.

Whenever there are such synapses there is usually some processing of information that occurs. In the sensory relay nuclei, incoming sensory afferent fibers make synaptic connections with higher-order afferent fibers, which also make connections with other afferent fibers. In many cases the synaptic connections between ascending afferent fibers of the same order are inhibitory. That is, one sensory afferent fiber inhibits the activity of adjacent fibers. This property is known as *lateral inhibition*, and it serves to sharpen sensory acuity.

To illustrate how lateral inhibition sharpens acuity, consider the following (Fig. 3-15). Sensory fibers in the CNS generally display some spontaneous activity in the absence of stimulation. Now, consider three sensory afferent fibers arriving at a relay nucleus. If only one of the three fibers received stimulation from an incoming fiber (2, in Fig. 3-15B), it would be firing APs at a higher rate than the others. Moreover, the postsynaptic cell receiving inputs from fiber 2 would inhibit the activity of the adjacent two fibers and reduce their spontaneous activity. At higher levels of the nervous system, the high level of activity in one input fiber and lack of activity in other fibers are perceived as stimulation of a restricted region of the body. Thus the lateral inhibition between afferent fibers accentuates the difference in firing rates among them. It is then easier for the sensory perception mechanisms of the CNS to determine the precise site of stimulation on the body. Without such mechanisms, the acuity of sensory discrimination would be much less than it is.

Another property of sensory fibers related to lateral inhibition is the "receptive field." Each sensory receptor at the periphery is excited only by stimuli that impinge on some part of the receptor process itself. Many free nerve endings in the skin have multiple endings that branch out in several directions and may extend several millimeters. Stimulation at any spot innervated by this network excites the receptor. It could be said then that the area of the body served by this network of branching fibers is that receptor's "receptive field." A *receptive field* may then be defined as that area of the body which when stimulated excites a particular receptor. At higher levels of the nervous system, the higher-order afferent fibers also have receptive fields that may be smaller or larger than that of

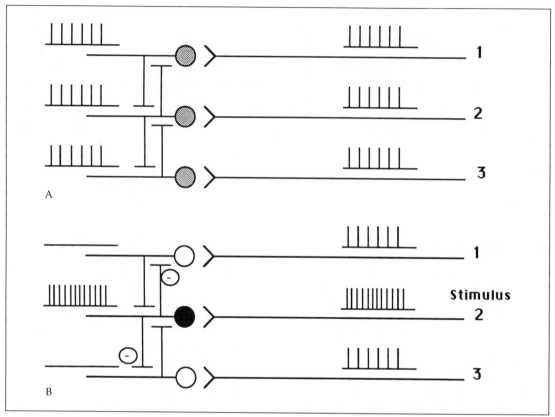

Fig. 3-15. Lateral inhibition. A. Fibers 1, 2, and 3 are not stimulated and each fires at the same frequency. The postsynaptic fibers on the left fire at the same frequency as the presynaptic fibers. B. Fiber 2 is stimulated; inhibition of fibers 1 and 3 at the synapse causes a further reduction in discharge rate of the postsynaptic fibers.

the peripheral receptors. By the mechanism of lateral inhibition at the sensory relay nuclei, adjacent cells inhibit one another and define receptive fields for each cell along the pathway.

The lateral inhibition seen in such sensory systems also leads to receptive fields of various shapes and complexities. For example, in the visual system, ganglion cells of the retina, cells in the lateral geniculate nucleus, and some cortical cells have circular receptive fields. A receptive field in the visual system refers to an area of the visual field that when stimulated excites a particular cell at some level of the neural visual system. The circular receptive fields in the visual system also have a center and an antagonistic surround. That is, if a stimulus to the center of the receptive field excites a cell, stimulation of the surrounding area inhibits it. There also are cells that are inhibited by a stimulus in the center of the field and excited by a stimulus in the surrounding area. In the visual cortex, cells with circular receptive fields make synaptic connections with other cells that have "rod"-

shaped receptive fields. The rod shape is derived from the inputs of several cells with circular receptive fields oriented in a line. Cells with rod-shaped receptive fields project to other cells that have even more complex receptive fields.

In addition to the lateral inhibition between ascending afferent fibers that occurs at the relay nuclei, these nuclei serve another function. Many fibers descending from the cerebral cortex terminate at these relay nuclei. These descending fibers can inhibit some ascending sensory afferent fibers. Through this inhibition, the cortex can modulate the flow of sensory inputs into the cortex. This form of inhibition probably underlies part of the ability to "pay attention" to some stimuli and to "ignore" others.

HIGHER FUNCTIONS

The basic properties of individual cells, their interactions through synapses, and small networks of cells constituting simple reflexes have been discussed. The functions of some of the major areas of the brain involved in the control of activities such as speech are now described in a simplified way. For the purposes of this discussion, the cerebral cortex, basal ganglia, and cerebellum are discussed separately. This discussion of necessity, however, mentions the interconnections between these three major systems, as they are of the utmost importance for normal brain function. The reader will find it helpful to have read Chapter 2, Basic Neuroanatomy, prior to reading this section.

CEREBRAL CORTEX

The cerebral cortex, being the largest and probably most highly evolved component of the human brain, is also perhaps the most difficult to study and understand. As discussed in other chapters, the cerebral cortex plays key roles in sensory perception, language, cognition, and speech motor control. The present chapter discusses sensory processing and aspects of cortical control of movement.

The cerebral cortex consists of six layers of cell bodies, as described in Chapter 2. The layering is due to the presence of different types of cells or fibers in each layer. Moreover, the relative thickness of the layers varies from one cortical area to another. Several investigators have studied the layered structure of the cortex, the best known of whom was Brodmann, who identified 52 cortical areas based on their laminated structure (Fig. 3-16). Most researchers now use Brodmann's numbering scheme to identify the various cortical areas. Although specific functions have not yet been identified for each of the structurally unique areas of the cortex, some areas seem to have relatively specific functions (see below).

Despite the different patterns of the cortical layers, each layer has a specific function no matter where in the cortex it is found. Thalamic inputs terminate in layer IV of the cortex. Stellate

cells in this layer receive thalamic inputs and transmit information through their profusely branching axons to other cells in the immediate area. Larger pyramidal cells in layer V send their axons to subcortical structures such as the basal ganglia, brainstem, and spinal cord. Cells in layers II and III project to other sensory and motor areas of the parietal cortex. Cells in layer VI project back to the thalamus.

SOMATOSENSORY CORTEX

From the early physiologic studies of the somatosensory cortex, it became evident that the

Fig. 3-16. Lateral (A) and mesial (B) views of the human cerebral cortex. Symbols covering different areas of the cortex illustrate that the areas have similar cytoarchitectonic structure as defined by Brodmann. Numbers accompanying the areas are generally described as Brodmann's areas. (From Kandel, E., and Schwartz, J. *Principles of Neural Science,* 2nd ed. New York: Elsevier, 1985. With permission.)

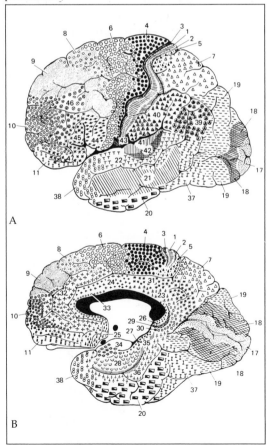

electrical activity of the surface of the sensory cortex was altered if different portions of the body were stimulated (Kandel and Schwartz, 1985). Subsequently, experiments on humans and in animals showed a consistent, topographic relation between areas of the body stimulated and responsive areas in the sensory cortex. Figure 3-17 illustrates this topographic relation in the form of a "homunculus." Of importance is the fact that body areas with a fine degree of sensibility are represented by larger cortical areas than body areas with low sensibility.

In later years, as investigators began studying the activity of single neurons, several organizational principles of the sensory (and motor) cortices were learned. One of the first things learned was that the sensory cortex may be divided into primary (SI) and secondary (SII) cortices. SII lies lateral to SI on the upper bank of the sylvian fissure; it receives bilateral inputs, whereas SI receives contralateral inputs.

It also became evident that each cell in the sensory cortex has its own receptive field. Within each of the sensory areas 1, 2, 3a, and 3b there are receptive fields of various sizes representing all surfaces of the body. Those parts of the body surface having the greatest degree

of sensory acuity have the largest number of receptive fields, and each receptive field is relatively small. Areas of the body with poor sensory acuity have fewer receptive fields, and each is relatively large. The smallest and most numerous receptive fields are located on the fingertips, tongue, and lips, areas with a high degree of sensibility. Larger receptive fields are found in other areas of the body (Dreyer Loe, Metz, and Whitsel, 1975; Kaas, Nelson, Sur, Lin, & Merzenich, 1979).

Within the different sensory areas, there is a complete somatotopic map of the body (Fig. 3-18). That is, a set of receptive fields covering the entire body surface can be found in each of areas 1, 2, 3a, and 3b (Kaas et al., 1979). Within each area, however, the nature of the receptive fields differs. Area 3a receives inputs from deep tissues and muscle spindles. Area 3b receives relays from slowly and rapidly adapting receptors located superficially in the skin. Cells in area 2 are excited by deep pressure (Kaas et al.,

Fig. 3-17. Relative amounts of cortical tissue devoted to control of different body areas, as depicted by figures called "homunculi." A. Precentral gyrus, motor cortex. B. Postcentral gyrus, somatosensory cortex. (From Warwick, R., and Williams, P. L. *Gray's Anatomy*, 35th British Edition. Edinburgh: Churchill-Livingstone, 1973. With permission.)

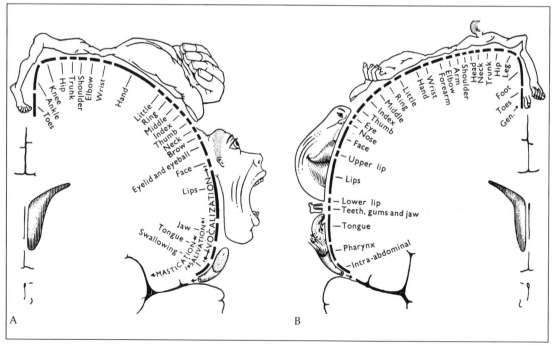

A   B

1979), whereas cells in area 1 are responsive to rapidly adapting cutaneous receptors. Areas 3a and 3b also project to areas 1 and 2. About 6 percent of the cells in areas 1 and 2 respond to more complex stimuli, such as movement in one direction over a patch of skin. From experiments in behaving animals, it has been found that some cells of the sensory cortex are responsive to position and torque and are probably intimately involved in the precise control of movements (Fromm and Evarts, 1982; Jennings, Lamour, Solis, and Fromm, 1983). Many cells of the sensory cortex also may be involved in modulating sensory inputs in the brainstem or spinal cord.

It also has been learned that the sensory cortex may be organized functionally into columns that extend through all six layers of the cortex. Each column is approximately 1 mm in diameter, and all the cells in a column have closely related receptive fields and respond to the same sensory modality. Adjacent cortical columns may have receptive fields that overlap one another to some extent. It has been suggested that a column constitutes a basic element of cortical organization (Kandel and Schwartz, 1985).

From sensory areas 1, 2, 3a, and 3b, cells project bilaterally to sensory areas 5 and 7 of the parietal lobe as well as to the motor cortex. Areas 5 and 7 represent a higher order of sensory processing in which information from the somatic sensory cortex is integrated with sensory information from other modalities, e.g., the visual system, to provide a sense of body and extrapersonal space. Cells in these areas also have complex receptive fields that may involve two or more joints; such cells respond best to coordinated movements between limbs, as in walking. In area 5, some neurons discharge only as an animal reaches for an object in the immediate surroundings but are quiet when the limb is passively manipulated. Other

Fig. 3-18. Receptive fields in the somatosensory cortex related to the fingers and hand recorded in macaque monkeys. A. Segment of the exposed cortex is shown with receptive fields of the digits corresponding to the drawings of the fingers. B. Receptive fields in areas 1 and 2, again showing the cortical areas of the fields and the fingers. (From Kaas, J. H., Nelson, R. J., Sur, M., Lin, C. S., and Merzenich, M. M. Multiple representations of the body within the primary somatosensory cortex of primates. *Science* 204:521, 1979. With permission.)

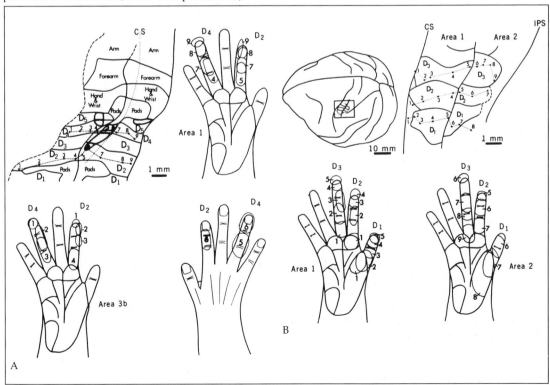

neurons are active only if an animal explores an object with his hands (Duffy and Burchfiel; 1971). Cells in area 7 respond best to activation of both somatosensory and visual information, such as when an animal makes reaching movements toward a target or brings food toward its mouth (Leinonen and Nyman, 1979). In area 7 the units depend more on the visual component and respond best when the eyes focus on an object of interest (Kandel and Schwartz, 1985).

Another important feature about cells in the sensory cortex is that many of them respond to peripheral stimulation in the same way as the receptors themselves. For example, a rapidly adapting receptor synaptically projects through relay nuclei to cells in SI that also rapidly adapt to stimuli. This feature of continuity in responsiveness of the sensory "chain" ensures that the information transduced by the receptor is accurately relayed to the cortex, where sensory perception occurs (Kandel and Schwartz, 1985).

In addition to a study of neuronal responsiveness to various stimuli, a functional understanding of various cortical areas has been learned from studies of traumatic injuries in humans or experimental lesions made in the brains of animals. Lesions of area 3b produce deficits in the ability to discriminate objects on the basis of size, texture, and shape. Lesions of area 1 affect only the ability to make discriminations on the basis of texture, and lesions of area 2 affect the ability to discriminate objects on the basis of size and shape. The effects seen with lesions of areas 1 and 2 are logical, as these areas receive projections from area 3b (Kandel and Schwartz, 1985). Lesions of area SII also result in deficits in learning tactile discrimination tasks (Garcha and Ettlinger, 1980). Lesions of areas 5 and 7 in monkeys and humans result in deficits in reaching toward objects in space (Deuel, 1977; Kolb and Milner, 1981). In humans these deficits manifest as patients having difficulty operating simple hand-held objects, as when eating with a knife or fork, or when reaching toward objects such as a doorknob.

From this review of the somatosensory cortex, it was seen that afferents from the periphery ascend through relays in the dorsal column nuclei and thalamus. From the thalamus, cells project most heavily to areas 3, 1, and 2 of the parietal cortex. Cells of these areas are responsive to specific sensory modalities, and they project to the motor cortex and areas 5 and 7. The latter areas represent a higher level of sensory processing and seem to be involved in the utilization of various forms of sensory feedback for the control of coordinated movements. Thus functionally, it can be seen that some areas of the somatosensory cortex are related to specific stimuli of a restricted area of the body (small receptive field). At other levels, cells are more generally related to complex stimulation involving larger areas of the body. From areas 5 and 7, cells project to the motor cortex (area 4), premotor cortex (area 6), and supplementary motor cortex (Petrides and Pandya, 1984).

MOTOR CORTEX

Motor control of actions depends not only on the sensory and motor cortices but also on the integrative function of various substructures of the CNS. Later sections briefly review some important subcortical structures involved in motor control. As for the cortical structures involved in motor functions, it shall be seen that different levels of functional complexity exist in a fashion analogous to that seen in the somatosensory system. The premotor (area 6) and supplementary cortex are related to movements of a general nature, whereas the motor cortex (area 4) is related to specific movements.

The primary motor cortex (area 4) lies just anterior to the central sulcus (Fig. 3-16). It receives inputs from the sensory cortex, thalamus and premotor cortex, and supplementary motor cortex. Within area 4 are found the giant Betz cells, which are large pyramid-shaped neurons that project to the brainstem and spinal cord and may monosynaptically impinge on motoneurons. This cortical area is the only one containing Betz cells (Kandel and Schwartz, 1985).

In a general sense, studies of area 4 neurons have revealed findings analogous to those of the primary sensory cortex, i.e., a topographic and columnar organization. By using microelectrodes and either recording from single cells or stimulating them with very small electrical currents, it has been demonstrated that many area 4 neurons project directly to small groups of MNs of synergistic muscles (muscles that contract as a group to perform a single movement) (Asanuma and Rosen, 1972; Cheney and Fetz, 1984; McGuinnes, Siversten, & Allman, 1980; Zealear, Hast, and Kurago, 1985). It was also shown that cells in the motor cortex that excite a single muscle or small groups of muscles are themselves modulated by sensory stimulation of an area of the body that would naturally be stimulated if those same muscles contracted (Rosen and Asanuma, 1972). This observation reflects a rather tight coupling between sensory inputs to and motor outputs from the cortex and has led to the suggestion that, for the control of precise movements, cells in individual columns of the motor cortex excite synergistic groups of muscles; moreover, the sensory activation of the same cortical cells by stimulation of the body part being controlled, e.g., fingers or wrist, aids in the precise execution of the movement (Asanuma, 1973; Cheney and Fetz, 1984; Evarts and Fromm, 1977). Some of the sensory inputs to the motor cortex are projected from the sensory cortex, whereas in other cases thalamic inputs relayed from some muscle spindle afferent fibers project directly to area 4. Interestingly, some thalamic projections to the motor cortex arborize over an area of about 1 mm^2, the same size as the columns (Asanuma and Fernandez, 1974). Finally, the descending cortical projections to the spinal cord also make synapses on interneurons that are involved in segmental reflexes. This projection allows the cortex to regulate the sensitivity, or "gain," of reflexes so that in the execution of voluntary movements the elicitation of reflexive muscle contractions does not interfere with the planned movement.

Several discharge patterns may be observed within the motor cortex. Some neurons are normally rather quiet and then become active prior to a movement. It is thought that such cells may be involved in causing muscular contractions, and their activity has been correlated with the steady-state level of force of muscle contraction, the rate of change of force, and the timing of muscular contractions (Evarts, 1968, 1972; Hoffman and Luschei, 1980; Porter, 1972). It also has been suggested that cortical neurons phasically active with jaw movements may be involved in the indirect control of jaw muscles, or they may project to subcortical sensory nuclei where they modulate sensory responsiveness of neurons (Luschei, Gathwaite, and Armstrong, 1971).

In the control of movements, it is natural to think about the contractions of muscles necessary to execute a task. It is important also to remember that when one muscle contracts its antagonist must relax to accomplish the task. In this sense, it may be argued that many cortical cells that become active during a movement

may inhibit the contraction of muscles that are antagonistic to other muscles being excited. Other cells may be active and then become inactive prior to a movement; they also may be involved in maintaining contraction of muscles antagonistic to a particular movement. By the cessation of discharge, the latter cells may allow the antagonistic muscles to relax during a movement. An important point about cortical function is that much of the activity is important for the inhibition of muscular contraction. For example, when lesions of the motor cortex controlling jaw muscles were made in monkeys, the jaw closing muscles were tonically active and the monkeys were not able to open their jaws to eat (Larson, Byrd, Garthwaite, and Luschei, 1980).

The idea that sensory influences project to cells in the motor cortex led Phillips (1968) to hypothesize that there exists in higher mammals and humans a "transcortical servo loop." This loop is mediated by proprioceptors (e.g., muscle spindles) and mechanoreceptors that project through their relays to the somatosensory and motor cortex. At the cortex the influence of the sensory input is strong enough to excite groups of neurons, which in turn project to motoneurons and lead to muscle contractions. Phillips proposed that in higher mammals this loop has evolved to such an extent that it has become more important than the traditional reflexes mediated at the spinal cord for the correction of movements. Moreover, by traversing the cerebral cortex, this transcortical servo loop may be affected by learning and behavioral set (Evarts and Tanji, 1974). For example, if a person is expecting a certain type of mechanical disturbance to a limb during a voluntary act, he may be able to counteract the influence of the disturbance so that it does not interfere with performance of the act.

Most of the research on the motor cortex has been in relation to the spinal system using animal subjects. There are, however, a few studies that have dealt with the cranial nervous system. McGuinness et al. (1980) studied the facial area of the motor cortex in monkeys using microstimulation. These investigators found that stimulation of discrete areas with low electrical currents, presumably within a single column, would elicit a discrete movement of the face. These movements resulted from contraction of single facial muscles or parts of facial muscles. Stimulation over a wide area of the facial motor cortex elicited a variety of movements. This research suggests that the facial cortex is also comprised of columns, and that each column has a slightly different function. Excitation of several columns would lead to contractions of several muscles. It may be presumed that a particular facial expression or posturing of the lips for a specific speech sound would be caused by activation of cells in several columns of the lateral motor cortex.

In a similar series of studies, Zealear et al. (1985) explored a slightly more lateral region of the motor cortex to investigate motor control of the laryngeal system. They also found that microstimulation in discrete areas led to activation of discrete muscles or movements. However, insofar as the larynx is concerned, they were unable to demonstrate that stimulation of the cortex led to the single isolated contraction of a laryngeal muscle without concomitant contraction of pharyngeal, tongue, lip, or jaw muscles. It may be that monkeys have not evolved discrete control of laryngeal muscles in the same fashion that other muscles are controlled.

At the cortical level, cells in the motor cortex may be the most important for the direct, voluntary control of movements. When this area is damaged, the effects on voluntary motor acts are profound. In experimental situations, lesions in the fibers descending from the motor cortex in monkeys leads to marked paresis of the affected limbs. Following ample time for recovery from the surgical intervention, the primary deficit is the loss of skilled, fractionated use of the digits. That is, monkeys were unable to use a single digit or appose their thumb and a finger for a delicate task (Beck and Chambers, 1970). In the control of jaw muscles, which is more akin to a "speech-like" task, ablations of the face area of the motor cortex result in monkeys being unable to regulate the force of muscle contraction (Luschei and Goodwin, 1975). In this case, other neuronal systems, presumably subcortical, cause excitation of the muscles, which cannot be controlled or inhibited after the lesions.

In humans the effects of motor cortex ablations seem to be greater. There is a problem, however, when interpreting the results from human studies. These studies have analyzed motor disturbances following accidental injury to the cortex, and frequently the damage also affects other areas of the cortex or subcortical

structures. It is therefore difficult to ascertain if the deficits result from damage exclusively to area 4 or to other areas as well. Nevertheless, the evidence is clear that when area 4 is damaged the individual loses the ability to make skilled purposeful movements with the affected limb. Because cells in the motor cortex exert such a strong influence on motoneurons, and because their destruction leads to such devastating results, they are sometimes referred to as "upper motoneurons."

From this brief description of the motor cortex, it is clear that it is an important structure for motor control. Although relatively little research of the motor cortex has dealt with systems involved in speech control, observations from clinical cases indicate that the same mechanisms important for limb control are involved in the control of speech musculature. It may be suggested at this point that individual cells of the motor cortex project to motoneurons and interneurons of the brainstem and spinal cord and cause contractions of discrete muscles. What is lacking at this point is knowledge of how the individual cells of the motor cortex are controlled so that their combined output leads to coordinated muscular contractions and purposeful movements. Some structures involved in this "higher order" motor control are discussed next.

The supplementary motor cortex (SMA) lies on the mesial surface of the frontal lobe and is contiguous with area 6 of the dorsolateral cortical surface. It receives projections from area 5 and 7 and projects to areas 4 and 6 as well as the brainstem and spinal cord (Macpherson, Wiesendanger, Marangoz, and Miles, 1982; Petrides & Pandya, 1984). The SMA also receives inputs from the ventral lateral nucleus of the thalamus, which receives inputs from the globus pallidus. This fact may indicate that function of the SMA is related to the basal ganglia (Kandel and Schwartz, 1985). Anatomically, the SMA is in a position to receive afferents related to sensation and to affect motor output directly through its corticospinal connections or with the motor cortex.

Recordings of single units in the SMA indicate that it plays a role in motor function different from that of the motor cortex. By comparing potentials from the SMA and motor cortex, Tanji (1985) showed that SMA neurons are less related temporally to specific movements than are motor cortex neurons. However, when a specific sensory cue such as a visual or auditory stimulus was used to trigger the movement, the SMA neurons were highly active. It may be that the SMA is involved in the decision-making process of movement execution in response to triggering stimuli. In a study mapping regional cerebral blood flow, it has been shown that when people make repetitive movements, or rehearse repetitive movements without executing them, there is increased activity in the SMA, suggesting that this area is involved in programming repetitive motor sequences (Kandel and Schwartz, 1985).

The premotor cortex (area 6) lies anterior to the motor cortex. It receives inputs from sensory areas of the parietal cortex and ventral lateral nucleus of the thalamus and projects directly to the motor cortex. Studies of neuronal activity in monkeys indicate that cells respond to visual or auditory stimuli that serve as cues for the initiation of movement and for guiding limb movements in space (Godschalk, Lemon, Kuypers, and Van Der Steen, 1985; Ito, 1982). Other premotor cortex neurons are active in preparation for a movement, and this activity represents anticipation by the animal of execution of a specific movement (Mauritz and Wise, 1986).

The results from lesion experiments on premotor cortex are largely consistent with the unit recording studies. Lesions of the premotor cortex in monkeys lead to deficits in the execution of skilled movements involving eye–hand coordination (Deuel, 1977; Moll and Kuypers, 1977; Sasaki and Gemba, 1986). Passingham (1985) found that the impairment of movements in monkeys with lesions of area 6 depends on how the instructional cues are presented to them. In humans, involuntary grasping responses are elicited by tactile stimulation of the palmar surface in patients with premotor ablations (Kandel and Schwartz, 1985). Again, the involvement of sensation and movement execution seems to be a predominant sign when the premotor cortex is damaged.

Considered together, the results of experiments on the SMA and premotor cortex suggest that these areas are related to motor behavior in abstract ways. That is, motor acts requiring preparation—attention to relevant stimuli for particular behaviors—seem to be those most heavily dependent on these two motor areas.

There are important details still lacking on how the projections to other areas of the brain give rise to normal coordinated movements.

As discussed in other chapters, the cerebral cortex communicates with other areas of the brain through well-established neural pathways. In this context, it is important to realize that the cerebral cortex does not operate in isolation but interacts heavily with areas such as the basal ganglia, cerebellum, red nucleus, and reticular formation. For purposes of physiologic investigation, it is often convenient to study only one such area at a time, although the interactions among these areas must be remembered.

CEREBELLUM

The cerebellum appears to be more directly related to motor coordination than perhaps any other area of the brain, except the MNs themselves. There is some general topographic organization of the cerebellum, and damage to the various regions can affect all types of motor activity. The connections between cells in the cerebellum are consistent among animal species and throughout the regions of the cerebellum. This consistency has provided neuroscientists with the opportunity to learn more about the physiology of the cerebellum than perhaps any other area of the brain. The following discussion refers to Figure 3-19A, which describes the cerebellar connections.

This discussion proceeds from the inputs to the cerebellum, through their interconnections, and concludes with the outputs from the cerebellum. There are two types of afferent fiber to the cerebellum: mossy fibers and climbing fibers. The latter arise from cells in the inferior olivary nucleus of the medulla. These fibers enter the cerebellum through the inferior cerebellar peduncle and project to the contralateral cerebellum. The fibers give off collaterals to the deep cerebellar nuclei and then terminate on the Purkinje (P) cells of the cerebellar cortex. Each climbing fiber innervates about ten P cells, but each P cell receives only one climbing fiber. Climbing fibers discharge about once per second, causing the P cells to discharge with a burst of spikes (Llinas and Simpson, 1981).

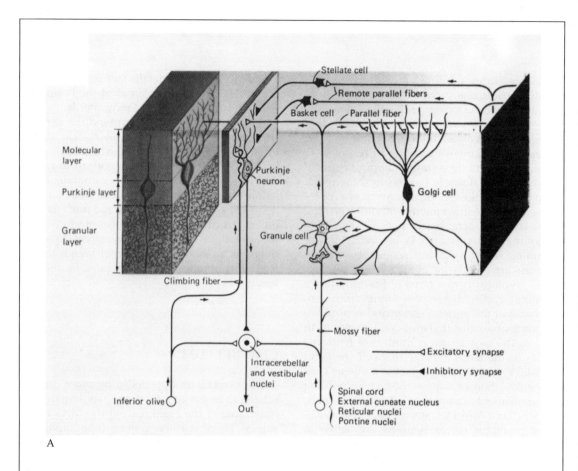

A

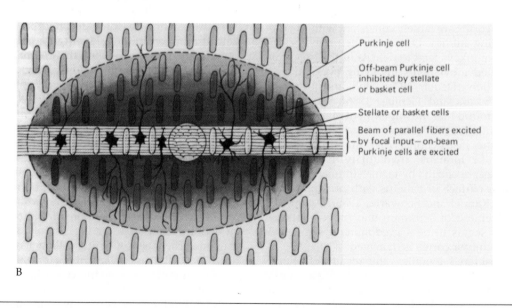

B

Fig. 3-19. A. Cells of the cerebellar cortex and their connections. B. Eccles' concept of how a band of parallel fibers would excite a narrow "beam" of Purkinje cell dendrites. By excitation of stellate and basket cells, the parallel fibers would cause adjacent Purkinje cells (off beam) to be inhibited. For details see text. (From Kandel, E., and Schwartz, J. *Principles of Neural Science,* 1st ed. New York: Elsevier, 1981. With permission.)

The mossy fibers arise from numerous sources, including the pontine nuclei, lateral reticular nuclei, and spinocerebellar tracts. These fibers also give off collaterals to the deep nuclei as well as project to the cerebellar cortex. The fibers end as glomeruli in the granular cell layer of the cortex. There, excitatory synapses are made with the dendrites of granule cells. The axons of granule cells project to the top of the folium (cortical "hill"), where they bifurcate into two branches in the molecular layer. Each branch, called the parallel fibers, proceeds longitudinally along the folium for about 2 mm. Along this route, the parallel fibers intersect the dendritic trees of about 50 P cells, giving off excitatory synapses to each. Each dendritic tree of the P cell is intersected by about 200,000 parallel fibers. The parallel fibers also excite stellate and basket cells, which send their axons in a perpendicular direction to the parallel fibers and inhibit P cells. The result of the excitatory mossy fibers' input to the cerebellum is that a bundle of parallel fibers causes a narrow focus of excitation to P cells along the length of a folium (termed "on beam") and lateral to this point is a stretch of inhibited P cells (termed "off beam") (Eccles, 1973). The parallel fibers also excite the Golgi cells, which in turn inhibit the granule cells (Fig. 3-19B).

The P cells thus receive excitatory inputs from the mossy fiber–parallel fiber system and climbing fibers. The P cells send inhibitory projections to the vestibular nuclei and the deep cerebellar nuclei. Thus the only output of the cerebellar cortex, the P cell, is inhibitory. It is thought that because the deep cerebellar nuclei receive excitation from the climbing and mossy fiber collaterals, they are continuously active. Therefore inhibition by P cells serves to modulate the activity of the deep cerebellar nuclei.

Although the physiology of the cerebellum is becoming understood, its functional relations are less clear. Recordings from cerebellar neurons in monkeys trained to make specific movements have revealed that discharge of the cells is correlated with various aspects of a movement, e.g., maintaining a position, starting a movement, or stopping a movement (Thach, 1978). Disruption of normal cerebellar function by temporary cooling has shown that monkeys make errors when stopping or starting a trained arm movement (Brooks, Kozlovskaya, Atkin, Horvath, and Uno, 1973). From clinical studies

it is widely recognized that the cerebellum is important for motor control and speech. Because the cerebellum receives sensory inputs from all areas of the body, it is likely that the cerebellum utilizes sensory information to aid in motor coordination. Some investigators (Allen and Tsukahara, 1974) have proposed that sensory feedback through the intermediate zone of the cerebellum assists in motor coordination. The intermediate zone, in turn, projects through the interposed nuclei of the cerebellum to the red nucleus and ventral lateral nucleus of the thalamus, and then to the motor cortex where connections are made with descending fibers to the MNs.

The lateral part of the cerebellum may be more involved in the planning and execution of movements. According to this scheme, the "idea" to move first arises in the association areas of the cerebral cortex, which project to the basal ganglia and lateral part of the cerebellum. The lateral cerebellum then projects through the dentate nuclei to the ventral lateral and ventral anterior nuclei of the thalamus to the motor cortex. The motor cortex then sends projections to the MNs. The cortical descending outputs also give off collaterals to the pontine nuclei, which in turn project back to the cerebellum and keep the cerebellum informed of the intended movements (Allen and Tsukahara, 1974). Thus through the sensory inputs and motor output collaterals through the pontine nuclei, the cerebellum aids in the continuous coordination and execution of movements.

The results of naturally occurring trauma to humans and the planned experiments in animals have provided additional insights into the function of the cerebellum in motor control. Early in this century, Holmes (1917) observed from casualties of World War I that damage to the cerebellum causes decomposition of movement, ataxia, and dysarthric speech. More recently, systematic investigations of the speech of cerebellum disordered patients have shown that slowness of movements, hypotonia, and inaccuracy of repetitive movements lead to speech characterized by slow rate, imprecise consonants, distorted vowels, excessive or equal stress, monopitch, and monoloudness (Brown, Darley, and Aronson, 1970). Together, this group of disorders is referred to as *ataxic dysarthria*.

BASAL GANGLIA

The basal ganglia are another group of CNS structures important for motor control. Most of the afferent input to the basal ganglia arrive at the caudate nucleus and putamen from wide areas of the cerebral cortex, intralaminar nucleus of the thalamus, and substantia nigra. The caudate nucleus and putamen project primarily to the internal and external parts of the globus pallidus. Most efferent fibers leave the basal ganglia from the globus pallidus and project to the ventral lateral and ventral anterior nuclei of the thalamus (recall that efferent fibers from the cerebellum dentate nucleus also project to these nuclei). Efferent fibers from the globus pallidus also project to the intralaminar nucleus of the thalamus and substantia nigra. Thus outputs from the basal ganglia do not project directly to MNs for their influence on motor control. Rather, by their projections back to the cerebral cortex through the thalamic relay, the basal ganglia affect motor control by influencing descending outputs from the cortex.

The connections made between the basal ganglia and other CNS structures have been studied widely; however, data on the role of the basal ganglia in motor control are fragmentary. By recording from neurons in the basal ganglia of animals trained to make specific movements, several important observations have been made. First, neurons of the globus pallidus and substantia nigra discharge prior to specific movements and therefore may be involved in the initiation and control of movement (Kandel and Schwartz, 1985). Some neurons of the globus pallidus also seem to be involved in making postural adjustments (Anderson, 1977). By relating basal ganglia neurons to specific parameters of movements, it has been found that they scale their discharge rate according to the magnitude, timing, and force of the movement (Anderson & Horak, 1985; DeLong, Crutcher, and Georgopoulos, 1983a). Units also have been recorded in the putamen of humans undergoing surgery, and they increase their discharge rate before movements of the arm and jaw. The units also are responsive to manipulation of the fingers (Martin-Rodriguez, Buno, and Garcia-Ausit, 1982). Interestingly, in the pars reticulata of the substantia nigra, a large proportion of the units have been found to change their discharge rates with licking and jaw movements but not with movements of other body parts (DeLong

et al., 1983b). The latter observation may be significant in that muscle systems innervated by the cranial nerves seem to be susceptible to a wide variety of disorders not common to muscles innervated by spinal nerves (e.g, myokymia, facial tics, hemifacial spasm, facial synkinesis, blepharospasm, Meige's syndrome, edentulous orodyskinesias, and drug-induced orodyskinesias) (Swanson, 1984). Therefore it must be assumed that some differences exist between the CNS control of facial muscles and of spinal muscles. It is possible that the area described by DeLong and colleagues (1983b) in the substantia nigra is one that when impaired may lead to one of the syndromes affecting the cranial facial area. From all of the above observations, it has been suggested that the basal ganglia may integrate information from various areas of the cerebral cortex for the determination of specific parameters of movement such as the direction or force of a movement (DeLong et al., 1983b).

The observations of patients with diseases affecting the basal ganglia conform with the above suggestion. Patients with diseases such as parkinsonism, Huntington's disease, athetosis, and chorea seem to exhibit signs of disorder in the control of parameters of movement. In hypokinetic dysarthria, resulting from basal ganglia damage, the range and extent of movement are reduced from normal. In hyperkinetic dysarthria, also resulting from basal ganglia damage, the range and extent of movements are excessive. In the milder forms of these diseases, patients can speak and execute movements, but precise control is impaired. In more severe cases the hypo- or hyperkinetic states can be severely debilitating.

Neurotransmitters play an exceedingly important role in all areas of the nervous system as discussed in Chapter 1. In the basal ganglia, relations between specific neurotransmitters and neurologic diseases have been linked closely. The following summary of connections between basal ganglia structures is provided to assist in the understanding of these relations. It is a brief review of information presented in Chapter 1. Within the dorsal part of the substantia nigra are found neurons that project to the neostriatum (putamen and caudate nucleus) and use dopamine as their neurotransmitter. In the striatum, neurons using ACh and γ-aminobutyric acid (GABA) as their transmitters project to the substantia nigra, globus pallidus, and thalamus. It is thought that some of the nigro-striatal projections are inhibitory (Coyle and Schwarcz, 1976). In parkinsonism, with the loss of dopamine neurons in the substantia nigra, there follows a loss of inhibition of the ACh (cholinergic) and GABA neurons in the striatum. The latter neurons may become overactive and lead to signs of parkinsonism. In some patients surgical ablation of the outputs of the striatum at the globus pallidus or thalamus alleviates some of the symptoms of parkinsonism. In other cases such surgical procedures are less effective. Because these surgical procedures yield inconsistent results, they are not universally advocated (Selby, 1967).

In Huntington's disease and chorea, the ACh and GABA neurons of the striatum are destroyed. Because these cells are inhibitory, there follows a disinhibition of neurons in the substantia nigra. The latter, in turn, become more active, resulting in excessive inhibition of pallidal neurons projecting to the thalamus. To support this scheme and illustrate the complexities arising from drug therapy in the CNS, administration of cholinergic or antidopaminergic drugs relieves signs of chorea and may produce side effects with signs such as those of parkinsonism. On the other hand, administration of anticholinergic or dopaminergic drugs alleviates some signs of parkinsonism but may produce signs like those of chorea (Penney and Young, 1983).

To summarize, the literature on function of the basal ganglia in motor control is still incomplete. Animal studies have revealed rough correlations between activity of cells and certain parameters of movement. Clinical studies in humans have shown disruption in the control of parameters of movement. Together, the literature suggests that basal ganglia are important for control of movement. Just how the basal ganglia interfaces with other areas of the brain in terms of motor control is not yet fully understood.

DESCENDING MOTOR SYSTEMS

As discussed in Chapter 2, neuroscientists traditionally have divided the motor system into two components: the pyramidal and extrapyramidal systems also called the direct and indirect motor systems respectively. According to this classification, the pyramidal system arises from the motor cortex and descends to the MNs; and the extrapyramidal system includes all other structures (e.g., cerebellum, basal ganglia, and thalamus) whose influence eventually impinges on the MNs. This classification may be somewhat unfortunate, however, because of the close relations between various structures and the fact that within the classically defined extrapyramidal system there appear to be major differences in function.

Considering first the pyramidal, or direct, system, about 30 percent of the one million fibers (in humans) in this pathway originate in the precentral gyrus, 30 percent arise from the premotor cortex, and about 40 percent arise from the sensory cortex (Kandel and Schwartz, 1985). Only about 3 percent of the fibers from the precentral gyrus arise from Betz cells and are thought to make monosynaptic connections with MNs of the distal and orofacial musculature in higher primates. Collaterals from pyramidal tract fibers also project to the striatum, thalamus, red nucleus, brainstem reticular formation, pontine nuclei, and sensory relay nuclei of the dorsal columns. The extrapyramidal, or indirect, system is generally described as including the basal ganglia, thalamus, cerebellum, substantia nigra, subthalamic nucleus, red nucleus, reticular formation, and the connections between them. Because the basal ganglia and cerebellum exert most of their influence on the motor system by projecting back to the cerebral cortex, there is considerable interaction between the classically defined extrapyramidal system and the pyramidal system. The distinction between these two systems is therefore misleading.

Despite the above cautions, people still tend to regard the output of the cerebral cortex as the most important for motor control. These feelings no doubt arise from the severe disturbances in motor behavior, language, and cognition resulting from damage to the cerebral cortex. Even though cortical damage can cause such impairments, not all of the deficits necessarily can be attributed solely to direct cortical projections to the MNs. In controlled experiments on animals, it has been found that following lesions of the pyramidal tract the only long-lasting impairment in motor control is the loss of fractionated movements of the digits (Beck and Chambers, 1970). Although one might suspect greater damage in humans, recall that only a small percentage of pyramidal tract fibers actually arise from the motor cortex, and many of the pyramidal tract fibers give off collaterals to other subcortical nuclei.

Descending pathways orginating from these subcortical nuclei are also important in motor control. Studies have shown that cells in the red nucleus are highly correlated with amplitude and velocity of movements of the wrist and hand in monkeys (Gibson, Hauk, and Kohlerman, 1985). Moreover, lesions of the rubrospinal tract in animals result in impairment of distal limb flexion movements (Schwindt, 1981). The vestibulospinal tract projects primarily to axial muscles and extensor muscles of the limbs. It seems to be mainly concerned with the oculomotor system, balance, and postural adjustments. Descending projections in the reticulospinal tract are not clearly understood, but some studies indicate that they facilitate flexor MNs and inhibit extensor MNs of the limb musculature (Schwindt, 1981). Additionally, within the midbrain there appears to be an area capable of producing locomotion when stimulated, termed the mesencephalic locomotion center (Garcia-Rill, Skinner, Jackson, and Smith, 1983). It is unclear how this system may function in normal awake animals and humans. Located near this region is the periaqueductal gray matter. Experiments indicate that parts of this region are important in some types of vocalization and may influence other brainstem nuclei involved in coordinating different groups of muscles during vocalization (Larson and Kistler, 1986).

In general, there are several descending systems that affect motor activities. Experimental evidence for the precise role of some of these systems is fragmentary at present, whereas in other cases (e.g., for the cerebral cortex and red nucleus) understanding is rapidly improving. Nevertheless, it must be stressed that a great deal needs to be learned before definitive statements can be made regarding the precise role each of the these systems plays in motor control. At the very least it should be stressed that a great deal of interaction between the various motor systems takes place subcortically.

As a final point, it must also be mentioned that much of the interaction between the descending motor pathways probably occurs at the MNs themselves. Each MN receives thousands of synaptic inputs from descending motor pathways. The net excitatory or inhibitory balance of the EPSPs and IPSPs determines if an MN generates an action potential and causes muscular contraction. If a particular type of input is missing or nonfunctional, e.g., from the cerebral cortex, the MN responds to the other inputs, and the contraction of muscles reflects both the loss of cortical inputs and the activity of other descending pathways. It also must be remembered, however, that each of the other descending pathways is itself influenced by the cerebral cortex, and so it may behave abnormally as well. It should be obvious that the control of motor behavior with the influence of sensory input is complex and poorly understood. Nevertheless, through continued research into the basic mechanisms of motor control and sensory input, the contribution of each component of the system as well as how the different components interact with each other will be learned.

REFERENCES

Allen, G. I., and Tsukahara, N. Cerebrocerebellar communications systems. *Physiol. Rev.* 54:957, 1974.

Anderson, M. E. Discharge of basal ganglia neuron during active maintenance of postural stability and adjustment to chair tilt. *Brain Res.* 143:325, 1977.

Anderson, M. E., and Horak, F. B. Influence of the globus pallidus on arm movements in monkeys. III. Timing of movement-related information. *J. Neurophysiol.* 54:433, 1985.

Asanuma, H., and Rosen, I. Topographical organization of cortical efferent zones projecting to distal forelimb muscles in the monkey. *Exp. Brain Res.* 14:243, 1972.

Asanuma, H. Cerebral cortical control of movement. *Physiologist* 16:143, 1973.

Asanuma, H., and Fernandez, J. J. Organization of projection from the thalamic relay nuclei to the motor cortex in the cat. *Brain Res.* 71:515, 1974.

Beck, C. H., and Chambers, W. W. Speed, accuracy and strength of forelimb movement after unilateral pyramidotomy in rhesus monkeys. *J. Comp. Physiol. Psychol.* 70:1, 1970.

Brooks, V. B., Kozlovskaya, I. B., Atkin, A., Horvath, F. E., and Uno, M. Effects of cooling dentate nucleus on tracking-task performance in monkeys. *J. Neurophysiol.* 36:974, 1973.

Brown, J. R., Darley, F. L., and Aronson, A. E. Ataxic dysarthria. *Int. J. Neurol.* 7:302, 1970.

Byers, M. R., and Yeh, Y. Fine structure of subepithelial free and corpuscular trigeminal nerve endings in anterior hard palate of the rat. *Somatosens. Res.* 3:265, 1984.

Carpenter, M. B., and Sutin, J. *Human Neuroanatomy.* Baltimore: Williams & Wilkins, 1983.

Cheney, P. D., and Fetz, E. E. Corticomotoneuronal cells contribute to long-latency stretch reflexes in the rhesus monkey. *J. Physiol. (Lond)* 349:249, 1984.

Coyle, J. T., and Schwarcz, R. Lesion of striatal neurones with kainic acid provides a model for Huntington's chorea. *Nature* 263:244, 1976.

DeLong, M. R., Crutcher, M. D., and Georgopoulos, A. P. Relations between movement and single cell discharge in the substantia nigra of the behaving monkey. *J. Neurosci.* 3:1599, 1983a.

DeLong, M. R., Georgopoulos, A. P., and Crutcher, M. D. Cortico-basal ganglia relations and coding of motor performance. *Exp. Brain Res.* 7(suppl.):30, 1983b.

Deuel, R. K. Loss of motor habits after cortical lesions. *Neuropsychologia* 15:205, 1977.

Dreyer, D. A., Loe, P. R., Metz, C. B., and Whitsel, B. L. Representation of head and face on postcentral gyrus of the macaque. *J. Neurophysiol.* 38:714, 1975.

Duffy, F. H., and Burchfiel, J. L. Somatosensory system: organizational hierarchy from single units in monkey area 5. *Science* 172:273, 1971.

Eccles, J. C. The cerebellum as a computer: patterns in space and time. *J. Physiol. (Lond)* 229:1, 1973.

Evarts, E. V. Relation of pyramidal tract activity to force exerted during voluntary movement. *J. Neurophysiol.* 31:14, 1968.

Evarts, E. V. Activity of motor cortex neurons in association with learned movement. *Int. J. Neurosci.* 3:113, 1972.

Evarts, E. V., and Tanji, J. Gating of motor cortex reflexes by prior instruction. *Brain Res.* 71:479, 1974.

Evarts, E. V., and Fromm, C. Sensory responses in motor cortex neurons during precise motor control. *Neurosci. Lett.* 5:267, 1977.

Fromm, C., and Evarts, E. V. Pyramidal tract neurons in somatosensory cortex: central and peripheral inputs during voluntary movement. *Brain Res.* 238:186, 1982.

Garcha, H. S., and Ettlinger, G. Tactile discrimination learning in the monkey: the effects of unilateral or bilateral removals of the second somatosensory cortex (area SII). *Cortex* 16:397, 1980.

Garcia-Rill, E., Skinner, R. D., Jackson, M. B., and Smith, M. M. Connections of the mesencephalic locomotor region (MLR) I. Substantia nigra afferents. *Brain Res. Bull.* 10:57, 1983.

Gibson, A. R., Houk, J. C., and Kohlerman, N. J. Relation between red nucleus discharge and movement parameters in trained Macaque monkeys. *J. Physiol. (Lond)* 358:551, 1985.

Godschalk, M., Lemon, R. N., Kuypers, H. G. J. M., and Van Der Steen, J. The involvement of monkey premotor cortex neurones in preparation of visually cued arm movements. *Exp. Brain Res.* 18:143, 1985.

Halata, Z., and Munger, B. L. The sensory innervation of primate facial skin. II. Vermilion border and mucosa of lip. *Brain Res. Rev.* 5:81, 1983.

Henneman, E., Somjen, G., and Carpenter, D. O. Functional significance of cell size in spinal motoneurons. *J. Neurophysiol.* 28:599, 1965.

Hille, B. *Ionic Channels of Excitable Membranes.* Sunderland, Mass.: Sinauer, 1984.

Hodgkin, A. L., and Huxley, A. F. Currents carried by sodium and potassium ions through the membrane of the giant axon of Loligo. *J. Physiol. (Lond)* 116:449, 1952.

Hoffman, D. S., and Luschei, E. S. Responses of monkey precentral cortical cells during a controlled jaw bite task. *J. Neurophysiol.* 44:333, 1980.

Holmes, G. The symptoms of acute cerebellar injuries due to gunshot injuries. *Brain* 40:461, 1917.

Houk, J., and Henneman, E. Responses of Golgi tendon organs to active contractions of the soleus muscle of the cat. *J. Neurophysiol.* 30:467, 1967.

House, E. L., and Pansky, B. *A Functional Approach to Neuroanatomy.* New York: McGraw-Hill, 1967. P. 238.

Ito, S-I. Prefrontal activity of macaque monkeys during auditory and visual reaction time tasks. *Brain Res.* 247:39, 1982.

Jennings, V. A., Lamour, Y., Solis, H., and Fromm, C. Somatosensory cortex activity related to position and force. *J. Neurophysiol.* 49:1216, 1983.

Kaas, J. H., Nelson, R. J., Sur, M., Lin, C. S., and Merzenich, M. M. Multiple representations of the body within the primary somatosensory cortex of primates. *Science* 204:521, 1979.

Kandel, E. R., and Schwartz, J. H. *Principles of Neural Science* (2nd ed.). New York: Elsevier, 1985.

Kolb, B., and Milner, B. Performance of complex arm and facial movements after focal brain lesions. *Neuropsychologia* 19:491, 1981.

Larson, C. R., Byrd, K. E., Garthwaite, C. R., and Luschei, E. S. Alterations in the pattern of mastication after ablations of the lateral precentral cortex in rhesus macaques. *Exp. Neurol.* 70:638, 1980.

Larson, C. R., and Kistler, M. K. The relationship of periaqueductal gray neurons to vocalization and laryngeal EMG in the behaving monkey. *Exp. Brain Res.* 63:596, 1986.

Leinonen, L., and Nyman, G., II. Functional properties of cells in anterolateral part of area 7 associative face area of awake monkeys. *Exp. Brain Res.* 34:321, 1979.

Llinas, R. R., and Simpson, J. I. Cerebellar control of movement. In A. L. Towe and E. S. Luschei (eds.), *Handbook of Behavioral Neurobiology, Vol. 5: Motor Coordination.* New York: Plenum, 1981.

Luschei, E. S., Garthwaite, C. G., and Armstrong, M. E. Relationship of firing patterns of units in face area of monkey precentral cortex to conditioned jaw movements. *J. Neurophysiol.* 34:552, 1971.

Luschei, E. S., and Goodwin, G. M. Role of monkey precentral cortex in control of voluntary jaw movements. *J. Neurophysiol.* 38:146, 1975.

Macpherson, J., Wiesendanger, M., Marangoz, C., and Miles, T. S. Corticospinal neurones of the supplementary motor area of monkeys: a single unit study. *Exp. Brain Res.* 48:81, 1982.

Marlow, C. D., Winkelmann, R. K., and Gibilisco, J. A. General sensory innervation of the human tongue. *Anat. Rec.* 152:503, 1965.

Martin-Rodriguez, J. G., Buno, W., and Garcia-Ausit, E. Human pulvinar units, spontaneous activity and sensory-motor influences. *Electroencephalog. Clin. Neurophysiol.* 54:388, 1982.

Matthews, P. B. C. *Mammalian Muscle Receptors and Their Central Actions.* Baltimore: Williams & Wilkins, 1972.

Mauritz, K-H., and Wise, S. P. Premotor cortex of the rhesus monkey: neuronal activity in anticipation of predictable environmental events. *Exp. Brain Res.* 61:229, 1986.

McGuinness, E., Siversten, D., and Allman, J. M. Organization of the face representation in Macaque motor cortex. *J. Comp. Neurol.* 193:591, 1980.

Moll, L., and Kuypers, H. G. J. M. Premotor cortical ablations in monkeys: contralateral changes in visually guided reaching behavior. *Science* 198:317, 1977.

Munger, B. L., and Halata, Z. The sensory innervation of primate facial skin. I. Hairy skin. *Brain Res. Rev.* 5:45, 1983.

Passingham, R. E. Premotor cortex: sensory cues and movement. *Behav. Brain Res.* 18:175, 1985.

Penney, J. B., and Young, A. B. Speculations on the functional anatomy of basal ganglia disorders. *Annu. Rev. Neurosci.* 6:73, 1983.

Petrides, M., and Pandya, D. N. Projections to the frontal cortex from the posterior parietal region in the rhesus monkey. *J. Comp. Neurol.* 228:105, 1984.

Phillips, C. G. The Ferrier lecture: motor apparatus of the baboon's hand. *Proc. R. Soc.* [B] 173:141, 1968.

Porter, R. Relationship of the discharges of cortical neurones to movements in free-to-move monkeys. *Brain Res.* 40:39, 1972.

Rosen, I., and Asanuma, H. Peripheral afferent inputs to the forelimb area of the monkey motor cortex: input-output relations. *Exp. Brain Res.* 14:257, 1972.

Ruch, T. C., and Patton, H. D. *Physiology and Biophysics.* Philadelphia: Saunders, 1965.

Sasaki, K., and Gemba, H. Effects of premotor cortex cooling upon visually initiated hand movements in the monkey. *Brain Res.* 374:278, 1986.

Schwindt, P. C. Control of motoneuron output by pathways descending from the brain stem. In A. L. Towe and E. S. Luschei (eds.), *Handbook of Behavioral Neurobiology, Vol. 5: Motor Coordination.* New York: Plenum, 1981.

Selby, G. Stereotaxic surgery for the relief of Parkinson's disease. I. A critical review. *J. Neurol. Sci.* 5:315, 1967.

Stein, R. B. *Nerve and Muscle: Membranes, Cells and Systems.* New York: Plenum, 1980.

Swanson, P. D. *Signs and Symptoms in Neurology.* Philadelphia: Lippincott, 1984.

Tanji, J. Comparison of neuronal activities in the monkey supplementary and precentral motor areas. *Behav. Brain Res.* 18:137, 1985.

Thach, W. T. Correlation of neural discharge with pattern and force of muscular activity, joint position, and direction of intended next movement in motor cortex and cerebellum. *J. Neurophysiol.* 41:654, 1978.

Wyke, B. D., and Kirchner, J. A. Neurology of the larynx. In R. Hinchcliffe and D. Harrison (eds.), *Scientific Foundations of Neurology.* Chicago: Year Book Medical Publishers, 1976.

Zealear, D. L., Hast, M. H., and Kurago, Z. The functional organization of the primary motor cortex controlling the face, tongue, jaw, and larynx in the monkey. In I. R. Titze and R. C. Scherer (eds.), *Vocal Fold Physiology: Biomechanics, Acoustics and Phonatory Control.* Denver: Denver Center for the Performing Arts, 1985.

CHAPTER 4

Developmental Neuro-anatomy and Neurophysiology

Paul C. Bunger

❏ Basic Development

❏ Myelination

❏ Speech

❏ Hearing

❏ Language

❏ Comparative Myelination of Speech, Hearing, and Language Structures

When one evaluates the neurologic bases of speech, hearing, and language, it is essential to consider the maturational sequence of these functions. Maturation of function can be evaluated in several ways. One method is to assess the performance of individuals on a time scale to see what capabilities they may have at certain points in time. One of the advantages of this system is that a given individual can be reevaluated at a later time, and the change in performance can be specifically correlated in that individual.

A second method for evaluating maturation is to study anatomic development. The advantage of this method is that many measurements of anatomic maturity can be precisely measured or quantified. However, an important disadvantage is that in most anatomic studies the data collection is conducted at autopsy or during biopsy. In either case, it is not clear if the specific structures evaluated were normal. A second disadvantage is that anatomic comparisons are made among individuals to determine a norm for a given population, and consequently the individual variation factor may be obscured when in fact it should always be kept in mind.

In this chapter the anatomic and physiologic development of the structures involved in speech, hearing, and language are summarized. An effort is made to correlate, where possible, the identifiable anatomy with the measurements of function. Remember that the data gathered are almost always from two populations of individuals. Functional data are derived from the living, whereas anatomic data are from biopsy or autopsy records. Therefore precise prediction of parallels between anatomy and physiology remains somewhat tenuous.

On the cellular level there are seven steps of development (Cowan, 1978). These steps appear to apply to all areas of development of the central nervous system (CNS), particularly the organization of the nuclear areas and gray matter: (1) production of an initial group of neurons and glial, or support, cells; (2) migration of cells to a more definitive location; (3) a selective gathering of cells that will form more definitive functional groups; (4) cytodifferentiation including formation of an axon, several dendrites, and early synaptic patterns; (5) selective death of some of the cells in the groups; (6) outgrowth of axons to specific target cells and establishment of appropriate connections; and (7) elimi-

nation of certain connections and functional stabilization of others.

This pattern of development takes place in areas associated with all functions including speech, hearing, and language. Myelination and further modifications of synapses bridge the gap between anatomic connections and functionally mature pathways.

BASIC DEVELOPMENT

NEURAL TUBE

During the third week of gestation the nervous system first appears as a neural plate lying on either side of a central axis and toward the head, or cranial, end of the developing embryo (Fig. 4-1). This neural plate undergoes dorsal folding followed by fusion to form a neural fold and finally a neural tube (Fig. 4-2). The neural tube forms first in the region that will become the cervical area and then closes like a zipper with progression passing both cranially and

Fig. 4-1. Embryonic disc at 18 days' gestation, dorsal view. The dotted area is neural tissue. The neural plate widens and then folds so that its right and left edges come together.

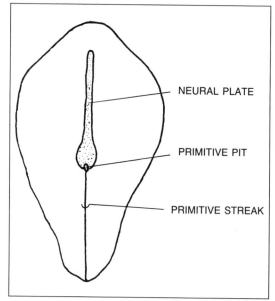

NEURAL PLATE

PRIMITIVE PIT

PRIMITIVE STREAK

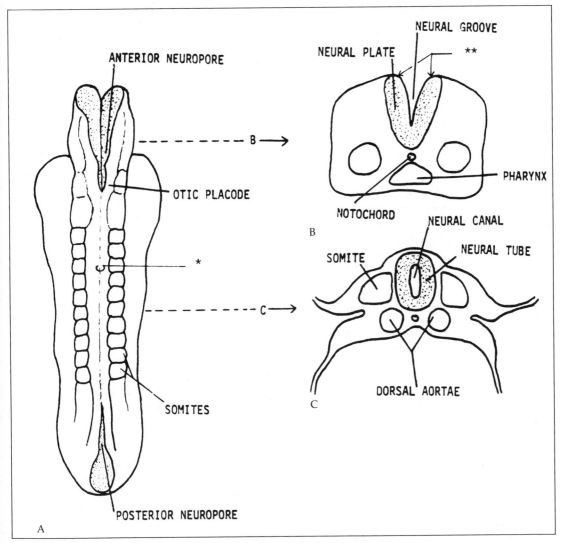

Fig. 4-2. Embryo at 22 days' gestation. Dotted area is neural tissue. A. Dorsal view. Note that the anterior and posterior neuropores are open. (*) The site of fusion resulting in formation of the neural tube. B. Transverse slice at level B. Note that the neural plate is still folding. (**) These edges of the neural plate fuse to form the neural tube. The space labeled "neural groove" becomes enclosed as the neural canal. C. Transverse slice at level C. Note that at the midsection of the body the neural plate has formed the neural tube and neural canal.

caudally, or toward the tail end of the embryo. The opening at the cranial end is called the anterior neuropore, and the one at the caudal end is the posterior neuropore. Closure of the anterior neuropore by day 24 and the posterior neuropore by day 26 completes the formation of the primitive CNS (Table 4-1). Essentially the CNS is now a hollow, tubular structure closed at both ends. The wall of this tube forms the substance of the nervous system and is called the neural tube. The fluid-filled cavity of this tube is called the neural canal, and it develops into the ventricular system of the brain and the central canal of the spinal cord. A small group of cells is pinched off at the site of fusion and migrates laterally to form the neural crest. The neural

TABLE 4-1. SEQUENCE OF APPEARANCE OF STRUCTURES

Gestational age (days)	Structure
18	Neural groove in neural plate
18	Optic disc, groove, and pit
22	Neural tube
24	Anterior neuropore closure
26	Otocyst formation
26	Caudal neuropore closure
26	Hypoglossal roots
28	Intramedullary roots of CN V, VII, IX, X, XI
32	Vestibular ganglion
32	Occipital somites merge
32	Medial longitudinal fasciculus
32	First sign of organized tectum
33	Hypoglossal roots united
33	First sign of marginal layer in cortex
33	Fibers of CN VIII reach otic vesicle
33 (50% of cases)	Cochlear ganglion cells separate from vestibular ganglion
33	Thalamus begins to organize

From O'Rahilly, R., Müller, F., Hutchins, G. M., and Moore, G. W. Computer ranking of the sequence of appearance of 100 features of the brain and related structures in staged human embryos during the first 5 weeks of development. *Am. J. Anat.* 171:243, 1984. With permission.

crest cells give rise to the autonomic ganglia, sensory ganglia, adrenal medulla, and many other structures.

The cranial end of the primitive neural tube forms three primary dilations during the fourth week of gestation (Fig. 4-3). From cranial to caudal, these structures are called the prosencephalon, the mesencephalon, and the rhombencephalon. By 5 weeks the prosencephalon has further subdivided into the bilaterally projecting telencephalon and the more medially located diencephalon. Shortly thereafter, the rhombencephalon divides into the metencephalon and myelencephalon. There are five secondary brain vesicles at this stage (Fig. 4-3).

MAJOR DIVISIONS OF THE SECONDARY VESICLES

As the brain continues to differentiate, the telencephalon gives rise to the frontal, parietal, occipital, temporal, and limbic lobes as well as

to the insula. Table 4-2 shows the major derivatives of each of the primitive parts of the brain. The telencephalon includes not only the cortical areas on the surface of these lobes but also the deeper white matter with its interwoven association, commissural and projection fibers, and deep telencephalic or subcortical nuclei including the amygdala, caudate nucleus, putamen, and perhaps the globus pallidus. Some authorities believe that the globus pallidus is a derivative of the diencephalon. This difference of opinion can be used to point out one of the useful principles about the nervous system: the system normally functions as a unit. Dividing it into named areas is done as a matter of convenience to enable scientists to formulate a better understanding of the complexities of nervous system function.

The most cranial part of the telencephalon is the primitive lamina terminalis (Fig. 4-3). This region gives rise to the commissures between the hemispheres, with a small portion of the original structure persisting as the definitive lamina terminalis.

The telencephalic portions of the primitive neural canal become the lateral ventricles (Table 4-2). These ventricles expand laterally with the telencephalon and subsequently take on their characteristic shape by following internally the growth of the frontal, parietal, temporal, and occipital lobes.

The diencephalon is prominent during the second month. However, as growth of the telencephalic vesicles continues, the diencephalon soon becomes hidden. The walls of the diencephalic vesicle develop into the thalamus, hypothalamus, epithalamus, and subthalamus. The mesencephalon becomes the midbrain, the metencephalon forms the pons and cerebellum, and the myelencephalon becomes the medulla. The dilated neural canal becomes the slit-like third ventricle in the diencephalon, the narrow cerebral aqueduct in the midbrain, and the widened fourth ventricle in the pons and cranial part of the medulla.

TELENCEPHALIC SUBDIVISIONS

The telencephalon develops by laterally directed growth of the cranial portion of the prosencephalon beginning during the seventh week. The basal portion soon becomes much

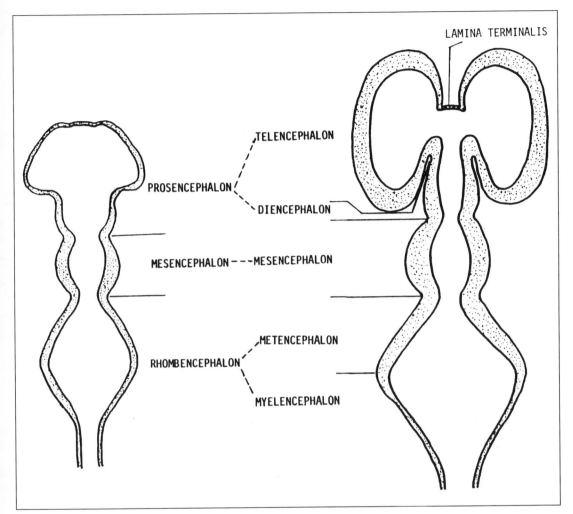

Fig. 4-3. Left. Dorsal view of the developing nervous system in coronal section. The dotted area is neural tissue, and the clear area is the developing ventricular cavity. During the fourth week the nervous system has three primary brain vesicles. Right. Dorsal view of the nervous system in coronal section at 5 weeks. Note that there are now five secondary brain vesicles. The two sides of the telencephalon have grown laterally and will become the cerebral hemispheres.

thicker than the dorsal and lateral parts. The basal portion gives rise to the caudate and lentiform nuclei, and the dorsal and lateral parts become the cerebral cortex. Soon the hippocampi can be seen as bulges along the medial walls of the dorsally adjacent telencephalic vesicles. The neocortex develops dorsal to these regions. The neocortex eventually comprises the major surface areas of the telencephalon and gives origin and termination to projection fibers from all parts of the body via the internal capsule.

Lateral to the caudate and lentiform nuclei the paleocortex develops, which gives rise to the areas of the anterior medial temporal lobe associated with the olfactory system. As these dilations expand laterally, the eventual regions of the frontal, parietal, occipital, and temporal lobes become identifiable. The olfactory bulb forms at the medial base of the frontal lobe area and attaches laterally to the anterior medial part of the temporal lobe.

It is possible to begin seeing the various lobes of the brain during weeks 10 to 14. This division comes about by the sequential appearance of the major sulci. The interhemispheric (longitudinal) fissure is the first to appear (at 10 weeks)

TABLE 4-2. DERIVATIVES OF THE BRAIN VESICLES

Primary vesicle	Secondary vesicle	Adult structure	Subdivisions	Ventricular derivative	Cranial nerve
Prosencephalon	Telencephalon	Telencephalon	Cerebral cortex White matter Subcortical nuclei	Lateral ventricle	I
	Diencephalon	Diencephalon	Thalamus Hypothalamus Epithalamus Subthalamus	Third ventricle	II
Mesencephalon	Mesencephalon	Midbrain	Tectum Tegmentum Basis pedunculus	Cerebral aqueduct	III, IV
Rhombencephalon	Metencephalon	Pons	Tegmental pons Basal pons	Rostral fourth ventricle	V, VI, VII, VIII
		Cerebellum	Cortex White matter Deep nuclei		
	Myelencephalon	Medulla	Reticular Olive Pyramid	Caudal fourth ventricle Central canal	IX, X, XII (XI = spinal cord)

and then the lateral fissure (at 14 weeks). Table 4-3 shows the sequence of appearance of the major sulci or fissures, and Figure 4-4 shows the locations of most of these sulci.

The insula is first identifiable as the floor of the lateral fissure by 19 weeks. The insula is gradually overgrown by the frontal, parietal, and temporal lobes such that it becomes completely covered shortly after birth.

The central sulcus appears at around 20 weeks, with the right side usually preceding the left by 1 week. This sulcus then marks the division between the frontal and parietal lobes. Within the frontal lobe the precentral sulcus is identifiable by 24 weeks, followed by the inferior frontal sulcus by 28 weeks. At the same time the triangular gyrus and frontal operculum become identifiable along the anterior portion of the lateral fissure. Secondary and tertiary gyri are further subdivisions of these primary gyri. The frontal operculum shows secondary gyri by 32 weeks and tertiary gyri by 40 weeks. In a mature brain the tertiary gyri represent every identifiable bump on the surface that has a sulcus marking its boundaries. In some cases the tertiary gyrus is specific and named. However, in most cases a named gyrus has several subdivisions. It is important that one recognizes

that reference to a specific gyrus may not always be to a single, specific bump on the surface of the brain; it may refer to the general limits of a primary or secondary gyrus as well.

In the parietal lobe the postcentral sulcus appears at 25 weeks and the intraparietal sulcus by 26 weeks. The supramarginal and angular gyri become identifiable by 28 weeks. Again development on the right side precedes that on the left side. By 33 weeks secondary gyri form, and by 39 weeks tertiary gyri are visible.

The temporal lobe remains smooth until about 23 weeks' gestation. The superior temporal sulcus appears at this time, with the right side preceding the left side. By 26 weeks the middle temporal sulcus and gyrus are visible. Secondary gyri appear by 34 weeks.

The transverse temporal gyri (Heschl) appear by 31 weeks, with the right side usually preceding the left by as much as 2 weeks. The gyrus also extends farther in the anterior direction on the right side and more posterior on the left. The left gyrus is shorter and angled more away from the anterior-posterior axis of the brain than is the right gyrus.

The planum temporale is longer on the left side, as is the lateral fissure. These dimensions become more asymmetric as gestation contin-

TABLE 4-3. DEVELOPMENT OF GYRI AND SULCI

Gestational age (weeks)	Fissure/Sulcus	Gyrus
10	Longitudinal	Separates hemispheres
14	Lateral	Separates lobes
16	Parietooccipital	Separates lobes
16	Calcarine	Superior and inferior occipital lobules
18	Circular	Insula
18	Cingulate	Cingulate
20	Central	Separates lobes
23	Superior temporal	Superior temporal
24	Precentral	Precentral
25	Postcentral	Postcentral
25	Superior frontal	Superior frontal
26	Intraparietal	Superior and inferior parietal lobules
26	Middle temporal	Middle temporal
27	Middle frontal	Middle frontal
28	Inferior frontal	Triangular
28		Angular
28		Supramarginal
31		Transverse temporal

From Dooling, E. C., Chi, J. G., and Gilles, F. H. Telencephalic development: changing gyral patterns. In F. H. Gilles, A. Leviton, and E. C. Dooling (eds.), *The Developing Human Brain*. Boston: John Wright, 1983. Pp. 105–116. With permission.

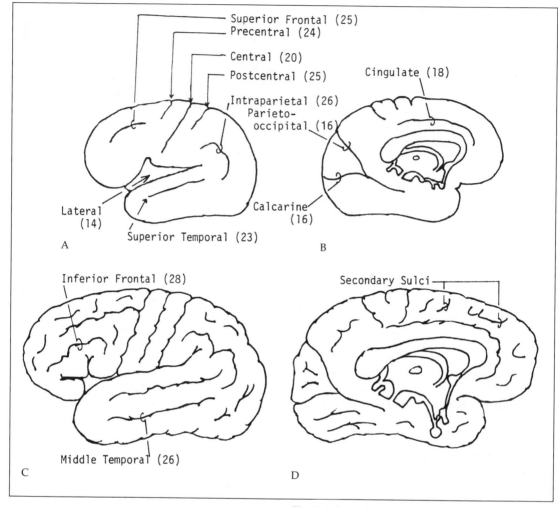

Fig. 4-4. Lateral (A) and medial (B) views of a brain at 26 weeks' gestation. C and D. Near the time of birth. The sulci, or fissures, have numbers to indicate the week of gestation when the structure begins to appear. There are many secondary and tertiary gyri present at birth, but they are not represented here.

ues. Secondary transverse temporal gyri appear after 36 weeks. In about one-half of the cases in one study (Jammes and Gilles, 1983), there were two gyri on the right and one on the left. In about 20 percent of the individuals the pattern was reversed, and in the remainder there was either one on both sides or two on both sides. Obviously, these differences would be noticeable during development as well, at least after the thirty-first week. However, it was noted that the transverse temporal gyri on the right tended to be more complex. In general, the frontal and temporal formation of secondary and tertiary gyri precedes that of the orbital areas and the occipital lobe.

During the later stages of gestation the opercula or folds of tissue covering the frontal, pa-

rietal, and temporal lobes begin to overgrow the insula. The opercula are of major significance in that attempts to localize function in specific areas of the brain show that these areas are involved in the processes of hearing, speech, and language. The temporal operculum contains the primary auditory cortex and the auditory association area. The parietal operculum is associated with language formation and integration of hearing and vision, as well as conduction of messages to the motor speech area. The portion of the sensorimotor strip associated with the head and neck, including the pharynx and larynx, marks the adjacent boundaries of the frontal and parietal opercula. The motor speech area is located in the frontal operculum.

DIENCEPHALIC SUBDIVISIONS

The diencephalon continues to develop primarily from the thickened lateral walls of the more caudal portion of the prosencephalon. It eventually becomes the four components of the diencephalon: thalamus, hypothalamus, epithalamus, and subthalamus. The diencephalon gradually shows formation of its largest nuclear mass, which forms the thalamus. This region transmits the fibers of the internal capsule as they pass between the telencephalon and midbrain. As the thalamus continues to differentiate, the major nuclear groups developing from the marginal zone can be seen: anterior, medial, ventral, and dorsal nuclei. In addition, the medial and lateral geniculate nuclei form as caudal extensions of the ventral group and lie inferior to the pulvinar, which in turn is a part of the dorsal group. The geniculates are a part of a phylogenetically newer division of the thalamus and consequently develop later than do the more primitive portions of the thalamus. The dorsal thalamic nuclei and the pulvinar show a rapid enlargement phase that begins during weeks 24 to 26 (Cooper, 1950).

The thickened lateral walls of the diencephalon are subdivided by a longitudinal hypothalamic sulcus. Dorsal to this sulcus the definitive thalamus forms, and ventrally and anteriorly the hypothalamus begins to differentiate. The hypothalamus further divides into the mamillary nuclei more caudally, the infundibulum at its ventral midpoint, and the optic chiasm at its more cranial end.

The subthalamus forms immediately caudal to the hypothalamus, with the epithalamus, including its habenular complex and pineal gland, forming dorsally and caudally. The hypothalamus and epithalamus begin to differentiate earlier than the thalamus. The pineal gland can be seen by 7 weeks. In the roof plate area near the pineal gland, two commissures form: The habenular commissure forms dorsal to the pineal, and the posterior commissure forms ventral to the pineal.

GENERAL PATTERN OF BRAIN GROWTH

The overall changes in the weight of the brain throughout gestation follow a curvilinear pattern, with an acceleration of growth rate during the twenty-fourth and twenty-fifth weeks. The growth of the cerebral cortex proper is relatively slow from 8 weeks through midgestation. A dramatic increase in the rate of growth coincides in part with the brain weight changes beginning during week 21 and continuing through week 26. The growth rate is much faster for the remainder of the fetal period than during the earlier weeks. The cortex does not show a left or right asymmetry of growth even though there is a hemispheral difference in the formation of sulci and gyri.

Studies of DNA in the brain during development show that there are two stages during which there is a marked increase in DNA content (Trevarthen, 1979). The first is during the twelfth to twentieth weeks of gestation, which coincides with formation of the cortical gray matter. A second, more prolonged increase in DNA content occurs from the thirtieth week of gestation up to about 3 months of age, which coincides with dramatic increases in myelination, dendritic growth, and glial cell proliferation.

The tubular structure of the developing CNS can be divided regionally into a roof plate and floor plate with an alar plate and a basal plate lying between them (Fig. 4-5). The floor plate and basal plate do not provide derivatives cranial to the midbrain. The roof plate has a consistent nonneuronal derivation in the brain and brainstem. In these regions the roof plate thins and is invaginated by blood vessels to form the tela choroidea. The tela choroidea further differentiates into the choroid plexus for production of cerebrospinal fluid. There is a choroid plexus associated with each of the ventricles. The choroid plexus lies in the groove between the tail of the caudate and the thalamus, within the lateral ventricle. It is continuous through the interventricular foramen to form the choroid plexus of the third ventricle, which lies along the dorsal and medial aspect of the thalamus. In the fourth ventricle it is located laterally and projects through the lateral aperture.

The alar plate gives rise to virtually all of the substance of the diencephalon. Because the alar plate consists primarily of sensory and associa-

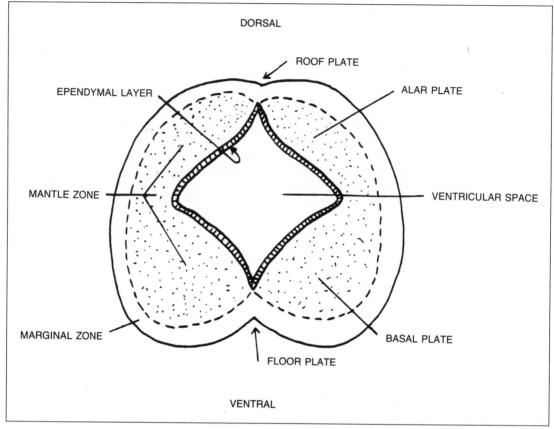

Fig. 4-5. Transverse view of the central nervous system during the fourth week of development. The alar plate is the most important for development of telencephalic and diencephalic gray matter.

tion neurons, this outcome is a logical developmental expectation.

Histologically, the CNS develops as a tubular structure with three layers: an inner ependymal layer, an intermediate mantle layer, and a more superficial marginal layer (Fig. 4-5). In the region of the telencephalon, the ependymal layer expands during the early weeks of fetal life to form a layer of germinal matrix. The germinal matrix zone gives rise to nerve cells and glial cells. This layer increases in size between 13 and 26 weeks; then, as differentiation proceeds, it begins suddenly to lose its volume. It is reduced to one-half its previous size by 28 weeks and gradually regresses after that. The cells from the germinal matrix zone adjacent to the ventricle remain as the ependymal layer of the newborn and adult brain.

The marginal layer gives rise to the white matter, which consists of projection fibers passing to and from the cortex, the long association bundles that interconnect major lobes in the same hemisphere, and commissures that interconnect the two cerebral hemispheres. In addition, short association fibers interconnect adjacent gyri and further contribute to the substance of the brain.

In the telencephalon, some cells of the mantle zone migrate to the surface and form a cortical zone. The cortical zone begins with a deeper pyramidal layer that eventually gives rise to layers II through VI of the mature cortex. The outermost layer or layer I, develops from the plexiform layer of the cortical zone.

The pyramidal layer is at first composed of cells called neuroblasts, which eventually become mature neurons. The glial cells appear later. As more neuroblasts are formed, the newer ones migrate farther toward the surface. Consequently, the cells in the deeper layers develop before those in the more superficial layers. The most massive migration of cells into these outer layers begins at around 12 weeks' gestation. The migration of cells at an earlier age may give the appearance of superficial to deep striation of the cortex (Larroche, 1966). After 26 to 28 weeks the horizontal interconnections of the layers begin to be more prominent. Although little information is available on the timing of this neuronal migration, the potential for identifying the timing of basic insult to the developing system is remarkable. Obviously, the development of layering in specific gyri would be of great interest and value to many areas of research.

SPECIFIC PATTERNS OF BRAIN GROWTH

Internally, the corpus striatum, which consists of the caudate and lentiform nuclei, develops by marked proliferation of the germinal zone at the basal lateral part of each telencephalic vesicle. Before long there is a division of medial and lateral components. As the temporal horn grows, it carries with it the ventricle and caudate nucleus to form their typical C-shaped configuration. Consequently, the caudate nucleus lies on the floor of the superior horn of the lateral ventricle and on the roof of the temporal horn.

While the caudate nucleus is developing, fibers going to and from the cortex pass in a major bundle between the caudate nucleus and the lentiform nucleus. This fiber bundle forms the internal capsule. Lying medial to the internal capsule is the caudate nucleus, and lateral to the fiber tracts is the lentiform nucleus.

There is considerable variation in development from one region of the cortex to the other. The hippocampus is structurally the first part of the cortex to begin to develop, but the specific microscopic arrangement of its cellular layers occurs relatively late in fetal life. Mantle zone cells migrate into the marginal zone along the medial aspect of the developing hemispheres. As the temporal lobe forms, the hippocampus follows and then begins to roll inward to form its characteristic intertwined layering, as seen in coronal slices. At about this time the hippocampi of the two sides are joined by the hippocampal commissure. This commissure ac-

tually forms within the primitive lamina terminalis. There is some apparent regression of the hippocampus prior to the end of gestation.

After the hippocampus forms, the paleocortex appears. This structure is formed by cells migrating from the mantle zone near the upper lateral boundary of the corpus striatum. This migration helps account for the layering of cells in the definitive cortex. Eventually this area becomes the cortex of the uncus above or medial to the rhinal sulcus and part of the parahippocampal gyrus.

The neocortex forms from the wall of the telencephalic vesicle, which lies between the hippocampus and the paleocortex. With the formation of the temporal and frontal lobes, the neocortex soon dominates the lateral surface of the telencephalon.

During the eighth week some cells of the mantle layer of the neocortex begin to migrate into the marginal layer to form the more primitive superficial cortical layer. This process takes place first in the lateral wall and later along the dorsal and medial aspects of the hemisphere. By 12 weeks it extends to the frontal and occipital poles. The earliest definitive site of neocortical development is in the parietal lobe. The formation of the six-layered neocortex continues from 8 weeks' gestation until the time of birth. Motor areas develop prominent pyramidal cells, and sensory areas show predominantly granular cells. Final maturation of the outer three layers of cortex is not complete until middle childhood.

Three telencephalic commissures develop from the primitive lamina terminalis. The first to appear is the anterior commissure, which connects the anterior medial temporal lobes beginning at around week 12. The second to form is the hippocampal commissure. By 14 weeks there are nonolfactory fibers added to the dorsal aspect of the hippocampal commissure, which eventually becomes the corpus callosum. This corpus callosum soon becomes the largest commissure, and by the twenty-fourth week the rostrum, genu, body, and splenium of the corpus callosum are identifiable.

Table 4-1 lists several structures related to the functions of speech, hearing, and language as well as the time of their first appearance. Note that the otocyst is one of the earliest neural structures to develop (during week 4). Note also the general pattern of appearance of peripheral sensory and motor structures followed by the appearance of nerve roots and central reflex pathways.

MYELINATION

Any description of anatomic and functional maturity must include a discussion of myelination. Myelination provides a unique blending of an anatomically identifiable substance that directly relates to function. It appears that neurons can conduct an impulse prior to myelination, but the ability to conduct repetitive stimuli at a rapid rate requires myelin (Huttenlocher, 1970).

CHARACTERISTICS OF MYELINATION

When considering myelination one must bear in mind six characteristics: (1) Myelination is highly variable among individuals. In all aspects of development there are individual variations in timing, rate, and sequence. In fact, this statement may describe one of the more significant concepts of development. Consider not only the "normal" variations among genetically different individuals but also the environmental influences on both mother and fetus and later on the newborn. Thus when data are presented as typical, they may not represent the complete pattern of any one individual. (2) Myelination is characterized by differences in the rate of myelination for differing structures. The total time committed to the process of myelination varies, depending on the fiber tract involved. Some tracts may not complete myelination for several months or even years after others have completely matured. (3) The total amount of myelination necessary for any one structure to appear "mature" is variable. Complete maturity is difficult to pinpoint because some areas of the brain appear to continue the process of myelination for many years, even up to age 70 years or more (Yakovlev and Lecours, 1967). (4) Myelination is directional within a given tract. The process usually begins near the cell body and proceeds to the termination of the peripheral process. (5) Myelination is a contin-

uous sequence between its time of onset and its completion, which means that myelination increases with time and that this increase is gradual, not in stages. (6) In general, myelination follows a phylogenetic pattern. The structures that are analogues of more primitive forms of life are likely to myelinate earlier.

PROCESS OF MYELINATION

The process of myelination signals the onset of mature function. Although neurons are capable of conducting an impulse prior to myelination, it is generally agreed that the precision of function of a particular tract is characterized by its degree of myelination. Degrees of myelination are, however, relative to the maximum myelination known for that given tract, and some neurons remain unmyelinated.

The early formation of myelin in the brainstem is indicated by a change in the glial cells, which show an increase in the size of the nuclei and nucleoli with the accumulation of premyelin lipids in the cytoplasm (Chi, Gilles, Kerr, and Hare, 1976). As the myelin is deposited around the axon, cerebroside increases, esterified lipid decreases, and mature myelin accumulates. Glial cell nuclei are gradually displaced (Matthews and Duncan, 1971), and the oligodendrocytes take on a mature appearance.

Myelination takes place by a different mechanism in the CNS than in the peripheral nervous system (PNS). In the CNS a single oligodendrocyte extends several of its processes to wrap myelin sheaths around several adjacent axons (Bunge, Bunge, and Ris, 1961). In contrast, in the PNS Schwann cells group together to wrap around a single axon. Because there is a difference in this process there is also a significant difference in response to injury. In the PNS there is a process that allows regeneration of the axon. When that part of the axon surrounded by Schwann cells dies, the Schwann cells undergo mitosis, which provides a solid cord of these cells. The stump of the axon, which survives the injury, grows and sends its regenerating tip into the cord of Schwann cells, following this group of cells to its original destination. The Schwann cells then myelinate the newly grown axon. In the CNS the loss of one of the axons myelinated by oligodendrocytes does not result in the formation of a cord of cells, as the oligodendrocytes must remain functional to maintain the status of the undamaged axons.

SPEECH

When considering the developmental aspects of speech, it is important to first establish the distinction between speech and language. Second, one must consider speech from the point of view of how its maturation is measured. Third, speech output is a different function from speech formulation. For example, when an individual knows and plans what to say, *speech formulation* has taken place. The actual production of what was planned is the *speech output*. The integration of auditory input, multiple sensory input, and memory or experience are important contributors to speech formulation. Speech is discussed in this chapter in the sense of using the mechanisms of respiratory, laryngeal, pharyngeal, lingual, palatal, labial, and mandibular structures. Details concerning the mature neuroanatomy and neurophysiology of these structures are explored in Chapters 5 and 6. Development of facial expressions, gestures, and so on, which fit better into a category of nonverbal language, are not discussed.

Speech maturation is considered based on the neuroanatomic changes in structures known to be associated with production of speech as well as the neurophysiologic changes in these structures. No attempt is made to draw direct correlations between neuroanatomic and neurophysiologic changes in measurements of speech production in infants or children. It is significant to recognize that even though the timing of neurologic development may correlate closely in some areas with the timing of speech onset or the beginning of certain parameters of speech and language maturity, it is also true that some areas do not necessarily fit into such a clear picture. Finally, the mechanisms of how thoughts, ideas, or sensory input trigger a verbal plan and then carry out that plan with actual speech remain a mystery.

DEVELOPMENT OF CORTICAL AREAS

The triangular gyrus, or Broca's convolution, which is important for language formulation, shows formation and definition around the 28th week of gestation (see Table 4-3). By 32 weeks secondary gyri are visible, and by birth tertiary gyri are present (Dooling, Chi, and Gilles, 1983).

MYELINATION OF SPEECH PATHWAYS

Myelination of the telencephalon does not begin until around the time of birth. The precentral gyrus and premotor areas begin to myeli-

TABLE 4-4. TIME OF BEGINNING MYELINATION

Gestational age (weeks)	Structure
22	Ventral spinal nerve roots
22–24	Dorsal spinal nerve roots
24	Trapezoid bundle
24	Medial longitudinal fasciculus–pons and medulla
24–26	Vestibular nerve root (CN VIII)
26	Facial nerve root (CN VII)
26–28	Trigeminal nerve root (CN V)
26–28	Lateral lemniscus–pons
26–28	Medial lemniscus–medulla
28	Medial longitudinal fasciculus–midbrain
28	Cranial nerve roots (CN IX, X, XII)
28	Lateral lemniscus–midbrain
28–30	Medial lemniscus–pons and midbrain
30	Cochlear nerve root (CN VIII)
30	Inferior colliculus
36–38	Pyramidal tract–pons
36–38	Superior colliculus
36–38	Internal capsule
38–40	Ventral thalamus
38–40	Geniculocalcarine tract
40	Geniculotemporal tract

From Larroche, J-C. The development of the central nervous system during intrauterine life. In F. Falkner (ed.), *Human Development*. Philadelphia: Saunders, 1966. Pp. 257–276. With permission.

nate first at the postnatal age of 1 month. At the same time, the postcentral gyrus, the area around the calcarine fissure, and Heschl's gyrus show beginning myelination (Yakovlev and Lecours, 1967). The precentral and postcentral gyri, Heschl's gyrus, and the area around the calcarine fissure are the specific, or primary, areas of cortical function. A secondary area of cortical myelination includes the opercular and paralimbic zones. The last parts of the cortex to mature are Broca's convolution, the auditory association area, and the supramarginal and angular gyri.

In general, myelination in a tract progresses from the nuclear area of origin toward termination of the tract. Some areas, such as the corona radiata and internal capsule, do not always appear to follow such a sequence because they are composed of bundles of fibers passing in both directions. The corona radiata begins myelination as early as 24 weeks (Gilles, Shankle, and Dooling, 1983). There is then a dramatic increase, so that some individuals may have reached maturity of myelination by birth. The posterior limb of the internal capsule begins myelination in some individuals as early as 23 weeks' gestation, and some even show mature development by 37 weeks.

The specific projection tracts to spinal levels, and brainstem levels begin myelination near the cortex and progress toward the target neurons. In general, the corticospinal tracts to the spinal cord precede the corticonuclear (corticobulbar) tracts to the brainstem nuclei. The corticospinal tracts in the midbrain may begin to show myelination by 23 weeks, and some individuals show maturity at this level by 40 weeks. The corticonuclear tracts in the midbrain show onset of myelination around 27 weeks' gestation, but maturity occurs postnatally. In most individuals the maturity of the entire corticospinal and corticonuclear tracts actually begins only around the time of birth, and they may not be mature until after 8 months of age.

The corticopontine tracts, which are involved with the pathways of coordination through the cerebellum, myelinate much more slowly. Even though they begin to myelinate by 2 to 3 months of postnatal age, the process continues for 3 to 4 years (Yakovlev and Lecours, 1967).

Afferent, or sensory, fiber pathways usually myelinate throughout the brainstem before efferent, or motor, fiber pathways. In contrast, the motor roots of cranial nerves myelinate

sooner and at a faster rate than do the sensory roots (Yakovlev and Lecours, 1967). Even the relatively short portions of the cranial nerves that lie within the substance of the brainstem show myelination of motor fibers sooner than sensory fibers.

The cranial nerves myelinate in several stages. The earliest group includes the trigeminal (V), facial (VII), vestibulocochlear (VIII), glossopharyngeal (IX), vagus (X), spinal accessory (XI), and hypoglossal (XII) nerves. The second group includes the oculomotor (III), trochlear (IV), and abducens (VI) nerves. Myelination of the olfactory (I) nerve is next, and that of the optic (II) nerve is last. Thus the nerves involved with autonomic functions, balance, communication, and feeding behaviors mature earliest. The development of nerves controlling eye movements, olfactory functions, and vision comes later.

The myelination of cranial nerves involved in speech is also sequential (Larroche, 1966). At 26 weeks the facial (VII) nerve and possibly the trigeminal (V) nerve begin to show myelination. By 28 weeks the glossopharyngeal (IX), vagus (X), and hypoglossal (XII) nerves are also beginning myelination (Table 4-4).

HEARING

INNER EAR DEVELOPMENT

The development of the inner ear is intimately involved with the functions of both the vestibular system and the auditory system. The pattern of development of the cochlea must involve consideration of each of its components, including the cochlear duct, membranes, fluid-filled spaces, hair cells, and afferent and efferent connections with the cell processes of the cochlear nerve.

The first sign of inner ear development is present at the beginning of the fourth week of gestation when an otic placode can be identified. The placode invaginates from the surface and pinches off to form an otic vesicle. Between the fifth and the eighth weeks the cochlea develops by growth and coiling of an elongated evagination of the anterior and medial end of the otic vesicle. The posterior and lateral portion becomes slightly flattened in three planes to form the semicircular ducts, and the vestibule with its utricle and saccule remains located between the semicircular ducts and cochlea.

As the spiral of the cochlea forms, the internal structure of the cochlea also changes. Vacuoles appear in the mesenchyme surrounding the cochlear duct. When these vacuoles coalesce, they form the perilymphatic cavities of the scala vestibuli and the scala tympani. Meanwhile, the endolymphatic space, or cochlear duct, has flattened out slightly and becomes wedge-shaped in cross section, with the apex of the wedge directed medially and centrally in the spiral. This apex marks the site of nerve cell processes entering or leaving the cochlea.

During the eleventh week of gestation the organ of Corti begins to develop from the wall of the otic vesicle and projects toward the cavity of the scala tympani. As the cells thicken, the individual features of the mature organ of Corti become evident. Immature supporting cells are seen with hair cells embedded in them and a thin tectorial membrane lying along their surface. The area of the inner spiral sulcus is still filled with cells, which at this stage appear to have microvillous attachments to the inferior surface of the tectorial membrane (Thorn, Arnold, Schinko, and Wetzstein, 1979). By the fifth gestational month the pillar cells and the inner and outer hair cells can be identified. During the latter half of gestation the cells at the base of the inner spiral sulcus separate from the tectorial membrane, and geometric changes are seen in the position of pillar cells (Kraus and Aulbach-Kraus, 1981). This development forms, respectively, a definitive inner spiral sulcus and a more peripheral tunnel of Corti. It is also during this time that the basilar membrane thins out.

HAIR CELL DEVELOPMENT

The development of the single row of inner hair cells and the three to five rows of outer hair cells begins at around 5 months' gestation. At this stage the surface cuticular plate can be seen, as can the multiple stereocilia and a single large kinocilium (Fig. 4-6). Both the inner and outer hair cells appear to be flask-shaped at this time. The step-like arrangement of stereocilia can soon be identified; and the shortest cilia,

with the kinocilium, disappear shortly thereafter (Tanaka, Sakay, and Terayama, 1979).

At first the inner hair cells have many afferent and efferent connections. Afferent endings increase in size and distribution during development, and many of the efferent endings disappear. On the mature cells the afferent endings predominate. The efferent endings retain a few contacts primarily with the afferent endings, whereas most of their direct contacts with hair cells disappear (Fig. 4-6).

The outer hair cells show several contrasting features during their development. Although they begin with a shape similar to that of the inner hair cells, they soon become elongated and assume the shape of a cylinder. The innervation of these cells earlier in development is exclusively afferent, but efferent endings gradually appear. These efferent endings soon completely dominate the number of neuronal contacts such that in mature outer hair cells only a few afferent endings remain (Pujol, Carlier, and Devigne, 1979). In contrast to the flask-shaped inner hair cells, where the neuronal contacts surround the base of the cell and extend well up the side, the contacts on the cylinder-shaped outer hair cells are almost exclusively at the base.

MYELINATION OF THE VESTIBULOCOCHLEAR NERVE

Myelination of the peripheral neuronal processes within the bony modiolus takes place in an orderly fashion. Early in development these processes do not exhibit myelin sheaths. As the cells in the spiral ganglion mature, they become less densely packed, and several may show beginning myelination. By 30 weeks the cochlear division of the vestibulocochlear (VIII) nerve shows myelination (Larroche, 1966). The vestibular division of the vestibulocochlear (VIII) nerve is actually the first part of a cranial nerve to myelinate, with beginning evidence of the process by 24 weeks.

ANATOMIC MATURATION OF THE COCHLEA

Anatomic maturation of the cochlea begins near the base and proceeds toward both the

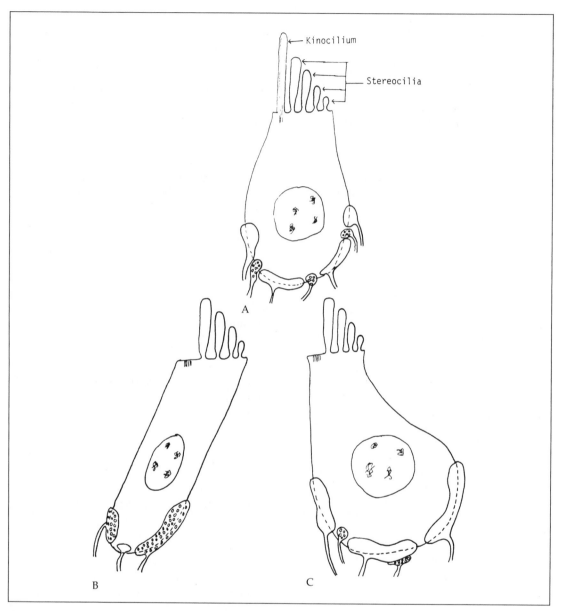

Fig. 4-6. A. Immature cell. B. Outer hair cell. C. Inner hair cell. The afferent endings in all three cells are clear; the efferent endings show synaptic vesicles. Note that the kinocilium degenerates, the efferent endings predominate on the cylinder-shaped outer hair cells, and the afferent endings predominate on the flask-shaped inner hair cells.

apex and the base (Bast and Anson, 1949). In the less mature areas the hair cells are closely packed, but later more supporting cells intervene (Tanaka et al., 1979). The immature hair cells have a single kinocilium with numerous small stereocilia. The more mature cells lose the kinocilium, and the stereocilia are greatly reduced in number. In addition, the inner row of hair cells matures earlier than the outer rows.

FUNCTIONAL MATURATION OF THE COCHLEA

Functional development of the cochlea goes through three stages (Romand, 1983). The first stage is before the onset of hearing. The second stage begins with the first measurement of function called the cochlear microphonic and ends with the appearance of an action potential in the vestibulocochlear (VIII) nerve. The third stage is characterized by modifications in both functions that allow more precise response to a given stimulus.

The first potentials in the inner ear relating to hearing are the cochlear microphonic and the summating potential. Prenatal measurements can be done only in experimental animals. As a result, the comparison with humans is by extrapolation. In mice, for example, the cochlear microphonic appears between 8 and 11 days' gestational age, depending on the strain of mouse, and the onset of action potentials is the next day. On the third day after onset of the cochlear microphonic, it appears that the fetal mice are capable of hearing. In humans onset of hearing is believed to occur late during the second trimester of pregnancy, during the twenty-second to twenty-fifth weeks (Johansson, Wendenberg, and Westin, 1964). In most experimental animals the onset of the cochlear microphonic shows the characteristics of increased threshold, narrow band width, and low amplitude (Romand, 1983). It is of interest to note that this rather restricted frequency range is uniform across many species and is usually in a range of 0.5 to 7.0 kHz.

CONTRASTS BETWEEN ANATOMY AND FUNCTION

There appears to be a significant contrast between the anatomic and the functional evidence of maturity. As previously stated, anatomic maturity starts near the basal turn of the cochlea, a region that eventually functions best for the higher frequencies. However, the evidence of functional maturity implies an earlier development toward the apex, where increased sensitivity to lower frequencies associated with speech is located.

It is accepted generally that the cochlear microphonic can be used to estimate cochlear function. Perhaps the apparent discrepancy between anatomic and functional maturation can be explained by the evidence that the cochlea is sensitive to low frequencies early, with peak sensitivity shifting toward the high frequencies later in development. It may also be that the structures being examined to identify anatomic maturity are not true indicators of functional maturity as measured by the cochlear microphonic. Further details of the cochlear potential are discussed in Chapter 8.

The origin of the cochlear microphonic is believed to begin at the top of the hair cell by the process of mechanical bending (Romand, 1983). However, it is also possible that it originates as a receptor potential. With the latter theory, the outer hair cells are responsible for the cochlear microphonic late in development, and the inner hair cells are responsible early. It is intriguing to speculate that the pattern of change in the cochlear microphonic may parallel the dominance of efferent fibers because it is known that efferent endings are prominent on the inner hair cells early and dominant on outer hair cells later.

The possibility that the thickness of the basilar membrane plays a role in functional maturity should be considered. The outer hair cells produce part of the cochlear microphonic based on the displacement of the basilar membrane, and the inner hair cells produce a cochlear microphonic proportional to the velocity of the displacement (Dallos, 1976). There is no doubt that the intricacies of development of the components of the cochlea could provide clues to the type of auditory stimulus available to the CNS at different stages of development.

MYELINATION OF AUDITORY NEURONS

Myelination of the neuroanatomic tracts associated with hearing show a sequential pattern. Myelination of the pathways below the medial geniculate nucleus appears to begin around the twentieth gestational week in the roots of the cochlear nerve (Yakovlev and Lecours, 1967). This myelination continues to involve successively higher levels, with gradual increases up to about 3 to 4 months' postnatal age.

The earliest tract of the auditory system within the brain stem to begin myelination is the trapezoid bundle, which is apparent around the twenty-third week of gestation (Gilles et al., 1983). The myelination of the trapezoid bundle is followed by that of the lateral lemniscus in the pons and then of the lateral lemniscus in the midbrain (Table 4-4). These tracts begin to myelinate during the twenty-fourth week, and their myelination is complete relatively early. It takes about 5 weeks for complete myelination of the trapezoid bundle and of the pontine level of the lateral lemniscus. The mesencephalic level of the lateral lemniscus has a 7-week cycle of myelination. It appears that in as many as 95 percent of fetuses myelination is nearly complete at all three of these brainstem sites at the time of birth (Gilles et al., 1983). It is noteworthy that myelination of the lateral lemniscus precedes the medial lemniscus by about 2 weeks (Yakovlev and Lecours, 1967).

The brachium of the inferior colliculus is the first fiber bundle to the thalamus to show myelination. The process begins at about 7 months' gestation and continues through the fourth postnatal month (Yakovlev and Lecours, 1967).

At levels above the medial geniculate nucleus, myelination occurs later. The geniculotemporal tract begins myelination around the time of birth and continues well into the fourth year of age. Although the auditory pathways develop earlier than the visual pathways in the brainstem, the geniculocalcarine tract completes myelination much sooner than the geniculotemporal tract.

This information demonstrates a contrast in that pregeniculate pathways myelinate relatively rapidly, whereas the postgeniculate tract myelinates over a completely different time frame. The pregeniculate pathways are nearly completely myelinated by birth, whereas the postgeniculate tract is just beginning to show myelination. Because the pregeniculate pathways are important for auditory reflexes, such as startle reflexes to loud noises, this pattern of myelination is consistent with earlier maturation of reflex pathways. In contrast, the postgeniculate pathways are more involved with cortical comprehension and conscious awareness of sounds, and these pathways mature and myelinate later.

As with virtually all major fiber systems in the CNS, there are minor nonlemniscal fiber tracts that go to the brainstem reticular area. In addition, there may be fiber tracts from a variety of areas of the nervous system that terminate in the same nucleus as the lateral lemniscus, an example being the nucleus of the inferior colliculus. These so-called minor fiber tracts have not been studied extensively but their importance to comprehensive auditory input, integration of function, and reflexes could be significant.

FUNCTIONAL MATURATION OF AUDITORY PATHWAYS

As with anatomic differences in sequences of maturation, there are also functional differences. It may be that complex functional abilities that are present early are more dependent on genetic predisposition, whereas those that appear later are more sensitive to environmental influence during critical periods of development.

The brainstem nuclei are important structures for study of auditory function. There are three cochlear nuclei encountered within the lower pons: the dorsal, posteroventral, and anteroventral nuclei. The anteroventral nucleus appears to function with rapid transmission of untransformed messages. The cell varieties in the dorsal and posteroventral nuclei indicate a potential for signal transformation at this level. These nuclei respond to both frequency and amplitude changes (Angelo, 1985). All three nuclei are capable of aiding in the process of pitch discrimination, which may include the interrelations of the frequencies used to detect distinctive features of speech. However, the medial geniculate nucleus appears to be much more capable of responding to the various acoustic features of speech (Angelo, 1985).

The complexities of functional development of the auditory system in the brainstem are illustrated by the development of the cochlear nuclei. There are nine cell types in the cochlear nuclei (Osen, 1969), and there is now evidence that they may each have specific functions and connections (Kiang, 1975; Kiang, Morest, Godfrey, Guinan, and Kane, 1973; Roth, Aitkin, Andersen, and Merzenich, 1978). Large cells appear first and intermediate sizes later. Some small granule cells appear postnatally. Other experimental evidence shows selective cell death in a cranial to caudal gradient (Rubel, Smith, and Miller, 1976). This evidence illustrates an often overlooked principle of normal development: Selective cell loss or degeneration is just as important as selective growth for proper function. In fact, specific degeneration of cells, cell processes, and even tracts is an important aspect of functional neuronal maturation (Cowan, Fawcett, O'Leary, and Stanfield, 1984).

Jhavari and Morest (1982a, 1982b) have shown that there are numerous dendritic branches in the immature cells of the cochlear nucleus. These branches withdraw as development progresses, leaving virtually no dendritic processes for establishing synapses with afferent fibers of the cochlear nerve in the mature cochlear nucleus. This selective loss permits a much more precise sorting of the auditory stimulus than would be possible with a large number of dendritic processes.

The two parts of the ventral cochlear nucleus change in size throughout life in humans (Konigsmark and Murphy, 1970, 1972), with volumes of about 5 mm^3 at birth, 12 mm^3 during the fifth decade, and returning to 8 mm^3 around age 90. This change is not in the number of neurons but appears to be related to cell body size, density of fibers entering or leaving the nucleus, and glial cells.

Functional maturation of the inferior colliculus has been studied extensively in the cat. Young kittens have an orderly tonotopic arrangement of cells, with the lower frequencies (0.5 kHz) represented near the surface. The higher frequencies increase with age. There is also an increase in the precision of tuning ability in the more mature inferior colliculus. There is some evidence from the cat that this tuning ability of the inferior colliculus lags behind that of the cochlear nerve (Carlier, Lenoir, and Pujol, 1979) and cochlear nucleus (Brugge, Javel, and Kitzes, 1978, and Brugge, Kitzes, and Javel, 1981). It is therefore possible that the sharpening of tuning function is related to the development of interneuronal connections (Brown, Grinnell, and Harrison, 1978) or the development of inhibitory neurons synapsing in the inferior colliculus.

Sharpened tuning may also be a result of reduced convergence of the auditory pathway in older animals. If many neurons synapse on one neuron, the level of convergence of stimuli is high. It results in much less precision of transmission because any number of stimuli can cause the single cell to be stimulated. Consequently, reduced convergence parallels in-

creased separation of function or precision. It may be possible that lower levels of auditory function undergo a parallel sharpening of tuning, which could help account for the overall increase in precision with age at the level of the inferior colliculus.

Altman and Bayer (1981) have shown that there is a cytogenic (cell development) sequence in the development of the auditory pathway. The sequence, or cytogenic gradient, begins in more cranial and lateral areas ventrally and continues in more caudal and medial areas dorsally. This pattern is similar to the pattern of neuronal function in the adult. High-frequency areas tend to overlap sites of earlier formed neurons, which are more sensitive to low frequencies. This information is consistent with the functional evidence of auditory maturity.

Thresholds in the inferior colliculus are generally high early in development and tend to decrease with maturity. The thresholds for low frequencies, however, tend always to remain relatively higher than the thresholds for higher frequencies.

The development of function of the auditory cortex is characterized by the length of time of the development of all processes. This fact is illustrated by the long latency period for stimuli to reach the cortex, which in turn is a reflection of the length of unmyelinated fibers. Even synaptic transmission seems to be relatively slow, which is due to the less effective immature enzymatic processes associated with neurotransmitters during development. Immature cortical areas exhibit the characteristics of low excitability and high threshold. In adults the stimulus thresholds for the various frequencies are fairly equal; consequently an increase in intensity of the stimulus produces a smaller net change in the mature cortex than in the immature cortex.

Another characteristic of the immature brain is its sensitivity to fatigue (Myslivecek, 1983). By way of illustration, the brainstem is able to produce higher rates of auditory evoked responses than the cortex. This neuronal evoked potential becomes more complex with increasing age. As development proceeds, the response to auditory stimuli is one of reducing the sensitivity of the pathway to fatigue while increasing the control of inhibitory capability. As in other functional areas of the nervous system, the ability to selectively modify afferent auditory stimuli with specific efferent control is a characteristic of the mature nervous system.

LANGUAGE

ATTEMPTS TO LOCALIZE LANGUAGE

When studying the development of the nervous system as it relates to language, several difficulties immediately emerge. Language is a combination of many aspects of function, including hearing, memory, experience, association, and speech production. Consequently, it is difficult to clearly define the process of language production.

A second difficulty is that in most cases where there is a clear functional loss in the nervous system a relatively specific region, area, tract, or nucleus can be identified as the site of the lesion producing that deficit. With language there are numerous components that work together to allow the advanced level of communication necessary for language formation. It becomes almost impossible to distinguish the specific functions anatomically.

In addition to the morphologic identity difficulty, there is no clear agreement on the type of mapping or model one should use to localize language (Buckingham, 1982). Some theories are precise in organizing the various cortical gyri into specific components of language. Others point to the interaction among Broca's area, Wernicke's area, the supplementary motor speech area, and diencephalic nuclei. Another model reflects a longitudinal building of language through the association bundles, and still others support a model of phylogenetic cortical type, building from limbic levels to generalized neocortex to asymmetric neocortex, and finally to sensorimotor cortex.

PLASTICITY

There is also the complicating factor that infants and children have a much greater plasticity of the brain and consequently can tolerate lesions and recover function much better than can adults. It is apparent that following injury in young individuals the brain still has the option of using parts of the cortex for development of language not normally associated with this function. Once the language becomes somewhat localized, the potential for recovery of function following insult is dramatically reduced.

MATURATION SEQUENCE

With these difficulties in mind, an attempt is made here to identify some evidence for a sequence of maturation. Because language is considered to be a function of the highest order in the nervous system, it is reasonable to assume that language function resides in those parts of the nervous system that develop later. In general, large neurons are associated with the projection pathways to and from the cortex, and these neurons develop early. Later the smaller and much more numerous interneurons develop. It may be that these smaller neurons are more responsive to experience or environmental influence (Jacobson, 1975). Consequently, the basic innate ability to activate the larynx, for example, may reside in the larger neurons, and the individual skills of symbolic and cognitive language may reside in the smaller neurons.

When analyzing the cortex, the large pyramidal cells of layer V develop first. Successive layers are then added to the surface. Within the layers, the last cells to develop a mature appearance are the stellate cells. These cells mature sooner in the deeper layers and later in the outer layer.

One significant feature of this pattern of development is that each type of neuron has a time during which it undergoes functional maturation. Signs of functional maturity include branching of axons and much growth and branching of the dendrites. Some degree of myelination also may occur. As the cells continue to mature, they appear to have a time during which they become more committed to a specific function. If this time period is short and the selective process of establishing synaptic fields does not proceed properly, the process may not be reversible and the opportunity to develop the full potential is gone (Jacobson, 1969).

It is significant that specific synaptic connections within a synaptic field are neither preselected nor permanent. Synapses form in excess early in the development of a region and then, gradually, only those that are needed survive (Cowan et al., 1984). In addition, synapses are dynamic, showing an ability to change position or contact site apparently as needed (Cowan et al., 1984; Jacobson, 1975).

Studies of regional cortical metabolic activity have demonstrated that changes in interrelations among functional areas may be responsible for deficits, in pathologic cases, rather than the loss of one specific site of function (Metter, Riege, Hanson, Phelps, and Kuhl, 1984). It may be that language also develops not as a specific site of maturity but, rather, as a gradually modified pattern of interrelations among many areas of the brain, including not only cortical areas but also subcortical nuclei and diencephalic nuclei. In fact, it may be that the subcortical nuclei coordinate the regional interrelations of the cortex (Metter et al., 1984). If this hypothesis is accurate, the relative maturation of the various components of the telencephalon and diencephalon would be contributing factors in the total process of language development.

COMPARATIVE MYELINATION OF SPEECH, HEARING, AND LANGUAGE STRUCTURES

The myelination patterns of the important anatomic structures associated with hearing, speech, and language are shown in Figure 4-7. The lower time line represents the beginning of myelination of that structure and the upper time line represents completed myelination. Where ranges of time of completion were available, the younger age was used for the graphic display. At birth and at 1 year postnatal age the scale on the time line changes. Consequently, the lines have angles at those changes to allow the slope of the line to be used to compare the differing myelination rates among structures within that time frame. The letters are selected for sequence of beginning myelination within the categories of hearing, speech, and language.

There are four significant patterns evidenced in this graph.

1. Structures involved with hearing tend to myelinate earlier than those involved with speech, and both precede structures involved with language. This pattern is logical and parallels the pattern of normal functional development.
2. Brainstem level structures (a–f, h) myelinate earlier than structures at higher levels of the nervous system. This sequence follows a pattern of maturation of reflex function prior to maturation of selective control of function or conscious awareness of function.
3. Specific tracts or pathways (a–c, e–i) myelinate prior to nonspecific association areas (j–m), and these areas both precede the nonspecific intercommunication between cortical layers (n). This sequence is consistent with a pattern of development that first involves individual specifics in language, later assimilates generalizations based on hearing and vision, and finally incorporates the nonspecific areas of judgment, experience, and emotion.
4. There are two structures whose myelination patterns cross the lines of myelination of other structures. The tectum (d) and striatum (l) begin to myelinate slightly after the initial myelination of functionally related structures but complete that myelination rather quickly, sooner than related structures. The tectum is an area where auditory information is integrated with other information, such as visual and somatic information. The concept of the striatum serving as a functional integration center for language production is consistent with studies that show increased metabolic activity in this area in association with language production (Metter et al., 1984).

It is important to recognize that, although many areas of hearing, speech, and language development have been investigated, others remain a mystery. Even though assumptions have been made about structure and function, it is important to remember that when a brain lesion occurs the functions of that brain are the result of the interactions of the remaining struc-

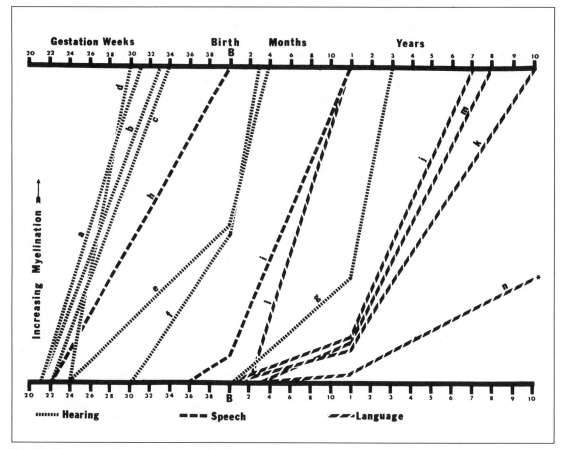

Fig. 4-7. Sequence and rate of myelination. Note the change of scale at birth and at 1 year. The structures normally associated with hearing, speech, and language are distinguished by the different patterns of lines. Structures associated with hearing: a = trapezoid bundle; b = lateral lemniscus in the pons; c = lateral lemniscus in the midbrain; d = tectum; e = sensory roots of the vestibulocochlear (VIII) nerve; f = brachium of the inferior colliculus; g = geniculotemporal tract. Structures associated with speech: h = motor roots of cranial nerves; i = corticonuclear (corticobulbar) tracts. Structures associated with language: j = short and then long association bundles; k = reticular areas; l = striatum; m = nonspecific thalamic radiations; n = intracortical neuropil (* = myelination of these areas continues at least into the third decade). See text for further explanations. (Data from Yakovlev and Lecours, 1967; Lecours, 1975; and Gilles et al., 1983.)

tures. Consequently, there is still no clear understanding of where many of these functions are located in the nervous system, particularly in relation to language. However, as continued efforts are made to identify functional changes in normal individuals and to correlate these changes with functional changes in normal development, there is hope for increasing the capabilities of reducing or preventing permanent deficits in future generations.

REFERENCES

Altman, J., and Bayer, S. A. Time of origin of neurons of the rat inferior colliculus and the relations between cytogenesis and tonotopic order in the auditory pathway. *Exp. Brain Res.* 42:411, 1981.

Angelo, R. M. Physiologic acoustic basis of speech perception. *Otolaryngol. Clin. North Am.* 18:285, 1985.

Bast, T. H., and Anson, B. J. *The Temporal Bone and the Ear*. Springfield, IL: Charles C Thomas, 1949. Pp. 87–92.

Brown, P. E., Grinnel, A. D., and Harrison, J. B. The development of hearing in the pallid bat Antrozous pallidus. *J. Comp. Physiol. [A]* 126:169, 1978.

Brugge, J. F., Javel, E., and Kitzes, L. M. Signs of functional maturation of the peripheral auditory system in discharge patterns of neurons in the anteroventral cochlear nucleus of kitten. *J. Neurophysiol.* 41:1557, 1978.

Brugge, J. F., Kitzes, L. M., and Javel, E. Postnatal development of frequency and intensity sensitivity of neurons in the anteroventral cochlear nucleus of kittens. *Hearing Res.* 5:217, 1981.

Buckingham, H. W., Jr. Neuropsychological models of language. In N. J. Lass, L. V. McReynolds, J. L. Northern, and D. E. Yoder (eds.), *Speech, Language and Hearing* (Vol. 1). Philadelphia: Saunders, 1982. Pp. 323–347.

Bunge, M. B., Bunge, R. P., and Ris, H. Ultrastructural study of remyelination in an experimental lesion in adult cat spinal cord. *J. Biophys. Biochem. Cytol.* 10:67, 1961.

Carlier, E., Lenoir, M., and Pujol, R. Development of cochlear frequency selectivity tested by compound action potential tuning curves. *Hearing Res.* 1:197, 1979.

Chi, J., Gilles, F., Kerr, C., and Hare, C. Sudanophilic material in the developing nervous system. *J. Neuropathol. Exp. Neurol.* 35:119, 1976.

Cooper, E. R. A. The development of the thalamus. *Acta Anat. (Basel)* 9:201, 1950.

Cowan, W. M. Aspects of neural development. In R. Porter (ed.), *International Review of Physiology, Neurophysiology III* (Vol. 17). Baltimore: University Park Press, 1978. Pp. 149–191.

Cowan, W. M., Fawcett, J. W., O'Leary, D. D. M., and Stanfield, B. Regressive events in neurogenesis. *Science* 225:1258, 1984.

Dallos, P. Cochlear receptor potentials. In R. J. Ruben, C. Eberling, and G. Salomon (eds.), *Electrocochlearography*. Baltimore: University Park Press, 1976. Pp. 5–21.

Dooling, E. C., Chi, J. G., and Gilles, F. H. Telencephalic development: changing gyral patterns. In F. H. Gilles, A. Leviton, and E. C. Dooling (eds.), *The Developing Human Brain*. Boston: John Wright, 1983. Pp. 105–116.

Gilles, F. H., Shankle, W., and Dooling, E. C. Myelinated tracts: growth patterns. In F. H. Gilles, A. Leviton, and E. C. Dooling (eds.), *The Developing Human Brain*. Boston: John Wright, 1983. Pp. 117–183.

Huttenlocher, P. R. Myelination and the development of function in the immature pyramidal tract. *Exp. Neurol.* 29:405–415, 1970.

Jacobson, M. Development of specific neuronal connections. *Science* 163:543, 1969.

Jacobson, M. Brain development in relation to language. In E. H. Lenneberg and E. Lenneberg (eds.), *Foundations of Language Development* (Vol. 1). New York: Academic Press, 1975. Pp. 105–119.

Jammes, J. L., and Gilles, F. H. Telencephalic development: matrix volume and isocortex and allocortex surface areas. In F. H. Gilles, A. Leviton, and E. C. Dooling (eds.), *The Developing Human Brain*. Boston: John Wright, 1983. Pp. 87–93.

Jhavari, S., and Morest, D. K. Sequential alterations of neuronal architecture in nucleus magnocellularis of the developing chicken: a Golgi study. *Neuroscience* 7:837, 1982a.

Jhavari, S., and Morest, D. K. Sequential alterations of neuronal architecture in nucleus magnocellularis of the developing chicken: an electron microscopic study. *Neuroscience* 7:855, 1982b.

Johansson, B., Wendenberg, E., and Westin, B. Measurement of time response by the human fetus. *Acta Otolaryngol. (Stockh)* 57:188, 1964.

Kiang, N. Y. S. Stimulus representation in the discharge patterns of auditory neurons. In D. B. Tower (ed.), *The Nervous System, Vol. 3: Human Communication and Its Disorders*. New York: Raven Press, 1975. Pp. 81–96.

Kiang, N. Y. S., Morest, D. K., Godfrey, D. A., Guinan, J. J., Jr., and Kane, E. C. Stimulus coding at caudal levels of cats auditory nervous system. I. Response characteristics of single units. In A. R. Moller (ed.), *Basic Mechanisms in Hearing*. New York: Academic Press, 1973. Pp. 455–478.

Konigsmark, B. W., and Murphy, E. A. Neuronal populations in the human brain. *Nature* 228:1335–1336, 1970.

Konigsmark, B. W., and Murphy, E. A. Volume of the ventral cochlear nucleus in man: its relationship to neuronal population with age. *J. Neuropathol. Exp. Neurol.* 31:304–316, 1972.

Kraus, H-J., and Aulbach-Kraus, K. Morphological changes in the cochlea of the mouse after onset of hearing. *Hearing Res.* 4:89, 1981.

Larroche, J-C. The development of the central nervous system during intrauterine life. In F. Falkner (ed.), *Human Development*. Philadelphia: Saunders, 1966. Pp. 257–276.

Lecours, A. R. Myelogenetic correlates of the development of speech and language. In E. H. Lenneberg and E. Lenneberg (eds.), *Foundations of Language Development*. New York: Academic Press, 1975. Pp. 121–135.

Matthews, M. A., and Duncan, D. A quantitative study of morphological changes accompanying the initiation of progress of myelin production in the dorsal funiculus of the rat spinal cord. *J. Comp. Neurol.* 142:1, 1971.

Metter, J. E., Riege, W. H., Hanson, W. R., Phelps, M. E., and Kuhl, D. E. Local cerebral metabolic rates of glucose in movement and language disorders from positron tomography. *Am. J. Physiol.* 246:R-897, 1984.

Myslivecek, J. Development of the auditory evoked responses in the auditory cortex in mammals. In R. Romand (ed.), *Development of Auditory and Vestibular Systems*. New York: Academic Press, 1983. Pp. 167–209.

Osen, K. K. Cytoarchitecture of the cochlear nuclei in the cat. *J. Comp. Neurol.* 136:453, 1969.

Pujol, R., Carlier, E., and Devigne, C. Significance of presynaptic formations in early stages of cochlear synaptogenesis. *Neurosci. Lett.* 15:97, 1979.

Romand, R. Development of the cochlea. In R. Romand (ed.), *Development of Auditory and Vestibular Systems*. New York: Academic Press, 1983. Pp. 47–88.

Roth, G. L., Aitkin, L. M., Andersen, R. A., and Merzenich, M. M. Some features of the spatial organization of the central nucleus of the inferior colliculus of the cat. *J. Comp. Neurol.* 182:661, 1978.

Rubel, E. W., Smith, D. J., and Miller, L. C. Organization and development of brain stem auditory nuclei of the chicken: ontogeny of n. magnocellularis and n. laminaris. *J. Comp. Neurol.* 166:469, 1976.

Tanaka, K., Sakay, N., and Terayama, Y. Organ of Corti in the human fetus: scanning and transmission electron microscope studies. *Ann. Otol. Rhinol. Laryngol.* 88:749, 1979.

Thorn, L., Arnold, W., Schinko, I., and Wetzstein, R. The limbus spiralis and its relationship to the developing tectorial membrane in the cochlear duct of guinea pig fetus. *Anat. Embryol.* 155:303, 1979.

Trevarthen, C. Neuroembryology and the development of perception. In F. Falkner and J. M. Tanner (eds.), *Human Growth, Vol. 3: Neurobiology and Nutrition*. New York: Plenum Press, 1979. Pp. 3–96.

Yakovlev, P. I., and Lecours, A-R. The myelogenetic cycles of regional maturation of the brain. In A. Minkowski (ed.), *Regional Development of the Brain in Early Life*. Oxford: Blackwell Scientific Publications, 1967. Pp. 3–65.

CHAPTER 5

Neuroanatomy of Speech

Jesse G. Kennedy III • David P. Kuehn

❏ Functional Elements

❏ Respiratory Mechanism

❏ Laryngeal Mechanism

❏ Supralaryngeal Mechanisms

The systematic peripheral neuroanatomy of the speech production mechanism is described in this chapter, not from the frequently utilized perspective of nervous system divisions but, rather, from the perspective of the involved muscles and sensory receptors. The discussion does not, for example, list a cranial nerve (CN) and then indicate the structures it innervates. Rather, the discussion is organized about the classic concept of a sound generator that requires an energy source (respiratory mechanism), a sound source (laryngeal mechanism), and a sound shaper (supralaryngeal articulatory mechanism). From this organizational schema the discussion proceeds to relate the elements of the motor systems with their innervation, as well as the functional elements of the sensory systems with their innervation. The discussion provided by this chapter concentrates on elements that experimental data indicate are directly related to speech production and related functions.

FUNCTIONAL ELEMENTS

The complex structural movements and deformations that ultimately produce the acoustic signal identified as speech are primarily generated and controlled by two functional elements: muscles and sensory receptors.

MUSCLE

Striated (voluntary, skeletal) muscles, working in a constantly changing three-dimensional field of opposing and assisting forces, are primarily responsible for generating the movements and deformations of the speech production mechanism. Muscles are comprised of muscle fibers of varying geometric pattern. The fibers might be aligned in a form that is parallel, or fusiform (e.g., intercostal muscles), radiating (e.g., pectoralis major), pennate (e.g., mylohyoid), or circumpennate (e.g., diaphragm). Each of the muscle fibers consists of many myofibrils, and each myofibril consists of many long protein molecules (thick myosin and thin actin)

forming myofilaments interconnected by numerous crossbridges.

In response to a propagated muscle action potential the geometry of the attachments of the crossbridges changes, causing the myofilaments to slide past each other in a series of mechanical events best described by the sliding filament theory of muscle contraction. As the myofilaments slide past each other, mechanical force is generated. If the force generated is greater than the opposing load on the muscle, the muscle exhibits concentric activity, that is, it shortens, in an auxotonic (isotonic) contraction. If the muscle force is equal to the opposing load on the muscle, the overall muscle length changes only negligibly in an isometric contraction. If the muscle force is less than the opposing load on the muscle, the muscle exhibits eccentric activity, that is, it lengthens, while still generating mechanical force.

The muscles that are active during speech production demonstrate a wide range of structural characteristics. At one end of a continuum of structure are the muscles of the trunk that actuate the respiratory mechanism. These muscles share many similarities with those of the limb, differing primarily in the frequency of relatively thin, sheet-like muscles characteristic of the respiratory musculature. At the other end of the structural continuum are the muscles of the circumoral muscles of the articulatory mechanism. These muscles of the face seldom attach directly to underlying bone via a distinct tendon. Instead, they attach through a series of smaller bundles to a superficial musculoaponeurotic system. The circumoral muscles demonstrate extensive muscle fiber interdigitation. Isolation of distinct muscles is made difficult because of an absence of encapsulating muscle fascia.

The musculature of the speech production mechanism differs from the more extensively studied limb musculature not only in some structural aspects but also in many basic functional aspects. The limb musculature typically acts with bilateral asymmetry to move significant externally applied loads located distal to the joint influenced by muscle activity. With the exception of the muscles of the respiratory mechanism, the muscles of the speech production mechanism typically act with bilateral symmetry and seldom interact with externally applied loads.

SENSORY RECEPTORS

The speech production mechanism shares a complement of sensory receptors capable of providing a continuous supply of information describing the constantly changing status of the internal and external environments during ongoing speech production. This sensory information is differentially distributed throughout the various subsystems. For example, the circumoral musculature of the articulatory mechanism lacks muscle spindles (presenting only the *atypische Muskelspindel* described by Kadanoff in 1956), whereas the masticatory, laryngeal, and respiratory muscle systems demonstrate variable populations of muscle spindles. Furthermore, the muscles innervated by the cranial nerves frequently lack the tendinous muscle attachment characteristic of the muscles of the limbs.

RESPIRATORY MECHANISM

The respiratory mechanism may be considered to be the primary energy source of the speech production mechanism. The mechanism consists of a complex air-filled, variable-volume cavity. Classically, the muscles of the respiratory mechanism are divided into two distinct groups: muscles of inspiration and muscles of expiration. The muscles of inspiration are capable of increasing the volume of the cavity, thereby decreasing the air pressure within the cavity relative to the external environment, which typically leads to inward airflow. The muscles of expiration have the functional potential of decreasing the cavity volume, thereby increasing cavity air pressure, which typically leads to outward airflow. This classic division is an oversimplification because of the difficulty of demonstrating consistent functional muscle categorization. Nevertheless, it is convenient to discuss the peripheral innervation of this system by functional grouping, as in this chapter.

The peripheral innervation of both motor and sensory components of the respiratory mechanism is characterized by the presence of neural plexuses. These intertwined networks of nerves are embryologic remnants of primitive muscle innervation. The plexuses are formed when simple muscles innervated by single spinal nerves fuse to form complex muscles that are supplied by two or more interwoven spinal nerves. Progressing distally from the spinal cord, a plexus divides from ventral rami to trunks, then divisions, then cords, and finally terminal branches called nerves. The primary nerve plexuses of the respiratory mechanism include the cervical plexus and the brachial plexus.

CERVICAL PLEXUS

The cervical plexus is a nerve network of the peripheral nervous system that is located deep to the sternocleidomastoid muscle lateral to the upper four cervical vertebrae. Formed by the ventral rami of the upper four cervical nerves (C1, C2, C3, C4), all but the first cervical nerve divide into superior and inferior branches that unite to form a series of three irregular loops, as shown in the upper portion of Figure 5-1. The general sensory distribution of the cervical plexus innervates the cutaneous nerves of the neck, shoulder, and lateral portions of the back of the head. The motor elements of the cervical plexus serve the deep muscles of the cervical spinal column, the infrahyoid and sternocleidomastoid muscles, and the trapezius and diaphragm muscles. The nerves in the cervical plexus are divided into superficial and deep branches. The superficial nerve branches include (1) lesser occipital (C2 and C3); (2) greater auricular (C2 and C3); (3) transverse colli (C2 and C3); and (4) supraclavicular (C3 and C4) nerves. Deep (muscular) nerve branches include (1) phrenic (primarily C4 with some elements of C3 and C5); (2) accessory phrenic (a variable contribution of C5); (3) ansa cervicalis (highly variable in position with contributions from C1 to C3); and (4) muscular (including rectus capitis, longus capitis and colli, and hyoid branches). The hyoid branches are branches of the hypoglossal (XII) cranial nerve. However, they originate in the cervical segments of the spinal cord, not from the hypoglossal nucleus in the brainstem.

The cervical plexus also has communications with the vagus (X), hypoglossal (XII), and spi-

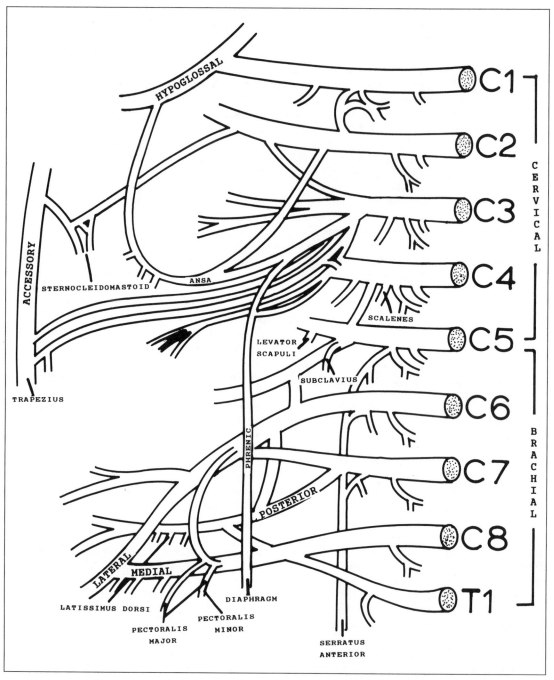

Fig. 5-1. Innervation of the cervical plexus and brachial plexus.

nal accessory (XI) cranial nerves. The communication with the vagus (X) nerve occurs in the loop formed between the first and second cervical nerves and the inferior ganglion of the vagus (X) nerve. The communication with the hypoglossal (XII) nerve consists of a small bundle of fibers, derived primarily from the first cervical nerve and secondarily from the second cervical nerve, that courses with the hypoglossal (XII) nerve a short distance before exiting as the descending hypoglossal nerve. The spinal accessory (XI) nerve includes communications from the cervical plexus from three areas: (1) the second and third cervical nerves, which join elements of the spinal accessory (XI) nerve innervating the sternocleidomastoid muscle; (2) the third cervical nerve, which joins elements of the spinal accessory (XI) nerve innervating the trapezius muscle; and (3) a group of proprioceptive sensory fibers that exit the fourth cervical nerve.

BRACHIAL PLEXUS

The brachial plexus is a nerve network of the peripheral nervous system situated partly in the lower part of the neck and extending to the axilla (armpit). This plexus mainly supplies nerves to the upper limb. As shown in the lower portion of Figure 5-1, it originates from the anterior branches of the lower four cervical spinal nerves (C5, C6, C7, C8) and the ventral branch of the first thoracic nerve (T1). Communication loops from C4 to C5 and from T1 to T2 may contribute to the plexus. Composed of ventral spinal nerve rami, the brachial plexus may be divided into two major parts: (1) the supraclavicular part near the subclavian artery and (2) the infraclavicular part behind the clavicle and extending inferiorly to the axilla in relation to the axillary artery. The supraclavicular portion is the origin of the following nerves: (1) dorsal scapular nerve (from the dorsal region of C5); (2) long thoracic nerve (from the dorsal surface of C5, C6, and C7); (3) subclavius nerve (C5); and (4) suprascapular (C4, C5, and C6) nerve. The infraclavicular portion is the origin of the following nerves: (1) medial and lateral pectoral (C5 to T1); (2) medial brachial cutaneous (medial cord of T1); (3) medial antebrachial cutaneous (C8 and T1); (4) median (C6 to T1); (5) ulnar (C7 to T1); (6) radial (C5 and T1); (7) subscapular (C5 to C8); (8) thoracodorsal (middle or long subscapular nerve, C6 to C8); (9) musculocutaneous (C5 to C7); and (10) axillary (C5 and C6).

MOTOR SYSTEM

As summarized in Figure 5-2, the muscles of the respiratory mechanism are innervated by a system involving the multiple innervation patterns provided by the neural plexuses described above and direct spinal nerves, which independently innervate muscles without the multiple nerve integration provided by plexuses. The categorization of musculature used is based primarily on published concepts of functional potential, often awaiting physiologic or neurophysiologic confirmation.

INSPIRATORY MUSCLE INNERVATION

The three primary muscles of inspiration include the diaphragm, external intercostals, and interchondral portion of the internal intercostals. The inspiratory activity of these muscles is supplemented during active inspiration by a number of accessory muscles capable of elevating the shoulders and ribs.

Diaphragm

Many investigators, such as Campbell, Agostoni, and Davis (1970), Draper, Ladefoged, and Whitteridge (1959), and Tokizane, Kawamata, and Tokizane (1952), described the vertical enlargement of the thorax provided by diaphragm muscle contraction as being the most significant maneuver during inspiration. The motor innervation of this muscle is derived from the phrenic nerve of the cervical plexus conveying fibers mainly from C4 but also from C3 and C5. The phrenic nerve demonstrates structural asymmetry, with the left nerve being more superficial and longer than that on the right. This pattern of ipsilateral phrenic nerve innervation appears to be consistent for the crural muscle fibers that attach to the lumbar vertebrae on both right and left aspects of the esophageal hiatus (Williams and Warwick, 1980).

External Intercostal Muscles

Campbell (1955) and Draper et al. (1959) observed activity in the external intercostal muscles during both quiet and active inspiratory maneuvers. This muscle might also be active

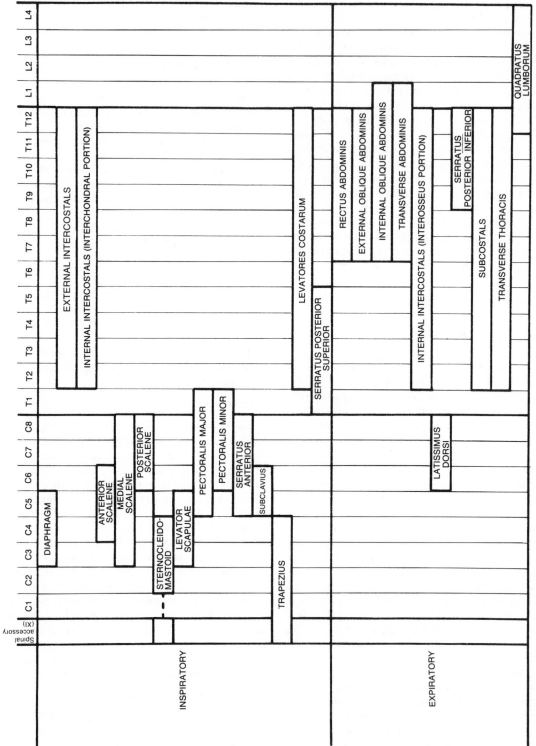

Fig. 5-2. Innervation of the respiratory musculature.

during the initial phase of expiration (Agostoni, 1964). Innervation is provided primarily by: (1) the thoracic intercostal nerves T2 through T6, numbered by the adjacent intercostal space (i.e., the fourth intercostal nerve innervates the intercostal space between the fourth and fifth ribs); (2) the thoracoabdominal intercostal nerves (T7 through T11); and (3) the subcostal nerve (T12) (Clemente, 1985).

Internal Intercostal Muscles (Interchondral Portion)

Campbell (1955) documented the activity of the interchondral portion of the internal intercostal muscles (with the external intercostals) during both quiet and active inspiration. These muscles share the innervation patterns of the external intercostals, deriving their motor innervation from the thoracic intercostal nerves, thoracoabdominal intercostal nerves, and subcostal nerve.

Scalene Muscles (Anterior, Medial, Posterior)

The scalenes function as accessory muscles of inspiration and are most active during forced inspiration at high lung volumes (Campbell et al., 1970). The anterior scalene is innervated by branches of C4 to C6. The medial scalene is innervated by branches from C3 to C8, with most of the fibers coming from the muscular branch of the cervical plexus derived from C3 and C4. The posterior scalene is innervated by C6 to C8. The innervation of the smallest scalene muscle (scalenus minimus, a variation observed in about 30 percent of cases) is not yet documented (Bergman, Thompson, and Afifi, 1984).

Sternocleidomastoid Muscle

Derived from the fusion of elements of two myotomes (the muscle plates of an embryonic somite from which striated muscle is developed), the sternocleidomastoid is an accessory muscle of inspiration. It is active with the scalenes at high lung volumes and assists in elevating the sternum and increasing the anteroposterior dimension of the thorax (Kahane, 1982). The motor innervation for this muscle is derived from the spinal part of the spinal accessory (XI) nerve, which traverses the muscle, and from branches of C2 and C3 with a possible contribution from C4. The spinal accessory (XI) nerve fibers are derived from a cell column of the anterior horn, which extends from the level of C5 or C6 to the pyramidal decussation superiorly. The cervical innervation, previously considered to be proprioceptive, is suggested to contain significant motor components (Williams and Warwick, 1980).

Levator Scapulae Muscle

A strap-like muscle, the levator scapulae is attached to the scapula and assists during forced inspiration by stabilizing the position of the scapula (Clemente, 1985). Its motor innervation is received directly from C3 and C4 of the cervical plexus, with the inferior muscle fibers frequently receiving fibers indirectly from C5 via the dorsal scapular nerve. The dorsal scapular nerve deviates from its usual course along the deep surface of the levator scapulae and pierces the muscle (Bergman et al., 1984).

Pectoralis Major Muscle

The pectoralis major is active during forced inspiration (Campbell et al., 1970; Grombeck and Skouby, 1960). Its motor innervation is mediated by the brachial plexus. The clavicular and cranial sternocostal parts of the pectoralis major receive motor innervation from C5 and C6 of the brachial plexus via the lateral (superior) pectoral nerve that pierces the clavipectoral fascia. The medial (inferior) pectoral nerve carries fibers from C7, C8, and T1 to innervate the caudal sternocostal portion of the muscle.

Pectoralis Minor Muscle

The pectoralis minor constitutes the major portion of the deep layer of the pectoral muscle sheet and is active during forced inspiratory activity. There is no widespread agreement on the motor innervation of this highly variable muscle. Many authors agree that the motor innervation of the pectoralis minor is derived from the medial (inferior) pectoral nerve of the lower trunk of the brachial plexus, which enters the deep surface of the muscle-carrying fibers from C8 and T1 (Clemente, 1985), and perhaps fibers from both the lateral and medial pectoral nerves including C6, C7, and C8 (Williams and Warwick, 1980).

Serratus Anterior Muscle

A thin quadrangular muscle, the serratus anterior appears to have the functional potential to elevate the ribs when the pectoral girdle is stabilized. Motor innervation is derived from the brachial plexus via the long (posterior) thoracic nerve (external respiratory nerve of Bell), which contains fibers from C5 and C6 and occasionally C7 and C8 (Bergman et al., 1984). This nerve courses caudally from the brachial plexus along the external surface of the muscle, giving off branches from C5 to the superior muscle fibers, C6 to the middle fibers, and C7 to the lower part of the muscle.

Subclavius Muscle

The subclavius muscle is a variable derivative of the deep pectoral muscle sheet that may receive fibers from the pectoralis minor muscle. Coursing deep and parallel to the clavicle, this muscle is not easily accessible to either palpation or electromyography (EMG) electrode implantation. This location may impede the gathering of experimental data, confirming that this muscle is capable of aiding forced inspiratory maneuvers by elevating the first rib when the clavicle is fixed. The subclavius muscle derives its primary motor innervation from a small branch of the lateral trunk of the brachial plexus, which contains fibers of C5 and C6. The primary innervation may be supplemented by an accessory phrenic nerve.

Trapezius Muscle

The trapezius muscle is a compound muscle consisting of three distinct bundles of fibers and described by Campbell (1954) as being active during the end phases of maximum inspiration. Its motor innervation is derived mainly from the upper spinal portion of the spinal accessory (XI) nerve with additional motor fibers from C1, C2, C3, and C4 (Brendler, 1968; Carpenter, 1976). An infrequent variation is observed when the spinal accessory (XI) nerve supplies only the sternocleidomastoid muscle. In these cases the trapezius muscle is supplied by C3 and C4 (Bergman et al., 1984).

Levatores Costarum

Relatively small muscles, the levatores costarum are found on the posterior surface of the rib cage and course from a vertebra above to near the angle of the rib below. Their functional potential to elevate the ribs has yet to be confirmed experimentally. Mirroring the external intercostal muscles, their innervation is primarily derived from the lateral muscular branches of the dorsal rami of the adjacent thoracic intercostal nerves (T2 through T12).

Serratus Posterior Superior Muscle

Found on the superoposterior aspect of the thorax, the serratus posterior superior muscle forcibly elevates the ribs during deep inspiration (Clemente, 1985). These muscles are innervated by the ventral primary divisions of the thoracic intercostal nerves T1 through T4 and perhaps T5 (Williams and Warwick, 1980).

EXPIRATORY MUSCLE INNERVATION

The primary muscles of expiration include the major abdominal muscles (rectus abdominis, external oblique abdominis, internal oblique abdominis, and transversus abdominis) supplemented by the action of the interosseus portion of the internal intercostal muscle. These primary muscles are supplemented by the action of a number of accessory muscles that act to reduce the volume of the thoracic cavity.

Rectus Abdominis Muscle

Roughly parallel and adjacent to the midline, the rectus abdominis muscle of the anterior abdominal wall contributes to the costal depression and visceral compression produced by the abdominal musculature. Draper et al. (1959) electromyographically observed contractile activity in the rectus abdominis muscle at end-expiration and during loud speech, initiating activity after the internal intercostal and before the external oblique abdominis muscles. The rectus abdominis muscle receives its motor innervation from both the thoracoabdominal intercostal (T7 through T11) and subcostal (T12) nerves. Segment T7 of the thoracoabdominal intercostal nerve innervates the uppermost section of the rectus abdominis muscle in the region superior to the first tendinous intersection. Segment T8 innervates the region between the first and second muscular regions, and segment T9 innervates the region between the lower two intersections.

External Oblique Abdominis Muscle

The external oblique abdominis muscle forms the outermost sheet of abdominal muscles and is capable of lowering the ribs and compressing the abdominal viscera. This muscle is variable in its attachments to the ribs and may present direct attachments to the pectoralis major, serratus anterior, latissimus dorsi, and serratus posterior inferior muscles. The external oblique abdominis muscle is mainly innervated by the thoracoabdominal intercostal nerve (T7 through T11) of the lower thoracic group and the subcostal nerve (T12), with a potential contribution from T6.

Internal Oblique Abdominis Muscle

Located deep to the external oblique abdominis muscle in the anterolateral abdominal wall, the internal oblique abdominis muscle contributes to the depression of the ribs and visceral compression, which is a significant component of expiratory maneuvers. This muscle is innervated by motor branches of T7 through T12 (thoracoabdominal intercostal and subcostal nerves) supplemented with fibers from the iliohypogastric and ilioinguinal branches of the first lumbar nerve (L1) (Clemente, 1985).

Transversus Abdominis Muscle

The deepest component of the abdominal wall, the transversus abdominis muscle courses horizontally to surround the abdominal viscera. Campbell et al. (1970) suggested that the muscle functions to supplement the expiratory activity of the external and internal oblique abdominis muscles. The transverse abdominis muscle shares the innervation complex of the other anterolateral abdominal muscles, deriving its motor innervation from the thoracoabdominal intercostal nerves, subcostal nerves, and iliohypogastric and ilioinguinal branches of the first lumbar nerve.

Internal Intercostal Muscles (Interosseus Portion)

Coursing between the ribs deep to the external intercostal muscles, the interosseus internal intercostal muscles were described by Draper et al. (1959) as increasing contractile activity during end-expiration. These muscles are innervated by the adjacent muscular branches of the (1) thoracic intercostal nerves (T2 through T6), which course between the internal and external intercostal muscles before emerging in the region of the costal cartilages; (2) thoracoabdominal intercostal nerves (T7 through T11); and (3) subcostal nerve (T12), which is larger than its superior counterparts and courses along the inferior border of the twelfth rib.

Latissimus Dorsi Muscle

The latissimus dorsi is a broad muscle located in the lower half of the back. The highly variable anatomy of this muscle (Bergman et al., 1984) may be partially responsible for the contradictory reports regarding its functional potential. Tokizane et al. (1952) observed no respiratory function, whereas Draper et al. (1959) reported EMG activity during end-expiration. Clemente (1985) described the muscle as being active during deep expiration and inspiration. The motor innervation of this muscle is derived from fibers of C6 to C8 via the posterior branch of the brachial plexus, forming the thoracodorsal (middle or long subscapular) nerve. The nerve follows the course of the subscapular and thoracodorsal arteries along the posterior axilla and terminates deep to the muscle (Clemente, 1985).

Serratus Posterior Inferior Muscle

The serratus posterior inferior muscle courses inferiorly from the lower two thoracic vertebrae and upper two lumbar vertebrae to attach to the lateral aspect of the lower four ribs. Kaplan (1960) and Clemente (1985) considered this muscle to have the functional potential to depress the lower four ribs during forced expiration. This muscle receives its motor innervation from the last three muscular branches of the thoracoabdominal intercostal nerves (T9 through T11) and the subcostal nerve (T12).

Subcostal Muscles

Highly variable in size and number, the muscle bundles known as subcostal muscles course deep and parallel to the internal intercostal muscles and may lower the ribs during forced expiration when the twelfth rib is fixed by contraction of the quadratus lumborum. Motor innervation is from the adjacent intercostal nerves.

Transverse Thoracis Muscle

The transverse thoracis muscle courses from the sternum laterally and superiorly to attach to the posterior surfaces of the second through sixth costal cartilages. In reference to this muscle, Kaplan (1960) stated, "This is the only truly thoracic muscle which is definitely expiratory," EMG data from Taylor (1960) suggested that this muscle supplements the contractile activity of the interosseous internal intercostals. Similar to the intercostal muscles, the transverse thoracis muscle derives its motor innervation from the thoracic intercostal, thoracoabdominal intercostal, and subcostal nerves.

Quadratus Lumborum Muscle

The quadratus lumborum muscle is a thin muscular sheet located deep in the posterior abdominal wall coursing from the twelfth rib inferiorly to the iliac crest. During contraction the muscle stabilizes the position of the twelfth rib, aiding not only the production of visceral compression by contraction of the diaphragm (Boyd, Blincoe, and Hayner, 1965) but also controlled relaxation of the diaphragm (Taylor, 1960). The quadratus lumborum muscle is innervated by the ventral rami of the subcostal nerve (T12) and by fibers of the upper three or four lumbar nerves.

SENSORY SYSTEM

CONTRACTILE ELEMENT INNERVATION

The muscles of the respiratory mechanism receive not only motor innervation but also sensory innervation, which provides proprioceptive information describing the contractile status of the muscles. The sensory system innervation may include both afferent and efferent elements subserving sensory receptors, such as muscle spindles.

In general, the population of proprioceptors in the diaphragm muscle is small. The sternal portion of the diaphragm demonstrates few if any muscle spindles, and the crural (spinal) muscle fibers that descend to insert on the lumbar vertebrae and arcuate ligaments also present few muscle spindles (Corde, Euler, and Lennerstrand, 1965; Euler, 1979). Examination of the muscle fibers and central tendon of the diaphragm indicates that there are more Golgi tendon organs than muscle spindles. Specifically, von Euler (1979) observed a ratio of spindles to tendon organs of 0.8, compared with 2.9 for the intercostal muscles. Fibers from C2 and C3 derived from the muscular branch of the cervical plexus may join the spinal accessory (XI) nerve and are proprioceptive sensory for the sternocleidomastoid muscle (Corbin and Harrison, 1938). The trapezius muscle receives proprioceptive innervation from fibers of C3 and C4, which course through the muscular branch of the cervical plexus.

NONCONTRACTILE ELEMENT INNERVATION

Trachea

The sensory nerves that innervate the trachea are derived from the recurrent laryngeal branch of the vagus (X) nerve (Sant'Ambrogio and Mortola, 1977; Sant'Ambrogio, Bartlett, and Mortola, 1977) and from sympathetic (thoracolumbar) nerve trunks that connect with the thoracic and upper lumbar segments of the spinal cord. The nerves originate from the tracheal muscle and the mucous membrane, with many small groups of nerve cell bodies (ganglia) found in the autonomic plexuses of both the tracheal and bronchial walls (Williams and Warwick, 1980).

Pleurae

The innervation of the pleurae of the thorax is derived from: (1) the adjacent intercostal nerves, including the thoracic intercostal nerves (T1 through T6), thoracoabdominal nerves (T7 through T11), and subcostal nerve (T12); and (2) the phrenic nerve (C4 augmented by fibers from C3 and C5). The intercostal and phrenic nerves innervate the parietal pleura on the inner lining of the thorax. Specifically, the intercostal nerves innervate the parietal pleura that lines (1) the deep surface of the ribs and the intercostal muscles (the costal pleura) and (2) the peripheral portion of the diaphragm muscle (the diaphragmatic pleura). The phrenic nerve innervates the parietal pleura that lines (1) other thoracic viscera (the mediastinal pleura) and (2) the central portion of the diaphragm muscle (diaphragmatic pleura). The parietal pleura lining the apex of the lung (cervical pleura) and the mediastinal pleura in the region of the apex of the lung are innervated by very fine filaments of the pleural branch of the phrenic nerve derived from the cervical plexus. The visceral pleura covering the outer surface of the lungs is innervated by autonomic nerves, which also innervate the lungs and bronchial vessels.

Lungs

The lungs are innervated by the anterior and posterior pulmonary plexuses, which are derived from branches of the sympathetic and vagus (X) nerves. Containing both efferent (to bronchial muscle and glands) and afferent (from the mucous membrane and alveoli of the lung) components, the nerve fibers follow the bronchial tubes and include numerous small ganglia along their course. The motor innervation of the bronchoconstrictors is derived primarily from the vagus (X) nerve.

LARYNGEAL MECHANISM

The laryngeal mechanism generates a complex glottal tone that serves as the primary sound source for all voiced sounds. Driven by the air pressures and flows generated by the respiratory mechanism, the larynx consists of valves controlling the opening to and from the lungs below. The valves mainly consist of mucous membrane-covered folds of tissue connected to a cartilaginous framework. The folds may be moved either toward or away from the midline to produce varying degrees of glottal resistance. In addition, the entire laryngeal valve complex may be moved superiorly or inferiorly. Traditionally, the muscles controlling the state of the valves may be divided into: (1) intrinsic muscles that control the position and state of the valves, and (2) extrinsic muscles that control the vertical position of the larynx (Fig. 5-3).

MOTOR SYSTEM

INTRINSIC MUSCLE INNERVATION

The intrinsic laryngeal musculature is attached to, and courses between, the cartilaginous structures of the larynx. These muscles may be grouped functionally as: (1) an abductor that increases the area of the glottis by displacing the vocal folds away from the midline, and (2) adductors that decrease the area of the glottis by moving the vocal folds toward the midline, and (3) longitudinal adjustors that modify and maintain the length–tension state of the vocal folds.

The intrinsic laryngeal muscles are innervated by branches of the vagus (X) nerve, shown in Figure 5-4. The lower motor neurons have their cell bodies in the nucleus ambiguus of the medulla oblongata. Szentagothai (1943) observed a spatial organization in this nucleus

in which lower motor neurons to the cricothyroid muscle were situated rostrally, followed by neurons to the posterior cricoarytenoid, thyroarytenoid, lateral cricoarytenoid, and, most caudally, interarytenoid muscles. The myelinated nerve fibers to these muscles range in size from 6 to 20 μm and demonstrate conduction velocities of 50 to 60 meters per second (Strong and Vaughan, 1981); they supply motor units with an estimated 30 muscle fibers to each motor neuron (English and Blevins, 1969). The fibers from this motor nucleus course dorsomedially and then turn laterally to join and exit with the vagus (X) nerve.

The recurrent (inferior or recurrent laryngeal) nerve of the vagus (X) nerve courses along the laryngeal branch of the inferior thyroid artery and passes under the caudal border of the inferior constrictor muscle; it divides into a motor and sensory branch prior to entering the larynx (Williams, 1954). Entering the larynx deep to the inferior cornu of the thyroid cartilage, immediately behind the cricothyroid joint, the recurrent nerve innervates the intrinsic muscles that control the abduction/adduction of the vocal folds. The external branch of the superior laryngeal nerve of the vagus (X) nerve innervates the muscles capable of changing the pitch of the voice by controlling the length–tension relation of the vocal folds (Shipp, 1982).

Posterior Cricoarytenoid Muscle

The posterior cricoarytenoid muscle rocks the arytenoid cartilage posteriorly and laterally and in so doing is the sole abductor of the vocal folds (Strong and Vaughan, 1981). The lower motor neurons are part of the inferior branch of the recurrent laryngeal nerve, which innervates the posterior surface of the posterior cricoarytenoid muscle facing the pharyngeal lumen. Faaborg-Andersen (1957) observed an innervation ratio of 116 muscle fibers per motor neuron in this muscle.

Lateral Cricoarytenoid Muscle

Confirmed by EMG evidence, the lateral cricoarytenoid muscle is capable of rocking the arytenoid cartilage forward, an action that may, because of the orientation of the articulating facet of the cricoarytenoid joint, adduct the vocal folds. Data presented by Hirano (1981) documented lateral cricoarytenoid muscle activity during pitch change. The innervation of this

		TRIGEMINAL (V)	FACIAL (VII)	GLOSSO-PHARYNGEAL (IX)	VAGUS (X)	SPINAL ACCESSORY (XI)	HYPOGLOSSAL (XII)	C1	C2	C3
INTRINSIC					POSTERIOR CRICOARYTENOID					
					LATERAL CRICOARYTENOID					
					INTERARYTENOIDS					
					CRICOTHYROID					
					THYROARYTENOID					
EXTRINSIC	SUPRAHYOID	ANTERIOR BELLY DIGASTRIC								
			POSTERIOR BELLY DIGASTRIC							
		MYLOHYOID								
			STYLOHYOID							
								GENIOHYOID		
	INFRAHYOID							THYROHYOID		
								STERNOTHYROID	STERNOTHYROID	STERNOTHYROID
								STERNOHYOID	STERNOHYOID	STERNOHYOID
								OMOHYOID	OMOHYOID	OMOHYOID

Fig. 5-3. Innervation of the laryngeal musculature.

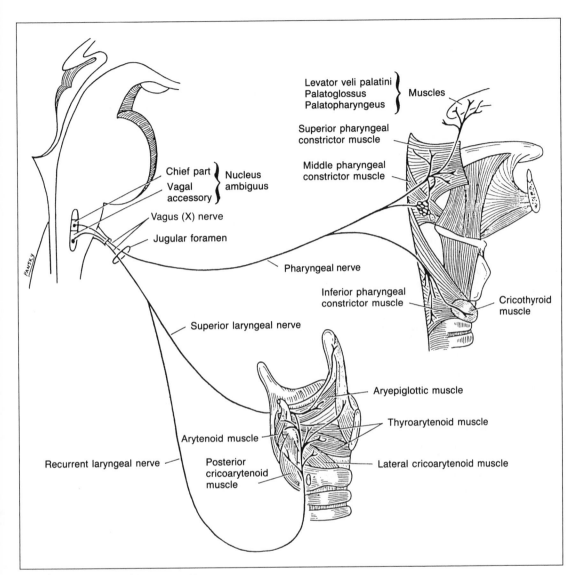

Fig. 5-4. Distribution of the vagus (X) nerve.

muscle is most frequently described as being derived from the inferior branch of the recurrent laryngeal nerve of the vagus (X) nerve. There is also evidence that this muscle might be innervated by the caudal portion of the internal branch of the superior laryngeal nerve, which is connected to the recurrent laryngeal nerve by a communicating nerve (Bergman et al., 1984; Dubner, Sessle, and Storey, 1978).

Interarytenoid Muscles

The interarytenoid muscles (transverse and oblique interarytenoids) adduct the vocal folds (especially the posterior region). Hirano (1981) presented data collected from one subject indicating limited interarytenoid activity during both pitch and intensity change. The interarytenoid muscles share motor innervation from the inferior branch of the recurrent laryngeal nerve of the vagus (X) nerve. Faaborg-Andersen (1957) estimated a ratio of 247 muscle fibers per motor neuron in the transverse interarytenoid muscle.

There is also evidence that a portion of the innervation of the interarytenoid muscles may be derived from a caudal offset of the internal branch of the superior laryngeal nerve that communicates with the recurrent laryngeal nerve (Dubner et al., 1978) and that the transverse interarytenoid muscle might receive special visceral motor fibers directly from the internal branch of the superior laryngeal nerve (Williams, 1951). The cranial extension of the oblique interarytenoid muscle, sometimes described as a distinct aryepiglottic muscle, receives its motor innervation from the inferior branch of the recurrent laryngeal nerve (Clemente, 1985).

Cricothyroid Muscle

Contracting in opposition to the thyroarytenoid muscle, the cricothyroid muscle draws the thyroid cartilage and the cricoid cartilage together anteriorly. Contracting in isolation, this muscle is capable of reducing the vibrating mass of the vocal fold and the thickness of the covering membrane as well as increasing the longitudinal tension of the vocal folds (Strong and Vaughan, 1981). Hirano (1981) and Shipp (1982) provided EMG data indicating that the cricothyroid muscle is directly involved in raising the pitch of the glottal tone, and that it is involved in providing compensatory adjustments that maintain constant pitch levels as vocal intensity changes. Motor innervation is provided by the pharyngeal and caudal ramus of the external branch of the superior laryngeal nerve of the vagus (X) nerve. This branch courses inferiorly along the larynx, deep to the sternothyroid muscle, and supplies both the cricothyroid and part of the inferior constrictor muscles (Clemente, 1985). In human muscle the innervation ratio has been reported variably as being 166 muscle fibers per motor unit (Faaborg-Andersen, 1957) and approximately 30 muscle fibers per motor unit (English and Blevins, 1969).

Thyroarytenoid Muscle

The thyroarytenoid muscle is a complex muscle forming the bulk of the vocal folds. Sonnesson (1960) described the division of the thyroarytenoid muscle into superior and inferior muscle bundles. The muscle fibers exhibit extensive interdigitation by elastic fibers of the conus elasticus (Hirano, 1974). Extensions of the thyroarytenoid muscle also course to the aryepiglottic fold (forming the thyroepiglotticus muscle) and the wall of the ventricle (forming the ventricularis muscle) (Clemente, 1985). The

most medial part of the muscle, those fibers coursing longitudinally within each vocal fold, is frequently referred to as the vocalis muscle. With the arytenoids fixed in place, unopposed contraction of the thyroarytenoid rocks the thyroid cartilage posteriorly, increasing the vibrating mass and decreasing the tension of the vocal folds (Strong and Vaughan, 1981). The motor innervation of the thyroarytenoid muscle is supplied by a portion of the inferior branch of the recurrent laryngeal nerve. That specific nerve is derived from a cephalic offset of the internal branch of the superior laryngeal nerve that communicates with the recurrent laryngeal nerve (Bergman et al., 1984; Dubner et al., 1978).

EXTRINSIC MUSCLE INNERVATION

The extrinsic laryngeal musculature connects the laryngeal cartilages and hyoid bone to the skull and mandible above by the suprahyoid musculature and to the thorax below by the infrahyoid musculature. This muscle group has the functional potential to: (1) elevate or lower the larynx; (2) fix the larynx in position; (3) aid the formation of mucosal folds within the larynx; and (4) rock the thyroid cartilage anteriorly, thereby increasing the tension of the vocal folds (Fink, 1975; Strong and Vaughan, 1981).

The motor innervation to these muscles is provided mainly by branches of three cranial nerves: the trigeminal (V) nerve, shown in Figure 5-5; the facial (VII) nerve, shown in Figure 5-6; and the hypoglossal (XII) nerve shown in Figure 5-7. The motor branches of the hypoglossal (XII) nerve communicate with the first, second, and third cervical nerves.

Suprahyoid Musculature

Digastric Muscle. The digastric muscle frequently is described as a paired muscle with an anterior and a posterior belly. However, consideration of function, derivation, and innervation indicates that it is more appropriate to consider the anterior and posterior bellies of the digastric muscle as separate muscles.

The anterior belly of the digastric muscle (ABD) connects the symphysis of the mandible with the hyoid bone and is potentially capable of: (1) drawing the hyoid bone (and hence the larynx) superiorly and anteriorly; and (2) open-

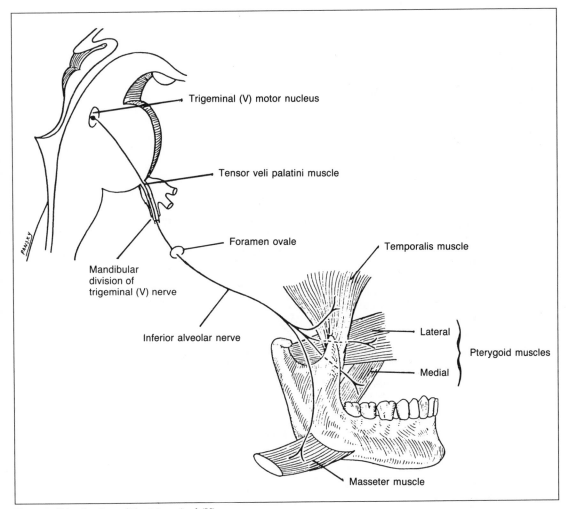

Fig. 5-5. Distribution of the trigeminal (V) nerve.

ing and retracting the mandible when the hyoid is fixed in position. The ABD often shares muscle fibers, and occasionally becomes totally fused, with the mylohyoid muscle. The ABD is formed from mesenchyme of the first (mandibular) branchial arch. Motor innervation is provided by the mylohyoid branch of the inferior alveolar nerve of the mandibular division of the trigeminal (V) nerve. The mylohyoid branch courses inferiorly and anteriorly in the mylohyoid groove of the mandible; and on exiting the groove, near the posterior border of mylohyoid, the nerve gives off several branches to the ABD.

The posterior belly of the digastric muscle

(PBD) connects the mastoid process of the temporal bone with the hyoid bone. This muscle has the functional potential to draw the hyoid bone superiorly and posteriorly. The PBD often is merged with the stylohyoid muscle when either muscle fails to separate from the common mass from which both of them are derived (Bergman et al., 1984). This muscle is formed from the second (hyoid) branchial arch and derives its innervation from the digastric branch of the facial (VII) nerve, which enters the deep surface of the muscle at a midpoint along its length.

Mylohyoid Muscle. Closely related to the ABD (sharing both derivation and innervation), the mylohyoid muscle forms the muscular floor of

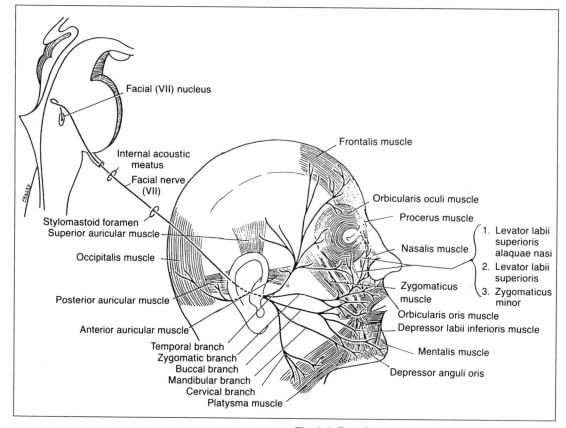

Fig. 5-6. Distribution of the facial (VII) nerve.

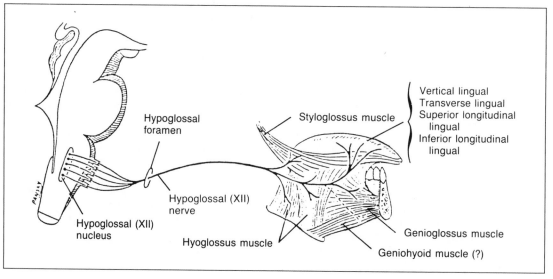

Fig. 5-7. Distribution of the hypoglossal (XII) nerve.

the mouth. Muscular contraction has the potential to: (1) change the position of the tongue by elevating the floor of the mouth; (2) lower the mandible if the hyoid bone is fixed in place; and (3) move the hyoid bone superiorly and anteriorly if the mandible is fixed in place. The motor innervation of the mylohyoid muscle is derived from the mylohyoid nerve. The mylohyoid nerve branches from the inferior alveolar nerve just prior to the passage of the inferior alveolar nerve through the mandibular foramen. The inferior alveolar nerve is a branch of the mandibular division of the trigeminal (V) nerve.

Stylohyoid Muscle. As stated above, the stylohyoid muscle is related closely to the PBD in both derivation and innervation. Capable of elevating and retracting the hyoid bone in a manner similar to the PBD, the stylohyoid muscle assists in fixing the vertical and horizontal position of the hyoid. The motor innervation is derived from the stylohyoid branch of the facial (VII) nerve, which enters the muscle at its midpoint after passing close to the parotid gland (Hiatt and Gartner, 1982).

Geniohyoid Muscle. The geniohyoid muscle is a paired muscle that courses parallel to the ABD and deep to the mylohyoid muscle. Like ABD, the geniohyoid muscle elevates the hyoid bone and draws it forward with the mandible fixed in position. As the lower motor neurons of the muscular branch of the hypoglossal (XII) nerve approach the posterior border of the hyoglossus muscle, they divide into numerous branches that enter the tongue to supply the intrinsic tongue muscles. Most of these small branches contain true hypoglossal (XII) nerve fibers, but those innervating the geniohyoid muscle are derived from the first cervical nerve (C1) (Clemente, 1985; Williams and Warwick, 1980).

Thyrohyoid Muscle. Coursing from the greater cornu of the hyoid bone inferiorly to the superior aspect of the oblique line (ligament) of the thyroid cartilage, the thyrohyoid muscle appears to be a superior extension of the sternothyroid muscle. During contraction, the thyrohyoid muscle controls the distance between the hyoid bone and the thyroid cartilage. Like the geniohyoid muscle, the thyrohyoid muscle receives its motor innervation from fibers of the first cervical nerve (C1), which course with fibers of the hypoglossal (XII) nerve and branch from it near the posterior border of the hyoglos-

sus muscle, proximal to the exit of the superior root of the ansa cervicalis (Clemente, 1985).

Infrahyoid Musculature

The motor innervation of the infrahyoid muscles is derived from branches of the ansa cervicalis loop nerve (Fig. 5-1). The superior root (descending hypoglossal nerve) of the ansa cervicalis nerve loop is derived from the first and second cervical nerves (C1 and C2). At the level of the first cervical vertebra (atlas) the superior root joins the hypoglossal (XII) nerve and travels as an independent functional unit with it for a short distance, branching from it near the external carotid artery. Upon leaving the hypoglossal (XII) nerve, the superior root divides into two small branches carrying fibers from C1 that will innervate the geniohyoid and thyrohyoid muscles. The inferior root is derived from the second and third cervical nerves (C2 and C3). Near the middle level of the neck the inferior root joins the superior root to form the characteristic loop (ansa) from which the name "ansa cervicalis" is derived.

Sternothyroid Muscle. Attached to the inferior portion of the oblique line (ligament) of the thyroid cartilage, the sternothyroid muscle connects the cartilaginous larynx with the manubrium of the sternum and first costal cartilage. Some of the fibers of the sternothyroid muscle may continue superiorly and posteriorly past the thyroid cartilage to interdigitate with the fibers of the inferior pharyngeal constrictor muscle (Zenker and Zenker, 1960). During contraction the sternothyroid muscle is capable of depressing the thyroid cartilage, stabilizing the position of the cartilaginous larynx, and enlarging the pharynx by drawing the larynx anteriorly and inferiorly. The motor innervation for the sternothyroid muscle is derived from a branch of the ansa cervicalis nerve loop, which contains fibers from the first, second, and third cervical nerves (C1, C2, and C3). The branch leaves the convexity of the loop of the ansa cervicalis nerve and courses as either a single nerve or separate nerve filaments along the superficial surface of the carotid artery before entering the muscle (Clemente, 1985).

Sternohyoid Muscle. The sternohyoid muscle (with the omohyoid muscle) is one of the "strap" muscles of the neck. The development of the sternohyoid muscle is variable and may be continuous with the other infrahyoid muscles (Bergman et al., 1984). This muscle courses vertically from the sternal manubrium and the clavicle to the body of the hyoid bone. During contraction the sternohyoid muscle may either depress the hyoid bone or fix it in position during active jaw opening. Similar to that of the sternothyroid muscle, the motor innervation is derived from a branch of the ansa cervicalis nerve loop that contains fibers of the first, second, and third cervical nerves (C1, C2, C3), which exit the convexity of the loop (Williams and Warwick, 1980).

Omohyoid Muscle. The omohyoid muscle forms the other portion of the "strap" muscles of the neck. Following a complex course, the omohyoid muscle first runs inferiorly from the greater cornu of the hyoid bone; then, near the sternum, it turns and courses laterally to attach to the upper border of the scapula. During contraction the omohyoid muscle may depress the hyoid bone; and it may stabilize the structures of the neck during deep inspiration (Zemlin, 1981). The upper portion (superior belly) of the omohyoid muscle derives its motor innervation from fibers of the first cervical nerve (C1) via the superior root of the ansa cervicalis nerve prior to the loop. The lower portion (inferior belly) of the omohyoid muscle is innervated by fibers from the second and third cervical nerves (C2 and C3), which leave the convexity of the loop of the ansa cervicalis nerve and run laterally, deep to its intermediate tendon, before entering the muscle (Clemente, 1985).

SENSORY SYSTEM

CONTRACTILE ELEMENT INNERVATION

The presence of muscle spindles in the intrinsic muscles of the human larynx appears to be somewhat variable in distribution but well documented (Baken, 1971; Baken and Noback, 1971; Grim, 1967; Lucas-Keene, 1961; Rossi and Cortesina, 1965).

Ganglion cells related to the mesencephalic nucleus of the trigeminal (V) nerve that are found along the motor root innervate muscle spindles found in the digastric and mylohyoid muscles (Carpenter, 1976). The superior root of the hypoglossal (XII) nerve communicates with the cervical plexus and provides proprioceptive innervation for the geniohyoid and thyrohyoid

muscles and the superior belly of the omohyoid muscle (Clemente, 1985). The contribution of the proprioceptive information conveyed by muscle spindles is uncertain, given data indicating that the population of muscle spindles in the muscles of this region is low (Dubner et al., 1978).

NONCONTRACTILE ELEMENT INNERVATION

Mucosa

The mucosa of the larynx is primarily innervated by the internal laryngeal branch of the superior laryngeal nerve of the vagus (X) nerve. This nerve branch is probably entirely sensory. However, Williams (1951) indicated that it may contain a few special visceral motor fibers that innervate the transverse interarytenoid muscle. The internal laryngeal branch pierces the posteroinferior portion of the thyrohyoid membrane immediately superior to the superior laryngeal artery. Deep to the thyrohyoid membrane the internal laryngeal branch divides into three parts, which form subepithelial plexuses and extend to innervate (1) both surfaces of the epiglottis; (2) the aryepiglottic fold; and (3) the mucous membrane of the posterior larynx to the level of the vocal folds. The division that innervates the epiglottis demonstrates differential distribution, with more free nerve endings and chemoreceptors on the laryngeal than on the lingual surface of the epiglottis. Furthermore, the lingual surface might receive a small contribution from the glossopharyngeal (IX) nerve (Clemente, 1985; Dubner et al., 1978). The division that innervates the mucous membrane of the posterior larynx is the largest part and communicates directly with the recurrent laryngeal nerve. The recurrent laryngeal nerve accompanies the laryngeal branch of the inferior thyroid artery and provides sensory innervation to the mucous membrane of the larynx below the level of the vocal folds (Dubner et al., 1978). The mucous membrane of the anterior larynx below the vocal folds is innervated by fibers of the external superior laryngeal nerve (Suzuki and Kirchner, 1968).

Joints

The fibrous capsules (not the synovial tissues) of the laryngeal joints contain numerous lamellated nerve endings (pacinian corpuscles) and few Ruffini endings and free nerve endings (Dubner et al., 1978; Kirchner and Wyke, 1965). These nerve endings are innervated primarily by branches of the recurrent laryngeal nerve (Psenicka, 1966).

Cartilages

The perichondrium of the epiglottis and arytenoid cartilages receives a dense distribution of free and organized endings. These nerve endings are innervated by perichondrial nerves from the internal laryngeal branch of the superior laryngeal nerve of the vagus (X) nerve, which penetrate adjacent muscles and tendons and terminate in the perichondrium of adjacent cartilages (Dubner et al., 1978).

SUPRALARYNGEAL MECHANISMS

The supralaryngeal mechanisms consist of the convoluted supraglottal airways and cavities and the structural boundaries of those airways and cavities. During the complex motor act of speech the supralaryngeal mechanisms function not only as acoustic resonators but also as supraglottal sound generators. The supralaryngeal mechanisms consist of: (1) the conduit formed by the pharynx; (2) the velopharynx, which forms the velopharyngeal valve; (3) the tongue, which forms the most mobile articulator; (4) the craniomandibular complex, controlled by the temporomandibular joint; and (5) the circumoral complex, which largely determines the radiation characteristic of the vocal tract. The motor innervation of the supralaryngeal mechanism is summarized in Figure 5-8.

PHARYNX

MOTOR SYSTEM

The pharynx is a musculomembranous tube located posterior to the nasal and oral cavities and superior to the larynx. The pharynx serves as a channel connecting the external environment with the lower airways during respiration and speech and with the esophagus during deglutition. During speech the pharynx functions as a variable volume resonator and aids in the opening and closing of the velopharyngeal port. The musculature of the pharynx traditionally may be divided into two groups: (1) pharyngeal elevators, found on the internal surface of the pharyngeal tube, which shorten and perhaps widen the pharynx by drawing the lateral pharyngeal walls superiorly and laterally; and (2) pharyngeal constrictors, found on the external surface of the pharyngeal tube, which narrow the lumen of that tube.

The principal motor innervation of the pharynx is derived from the vagus (X) nerve (see Fig. 5-4) supplemented by fibers from the glossopharyngeal (IX) nerve (Fig. 5-9) and the spinal accessory (XI) nerve (Fig. 5-10). The pharyngeal branch of the vagus (X) nerve carries motor fibers derived from the cranial root of the spinal accessory (XI) nerve and sensory fibers from the inferior ganglion as it passes between the external and internal carotid arteries (Clemente, 1985). Approaching the superior border of the external surface of the middle pharyngeal constrictor muscle, the pharyngeal nerve divides into numerous filaments that join with fibers from the glossopharyngeal (IX) nerve and with the external branch of the superior laryngeal branch of the vagus (X) nerve to form the pharyngeal plexus. Through this plexus fibers of the vagus (X) nerve are distributed to the muscles and mucous membrane of the pharynx and soft palate (except the tensor veli palatini muscle). Although the innervation of the upper pharynx is described consistently as involving the pharyngeal plexus of fibers, the exact contribution to the plexus from specific cranial nerves has been questioned (Dickson, 1975).

Pharyngeal Elevator Muscle Innervation

Stylopharyngeus Muscle. The stylopharyngeus muscle is located on the internal surface of the mid to lower pharynx, coursing from the styloid process inferiorly to attach to the lateral pharyngeal wall. It gains entrance to the inner aspects of the pharynx between the superior and middle pharyngeal constrictor muscles. The stylopharyngeus muscle shortens and dilates the pharynx (Kahane, 1982). Motor innervation to this muscle is derived from fibers of the glossopharyngeal (IX) nerve, which are derived from the rostral parts of the nucleus ambiguus (Clemente, 1985).

			TRIGEMINAL (V)	FACIAL (VII)	GLOSSO-PHARYNGEAL (IX)	VAGUS (X)	SPINAL ACCESSORY (XI)	HYPOGLOSSAL (XII)
PHARYNX	ELEVATORS				STYLO-PHARYNGEUS			
					SALPINGOPHARYNGEUS			
	CONSTRICTORS				SUPERIOR PHARYNGEAL CONSTRICTOR			
					MIDDLE PHARYNGEAL CONSTRICTOR			
					INFERIOR PHARYNGEAL CONSTRICTOR			
VELUM	INTRINSIC						UVULAE	
	EXTRINSIC		TENSOR VELI PALATINI					
							LEVATOR VELI PALATINI	
							PALATO-PHARYNGEUS	
							PALATOGLOSSUS	
TONGUE	INTRINSIC							SUPERIOR LONGITUDINAL
								INFERIOR LONGITUDINAL
								TRANSVERSE LINGUAL
								VERTICAL LINGUAL
	EXTRINSIC							STYLOGLOSSUS
								HYOGLOSSUS
								GENIOGLOSSUS
							PALATOGLOSSUS	
CRANIOMANDIBULAR COMPLEX	ABDUCTORS		LATERAL PTERYGOID					
			DIGASTRIC (ANTERIOR BELLY)					
			MYLOHYOID					
	ADDUCTORS		TEMPORALIS					
			MASSETER					
			MEDIAL PTERYGOID					
CIRCUMORAL COMPLEX	GROUP I			ZYGOMATICUS MAJOR				
				LEVATOR ANGULI ORIS				
				DEPRESSOR ANGULI ORIS				
				ORBICULARIS ORIS				
				BUCCINATOR				
				RISORIUS				
	GROUP II			LEVATOR LABII SUPERIORIS ALAEQUE NASI				
				LEVATOR LABII SUPERIORIS				
				ZYGOMATICUS MINOR				
	GROUP III			DEPRESSOR LABII INFERIORIS				
				MENTALIS				

Fig. 5-8. Innervation of the supralaryngeal musculature.

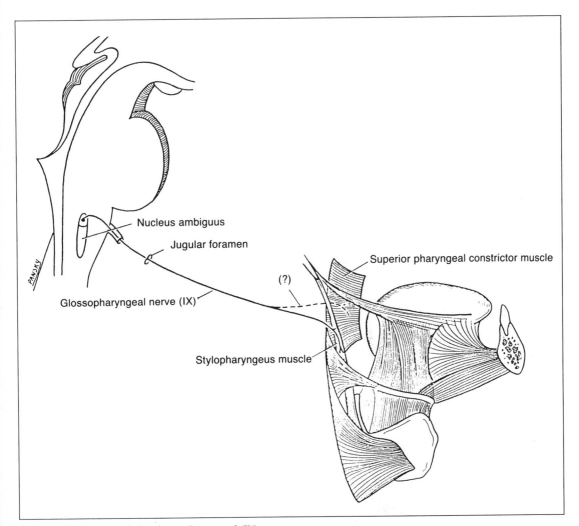

Fig. 5-9. Distribution of the glossopharyngeal (IX) nerve.

Salpingopharyngeus Muscle. The salpingopharyngeus muscle is a small muscle of the internal pharynx, often absent, that consists of a few muscle fibers coursing from the torus tubarius above to attach to the mucous membrane of the lower pharyngeal wall. The nerves of the pharyngeal plexus provide motor innervation to this muscle.

Pharyngeal Constrictor Muscle Innervation

Superior Pharyngeal Constrictor Muscle. The superior pharyngeal constrictor muscle courses horizontally along the external surface of the pharynx from the soft palate, pterygomandibular raphe, mandible, and tongue to the posterior median raphe (pharyngeal raphe). This muscle frequently is divided into distinct muscle fiber bundles, each provided a distinct name (i.e., pterygopharyngeus, buccopharyngeus, mylopharyngeus, glossopharyngeus) (Bergman et al., 1984). During contraction the superior pharyngeal constrictor muscle may move the lateral pharyngeal walls medially and the posterior pharyngeal walls anteriorly to reduce the cross-sectional area of the pharynx. The motor innervation of this muscle is from fibers derived from the vagus (X) nerve that pass through the pharyngeal plexus (Williams and Warwick, 1980). These motor fibers might be supplemented by direct fibers of the glossopharyngeal (IX) nerve (Clemente, 1985).

Middle Pharyngeal Constrictor Muscle. One of

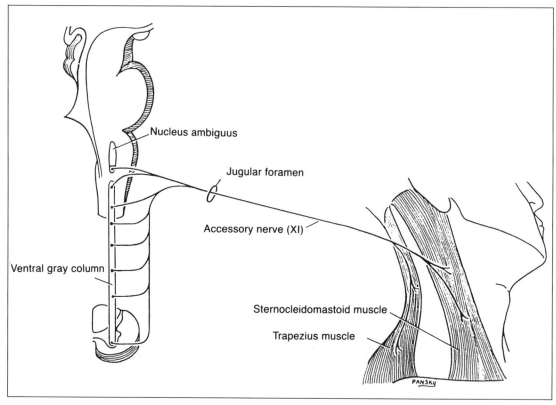

Fig. 5-10. Distribution of the spinal accessory (XI) nerve.

the outer layer of pharyngeal muscles, the middle pharyngeal constrictor muscle courses transversely from the hyoid bone and stylohyoid ligament to the median pharyngeal raphe. The fibers of the middle pharyngeal constrictor muscle may show considerable independence, so that those fibers that attach to the greater cornu of the hyoid bone may be called the ceratopharyngeus muscle, and the fibers that attach to the lesser cornu and stylohyoid ligament may be called the chondropharyngeus muscle. The hyoid attachment has led some investigators to consider the middle pharyngeal constrictor muscle a suprahyoid extrinsic laryngeal muscle. As the muscle shortens during contraction, the pharyngeal tube narrows and perhaps draws the hyoid bone posteriorly (Dickson and Maue-Dickson, 1982). The middle pharyngeal constrictor muscle is innervated by the pharyngeal branch of the vagus (X) nerve and perhaps some small fibers of the glossopharyngeal (IX) nerve as the fibers join to form the pharyngeal plexus of the vagus (X) nerve.

Inferior Pharyngeal Constrictor Muscle. The most caudal of the muscles that make up the outer constrictor layer of the pharynx, the inferior pharyngeal constrictor muscle courses from the oblique line of the thyroid cartilage and the arch of the cricoid cartilage to the median pharyngeal raphe. The independence of the anterior attachments has led to the description of two parts of the inferior pharyngeal constrictor muscle: (1) the thyropharyngeus muscle arising from the thyroid cartilage, and (2) the cricopharyngeus muscle arising from the cricoid cartilage. The nature of the anterior muscle attachment to the cartilaginous larynx has led to consideration of the inferior pharyngeal constrictor muscle as an infrahyoid extrinsic laryngeal muscle (Strong and Vaughn, 1981). Constricting the pharyngeal tube lumen and perhaps modifying the thyroid angle, the inferior constrictor muscle is innervated by two branches of the vagus (X) nerve. The external laryngeal branch of the superior laryngeal nerve of the vagus (X) nerve provides motor innervation to part of the muscle, and the pharyngeal branch of the recurrent laryngeal nerve of the vagus (X) nerve innervates the other part of the inferior pharyngeal constrictor muscle (Clemente, 1985).

SENSORY SYSTEM

Contractile Element Innervation

Kuehn, Frederick, and Maynard (1981), after a careful search, found no muscle spindles in the superior constrictor muscle in human specimens. Bossy and Vidic (1967) also indicated that there is no compelling evidence supporting the presence of proprioceptive nerve endings in the muscles of the pharynx.

Noncontractile Element Innervation

The major sensory nerves innervating the pharyngeal mucosa include the trigeminal (V), glossopharyngeal (IX), and vagus (X) nerves. The pharyngeal and palatine branches of the maxillary nerve of the trigeminal (V) nerve innervate the superior portion of the pharynx, including the mucous membrane of the nasopharynx and the anterior part of the soft palate (Dubner et al., 1978). The greater petrosal branch of the facial (VII) nerve provides innervation overlapping that of the trigeminal (V) nerve in the region of the faucial arches. The pharyngeal branch of the glossopharyngeal (IX) nerve innervates the touch and pressure receptors in the mucous membrane of the lateral pharyngeal wall adjacent to the posterior third of the tongue. The pharyngeal branches of the vagus (X) nerve that form the pharyngeal plexus also innervate the mucous membrane of the pharynx.

VELUM

The velopharyngeal port is formed by the velum (soft palate) and the adjacent pharyngeal walls. It acts as a valve capable of separating the nasal cavity and nasopharynx from the airways below. The action of this valve is not strictly binary, having only a completely open or a completely closed state. Instead, the velopharyngeal port provides many degrees of opening, each offering a different amount of resistance to airflow. The five pairs of muscles associated with the velopharyngeal port are traditionally

divided into an intrinsic muscle contained entirely within the velum and four extrinsic muscles that displace the velum and the walls of the upper pharynx. Except for the tensor veli palatini muscle, which is innervated by the trigeminal (V) nerve, the muscles that control the velopharyngeal port are innervated by fibers of the pharyngeal plexus.

MOTOR SYSTEM

Intrinsic Muscle Innervation

Uvulae Muscle. The only intrinsic muscle of the velum, the uvulae muscle courses from the palatal aponeurosis to the uvula. This muscle is in a favorable position to aid in velopharyngeal port closure (Azzam and Kuehn, 1977). Kuehn, Folkins, and Linville (1988) hypothesized that, upon contraction, the uvular muscle increases the stiffness of the velum, thus facilitating more rapid movement control and preventing distortion of the velum by the extrinsic velar muscles.

The uvulae muscle is innervated by the fibers of the cranial portion of the spinal accessory (XI) nerve. These spinal accessory nerve fibers join fibers from the vagus (X) nerve distal to the jugular foramen to form the ramus internus and are distributed to the uvulae muscle from the pharyngeal plexus via the pharyngeal branch of the vagus (X) nerve (Clemente, 1985).

Extrinsic Muscle Innervation

Tensor Veli Palatini Muscle. The tensor veli palatini muscle has superior attachments to the medial pterygoid plate and attaches to the lateral aspects of the auditory tube. The muscle fibers course inferiorly to terminate in a tendon that wraps around the pterygoid hamulus and courses medially to form the anterior palatal aponeurosis (Kahane, 1982). In view of the complex geometry of the tensor veli palatini muscle, it has been assigned a number of functions including (1) tensing the anterior velum (Judson and Weaver, 1965); (2) lowering the anterior velum (Judson and Weaver, 1965; Morley, 1970); (3) elevating the anterior velum (Kaplan, 1960); and (4) dilating the auditory tube (Rood and Doyle, 1978). The motor innervation of the tensor veli palatini muscle is derived from the mandibular branch of the trigeminal (V) nerve. Specifically, the innervation is derived either directly from the medial pterygoid nerve of the mandibular branch or from a nerve root that arises close to the origin of the medial pterygoid nerve. The medial pterygoid nerve passes between the tensor veli palatini muscle and the lateral pterygoid muscle (Dubner et al., 1978).

Levator Veli Palatini Muscle. Coursing from the petrous portion of the temporal bone above to the midline of the velum below, the levator veli palatini muscle forms a muscular sling through the velum. Dickson and Maue-Dickson (1982) observed that fibers of the superior pharyngeal constrictor muscle interdigitate with those of the levator veli palatini muscle. During auxotonic contraction the levator veli palatini muscle elevates the velum, displacing it superiorly and posteriorly. Fibers of the cranial portion of the spinal accessory (XI) nerve that form part of the pharyngeal plexus innervate the levator veli palatini muscle.

Palatopharyngeus Muscle. The palatopharyngeus muscle courses from the velum above to have its superior fibers interdigitate with fibers from the superior pharyngeal constrictor muscle before attaching to the pharyngeal walls. Its inferior fibers course downward to form the palatopharyngeal (posterior faucial) arch prior to attaching to the inferior pharyngeal walls. Contraction of the palatopharyngeus muscle draws the velum inferiorly and may assist the pharyngeal constrictor muscles in displacing the pharyngeal walls inward. Innervation is provided by fibers of the cranial portion of the spinal accessory (XI) nerve via the pharyngeal plexus.

Palatoglossus Muscle. In forming the palatoglossal (anterior faucial) arch the palatoglossus muscle courses from a superior attachment extending through the velum to insert into the muscles of the lateral aspect of the tongue (DiFoggio, 1984; DiFoggio and Kennedy, 1984; Kuehn and Azzam, 1978). The palatoglossus muscle may open the velopharyngeal port by drawing the velum inferiorly and anteriorly. It also has the potential of assisting in tongue dorsum elevation. Like the palatopharyngeus muscle, the palatoglossus muscle receives motor innervation from fibers of the cranial portion of the spinal accessory (XI) nerve via the pharyngeal plexus.

Other Possible Sources of Motor Innervation

In general, the description of motor nerve supply to the velopharyngeal (velum plus pharynx) region tends to be fairly consistent in the literature. Specifically, the tensor veli palatini

muscle receives its nerve supply from the mandibular branch of the trigeminal (V) nerve, and the other velopharyngeal muscles are supplied through the pharyngeal plexus, whose source is probably a combination of the glossopharyngeal (IX), the vagus (X), and the cranial portion of the spinal accessory (XI) nerves.

Other nerves have been implicated in the innervation of the velopharyngeal region. Broomhead (1957) described innervation to the uvulae muscle as being derived from the lesser palatine nerve, which is a branch of the maxillary division of the trigeminal (V) nerve. However, the lesser palatine nerve typically is considered sensory, and it is doubtful that it provides motor innervation to the velum. Also, Nishio, Matsuya, Machida, and Miyazaki (1976) demonstrated that the facial (VII) nerve, as well as the glossopharyngeal (IX) and vagus (X) nerves innervate the uvulae, levator veli palatini, and superior pharyngeal constrictor muscles in rhesus monkeys. Whether the facial (VII) nerve also innervates velopharyngeal muscles in humans remains to be determined.

SENSORY SYSTEM

Contractile Element Innervation

Investigation of the presence and distribution of the proprioceptive innervation of the muscles of the soft palate has been limited. Winkler (1964) provided data collected from human material indicating the presence of numerous muscle spindles in the vertical portion of the tensor veli palatini muscle (a palatal muscle innervated by the trigeminal nerve). Evidence indicates that the other muscles of the soft palate, innervated by the vagus (X) and spinal accessory (XI) nerves, present few if any typical muscle spindles in humans (Dubner et al., 1978). In the most comprehensive investigation of spindles in the human velopharyngeal region, Kuehn and colleagues (1981) found numerous spindles in the tensor veli palatini, very few in the palatoglossus muscle, and none in the levator veli palatini, palatopharyngeus, uvulae, salpingopharyngeus, and superior pharyngeal constrictor muscles.

Noncontractile Element Innervation

The primary sensory innervation of the noncontractile elements of the palate are derived from the trigeminal (V), facial (VII), and glossopharyngeal (IX) nerves. The sensory supply of the mucous membrane is derived from the greater and lesser palatine branches that divide from the pterygopalatine nerves of the maxillary division of the trigeminal (V) nerve. The greater palatine branch emerges from the greater palatine foramen and divides into branches innervating the mucosa of the hard palate and the palatine gingiva. The lesser palatine nerves emerge from the lesser palatine foramen and are distributed to the mucous membrane of the soft palate, uvulae, and the upper pole of the palatine tonsil. Sensory fibers of the greater petrosal nerve of the facial (VII) nerve frequently accompany the trigeminal (V) nerve fibers. The tonsillar branch of the glossopharyngeal (IX) nerve innervates the palatine tonsil, soft palate, and mucous membrane of the faucial arches. The lingual branch of the glossopharyngeal (IX) nerve innervates the mucous membrane on the posterior tongue (Larson and Pfingst, 1982).

TONGUE

The tongue is perhaps the most significant articulator. Dynamically capable of forming partitioning constrictions of the oral cavity and influencing the oropharynx, the tongue is importantly involved in establishing and maintaining vocal tract resonances. In addition, by forming constrictions with other oral cavity structures the tongue can control airflow and pressure and thereby act as a sound source for many consonants.

Traditionally, the lingual muscles are divided into intrinsic and extrinsic muscle groups. Both the intrinsic and extrinsic muscles of the tongue (except the palatoglossus muscle) are innervated by the hypoglossal (XII) nerve, shown in Figure 5-7. The hypoglossal (XII) nerve exits the cranium through the hypoglossal canal. After it emerges from the canal, the hypoglossal (XII) nerve is tightly bound to the vagus (X) nerve and descends to the level of the lower border of the digastric muscle. At that point the hypoglossal (XII) nerve curves anteriorly and superiorly to innervate the hyoglossus muscle and continues past the deep surface of the stylohyoid muscle to enter the oral cavity near the posterior border of the mylohyoid muscle. On entering the oral cavity the hypoglossal (XII) nerve exchanges fibers with the lingual nerve of the mandibular division of the trigeminal (V) nerve and splits into numerous branches as it courses along the genioglossus muscle as far as the tip of the tongue (Sicher and DuBrul, 1970). In addition to innervating the muscles of the tongue, the hypoglossal (XII) nerve may send branches to the mylohyoid, digastric, and stylohyoid muscles (Bergman et al., 1984).

MOTOR SYSTEM

Intrinsic Muscle Innervation

The intrinsic lingual muscles are contained entirely within the structure of the tongue and are characterized by their extensive interdigitation (Kraus, Kitamura, and Latham, 1966). The intrinsic muscles change the shape of the tongue body by lifting the tongue tip, lowering the tongue tip, and flattening and narrowing the tongue blade.

Superior Longitudinal Lingual Muscle. The unpaired superior longitudinal lingual muscle covers the dorsum of the tongue as it courses posteriorly from the tongue tip and medial septum to the epiglottis and hyoglossal membrane (Abd-El-Malek, 1939). During auxotonic contraction the superior longitudinal muscle shortens the tongue, elevates the tongue tip and sides, and forms a concavity in the tongue dorsum (Kahane, 1982). The motor innervation of this muscle is derived from the muscular branch of the hypoglossal (XII) nerve.

Inferior Longitudinal Lingual Muscle. The inferior longitudinal lingual muscle is a variably paired muscle deep within the body of the tongue. It courses posteriorly from the mucous membrane of the inferior tongue tip through the lateral aspects of the body and attaches to the greater cornu of the hyoid bone. The inferior longitudinal lingual muscle may shorten the tongue and lower both the tongue tip and sides. This muscle is innervated by the muscular branch of the hypoglossal (XII) nerve.

Transverse Lingual Muscle. The transverse lingual muscle arises from the median septum (which is penetrated by some of the muscle fibers) and courses transversely to attach to the lamina propria of the mucous membrane of the lateral aspect of the tongue body. Drawing the lateral aspects of the tongue medially, the transverse lingual muscle narrows and increases the height of the tongue. Innervation of this muscle is provided by the muscular branch of the hypoglossal (XII) nerve.

Vertical Lingual Muscle. Arising from the lamina propria of the mucous membrane of the tongue dorsum the fibers of the vertical lingual muscle course directly inferiorly to terminate within the tongue body or on the lamina propria of the inferior aspect of the tongue blade. By approximating the superior and inferior surfaces of the tongue body, the vertical lingual muscle flattens and widens the tongue. The muscular branch of the hypoglossal (XII) nerve innervates the vertical lingual muscle.

Extrinsic Muscle Innervation

The paired extrinsic lingual muscles connect the tongue body with the skeletal support structures of the mandible and hyoid bone below and the cranium and soft palate above. The extrinsic muscles displace the tongue body both inside and outside the oral cavity and in doing so change the shape of the vocal tract and may produce limited alterations of the shape of the tongue as well.

Genioglossus Muscle. Composed of at least two and probably three distinct muscle bundles, the paired genioglossus muscle courses from its anterior attachment on the superior genial tubercles of the internal mandibular symphysis to the lamina propria of the dorsum of the tongue. The anterior bundle of the genioglossus muscle may retract and depress the tongue tip, the intermediate bundle may depress the middle of the tongue and draw the tongue forward, and the posterior bundle has the potential to draw the tongue body anteriorly. Motor innervation is provided by the muscular branch of the hypoglossal (XII) nerve.

Styloglossus Muscle. The styloglossus muscle arises from the styloid process and courses anteriorly and inferiorly in a fan-shaped sheet along the inferolateral aspects of the tongue, eventually spreading along the medial lingual septum in the posterior to anterior regions of the tongue body (DiFoggio, 1984; DiFoggio and Kennedy, 1984). Auxotonic contraction of the styloglossus muscle may elevate and retract the tongue body and perhaps (via its anterior fibers) elevate the tongue tip. Innervation is provided by the muscular branch of the hypoglossal (XII) nerve.

Hyoglossus Muscle. Coursing superiorly from the body and greater cornu of the hyoid bone,

the hyoglossus muscle interdigitates with the fibers of the styloglossus muscle and terminates within the side of the posterior tongue body (DiFoggio, 1984; DiFoggio and Kennedy, 1984). During contraction the hyoglossus muscle draws the tongue inferiorly and posteriorly, and perhaps elevates the hyoid bone (Kaplan, 1960). Innervation is provided by the muscular branch of the hypoglossal (XII) nerve.

Palatoglossus Muscle. The palatoglossus muscle innervation is provided by fibers of the spinal accessory (XI) nerve via the pharyngeal plexus. This pattern of innervation leads to the classification of the palatoglossus muscle as one of the complement of extrinsic muscles of the velopharyngeal port. However, the palatoglossus muscle may assist in tongue elevation if the velum is fixed in place, especially in those individuals with a more anterior velar attachment (Kuehn and Azzam, 1978). A description of innervation of the palatoglossus muscle is provided in the section of this chapter that discusses the muscles of the velum.

SENSORY SYSTEM

Contractile Element Innervation

The existence of a proprioceptive apparatus in the lingual musculature has been the source of discussion and description for many years. The presence of muscle spindles has been documented in the monkey tongue (Bowman, 1968, 1971; Fitzgerald and Sachithananadan, 1977, 1978, 1979) and human tongue (Cooper, 1953; Kubota, Negishi, and Nasegi, 1975; Nakayama, 1944). The sensory innervation of the proprioceptor nerve endings of the intrinsic and extrinsic lingual musculature exits the tongue primarily via fibers from the hypoglossal (XII) nerve supplemented by fibers of the lingual branch of the mandibular division of the trigeminal (V) nerve. The sensory fibers then branch from these nerves and enter the second (C2) and third (C3) cervical nerves (Landgren and Olsson, 1982).

Noncontractile Element Innervation

The sensory innervation of the tongue is provided by portions of the trigeminal (V), facial (VII), glossopharyngeal (IX), and vagus (X) nerves. The lingual nerve of the mandibular branch of the trigeminal (V) nerve serves general sensation from the anterior two-thirds (presulcal region) of the tongue. The chorda tympani is derived partially from the intermediate nerve of the facial (VII) nerve and provides taste sensation from the mucous membrane of the presulcal region (except the vallate papillae). The lingual branch of the glossopharyngeal (IX) nerve has two segments: one segment that supplies the vallate papillae with afferent fibers for taste and the mucous membrane near the sulcus terminalis for general sensation, and another segment that serves the mucous membrane of the postsulcal region for general sensation. The internal laryngeal nerve, which is derived from the superior laryngeal branch of the vagus (X) nerve, receives general sensation from the region of the tongue immediately anterior to the epiglottis (Williams and Warwick, 1980).

CRANIOMANDIBULAR COMPLEX

MOTOR SYSTEM

The craniomandibular complex is formed by the mandible, maxilla, and the temporomandibular joint (TMJ), at which the mandible and temporal bones interface. This structural complex directly influences both the vertical position of the tongue by controlling the position of its base and the oral opening by controlling the inferior attachment of many of the muscles of the circumoral complex.

The TMJ limits the degrees of freedom of movement of the mandible. It differs from many joints of the body in that: (1) the condyle not only rotates but also translates jaw motion; (2) the adult mandible is a single bone, so TMJs function as bilaterally coupled joints, with the sensory input from both joints integrated in a manner similar to the paired vestibular organs; (3) the articular surfaces are not covered by hyaline cartilage; (4) an interposed articular disc divides the joint into an upper arthrodial (sliding) portion lacking a cartilage layer and a lower ginglymoid (rotating) portion lacking a fixed articular bone; (5) muscle action, rather than the configuration of the articular fossa, determines joint motion; and (6) the fully adducted (closed) position of the mandible is determined by dental approximation (Dubner et al., 1978; Kahane, 1982).

The muscles of the craniomandibular complex may be divided into abductor (jaw opening) and adductor (jaw closing) groups. The motor innervation for all the muscles of the region is provided by branches of the trigeminal (V) nerve.

Abductor Muscle Innervation

Assisted by gravitational force, the abductor muscles of the craniomandibular complex increase the distance between the mandible and maxilla. The increase in vertical distance may lower the tongue and dilate the oral opening.

Lateral Pterygoid Muscle (Inferior Head). The inferior head of the lateral pterygoid muscle originates from the lateral surface of the lateral pterygoid plate. It courses posteriorly and converges with the superior head of the lateral pterygoid muscle complex prior to attaching to the articular disk of the condyle of the mandible. During auxotonic contraction the inferior head may protrude the mandible. If contracting unilaterally, it may pull the mandible to one side. The muscle might initiate mandibular opening by pulling the condyle anteriorly and inferiorly. The motor innervation of the lateral pterygoid muscle is supplied by the lateral pterygoid nerve, which arises from the anterior trunk of the mandibular division of the trigeminal (V) nerve. It may arise from the mandibular division in conjunction with the buccal nerve, which is a branch of the mandibular division.

Digastric Muscle (Anterior Belly). Previously described as an extrinsic laryngeal muscle, the anterior belly of the digastric muscle has the functional potential to aid mandibular abduction by generating a "hinge" movement at the TMJ that decreases the distance between the hyoid bone and the mandibular symphysis. Motor innervation is provided by the mylohyoid branch of the inferior alveolar nerve of the mandibular division of the trigeminal (V) nerve.

Mylohyoid Muscle. The mylohyoid muscle, like the anterior belly of the digastric muscle, has been described previously as an extrinsic laryngeal muscle. The mylohyoid muscle may aid mandibular abduction by supplementing a "hinge" movement in the TMJ that draws the anterior portion of the mandible downward when the hyoid bone is fixed in place. The mylohyoid muscle is innervated by the mylohyoid branch of the inferior alveolar nerve derived from the mandibular division of the trigeminal (V) nerve.

Geniohyoid Muscle. Previously described as an extrinsic laryngeal muscle, the paired geniohyoid muscle also influences the movement of the mandible. The paired components of the geniohyoid lie adjacent to each other at the midline and frequently share muscle fascicles to the extent that they appear to constitute a single muscle (Kennedy and DiFoggio, 1985). Situated immediately deep to the mylohyoid, the geniohyoid may aid in depressing the anterior portion of the mandible when the hyoid bone is fixed in place. The geniohyoid muscle is innervated by a branch of the first cervical nerve (C1) through the hypoglossal (XII) nerve (Clemente, 1985).

Adductor Muscle Innervation

The extremely powerful adductor muscles of the craniomandibular complex decrease the vertical distance between the mandible and the maxilla. When raising the mandible, the adductor muscles elevate the platform on which the tongue rests, which may decrease the amount of oral opening and may bring the dentition into complete occlusion.

Temporalis Muscle. Embryologically derived from a muscle mass common with the other muscles of mastication, the temporalis muscle often shares fiber bundles with surrounding muscles (e.g., the masseter and lateral pterygoid muscles) (Bergman et al., 1984). From a broad, fan-shaped origin on the lateral surface of the cranium, the temporalis muscle fibers converge as they course inferiorly to attach to the coronoid process and anterior portion of the ramus of the mandible. During contraction the temporalis muscle may elevate, retract, and produce ipsilateral deviation of the mandible (Kahane, 1982).

The motor innervation of the temporalis muscle is derived from the anterior and posterior deep temporal nerves of the anterior trunk of the mandibular division of the trigeminal (V) nerve (Clemente, 1985). The anterior branch of the deep temporal nerve is often derived from the buccal nerve. The buccal nerve itself is a branch of the mandibular division of the trigeminal (V) nerve. That anterior branch ascends along the superior head of the lateral pterygoid muscle prior to its muscular termination. The smaller posterior branch may arise with the masseteric nerve, a branch of the trigeminal (V) nerve and course through the posterior part of the temporal fossa. A third, intermediate branch may be observed (Williams and Warwick, 1980).

Masseter Muscle. Composed of a superficial and deep portion, and segmented into many subdivisions, the massive masseter muscle courses along the external surface of the ramus of the mandible. The superficial portion courses from the anterior portion of the zygomatic arch inferiorly to the superficial surface of the angle of the mandible. The deep portion runs deep to the superficial portion extending from the zygomatic arch to the lateral surface of the mandibular ramus and coronoid process. During auxotonic contraction the masseter muscle elevates the mandible.

Motor innervation is derived from the masseteric branch of the anterior trunk of the mandibular division of the trigeminal (V) nerve. The masseteric branch has been estimated to supply as many as 1,021 muscle fibers per motor nerve fiber (Buchthal and Schmalbruch, 1980). The masseteric branch passes above the superior head of the lateral pterygoid muscle, anterior to the TMJ (to which it may give a filament) and posterior to the tendon of the temporalis muscle. From there it passes through the mandibular notch and ramifies the deep surface of the masseter muscle.

Medial Pterygoid Muscle. The medial pterygoid muscle parallels the masseter muscle on the medial surface of the ramus of the mandible. In conjunction with the masseter muscle it forms the "mandibular sling" around the angle of the mandible. From its superior attachment at the medial surface of the lateral pterygoid plate and palatine bone, the muscle courses inferiorly to the angle of the mandible. During contraction this muscle may elevate the mandible and produce contralateral mandibular deviation.

The motor innervation is derived from the slender medial pterygoid branch of the mandibular division of the trigeminal (V) nerve. The medial pterygoid branch separates from the main nerve proximal to the point at which the mandibular division divides into anterior and posterior trunks.

Lateral Pterygoid Muscle (Superior Head). The superior head of the lateral pterygoid muscle originates from the infratemporal crest and greater wing of the sphenoid bone. From that superior attachment the muscle bundle courses posteriorly, converging with the inferior head, and attaches to the articular capsule of the condyle of the mandible. Contraction of the superior head may stabilize and aid adduction of the mandible, especially if co-contracting with other mandibular adductors (Folkins, 1981; Kahane, 1982). The motor innervation of the superior head of the lateral pterygoid muscle is the same as the inferior head and is provided by the lateral pterygoid nerve of the anterior trunk of the mandibular division of the trigeminal (V) nerve.

SENSORY SYSTEM

Contractile Element Innervation

The distribution of contractile element sensory receptors in the muscles of the human craniomandibular complex apparently follows functional lines. The abductor muscles have either no or few muscle spindles (Gill, 1971; Kubota and Masegi, 1977; Lennartsson, 1979; Maier, 1979). On the other hand, the adductor muscles that generate high closing forces are provided with a large complement of muscle spindles (Freimann, 1954; Smith and Marcarian, 1967). The afferent fibers arising from muscle spindles and other proprioceptors, such as nerve endings in the dental complex, periodontium, hard palate, and joint capsules, have their first-order neuron cell bodies in the mesencephalic nucleus of the trigeminal (V) nerve and terminate on other cranial nerve nuclei (Carpenter, 1976).

Noncontractile Element Innervation

The sensory receptors of the noncontractile element of the craniomandibular complex include (1) the fascia of the temporal and masseter muscles containing both slowly and rapidly adapting mechanoreceptors (Sakada, 1971); (2) extremely sensitive mechanoreceptors in the periodontal ligament (Dubner et al., 1978); (3) vibration-sensitive mechanoreceptors in the periosteum of the jaw and hard palate (Sakada, 1971); and (4) a large distribution of sensory receptors in the joint capsule of the TMJ. It has been reported that the density of cutaneous sensory innervation decreases from the anterior to the posterior oropharyngeal cavity (Grossman and Hattis, 1964; Kanagasuntheram, Wong, and Chan, 1969).

Mucosa, Periodontium, Periosteum. The sensory receptors of the region comprising the mucosa, periodontium and periosteum primarily are innervated by branches of the trigeminal (V) nerve. The buccal nerve of the anterior trunk of the mandibular division innervates the mucous membrane of the posterior buccal surface of the alveolar ridge. Branches of the lingual nerve of the posterior trunk of the mandibular division innervate the mucous membrane of the floor of the mouth and the lingual surface of the alveolar ridge (Williams and Warwick, 1980). The periodontal ligaments of the mandible are served by various branches of the inferior alveolar nerve of the posterior trunk of the mandibular division. The branches of the inferior alveolar nerve include (1) the mylohyoid nerve, which innervates the mandibular molar and premolar teeth and the adjacent mucous membrane; and (2) the incisive nerve to the canine and incisor teeth and adjacent mucous membrane. Three branches of the superior alveolar nerve of the maxillary division innervate the maxillary dentition: (1) the posterior branch, which supplies the molars and adjacent mucous membrane; (2) the middle branch, which supplies the premolars; and (3) the anterior branch from the incisor and canine dentition.

Temporomandibular Joint. The sensory receptors of the primate TMJ are innervated by branches of the mandibular division of the trigeminal (V) nerve. The posterior and lateral portions of the joint capsule are innervated by the large auriculotemporal branch of the posterior trunk of the mandibular division. The anterior portion of the joint capsule is innervated by the masseteric branch of the anterior trunk of the mandibular division and may be supplemented by the deep temporal branch of the same trunk (Dubner et al., 1978). The medial portion of the TMJ capsule is supplied by the masseteric and auriculotemporal branches of the anterior trunk of the mandibular division of the trigeminal (V) nerve.

CIRCUMORAL COMPLEX

MOTOR SYSTEM

Located between inner and outer boundary elements, the muscles of the circumoral complex form the middle layer of the flexible labial lamina and control the oral opening of the acoustic conduit. Coursing from the bones and ligaments of the mandible and cranium, these muscles demonstrate a number of unique qualities including (but not restricted to): (1) their organization into sheets of muscle that follow the contours of the underlying muscle and tissue; (2) muscles that course through an adipose layer connecting deep tissues with a superficial musculoaponeurotic system; (3) an absence of fascial sheaths; (4) extreme variability; (5) superficial, rather than deep, motor nerve entry; (6) a contractile environment characterized by the absence of externally opposed loads; (7) sequence-dependent muscle contraction; and (8) transverse contractile force distribution (Kahane, 1982; Kennedy and Abbs, 1979; Kennedy and DiFoggio, 1985).

Sequence-dependent muscle contraction means that the effect of the contractile effort depends on the status of the system at the time the muscle is activated. For example, if the modiolus (the muscle mass lateral to the oral angle, or "corner" of the mouth) is fixed in place, contraction of the orbicularis oris muscle compresses the lips against the dental arch. On the other hand, if the modiolus is free to move, the same degree of contractile force draws the modiolus and oral angles medially. Because these muscles do not contract in isolation and they exhibit sequence dependence, it is difficult to provide the traditional muscle action description.

The complexity of circumoral muscle function leads to a description involving muscle location rather than function. Group I muscles include those that are directly attached to and form the muscular modiolus. Group II muscles are located lateral to the nose and directly influence the upper lip medial to the modiolus. Group III muscles are located medial to the modiolar muscles and influence the lower lip.

As discussed by Folkins, Kennedy, and Loncarich (1978), the nomenclature for the circumoral musculature is variable in the anatomic literature. The muscle names that follow the Paris Nomina Anatomica, as suggested by Folkins et al. (1978), are used in this chapter.

The muscles of the circumoral complex receive their motor innervation from branches of the facial (VII) nerve. The pathway followed by the branches of the facial (VII) nerve is highly variable (Bernstein and Nelson, 1984). The lower motor neurons of the facial (VII) nerve demonstrate a spatial organization defining the muscles they innervate (Podvinec and Pfaltz, 1976). The buccal branch of the facial (VII) nerve courses directly anteriorly from the stylomas-

toid foramen and is distributed through (1) superficial, (2) upper deep, and (3) lower deep divisions to the region below the eye orbit and around the oral aperture. The mandibular branch of the facial (VII) nerve courses anteriorly inferior to the angle of the mandible deep to the platysma muscle to innervate the muscles of the lower lip and chin.

Group I: Modiolar Muscle Innervation

Orbicularis Oris Muscle. The orbicularis oris is a complex muscle frequently described as a sphincter yet demonstrating no sphincteric fiber continuity. The orbicularis oris muscle consists of fibers that course not only concentrically around the oral opening but also perpendicular to the opening, and from the deep mucosa to the superficial skin layer. The three-dimensional muscle complex referred to as the singular entity of the orbicularis oris muscle also includes the less developed incisivus labii superioris, incisivus labii inferioris, nasolabialis, and labii proprius muscles. Unopposed, isolated, auxotonic contraction of this muscle might protrude the lips, compress the lips against the maxilla, draw the oral angles medially, or approximate the midline of the upper and lower lips. Motor innervation is provided by the lower deep nerve of the buccal branch and by the marginal mandibular branch of the facial (VII) nerve.

Zygomaticus Major Muscle. The zygomaticus major muscle courses from the zygomatic bone to attach to and interdigitate with the muscles of the superficial surface of the superolateral aspect of the muscular modiolus. Isolated auxotonic contraction draws the oral angle toward the zygomatic bone. Motor innervation is supplied by the upper deep nerve of the buccal branch of the facial (VII) nerve, which passes the deep surface of the muscle.

Levator Anguli Oris Muscle. Coursing inferiorly from its attachment in the canine fossa of the maxilla to the muscles of the modiolus lateral to the oral angle, the levator anguli oris muscle has the potential to elevate the oral angle during auxotonic muscle contraction. The lower motor neuron innervating this muscle is derived from the upper deep nerve of the buccal branch of the facial (VII) nerve.

Depressor Anguli Oris Muscle. The depressor anguli oris muscle is the inferior counterpart of the levator anguli oris muscle and demonstrates muscle fibers continuous with the fibers of the levator anguli oris. The depressor anguli oris muscle courses from the oblique line of the mandible to and beyond the muscular modiolus. This muscle also frequently has a portion called the transversus menti consisting of muscle fibers that continue below the chin to become continuous with the contralateral muscular counterpart, forming a "mental (chin) sling." Isolated auxotonic contraction of this muscle might depress the oral angle. Motor innervation is derived from the marginal mandibular branch of the facial (VII) nerve, which courses anteriorly along the margin of the mandible deep to the platysma muscle and enters the deep surface of the depressor anguli oris muscle.

Buccinator Muscle. The buccinator muscle forms the major muscular component of the cheek as it courses from the maxilla, pterygomandibular raphe, and mandible anteriorly to attach to and extend beyond the muscular modiolus. Isolated auxotonic muscle contraction might retract the oral angles and compress the cheek against the buccal dental arches. The innervation of the buccinator muscle is provided by the lower deep branches of the facial (VII) nerve.

Risorius Muscle. Variable in expression, the risorius muscle sweeps from the fascia over the masseter muscle anteriorly to interdigitate with the muscle fibers of the posterior and inferior border of the modiolus. Contracting in isolation, this slight muscle might apply torque (rotational force) to the muscular modiolus. The lower motor neurons innervating this muscle are derived from the marginal mandibular branch of the facial (VII) nerve.

Group II: Superior Labial Muscle Innervation

Levator Labii Superioris Alaeque Nasi Muscle. A highly variable, small muscle bundle, the levator labii superioris alaeque nasi muscle (also called the angular head of the levator labii superioris) courses from the frontal process of the maxilla inferiorly to interdigitate with the muscle fibers of the medial portion of the upper lip. This muscle has the potential to aid elevation of the upper lip. Motor innervation is provided by the upper deep nerves of the buccal branch of the facial (VII) nerve.

Levator Labii Superioris Muscle. Extending from the inferior border of the orbit inferiorly to attach to the muscle tissue of the upper lip lateral to the nose, the levator labii superioris muscle (also called the infraorbital head of the levator labii superioris) has the potential to elevate the upper lip. The upper deep nerves of the buccal branch of the facial (VII) nerve innervate this muscle.

Zygomaticus Minor. The zygomaticus minor muscle (also called the zygomatic head of the levator labii superioris) has a lateral attachment to the zygomatic bone, from which it courses inferiorly and medially to attach to: (1) the skin in the region of the nasolabial fold and (2) the muscle tissue immediately medial to the modiolus. During an isolated contraction the zygomaticus minor may aid elevation and retraction of the upper lip in the region of the oral angle. Often absent or fused with the zygomaticus major muscle (Bergman et al., 1984), this muscle is innervated by the upper deep nerve of the buccal branch of the facial (VII) nerve.

Group III: Inferior Labial Muscle Innervation

Depressor Labii Inferioris Muscle. A thin muscle sheet of the lower lip, the depressor labii inferioris muscle extends from the oblique line of the mandible (medial to the attachment of the depressor anguli oris muscle) superiorly to attach to the muscle tissue and skin of the lower lip. Isolated auxotonic muscle contraction could lower the lower lip and may provide some lower lip eversion. Motor innervation is provided by the marginal mandibular branch of the facial (VII) nerve with numerous communications with the mental nerve of the mandibular branch of the trigeminal (V) nerve.

Mentalis Muscle. The paired mentalis muscles course from the incisive fossa of the mandible to the skin of the chin. If the lower lip is everted, contraction may draw the lower lip inferiorly and compress the skin against the mandible. If the lower lip is at rest against the mandible, contraction of the mentalis muscle may draw the lower lip superiorly and evert it. The marginal mandibular branch of the facial (VII) nerve provides motor innervation to the mentalis muscle.

SENSORY SYSTEM

Contractile Element Innervation

Relying on anatomic investigation, Kadanoff (1956) indicated that few if any typical muscle spindle sensory receptors exist in the circumoral muscles. In a physiologic study, Folkins and Larson (1978) supported this view, reporting the absence of vibratory reflex in the lips. The deep sensibility that has been reported in facial and extraocular muscles is suggested to enter the brainstem through the trigeminal (V) nerve (Cooper, Daniel, and Whitteridge, 1953a,b). The lack of developed tendinous attachments within the muscles of the circumoral complex would greatly restrict the presence of traditional tendon sensory receptors.

Noncontractile Element Innervation

Although the muscles of the circumoral complex apparently lack the complement of intramuscular sensory receptors found in skeletal muscles, it must be remembered that the muscles of this system are inseparably attached to the overlying boundary elements of skin and mucous membrane by a superficial musculoaponeurotic system. The muscles of the circumoral complex cannot contract without directly distorting the overlying boundary elements. These boundary elements are provided with an extremely dense sensory representation. As reviewed in detail by Darian-Smith (1973) and Munger (1975), the complement of mechanoreceptors includes (but is not restricted to) free nerve endings, Ruffini-type endings, Meissner corpuscles, Merkel cell-neurite endings, Krause end bulbs, Ruffini endings, and an array of receptors characteristic of both glabrous and hairy skin.

The sensory neurons innervating the many receptors of the circumoral complex are supplied by the maxillary and mandibular divisions of the trigeminal (V) nerve. The maxillary division of the trigeminal (V) nerve (called the infraorbital nerve when it passes through the inferior orbital fissure) divides into cranial, pterygopalatine, infraorbital, and facial nerve groups that innervate the maxillary region of the head. The pterygopalatine group separates from the infraorbital nerve in the pterygopalatine fossa and is divided into the zygomatic nerve, pterygopalatine nerves, and posterior superior alveolar branches. The zygomatic nerve divides into two branches, one of which (the zygomaticofacial branch) innervates the skin of the prominence of the cheek. The pterygopalatine nerves divide into four groups: orbital, palatine, posterior superior nasal, and pharyngeal. The greater palatine nerve of the palatine group supplies the mucous membrane of

the alveolar processes, hard palate, and parts of the soft palate. The pharyngeal branch of the palatine group innervates the mucous membrane of the posterior nasopharynx. The posterior superior alveolar branch of the pterygopalatine group innervates the mucous membrane of the posterior cheek and the molar teeth. The infraorbital group separates from the maxillary division of the trigeminal (V) nerve in the infraorbital canal. The infraorbital group innervates the premolar teeth (via the middle superior alveolar branch) and the incisor and canine teeth (via the anterior superior alveolar branch).

Separating from the maxillary division after it exits the infraorbital foramen, the facial group includes the inferior palpebral, external nasal, and superior labial branches. The superior labial branch is the largest branch and innervates the sensory receptors of the skin of the upper lip and mucous membrane of the mouth.

The mandibular division of the trigeminal (V) nerve divides into four parts: (1) meningeal branch; (2) medial pterygoid nerve; (3) anterior trunk; and (4) posterior trunk. These parts innervate the sensory receptors of the cheek, lower lip, teeth, alveolar process, and face, as well as the temporomandibular joint.

The anterior trunk of the mandibular nerve has a small sensory component, including the masseteric nerve, which innervates the temporomandibular joint, and the buccal nerve, which innervates the sensory receptors of the skin and mucous membrane of the buccal cheek and alveolar process of the mandible. The posterior trunk of the mandibular nerve is mainly sensory and divides into the auriculotemporal, lingual, and inferior alveolar nerves. The auriculotemporal nerve communicates with the facial (VII) nerve and provides sensation from the skin overlying the zygomatic, buccal, and mandibular branches of the facial (VII) nerve. The articular branch of the auriculotemporal nerve innervates the posterior portion of the temporomandibular joint.

The lingual nerve of the posterior trunk supplies the sensory receptors of the mucous membrane of the anterior two-thirds of the tongue and adjacent oral cavity and the mandibular alveolar processes. The inferior alveolar nerve divides to terminate as the mylohyoid and mental nerves. The mylohyoid nerve includes an incisive branch that innervates the mandibular canine and incisor teeth. The mental nerve is distributed to the skin of the chin and lower lip and the mucous membrane of the lower lip.

CONCLUSION

The complexity of the speech production process is reflected in its coordination among systems of significantly different anatomy and physiology. The muscles of the speech production mechanism are distributed across two major systems: (1) the muscle system of the neck and torso characterized by sheathed muscles and tendinous attachments to bone and cartilage, and (2) the cranial muscle system characterized by interdigitating muscles that frequently attach to skin and mucosa without a developed tendon.

The innervation of the speech musculature is distributed across two major systems: (1) the spinal nervous system with relatively consistent division into sensory and motor elements; and (2) the cranial nervous system with cranial nerve nuclei that may be motor, sensory, or mixed in function. In view of such a diverse structural and functional arrangement, it is understandable that much remains to be learned about the intricacies of innervation involving the speech mechanism.

REFERENCES

Abd-El-Malek, S. Observations on the morphology of the human tongue. *J. Anat.* 73:201, 1939.

Agostoni, E. Action of respiratory muscles. In W. Fenn and H. Rahn (eds.), *Handbook of Physiology, Sect. 3: Respiration* (Vol. 1). Washington, DC: American Physiological Society, 1964.

Azzam, N., and Kuehn, D. The morphology of musculus uvulae. *Cleft Palate J.* 14:78, 1977.

Baken, R. Neuromuscular spindles in the intrinsic muscles of a human larynx. *Folia Phoniatr. (Basel)* 23:204, 1971.

Baken, R., and Noback, C. Neuromuscular spindles in the intrinsic muscles of a human larynx. *J. Speech Hear. Res.* 14:513, 1971.

Bergman, R., Thompson, S., and Afifi, A. *Catalog of Human Variation.* Baltimore: Urban & Schwarzenberg, 1984.

Bernstein, L., and Nelson, R. Surgical anatomy of the extraparotid distribution of the facial nerve. *Arch. Otolaryngol.* 110:177, 1984.

Bossy, J., and Vidic, B. Existe-il une innervation proprioceptive des muscles du pharynx chez l'homme? *Arch. Anat. Histol. Embryol.* 50:273, 1967.

Bowman, J. Muscle spindles in the intrinsic and extrinsic muscles of the rhesus monkey's tongue. *Anat. Rec.* 161:483, 1968.

Bowman, J. *The Muscle Spindle and Neural Control of the Tongue: Implications for Speech.* Springfield, IL: Charles C Thomas, 1971.

Boyd, W., Blincoe, H., and Hayner, J. Sequence of action of the diaphragm and quadratus lumborum during quiet breathing. *Anat. Rec.* 151:579, 1965.

Brendler, S. The human cervical myotomes: functional anatomy studied at operation. *J. Neurosurg.* 28:105, 1968.

Broomhead, I. The nerve supply of the soft palate. *Br. J. Plast. Surg.* 10:81, 1957.

Buchthal, F., and Schmalbruch, H. Motor units of mammalian muscle. *Physiol. Rev.* 60:90, 1980.

Campbell, E. The muscular control of breathing in man. Ph.D. dissertation, University of London, 1954.

Campbell, E. An electromyographic examination of the role of the intercostal muscles in breathing in man. *J. Physiol. (Lond)* 129:12, 1955.

Campbell, E., Agostoni, E., and Davis, J. *The Respiratory Muscles, Mechanics and Neural Control.* Philadelphia: Saunders, 1970.

Carpenter, M. *Human Neuroanatomy* (7th ed.). Baltimore: Williams & Wilkins, 1976.

Clemente, C. (ed.), *Gray's Anatomy of the Human Body* (30th American ed.). Philadelphia: Lea & Febiger, 1985.

Cooper, S. Muscle spindles in the intrinsic muscles of the human tongue. *J. Physiol. (Lond)* 122:193, 1953.

Cooper, S., Daniel, P., and Whitteridge, D. Nerve impulses in the brainstem of the goat: short latency responses obtained by stretching the extrinsic eye muscles and the jaw muscles. *J. Physiol. (Lond)* 120:471, 1953a.

Cooper, S., Daniel, P., and Whitteridge, D. Nerve impulses in the brainstem of the goat: responses with long latencies obtained by stretching the extrinsic eye muscles. *J. Physiol. (Lond)* 120:491, 1953b.

Corbin, K., and Harrison, F. Proprioceptive components of cranial nerves: the spinal accessory nerve. *J. Comp. Neurol.* 69:315, 1938.

Corda, M., Euler, C. von, and Lennerstrand, G. Proprioceptive innervation of the diaphragm. *J. Physiol. (Lond)* 178:161, 1965.

Darian-Smith, I. The trigeminal system. In A. Iggo (ed.), *Handbook of Sensory Physiology, Vol. 2: Somatosensory System.* Berlin: Springer-Verlag, 1973.

Dickson, D. Anatomy of the normal velopharyngeal mechanism. *Clin. Plast. Surg.* 2:235, 1975.

Dickson, D., and Maue-Dickson, W. *Anatomical and Physiological Bases of Speech.* Boston: Little, Brown, 1982.

DiFoggio, J. An anatomical investigation of the extrinsic lingual musculature. M. S. thesis, University of Wisconsin, 1984.

DiFoggio, J., and Kennedy, J. The extrinsic lingual musculature. *ASHA* 26:84, 1984.

Draper, M., Ladefoged, P., and Whitteridge, D. Respiratory muscles in speech. *J. Speech Hear. Res.* 2:16, 1959.

Dubner, R., Sessle, B., and Storey, A. *The Neural Basis of Oral and Facial Function.* New York: Plenum, 1978.

English, D., and Blevins, C. Motor units of laryngeal muscles. *Arch. Otolaryngol.* 89:778, 1969.

Faaborg-Andersen, K. Electromyographic investigations of intrinsic laryngeal musculature in humans. *Acta Physiol. Scand.* 41:140, 1957.

Fink, B. *The Human Larynx. A Functional Study.* New York: Raven Press, 1975.

Fitzgerald, M., and Sachithananadan, S. Proprioceptive nerve endings in the primate tongue. *J. Anat.* 124:500, 1977.

Fitzgerald, M., and Sachithananadan, S. The proprioceptive innervation of the tongue. *Ir. J. Med. Sci.* 147:157, 1978.

Fitzgerald, M., and Sachithananadan, S. The structure and source of lingual proprioceptors in the monkey. *J. Anat.* 128:523, 1979.

Folkins, J., Kennedy, J., and Loncarich, P. Standardization of lip muscle nomenclature. *J. Speech Hear. Res.* 21:603, 1978.

Folkins, J., and Larson, C. In search of a tonic vibration reflex in the human lip. *Brain Res.* 151:409, 1978.

Folkins, J. Muscle activity for jaw closing during speech. *J. Speech Hear. Res.* 24:601, 1981.

Freimann, R. Untersuchungen uber Zahl und Anordnung der Muskelspindeln in den Kaumuskeln des Menschen. *Anat. Anz.* 100:258, 1954.

Gill, H. Neuromuscular spindles in human lateral pterygoid muscles. *J. Anat.* 109:157, 1971.

Grim, M. Muscle spindles in the posterior cricoarytenoid muscle of the human larynx. *Folia Morphol. (Praha)* 15:124, 1967.

Grombeck, P., and Skouby, A. The activity pattern of the diaphragm and some muscles of the neck and trunk in chronic asthmatics and normal controls: a comparative electromyographic study. *Acta Med. Scand.* 168:413, 1960.

Grossman, R., and Hattis, B. Oral mucosal sensory innervation and sensory experience. In J. Bosma (ed.), *First Symposium on Oral Sensation and Perception.* Springfield, IL: Charles C Thomas, 1964.

Hiatt, J., and Gartner, L. *Textbook of Head and Neck Anatomy.* New York: Appleton-Century-Crofts, 1982.

Hirano, M. Morphological structure of the vocal cord as a vibrator and its variations. *Folia Phoniatr. (Basel)* 26:89, 1974.

Hirano, M. The function of the intrinsic laryngeal muscles in singing. In K. Stevens and M. Hirano (eds.), *Vocal Fold Physiology.* Tokyo: University of Tokyo, 1981.

Judson, L., and Weaver, A. *Voice Science* (2nd ed.). New York: Appleton-Century-Crofts, 1965.

Kadanoff, D. Die sensiblen nervendigungen in der mimschen Muskulatur des Menschen. *Z. Mikrosk. Anat. Forsch.* 62:1, 1956.

Kahane, J. Anatomy and physiology of the organs of the peripheral speech mechanism. In N. Lass, L. McReynolds, J. Northern, and D. Yoder (eds.), *Speech, Language, and Hearing. Vol. I: Normal Processes.* Philadelphia: Saunders, 1982.

Kanagasuntheram, R., Wong, W., and Chan, H. Some

observations on the innervation of the human nasopharynx. *J. Anat.* 104:361, 1969.

Kaplan, H. *Anatomy and Physiology of Speech.* New York: McGraw-Hill, 1960.

Kennedy, J., and Abbs, J. Anatomical studies of the perioral motor system: foundations for studies in speech physiology. In N. Lass (ed.), *Speech and Language: Advances in Basic Research and Practice* (Vol. 1). New York: Academic Press, 1979.

Kennedy, J., and DiFoggio, J. Directional variability in the anatomy of selected cranial muscles. *ASHA* 27:153, 1985.

Kirchner, J., and Wyke, B. Articular reflex mechanisms in the larynx. *Ann. Rhinol. Laryngol.* 74:749, 1965.

Kraus, B., Kitamura, H., and Latham, R. *Atlas of Developmental Anatomy of the Face.* New York: Harper & Row, 1966.

Kubota, K., Negishi, T., and Nasegi, T. Topological distribution of muscle spindles in the human tongue. *Bull. Tokyo Med. Dent. Univ.* 22:235, 1975.

Kubota, K., and Masegi, T. Muscle spindle supply to the human jaw muscles. *J. Dent. Res.* 56:901, 1977.

Kuehn, D., and Azzam, N. Anatomical characteristics of palatoglossus and the anterior faucial pillar. *Cleft Palate J.* 15:349, 1978.

Kuehn, D., Frederick, P., and Maynard, J. Muscle spindles in the velopharyngeal musculature of humans. Presented at the annual meeting of the American Speech-Language-Hearing Association, Los Angeles, 1981.

Kuehn, D., Folkins, J., and Linville, R. An electromyographic study of the musculus uvulae. *Cleft Palate J.* 25:348, 1988.

Landgren, S., and Olsson, K. Oral mechanoreceptors. In S. Grillner, B. Lindblom, J. Lubker, and A. Persson (eds.), *Speech Motor Control.* New York: Pergamon, 1982.

Larson, C., and Pfingst, B. Neuroanatomic bases of hearing and speech. In N. Lass, L. McReynolds, J. Northern, and D. Yoder (eds.), *Speech, Language, and Hearing, Vol. I: Normal Processes.* Philadelphia: Saunders, 1982.

Lennartsson, B. Number and distribution of muscle spindles in the masticatory muscles: a histological and electromyographic study. Thesis, University of Göteborg, 1979.

Lucas-Keene, M. Muscle spindles in human laryngeal muscles. *J. Anat.* 95:25, 1961.

Maier, A. Occurrence and distribution of muscle spindles in masticatory and suprahyoid muscles of the rat. *J. Anat.* 155:483, 1979.

Morley, M. *Cleft Palate and Speech* (7th ed.). Baltimore: Williams & Wilkins, 1970.

Munger, B. Cytology of mechanoreceptors in oral mucosa and facial skin of the rhesus monkey. In B. Tower (ed.), *The Nervous System. Vol. 1: The Basic Neurosciences.* New York: Raven Press, 1975.

Nakayama, M. Nerve terminations in the muscle spindle of the human lingual muscles. *Tohuku Med. J.* 34:367, 1944.

Nishio, J., Matsuya, T., Machida, J., and Miyazaki, T. The motor nerve supply of the velopharyngeal muscles. *Cleft Palate J.* 13:20, 1976.

Podvinec, M., and Pfaltz, C. Studies on the anatomy

of the facial nerve. *Acta Otolaryngol. (Stockh)* 81:173, 1976.

Psenicka, P. Beitrag zur Kenntnis der Innervation der Kehlkopfgelenke. *Anat. Anz.* 118:1, 1966.

Rood, S., and Doyle, W. Morphology of tensor veli palatini, tensor tympani, and dilator tubae muscles. *Ann. Otol. Rhinol. Laryngol.* 74:645, 1978.

Rossi, G., and Cortesina, G. Morphological study of the laryngeal muscles in man. *Acta Otolaryngol. Scand.* 59:575, 1965.

Sakada, S. Response of Golgi-Mazzoni corpuscles in the cat periosteum to mechanical stimuli. In R. Dubner and Y. Kawamura (eds.), *Oral-Facial Sensory and Motor Mechanisms.* New York: Appleton-Century-Crofts, 1971.

Sant'Ambrogio, G., and Mortola, J. Behavior of slowly adapting stretch receptors in the extrathoracic trachea of the dog. *Respir. Physiol.* 31:377, 1977.

Sant'Ambrogio, G., Bartlett, D., and Mortola, J. Innervation of stretch receptors in the extra-thoracic trachea. *Respir. Physiol.* 29:93, 1977.

Shipp, T. Aspects of voice production and motor control. In S. Grillner, B. Lindblom, J. Lubker, and A. Persson (eds.), *Speech Motor Control.* New York: Pergamon Press, 1982.

Sicher, H., and DuBrul, E. *Oral Anatomy.* St. Louis: Mosby, 1970.

Smith, R., and Marcarian, H. The neuromuscular spindles of the lateral pterygoid muscle. *Anat. Anz.* 120:47, 1967.

Sonnesson, B. On the anatomy and vibratory pattern of the human vocal folds. *Acta Otolaryngol. [Suppl] (Stockh)* 156:1, 1960.

Strong, M., and Vaughn, C. The morphology of the phonatory organs and their neural control. In K. Stevens and M. Hirano (eds.), *Vocal Fold Physiology.* Tokyo: University of Tokyo Press, 1981.

Suzuki, M., and Kirchner, J. Afferent nerve fibers in the external branch of the superior laryngeal nerve in the cat. *Ann. Otol. Rhinol. Laryngol.* 77:1059, 1968.

Szentagothai, J. Die lokalisation der Kehlkopfmuskulatur in den Vaguskernen. *Z. Anat. Entwicklungsgesch.* 112:704, 1943.

Taylor, A. The contribution of the intercostal muscles to the effort of respiration in man. *J. Physiol. (Lond)* 151:390, 1960.

Tokizane, T., Kawamata, K., and Tokizane, H. Electromyographic studies on the human respiratory muscles. *Jpn. J. Physiol.* 2:232, 1952.

Von Euler, C. On the neural organization of the motor control of the diaphragm. *Am. Rev. Respir. Dis.* 119:45, 1979.

Williams, A. Nerve supply of laryngeal muscles. *J. Laryngol. Otol.* 65:343, 1951.

Williams, A. Recurrent laryngeal nerve and the thyroid gland. *J. Laryngol. Otol.* 68:719, 1954.

Williams, P., and Warwick, R. (eds.), *Gray's Anatomy* (36th British ed.). Philadelphia: Saunders, 1980.

Winkler, G. L'equipment nerveux du muscle tenseur du voile de palais. *Arch. Anat. Histol. Embryol.* 47:311, 1964.

Zemlin, W. *Speech and Hearing Science* (2nd ed.). Englewood Cliffs, NJ: Prentice-Hall, 1981.

Zenker, W., and Zenker, A. Uber die Regelung der Stimmlippenspannung durch von assen eingreifende Mechanismen. *Folia Phoniatr. (Basel)* 12:1, 1960.

CHAPTER 6

Neurophysiology of Speech

Steven M. Barlow • *Glenn R. Farley*

- ❏ Speech as a Phylogenetically Advanced Motor Skill

- ❏ Neural Movement Control System

- ❏ Neural Control of Laryngeal-Vocalization Systems

- ❏ Neural Control of Supralaryngeal Systems

- ❏ Central Processes Underlying Speech Movements

- ❏ Summary and Research Directions

This work was supported by National Institutes of Health research grants NS-19624-04 (Boys Town National Institute) and NS-23825-01 (S. M. Barlow) and in part by the Moody Foundation of Galveston, Texas. Special thanks to Dr. Ronald Netsell for his editorial comments and to Ms. Mary Burton and Ms. Carole Dugan for expert technical support.

SPEECH AS A PHYLOGENETICALLY ADVANCED MOTOR SKILL

More than a century ago, John Hughlings Jackson made several remarkable clinical observations concerning the function of the human cerebral cortex. Perhaps most controversial was his contention that "convolutions [of the cerebral cortex] contain nervous arrangements representing movements" (1874). At about the same time, pioneering experiments on the electrically excitable motor cortex of the dog (Fritsch and Hitzig, 1870) and monkey (Ferrier, 1873)

made it clear that a disproportionate part of the precentral motor cortex was allocated to control a very small proportion of select muscles involved in the fine, precise movements of the body (Evarts, 1981a,b). As shown in Figure 6-1, the proportion of motor responses evoked from human precentral and postcentral gyri in a series of neurosurgical explorations is dominated by distal limb and vocal tract structures (Penfield and Rasmussen, 1950; Rasmussen and Penfield, 1947). A portion of the efferents originating from these cortical areas form direct monosynaptic projections to brainstem and spinal lower motor neurons (Kuypers, 1964, 1973; Phillips and Porter, 1977). Thus phylogenetic elaboration of the motor cortex has evolved to provide finer motor control of existing muscles in new movement patterns.

One such movement pattern special to humans, involving neocortical structures, is speech. As a motor skill, speech is performed with speed and accuracy, improves with practice, is flexible in achieving spatiotemporal goals, and is virtually relegated to automaticity

Fig. 6-1. Motor-sensory homunculus. Sensory and motor sequences in cerebral cortex of human as determined by electrical stimulation. The extent of cortex devoted to each part of the body is indicated by the length of the heavy black lines. (From Rasmussen, T., and Penfield, W. Further studies of sensory and motor cerebral cortex of man. *Fed. Proc.* 6:452, 1947.)

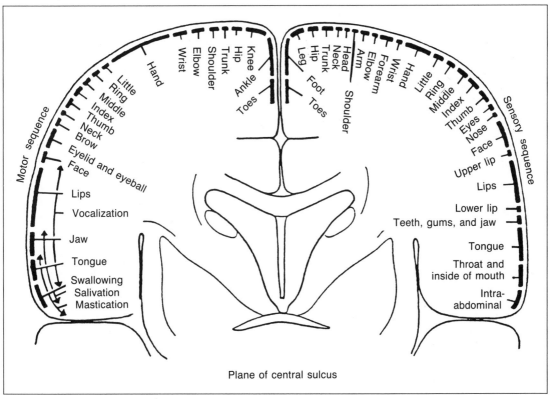

Plane of central sulcus

in the mature speaker (Netsell, 1982). Speech is often regarded as a highly adaptive, afferent guided motor control system (Abbs and Cole, 1982; Barlow and Netsell, 1986b,c; Evarts, 1982; Gracco and Abbs, 1985; Grillner, 1982; Lubker and Gay, 1982; Lund, Appenteng, and Seguin, 1982; McClean and Smith, 1982; Smith, Moore, McFarland, and Weber, 1985). In contrast to our present understanding of limb motor control, relatively little is known about the neurophysiology of speech production, due in large part to: (1) the biomechanical complexities of the vocal tract; (2) the complex nature of the nervous system involved in sensorimotor control of vocal tract structures; (3) the complexity of speech as a motor behavior; (4) the absence of an animal homologue for neurobiologic research; and (5) the relatively small number of neuroscientists investigating neural control mechanisms relevant to speech.

NEURAL MOVEMENT CONTROL SYSTEM

In the following sections, speech neurophysiology is explored first by considering the functional organization and response properties of neural subsystems considered important for movement control. The significance of these subsystems is then evaluated in terms of their functional connectivity, their response to electrical and natural stimulation, the effects of lesions, and their potential role in speech movement control.

PRIMARY MOTOR CORTEX

Current ideas about the extent and subdivision of the primate sensorimotor cortex come largely from the work of Woolsey and his colleagues (1951). The primary motor cortex (MI, consisting of Brodmann's area 4 and possibly the posterior strip of area 6) is cytoarchitectonically distinct from the primary sensory cortex. MI is dominated by somatosensory input with pyramidal tract neurons as summing points of central command signals and peripheral feedback signals, allowing for rapid adaptations

imposed by the environment (Wiesendanger, Hummelsheim, and Bianchetti, 1985). Posteriorly, MI is bounded by the primary sensory cortex (SI). For example, areas 3a, 3b, 1, and 2 of the SI receive thalamic inputs from ventralis posterior lateralis pars caudalis, whereas the MI receives inputs from nuclei ventralis posterior lateralis pars oralis and ventralis lateralis caudalis (Friedman and Jones, 1981).

PRIMARY SENSORY CORTEX

Neurons in the somatosensory cortex are arranged in modality-specific, vertical columns (Mountcastle, 1957). Within the postcentral gyrus of the cerebrum lie the primary receiving areas for somatosensory information originating from mechanoreceptors located within skin, joints, and muscle. The work of Pandya and Kuypers (1969) and Jones and Powell (1970), using degeneration methods, have shown that the subareas of SI are interconnected. More recent tract tracing methods employing horseradish peroxidase and tritiated amino acids in primates have led to the identification of subareas 3a, 3b, 1, 2, and 5 (Evarts, 1981a; Merzenich, Kaas, Sur, and Lin, 1978). Each subarea receives different types of somatosensory information. Area 3a responds to stimulation of group I muscle afferents, area 3b is activated by slowly adapting mechanoreceptors in the skin, area 1 is activated by rapidly adapting cutaneous mechanoreceptors, and area 2 is primarily activated by joint movements.

The somatosensory cortex has been shown to contain a number of complete somatotopic representations in a number of species of primates (Kaas, Nelson, Sur, Lin, and Merzenich, 1979; Merzenich et al., 1978; Paul, Merzenich, and Goodman, 1972). The region spanning cytoarchitectural areas 3a, 3b, 2, and 1, traditionally called SI, contains at least three complete representations and possibly a fourth, although the organization of 3a is still somewhat ambiguous (Kaas et al., 1979). Each complete map of the body corresponds to one cytoarchitectural area. Although there are discontinuities, the organization within each area is basically topographic.

The thalamus is one of the major relays to the somatosensory cortex. The lesser thalamic input (ventrobasal complex) to areas 1 and 2, compared with area 3b, is correlated with a relatively thin internal granular layer in these cytoarchitectonic areas (Jones, 1975). The work of Vogt and Pandya (1978) and Jones, Coulter, and Hendry (1978) shows that there is in fact an inverse relation between the strength of thalamocortical inputs to the subsectors of SI and the input of corticocortical projections to these subsectors. According to Jones et al. (1978), area 3b, which receives a dense thalamocortical input, receives relatively slight corticocortical inputs from areas 1, 2, and 4. It is thus apparent that area 3b is dominated by primary afferent input from the thalamus with relatively little input from other cortical areas. The output of area 3b via corticocortical projections is directed back into areas 1 and 2, but this projection is not reciprocated: Instead of projecting back to area 3b, the major projection of areas 1 and 2 is to area 5 and MI. Thus mechanoreceptor information reaching area 3b is not sent directly on to MI but is further processed in area 2, which also receives dense corticocortical input from areas 3b and 1.

SOMATOTOPY OF OROFACIAL/ LARYNGEAL STRUCTURES

Maintenance of continuity in the neural representation of body parts, termed *somatotopy*, is a feature of numerous structures within the nervous system, including the primary sensorimotor cortex (Woolsey et al., 1951). The amount of cortex devoted to a given muscle is presumed to reflect the frequency and intensity of the use of a muscle in normal behavior (Penfield and Rasmussen, 1950). Examples of body structures mapped to relatively large areas of the sensorimotor cortex include the fingers and hand for *manipulation* and the lips, tongue, jaw, velopharynx, larynx, and chest wall for *speech production*. Discrete activation of individual muscles (*individuation*) in a finely graded manner (*fractionation*) are characteristics of skilled movements that have evolved with the elaboration of MI (Evarts, 1985; Kuypers, 1964; Phillips and Porter, 1977).

Detailed information on the microorganization of the motor cortex involved in the fine control of the vocal tract (Clark and Luschei, 1973; McGuinness, Siversten, and Allman, 1980; Sessle and Wiesendanger, 1982; Sirisko and Sessle, 1981, 1982, 1983; Zealear, Hast, and Kur-

ago, 1983) has been obtained using intracortical microstimulation (ICMS) (Asanuma and Sakata, 1967). In primates, the neural representation of facial muscles is clustered together in the posterior and anterior portions of the precentral gyrus, with tongue movements represented in the intervening region and along the lateral extent. Within each cluster there are multiple representations of individual muscle movements (McGuinness et al., 1980). It appears that at least two somatotopic representations of the facial musculature exist in primates (McGuinness et al., 1980; Zealear et al., 1983) and cats (Iwata, Itoga, Ikukawa, Hanashima, and Sumino, 1985).

For orofacial representations, threshold currents typically yield responses limited to a small focus of movement in part of a muscle. Successive stimulation points separated by as little as 50 μm yield different muscle responses (McGuinness et al., 1980). The discrete nature of these responses is explained, in part, by the columnar organization of the motor cortex (Asanuma, 1973; Asanuma and Arnold, 1975; Asanuma and Rosen, 1972; Asanuma and Sakata, 1967; Mountcastle, 1957). As described by McGuinness and her colleagues (1980), the columns within the orofacial motor regions are roughly cylindrical and take the form of narrow, curving bands running mediolaterally across the cortex. Adjacent muscles tend to occur together and approximately topographic in relation to the morphologic structure of the muscles themselves.

Zealear and colleagues (1983) found that activation of neurons within a single orthogonal column of MI projecting to orofacial or jaw muscles yields a unitary response. Using these physiologic criteria, it appears that individual facial muscles are represented repeatedly within each field. Ipsilateral muscles are represented primarily in the posterior field of the primary motor cortex, whereas the anterior field contains the representation of contralateral medial muscles. Consistent with these physiologic findings is anatomic evidence indicating that projections from MI to the lower facial motor nuclear region are direct and predominantly contralateral in nature (Jenny and Saper, 1987).

The neural representation of the tongue occupies the center of the precentral gyrus and extends from above inferiorly into the ovoid region of the laryngeal representation. The tongue and laryngeal regions are flanked by an anterior and a posterior face field, which are bridged in the middle, forming a horseshoe-shaped face representation as outlined in Figure 6-2. The more exterior or lateral aspect of each face field represents the more lateralized muscles of the face, such as the zygomaticus; and the central bridge area represents the more midline face muslces, such as the orbicularis oris and mentalis (Zealear et al., 1983).

The discrete nature of responses evoked in orofacial structures using ICMS is not apparent in the laryngeal musculature (Zealear et al., 1983). All the zones encountered in the laryngeal region are multimuscle zones involving the posterior cricoarytenoid (PCA) and one or more adductor or extrinsic muscles. The widespread cortical representation of PCA is consistent with its postural stabilizing action on the arytenoid during the sliding phases of adduction and abduction (Fink and Demarest, 1978). Neural in-

structions arising from the ovoid region may be important for voluntary laryngeal activities requiring modification of the glottis. Apparently, the motor cortex does not exert direct control over individual laryngeal muscles as suggested by the long electromyographic (EMG) latencies following cortical microstimulation. The apparent reciprocal relation between the abductor and adductor responses during cortical microstimulation lend further support for the idea

Fig. 6-2. Somatotopy of orofacial structures. Map of face, tongue, jaw, and larynx zones for monkey obtained using intracortical microstimulation. Triangles indicate laryngeal zones (large triangles = thresholds less than 10 μA, small triangles = thresholds 6 to 10 μA). F = face; T = tongue; J = jaw zones. (From Zealear, D. L., Hast, M. H., and Kurago, Z. Functional organization of the primary motor cortex controlling the face, tongue, jaw, and larynx in the monkey. In I. R. Titze and R. C. Scherer (eds.), *Vocal Fold Physiology: Biomechanics, Acoustics and Phonatory Control.* Denver: Denver Center for the Performing Arts, 1983.)

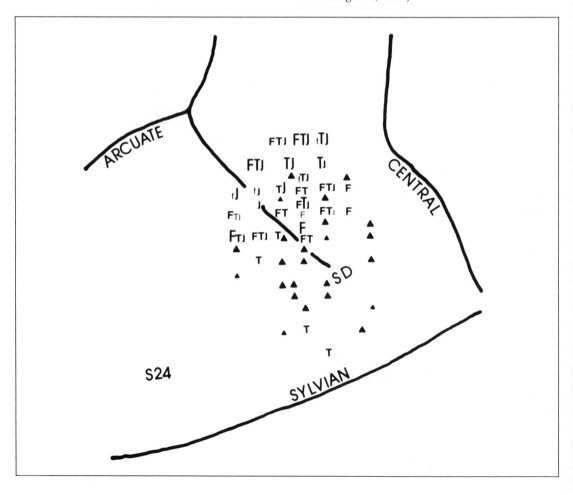

that the cortical influence is mediated through reticular inspiratory and expiratory interneurons (Zealear et al., 1983).

FRONTAL LOBE INPUTS TO PRIMARY MOTOR CORTEX

One of the classic concepts concerning the cortical control of movement is that "premotor" areas exist in the frontal lobe that have bilateral and direct access to the primary motor cortex (Matsumura and Kubota, 1979; Muakkassa and Strick, 1979; Pandya and Vignolo, 1971; Von Bonin and Bailey, 1947). These "premotor" areas are thought to contribute to the organization of skilled movement and the programming of motor cortex output. One study, using a retrograde tracer (horseradish peroxidase: HRP) in

Fig. 6-3. Frontal lobe inputs to MI. A. Location and approximate spatial extent of the four "premotor" areas that project to the primary motor cortex in primates are indicated by symbols: posterior arcuate (•); precentral sulci (△); SMA (■); cingulate sulcus (○). B. Body representation in each of the four "premotor" areas depicted in A is indicated by the words "face," "arm," and "leg." (From Muakkassa, K. F., and Strick, P. L. Frontal lobe inputs to primate motor cortex: evidence for four somatotopically organized "premotor" areas. *Brain Res.* 177:176, 1979.)

primates (Muakkassa and Strick, 1979), revealed the location of four spatially separate and somatotopically organized premotor areas with projections to the primary motor cortex (Fig. 6-3). Following HRP injections into the face area of the motor cortex, labeled neurons were found in various areas of the frontal lobe, including: (1) the inferior limb of the arcuate sulcus (caudal bank); (2) rostrally in the supplemental motor area; (3) rostrally in the ventral bank of the cingulate sulcus; and (4) the lateral bank of the inferior precentral sulcus. The densest projections originate from the premotor cortex and the supplementary motor area. These premotor areas represent elements in parallel pathways that may separately influence motor cortex output and motor behavior.

SUPPLEMENTAL MOTOR AREA

The supplementary motor area (SMA) occupies the medial portions of area 6 and is generally considered to function in the programming of motor sequences, including preparatory states for forthcoming movements (Kornhuber and Deecke, 1965; Orgogozo and Larsen, 1979; Roland, Larsen, Lassen, and Skinhoj, 1980; Wiesendanger et al., 1985). Electrical stimulation of the SMA results in complex, coordinated movements of the contralateral limbs and

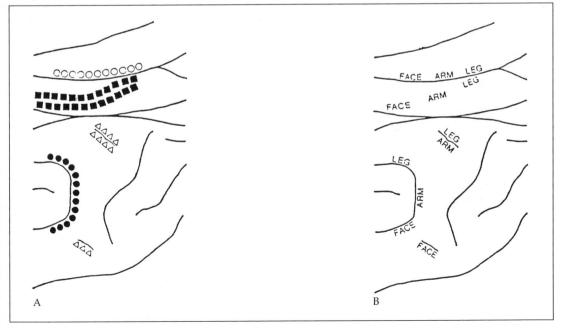

A   B

body, with occasional ipsilateral limb movements (Bancaud and Talairach, 1967; Penfield and Welch, 1951). This situation is in sharp contrast to the MI, where focal stimulation elicits highly localized and discrete movements of the contralateral musculature (Tanji, 1985). Studies of movement disturbance after ablation of the SMA have shown that the effects are subtle, often transient, and with no apparent paralysis, again contrasting remarkably with effects of primary motor cortex lesions.

Approximately 30 percent of the neurons sampled in the SMA show time-locked responses to either visual or auditory signals during simple movements of the wrist (Wiesendanger et al., 1985). Some SMA neurons are activated by tactile inputs, although the magnitude of such responses is smaller than that observed in the motor cortex. SMA units responsive to passive arm displacements have been identified in the posterior region, where microstimulation effects in arm muscles can be elicited. The shortest latencies are around 15 ms (Wiesendanger et al., 1985). Because of the smaller magnitude of the movement-related activity and the lack of strong correlations of neuronal activity with movement onset, the SMA is functionally more remote from the peripheral motor apparatus than the primary motor cortex (Wise and Tanji, 1981). SMA neurons are also responsive to visual and auditory signals at significantly shorter latencies than those of the precentral cortex. The functional significance of these inputs remains to be studied.

Tanji and coworkers have found that a significant number of SMA neurons manifest instruction-induced changes of activity during the period intervening between the instruction and a perturbation-triggered movement. These particular SMA neurons, however, are not active in association with the movement itself. It appears that SMA neurons may function in a conditional manner, depending on the behavioral context or intentional set, or as triggered premotor inputs to summing pyramidal tract neurons in the primary motor cortex (Evarts, Shinoda, and Wise, 1984; Tanji, Taniguchi, and Saga, 1980).

Although several functions have been suggested for the SMA, including its involvement in the control of posture, gating motor cortical reflexes, and initiating motor cortex output and movement (Brinkman and Porter, 1978; Pandya and Vignolo, 1971; Tanji and Taniguchi, 1978;

Wiesendanger, Seguin, and Kunzle, 1973), the exact role of this region for speech motor control is unknown. However, the somatotopic organization of vocal tract structures within the SMA (Brickman and Porter, 1978; Muakkassa and Strick, 1979) combined with its considerable sensitivity to somatosensory inputs is consistent with its hypothesized importance for speech production.

PREMOTOR CORTEX

The lateral portion of area 6 is known as the premotor cortex (PMC) in humans and as the arcuate premotor area in monkeys. This region of the cerebral cortex receives inputs from the primary visual cortex (Pandya and Kuypers, 1969) and is considered to be involved in visually guided movements (Haaxma and Kuypers, 1975; Kubota and Hamada, 1978; Moll and Kuypers, 1977; Wiesendanger et al., 1985). In addition to visual inputs, some neurons in the PMC are responsive to somatosensory input resulting from passive limb displacement, with minimal latencies ranging from 13 to 15 ms (Wiesendanger et al., 1985). As with SMA neurons, only a few of all the responsive PMC neurons have direction-specific responses. Similar to SMA neurons, some of the PMC neurons are active when a monkey is grasping for food. Approximately 65 percent of the neurons reacting to kinesthetic stimuli are also responsive to visual inputs (Bignall and Imbert, 1969; Rizzolatti, Scandolara, Matelli, and Gentilucci, 1981a,b).

Similar to the SMA, the overall responsiveness of PMC neurons to somatosensory stimuli is weaker than for neurons in MI. Wiesendanger and others have suggested that the somatosensory input is focalized primarily to neurons at the input stage of the cortical compartment and perhaps less to the output neurons. Because most cells within the PMC are responsive to visual inputs, this region of the brain may be less important for speech production because this motor behavior typically is less dependent on visual feedback.

SUBCORTICAL-THALAMO-CORTICAL RELATIONS
BASIC ORGANIZATION

A question of special significance in movement control concerns how two of the major subcortical motor systems, the cerebellum and the basal ganglia, differentially influence the premotor areas and motor cortex. For the most part, efferents originating from cerebellar, pallidal, and nigral nuclei are highly segregated, manifesting little overlap in their projections to the ventrolateral thalamus (Asanuma, Thach, and Jones, 1983c; Carpenter, Nakano, and Kim, 1976; DeVito and Anderson, 1982; Kalil, 1981; Kim, Nakano, Jayarman, and Carpenter, 1976; Kuo and Carpenter, 1973; Mehler, 1971; Percheron, 1977; Stanton, 1980). The basic pattern of termination of subcortical efferents in the thalamus includes (1) rostral portions of the deep cerebellar nuclei projecting to the motor cortex via the nucleus ventralis posterior lateralis (VPLo); (2) caudal portions of the deep cerebellar nuclei projecting to the PMC via area X; and (3) the globus pallidus projecting to the SMA via the nucleus ventralis lateralis (VLo) (Asanuma, Thach, and Jones, 1983b; Jones, Wise, and Coulter, 1979; Kalia, 1981; Kusama, Mabuchi, and Sumino, 1971; Percheron, 1977). Schell and Strick (1984), using retrograde transport in primates, demonstrated that the SMA, arcuate premotor area (PMC in humans), and MI receive thalamic input from separate, cytoarchitectonically well defined subdivisions of the ventrolateral thalamus (Fig. 6-4). Thus each thalamocortical pathway is associated with a distinct subcortical input (Schell and Strick, 1984).

BASAL GANGLIA-THALAMIC-CORTICAL RELATIONS

The principal efferents from the basal ganglia include those originating from the globus pallidus and the substantia nigra. Efferents from the internal segment of the globus pallidus (GPi) terminate in three subdivisions of the ventrolateral thalamus: the VLo, parts of the parvocellular division of the ventroanterior nucleus (VApc), and the medial division of the ventrolateral nucleus (VLm) (DeVito and Anderson, 1982; Kim et al., 1976; Kuo and Carpenter, 1973; Nauta and Mehler, 1966). Nigrothalamic projections originate from the pars reticulata segment of the substantia nigra (SNpr) and terminate in two subdivisions of the ventrolateral thalamus: magnocellular division of the ventroanterior nucleus (VAmc) and VLm (Carpenter and McMasters, 1964; Carpenter and Peter, 1972;

Carpenter and Strominger, 1967; Carpenter et al., 1976; Carpenter, Carleton, Keller, and Conte, 1981). Additional projections also terminate in the area of the medial dorsal thalamic nucleus paralaminar (MD). According to Schell and Strick, pallidal output is focused on subdivisions of the ventrolateral thalamus that project to the SMA (i.e., VLo and VLm), and part of the nigral output also is focused on thalamic regions that project to the SMA (i.e., VLm and MD). Anatomic evidence in monkeys indicates that the somatotopic organization of the pallidonigral system is maintained in its thalamic projections. For example, the "face" representation in SNpr projects to a "face" representation in VLm, which in turn projects to the "face" representations in the SMA. Interestingly, neither pallidal nor nigral efferents appear to terminate in thalamic regions that project to the arcuate premotor area or the motor cortex. Of the cortical areas concerned with movement, the pallidonigral system is most directly connected to the SMA. The pallidonigral-thalamo-SMA-MI pathway is considered by some (Evarts, 1985; Schell and Strick, 1984) possibly to mediate the transcortical reflex (discussed later), which is thought to be active during manipulation and speech.

CEREBELLOTHALAMIC-CORTICAL RELATIONS

Cerebellothalamic projections originate from all deep cerebellar nuclei, including the dentate, interpositus, and fastigial nuclei (Asanuma et al., 1983a,c; Brooks and Thach, 1981). There are two major cerebellothalamic systems that ultimately influence separate cortical areas, including the APA (PMC) and MI (Sasaki, Jinnai, Gemba, Hashimoto, and Mizuno, 1979; Sasaki, Kawaguchi, Oka, Sakai, and Mizuno, 1976; Schell and Strick, 1984). One system, located in rostral portions of the deep nuclei projects largely to the VPLo, which in turn influences the motor cortex. A second system, located in caudal portions of the deep nuclei, projects in a somatotopic fashion to medial portions of the ventrolateral thalamus in area X and on to the PMC (Asanuma et al., 1983a; Brooks and Thach, 1981). Therefore "face" efferents from caudal regions of the deep nuclei projecting to area X of the thalamus have access to neurons in the face representation of the motor cortex.

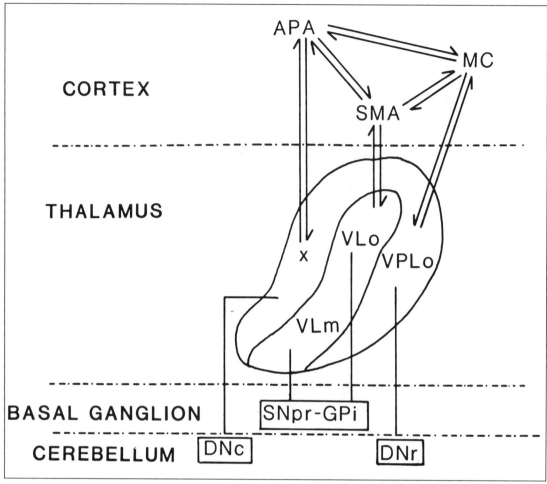

Fig. 6-4. Subcortico-thalamo-cortical relations. Summary of anatomic relations among cerebellar and basal ganglia efferents and motor and premotor cortical areas in primates. This diagram shows (1) the pathway from caudal portions of the deep cerebellar nuclei (DNc) to area X and arcuate premotor area (APA, analogous to the PMC in humans); (2) the pathways from the pars reticulata of the substantia nigra (SNpr) and the internal segment of the globus pallidus (GPi) to VLm and VLo and the supplementary motor area (SMA); (3) the pathway from rostral portions of the deep cerebellar nuclei (DNr) to VPLo and the motor cortex (MC); and (4) the reciprocal connections between the MC, APA, and SMA. (From Schell, G. R., and Strick, P. L. The origin of thalamic inputs to the arcuate premotor and supplementary motor areas. *J. Neurosci.* 4:539, 1984.)

SYNTHESIS ON SUBCORTICAL-THALAMIC-CORTICAL SYSTEMS

Outputs from the cerebellum and basal ganglia form three parallel systems of subcortical efferents to the ventrolateral thalamus that project, in a segregated fashion, to motor and premotor areas of the cerebrum (Schell and Strick, 1984). One parallel pathway originates in the caudal portions of the deep cerebellar nuclei and most directly influences the PMC. A second pathway originates in the SNpr and GPi with direct access to the SMA. The third pathway originates in rostral portions of the deep cerebellar nuclei and most directly influences the primary motor cortex. These systems, which form parallel pathways to motor and premotor cortical areas, are thought to contribute to the programming of skilled movement and the sequencing of motor tasks.

Additional lines of evidence in support of three distinct efferent systems that are driven by largely separate subcortical nuclei are available from lesion studies. For example, the anatomic relation between the basal ganglia and the SMA suggests that some of the movement disorders associated with basal ganglia dysfunction might be mediated by the SMA. Akinesia, which is associated with basal ganglia disorders (Denny-Brown, 1980), also is produced by lesions involving the SMA in humans (Damasio and Van Hoesen, 1980; LaPlane, Talairach, Meininger, Bancaud, and Orgogozo, 1977).

Frontal lobe lesions in humans, involving the PMC, can result in a complex disorder of learned skilled movements termed *apraxia* (Geschwind, 1965; Heilman, 1979). The anatomic relation between the cerebellum and the PMC suggests the possibility of cerebellar involvement in the motor functions of the frontal lobe. Future studies might search for "apraxic-like" symptoms following lesions that involve caudal cerebellar efferent systems.

RESPONSE PROPERTIES

ACTIVITY OF NEURONS IN THE PRECENTRAL MOTOR CORTEX

The motor cortex is an important structure, serving as the final relay station for other areas of the cerebral cortex involved in the initiation, planning, and programming of speech movements (Eccles, 1977). The pyramidal cells of the motor cortex are strategically situated in the speech movement control system. In addition to functioning as a summing point for a variety of prefrontal and somatosensory inputs, the pyramidal cells of the motor cortex also provide a direct output channel from the brain to the lower motoneurons that are mapped to muscles of the vocal tract, including the tongue, lips, jaw, pharynx, larynx, and chest wall. Therefore special consideration is given in the following paragraphs to the neurophysiology of the motor cortex in relation to fine motor control.

Most neurons recorded in the hand area of primate MI manifest changes in discharge frequency correlated with wrist load and the

pattern of muscle contraction, in contrast to changes in wrist position (Evarts, 1968). MI firing patterns are more especially correlated with force, including the rate of force change (A. M. Smith, Hepp-Reymond, and Wyss, 1975), than with other movement parameters (Humphrey, Schmidt, and Thompson, 1970). Averaging the EMG activity following the discharge of MI corticomotoneurons (CMs), which covary with flexion-extension movements of the wrist, allows classification of CMs into one of four basic types: phasic-tonic (59 percent), tonic (28 percent), phasic-ramp (8 percent), and ramp (5 percent) (Fetz, Cheney, and German, 1976). The main conclusion derived from the experiments reviewed in this section is that most pyramidal tract neurons recorded from MI manifest a stronger relation to the *rate of force change* than to static force.

Another prominent feature of MI pyramidal tract neurons (PTNs) is an increased activity level when the force changes about the wrist are limited to small steps between 0.1 and 1.0 newton. It has been hypothesized that force encoding by MI cells involves the recruitment of additional cortical cells as the demands for greater absolute force levels are incorporated into the motor program (Hepp-Reymond, Wyss, and Anner, 1978). The evidence in favor of this force encoding scheme is based on the fact that (1) the linear covariation of the firing rate with the force is limited to a certain force operating range, (2) the time constants for changes in discharge frequency with force show a large interneuronal variability, and (3) a few neurons coding force are active only above a certain threshold force level (Hepp-Reymond et al., 1978).

The behavior of CM cells projecting to jaw muscles is consistent with observations reported for the hand and wrist. During a controlled biting task in monkeys, involving steady forces ranging from 1 to 70 newtons, there is a clear relation between the rate of maintained discharge and the force output of jaw-closing muscles for 25 percent of the cells tested (Hoffman and Luschei, 1980). Investigation of MI neuron activity during chewing and operantly conditioned biting revealed that most CMs for the jaw failed to exhibit modulation with chewing. This observation is important because it points to a greater role for MI in controlling operantly conditioned or learned movements and to a lesser role for MI in controlling automatic movements using the same muscles (Evarts, 1981a,b; Phillips and Porter, 1977).

RESPONSES OF THE PRIMARY MOTOR CORTEX TO AFFERENT INPUT

Neurons in MI receive somatosensory input from muscle spindle afferents (Albe-Fessard and Liebeskind, 1966; Malis, Pribram, and Kruger, 1953) and cutaneous mechanoreceptors (Welt, Aschoff, Kameda, and Brooks, 1967). There appears to be more than one route by which somatosensory information can influence MI activity. The functional significance of these afferent inputs that influence MI from thalamus versus primary somatosensory cortex (SI) is considered in the following paragraphs.

Neurons in thalamic nucleus ventralis posterior lateralis pars oralis (VPLo) receive short latency (6 to 10 ms) inputs from the arm and transmit these signals to the arm area of MI (Horne and Tracey, 1979; Lemon and van der Burg, 1979). Electrical stimulation and HRP injections confirmed these connections. On the other hand, SI receives somatosensory inputs via the ventrobasal complex, which receives projections from the medial lemniscus. This latter pathway is important because neural activity in MI is dependent on dorsal column function, and lesions of the dorsal column or postcentral gyrus significantly diminish MI responses to somatosensory stimulation (Friedman and Jones, 1981).

These findings are supported by the fact that massive fiber projections link areas of the postcentral cortex (SI, SII, area 5) to MI. It should be noted that inputs to SI are not directly transmitted to MI; rather, a hierarchic organization within SI suggests that somatosensory information is sequentially processed prior to transmission to MI. Inputs to areas 3a, 3b, and 1 are down-loaded to areas 1, 2, and 5 for additional signal processing before transmission to area 4 of the primary motor cortex. At this point it becomes possible for lemniscal inputs mediated by SI to interact with nonlemniscal inputs mediated by the VPL nuclei of the thalamus.

Summary of Primary Motor Cortex Response Properties

In summary, there are a number of features of movement to which MI output might be related, including force level, rates of force change, position, and velocity (Evarts, 1981a,b).

Actions of the primary motor cortex appear to be under the influence of premotor and somatosensory areas, which apparently modify MI output according to set, goal, and intention. Some of the most notable response properties of motor cortex include the following.

1. The discharge frequencies of MI neurons change with different levels of force. The proportion of force-related neurons is high in certain classes of MI neurons (those sending axons to contact lower motoneurons) and low in other classes (those sending axons to the red nucleus).
2. MI activity is related to the magnitude of muscular contraction underlying this force. Because of the length–tension properties of muscle, more muscle discharge is required to exert a given force against an external object when the muscle is short than when it is long.
3. Unlike spinal cord and brainstem motoneurons, which are silent during skeletal muscle relaxation, most MI neurons are spontaneously active at rest. As the set or intention of the subject changes, there may be corresponding changes in the level of this spontaneous discharge.
4. MI neurons related to force exhibit marked changes in discharge frequencies for small changes of force near the zero-force level, as has been seen for fingers, jaw, and arm. It points to the special role of MI output for controlling the early-recruited portion of the motoneuron pool in fine motor control.
5. MI neurons are responsive to a variety of somatosensory inputs originating from muscle spindle afferents, joint receptors, and cutaneous mechanoreceptors.
6. Lemniscal somatosensory information is preprocessed by well defined areas in the postcentral gyrus (areas 3, 1, 2, 5) before transmission to MI.
7. Nonlemniscal inputs to MI are mediated by the thalamic nucleus ventralis posterior lateralis.

TRANSCORTICAL REFLEXES

Corticomotoneurons can be activated and modulated by peripheral afferent input emanating from deep receptors (Strick and Preston, 1978; Tanji and Wise, 1981), cutaneous afferents, and postcentral gyrus outputs (Evarts,

1985). This form of MI activation is known as a *transcortical reflex*. It should be noted that the transcortical reflex was originally referenced to an output from motor cortex CMs rather than to any particular component of a muscle response (Phillips, 1969). For the transcortical reflex, the phylogenetically recent CM projection represents the efferent limb.

In primates, CMs have two phases of activity following a limb displacement. The first phase (20 ms latency) is analogous to a segmental stretch reflex that depends on the direction of limb displacement, whereas the second phase (40 ms latency) depends on motor set. These two phases of motor cortex output have different properties and different functional roles. The first phase follows the rules of a closed-loop negative feedback control system and is especially important for the maintenance of postural stability, whereas the second phase operates according to open-loop principles and is considered important in goal-directed movements that occur from a variety of starting positions using multiple articulators such as the system for speech production (Evarts, 1985). Therefore the properties of motor cortex CM responses are different, depending on the extent to which one or the other of these two control modes is dominant. For a more complete discussion of the dynamic processes involving closed-loop and open-loop modes in MI, refer to Wiesendanger (1981) and Wiesendanger and Miles (1982). As to the pathways mediating the transcortical reflex, Asanuma et al. (1983a,b,c) considered the current state of knowledge and summarized evidence showing that there are several routes (corticocortical and thalamocortical) over which sensory inputs may activate MI in the closed-loop mode.

PERIPHERAL NEURAL ELEMENTS IMPORTANT FOR SPEECH

An understanding of the organization and workings of neural networks in cortical and subcortical structures is not complete unless one also considers the specialized peripheral neural elements that reside within the tissues of the musculoskeletal system. The muscles and connective tissues of the human vocal tract are richly endowed with a variety of specialized sensory elements, including muscle spindles,

Golgi tendon organs, joint receptors, and mechanoreceptors. These *sensors* selectively transduce or convert mechanical energy (resulting from passive and active movement and force) into a neural signal that is encoded by the central nervous system. The response properties of muscle spindles and Golgi tendon organs are described in Chapter 3 and are not considered further in this chapter. Instead, the following discussion highlights some of the response properties of mechanoreceptors associated with rapidly conducting myelinated afferents known to exist in tissues of the vocal tract in primates (Halata and Munger, 1983; Munger and Halata, 1983) and humans (Darian-Smith, 1966). Similar to the proprioceptors, information transmitted by mechanoreceptive afferents to the central nervous system is considered important for speech motor control. The four mechanoreceptor types described in the following sections are based, in part, on the classification scheme of Johansson and Vallbo (1976).

RAPIDLY ADAPTING MECHANORECEPTORS

Rapidly adapting (RA) receptive fields are characterized by several (12 to 17) zones of maximal sensitivity with distinct borders and distributed over an approximately circular or oval area. The end-organs of the RA units are thought to be the Meissner corpuscles (Janig, 1970; Munger, 1971). These receptors seem particularly well suited for spatial discrimination and accurate localization of stimuli. Meissner corpuscles are selectively sensitive to low-frequency sinusoids in the range of 30 to 40 Hz (flutter). They show a brief discharge to a step indentation of the skin that adapts quickly if the step is maintained; a brief discharge is seen on release of the step, which again adapts quickly.

Another mechanoreceptor that is especially sensitive to transients is the pacinian corpuscle (PC). The pacinian nerve terminal is encapsulated by a multilamellated accessory structure of nonneural tissue. This encapsulation acts effectively as a high-pass filter for transmitting energy to the receptor terminal located deep in the corpuscle. PC receptors are difficult to excite even with large-amplitude sinusoidal displacements at frequencies below 40 to 60 Hz. Pacinian afferents are most sensitive to sinusoidal mechanical stimuli of high frequency, with a best frequency at about 250 Hz. At this frequency, stimuli of 0.1 to 0.2 μm peak-to-peak displacement elicit one impulse in phase with each sine wave. PC receptors respond best to the higher derivatives of movement, including acceleration and jerk. These receptors lack directionality, have short recovery cycles, and are resistant to fatigue.

SLOWLY ADAPTING MECHANORECEPTORS

Type I slowly adapting (SAI) units have small receptive fields with distinct borders and are found in both hairy and glabrous skin. Their afferent nerve fibers have conduction velocities ranging from 55 to 75 meters per second. The Merkel cell–neurite complexes have been identified as SAI units. These receptors appear to be well suited for spatial discrimination and accurate localization of stimuli. There is a double exponential time course to a steady rate of discharge. Adaptation in the Merkel cell–neurite complex has been attributed to changes in force at the skin interface due to viscous flow within the tissue. Both velocity and position associated with low-level stimulation (5 to 15 μm) are encoded by the discharge pattern in the afferent nerve serving the Merkel cell–neurite mechanoreceptor.

Type II slowly adapting (SAII) units are associated with the Ruffini corpuscle (Chambers, Andres, von During, and Iggo, 1972). Their afferent nerve fibers have conduction velocities ranging from 45 to 65 meters per second. They are most common in hairy skin. The Ruffini end-organs are thought to be anchored to the surrounding tissues by means of the collagenous fibers that extend from the two poles of the Ruffini receptor. This unique mode of linkage between the end-organ and neighboring soft tissue may partially explain the directional sensitivity of the Ruffini corpuscle (Johansson, 1976). Although definitive data are not available, mechanoreceptors with "SAII type" properties are logical candidates to mediate kinesthetic information from the interleaved network of skin and muscle comprising structures of the orofacial complex.

In summary, there are four types of specialized mechanoreceptors with rapidly conducting (A, alpha) afferent fibers having distinct functional properties. The RA and SAI units are particularly well suited for spatial discrimination and accurate localization of skin perturbations.

PC units, on the other hand, are sensitive to mechanical vibrations traveling through the skin. Of all cutaneous mechanoreceptors, SAII units are best suited to encode kinesthetic information.

NEURAL CONTROL OF LARYNGEAL-VOCALIZATION SYSTEMS

RESPIRATORY CONTROL SYSTEM

The respiratory system, in addition to providing the air source for sound production during speech, participates in a variety of other behaviors, including quiet and forced breathing and expulsive reflexes. Furthermore, the demands of these varied motor tasks are altered by such factors as postural orientation and gravitational load (Hixon, Mead, and Goldman, 1987). The neural control of the respiratory system is complex in nature, involving the interaction of phylogenetically new mechanisms (voluntary motor control) and phylogenetically older pathways (central pattern generators for automatic breathing). Unfortunately, only a preliminary understanding of the neurophysiology of speech breathing is available. A brief discussion of the mechanical constraints and physiologic mechanisms underlying these behaviors is presented in the following sections. The interested reader is referred to Hixon (1987; especially Chapters 1 and 4) and Von Euler (1982) for a more detailed treatment.

MECHANICAL CONSIDERATIONS AND MUSCULATURE

Breathing function is determined by an interaction between passive and active forces of the respiratory mechanism. The passive forces include the elasticity of the lungs, rib cage, and abdominal wall, and the surface tension of the thin liquid coating of the alveoli. For each degree of lung inflation or deflation, these passive forces of the respiratory mechanism combine to produce a unique alveolar pressure. The functional relation between the two is known as the *relaxation curve.* In the absence of muscular effort or a blocked airway, air flows between the lungs and the atmosphere until the lungs contain a *functional residual capacity* of air for which alveolar pressure just balances atmospheric pressure.

A variety of thoracic and abdominal muscles can actively change the lung volume, thereby altering alveolar pressure and respiratory airflow. These muscles include (1) the diaphragm, which expands the thoracic cavity by moving its lower wall downward; (2) intercostal (and other thoracic) muscles, which alter thoracic volume by changing the configuration of the rib cage; and (3) various abdominal muscles, which act indirectly, via the abdominal contents, to raise and lower the wall of the thoracic cavity. These various muscle groups appear to be differentially activated during quiet breathing and speech.

Quiet Metabolic Breathing

The primary function of quiet breathing is the efficient exchange of oxygen and carbon dioxide to maintain optimal levels of blood gases and extracellular pH. It is normally accomplished by a stereotyped breathing pattern that occurs periodically at 12 times or more per minute. Each inhalation starts at the resting expiratory capacity; the lungs are inflated by about one-sixth the available inflation volume, and exhalation then occurs, returning the lungs to their original volume (Hixon, Goldman, and Mead, 1973). The diaphragm appears to be the most important muscular contributor to quiet, metabolic breathing (Von Euler, 1982). Its EMG activity increases progressively during the inspiratory cycle, then rapidly decreases at the end of inspiration, although residual activity is maintained during a portion of the expiratory cycle to counteract the elastic recoil of the lungs and the rib cage. The external and parasternal intercostal muscles are generally secondary contributors to quiet breathing (Von Euler, 1982). The remaining thoracic and abdominal muscles have minimal involvement in most circumstances but can be recruited into the respiration process when more forceful or deeper breathing is required (Hixon et al., 1973).

Speech Breathing

Breathing patterns during speech depart radically from the normal quiet breathing pattern.

First, the goal of maintaining blood gas and pH balance is relaxed, and significant departures from the homeostatic set-points of these variables can be observed during speech production (Von Euler, 1982). Second, considerably higher lung inflation volumes are typically used, although exhalations below the resting expiratory capacity remain infrequent. In addition, the required air pressures and flows for speech production are highly variable, depending on both slowly varying linguistic features such as general loudness and prosody and more rapidly varying demands including syllabic stress and phonemic articulation.

Even for the relatively simple task of producing a steady-state vowel, the required airflows and pressures during exhalation depart at almost all lung volumes from those produced by passive relaxation, requiring that carefully graded muscular effort be continuously delivered to produce the required air stream. For normal speech, with rapidly varying phonemic and prosodic structure, additional rapid fluctuations in muscular forces are required.

Speech production generally uses a different set of muscles from that typically active during quiet breathing. The EMG activity of the diaphragm generally ceases at the onset of expiration, and the diaphragm remains inactive during the utterance. By contrast, both the inspiratory and expiratory intercostals show much increased activity. It has been speculated that this increased functional role during phonation may reside in the much richer muscle spindle innervation of the intercostal muscles relative to the diaphragm. In addition, there is significant involvement of abdominal muscles in speech production, depending on the speaker's posture relative to gravitational forces.

BRAIN SYSTEMS FOR RESPIRATORY CONTROL

Multiple Control Systems

The respiratory system appears to be controlled by at least two separable neural systems: one responsible for producing optimal metabolic breathing and the other providing control during vocalization and speech. As suggested by the discussion of the function of the various muscle groups, this differential control relies partly on control of different muscles, but it is also clear that the speech system can, to some extent, override metabolic breathing. Thus inferences about mechanisms of speech motor control from study of the metabolic control system are limited (Von Euler, 1982). Unfortunately, few data are available about this aspect of speech motor control.

Respiratory Motoneurons

The motoneurons responsible for respiratory control are found in the spinal cord distributed across most of the cervical and thoracic segments, and they project to the respiratory muscles through peripheral nerves. A detailed overview of this anatomy can be found in Chapter 5. Extensive interaction between metabolic and speech respiratory control occurs in these motoneurons. These neurons, with associated spinal interneurons, also participate in various expulsive, postural, and segmental reflexes.

Metabolic Breathing System

The basic pattern generators for quiet, metabolic breathing involve three bulbopontine nuclei shown in Figure 6-5 (Cohen, 1981; Kalia, 1981; Von Euler 1977, 1980, 1982). The nucleus tractus solitarius (NTS) contains two pools of neurons (Ia and Ib), both of which fire with an

Fig. 6-5. Respiratory central pattern generator. Major functional components and connections thought responsible for generating quiet metabolic breathing. Excitatory connections are indicated by solid lines and pluses; and the inhibitory connections by dotted lines and minuses. Anatomic entities presumed responsible for these functions are indicated in parentheses. Also depicted (dashed lines) are sources and targets of descending influences that modulate pattern generating activity. PAG = periaqueductal gray; PBM = nucleus parabrachialis medialis; Bot. C. = Botzinger complex; NTS = nucleus of the solitary tract; Ia, Ib = cell types within the NTS. (Based on von Euler, C. Central pattern generation during breathing. *Trends Neurosci.* 3:275, 1980.)

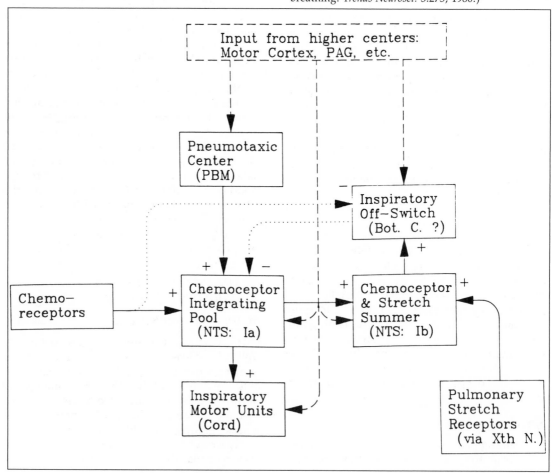

increasing rate during inspiration but have different responses to sensory feedback. These neurons receive sensory information from the lungs and other parts of the airway via the vagus (X) nerve (Kalia, 1981). However, their cyclic inspiratory activity does not require these inputs because they also integrate chemical information (PCO_2, PO_2, and pH) and neural information from cortical and bulbopontine centers. A second, less studied column of respiratory-related neurons includes the Botzinger complex, nucleus paraambiguus (NPA), and nucleus retroambigualis (NRA). Although the function of these neurons is less clear, the Botzinger complex has been demonstrated to fire during expiration and may have an important role in switching off the inspiratory activity of NTS neurons. Finally, the nucleus parabrachialis medialis (NPBm) has been identified as the "pneumotaxic center." A lesion of this nucleus results in abnormally deep and prolonged inspirations. It contains three types of respiratory neuron through which neural activity is thought to cycle: (1) inspiratory units; (2) phase-spanning inspiratory-expiratory units; and (3) expiratory units (Hugelin, 1977). All three of these major respiratory centers appear to send connections directly to the spinal respiratory motoneurons (Kalia, 1981).

Neural Control of Respiration During Vocalization

In contrast, respiratory control during vocalization is thought to involve a multitude of vocalization-related brain structures, including anterior cingulate cortex, periaqueductal gray, cerebellum, and direct and indirect motor cortical projections to the spinal motoneurons. The direct motor cortical control of the respiratory motoneurons appears to achieve greatest significance in human speech control. The effects on vocal behavior of stimulating and lesioning these regions and neural firing patterns during vocalization are beginning to be understood and are discussed in more detail below. However, the role of each of these regions in respiratory control, per se, remains largely a matter of speculation.

LARYNGEAL SYSTEM

The larynx, by virtue of its unique position in the vocal tract, constitutes a microcosm of the entire speech production system. It acts in a coordinated manner with the respiratory system to produce a frequency-modulated sound source during vocalization while at the same time acting in coordination with the rapidly acting articulatory structures of the upper airway (Barlow, Netsell, and Hunker, 1986). It thus may provide a particularly interesting system to study for determining the neural mechanisms of vocal control.

EFFECTS OF VARIOUS LARYNGEAL MUSCLES

The various extrinsic and intrinsic laryngeal muscles are differentially innervated and serve a variety of functions (see Chapter 5). Figure 6-6 summarizes the differential function of some of these muscle groups during speech. It should also be noted that there may be different roles for these muscles in different voice registers, and individual speakers appear to show individual strategies for their use.

Pure Abductor/Adductors

The posterior cricoarytenoid (PCA) muscles have EMG activity that appears to correlate best with vocal fold abduction. They contract during respiration (especially the inspiratory phase) and have minimal activity during phonation (Dickson and Maue-Dickson, 1982). The interarytenoid muscles contract mainly during glottal closure and thus serve a function antagonistic to that of the PCAs. Interarytenoid EMG activity tends to be held constant during phonation, however, and does not correlate with changes in fundamental frequency.

Mixed Function

By contrast, several muscles, including the thyroarytenoid, lateral cricoarytenoid, and cricothyroid muscles, have EMG activity that correlates fairly well with both vocal fold adduction and increases in fundamental frequency (Baer, 1981; Hast and Globus, 1971; Hirano, Vennard, and Ohala, 1970; Larson and Kempster, 1983). However, the actual relative roles of these muscles in independent control of these two functions remains to be determined. Cricothyroid activity, in particular, correlates most consistently with fundamental frequency changes (Sapir, McClean, and Luschei, 1984; Shipp, 1982). Thyroarytenoid activity correlations with fundamental frequency tend to vary

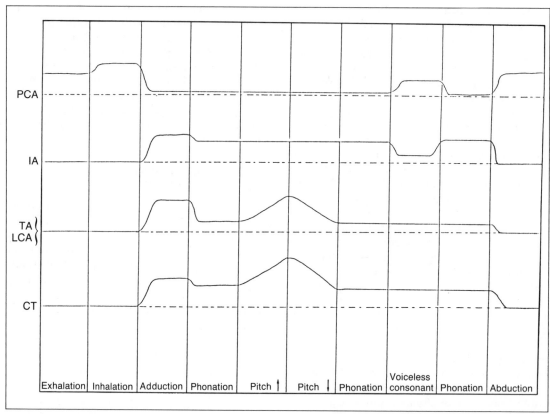

Exhalation | Inhalation | Adduction | Phonation | Pitch ↑ | Pitch ↓ | Phonation | Voiceless consonant | Phonation | Abduction

Fig. 6-6. Intrinsic laryngeal muscle patterns. Extent of activity of the intrinsic laryngeal muscles. PCA = posterior cricoarytenoid muscle; IA = interarytenoid muscles; TA = thyroarytenoid muscle; LCA = lateral cricoarytenoid muscle; CT = cricothyroid muscle. (From Dickson, D. R., and Maue-Dickson, W. *Anatomical and Physiological Bases of Speech.* Boston: Little, Brown, 1982.)

considerably among subjects, whereas the lateral cricoarytenoid appears to be more strongly correlated with adduction than fundamental frequency control (Shipp, 1982).

Other Fundamental Frequency Control

Other, extrinsic laryngeal musculature may play a role in determining voice fundamental frequency. These muscles can raise and lower the larynx from its resting position and thus indirectly produce fundamental frequency changes (Shipp, 1982). In addition, changes in subglottal air pressure, partially under control of the lower respiratory musculature, can produce small fundamental frequency alterations (Hixon, Mead, and Klatt, 1971; Shipp, 1982).

PERIPHERAL AFFERENT INNERVATION AND REFLEXES

Afferent information from the larynx is derived from several types of receptor, including rapidly and slowly adapting corpuscular receptors located in the subglottic mucosa, a limited number of muscle spindles and many spiral nerve endings wrapped around muscle fibers within the laryngeal muscles, and corpuscular receptors located within the laryngeal joint capsules. Much of the sensory information from these receptors is conveyed through the internal branch of the superior laryngeal nerve, then the vagus (X) nerve, to the nucleus tractus solitarius (NTS).

Information from these receptors is considered to play an important role in reflexive modulation of vocal fold adduction during speech (Wyke, 1983). However, for electrically stimulated vocalizations in anesthetized cats, subglottal air pressure changes do not elicit reflexive laryngeal EMG activity (Garrett and Luschei, 1987), although such reflexes can be produced by mechanical stimulation of the larynx (Garrett and Luschei, 1987; Kirchner and Suzuki, 1968). In addition, unilateral and bilateral transection of the superior laryngeal nerve internal branch produces little change in electrically elicited monkey call acoustic structure (Jurgens and Kirzinger, 1985). Thus the functional significance of these reflexes during vocalization is open to question.

There also appear to be extrinsic reflexes operating to control the laryngeal musculature. The first of these reflexes involves inputs from a variety of pulmonary receptors thought to serve predominantly nonvocalization protective functions (Wyke, 1983). However, information from the lungs can provide powerful control of the expiratory drive and laryngeal adduction during both normal expiration (Green and Neil, 1955) and electrically elicited vocalization (Garrett and Luschei, 1987). There is also short latency input from auditory centers that may provide the means for acoustically based adjustments of the vocal tract during phonation (Barlow, 1980; Cole and Abbs, 1983; McClean, 1977; Wyke, 1983).

BASIC CNS NUCLEI, PATHWAYS, AND PHYSIOLOGY

Laryngeal Motoneurons

Functional Organization. The motoneurons controlling the laryngeal, as well as the pharyngeal and esophageal, musculature are located in a long, ill-defined brainstem cell column that includes the nucleus ambiguus and the retrofacial nucleus (Lawn, 1966a,b; Davis and Nail, 1984; Schweizer, Ruebsamen, and Ruehle, 1981; Yoshida, Mitsumasu, Hirano, Morimoto, and Kanaseki, 1987; Yoshida, Miyazaki, Hirano, and Kanaseki, 1983; Yoshida, Miyazaki, Hirano, Shin, Totoki, and Kanaseki, 1982). These neurons are functionally arranged so that esophageal and pharyngeal constrictor muscles are represented in the rostral half of the cell column, with the laryngeal muscles (except the cricothyroid) in the caudal half of the column (Yoshida et al., 1983). The cricothyroid is represented by more ventrally located cells of the caudal portions of the rostral half of the nucleus ambiguus. There is partial segregation of neural input to different muscles in the dorsoventral and mediolateral dimensions as well. A summary of this organization is presented in Figure 6-7.

Physiologic Studies. Little is known about the activity of these laryngeal motoneurons. Delgado-Garcia and colleagues (1983) recorded activity from laryngeal motoneurons during breathing and tested projection patterns physiologically by stimulating the laryngeal nerves and descending tracts to the spinal cord. They were able to distinguish four types of neuron, including motoneurons active during inspiration and expiration, inspiratory interneurons that send axons into the spinal cord, and interneurons without any obvious respiratory function (Delgado-Garcia, Lopez-Varneo, Serra, and Gonzalez-Baron, 1983). Zealear and Larson (1987) identified three types of laryngeal motor neuron in the thyroartenoid region of the nucleus ambiguus. The most common type was recruited only during swallowing and vocalization; the other two types were involved in expiratory and inspiratory respiration, respectively. Additional study is needed of how these and other laryngeal motor neurons act to control vocal output.

Brainstem Nuclei

Anatomic Overview of Nuclei. Only preliminary observations are available concerning the brain regions connecting to laryngeal motoneurons. Yoshida et al. (1987) and Kobler (1983) have studied this issue using horseradish peroxidase (HRP) transport in the cat and bat, respectively. A large number of brainstem regions were labeled in these studies, including contralateral nucleus ambiguus cell columns. However, three regions had the most consistent inputs to the nucleus ambiguus/retrofacial nucleus: the nucleus tractus solitarius (NTS), which is a primary target for sensory feedback from the larynx; the nucleus parabrachialis (NPB), which may perform second-order sensory processing on somatosensory information from the larynx; and the periaqueductal gray (PAG) near the inferior colliculus, a region implicated in vocalization control by various physiologic techniques. It is important, however, to remember the role of NTS and NPB (medial division) in metabolic respiration; their role in vocalization control remains to be delineated.

Also worthy of note is the report (Thoms and Jurgens, 1987) identifying brain regions that project to multiple motor nuclei controlling each of the vocal tract effectors. Such regions, which include parts of the lateral pontine and medullary reticular formation, may be key

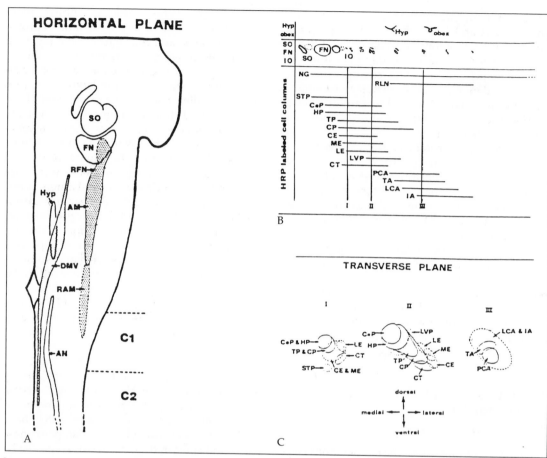

Fig. 6-7. Functional organization of laryngeal motoneurons. A. Location of HRP-labeled cells in the caudal brainstem and the cervical cord of cats following HRP injection of the nodose ganglion (a thickening of the vagus nerve near the brainstem in which all vagal fibers innervating the vocal tract are present). SO = superior olivary nucleus; FN = facial nucleus; RFN = retrofacial nucleus; AM = nucleus ambiguus; Hyp = hypoglossal nucleus; DMV = dorsal motor vagal nucleus; RAM = retroambigualis nucleus; AN = accessory nucleus. B. Level of labeled cell columns for the nodose ganglion, the recurrent laryngeal nerve, and the muscles in the rostrocaudal direction. The level in the brainstem is indicated with the shape of the hypoglossal nucleus (Hyp), obex, the superior olivary nucleus (SO), and inferior olivary nucleus (IO). C. Outline of somatotopic arrangement of the labeled motoneurons for each muscle in the transverse plane of the nucleus ambiguus at the three levels (I, II, III) indicated in B. NG = nodose ganglion; RLN = recurrent laryngeal nerve; STP = stylopharyngeal muscle; CeP = cephalopharyngeal (or superior constrictor) muscle; HP = hyopharyngeal (or middle constrictor) muscle; TP = thyropharyngeal (or inferior constrictor) muscle; CP = cricopharyngeal muscle; CE = cervical esophagus muscle; ME = middle part of thoracic esophagus muscle; LE = lower part of thoracic esophagus muscle; LVP = levator veli palatini muscle; CT = cricothyroid muscle; PCA = posterior cricoarytenoid muscle; TA = thyroarytenoid muscle; LCA = lateral cricoarytenoid muscle; IA = interarytenoid muscle. (A. Adapted from Miyazaki, T. Somatotopical organization of the motoneurons in the nucleus ambiguus of cats—the horseradish peroxidase method. *Otologia [Fukuoka]* 28:649, 1982.) B,C. From Yoshida, Y., Miyazaki, T., Hirano, M., and Kanaseki, T. Localization of the laryngeal motoneurons in the brain stem and myotopical representation of the motoneurons in the nucleus ambiguus of cats—an HRP study. In E. R. Titze and R. C. Scherer (eds.), *Vocal Fold Physiology: Biomechanics, Acoustics and Phonatory Control.* Denver: Denver Center for the Performing Arts, 1983.

structures for coordinating function of the various vocal tract systems during vocalization.

Physiologic Recording Studies. There is also little known about the firing patterns of neurons in these brainstem centers, especially during vocal control. Larson and Kistler (1984) and Larson (1985) reported that neurons in a small portion of PAG neurons fire during the interval immediately preceding vocalization onset and appear to have no activity correlated with the respiratory cycle. Neural firing is generally uncorrelated with vocalization intensity, but a few of the units fire preferentially before certain types of vocalization (Sandrew and Poletti, 1984).

Stimulation and Lesion Studies. Stimulation experiments appear also to have concentrated on periaqueductal gray. Stimulation of selected small loci in or near the PAG has been reported to cause vocalizations in both anesthetized monkeys (Larson, 1985; Magoun, Atlas, Ingersoll, and Ranson, 1937) and cats (Garrett and Luschei, 1987; Larson, Wilson, and Luschei, 1983; Magoun et al., 1937), with concomitant EMG activity in vocal tract musculature at all levels of the airway (Larson, 1985), and to alter parameters of ongoing calls in awake, vocalizing monkeys (Larson, 1985). The loudness of the electrically elicited vocalizations is controllable by the intensity of the stimulation (Larson, 1985), whereas for decerebrate cats fundamental frequency is weakly correlated with stimulus frequency (McGlone, Richmond, and Bosma, 1966). The elicited behavior is bilateral and has at least some resemblance to that of normal calls (Larson, 1985). In monkeys, more dorsal anterior stimulating sites produce clear calls, e.g., "coos," whereas stimulating more posteriorly produces rougher calls (e.g., "barks") (deRosier, Ortega, Park, and Larson, 1987). Monkey calls have also been elicited by chemical stimulation of PAG with excitatory amino acids (Jurgens and Richter, 1986; Richter and Jurgens, 1986), suggesting that stimulation effects cannot be attributed to stimulation of fibers of passage.

Lesions of PAG have also been reported to disrupt vocal output. In both humans (Botez and Barbeau, 1971) and cats (Adametz and O'Leary, 1959), PAG destruction is reported to produce mutism. In monkeys, both unilateral and bilateral lesions of the NTS seriously disrupt the acoustic structure of electrically elicited vocalizations, whereas destruction of the NPB

has no discernible effect (Jurgens and Kirzinger, 1985).

Neocortical Areas

Sensorimotor Cortex. It is generally thought that the primary somatosensory and motor cortices play a major role in laryngeal control during speech and that damage typically produces considerable loss of phonatory control (see Barlow et al., 1986 for review). It has been suggested that lesions of different lateral precentral regions produce different deficits (Abbs and Welt, 1985). However, these cortical areas are thought to play a much smaller role in animal vocalization control. This suggestion is based in part on the relative lack of direct descending projections to the nucleus ambiguus from the motor cortex in all but anthropoid apes and humans (Kuypers, 1958a,b,c, 1964), although direct projections appear to be present to the NTS, PAG, and NPB—nuclei that directly connect to the nucleus ambiguus (Jurgens and Pratt, 1979; Kuypers, 1958b,c). There is also an apparent lack of motor cortex lesion effect on nonhuman vocalizations. Destruction of somatosensory areas likewise produces little effect on monkey call acoustic structure (Jurgens and Kirzinger, 1985). In addition, stimulation of the motor cortex can produce vocal output in humans (Penfield and Rasmussen, 1950) and anthropoid apes (Dusser de Barenne, Garol, McCulloch, 1941) but generally does not do so in other species, although laryngeal EMG activity is often affected (Clark and Luschei, 1973; Craggs, Rushton and Clayton, 1976; Hoffman and Luschei, 1980; Larson et al., 1983; McGuinness et al., 1980).

Nonetheless, at least slow potential shift physiologic activity (which may be related to motor system preparation) can be recorded from the motor cortex prior to animal vocalization onset (Szirtes, Marton, and Urban, 1977). It is also interesting to note that cortical stimulation can affect laryngeal EMG output during PAG-stimulation-elicited vocal behavior (Larson et al., 1983). It thus may be that the motor cortex plays a supportive but not obligatory role in laryngeal control in animals.

Other Neocortical Regions. There are also other cortical areas involved with vocal production in humans. Generally they seem not to have been particularly studied from the aspect of laryngeal control. Stimulation of supplementary motor areas in humans can produce vocal output (Penfield and Welch, 1951). Vocal output is little affected by lesioning monkey homologues of Broca's, Wernicke's, and other association areas implicated in human speech (Sutton, Larson, and Lindeman, 1974).

Limbic Areas

Anterior Cingulate Gyrus. Anterior portions of the cingulate gyrus appear to play a major role in animal vocalization control (Jurgens, 1983) and to be relatively independent of reinforcement potential (Jurgens, 1976). Electrical stimulation of these regions can produce normal-appearing vocalizations in animals (Jurgens and Ploog, 1970: Jurgens and Pratt, 1979; Robinson, 1967a,b; W. K. Smith, 1945), although excitatory amino acid injections appear to be without effect (Jurgens and Richter, 1986; Richter and Jurgens, 1986). Lesions of the regions usually do not disrupt an animal's ability to spontaneously vocalize (Franzen and Myers, 1973; Kirzinger and Jurgens, 1982; Trachy, Sutton, and Lindeman, 1981), but monkeys conditioned to vocalize lose that ability following destruction of this area (Aitken, 1981; Sutton et al., 1974; Trachy et al., 1981). In humans, bilateral anterior cingulate lesions have been reported to produce deficits in volitional control of emotional intonation (Jurgens and von Cramon, 1982) and in some cases major or complete loss of speech articulation capability (Botez and Barbeau, 1971). The anterior cingulate gyrus is richly connected with other cortical and subcortical regions thought to be involved in emotion, vocal control, or both (Jurgens, 1983).

Other Limbic Areas. Stimulation of many other limbic areas, including the amygdala, the lateral, dorsomedial, and periventricular hypothalamic areas, and the mediodorsal thalamus, can produce vocalizations in monkeys, probably as a consequence of emotional, motivational, or pain/pleasure concomitants of stimulation (Jurgens, 1976; Ploog, 1981). Some of these regions connect with structures such as anterior cingulate cortex and periaqueductal gray, which appear to control vocalization more directly.

Cerebellum

In both humans and animals there is evidence that the cerebellum plays a coordinating role in vocalization control. Destruction of portions of the cerebellum in humans produces "ataxic dysarthria" characterized by excessive variations in fundamental frequency and intensity, with reductions in lip and jaw movement velocities during speech production (Barlow et al., 1986; Hirose, Kiritani, Ushijima, and Sawashima, 1978; Kent and Netsell, 1975; Kent, Netsell, and Abbs, 1979). Evoked potentials can be recorded from the paramedian lobes and the ansiform lobes adjacent to the vermis on stimulation of the recurrent laryngeal nerve (Lam and Ogura, 1952; Larson, Sutton, and Lindeman, 1978). Destruction of the cerebellum or deep cerebellar nuclei in animals has been reported to alter call structure but not frequency. Changes are noted in intensity, fundamental frequency, call duration, and more complex interactions between these features (Larson et al., 1978). Generally, these observations are consistent with a cerebellar role in coordination, but not initiation, of vocal output.

Basal Ganglia

Lesions involving the basal ganglia produce a number of speech defects involving the laryngeal system. They include breathiness, roughness, tremor, hoarseness, alterations of fundamental frequency control, and deficits in the ability to rapidly adduct/abduct the vocal folds (Barlow et al., 1986). Complementary studies have not been done in animals but could be interesting as such effects are probably indirect, through the motor cortex, and might bear on its role in animal vocal control.

Thalamus

Thalamic centers, especially ventrolateral and ventroposteromedial, are integral parts of the motor control systems involving basal ganglia, cerebellum, and motor cortex, and thus are undoubtedly involved in speech motor control in humans. However, VPM thalamus seems to be dispensable in electrically elicited monkey vocalizations (Jurgens and Kirzinger, 1985).

SUMMARY: MULTIPLE CONTROL SYSTEMS AND HOMOLOGY

The major neural systems involved in the control of the larynx and chest wall are highlighted in Figure 6-8. The primary motoneurons represent a final common pathway for descending influences and participate as well in relatively direct reflexes involving these vocal tract

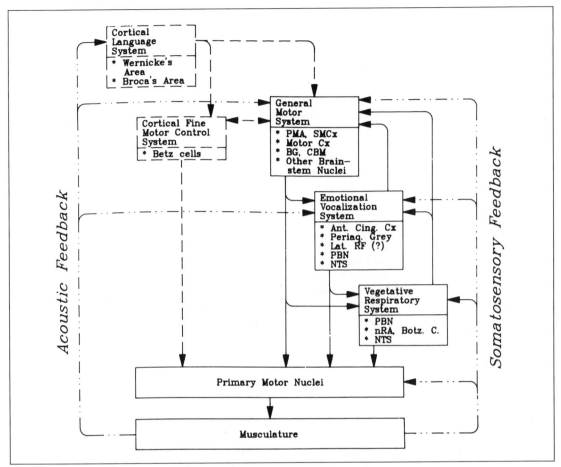

Fig. 6-8. CNS control of phonation. Hypothesized functional subsystems and their general connectivity. Major neural structures that appear to be involved are listed, but details of their interconnections are omitted. Blocks diagrammed with solid lines are thought to be present in all mammals; broken lines are used to represent functional components more characteristic of humans. Also presented without listing the neural structures involved are somatosensory and auditory feedback pathways (dash–dotted lines). PMA = premotor areas; SMCx = supplementary motor cortex; Cx = cortex; BG = basal ganglia; CBM = cerebellum; Ant. Cing. Cx = anterior cingulate cortex; Periaq. Gray = periaqueductal gray; Lat. RF = lateral reticular formation; PBN = parabrachial nucleus; NTS = nucleus of the solitary tract; nRA = nucleus retroambigualis; Botz. C. = Botzinger complex.

structures. Next, three relatively separable systems common to all mammalian species can be distinguished. The first is the central pattern generator for quiet, metabolic breathing that can function in the absence of, but is subject to modulation by, higher control centers. The second, "emotional vocalization," system appears to be responsible for initiation or production of nearly all animal vocalizations. This system is generally associated with limbic areas. A third, "general motor," system, described in more detail in other parts of this chapter, includes structures that probably subserve more volitional or operant motor behaviors. This system has been most studied by motor physiologists interested in limb and orofacial control, and its role in vocalization control remains sketchy. In addition, two systems characteristic of humans are depicted: (1) a direct motor cortical projection to primary motoneurons that subserves fine speech motor control, and (2) an elaboration of association cortical areas concerned with language function. The presence of auditory and somatosensory feedback is also indicated, although in less detail than descending control systems. Clearly, many aspects of these functional systems remain to be understood. Included are some basic data about connectivity and physiologic activity that presently can be studied only in animals.

Obviously, there are questions concerning the applicability of animal data to human speech production mechanisms. Available data suggest that human speech production is under direct motor cortical control, whereas animal vocalizations appear to be controlled by more primitive, emotive systems (Myers, 1976; Netsell, 1982), including the anterior cingulate cortex and the periaqueductal gray. This primitive system is thought by some also to control human emotional vocalizations but to be "gated out" during speech, much as the more primitive metabolic respiratory control system may be deactivated during phonation. Nonetheless, the emotional vocalization control system may play some role in any or all of the following: (1) speech production; (2) interfering with speech production; or (3) development of speech and language.

NEURAL CONTROL OF SUPRALARYNGEAL SYSTEMS

UPPER AND LOWER LIP CONTROL SYSTEMS

The lips are composed of approximately ten muscles originating on the bony surfaces of the maxilla and mandible. Nearly all muscles make insertion into the integument surrounding the mouth and therefore are remarkably different from most other skeletal muscles (Kennedy and Abbs, 1979). There is essentially no fascia within the labial muscles and no tendons. The fibers of the muscle orbicularis oris form the major bulk of the upper and lower lips. It has been described as a sphincter-like muscle with the fibers generally coursing from one corner of

the mouth to the other and whose action contributes to compression and rounding of the lips (Gray, 1977; Kennedy and Abbs, 1979; Muller, Abbs, Kennedy, and Larson, 1977; Muller, Milenkovic, and MacLeod, 1984). Assisting the orbicularis oris for lower lip closure is the mentalis muscle, which is optimally situated to provide a high degree of mechanical advantage in achieving forceful lower lip elevation (Barlow and Rath, 1985). The upper lip, for all practical purposes, lacks a mentalis homologue.

Fundamental differences between the upper and lower lips are not limited to musculoskeletal anatomy but extend to fine motor control. Modeled as an elastically assisted mass (Muller et al., 1977), the surfaces of the lips are displaced at movement velocities in the range of 5 to 20 cm per second during speech. The relative contribution of each lip during speech production can be significantly different. For example, during the production of [p], [b], and [m], the lower lip typically travels a distance that is roughly twice that of the upper lip (Barlow, 1984; Hughes and Abbs, 1976; Kuehn and Moll, 1976; Netsell, Kent, and Abbs, 1980; Sussman, MacNeilage, and Hanson, 1973). To maintain temporal synchronization with the upper lip, peak velocity for the lower lip is approximately twice that of the upper lip (Barlow, 1984; Netsell et al., 1980). The lower lip dental contrast for [f] production is obvious evidence that the upper and lower lips can be activated separately.

The organization of somatic sensory receptors is equally unique for this musculature. Morphologic equivalents of muscle spindles and Golgi tendon organs, which mediate proprioceptive information in limb muscles, have not been found in facial muscles (Folkins and Larson, 1978; Lovell, Sutton, and Lindeman, 1977). However, examination of the unique linkage between muscle and skin provides an alternative anatomy for proprioception in the face. The attachments of the perioral muscles are made by small fascicles that can be widely distributed (Blair and Smith, 1986). Because of this unique relation between skin and muscle, nerve endings and mechanoreceptors become logical candidates to mediate proprioceptive information. Several tissue–mechanoreceptor configurations have been identified in human skin that appear capable of providing proprioceptive information (displacement, velocity, force, rate of force change, acceleration) (Johansson, 1976; Johansson and Olsson, 1976). Reflex sensitivity to small mechanical inputs applied to the perioral region indicates a high degree of sensorimotor coupling and is discussed at greater length later in the chapter.

MECHANOSENSITIVITY OF THE PERIORAL SYSTEM

The speech and masticatory systems have common features because both involve use of the mouth, tongue, anterior teeth, lips, and jaw. Because these motor behaviors use the same body parts, they probably use information from the same sensory receptors, although the importance of the various types of sensory afferents and the way in which this information is used may be different (Lund et al., 1982).

The findings of Lund and his colleagues provide a basis for speculating about the patterns of sensory inputs generated during speech. First, most mucosal and cutaneous afferents seem to be silent in the absence of movement. According to Lund et al., most skin and intraoral afferents are not excited by small local distortions of the skin but only by direct contact with their receptive fields. This observation is consistent with the relatively high reflex sensitivity of perioral muscles to mechanical stimulation of the labial mucosa (Barlow, 1988). Conceivably, no signals would be sent from the surface of the closing lower lip or protruding tongue until they touch another surface. In contrast, hair afferents could provide a continuous velocity signal during speech.

A promising line of study into the mechanosensory properties of afferent nerve endings in skin and other soft tissues involves the application of psychophysics (Barlow, 1987; Essick and Whitsel, 1985; Essick, Afferica, Aldershof, Nestor, Kelly, and Whitsel, 1988; Essick and McGuire, 1988; Fucci, 1972; Mountcastle, LaMotte, and Carli, 1972; Verrillo, 1966a,b,c). The results of an investigation on the mechanical frequency detection thresholds of human perioral skin indicate that the distribution and class of mechanoreceptors present in the lips and surrounding skin are remarkably different from the afferents that innervate the glabrous surfaces of the hand (Barlow, 1987). As shown in Figure 6-9, threshold functions for facial skin sites to sinusoidal mechanical stimulation lack the characteristic "dip" at 250 Hz that is correlated with the pacinian corpuscular afferent. The significance of this difference in mechano-

sensitivity between hand and orofacial structures may be due, in part, to their kinematic roles in fine movement control.

Another remarkable example of mechanosensory specialization in the face can be found in the work of Essick and colleagues (Essick and McGuire, 1988; Essick, Franzen, and Whitsel, 1988). These experiments involved the use of more complex mechanical stimuli in which subjects were required to psychophysically scale the velocity of an external probe moving across the skin at a relatively constant force. Interestingly, the velocity tuning is greatest when the stimuli are delivered to the facial skin, in contrast to the skin of the arm or hand (Essick, Starr, Dolan, and Afferica, 1987). The optimal velocity range in the face is 4 to 8 cm per second. These psychophysical estimates of velocity detection may bear direct relation to velocity characteristics of perioral structures during speech, as most lip and jaw movements occur within this range. Future studies might attempt to relate the velocity of tissue shear in this region of the face during speech to the psychophysical estimates of velocity tuning. In light of these insightful studies, it seems likely that spatiotemporal integration associated with cutaneous and subcutaneous motion perception may be an important signal source encoded by the brain for the maintenance and timing of vocal tract movements for speech.

FINE FORCE CONTROL

Significant differences exist in lip function during fine motor control. For example, fine force control in the lower lip is significantly more stable and recruited at higher rates than the upper lip (Barlow and Netsell, 1986a). Several factors may account for the observed differences in fine motor control between the upper and lower lips. First, elevation of the lower lip results primarily from contraction of two muscle groups: orbicularis oris inferior (OOI) and mentalis. Located inferior to the OOI, the mentolis is optimally situated to provide a high degree of mechanical advantage for assisting the OOI achieve forceful lower lip elevation (Barlow and Rath, 1985). In contrast, the upper lip lacks a significant homologue to the mentolis for assisting the orbicularis oris superior (OOS) during forceful closure of the upper lip. On musculoskeletal grounds, the lower lip is particularly well suited for assuming a greater pro-

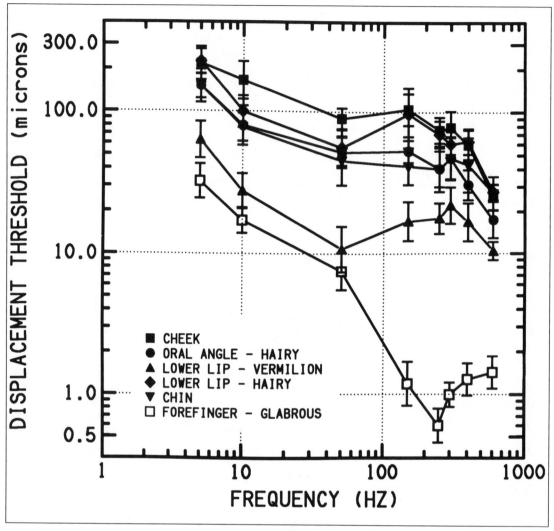

Fig. 6-9. Mean vibrotactile threshold values for the face and hand using the same stimulator probe-surround configuration. The vertical bars represent 95 percent confidence intervals for the mean. (From Barlow, S. M. Mechanical frequency detection thresholds in the human face. *Exp. Neurol.* 96:253, 1987.)

portion of the kinematic demands involved in achieving lip closure.

It is important to note that the force behaviors described above are not purely isometric because it is not possible to hold muscle length constant in the soft tissues of the face. It is especially true within the orofacial complex, given the unique modes of insertions and origins of these muscles. An additional point concerns the definition of force. The force of contraction, as sampled in vivo, is more accurately described by the term *resultant force*. As reported in this chapter, they are resultant forces at the surface of the lip. As defined by Dull, Metcalfe, and Williams (1963), "When two or more forces act

concurrently (simultaneously) at a point, the resultant force is that single force applied at the same point which would produce the same effect."

As reviewed earlier, the lower lip typically moves twice as far and twice as fast as the upper lip for bilabial contact. When forming light contact with the upper teeth for [f] and [v] productions, the lower lip also performs endpoint control independent of upper lip activity. Additionally, movement of the lower lip depends on the excursion of the jaw during speech. Many of the lower lip movements are in the opposite direction of the jaw, and the former is presumed to have evolved a high degree of fine motor control to execute movement with maximal degrees of freedom from the jaw. The higher velocities associated with lower lip displacement for bilabial contact also require the capability for higher rates of force recruitment in this structure. The differences in fine force control between the upper and lower lips (Barlow and Netsell, 1986a) are consistent and predictive of their kinematic role during speech.

LOAD PERTURBATION

For more than three decades the investigation of motor control in human subjects has focused, to a large extent, on studies of reflex EMG activity elicited by muscle stretch or electrical stimulation (Lee and Tatton, 1978). Some of the earlier studies were concerned with mono- or polysynaptic spinal reflex mechanisms. They were followed by investigations of long-loop reflexes involving supraspinal structures (Hammond, 1955, 1956). Based on the relatively long latency of this response (e.g., 60 ms) it was suggested that the late response might be mediated by feedback over a transcortical servo loop (Phillips, 1969). Therefore the perturbation paradigm represents a special investigative tool useful for expanding our understanding of both segmental and suprasegmental sensorimotor pathways in man and subhuman primates (Desmedt, 1978).

Logically, this paradigm has been applied to the study of sensorimotor processes underlying speech production (Abbs and Gracco, 1981, 1983, 1984; Abbs, Gracco, and Cole, 1984; Barlow, 1980; Barlow and Abbs, 1978; Bauer, 1974; Folkins and Abbs, 1973, 1975, 1976; Folkins and Zimmerman, 1982; Gracco and Abbs, 1985; Kelso, Tuller, and Fowler, 1982; Kennedy, 1977; Lindblom, Lubker and Gay, 1979; Netsell and Abbs, 1975; Netsell et al., 1980). Some of the major findings from those studies employing unanticipated loads to orofacial structures are reviewed in the following paragraphs.

In one of the initial studies (Folkins and Abbs, 1975), resistive loads were applied to the jaw during speech production. These loads halted the normal jaw elevation movement

associated with coordinated labial-mandibular closure for [p]. Loads were initiated during the jaw closing movement associated with the production of bilabial stops, creating a situation in which bilabial closure would be disrupted if motor control were independent of peripheral feedback. Despite the mechanical load, subjects were able to achieve lip closure associated with the bilabial stop. Compensatory movements in both the upper and lower lips were associated with jaw loading. These authors concluded that on-line afferent feedback is capable of contributing to the compensatory motor reorganization of the lips and the jaw during speech production. Subsequent reinterpretation offered by Abbs and his colleagues suggests that these data indicate the operation of open-loop, sensorimotor mechanisms inasmuch as compensation was absent in the jaw, where the loads were introduced, but was present in the lips. The interested reader is referred to the literature for a more detailed discussion of open-loop neural control mechanisms (Arbib, 1981; Houk and Rymer, 1981; Ito, 1975; Miles and Evarts, 1979; Rack, 1981).

Using a more sophisticated stimulus control system, Gracco and Abbs (1985) examined the afferent contributions to the motor control of speech by applying unanticipated loads to the lower lip during the production of the bilabial /b/. The loads were considered to be within the normal range of forces and movements involved in lip actions during speech. Kinematic adjustments of the upper and lower lips to these perturbations were examined in detail.

In the five subjects studied, load-induced changes in upper and lower lip displacement, movement time, and closing velocity were statistically significant and observed the first time a perturbation was introduced. Even in the presence of a mechanical perturbation, subjects were able to complete the speech gesture with little or no degradation of the speech output. Load timing variations within the target interval resulted in systematic changes in the site of the compensatory adjustments (upper versus lower lip) and in the magnitude of the kinematic responses. These kinematic changes appeared to reflect the dynamic nature of underlying control processes and clearly contrasted the response characteristics of autogenic (lower lip: perturbed structure) and nonautogenic (upper lip: nonperturbed structure) compensatory actions. An example of compensatory actions of lip muscles associated with control and loaded trials is shown in Figure 6-10.

Although both upper and lower lip adjustments contributed to perturbation compensations, autogenic responses were found to predominate when loads occurred 20 to 55 ms before muscle activation. For these early loads, autogenic responses provided approximately 75 percent of the total compensation. For later loads, when the evolving speech motor action was more time-constrained, nonautogenic (thought to be open-loop) compensations predominated, providing approximately 65 percent of the total compensation.

Overall, the degree of compensation is related to the magnitude of the perturbation displacement, especially for loads introduced prior to agonist muscle onset, reflecting a well calibrated readjustment. Responses to later loads are less consistently related to perturbation displacement. For speech motor control, both corrective feedback and open-loop predictive processes may be operating, with the latter involved in the control of coordination among multiple-movement subcomponents (Abbs and Gracco, 1984).

The compensatory responses reported by Abbs and Gracco (1984) are consistent with observations of parallel motor equivalence trade-off between the upper lip, lower lip, and jaw movements observed during speech (Hase-

gawa, McCutcheon, Wolf, and Fletcher, 1976; Hughes and Abbs, 1976) and observations that perturbation of the jaw induces compensation in the upper and lower lips (Folkins and Abbs, 1975). Comparable trade-offs have been observed between the abdomen and rib cage in their synergistic contributions to speech pleural pressures (Hixon et al., 1973; Hixon, Mead, and Goldman, 1976; Hunker and Abbs, 1982).

PERIORAL REFLEX PHYSIOLOGY

Sensory information derived from mechanoreceptors located within skin, muscle, and joints of the vocal tract is considered important in the development and maintenance of speech motor control (Evarts, 1981a; Mountcastle, 1980). One approach that has been used to study the sensorimotor organization of trigeminofacial systems during motor control involves the use of facial reflexes (Barlow and Netsell, 1986a,b; Larson, 1977; McClean, 1978, 1986; McClean and Smith, 1982; Netsell and Abbs,

Fig. 6-10. Load perturbation. A. Movements of the upper and lower lips for three normal trials and three loaded trials. B. Comparison of a pair of control/loaded trials illustrating the compensatory actions of the lip muscles and movement changes in the upper lip. Compensation in shaded areas. (From Abbs, J. H., and Gracco, V. L. Control of complex motor gestures: orofacial muscle responses to load perturbations of the lip during speech. *J. Neurophysiol.* 51:705, 1984.)

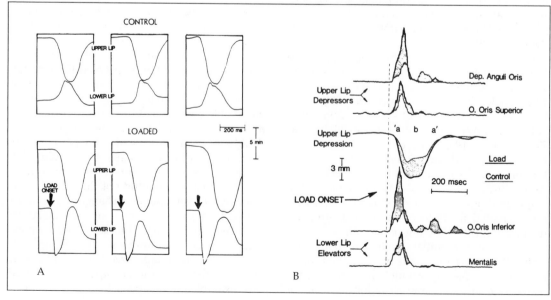

1975; Netsell and Barlow, 1986; Smith, Mc-Farland, Weber, and Moore, 1987; Weber and Smith, 1987). The perioral reflex is elicited by a brisk mechanical tap or stretch applied to the perioral region or by electrical stimulation of trigeminal nerve branches (Ekbom, Jernelius, and Kugelberg, 1952; Gandiglio and Fra, 1967; Kugelberg, 1952; Larson, Folkins, McClean, and Muller, 1978). The perioral reflex is classically described from gross EMG recordings as a two-component excitatory response (Fig. 6-11). In the orbicularis oris muscle, the reflex is composed of an early (10 to 15 ms) component that is present on repeated stimulation and a late (30 to 45 ms) component that adapts or decays rapidly. The neural pathways mediating the early component are thought to be restricted primarily to the brainstem and to involve at least two synapses (Fig. 6-12). The pathways involved in mediating the late component are not well understood, although ablation of area 3a in the monkey (Larson, 1977) has been shown to abolish this component of the perioral reflex.

Several investigations on the properties of facial reflexes have demonstrated clearly the exquisite sensitivity of the perioral system to non-noxious mechanical stimuli (Bratzlavsky, 1979; Lund et al., 1982). For example, displacing a smooth metal disk in light contact with the skin of the upper lip effectively elicits a reflex in the

lower lip muscles of humans (A. Smith et al., 1985). McClean and Smith (1982) generated consistent perioral reflex responses using a 0.5-mm stretch applied to the corner of the mouth. Larson and associates (1978) used a 1.0- and 3.0-mm stretch to evoke the perioral reflex. Efforts have also been successful in generating reflex responses in perioral muscles during fine force control using low-amplitude taps (100 μm) applied to the mucosal surfaces of the lip (Barlow, 1988; Barlow and Netsell, 1986a,b; Netsell and Barlow, 1986). The functional properties of this sensorimotor process are considered in greater detail in the following sections.

Response Specificity

McClean and Smith (1982) have reported that mechanical stimulation of the skin of the upper or lower lip produces reflex responses of local sign in both inferior (OOI) and superior (OOS) divisions of the orbicularis oris muscle. For example, stimulation of remote structures (e.g., the chin) does not evoke the early reflex response in OOI motor units. Localization of the reflex is known as *response specificity*. Further evidence of response specificity among facial structures also has been demonstrated in a report by Netsell and Barlow (1986). They sampled EMG activity simultaneously from muscles surrounding the mouth and eyes. A mechanical stretch ranging from 0.5 to 2.0 mm was applied to the lower lip. As shown in Figure 6-13, reflex responses were found only ipsilateral to the me-

Fig. 6-11. Perioral reflex R1/R2: the two-component EMG perioral reflex response. The early and late components are designated R1 and R2, respectively.

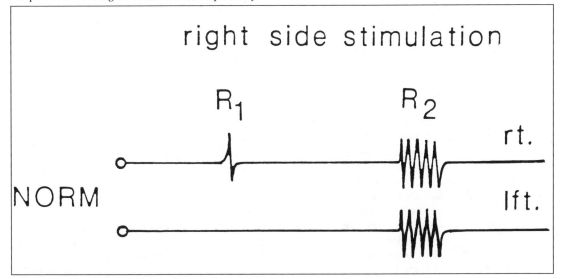

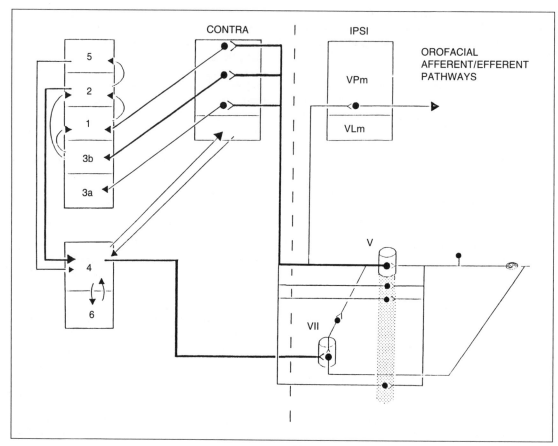

Fig. 6-12. Bulbar and suprabulbar pathways thought to be involved in the "early" (R1) and "late" (R2) components of the perioral reflex. V = trigeminal nuclei; VII = facial nucleus; VPm = ventroposteromedial nucleus of the thalamus; VLm = ventrolateral nucleus of the thalamus. Areas 5, 2, 1, 3b, and 3a constitute primary somatosensory zones of postcentral cortex; and areas 4 and 6 represent motor zones of the precentral cortex. R1 is thought to be mediated over the brainstem pathway involving trigeminal and facial relays. R2 is presumed to involve thalamic and sensorimotor cortices.

chanical stimulus and confined to the lower face. The high degree of response specificity observed in these experiments is likely due to the physiologic nature of the mechanical stimulus and the nature of the motor task performed by the subject. The fact that different populations of labial motor units have different reflex responses to mechanical stimulation at one site suggests that trigeminofacial projections are muscle-specific within the sensory and motor nuclei of the brainstem (Barlow and Netsell, 1986b,c; McClean and Smith, 1982).

The following example illustrates the high degree of response specificity possible within a group of facial muscles involved in lip movements. Perioral motor unit signals from five sites in the lower face, including the right medial portion of the OOI, the right lateral segment of the OOI, the right side of the mentalis muscle, the right lateral segment of the OOS, and a contralateral OOI are shown in Figure 6-

14 in relation to the displacement signal corresponding to a skin tap on the right lower lip. In this example, reflex responses were localized to lateral placements in the orbicularis oris and mentalis muscles. There was no activity in the medial OOI placement. In general, reflexive activation of muscles contralateral to the mechanical stimulus was not observed when the amplitude of the tap stimulus was kept below 2 mm. Typical latencies between stimulus onset and the evoked perioral muscle activation range

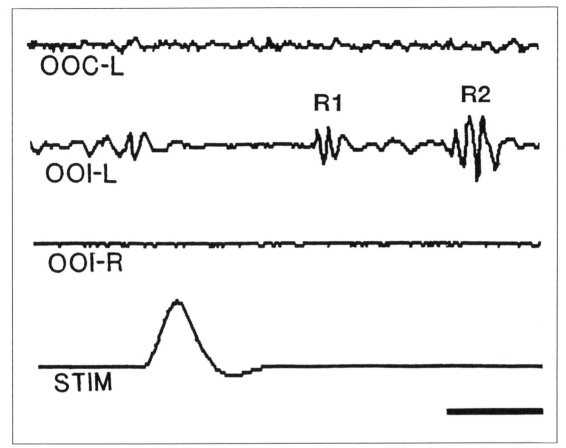

Fig. 6-13. Reflex specificity. An example of the R1 and R2 reflex components recorded ipsilaterally from a bipolar hook-wire electrode located within the lateral part of the orbicularis oris inferior muscle (OOI). The eliciting stimulus was a 1.0-mm tap applied to the left side of the lower lip. OOC-L = orbicularis oculi (left side); OOI-R = orbicularis oris inferior (right side). Time bar = 10 ms.

from 12 to 15 ms. Intermuscle latency differences are apparent between orbicularis oris and mentalis muscles. This finding is consistent with the observation that the perioral reflex is actually composed of a set of responses from select motor unit populations (Blair and Smith, 1986; McClean and Smith, 1982).

Response Modulation

An important issue in studies of sensorimotor integration is whether the gain of a reflex pathway is modulated before or during movement (McClean and Smith, 1982). Experiments on reflex sensitivity to a mechanical stimulus simul-taneous with subject-generated perioral force have provided a direct test of this hypothesis (Barlow, 1988; Barlow and Netsell, 1986b,c; Netsell and Abbs, 1975; Netsell and Barlow, 1986). An example of perioral reflex modulation during lip force control is shown in the EMG/force waterfall displays of Figure 6-15. In this experiment, rectified and integrated (2.5 ms time constant) EMG signals recorded from bilateral portions of the OOI, OOS, and an ipsilateral portion of the mentalis muscle were averaged (n = 128 sweeps) in reference to the onset of a mechanical stimulus (2-mm tap) applied to the right lower lip. Consistent perioral reflexes in recording sites ipsilateral to the stimulus again illustrate the specificity of these responses. Additionally, these responses depend on the level of lower lip force generated by the subject. This feature of response growth is defined as *modulation*. The degree of modulation varies for different muscle recording sites. In the present ex-

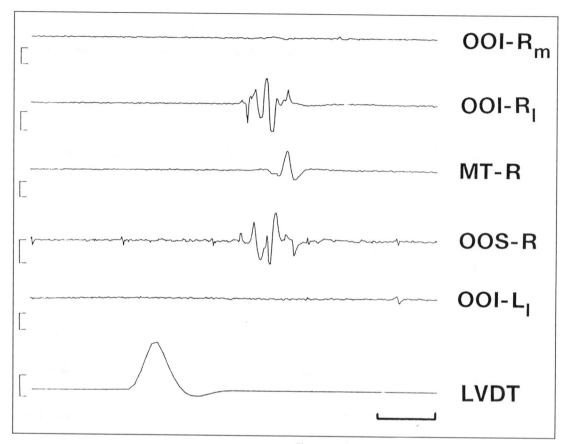

Fig. 6-14. Specificity within lower face to a skin tap on the right lower lip. Multiunit EMG responses from several recording sites in the lower face are shown. EMG cals = 100 μV. LVDT cal = 0.5 mm. Time bar = 10 ms.

ample, a well defined reflex response is present at the OOI-R (OOI, right side) muscle site during rest. On the other hand, the mentalis muscle, right side, site is quiescent at this force level and does not recruit until the subject generates lip forces above the 0.05 newton level. Because both muscles are involved in generating lower lip closing forces (Abbs et al., 1984; Barlow and Netsell, 1986a; Barlow and Rath, 1985; Blair and Smith, 1986), the trade-offs in reflex sensitivity between the OOI and the mentalis muscle may reflect a fundamental property of their neuromotor organization for coordination and fine control.

Concerning the dynamics of perioral reflex action, Smith and her colleagues suggested that "this reflex pathway is not suppressed during phonation or speech. However, the response appears to be suppressed or absent because the amplitude of the observed response depends upon the activation levels of the various muscles of the lower lip and, therefore, indirectly on

the nature of the gesture the subject is instructed to produce." This finding supports an earlier notion by McClean and Smith (1982) in which they emphasized that the question of perioral reflex amplitude (i.e., modulation) during speech and vocalization may require evaluation in terms of the specific muscle groups that are active.

Short-Term Adaptation

Following the presentation of consecutive stimuli to the face of the cat, Lindquist and Martensson (1970) noted a substantial decrease in the amplitude of early reflex component between the first and second tap. In physiologic systems this property is known as *short-term adaptation* and is defined as the rapid exponential decay in the evoked motor response immedi-

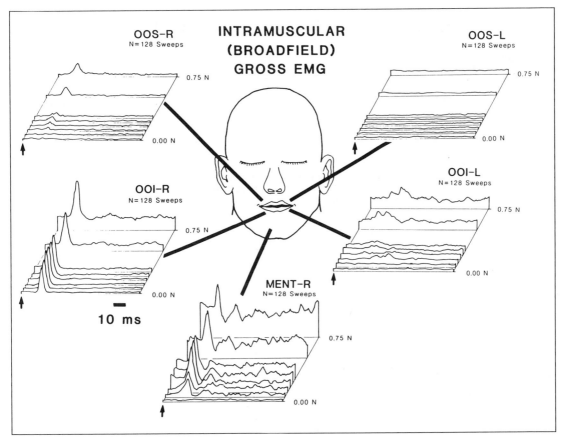

Fig. 6-15. Reflex modulation. A waterfall display of rectified, integrated (2.5 ms time constant), and signal-averaged (128 sweeps) EMG from the orbicularis oris inferior (OOI), orbicularis oris superior (OOS), and mentalis (MENT) electrode sites in response to mechanical stimulation of the right lower lip simultaneous with subject-generated lower lip closing forces. Time bar = 10 ms. Vertical arrow indicates onset of the mechanical stimulus. (From Netsell, R., and Barlow, S. M. Specificity of perioral reflexes. *Abstr. Assoc. Res. Otolaryngol.* 169:135, 1986.)

ately following stimulation. This phenomenon should not be confused with *fatigue*, which is defined as the slow decline in response that occurs with continuous stimulation over a period of minutes (Harris, 1977; Kiang, Watanabe, Thomas, and Clark, 1965; R. L. Smith, 1973, 1977; Young and Sachs, 1973).

As it turns out, the human perioral reflex manifests adaptation following the presentation of consecutive stimuli. The example given in Figure 6-16 illustrates short-term adaptation of the perioral reflex to train stimulation (Barlow and Netsell, 1986b). A train consists in five me-

chanical taps. Within a train, the tap presentation rate may vary from 2 to 40 Hz. Individual trains are separated by intervals ranging from 2.5 to 5.0 seconds. For the examples shown in Figure 6-17, individual reflex responses are averaged (n = 64 sweeps) according to their corresponding position in the stimulus train. The normalized amplitude of the short-latency reflex response recorded from the medial and lateral segments of the OOI and the lateral portion of the mentalis muscle are plotted as a function of position within the stimulus train for lower lip bias forces of 0, 0.10, 0.20, and 0.50 newton. The intertap interval corresponded to a stimulus rate of 20 taps per second. For each of the recording sites, the amplitude of the early reflex component was reduced between the first and second tap when the lower lip was at rest. As subject-generated lip force increases, the amplitude functions for the early response flatten, indicating a reduction in the degree of adaptation. The pattern of early component short-term ad-

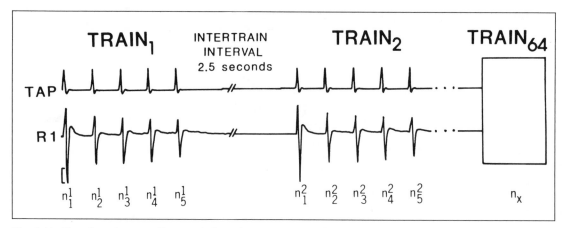

Fig. 6-16. The adaptation paradigm, including the tap stimuli and EMG responses, is shown for a five-tap sequence. Individual R1 responses were averaged according to position in the train, as indicated by the subscript notation.

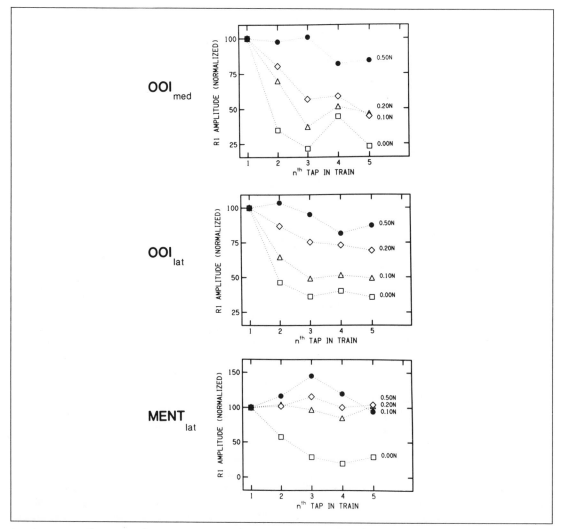

Fig. 6-17. Adaptation of perioral reflex for medial OOI, lateral OOI, and MENT electrode sites. Stimulus conditions: 2-mm tap to the right corner of the mouth at a rate of 20 per second within the train. Intertrain interval is 2.5 seconds.

aptation for the mentalis muscle recording site appears to be remarkably different from either of the OOI placements. The degree and nature of short-term adaptation for a particular muscle recording site is hypothesized to reflect an aspect of temporal resolution for somatic-motor function. As yet, the significance of this phenomenon for speech motor control remains unknown.

JAW SYSTEM

The mandible is part of a bilateral mechanically linked musculoskeletal system that is involved in mastication, object manipulation, and speech (Luschei and Goldberg, 1981). As detailed in Chapter 5, the muscles that move the mandible can be grouped into the opening muscles or flexors (digastric, lateral pterygoid, suprahyoid) and the closing muscles, or extensors (temporalis, masseter, medial pterygoid). These muscles originate from several bones of the skull, including the maxilla, sphenoid, pterygoid, and palatine, and are heavily sheathed with fascia and organized into three to five compartmentalized planes above the temporomandibular joint. Jaw velocities during speech (2 to 10 cm/second) (Barlow, 1984) generally are slower than those typical of the lips and tongue (Kuehn and Moll, 1976). It has been well documented that muscle spindles, joint receptors, tendon organs, and a variety of mechanoreceptors in the periodontal ligament are present in the jaw system (Bratzlavsky, 1976; Goodwin, Hoffman, and Luschei, 1978; Harrison and Corbin, 1942; Karlsson, 1976; Luschei and Goldberg, 1981). The neural control system for the jaw appears to have multiple components, including a central pattern generator for mastication (discussed later in the chapter), reflex regulation, and "command inputs" that can modulate the activity of rhythmic movement or exert direct purposive control for speech and oral manipulation (Luschei and Goldberg, 1981). The following sections briefly review some of the features of the mandibular neural control system.

SENSORIMOTOR CONTROL OF THE JAW

A number of reflexes, possibly involved in mastication, can be evoked from mammalian jaw muscles using electrical or mechanical stimulation. The first reflex considered is the jaw stretch reflex. Jaw closing muscles are well endowed with muscle spindles, whereas jaw opening muscles have few. Afferents from the spindles of jaw-closing muscles make monosynaptic excitatory connections, via the trigeminal mesencephalic nucleus, with the motoneurons of closing muscles (Harrison and Corbin, 1942; Lund, Richmond, Touloumis, Patry, and Lamarre, 1978a). Primary and secondary muscle spindle afferents have been recorded in cats during chewing and lapping (Cody, Harrison, and Taylor, 1975; Taylor and Cody, 1974; Taylor, Appenteng, and Morimoto, 1981) and in monkeys during chewing (Goodwin and Luschei, 1975).

Spindle primaries fire phasically and are most sensitive to the velocity of muscle lengthening during opening. Their activity results in part from the effects of fusimotor neurons, which are active before and during biting and rhythmic movements (Appenteng, Morimoto, and Taylor, 1980; Lund, Smith, Sessle, and Murakami, 1979; Taylor et al., 1981).

Muscle spindle secondaries are mainly sensitive to length changes, and their firing frequency generally is proportional to the distance between the incisor teeth during the performance of slow movements. The displacement information encoded by secondary endings, if operative in humans, may explain partially the ability of the speech motor control system to reprogram lip and tongue movements for vowel production under jaw-blocked conditions.

The second major reflex considered is the jaw opening reflex. Mechanoreceptors in the periodontal ligament are strongly activated during chewing. Electrical or mechanical stimulation of the oral mucosa or direct electrical stimulation of nerves innervating the oral mucosa results in brisk opening of the jaw. This response, better known as the jaw opening reflex (JOR), is effected by excitation of jaw opening muscles and inhibition of jaw closing muscles. The JOR is thought to be mediated by large-diameter, rapidly conducting afferents in the lingual, inferior alveolar, and superior dental nerves with conduction velocities of approximately 40 to 60 meters per second. Unlike reflex organization of limb muscles, there does not appear to be reciprocal inhibition of motoneurons of antagonistic muscles.

A central question concerning the role of reflexes in mastication is whether they modulate motoneuron activity within a central neural circuit or are themselves the source for the basic pattern (Luschei and Goldberg, 1981). A model of mastication based purely on reflexes is not plausible because decerebrate cats do not masticate. Likewise, deafferentation does not abolish the basic pattern of mastication. Therefore the basic pattern of excitation to jaw-closing motoneurons during mastication does not originate from muscle spindles (Cody et al., 1975; Goodwin and Luschei, 1975). Rather, the basic pattern of jaw movement during mastication appears to result from central mechanisms that may be activated by commands originating from the sensorimotor cortex or modified by afferent signals conducted by the trigeminal system. The influence of spindle-mediated afferent mechanisms appears to be greater for finely graded, low-force control of the jaw (Goodwin et al., 1978; Lund et al., 1979).

This conclusion leads into a discussion of jaw reflexes and load compensation. The responses to rapid loading and unloading of the jaw closing muscles are asymmetric. Rapid stretch evokes a single response that corresponds in latency with the monosynaptic jaw jerk reflex (5 to 10 ms). The stretch response is followed 6 to 10 ms later by an increase in the velocity of closure. The velocity depends on EMG peak amplitude (Lamarre and Lund, 1975). Unloading the jaw is followed by a decrease in EMG activity occurring at monosynaptic latency but with later phases of depression beginning at about 30 and 60 ms (Hannam, Matthews, and Yemm, 1968; Lund et al., 1982). If suprasegmental long-loop load compensatory mechanisms are functional in this system (Lamarre and Lund, 1975), they appear to be of importance only for unloading (Lund et al., 1982).

Although short latency load compensatory reflexes may play a role in voluntary biting and mastication, the need for them in speech production is not evident because of the absence of large load variations (Lund et al., 1982). Furthermore, muscle spindle sensitivity is apparently low during speech gestures involving closing movements of the jaw. A number of investigators have reported that it is difficult to obtain consistent load responses in jaw closing muscles during speech (Folkins and Abbs, 1975, 1976; Lamarre and Lund, 1975; Lund, Smith, and Lamarre, 1978b).

Subcortical Mastication Pattern Generator

The evidence in support of a central pattern generator for mastication is derived largely from experiments that have used random electrical stimulation of the cerebral cortex in the presence of a drug that selectively blocks intra- and extrafusal muscle fibers. Under the blocked condition, rhythmic activity is present in the efferent nerves to the jaw and tongue muscles of the rabbit (Dellow and Lund, 1971) and the cat (Nakamura, Kubo, Nozaki, and Takatori, 1976). These results suggest that the brainstem mechanism, located in the medial bulboreticular formation, can generate a rhythmic pattern of activity without peripheral input. Lund and Rossignol (1980) suggested that the masticatory pattern generator regulates the reflex amplitude by phasically modulating the excitability of interneurons along the reflex pathway.

Purposive Jaw Movements for Speech

From the preceding discussion, it is apparent that a substantial portion of the neural control system of the jaw is designed for mastication. Of special importance to the student of speech neurophysiology is how the nervous system controls the jaw for speech. There are no clear answers to this intriguing question. An examination of voluntary jaw control represents a starting point for advancing our understanding of this structure during speech.

One structure that is consistently implicated in voluntary jaw control is the sensorimotor cortex, due in part to its connectivity and short latency effects (8 to 40 ms in primates) on motoneurons of the jaw (Chase, Sterman, Kubota, and Clemente, 1973). Reports have shown a strong relation between the activity of neurons in the precentral motor cortex and controlled (voluntary) bite responses in monkeys. Approximately 50 percent of the cells studied in the face motor cortex of monkeys increased their rate of firing during the dynamic phase of the bite response (Hoffman, 1977). These corticomotoneurons are known as "phasic-tonic" cells. Another class of cells, termed "tonic," are principally related to the static or sustained phase of voluntary bite. As described earlier in the chapter, the activity of corticomotoneurons can be modified by sensory input. Hoffman found that most activated cells exhibit phase-related changes in firing rate during imposed displacements of the jaw.

An evolving concept on the role of the sensorimotor cortex suggests that this cortical region functions primarily to coordinate the complex movements of the tongue, lips, and jaw during mastication and voluntary activity (Lund and Lamarre, 1974). For example, the tongue must be carefully guided to avoid being crushed by the teeth during motor behaviors involving the jaw. Motoneurons controlling the tongue may facilitate the jaw-opening muscles and provide inhibitory inputs to the jaw-closing muscles (Luschei and Goldberg, 1981). The fact that the mandible can be used independently from the lips and tongue indicates that neural inputs to the jaw muscles are highly organized. At least a portion of the voluntary control system for the jaw as well as other orofacial structures is represented by neurons located within the face area of the precentral cortex. Sensory inputs originating from temporomandibular joint afferents may provide both velocity and displacement signals over the range of movement encountered in human speech and mastication (Lund et al., 1982).

TONGUE SYSTEM

The tongue is capable of mass reorganization through multivectorial muscle contractions of intrinsic and extrinsic muscles. Movement velocities ranging from 5 to 20 cm per second are typical during speech. A rich supply of mechanoreceptors is distributed in cutaneous and subcutaneous structures of the tongue. Muscle spindles have been found in the lingual muscles of humans (Cooper, 1953; Kubota, Negishi and Hasegi, 1975; Nakayama, 1944; Walker and Rajagopal, 1959) and monkeys (Bowman, 1968; Fitzgerald and Sachitanandan, 1979). However, lingual spindle afferents, derived from distal portions of the hypoglossal nerve, do not appear to project directly to the cerebellum (Bowman, 1982; Egel, Bowman, and Combs, 1969; Bowman and Combs, 1969a,b; Oscarsson, 1965). Rather, lingual spindle information projects to the cerebral cortex via a fast conducting pathway synapsing in the thalamic ventral posteromedial nucleus (Bowman and Combs, 1969a,b). Contralateral projections have been

identified in the medial portion of the pontine reticulotegmental nucleus, a precerebellar relay nucleus (Bowman, 1982). Unlike the limbs, deep (proprioceptive) and superficial (tactile) mechanoreceptive input from the tongue enters the central nervous system over separate routes. Tactile afferents project centrally in the lingual branch of the trigeminal nerve, whereas the proprioceptive afferents after first being incorporated in the hypoglossal nerve, depart from it to enter the central nervous system over upper cervical dorsal roots (Bowman, 1971).

SOME EFFECTS OF CNS LESIONS ON VOCAL TRACT CONTROL

Damage to certain regions of the brain can have devastating effects on speech production. Dysarthria is a speech disorder resulting from damage to neural mechanisms that regulate speech movements (Netsell, 1984a). Dysarthria resulting from damage to the basal ganglia or the cerebral cortex represents two major neurologic populations that have been studied by speech neuroscientists using quantitative physiologic methods. Several of these investigations are reviewed in the following sections. Because a detailed treatment of the physiologic bases of dysarthria is beyond the scope of this chapter, the interested reader is referred to the works of Netsell (1982, 1983, 1984a,b, 1985, 1986) for a comprehensive review.

LESIONS OF MOTOR-SENSORY CORTEX

Several types of motor impairment are typically associated with precentral motor cortex lesions, including paralysis, hypertonia, and spasticity (Fulton, 1949; Tasker, Gentili, Hwang, and Sogabe, 1980). Perhaps more striking are the persisting deficits in fine motor control that manifest primarily in phylogenetically advanced neural systems controlling limb muscles (Denny-Brown, 1980; Tower, 1940; Travis, 1955) and orofacial musculature (Barlow and Abbs, 1982a,b, 1984, 1986; Neilson and O'Dwyer, 1981; Netsell, 1982). Clinical observations suggest that the least automatic and most highly differentiated movements, including manipulation and speech, suffer first and most (Jackson, 1880). In monkeys with lesions of the precentral cortex or pyramidal tract, movements are slow but accurate; the inability to make rapid adjustments in the distal musculature controlling the hand constitute a permanent deficit (Gilman and Marco, 1971; Gilman, Marco, and Ebel, 1971; Lawrence and Kuypers, 1968a,b; Travis, 1955). Thus the corticospinal and corticobulbar pathways represent the main sources of descending input, terminating directly on those motoneurons principally innervating the distal muscles of the hand and the complex arrangement of muscles in the vocal tract.

Investigation of the pathophysiology of speech subsystems in patients with lesions ostensibly involving the motor cortex has focused on the fine force and position control of the most accessible orofacial structures (Barlow and Abbs, 1984, 1986; Barlow and Burton, 1988). Similar to reports in primates, impairments in motor control include a reduction in the rate of force change associated with generating fine levels of force in the upper lip, lower lip, tongue, and jaw. These measures are highly related to impairments in movement velocity in these same structures. Endpoint accuracy, defined as the ability to generate specified target levels for both force and position, is relatively well preserved in these structures. Moreover, the measures of orofacial force and position dynamics used in these experiments were found to be related to impairment in speech intelligibility. Considerably more information is needed about the nature of impaired force control and resultant movement before a cause–effect relation on speech intelligibility can be accurately specified. At this juncture, it is certainly the case that quantitative physiologic measures of force and movement control are considerably more sensitive than conventional methods for determining the distribution and nature of orofacial motor impairments that degrade fine motor performance.

LESIONS OF BASAL GANGLIA

The temporal aspects of voluntary movements in patients with Parkinson's disease are impaired with considerable individual variation. It is due, in part, to the tremor, rigidity, and dyskinesia that accompany disease of the basal ganglia. Parkinsonian dysarthrics manifesting tremor and minimal rigidity have increased reaction times and near-normal movement times for orofacial and finger control

systems (Hunker and Abbs, 1985). By contrast, in a second group manifesting rigidity with minimal tremor, reaction times were normal but movement times were elongated. These results indicate that the pathologic mechanisms involved in tremor and muscle rigidity may account, in part, for the movement aberrations of dyskinesia and bradykinesia, respectively. Hence two distinctly different pathologic mechanisms (viz., abnormal oscillatory activity and increased muscle stiffness) may hypothetically underlie increased movement time in Parkinson's disease (also see Netsell et al., 1975).

The delays in movement initiation common to parkinsonian patients with resting tremor may be due to an inability to initiate a voluntary muscle contraction until synchronized with the excitatory EMG phase of the tremor cycle in agonist muscles of the limbs (Hallet, Shahani and Young, 1977) and orofacial structures (Hunker and Abbs, 1984).

Another feature of movement control following damage to the basal ganglia (parkinsonism) is a reduction of both voluntary and automatic movement, i.e., hypokinesia. Similar results have been found in the monkey (Hore and Vilis, 1984). The possibility that rigidity causes hypokinesia in the orofacial complex has been supported indirectly (Hunker, Abbs, and Barlow, 1982). Lee and Tatton (1978) suggested that parkinsonian rigidity is a manifestation of increased sensitivity in a transcortical reflex loop. They found that parkinsonian patients, unlike normal subjects, could not reduce the amplitude of the later posttendon jerk EMG response (M2). This increased feedback gain over transcortical pathways was subsequently correlated with the degree of muscle rigidity in parkinsonian patients.

DIFFERENTIAL IMPAIRMENT

Lesions of the central nervous system (CNS) that disrupt speech motor control are usually characterized by differential sensorimotor impairment to vocal tract structures. The neurology of dysarthria therefore necessitates systematic evaluation of several components of the vocal tract, including respiratory, laryngeal, velopharyngeal, and orofacial structures. The following examples illustrate some general patterns of impairment that may accompany dysarthrias of central origin.

Upper and Lower Lips

Clinical observations of motor function following damage to the CNS suggest that structures normally capable of finer control manifest disproportionately greater impairment in generating precise forces and displacements (Denny-Brown, 1980; Jackson, 1958). It logically follows that the lower lip, because of its dominant kinematic role during speech, manifests proportionately greater deficits in fine motor control following CNS damage than its counterpart, the upper lip. This pattern of impairment is shown in the following examples.

Leanderson and Persson (1972) suggested that with increased background activity and disturbed reciprocal activation the labial muscles alter their normal coordination for speech. Hunker et al. (1982) extended this observation and quantified stiffness (change in force/change in displacement) in the lip muscles of parkinsonian adults with dysarthria. The perioral musculature was found to be differentially impaired in that the lower lip manifested the more significant deficits in range of displacement and larger increases in muscle stiffness in regard to the upper lip.

Tremors in the force or movement domain have been found in a variety of vocal tract structures including the chest wall, larynx, velopharynx, and orofacial structures. Although it has been reported that tremor frequencies are uniform among orofacial structures and the index finger within the same parkinsonian subject (Hunker and Abbs, 1983), significant deviations in frequency and amplitude may exist between the upper lip, lower lip, and index finger in Parkinson's disease (Fig. 6-18). For this parkinsonian man the amplitude of lower lip force tremor during a 2-newton contraction was approximately an order of magnitude greater than the tremor associated for a 2-newton contraction performed using the upper lip (Barlow and Hunker, 1988). The difference in the magnitude of the 8.06 Hz force tremor between the upper and lower lip is an example of differential involvement in *degree*. In this same parkinsonian patient, the spectral peak associated with the force tremor for the lips and index finger was remarkably different, suggesting a difference in the *nature* of the underlying neural mechanism contributing to the motor impairment. As shown in Figure 6-18, the primary frequency

component of force tremor in the index finger is centered at approximately 4.88 Hz.

Differential motor involvement of the perioral musculature also was described by Barlow and colleagues (Barlow, 1984; Barlow and Abbs, 1986) in a group of patients with a congenital form of the upper motor neuron syndrome (Landau, 1974, 1980). In particular, the ability to recruit force and achieve normal movement velocity was severely compromised in these patients. Similar results have been found in lesioned monkeys (Travis, 1955). Consistently greater deficits in fine force and position control were found in the lower lip compared to the upper lip. The pattern and degree of these fine motor impairments were highly correlated with auditory-perceptual measures of speech intelligibility in these patients.

Jaw

Congenital lesions involving the motor cortex (known as cerebral palsy or congenital spasticity) can result in a variety of negative symptoms affecting jaw control, including a slowness of movement (reduced velocity) and unsteadiness during precise movements. Jaw force instability, quantified as the variability in force output over some specified period of time, is significantly increased in this patient population, especially at lower force levels (Barlow and Abbs, 1984; 1986). Similar impairments occur in monkeys following lesions to the face area of the precentral cortex (Luschei and Goodwin, 1975).

Tongue

The tongue, because of its relative inaccessibility, is more difficult to study during speech production. Therefore experiments have quantified tongue forces and movements under highly controlled conditions. These studies revealed several interesting patterns of deficit that depend on the site of lesion. For example, in parkinsonian patients the instability associated with generating a steady, low-level force is disproportionately greater in the tongue than in the lips or jaw (Abbs, Hunker, and Barlow, 1983; Barlow and Abbs, 1983). In patients with the upper motor neuron syndrome, the most significant deficit in tongue force control is a reduction in the rate of force change, paralleled by a decrease in movement velocity (Barlow and Abbs, 1986). These findings are consistent

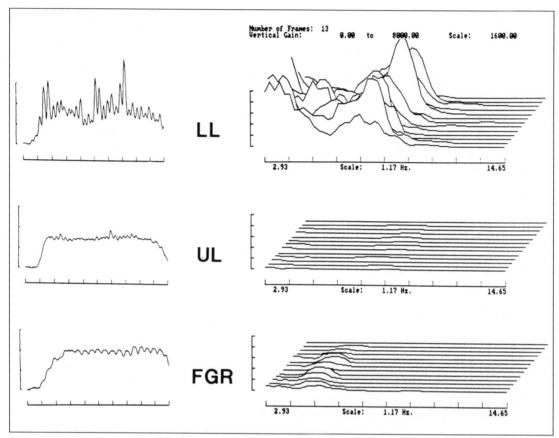

Fig. 6-18. Time domain waveforms and Fourier transforms of force signals sampled from the upper lip, lower lip, and index finger of an adult man with Parkinson's disease. Multiple Fourier transforms (right) were computed on force signals associated with individual contractions (examples at left) generated under visual feedback with a target at 2 newtons. The display gains and processing conditions are identical among the three structures. Force calibration: 1 newton/division. (Barlow, S. M., and Hunker, C. Unpublished data. Boys Town National Institute, Omaha, 1988.)

with the notion that the rate of force change is encoded by corticomotoneurons.

CENTRAL PROCESSES UNDERLYING SPEECH MOVEMENTS

SPATIOTEMPORAL GOALS

Speech is considered by many scientists to be a goal-oriented process. For example, the target of a vowel is thought to be encoded by the brain in terms of area–function features that yield particular acoustic end-products (Lubker and Gay, 1982). In kinematic terms, these area functions can be modeled by a series of constrictions along the length of the vocal tract that are executed using a large number of central mechanisms, including open-loop and feedback-dependent processes (Allen and Tsukahara, 1974; Eccles, 1977; Gurfinkel and Levik, 1979).

Evidence for goal orientation in the production of speech has been derived largely from research demonstrating that speakers are able to achieve articulatory and acoustic goals even in the face of considerable constraints placed on the articulators (Lubker and Gay, 1982). For example, the speech articulatory goal of lip rounding appears to be a learned, language-specific act (Abelin, Landberg, and Perrson, 1981). The motor goals represented by this act are chosen by the speaker as a part of learning his language. These speech motor goals are not "hard-wired" into the system at birth but are encoded within the CNS as the individual learns the communication system of the particular language into which he or she is born. A comparison of the lip rounding gesture in Swedish and American speakers indicates that Swedes move their lips farther, with greater velocity and with greater precision of goal achievement, than do American speakers. These data also suggest that different motor control strategies may be required when these labial movements are used in meaningful speech compared to when they are used in nonmeaningful vocalizations. These observations concerning the goals of labial protrusion are thought to be true for a number of other speech articulatory movements involving respiratory, laryngeal, velopharyngeal, and perioral structures.

Evarts (1982) suggested that afferent inputs mediated by forward-looking control systems (feed-forward) can give rise to articulatory compensations that are complete despite dynamic mechanical perturbations impinging on one or more components of the articulatory apparatus. The implication is that the brain encodes a representation of the goal of articulation and that afferent input is evaluated in terms of this goal. Therefore goal orientation is essential to voluntary movement because the articulatory movement goal depends on the coordination of a great variety of open-loop and closed-loop reflex processes (Jackson, 1874).

MOTOR EQUIVALENCE/ COMPENSATORY VOWEL ARTICULATION

Motor equivalence is defined as the capacity of a motor system to achieve the same end-product with considerable variation in the individual components that contribute to that output (Hebb, 1949). For achieving a particular vocal tract goal, the specific contributions of individual articulators may vary from one production of a particular element to another, so long as the desired end-product is achieved (Lashley, 1951; MacNeilage, 1970; Netsell et al., 1980).

Compensatory vowel articulation, presumably involving the operation of motor equivalence, is defined as the ability of speakers to generate acceptable vowel qualities despite a fixed position of the mandible. Producing vowels that require a relatively closed jaw position, such as /i/ or /u/, with a spacer held between the teeth to fix the jaw in an open position, confronts a speaker with a new, or at least a highly novel, task compared with producing the same vowel under normal, nonconstrained conditions. Several studies have shown that under such conditions speakers are able to produce vowels that are acoustically correct with regard to formant frequency locations already at the first glottal pulse (Gay, Lindblom, and Lubker, 1981; Lindblom and Sundberg, 1971; Lindblom, Lubker and Gay, 1979; Netsell, Kent, and Abbs, 1978). These studies have demonstrated that the tongue is capable of reorganizing motor output. An example of this phenomenon is shown in Figure 6-19. The reorganization in tongue height appears to be a goal-oriented process. In the example shown, compensatory adjustment in tongue height was maximum at points along the vocal tract where the normal vowel exhibited constrictions. At least for adult speakers, goal-oriented motor reorganization appears to require no learning, as speakers are able to produce the correct vowels under bite-block conditions on the first attempt, only a few seconds after inserting the bite-block, and being cued for what vowel to produce.

MOTOR PROGRAMS

Broadly defined, the term *motor program* refers to the differentiation of knowledge into an appropriate movement configuration for action. Early notions portrayed the motor program as operating independently of peripheral feedback (Keele, 1968). Contemporary hypotheses suggest that the motor program includes the organization and parameterization of muscle-specific forcing functions that can be influenced by afferent feedback (Evarts, Bizzi, Burke, DeLong, and Thach, 1971; Newell, 1978; Newell and Barclay, 1982; Sternberg, Monsell, Knoll, and Wright, 1978).

For the sake of discussion, consider the possibility that the motor program for speech is processed by the central nervous system in sub-

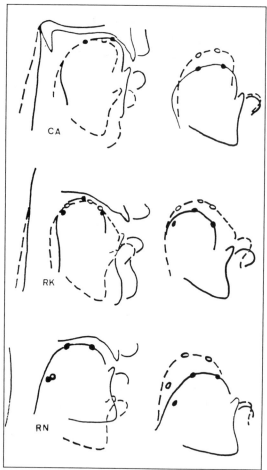

Fig. 6-19. Vowel reorganization. Midsagittal line drawings of the upper airway for /i/ vowel productions by three adult speakers. Left. Superimpositions of lips, tongue, and pharynx when the jaw was free to move (solid lines) and held in a fixed position (dashed lines). Right. Superimpositions of tongue shapes referenced to the jaw, showing the extent of adjustment made with the tongue to achieve the similar tongue positions on the left. (From Netsell, R., Kent, R. D., and Abbs, J. The organization and reorganization of speech movement. *Soc. Neurosci. Abstr.* 6:462, 1980.)

operation of motor programs is the mechanism of "switching" (Pearson, 1976). Pearson showed that "switching" the locomotion motor program from swing to stance is triggered by sensory input. Feedback during locomotion can be thought of as having two broad functions, the first being to switch the motor program from one phase to the next and the second being to modify the motor output within a single phase (Evarts, 1982). Tactile inputs are especially important for switching, and proprioceptive feedback provides continuous control of motoneuronal discharge during movement. From this example, one may hypothesize that the burst of afferent activity resulting from labial contact during the production of [p] may provide the triggering sensory input to "switch" the motor program to the next phase.

Another creative implementation of the "program" concept in the context of speech motor control has been offered by Grillner (1982). In this scheme, speech is modeled as a sequence of individual sounds, each of which is produced by highly automated learned motor programs. Learned and innate movements, in some cases, are thought to share common neural mechanisms. In the simplest case the neural substrate for a learned motor act may thus constitute only a slight modification of a basic innate motor program. Grillner's model implies that learned movements may result from a recombination of parts of different innate neural motor programs and other motor mechanisms.

units of varying complexity. As Evarts (1982) has suggested, central and peripheral sources of afferent information may be important for operation of the motor program. Additionally, afferent information may be involved in the selection, sequencing, and timing of subunits for motor planning and actual execution of the speech act.

Another interesting concept regarding the

OPEN-LOOP AND CLOSED-LOOP CONTROL SYSTEMS

Concerning closed-loop systems, Ito (1975) stated that: "Feedback control is the most basic form of engineering control wherein the output is returned to the input" (Fig. 6-20A). In contrast to closed-loop systems with outputs that nullify their inputs, open-loop control systems involve outputs that do not nullify the original signal but, instead, generate another signal (Fig. 6-20B). Applied to the orofacial complex, open-loop control would involve outputs from one structure (jaw) influencing the activity of another motor system (lips or tongue). In this scheme, information from any relevant receptor system available may be utilized, at the time a movement is planned, to "construct" an opti-

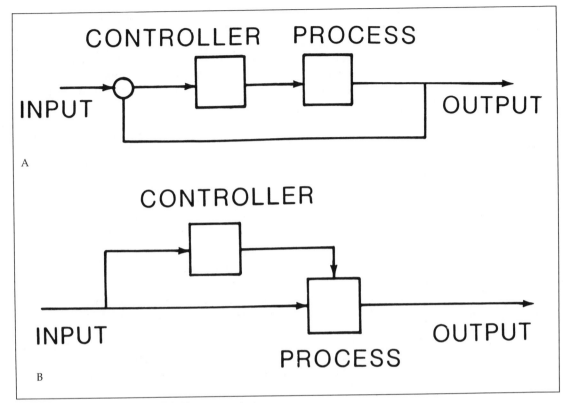

Fig. 6-20. Closed-loop versus open-loop control. A. Feedback (closed-loop) control system. B. Feedforward (open-loop) control system. (From Ito, M. The control mechanisms of cerebellar control systems. In F. O. Schmitt and F. G. Worden (eds.), *The Neurosciences: Third Study Program*. Boston: MIT Press, 1974.)

mized motor command (Ghez, 1979; Grillner, 1982; Weiss, 1941). Open-loop systems have the great advantage of speed; however, the precision of output in the affected structure depends on the internal calibration. Abbs and Gracco (1984) noted that "for control in a system where the boundaries are internal and hence extremely predictable (e.g., the coordinated movements for producing oral shapes for speech), open-loop prediction may be as precise as feedback with the additional advantages of speed and stability."

AFFERENT REGULATION OF MOTOR CORTEX OUTPUT

The notion that large, high-velocity movements and small, low-velocity movements may involve different control mechanisms is supported by the results of studies on motor cortex activity (Evarts and Fromm, 1978; Fromm and Evarts, 1977). Precentral neuron responses to kinesthetic stimuli are enhanced during accurate positioning and controlled fine movement but depressed just before and during ballistic movement. Thus there are marked changes in motor cortex responses to feedback depending on the movement strategy at the time feedback was delivered.

As reviewed earlier in this chapter, afferent feedback is especially important for modulating motor cortex output during precise control. During such fine movements motor cortex neurons are influenced by closed-loop negative feedback, as evidenced by their intense modulation to sensory feedback from the hand (Evarts, 1982). However, these motor cortex neurons may, depending on the context and goals of the situation, shift from being controlled by the negative feedback pathway to being controlled by central programs that are themselves triggered by afferent stimuli.

For movements of the articulatory apparatus, it is apparent that the initial set or preparatory state of the subject is of critical significance for determining the short latency responses that occur as a result of afferent inputs during movement. One must presume that each particular form of motor behavior has an associated central state that selects the afferent inputs to be employed in controlling movement. For articulation there is presumably an analogous process but with the difference that a great number of subunits of the motor program can be called up by any of a large number of different sorts of afferent stimuli.

EFFERENCE COPY

Efference copy provides the central nervous system with a comparator by which intended motor output can be compared with actual output (von Holst, 1954). Specifically, voluntary movements are thought to involve two sets of signals, both of which are feed-forward in operation. The first neural signal is directed to the effector organs (muscles), and a second simultaneous "copy" signal is sent to sensory systems that preset the sensory system for the anticipated consequences of the motor act (Kelso and Stelmach, 1976).

Considerable progress has been made concerning the pathways that may mediate an efference copy mechanism. Anatomic studies have shown that the input to the pontine nuclei (and other relays to cerebellum) is considerably stronger from sensorimotor cortex (SI and MI) than from association areas. This result in turn favors a major role for the cerebrocerebellar projection in relation to providing the cerebellum with efference copy signals from MI together with sensory feedback from SI (Evarts, 1982). As movement occurs, the efference copy signals from motor cortex to cerebellum would be compared to feedback signals reaching the cerebellum from SI, and error signals would be returned to MI via the dentate nucleus and ventrolateral thalamus (Dhanarajan, Ruegg, and Wiesendanger, 1977).

During efference copy, the nervous system utilizes information about issued motor commands (Grillner, 1982). During speech, rapid sequences of different motor acts (sounds and gestures) follow each other. Each motor act cor-

responds to a critical configuration of the oral cavity. The brain obviously "knows" not only which "speech gesture" it is planning but also which one is carried out at that particular instance. Information about the expected "oral configuration" in any given instance is thus continuously available. It would be surprising if the central nervous system did not utilize this information to "design" the command signal to reach the new target in the most expedient way. Efference copy information and afferent information used to "construct" movements are well suited for a system controlling rapid motor sequences (Grillner, 1982).

PATHWAYS TRANSMITTING CENTRAL PROGRAMS TO MI

In addition to cerebellum and basal ganglia, association areas of the cerebral cortex are potential sources of central programs reaching MI (Arbib, 1981). The planning and management role of the motor program is relatively unimpaired in the performance of Holmes' cerebellar patients despite the gross impairment of the feed-forward component of the pointing control system(s).

The lateral cerebellum is important for events occurring just before and after movement onset. Long-term goals are probably subserved by secondary motor areas or by the basal ganglia. As reviewed earlier in the chapter, cerebellar projections to the thalamus are directly relayed to MI via the thalamic nucleus VPLo, whereas regions of the thalamus receiving inputs from the globus pallidus project in large part to the premotor cortex (supplementary motor area and lateral area 6), areas that in turn project to MI via corticocortical connections. Therefore the initiation of movement involves prefrontal, temporal, and parietal association cortex projections via striatum and globus pallidus to the ventrolateral and ventroanterior regions of the thalamus and thence to premotor cortex (Brooks, 1979). This sequence implies that discharges of the premotor cortex would precede (for centrally programmed movement) activity in MI or deep cerebellar nuclei. Therefore during the initial phases of a centrally programmed movement it is possible for corticomotoneurons in MI to be influenced by cells in the premotor area (via corticocortical inputs) and from the cerebellum (via the cerebello-thalamo-cortical pathway). It is also possible for activity to occur in the dentate nucleus of the cerebellum prior to discharge of neurons in MI (via projections from premotor cortex-pontine nuclei-dentate), as observed by Thach (1975) in the case of ballistic arm movements in the monkey. This particular example illustrates the importance of prior instruction when selecting the appropriate neural pathways for reflex and intended movements.

A study examining the effects of cerebellar cooling on MI responses to limb displacements has provided further evidence for separate pathways underlying the reflex and intended components of MI discharge (Vilis, Hore, Meyer-Lohmann, and Brooks, 1976). MI neuron responses to limb displacements consist in an early reflex phase of discharge (20 to 50 ms) followed by a second phase of response (50 to 100 ms). This second phase corresponds to what has been referred to above as the intended or centrally programmed component of MI output. Cerebellar nuclear cooling did not affect the early component of the MI feedback-dependent response. Cerebellar nuclear cooling did, however, decrease the second phase of MI activity, thereby indicating a role for the cerebellum in the central programming of movement.

CENTRAL PATTERN GENERATION

A pattern generator may be thought of as a highly organized set of neurons that when activated yields a relatively stereotypic response such as locomotion or breathing. This concept has been applied to the control of more discrete, fractionated motor acts as well. For example, if all neurons in a given spinal network that normally act to flex and extend the upper limb are activated, locomotion results. If only some of these neurons are activated, another motor act results, e.g., finger movement or shoulder flexion. During evolution, more precise control of smaller fractions of pattern generators may account for the movement precision associated with manipulation and speech (Grillner, 1982).

There are well developed motor systems for mastication and swallowing, with the pattern-generating networks residing mainly in the brainstem (Lund et al., 1982). Sound production results from a concomitant control of the respiratory airflow and the shape of the oral cavity. Grillner (1982) suggested that the innate programs to control different sound sequences in animals may result from the coordinated actions of the respiratory brainstem pattern generator and fractions of the central pattern generators for mastication and swallowing. Given the diversity of sound production in humans, it logically follows that the central nervous system would require separate access to small fractions of the respective pattern generators and perhaps directly to some motoneurons. Grillner also stated that learning of a sound motor program for speech would involve learning to combine in time the appropriate fractions of the motor apparatus.

SUMMARY AND RESEARCH DIRECTIONS

Our understanding of the neural pathways involved in the planning and execution of simple voluntary movements is meager at best. The flow diagram shown in Figure 6-21 represents some of the key neural elements (relay nuclei and specialized areas of the brain) that are important for the planning, programming, and execution of movements, including those of the vocal tract for speech production. Neurophysiologic specification of speech movement control is limited, for the most part, to hypotheses and general principles adapted from limb motor control. In the future, collection of certain types of data should be emphasized to remedy this informational lacuna.

Physiologic studies in animals are especially needed to characterize the firing patterns of central nervous system neurons during natural oral communication behaviors (e.g., vocalization) and to relate those patterns to peripheral variables such as individual muscle contractions or parameters of the vocalization. Special emphasis should be placed on recordings during natural or conditioned vocalizations rather than using electrically elicited calls in anesthetized subjects, as there is serious question about the ability of electrical stimulation to produce patterns of normal vocal tract control. Anatomic studies are needed to determine cell classes

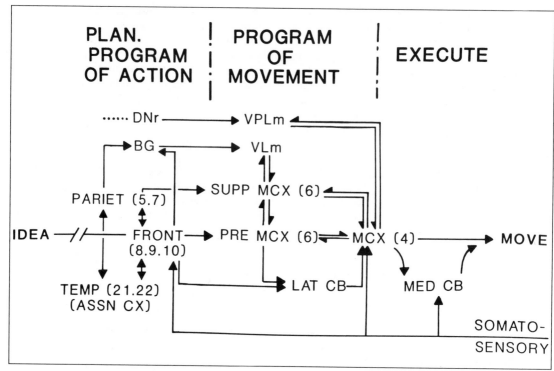

Fig. 6-21. Pathways for planning, control, and execution of voluntary movement. BG = basal ganglia; DNr = dentate nucleus of cerebellum; FRONT = frontal cortex (areas 8, 9, and 10); LAT CB = lateral cerebellum; MED CB = medial cerebellum; MCX = motor cortex (area 4); PARIET = parietal cortex (areas 5 and 7); PRE MCX = premotor cortex (area 6); SUPP MCX = supplementary motor cortex (area 6); TEMP = temporal association cortex (areas 21 and 22); VLm = medial part of the ventral lateral thalamic nucleus; VPLm = medial part of the ventral posterior lateral thalamic nucleus. (Modified from Allen, G. I., and Tsukahara, N. Cerebrocerebellar communication systems. *Physiol. Rev.* 54:957, 1974; and Kubota, K. An introduction to "voluntary movement and the brain." *Adv. Neurol. Sci.* 28:3, 1984.)

within the vocal tract controlling nuclei and the topography of connections between nuclei and specific cell types. A problem not adequately addressed in most anatomic studies is whether the tracer injections are labeling vocalization-specific neural pathways rather than other neurons and fibers of passage that happen to be in the same area. This problem is critical in some structures, such as the periaqueductal gray, where only a small portion of the nucleus appears to be devoted to vocal tract control. Anatomic tract tracing from physiologically characterized sites and the complementary use of anterograde and retrograde markers would probably be of particular utility here. In addition, studies aimed at understanding the physiologic and anatomic bases for coordination between vocal tract articulator systems may prove informative.

Finally, future studies of disordered speech motor control that combine modern brain imaging techniques (including magnetic resonance imaging, computed tomography, positron emission tomography) with basic and process-oriented studies of speech physiology are needed.

REFERENCES

Abbs, J. H., and Gracco, V. L. Compensatory responses to low magnitude loads applied to the lower lip during speech. *J. Acoust. Soc. Am.* 70(suppl. 1):S78, 1981.

Abbs, J. H., and Cole, K. L. Consideration of bulbar and suprabulbar afferent influences upon speech motor coordination and programming. In S. Grillner, B. Lindblom, J. Lubker, and A. Persson (eds.), *Speech Motor Control.* Oxford: Pergamon Press, 1982.

Abbs, J. H., and Gracco, V. L. Sensorimotor actions in the control of multimovement speech gestures. *Trends Neurosci.* 6:391, 1983.

Abbs, J. H., Hunker, C., and Barlow, S. M. Differential speech motor subsystem impairments in subjects with suprabulbar lesions: neurological framework and supporting data. In W. Berry (ed.), *Clinical Dysarthria.* San Diego: College-Hill Press, 1983.

Abbs, J. H., and Gracco, V. L. Control of complex motor gestures: orofacial muscle responses to load perturbations of the lip during speech. *J. Neurophysiol.* 51:705, 1984.

Abbs, J. H., Gracco, V. L., and Cole, K. J. Control of multimovement coordination: sensorimotor mechanisms in speech motor programming. *J. Motor Behav.* 16:195, 1984.

Abbs, J. H., and Welt, C. Lateral precentral cortex in speech motor control. In R. G. Daniloff (ed.), *Recent Advances in Speech Science.* San Diego: College-Hill Press, 1985.

Abelin, A., Landberg, I., and Perrson, L. A study of anticipatory labial coarticulation in the speech of children. In: *PERILUS 2. Phonetic Experimental Research at the Institute of Linguistics. University of Stockholm.* Stockholm: University of Stockholm, 1981.

Adametz, J., and O'Leary, J. L. Experimental mutism resulting from periaqueductal lesions in cats. *Neurology* 9:636, 1959.

Aitken, P. G. Cortical control of conditioned and spontaneous vocal behavior in rhesus monkeys. *Brain Lang.* 13:171, 1981.

Albe-Fessard, D., and Liebeskind, J. Origine des messages somato-sensitifs activant les cellules du cortex moteur chez le singe. *Exp. Brain Res.* 1:127, 1966.

Allen, G. I., and Tsukahara, N. Cerebrocerebellar communication systems. *Physiol. Rev.* 54:957, 1974.

Appenteng, K., Morimoto, T., and Taylor, A. Fusimotor activity in masseter nerve of the cat during reflex jaw movement. *J. Physiol. (Lond).* 305:415, 1980.

Arbib, M. A. Perceptual structures and distributed motor control. In V. B. Brooks (ed.), *Handbook of Physiology. The Nervous System* (Vol. 2, Sect. 1, Pt. 2). Bethesda: American Physiological Society, 1981.

Asanuma, H., and Sakata, H. Functional organization of a cortical efferent system examined with focal depth stimulation in cats. *J. Neurophysiol.* 30:35, 1967.

Asanuma, H., and Rosen, I. Topographical organization of cortical efferent zones projecting to distal forelimb muscles in the monkey. *Exp. Brain Res.* 14:243, 1972.

Asanuma, H. Cerebral cortical control of movement. *Physiologist* 16:143, 1973.

Asanuma, H., and Arnold, A. P. Noxious effects of excessive currents used for intracortical microstimulation. *Brain Res.* 96:103, 1975.

Asanuma, C., Thach, W. T., and Jones, E. G. Cytoarchitectonic delineation of the ventral lateral thalamic region in the monkey. *Brain Res. Rev.* 5:219, 1983a.

Asanuma, C., Thach, W. T., and Jones, E. G. Distribution of cerebellar terminations in the ventral lateral thalamic region of the monkey. *Brain Res. Rev.* 5:237, 1983b.

Asanuma, C., Thach, W. T., and Jones, E. G. Anatomical evidence for segregated focal groupings of efferent cells and their terminal ramifications in the cerebellothalamic pathway of the monkey. *Brain Res. Rev.* 5:267, 1983c.

Baer, T. Investigation of the phonatory mechanism: proceedings of the conference on the assessment of vocal pathology. *Am. Speech Hear. Assoc. Rep.* 11:38, 1981.

Bancaud, J., and Talairach, J. Organisation fonctionelle de l'aire motrice supplementaire: endeignements apportes par la stereo EEG. *Neurochirurgie* 13:343, 1967.

Barlow, S. M., and Abbs, J. H. Some evidence of auditory feedback contribution to the ongoing control of speech production. Presented at the American Speech and Hearing Association, San Francisco, 1978.

Barlow, S. M. Some effects of auditory sidetone disruption upon ongoing speech production. Master's thesis, University of Wisconsin, 1980.

Barlow, S. M. Impaired control of orofacial muscle force in congenital spasticity. Abstracts of the Society for Neuroscience. 8:953, 1982a.

Barlow, S. M., and Abbs, J. H. Impaired regulation of orofacial force in adults with congenital spasticity. Presented at the American Speech and Hearing Association Convention, Toronto, 1982b.

Barlow, S. M., and Abbs, J. H. Force transducers for the evaluation of labial, lingual, and mandibular motor impairments. *J. Speech Hear. Res.* 26:616, 1983.

Barlow, S. M. Fine force and position control of select limb and orofacial structures in the upper motor neuron syndrome. Doctoral dissertation, University of Wisconsin, 1984.

Barlow, S. M., and Abbs, J. H. Orofacial fine motor control impairments in congenital spasticity: evidence against hypertonus related performance deficits. *J. Neurol.* 34:145, 1984.

Barlow, S. M., and Rath, E. M. Maximum voluntary closing forces in the upper and lower lips of humans. *J. Speech Hear. Res.* 28:373, 1985.

Barlow, S. M., and Abbs, J. H. Fine force and position control of select orofacial structures in the upper motor neuron syndrome. *Exp. Neurol.* 94:699, 1986.

Barlow, S. M., and Netsell, R. Differential fine force control of the upper and lower lips. *J. Speech Hear. Res.* 29:163, 1986a.

Barlow, S. M., and Netsell, R. Force biasing of the perioral reflex. In: *Abstracts of the Association for Research in Otolaryngology,* 9:135, 1986b.

Barlow, S. M., and Netsell, R. Mechanically evoked responses of perioral muscles during fine force control. Abstract, 16th Annual Meeting of the Society for Neuroscience, Washington, DC, 16:1539, 1986c.

Barlow, S. M., Netsell, R., and Hunker, C. J. Phonatory disorders associated with CNS lesions. In C. W. Cummings, J. M. Fredrickson, L. A. Harker, E. J. Krause, and D. E. Schuller (eds.), *Otolaryngology—Head and Neck Surgery* (Vol. 3). St. Louis: Mosby, 1986.

Barlow, S. M. Mechanical frequency detection thresholds in the human face. *Exp. Neurol.* 96:253, 1987.

Barlow, S. M. The relation between probe contactor area and the mechanically evoked perioral reflex. Abstract for the Association for Research in Otolaryngology. February V.11:220, 1988.

Barlow, S. M., and Burton, M. Orofacial force control impairments in brain-injured adults. Abstract for the Association for Research in Otolaryngology. 11:218, 1988.

Barlow, S. M., and Hunker, C. Unpublished data. Omaha: Boys Town National Institute, 1988.

Bauer, L. Peripheral control and mechanical properties of the lips during speech. Master's thesis, University of Wisconsin, 1974.

Bignall, K. E., and Imbert, M. Polysensory and corticocortical projections to frontal lobe of squirrel and rhesus monkeys. *Electroencephalogr. Clin. Neurophysiol.* 26:206, 1969.

Blair, C., and Smith, A. EMG recording in human lip muscles: can single muscles be isolated? *J. Speech Hear. Res.* 29:256, 1986.

Botez, M. I., and Barbeau, A. Role of subcortical structures and particularly of the thalamus, in the mechanisms of speech and language. *Int. J. Neurol.* 8:300, 1971.

Bowman, J. P. Muscle spindles in the intrinsic and extrinsic muscles of the rhesus monkey's (Macaca mulatta) tongue. *Anat. Rec.* 161:483, 1968.

Bowman, J. P., and Combs, C. M. The cerebrocortical projection of hypoglossal afferents. *Exp. Neurol.* 23:291, 1969a.

Bowman, J. P., and Combs, C. M. The thalamic projection of hypoglossal afferents in the rhesus monkey. *Exp. Neurol.* 25:509, 1969b.

Bowman, J. P. *The Muscle Spindle and Neural Control of the Tongue. Implications for Speech.* Springfield, IL: Charles C Thomas, 1971.

Bowman, J. P. Lingual mechanoreceptive information. I. An evoked-potential study of the central projections of hypoglossal nerve afferent information. *J. Speech Hear. Res.* 25:348, 1982.

Bratzlavsky, M. The connections between muscle afferents and motoneurons of the muscles of mastication. In D. J. Anderson and B. Matthews (eds.), *Mastication*. Bristol: Wright, 1976.

Bratzlavsky, M. Feedback control of human lip muscle. *Exp. Neurol.* 65:209, 1979.

Brinkman, C., and Porter, R. Supplementary motor area in the monkey: activity of neurons during performance of a learned motor task. *J. Neurophysiol.* 42:681, 1978.

Brooks, V. B. Motor programs revisited. In R. E. Talbott and D. R. Humphrey (eds.), *Posture and Movement: Perspective for Integrating Sensory and Motor Research on the Mammalian Nervous System.* New York: Raven Press, 1979.

Brooks, V. B., and Thach, W. T. Cerebellar control of posture and movement. In V. B. Brooks (ed.), *Handbook of Physiology, Sect. 1: The Nervous System. Vol. 2: Motor Control.* Bethesda: American Physiological Society, 1981.

Carpenter, M. B., and McMasters, R. E. Lesions of the substantia nigra in the rhesus monkey: efferent fiber degeneration and behavioral observations. *Am. J. Anat.* 114:293, 1964.

Carpenter, M. B., and Strominger, N. L. Efferent fiber projections of the subthalamic nucleus in the rhesus monkey: a comparison of the efferent projections of the subthalamic nucleus, substantia nigra, and globus pallidus. *Am. J. Anat.* 121:41, 1967.

Carpenter, M. B., and Peter, P. Nigrostriatal and nigrothalamic fibers in the rhesus monkey. *J. Comp. Neurol.* 144:93, 1972.

Carpenter, M. B., Nakano, K., and Kim, R. Nigrothalamic projections in the monkey demonstrated by autoradiographic techniques. *J. Comp. Neurol.* 165:401, 1976.

Carpenter, M. B., Carleton, S. C., Keller, J. T., and Conte, P. Connections of the subthalamic nucleus in the monkey. *Brain Res.* 224:1, 1981.

Chambers, M. R., Andres, K. H., von During, M., and Iggo, A. Structure and function of the slowly adapting type II mechanoreceptor in hairy skin. *Q. J. Exp. Physiol.* 57:417, 1972.

Chase, M. H., Sterman, M. B., Kubota, K., and Clemente, C. D. Modulation of masseteric and digastric neural activity by stimulation of the dorsolateral cerebral cortex in the squirrel monkey. *Exp. Neurol.* 41:277, 1973.

Clark, R. W., and Luschei, E. S. Short latency jaw movement produced by low intensity intracortical microstimulation of the precentral face area in monkeys. *Brain Res.* 70:144, 1973.

Cody, F. W. J., Harrison, L. M., and Taylor, A. Analysis of activity of muscle spindles of jaw closing muscles during normal movements in the cat. *J. Physiol. (Lond)* 253:565, 1975.

Cohen, M. I. Central determinants of respiratory rhythm. *Annu. Rev. Physiol.* 43:91, 1981.

Cole, K. J., and Abbs, J. H. Intentional responses to kinesthetic stimuli in orofacial muscles: implications for the coordination of speech movements. *J. Neurosci.* 3:2660, 1983.

Cooper, S. Muscle spindles in the intrinsic muscles of the human tongue. *J. Physiol.* 122:193, 1953.

Craggs, M. D., Rushton, D. N., and Clayton, D. G. The stability of the electrical stimulation map of the motor cortex of the anaesthetized baboon. *Brain* 99:575, 1976.

Damasio, A. R., and Van Hoesen, G. W. Structure and function of the supplementary motor area. *Neurology* 30:359, 1980.

Darian-Smith, I. Neural mechanisms of facial sensation. *Int. Rev. Neurobiol.* 9:301, 1966.

Davis, P. J., and Nail, B. S. On the location and size of laryngeal motoneurons in the cat and rabbit. *J. Comp. Neurol.* 230:13, 1984.

Delgado-Garcia, J. A., Lopez-Varneo, J., Serra, R., and Gonzalez-Baron, S. Electrophysiological and functional identification of different neuronal types within the nucleus ambiguus in the cat. *Brain Res.* 177:231, 1983.

Dellow, P. G., and Lund, J. P. Evidence for central timing of rhythmical mastication. *J. Physiol. (Lond)* 215:1, 1971.

Denny-Brown, D. Preface: historical aspects of the relation of spasticity to movement. In R. G. Feldman, R. R. Young, and W. P. Koella (eds.), *Spasticity: Disordered Motor Control.* Chicago: Year Book Medical Publishers, 1980.

DeRosier, E. A., Ortega, J. D., Park, S., and Larson, C. R. Effects of PAG stimulation on laryngeal EMG and vocalization in the awake monkey. In: *Society for Neuroscience Abstracts, 1987.*

Desmedt, J. E. (ed.), *Cerebral Motor Control in Man: Long*

Loop Mechanisms, Vol. 4: Progress in Neurophysiology. Basel: Karger, 1978.

DeVito, J. L., and Anderson, M. E. An autoradiographic study of efferent connections of the globus pallidus in Macaca mulatta. *Exp. Brain Res.* 46:107, 1982.

Dhanarajan, P., Ruegg, D. G., and Wiesendanger, M. An anatomical investigation of the corticopontine projection in the primate (Saimiri sciureus): the projection from motor and somatosensory areas. *Neuroscience* 2:913, 1977.

Dickson, D. R., and Maue-Dickson, W. *Anatomical and Physiological Bases of Speech.* Boston: Little, Brown, 1982.

Dull, C. E., Metcalfe, H. C., and Williams, J. E. *Modern Physics.* New York: Holt, Rinehart & Winston, 1963.

Dusser de Barenne, J. G., Garol, H. W., and McCulloch, W. S. The motor cortex of the chimpanzee. *J. Neurophysiol.* 4:287, 1941.

Eccles, J. C. *The Understanding of the Brain* (2nd ed.). New York: McGraw-Hill, 1977.

Egel, R. T., Bowman, J. P., and Combs, C. M. Calibre spectra of the lingual and hypoglossal nerves of the rhesus monkey. *J. Comp. Neurol.* 134:163, 1969.

Ekbom, K., Jernelius, M., and Kugelberg, E. Perioral reflexes. *Nuerology* 2:103, 1952.

Essick, G. K., and Whitsel, B. L. Factors influencing cutaneous directional sensitivity: a correlative psychophysical and neurophysiological investigation. *Brain Res. Rev.* 10:213, 1985.

Essick, G. K., Starr, G. M., Dolan, P. J., and Afferica, T. S. Evaluation of directional sensitivity within the mental nerve distribution. *J. Dent. Res.* 66:157, 1987 (abstract 406).

Essick, G. K., Afferica, T., Aldershof, B., Nestor, J. Kelly, D., and Whitsel, B. Human perioral directional sensitivity. *Exp. Neurol.* 100:506, 1988.

Essick, G. K., Franzen, O., and Whitsel, B. L. Tactile velocity discrimination. *Somatosens. Res.* 1988 (in press).

Essick, G. K., and McGuire, M. H. Long-range and short-range processes in tactile motion perception. *J. Neurosci.* 1988 (in press).

Evarts, E. V. Relation of pyramidal tract activity to force exerted during voluntary movement. *J. Neurophysiol.* 31:14, 1968.

Evarts, E. V., Bizzi, E., Burke, E., DeLong, M., and Thach, W. T. Central control of movement. *Neurosci. Res. Prog. Bull.* Cambridge, MA: M.I.T. Press, 1971.

Evarts, E. V., and Fromm, C. The pyramidal tract neuron as summing point in a closed-loop control system in the monkey. In J. E. Desmedt (ed.), *Cerebral Motor Control in Man: Long Loop Mechanisms, Progress in Clinical Neurophysiology* (Vol. 4). Basel: Karger, 1978.

Evarts, E. V. Role of motor cortex in voluntary movements in primates. In V. B. Brooks (ed.), *Handbook of Physiology, Sect. 1: The Nervous System. Vol. 2: Motor Control.* Bethesda: American Physiological Society, 1981a.

Evarts, E. V. Functional studies of the motor cortex. In F. O. Schmitt, F. G. Worden, G. Adelman, and S. G. Dennis (eds.), *Organization of the Cerebral Cortex.* Cambridge, MA: MIT Press, 1981b.

Evarts, E. V. Analogies between central motor programs for speech and for limb movements. In S. Grillner, B. Lindblom, J. Lubker, and A. Persson (eds.), *Speech Motor Control.* Oxford: Pergamon Press, 1982.

Evarts, E. V., Shinoda, A., and Wise, S. P. *Neurophysiological Approaches to Higher Brain Functions.* New York: Wiley, 1984. P. 198.

Evarts, E. V. Transcortical reflexes: their properties and functional significance. In A. W. Goodwin and I. Darian-Smith (eds.) Hand Function and the Neocortex. Berlin: Springer-Verlag, 1985.

Ferrier, D. Experimental researches in cerebral physiology and pathology. *Western Riding Lunatics Asylum Medical Report* (Vol. 3). 1873. Pp. 30–96.

Fetz, E. E., Cheney, P. D., and German, D. C. Corticomotoneuronal connections of precentral cells detected by postspike averages of EMG activity in behaving monkeys. *Brain Res.* 114:505, 1976.

Fink, B. R., and Demarest, R. J. *Laryngeal Biomechanics.* Cambridge, MA: Harvard University Press, 1978.

Fitzgerald, M. J. T., and Sachithanandan, S. R. The structure and source of lingual proprioceptors in the monkey. *J. Anat.* 128:523, 1979.

Folkins, J., and Abbs, J. H. Lip and jaw motor control during speech: motor reorganization responses to external interference. Presented at the Acoustical Society of America meeting, Los Angeles, 1973.

Folkins, J., and Abbs, J. Lip and jaw motor control during speech: responses to resistive loading of the jaw. *J. Speech Hear. Res.* 18:207, 1975.

Folkins, J., and Abbs, J. Additional observations on responses to resistive loading of the jaw. *J. Speech Hear. Res.* 19:820, 1976.

Folkins, J. M., and Larson, C. R. In search of a tonic vibration reflex in the human lip. *Brain Res.* 151:409, 1978.

Folkins, J., and Zimmerman, G. Lip and jaw interaction during speech: responses to perturbation of lower-lip movement prior to bilabial closure. *J. Acoust. Soc. Am.* 71:1225, 1982.

Franzen, E. A., and Myers, R. E. Neural control of social behavior: prefrontal and anterior temporal cortex. *Neuropsychology* 11:141, 1973.

Friedman, D. P., and Jones, E. G. Thalamic input to areas 3a and 2 in monkeys. *J. Neurophysiol.* 45:59, 1981.

Fritsch, G., and Hitzig, E. Uber die elektrische Erregbarkeit des Grosshirns. *Arch. Anat. Physiol. Wiss. Med.* 37:300, 1870. [Translated by G. von Bonin. In W. W. Nowinski (ed.), *The Cerebral Cortex.* Springfield, IL: Charles C Thomas, 1960. Pp. 73–96.]

Fromm, C., and Evarts, E. V. Relation of motor cortex neurons to precisely controlled and ballistic movements. *Neurosci. Lett.* 5:259, 1977.

Fucci, D. Oral vibrotactile sensation: an evaluation of normal and defective speakers. *J. Speech Hear. Res.* 15:179, 1972.

Fulton, J. F. *Physiology of the Nervous System* (3rd ed.). New York: Oxford University Press, 1949.

Gandiglio, C., and Fra, L. Further observations on facial reflexes. *J. Neurol. Sci.* 5:173, 1967.

Garrett, D., and Luschei, E. S. Subglottic pressure modulation during evoked phonation in the anesthetized cat. In T. Baer, C. Sasaki, and K. Harris (eds.), *Laryngeal Function in Phonation and Respira-*

tion. Boston: College-Hill Press, 1987.

Gay, T., Lindblom, B., and Lubker, J. Production of bite-block vowels: acoustic equivalence by selective compensation. *J. Acoust. Soc. Am.* 69:802, 1981.

Geschwind, W. Disconnexion syndromes in animals and man. Part II. *Brain* 88:585, 1965.

Ghez, C. Contributions of central programs to rapid limb movement in the cat. In H. Asanuma and V. J. Wilson (eds.), *Integration in the Nervous System.* Tokyo: Igaku-Shoin, 1979.

Gilman, S., and Marco. L. A. Effects of medullary pyramidotomy in the monkey. I. Clinical and electromyographic abnormalities. *Brain* 94:495, 1971.

Gilman, S., Marco, L. A., and Ebel, H. C. Effects of medullary pyramidotomy in the monkey. II. Abnormalities of spindle afferent responses. *Brain* 94:515, 1971.

Goodwin, G. M., and Luschei, E. S. Discharge of spindle afferents from jaw-closing muscles during chewing in alert monkeys. *J. Neurophysiol.* 38:560, 1975.

Goodwin, G. M., Hoffman, D., and Luschei, E. S. The strength of the reflex response to sinusoidal stretch of monkey jaw closing muscles during voluntary contraction. *J. Physiol. (Lond)* 279:81, 1978.

Gracco, V. L., and Abbs, J. H. Dynamic control of the perioral system during speech: kinematic analyses of autogenic sensorimotor processes. *J. Neurophysiol.* 54:418, 1985.

Gray, H. *Gray's Anatomy* (15th ed.). New York: Bounty Books, 1977.

Green, J. H., and Neil, E. The respiratory function of the laryngeal muscles. *J. Physiol. (Lond)* 129:134, 1955.

Grillner, S. Possible analogies in the control of innate motor acts and the production of sound in speech. In S. Grillner, B. Lindblom, J. Lubker, and A. Persson (eds.), *Speech Motor Control.* New York: Pergamon Press, 1982.

Gurfinkel, V. S., and Levik, Y. S. Sensory complexes and sensorimotor integration. *Fiziol. Cheloveka* 5:399, 1979.

Haaxma, R., and Kuypers, H. G. J. M. Intrahemispheric cortical connexions and visual guidance of hand and finger movements in the rhesus monkey. *Brain* 98:239, 1975.

Halata, Z., and Munger, B. L. The sensory innervation of primate facial skin. II. Vermillion border and mucosa of lip. *Brain Res. Rev.* 5:81, 1983.

Hallett, M., Shahani, B. T., and Young, R. R. Analysis of stereotyped voluntary movements at the elbow in patients with Parkinson's disease. *J. Neurol. Neurosurg. Psychiatry* 40:1129, 1977.

Hammond, P. H. Involuntary activity in biceps following the sudden application of velocity to the abducted forearm. *J. Physiol. (Lond)* 127:23, 1955.

Hammond, P. H. The influence of prior instruction to the subject on an apparently involuntary neuromuscular response. *J. Physiol. (Lond)* 132:17, 1956.

Hannam, A. G., Matthews, B., and Yemm, R. The unloading reflex in masticatory muscles of man. *Arch. Oral Biol.* 13:361, 1968.

Harris, D. M. Forward masking and recovery from short-term adaptation in single auditory-nerve fibers. Doctoral dissertation, Northwestern University, 1977.

Harrison, F., and Corbin, K. B. The central pathway for the jaw-jerk. *Am. J. Physiol.* 135:439, 1942.

Hasegawa, A., McCutcheon, M. J., Wolf, M. B., and Fletcher, S. G. *J. Acoust. Soc. Am.* 59:S85, 1976.

Hast, M. H., and Globus, S. Physiology of the lateral cricoarytenoid muscle. *Pract. Otol. Rhinol. Laryngol.* 33:209, 1971.

Hebb, D. O. *The Organization of Behavior. A Neuropsychological Theory.* New York: Wiley, 1949.

Heilman, K. M. Apraxia. In K. M. Heilman and E. Valenstein (eds.), *Clinical Neuropsychology.* New York: Oxford University Press, 1979.

Hepp-Reymond, M-C., Wyss, U. R., and Anner, R. Neuronal coding of static force in the primate motor cortex. *J. Physiol. (Paris)* 74:287, 1978.

Hirano, M., Vennard, W., and Ohala, J. Regulation of register, pitch and intensity of voice: an electromyographic investigation of intrinsic laryngeal muscles. *Folia Phoniatr. (Basel)* 22:1, 1970.

Hirose, H., Kiritani, S., Ushijima, T., and Sawashima, M. Analysis of abnormal articulatory dynamics in two dysarthric patients. *J. Speech Hear. Disord.* 43:96, 1978.

Hixon, T., Mead, J., and Klatt, D. H. Influence of forced transglottal pressure changes on vocal fundamental frequency. *J. Acoust. Soc. Am.* 49:105, 1971.

Hixon, T. J., Goldman, M. D., and Mead, J. Kinematics of the chest wall during speech production: volume displacements of the rib cage, abdomen, and lung. *J. Speech and Hear. Res.* 16:78, 1973.

Hixon, T. J., Mead, J., and Goldman, M. D. Dynamics of the chest wall during speech production: function of the thorax, rib cage, diaphragm, and abdomen. *J. Speech Hear. Res.* 19:297, 1976.

Hixon, T. J. Respiratory function in speech. In T. J. Hixon (ed.), *Respiratory Function in Speech and Song.* Boston: College-Hill Press, 1987.

Hixon, T. J., Mead, J., and Goldman, M. D. Dynamics of the chest wall during speech production: function of the thorax, rib cage, diaphragm, and abdomen. In T. J. Hixon (ed.), *Respiratory Function in Speech and Song.* Boston: College-Hill Press, 1987.

Hoffman, D. S. Responses of monkey precentral cortical cells during a controlled jaw bite task. Dissertation, University of Washington, Seattle, 1977.

Hoffman, D. S., and Luschei, E. S. Responses of monkey precentral cortical cells during a controlled jaw bite task. *J. Neurophysiol.* 44:333, 1980.

Hore, J., and Vilis, T. Loss of set in muscle responses to limb perturbations during cerebellar dysfunction. *J. Neurophysiol.* 51:1137, 1984.

Horne, M. K., and Tracey, D. J. The afferents and projections of the ventroposterolateral thalamus in the monkey. *Exp. Brain Res.* 36:129, 1979.

Houk, J., and Rymer, W. Neural control of muscle length and tension. In V. B. Brooks (ed.), *Handbook of Physiology. The Nervous System.* (Vol. 2, Sect. 1, Pt. 1). Bethesda: American Physiological Society, 1981.

Hugelin, A. Anatomical organization of bulbopontine respiratory oscillators. *Fed. Proc.* 36:2390, 1977.

Hughes, O. M., and Abbs, J. H. Labial-mandibular coordination in the production of speech: implications for the operation of motor equivalence. *Phonetica* 33:199, 1976.

Humphrey, D. R., Schmidt, E. M., and Thompson, W. D. Predicting measures of motor performance from multiple cortical spike trains. *Science* 179:758, 1970.

Hunker, C. J., and Abbs, J. H. Respiratory movement control during speech: evidence for motor equivalence. *Soc. Neurosci. Abstr.* 8:946, 1982.

Hunker, C. J., Abbs, J. H., and Barlow, S. M. The relationship between parkinsonian rigidity and hypokinesia in the orofacial system: a quantitative analysis. *Neurology* 32:755, 1982.

Hunker, C. J., and Abbs, J. H. Parkinsonian resting tremor and its relationship to movement initiation delays. *Soc. Neurosci. Abst.*, 10:906, 1984.

Hunker, C. J., and Abbs, J. H. Reaction time and movement time deficits in parkinsonian patients. *Soc. Neurosci. Abst.*, 11:1165, 1985.

Hunker, C. J., and Abbs, J. H. The uniformity of parkinsonian resting tremor in the lips, jaw, tongue, and index finger. *Soc. Neurosci. Abst.*, 9:1036, 1983.

Ito, M. The control mechanisms of cerebellar control systems. In F. O. Schmitt and F. G. Worden (eds.), *The Neurosciences: Third Study Program.* Cambridge, MA: MIT Press, 1974.

Ito, M. The control mechanisms of cerebellar motor systems. In E. V. Evarts (ed.), *Central Processing of Sensory Input Leading to Motor Output.* Cambridge, MA: MIT Press, 1975.

Iwata, K., Itoga, H., Ikukawa, A., Hanashima, N., and Sumino, R. Movements of the jaw and orofacial regions evoked by stimulation of two different cortical areas in cats. *Brain Res.* 359:332, 1985.

Jackson, J. H. On the anatomical and physiological localization of movements in the brain. *Br. Med. J.* September 26, 1874. [In: *Selected Writings of John Hughlings Jackson.* New York: Basic Books, 1958. Pp. 37–76.]

Jackson, J. H. On temporary paralysis after epileptiform and epileptic seizures: a contribution to the study of dissolution of the nervous system. *Brain,* Vol. 3, 1880. [In Taylor, J. (ed.), *Selected Writings of John Hughlings Jackson* (Vol. 1). New York: Basic Books, 1958. Pp. 318–329.]

Janig, W. Morphology of rapidly and slowly adapting mechanoreceptors in the hairless skin of the cat's hind foot. *Brain Res.* 28:217, 1970.

Jenny, A. B., and Saper, C. B. Organization of the facial nucleus and corticofacial projection in the monkey: a reconsideration of the upper motor neuron facial palsy. *Neurology* 37:930, 1987.

Johansson, R. S. Skin mechanoreceptors in the human hand: receptive field characteristics. In Y. Zotterman (ed.), *Sensory Functions of the Skin in Primates.* Oxford: Pergamon Press, 1976.

Johansson, R. S., and Olsson, K. A. Microelectrode recordings from human oral mechanoreceptors. *Brain Res.* 118:307, 1976.

Johansson, R. S., and Vallbo, A. B. Skin mechanoreceptors in the human hand: an inference of some population properties. In Y. Zotterman (ed.), *Sensory Functions of the Skin in Primates.* Oxford: Pergamon Press, 1976.

Jones, E. G., and Powell, T. P. S. An anatomical study of converging sensory pathways within the cerebral cortex of the monkey. *Brain* 93:793, 1970.

Jones, E. G. Lamination and differential distribution of thalamic afferents within the sensory-motor cortex of the squirrel monkey. *J. Comp. Neurol.* 160:167, 1975.

Jones, E. G., Coulter, J. D., and Hendry, S. H. Intracortical connectivity of architectonic fields in the primate somatic sensory, motor and parietal cortex of monkeys. *J. Comp. Neurol.* 181:291, 1978.

Jones, E. G., Wise, S. P., and Coulter, J. D. Differential thalamic relationships of sensory-motor and parietal cortical fields in monkeys. *J. Comp. Neurol.* 183:833, 1979.

Jurgens, U., and Ploog, D. Cerebral representation of vocalization in the squirrel monkey. *Exp. Brain Res.* 10:532, 1970.

Jurgens, U. Reinforcing concomitants of electrically elicited vocalizations. *Exp. Brain Res.* 26:203, 1976.

Jurgens, U., and Pratt, R. The cingular vocalization pathway in the squirrel monkey. *Exp. Brain Res.* 34:449, 1979.

Jurgens, U., and von Cramon, D. On the role of the anterior cingulate cortex in phonation: a case report. *Brain Lang.* 15:234, 1982.

Jurgens, U. Afferent fibers to the cingular vocalization region in the squirrel monkey. *Exp. Neurol.* 80:395, 1983.

Jurgens, U., and Kirzinger, A. The laryngeal sensory pathway and its role in phonation: a brain lesioning study in the squirrel monkey. *Exp. Brain Res.* 59:118, 1985.

Jurgens, U., and Richter, K. Glutamate-induced vocalization in the squirrel monkey. *Brain Res.* 373:349, 1986.

Kaas, J. H., Nelson, R. J., Sur, M., Lin, C., and Merzenich, M. M. Multiple representations of the body within the primary somatosensory cortex of primates. *Science* 204:521, 1979.

Kalia, M. P. Anatomical organization of central respiratory neurons. *Annu. Rev. Physiol.* 43:105, 1981.

Kalil, K. Projections of the cerebellar and dorsal column nuclei upon the thalamus of the rhesus monkey. *J. Comp. Neurol.* 195:25, 1981.

Karlsson, U. L. The structure and function of muscle spindles and tendon organs in the masticatory muscles. In D. J. Anderson and B. Matthews (eds.), *Mastication.* Bristol: Wright, 1976.

Keele, S. W. Movement control in skilled motor performance. *Psychol. Bull.* 70:387, 1968.

Kelso, J. A. S., and Stelmach, G. E. Central and peripheral mechanisms in motor control. In G. E. Stelmach (ed.), *Motor Control: Issues and Trends.* New York: Academic Press, 1976.

Kelso, J. A. S., Tuller, B., and Fowler, C. The functional specificity of articulatory control and coordination. *J. Acoust. Soc. Am.* 72:S103, 1982.

Kennedy, J. Compensatory responses of the labial musculature to unanticipated disruption of articulation. Ph.D. thesis, University of Washington, Seattle, 1977.

Kennedy, J. G., and Abbs, J. H. Anatomic studies of the perioral motor system: foundations for studies in speech physiology. In N. Lass (ed.), *Speech and Language* (Vol. 1). New York: Academic Press, 1979.

Kent, R., and Netsell, R. A case study of an ataxic dysarthric: cinefluorographic and spectrographic observations. *J. Speech Hear. Disord.* 40:52, 1975.

Kent, R., Netsell, R., and Abbs, J. Acoustic characteristics of dysarthria associated with cerebellar disease. *J. Speech Hear. Res.* 22:627, 1979.

Kiang, N. Y. S., Watanabe, T., Thomas, E. C., and Clark, L. F. *Discharge Patterns of Single Fibers in the Cats Auditory Nerve.* Cambridge: MIT Press, 1965.

Kim, R., Nakano, K., Jayarman, A., and Carpenter, M. B. Projections of the globus pallidus and adjacent structures: an autoradiographic study in the monkey. *J. Comp. Neurol.* 169:263, 1976.

Kirchner, J. A., and Suzuki, M. Laryngeal reflexes and voice production. *Ann. NY Acad. Sci.* 155:98, 1968.

Kirzinger, A., and Jurgens, U. Cortical lesion effects and vocalization in the squirrel monkey. *Brain Res.* 233:299, 1982.

Kobler, J. B. The nucleus ambiguus of the bat, Pteronotus parnelli: peripheral targets and central inputs. Ph.D. thesis, University of North Carolina, 1983.

Kornhuber, H. H., and Deecke, L. Hirnpotentialanderungen bei Wilkurbewegungen und passiven Bewegungen des Menschen: Bereitschaftspotential und reafferente Potentiale. *Pflugers Arch. Ges. Physiol.* 284:1, 1965.

Kubota, K., Negishi, T., and Hasegi, T. Topological distribution of muscle spindles in the human tongue and its significance in proprioception. *Bull. Tokyo Med. Dent. Univ.* 22:235, 1975.

Kubota, K., and Hamada, I. Visual tracking and neuron activity in the post-arcuate area of monkeys. *J. Physiol. (Paris)* 74:297, 1978.

Kubota, K. An introduction to "voluntary movement and the brain." *Adv. Neurol. Sci.* 28:3, 1984.

Kuehn, D. P., and Moll, K. L. A cineradiographic study of VC and CV articulatory velocities. *J. Phonet.* 4:303, 1976.

Kugelberg, E. Facial reflexes. *Brain* 75:385, 1952.

Kuo, J. S., and Carpenter, M. B. Organization of pallidothalamic projections in rhesus monkey. *J. Comp. Neurol.* 151:201, 1973.

Kusama, T., Mabuchi, M., and Sumino, T. Cerebellar projections to the thalamic nuclei in monkeys. *Proc. Jpn. Acad.* 47:505, 1971.

Kuypers, H. G. J. M. An anatomical analysis of corticobulbar connexions to the pons and lower brain-stem in the cat. *J. Anat.* 92:198, 1958a.

Kuypers, H. G. J. M. Corticobulbar connections to the pons and lower brainstem in man: an anatomical study. *Brain* 81:364, 1958b.

Kuypers, H. G. J. M. Some projections from the pericentral cortex to the pons and lower brain stem in monkey and chimpanzee. *J. Comp. Neurol.* 110:221, 1958c.

Kuypers, H. G. J. M. The descending pathways to the spinal cord, their anatomy and function. In J. C. Eccles and J. P. Schade (eds.), *Progress in Brain Research. Organization of the Spinal Cord* (Vol. 2). Amsterdam: Elsevier, 1964.

Kuypers, H. G. J. M. The anatomical organization of the descending pathways and their contributions to motor control especially in primates. In J. E. Desmedt (ed.), *New Developments in Electromyography and Clinical Neurophysiology* (Vol. 3). Basel: Karger, 1973.

Lam, R. L., and Ogura, J. H. An afferent representation of the larynx in the cerebellum. *Laryngoscope* 62:486, 1952.

Lamarre, Y., and Lund, J. P. Load compensation in human masseter muscles. *J. Physiol. (Lond)* 253:21, 1975.

Landau, W. M. Spasticity: the fable of a neurological demon and the emperor's new therapy. *Arch. Neurol.* 31:217, 1974.

Landau, W. M. Spasticity: what is it? What is it not? In R. G. Feldman, R. R. Young, and W. P. Koella (eds.), *Spasticity: Disordered Motor Control* (Vol. 17). Chicago: Year Book Medical Publishers, 1980.

LaPlane, L., Talairach, J., Meininger, V., Bancaud, J., and Orgogozo, J. M. Clinical consequences of corticectomies involving the supplementary motor area in man. *J. Neurol. Sci.* 34:301, 1977.

Larson, C. R. Lesion effects on the perioral reflex in awake monkeys. Presented to the American Speech and Hearing Association, Chicago, 1977.

Larson, C. R., Folkins, J. W., McClean, M. D., and Muller, E. M. Sensitivity of the human perioral reflex to parameters of mechanical stretch. *Brain Res.* 146:159, 1978.

Larson, C. R., Sutton, D., and Lindeman, R. C. Cerebellar regulation of phonation in rhesus monkey (Macaca mulatta). *Exp. Brain Res.* 33:1, 1978.

Larson, C. R., and Kempster, G. B. Voice fundamental frequency changes following discharge of laryngeal motor units. In I. R. Titze and R. C. Scherer (eds.), *Vocal Fold Physiology: Biomechanics, Acoustics and Phonatory Control.* Denver: Denver Center for the Performing Arts, 1983.

Larson, C. R., Wilson, K. E., and Luschei, E. S. Preliminary observations on cortical and brainstem mechanisms of laryngeal control. In D. Bless and J. Abbs (eds.), *Vocal Fold Physiology: Contemporary Research and Clinical Issues.* San Diego: College-Hill Press, 1983.

Larson, C. R., and Kistler, M. K. Periaqueductal gray neuronal activity associated with laryngeal EMG and vocalization in the awake monkey. *Neurosci. Lett.* 46:261, 1984.

Larson, C. R. The midbrain periaqueductal gray: a brainstem structure involved in vocalization. *J. Speech Hear. Res.* 28:241, 1985.

Lashley, K. S. The problem of serial order in behavior. In L. A. Jeffress (ed.), *Cerebral Mechanisms in Behavior.* New York: Wiley, 1951.

Lawn, A. M. The localization in the nucleus ambiguus of the rabbit, of the cells of origin of motor nerve fibers in the glossopharyngeal nerve and various branches of the vagus nerve by means of retrograde degeneration. *J. Comp. Neurol.* 127:293, 1966a.

Lawn, A. M. The nucleus ambiguus of the rabbit. *J. Comp. Neurol.* 127:307, 1966b.

Lawrence, D. G., and Kuypers, H. G. J. M. The functional organization of the motor system in the monkey. I. The effects of bilateral pyramidal lesions. *Brain* 91:1, 1968a.

Lawrence, D. G., and Kuypers, H. G. J. M. The functional organization of the motor system in the monkey. II. The effects of lesions of the descending brainstem pathways. *Brain* 91:15, 1968b.

Leanderson, R., and Persson, A. The effect of trigeminal nerve block on the articulatory EMG activity of facial muscles. *Acta Otolaryngol. (Stockh)* 74:271, 1972.

Lee, R. G., and Tatton, W. G. Long loop reflexes in man: clinical applications. In J. E. Desmedt (ed.), *Progress in Clinical Neurophysiology, Vol. 4: Cerebral Motor Control in Man: Long Loop Mechanisms.* Basel: Karger, 1978.

Lemon, R. N., and van der Burg, J. Short-latency peripheral inputs to thalamic neurones projecting to the motor cortex in the monkey. *Exp. Brain Res.* 36:445, 1979.

Lindblom, B., and Sundberg, J. Neurophysiological representation of speech sounds. *Inst. Linguistic Papers (Stockh)* 1:16, 1971.

Lindblom, B., Lubker, J., and Gay, T. Formant frequencies of some fixed mandible vowels and a model of speech motor programming by predictive simulation. *J. Phonet.* 7:147, 1979.

Lindquist, C., and Martensson, A. Mechanisms involved in the cat's blink reflex. *Acta Physiol. Scand.* 80:149, 1970.

Lovell, M., Sutton, D., and Lindeman, R. Muscle spindles in the nonhuman primate extrinsic auricular muscles. *Anat. Rec.* 189:519, 1977.

Lubker, J., and Gay, T. Spatio-temporal goals: maturational and gross-linguistic variables. In S. Grillner, B. Lindblom, J. Lubker, and A. Persson (eds.), *Speech Motor Control.* Oxford: Pergamon Press, 1982.

Lund, J. P., and Lamarre, Y. Activity of neurons in the lower precentral cortex during voluntary and rhythmical jaw movements in the monkey. *Exp. Brain Res.* 19:282, 1974.

Lund, J. P., Richmond, F. J. R., Touloumis, C., Patry, Y., and Lamarre, Y. The distribution of Golgi tendon organs and muscle spindles in masseter and temporalis muscles of the cat. *Neuroscience* 3:259, 1978a.

Lund, J. P., Smith, A., and Lamarre, Y. Sensory control of mandibular movements and the modulation by set and circumstances. In J. H. Perryman (ed.), *Oral Physiology and Occlusion.* Elmsford, NY: Pergamon Press, 1978b.

Lund, J. P., Smith, A., Sessle, B. J., and Murakami, T. Activity of trigeminal and motoneurons and muscle afferents during performance of a biting task. *J. Neurophysiol.* 42:710, 1979.

Lund, J. P., and Rossignol, S. Modulation of the amplitude of the digastric jaw opening reflex during masticatory cycle. *Neuroscience* 6:95, 1980.

Lund, J. P., Appenteng, K., and Seguin, J. J. Analogies and common features in the speech and masticatory control systems. In S. Grillner, B. Lindblom, J. Lubker, and A. Persson (eds.), *Speech Motor Control.* Oxford: Pergamon Press, 1982.

Luschei, E. S., and Goodwin, G. M. Role of monkey precentral cortex in control of voluntary jaw movements. *J. Neurophysiol.* 38:146, 1975.

Luschei, E. S., and Goldberg, L. J. Neural mechanisms of mandibular control: mastication and voluntary biting. In V. B. Brooks (ed.), *Handbook of Physiology, Vol. 2, Sec. 1, Part 2, The Nervous System.* Bethesda: American Physiological Society, 1981.

MacNeilage, P. Motor control of serial ordering of speech. *Psychol. Rev.* 77:182, 1970.

Magoun, H. W., Atlas, D., Ingersoll, E. H., and Ranson, S. W. Associated facial, vocal and respiratory components of emotional expression: an experimental study. *J. Neurol. Psychopathol.* 17:241, 1937.

Malis, L. I., Pribram, K. H., and Kruger, L. Action potentials in "motor" cortex evoked by peripheral nerve stimulation. *J. Neurophysiol.* 16:161, 1953.

Matsumura, M., and Kubota, K. Cortical projection to hand-arm motor area from post-arcuate in macaque monkeys: a histological study of retrograde transport of horseradish peroxidase. *Neurosci. Lett.* 11:241, 1979.

McClean, M. Effects of auditory masking on lip movements during speech. *J. Speech Hear. Res.* 20:731, 1977.

McClean, M. Variation in perioral reflex amplitude prior to lip muscle contraction for speech. *J. Speech Hear. Res.* 21:276, 1978.

McClean, M. D., and Smith, A. The reflex responses of single motor units in human lower lip muscles to mechanical stimulation. *Brain Res.* 251:65, 1982.

McClean, M. D. Surface EMG recording of the perioral reflexes: preliminary observations on stutterers and nonstutterers. *J. Speech Hear. Res.* 30:283, 1987.

McGlone, R. E., Richmond, W. H., and Bosma, J. F. A physiological model for investigation of the fundamental frequency of phonation. *Folia Phoniatr. (Basel)* 18:109, 1966.

McGuinness, E., Siversten, D., and Allman, J. M. Organization of the face representation in macaque motor cortex. *J. Comp. Neurol.* 193:591, 1980.

Mehler, W. R. Idea of a new anatomy of the thalamus. *J. Psychiatr. Res.* 8:203, 1971.

Merzenich, M. M., Kaas, J. H., Sur. M., and Lin, C. S. Double representation of the body surface within cytoarchitectonic areas 3b and 1 in "SI" in the owl monkey (Aotus trivirgatus). *J. Comp. Neurol.* 181:41, 1978.

Miles, F. A., and Evarts, E. V. Concepts of motor organization. *Annu. Rev. Psychol.* 30:327, 1979.

Miyazaki, T. Somatotopical organization of the motoneurons in the nucleus ambiguus of cats—the horseradish peroxidase method. *Otologia (Fukuoka)* 28:649, 1982.

Moll, L., and Kuypers, H. G. J. M. Premotor cortical ablations in monkeys: contralateral changes in visually guided reaching behavior. *Science* 198:317, 1977.

Mountcastle, V. Modality and topographic properties of single neurons of cat's somatic sensory cortex. *J. Neurophysiol.* 20:408, 1957.

Mountcastle, V. B., LaMotte, R. H., and Carli, G. Detection thresholds for stimuli in humans and monkeys: comparison with threshold events in mechanoreceptive afferent nerve fibers innervating the monkey hand. *J. Neurophysiol.* 35:122, 1972.

Mountcastle, V. B. Neural mechanisms in somesthesis. In V. B. Mountcastle (ed.), *Medical Physiology.* St. Louis: Mosby, 1980.

Muakkassa, K. F., and Strick, P. L. Frontal lobe inputs to primate motor cortex: evidence for four somatotopically organized "premotor" areas. *Brain Res.* 177:176, 1979.

Muller, E. M., Abbs, J. H., Kennedy, J. G., and Larson, C. Significance of biomechanical variables in lip movements for speech. Presented at the annual convention of the American Speech, Language, and

Hearing Association, Chicago, 1977.

Muller, E. M., Milenkovic, P. H., and MacLeod, G. E. Perioral tissue mechanics during speech production. In C. DeLisi and J. Eisenfeld (eds.), *Proceedings of the Second IMAC International Symposium on Biomedical Systems Modeling.* Amsterdam: North Holland, 1984.

Munger, B. L. Patterns of organization of peripheral sensory receptors. In W. R. Lowenstein (ed.), *Handbook of Sensory Physiology* (Vol. 1). New York: Springer, 1971.

Munger, B. L., and Halata, Z. The sensory innervation of primate facial skin. I. Hairy skin. *Brain Res. Rev.* 5:45, 1983.

Myers, R. E. Comparative neurology of vocalization and speech: proof of a dichotomy. In S. R. Harnad, H. D. Steklis, and J. Lancaster (eds.), *Origins and Evolution of Language and Speech.* New York: New York Academy of Sciences, 1976.

Nakamura, Y., Kubo, Y., Nozaki, S., and Takatori, M. Cortically induced masticatory rhythm and its modification by tonic peripheral inputs in immobilized cats. *Bull. Tokyo Med. Dent. Univ.* 23:101, 1976.

Nakayama, M. Nerve terminations in the muscle spindle of the human lingual muscles. *Tohoku Med. J.* 34:367, 1944.

Nauta, W. J. H., and Mehler, W. R. Projections of the lentiform nucleus in the monkey. *Brain Res.* 1:3, 1966.

Neilson, P. D., and O'Dwyer, N. J. Pathophysiology of dysarthria in cerebral palsy. *J. Neurol. Neurosurg. Psychiatry* 44:1013, 1981.

Netsell, R., and Abbs, J. H. Modulation of perioral reflex sensitivity during speech movements. *J. Acoust. Soc. Am.* 58:Suppl 1, S41, 1975.

Netsell, R., Daniel, B., and Celesia, G. Acceleration and weakness in parkinsonian dysarthria. *J. Speech Hear. Disord.* 40:170, 1975.

Netsell, R., Kent, R., and Abbs, J. Adjustments of the tongue and lips to fixed jaw positions during speech; a preliminary report. Presented at the Conference of Speech Motor Control, Madison, WI, 1978.

Netsell, R., Kent, R. D., and Abbs, J. The organization and reorganization of speech movement. *Soc. Neurosci. Abstr.* 6:462, 1980.

Netsell, R. Speech motor control and selected neurologic disorders. In S. Grillner, B. Lindblom, J. Lubker, and A. Persson (eds.), *Speech Motor Control.* New York: Pergamon Press, 1982.

Netsell, R. Speech motor control: theoretical issues with clinical impact. In W. R. Berry (ed.), *Clinical Dysarthria.* San Diego: College-Hill Press, 1983.

Netsell, R. A neurobiologic view of the dysarthrias. In M. McNeil, J. Rosenbek, and A. Aronson (eds.), *The Dysarthrias: Physiology–Acoustics–Perception–Management.* San Diego: College-Hill Press, 1984a.

Netsell, R. Physiologic studies of dysarthria and their relevance to treatment. In J. C. Rosenbek (ed.), *Seminars in Speech and Language: Current Views of Dysarthria.* New York: Thieme-Stratton, 1984b.

Netsell, R. Construction and use of a bite-block in evaluating and treating speech disorders. *J. Speech Hear. Disord.* 50:103, 1985.

Netsell, R. *A Neurobiologic View of Speech Production and the Dysarthrias.* San Diego: College-Hill Press, 1986.

Netsell, R., and Barlow, S. M. Specificity of perioral reflexes. *Abstr. Assoc. Res. Otolaryngol.* 169:135, 1986.

Newell, K. M. Some issues on action plans. In G. E. Stelmach (ed.), *Information Processing in Motor Learning and Control.* New York: Academic Press, 1978.

Newell, K. M., and Barclay, C. R. Developing knowledge about action. In J. A. S. Kelso and J. E. Clark (eds.), *Development of Movement Control and Coordination.* New York: Wiley, 1982.

Orgogozo, J. M., and Larsen, B. Activation of the supplementary motor area during voluntary movement in man suggests it works as a supra-motor area. *Science* 206:847, 1979.

Oscarsson, O. Functional organization of the spino- and cuneocerebellar tracts. *Physiol. Rev.* 45:495, 1965.

Pandya, D. N., and Kuypers, H. G. J. M. Cortico-cortical connections in the rhesus monkey. *Brain Res.* 13:13, 1969.

Pandya, D. N., and Vignolo, L. A. Intra- and interhemispheric projections of the precentral, premotor, and arcuate areas in the rhesus monkey. *Brain Res.* 26:217, 1971.

Paul, R. L., Merzenich, M., and Goodman, H. Representation of slowly and rapidly adapting cutaneous mechanoreceptors of the hand in Brodmann's areas 3 and 1 of Macaca mulatta. *Brain Res.* 36:229, 1972.

Pearson, K. The control of walking. *Sci. Am.* 235:72, 1976.

Penfield, W., and Rasmussen, T. *The Cerebral Cortex of Man* (1st ed.). New York: Macmillan, 1950.

Penfield, W., and Welch, K. The supplementary motor area of the cerebral cortex. *Arch. Neurol. Psychiatry* 66:289, 1951.

Percheron, G. The thalamic territory of cerebellar afferents and the lateral region of the thalamus of the macaque in stereotaxic ventricular coordinates. *J. Hirnforsch.* 18:375, 1977.

Phillips, C. G. Motor apparatus of baboon's hand. *Proc. R. Soc. [B]* 173:141, 1969.

Phillips, C. G., and Porter, R. *Corticospinal Neurons: Their Role in Movements.* London: Academic Press, 1977.

Ploog, D. Neurobiology of primate audio-vocal behavior. *Brain Res. Rev.* 3:35, 1981.

Rack, P. M. H. Limitations of somatosensory feedback in control of posture and movement. In V. B. Brooks (ed.), *Handbook of Physiology. The Nervous System* (Vol. 2, Sect. 1, Pt. 1) Bethesda: American Physiological Society, 1981.

Rasmussen, T., and Penfield, W. Further studies of sensory and motor cerebral cortex of man. *Fed. Proc.* 6:452, 1947.

Richter, K., and Jurgens, U. A comparative study on the elicitability of vocalization by electrical brain stimulation, glutamate, aspartate and quisqualate in the squirrel monkey. *Neurosci. Lett.* 66:239, 1986.

Rizzolatti, G., Scandolara, C., Matelli, M., and Gentilucci, M. Afferent properties of periarcuate neurons in macaque monkeys. I. Somatosensory responses. *Behav. Brain Res.* 2:125, 1981a.

Rizzolatti, G., Scandolara, C., Matelli, M., and Gentilucci, M. Afferent properties of periarcuate neurons in macaque monkeys. II. Visual responses. *Behav. Brain Res.* 2:147, 1981b.

Robinson, B. W. Neurological aspects of evoked vocalizations. In S. A. Altmann (ed.), *Social Communication Among Primates.* Chicago: University of Chicago Press, 1967a.

Robinson, B. W. Vocalization evoked from forebrain in Macaca mulatta. *Physiol. Behav.* 2:345, 1967b.

Roland, P. E., Larsen, B., Lassen, N. A., and Skinhoj, E. Supplementary motor area and other cortical areas in organization of voluntary movements in man. *J. Neurophysiol.* 43:118, 1980.

Sandrew, B. B., and Poletti, C. E. Limbic influence on the periaqueductal gray: a single unit study in the awake squirrel monkey. *Brain Res.* 303:77, 1984.

Sapir, S., McClean, M. D., and Luschei, E. S. Time relations between cricothyroid muscle activity and the voice fundamental frequency (Fo) during sinusoidal modulations of Fo. *J. Acoust. Soc. Am.* 75:1639, 1984.

Sasaki, K., Kawaguchi, S., Oka, H., Sakai, M., and Mizuno, N. Electrophysiological studies on the cerebellocerebral projections in monkeys. *Exp. Brain Res.* 24:495, 1976.

Sasaki, K., Jinnai, K., Gemba, H., Hashimoto, S., and Mizuno, N. Projection of the cerebellar dentate nucleus onto the frontal association cortex in monkeys. *Exp. Brain Res.* 37:193, 1979.

Schell, G. R., and Strick, P. L. The origin of thalamic inputs to the arcuate premotor and supplementary motor areas. *J. Neurosci.* 4:539, 1984.

Schweizer, H., Ruebsamen, R., and Ruehle, C. Localization of brain stem motoneurons innervating the laryngeal muscles in the rufous horseshoe bat, Rhinolophus rouxi. *Brain Res.* 230:41, 1981.

Sessle, B. J., and Wiesendanger, M. Structural and functional definition of the motor cortex in the monkey (Macaca fascicularis). *J. Physiol. (Lond)* 323:245, 1982.

Shipp, T. Aspects of voice production and motor control. In S. Grillner, B. Lindblom, J. Lubker, and A. Persson (eds.), *Speech Motor Control: Proceedings of an International Symposium on the Functional Basis of Oculomotor Disorders.* Oxford: Pergamon Press, 1982.

Sirisko, M., and Sessle, B. J. Intracortical microstimulation and single neurone recording data related to face, jaw and tongue representations in sensorimotor cortex of Macaca fascicularis. *Soc. Neurosci. Abstr.* 7:564, 1981.

Sirisko, M., and Sessle, B. J. Superficial and afferent inputs to single neurones in the sensory and motor cortex of Macaca fascicularis. *Soc. Neurosci. Abstr.* 8:539, 1982.

Sirisko, M., and Sessle, B. J. Corticobulbar projections and orofacial muscle afferent inputs of neurons in primate sensorimotor cerebral cortex. *Exp. Neurol.* 82:716, 1983.

Smith, A., Moore, C., McFarland, D., and Weber, C. Reflex responses of human lip muscles to mechanical stimulation during speech. *J. Motor Behav.* 17:148, 1985.

Smith, A., McFarland, D. H., Weber, C. M., and Moore, C. A. Spatial organization of human perioral reflexes. *Exp. Neurol.* 98:233, 1987.

Smith, A. M., Hepp-Reymond, M-C., and Wyss, U. R. Relation of activity in precentral cortical neurons to

force and rate of force change during isometric contractions of finger muscles. *Exp. Brain Res.* 23:315, 1975.

Smith, R. L. Short-term adaptation and incremental responses of single auditory-nerve fibers. Ph.D. dissertation, Syracuse University, and special report LSC-S-11, Institute for Sensory Research, 1973.

Smith, R. L. Short-term adaptation in single auditory nerve fibers: some poststimulatory effects. *J. Neurophysiol.* 40:1098, 1977.

Smith, W. K. The functional significance of the rostral cingular cortex as revealed by its responses to electrical excitation. *J. Neurophysiol.* 8:241, 1945.

Stanton, G. B. Topographical organization of ascending cerebellar projections from the dentate and interposed nuclei in Macaca mulatta: an anterograde degeneration study. *J. Comp. Neurol.* 190:699, 1980.

Sternberg, S., Monsell, S., Knoll, R. L., and Wright, C. E. The latency and duration of rapid movement sequences: comparisons of speech and typewriting. In G. E. Stelmach (ed.), *Information Processing in Motor Control and Learning.* New York: Academic Press, 1978.

Strick, P. L., and Preston, J. B. Multiple representation in the primate motor cortex. *Brain Res.* 154:366, 1978.

Sussman, H. M., MacNeilage, P. F., and Hanson, R. J. Labial and mandibular dynamics during the production of bilabial consonants: preliminary observations. *J. Speech Hear. Res.* 16:397, 1973.

Sutton, D., Larson, D., and Lindeman, R. C. Neocortical and limbic lesion effects on primate phonation. *Brain Res.* 71:61, 1974.

Szirtes, J., Marton, M., and Urban, J. Cortical potentials associated with vocalization in the rhesus monkey. *Acta Physiol. Acad. Sci. Hung.* 49:89, 1977.

Tanji, J., and Taniguchi, K. Does the SMA play a part in modifying motor cortex reflexes? *J. Physiol. (Paris)* 74:317, 1978.

Tanji, J., Taniguchi, K., and Saga, T. Supplementary motor area: neuronal response to motor instructions. *J. Neurophysiol.* 43:60, 1980.

Tanji, J., and Wise, S. P. Submodality distribution in sensorimotor cortex of the unanesthetized monkey. *J. Neurophysiol.* 45:467, 1981.

Tanji, J. Differences of neuronal responses in two cortical motor areas in primates. In A. W. Goodwin and I. Darian-Smith (eds.), *Hand Function and the Neocortex.* Berlin: Springer-Verlag, 1985.

Tasker, R. R., Gentili, F., Hwang, P., and Sogabe, K. Animal models of spasticity and treatment of dentatectomy. In R. G. Feldman, R. R. Young, and W. P. Koella (eds.), *Spasticity: Disordered Motor Control.* Miami: Symposia Specialists, 1980.

Taylor, A., and Cody, F. W. J. Jaw muscle spindle activity in the cat during normal movements of eating and drinking. *Brain Res.* 71:523, 1974.

Taylor, A., Appenteng, K., and Morimoto, T. Proprioceptive input from the jaw muscles and its influence on lapping, chewing and posture. *Can. J. Physiol. Pharmacol.* 59:636, 1981.

Thach, W. T. Timing of activity in cerebellar dentate nucleus and cerebral motor cortex during prompt volitional movement. *Brain Res.* 88:233, 1975.

Thoms, G., and Jurgens, U. Common input of the cranial motor nuclei involved in phonation in squirrel monkey. *Exp. Neurol.* 95:85, 1987.

Tower, S. S. Pyramidal lesion in the monkey. *Brain* 33:36, 1940.

Trachy, R. E., Sutton, D., and Lindeman, R. C. Primate phonation: anterior cingulate lesion effects on response rate and acoustical structure. *Am. J. Primatol.* 1:43, 1981.

Travis, A. M. Neurological deficiencies after ablations of the precentral motor area in Macaca mulatta. *Brain* 78:155, 1955.

Verrillo, R. T. Effect of spatial parameters of the vibrotactile threshold. *J. Exp. Psychol.* 71:570, 1966a.

Verrillo, R. T. Specificity of a cutaneous receptor. *Percept. Psychophys.* 1:149, 1966b.

Verrillo, R. T. Vibrotactile sensitivity and the frequency response of the pacinian corpuscle. *Psychonom. Sci.* 4:135, 1966c.

Vilis, T., Hore, J., Meyer-Lohmann, J., and Brooks, V. B. Dual nature of the precentral responses to limb perturbations revealed by cerebellar cooling. *Brain Res.* 117:336, 1976.

Vogt, B. A., and Pandya, D. N. Cortico-cortical connections of somatic sensory cortex (areas 3, 1 and 2) in the rhesus monkey. *J. Comp. Neurol.* 177:179, 1978.

Von Bonin, G., and Bailey, P. *The Neocortex of Macaca mullata.* Urbana: University of Illinois Press, 1947. P. 163.

Von Euler, C. The functional organization of the respiratory phase-switching mechanisms. *Fed. Proc.* 36:2375, 1977.

Von Euler, C. Central pattern generation during breathing. *Trends Neurosci.* 3:275, 1980.

Von Euler, C. Some aspects of speech breathing physiology. In S. Grillner, B. Lindblom, J. Lubker, and A. Persson (eds.), *Speech Motor Control.* Oxford: Pergamon, 1982.

Von Holst, E. Relation between central nervous system and the peripheral organs. *Br. J. Anim. Behav.* 2:89, 1954.

Walker, L. B., and Rajagopal, M. D. Neuromuscular spindles in the human tongue. *Anat. Rec.* 133:438, 1959.

Weber, C. M., and Smith, A. Reflex responses in human jaw, lip, and tongue muscles elicited by mechanical stimulation. *J. Speech Hear. Res.* 30:70, 1987.

Weiss, P. Does sensory control play a constructive role in the development of motor coordination? *Schweiz. Med. Wochenschr.* 71:406, 1941.

Welt, C., Aschoff, J. C., Kameda, K., and Brooks, V. B. Intracortical organization of cat's motorsensory neurons. In M. D. Yahr and D. P. Purpura (eds.), *Neurophysiological Basis of Normal and Abnormal Motor Activities.* New York: Raven Press, 1967.

Wiesendanger, M., Seguin, J. J., and Kunzle, H. The supplementary motor area: a control system for posture? *Adv. Behav. Biol.* 7:331, 1973.

Wiesendanger, M. Organization of secondary motor areas of cerebral cortex. In V. B. Brooks (ed.), *Handbook of Physiology, Sect. 1: The Nervous System. Vol. 2:*

Motor Control. Bethesda: American Physiological Society, 1981.

Wiesendanger, M., and Miles, T. S. Ascending pathway of low-threshold muscle afferents to the cerebral cortex and its possible role in motor control. *Physiol. Rev.* 4:1234, 1982.

Wiesendanger, M., Hummelsheim, H., and Bianchetti, M. Sensory input to the motor fields of the agranular frontal cortex: a comparison of the precentral, supplementary motor and premotor cortex. *Behav. Brain Res.* 18:89, 1985.

Wise, S. P., and Tanji, J. Supplementary and precentral motor cortex: contrast in responsiveness to peripheral input in the hindlimb area of the unanesthetized monkey. *J. Comp. Neurol.* 195:433, 1981.

Woolsey, C. N., Settlage, P. H., Meyer, D. R., Sencer, W., Hamuy, T. P., and Travis, A. M. Patterns of localization in precentral and "supplementary" motor areas and their relation to the concept of a premotor area. *Res. Publ. Assoc. Res. Nerv. Ment. Dis.* 30:238, 1951.

Wyke, B. D. Reflexogenic contributions to vocal fold control systems. In I. R. Titze and R. C. Scherer (eds.), *Vocal Fold Physiology: Biomechanics, Acoustics and Phonatory Control.* Denver: Denver Center for the Performing Arts, 1983.

Yoshida, Y., Miyazaki, T., Hirano, M., Shin, T., Totoki, T., and Kanaseki, T. Arrangement of motoneurons innervating the intrinsic laryngeal muscles of cats as demonstrated by horseradish peroxidase method. *Acta Otolaryngol. (Stockh)* 94:329, 1982.

Yoshida, Y., Miyazaki, T., Hirano, M., and Kanaseki, T. Localization of the laryngeal motoneurons in the brain stem and myotopical representation of the motoneurons in the nucleus ambiguus of cats—an HRP study. In I. R. Titze and R. C. Scherer (eds.), *Vocal Fold Physiology: Biomechanics, Acoustics and Phonatory Control.* Denver: Denver Center for the Performing Arts, 1983.

Yoshida, Y., Mitsumasu, T., Hirano, M., Morimoto, M., and Kanaseki, T. Afferent connections to the nucleus ambiguus in the brainstem of the cat—an HRP study. In T. Baer, C. Sasaki, and K. Harris (eds.), *Laryngeal Function in Phonation and Respiration.* Boston: College-Hill Press, 1987.

Young, E., and Sachs, M. B. Recovery from sound exposure in auditory nerve fibers. *J. Acoust. Soc. Am.* 54:1535, 1973.

Zealear, D. L., Hast, M. H., and Kurago, Z. Functional organization of the primary motor cortex controlling the face, tongue, jaw, and larynx in the monkey. In I. R. Titze and R. C. Scherer (eds.), *Vocal Fold Physiology: Biomechanics, Acoustics and Phonatory Control.* Denver: Denver Center for the Performing Arts, 1983.

Zealear, D. L., and Larson, C. R. Microelectrode studies of laryngeal motoneurons in the nucleus ambiguus of the awake vocalizing monkey. *Soc. Neurosci. Abstr.* 13:1696, 1987.

CHAPTER 7

Neuroanatomy of Hearing

Robert V. Harrison • Ivan M. Hunter-Duvar

❏ Inner Ear: Cochlea

❏ Central Auditory Pathways

The authors express their gratitude to Richard Mount, Claudia Fleckeisen, and Genevieve Coutinho for their assistance in preparing this chapter.

Current knowledge about neuroanatomy of the auditory system is reviewed here, starting with a detailed description of the peripheral auditory system, that is, the cochlea and cochlear nerve. The central auditory pathways are then considered, from the cochlear nuclei of the brainstem to the auditory cortex and beyond.

INNER EAR: COCHLEA

The cochlea is the input device for the auditory system. Here mechanical vibrations of sound are converted into electrical signals that can be transmitted, in the form of neural impulses, to the central auditory system. The cochlear hair cells, which are *mechanoreceptors,* convert mechanical movement (displacement of hair cell stereocilia) into voltage changes inside the cell (receptor potentials), which in turn causes the release of neurotransmitter and activation of the cochlear neurons of the vestibulo-cochlear (VIII) nerve.

Strictly speaking, the only neural components in the cochlea are the sensory cells and their innervation. This sensory organ, however, is more than a simple transducer. The cochlea is exquisitely designed to *process* sound, whereby important features of acoustic stimuli are converted to meaningful patterns of neural activity within the neural array of the cochlear nerve. Those patterns can be further processed by the central auditory pathways. The sensory hair cells cannot operate independently of the other cells that make up the cochlea. The sound analysis carried out by the cochlea can be understood only by considering the cochlear anatomy in general. For these reasons this section includes a description of all cochlear components that contribute to its sensory function.

Studies of the structure of the inner ear have progressed according to the technologic development of microscopic techniques: Many of the early investigators, using light microscopy, are familiar to us because their names have become associated with cochlear structures, for example, Corti, Claudius, Hensen, Retzius, Deiters. With the introduction of transmission electron microscopy, more detailed ultrastructural studies of the cochlea became possible (Bredberg,

1968; Engström and Wersäll, 1958; Engström, Ades, and Anderson, 1966; Iurato, 1967; Kimura, 1975; Spoendlin, 1966). The development of the scanning electron microscope gave a new perspective to the study of the inner ear (Bredberg, Ades, and Engström, 1972; Hunter-Duvar, 1978a, 1983; Harada, 1983; Lim, 1969).

The mammalian inner ear consists of a series of membranous sacs and ducts (the membranous labyrinth) enclosed in a shell of bone (osseous labyrinth), which is largely embedded in the hard temporal bone of the cranium. The membranous labyrinth contains the vestibular and auditory sensory epithelia and is primarily filled with a fluid called *endolymph*. The ionic composition of endolymph is similar to that found intracellularly (notably high in potassium ions and low in sodium ions). Between the membranous and osseous labyrinth is a fluid called *perilymph*, which is high in sodium and low in potassium, similar therefore to extracellular and cerebrospinal fluid.

COCHLEAR ANATOMY

The spiral canal of the cochlea is anterior to the vestibular organs. In humans its axial length is about 5 mm, and the basal turn is about 10 mm across. Uncoiled it measures approximately 35 mm and has just over 2.5 turns around the central modiolus.

The mammalian cochlea is illustrated in Figure 7-1. The specimens shown are from the cat (Fig. 7-1A) and the chinchilla (Fig. 7-1B), but it should be emphasized that the structure of the cochlea, and indeed most of the neuroanatomy of the auditory system, is similar to that of the mammalian species of major interest, *Homo sapiens*. The spiral cochlea is divided into three spaces: *scala vestibuli* and *scala tympani*, which are filled with perilymph, and the *scala media*, which is part of the endolymphatic system. Scala media, its membranous boundary, the sensory epithelium, and supporting structures (organ of Corti) are sometimes collectively termed the membranous cochlear duct. The basal end of this duct communicates with the *saccule* of the vestibular organs via the *ductus reuniens*; the duct ends blindly at the cochlear apex. Conversely, scala vestibuli and scala tympani join at the helicotrema.

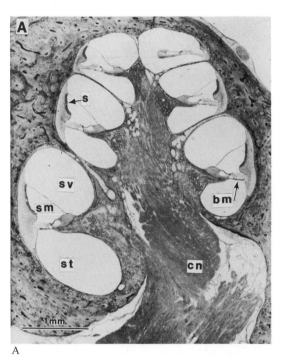

A

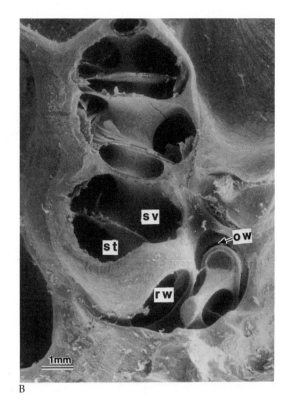

B

Fig. 7-1. A. Cross-sectional view of mammalian cochlea. B. Scanning electron micrograph of opened cochlea. bm = basilar membrane; cn = cochlear nerve; ow = oval window; rw = round window; s = stria vascularis; sm = scala media; st = scala tympani; sv = scala vestibuli.

The organ of Corti and related cochlear structures are seen in Figure 7-2. The cochlear duct is separated from the scala vestibuli by Reissner's membrane, a thin (2 to 3 μm) structure extending from the inner spiral limbus to the crest of the spiral ligament. Figure 7-3 shows, at high magnification, part of Reissner's membrane. In the adult it consists of two cellular layers between which is a thin basement membrane about 0.25 μm thick. On the endolymphatic surface there are numerous small extensions to the cell membrane called *microvilli*. The epithelial cells of Reissner's membrane are bonded to each other by *tight junctions*, which make the membrane an impermeable barrier and help maintain the special ionic environment of the scala media. Reissner's membrane possibly has a role in keeping the cochlea free of debris (Hunter-Duvar, 1978b).

The tectorial membrane is an acellular matrix essentially composed of filaments, fibrils, and perhaps a homogeneous ground substance. As shown in Figure 7-2, it extends from the spiral limbus to the outer margin of the organ of Corti (Iurato, 1960; Kronester-Frei, 1978; Lim, 1972, 1977). In the unfixed state, the membrane appears to be a soft gel, the thickness of which increases from the base to apex of the cochlea.

The underside of the tectorial membrane is seen in Figure 7-4 at different degrees of magnification. The outer zone of the tectorial membrane consists of a marginal band and a marginal net *(Randfasernetz)* attached to the outermost row of Deiters' or Hensen cells. It is not clear if the outer margin forms a complete seal with the reticular lamina. The main body of the membrane is occupied by fibers that radiate from the inner zone inclined at about 30 degrees toward the apical turn of the cochlea. Hensen's stripe is located (Fig. 7-4A) on the undersurface near the position of the inner hair cells. Small trabeculae may anchor the tectorial membrane to the inner hair cell region of the organ of

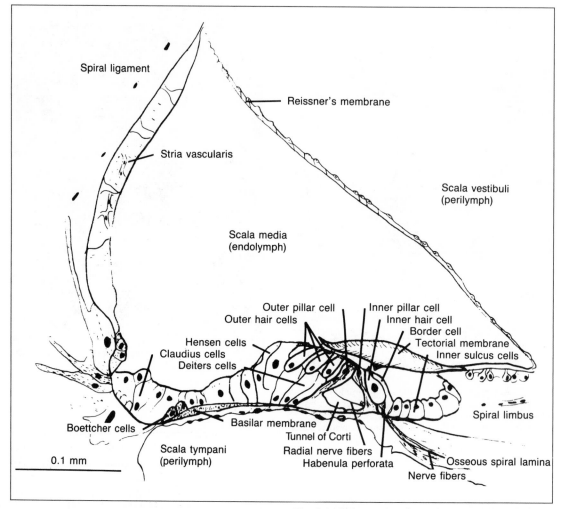

Fig. 7-2. Cross section through one cochlear turn.

Corti. Hardesty's membrane is positioned adjacent to the outer hair cell region.

It is now clear that the tallest row of stereocilia of the outer hair cells is in close contact with the tectorial membrane. Evidence of this positioning is seen in the hollows of W- or V-shaped patterns on the underside (Hardesty's membrane) of the tectorial membrane (Fig. 7-4) (Hoshino, 1977, Hunter-Duvar, 1977; Lim, 1972). The stereocilia are firmly embedded in the tectorial membrane, as is clear from Figure 7-4C, which shows stereocilia uprooted from their parent hair cell but still attached to the tectorial membrane. It is less clear if a similar attachment exists between the tectorial membrane and the inner hair cell stereocilia. If any contact exists, it is certainly less firm than for

the outer hair cell stereocilia. Over the upper surface of the tectorial membrane there appears to be a covering net (Fig. 7-5). However, it should be noted that such fine structure of the tectorial membrane is much influenced by fixative and staining procedures used in its examination. Tectorial membrane structure and function have been reviewed by Steel (1983).

The cochlear duct is enclosed on the scala tympani side by the basilar membrane, which is attached to the modiolus and laterally at the spiral ligament. The membrane is composed of fibrous material, ground substance, surface-covering cells and some capillaries. Figure 7-6 shows surface and cross-sectional views of the membrane. The division between the basilar

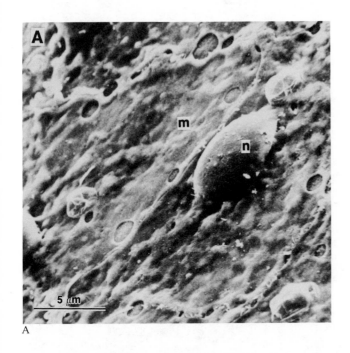

A

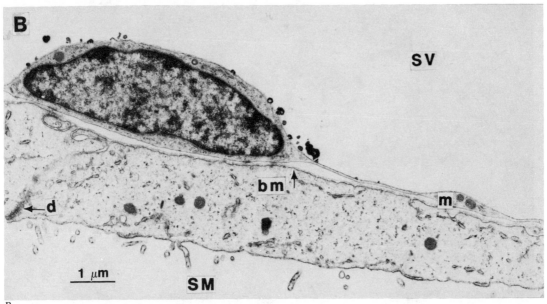

B

Fig. 7-3. A. Scanning electron micrograph of the surface (from scala vestibuli) of Reissner's membrane. B. Transmission electron micrograph through Reissner's membrane. bm = basement membrane; d = desmosome; m = mesothelial cell; n = nucleus of mesothelial cell; SM = scala media; SV = scala vestibuli.

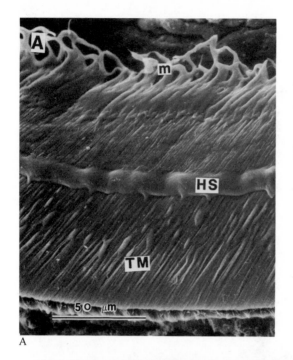

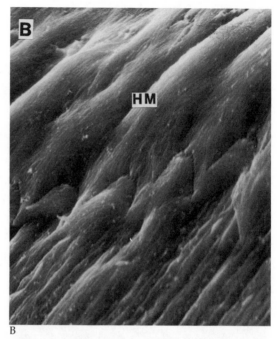

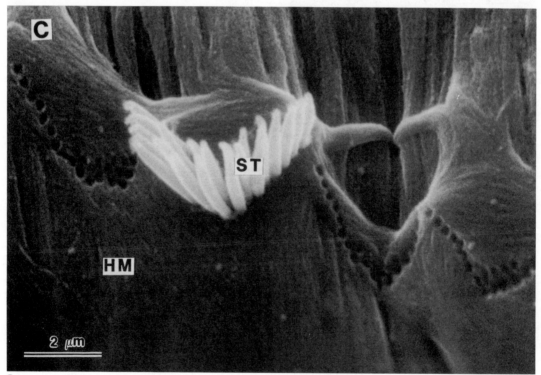

Fig. 7-4. Scanning electron micrographs of the underside of the tectorial membrane. A,B,C. Low, medium, and high magnifications, respectively. HM = Hardesty's membrane; HS = Hensen's stripe; m = marginal net; ST = stereocilia (plucked from hair cell during tissue preparation) embedded in the tectorial membrane (TM).

membrane and the organ of Corti is clear. The cells of the organ have a plasma membrane that appears to directly contact a thin basement membrane over the basilar membrane. The basilar membrane itself can be divided into two portions: the pars tecta, which extends from the region of the habenula perforata of the osseous spiral lamina to the duct of the outer pillar cells (see Fig. 7-2), and the pars pectinata, which stretches from outer pillar cells to the outer spiral ligament. Both regions contain fibrous layers separated by homogeneous matter. On the surface of the basilar membrane facing the scala tympani (Fig. 7-6A) are the elongated cells of the tympanic covering layer.

The structure of the basilar membrane shows graded differences along the cochlear length (Fig. 7-7). At the base, fiber bundles are densely packed, as is the tympanic covering layer. Toward the apex, the fiber bundles and covering cells are more loosely arranged. These structural factors contribute to a stiffness gradient along the basilar membrane that allows propagation of a traveling wave and contributes to the well known *place coding* of sound frequency.

Fig. 7-5. Scanning electron micrograph of the cochlear partition. OC = organ of Corti; rm = Reissner's membrane; SV = stria vascularis; tm = tectorial membrane.

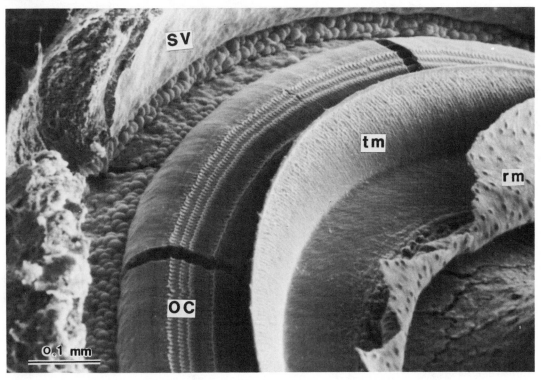

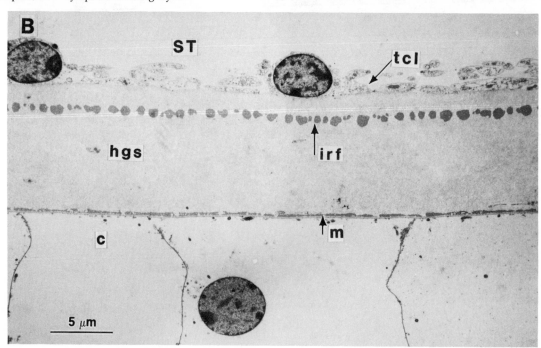

Fig. 7-6. A. Scanning electron micrograph of the surface of the basilar membrane as viewed from scala tympani. B. Cross-sectional view of basilar membrane. c = Claudius cell; hgs = homogeneous ground substance; irf = inner radial fibers; m = basement membrane; rf = radial fibers; ST = scala tympani; tcl = tympanic covering layer.

A

B

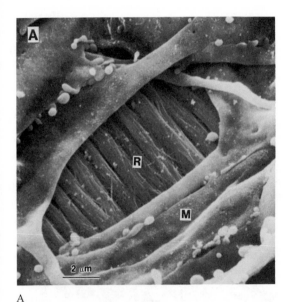

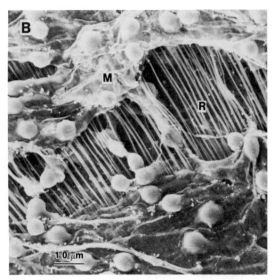

A

B

Fig. 7-7. Scanning electron micrographs of the surface of the basilar membrane at the cochlear base (A) and toward the apex of the cochlea (B). M = mesothelial cells of the tympanic covering layer; R = radial fibers.

ORGAN OF CORTI

The organ of Corti, which lies on the spiral basilar membrane, consists of sensory cells, supporting cells, and nerve fibers. A surface view of the (chinchilla) organ of Corti is shown in the scanning electron micrograph of Figure 7-5. Here the tectorial membrane has lifted away from the surface of the organ of Corti (recticular lamina) to reveal the hair cells and their stereocilia. Along the length of the organ of Corti are two hair cell types: The inner hair cells form one row, and the outer hair cells form three to four rows. In humans there are approximately 3,500 inner and 12,000 outer hair cells.

HAIR CELLS

The inner hair cell is flask-shaped with a narrow apical region and a large cell body that is inclined toward the tunnel of Corti. Figure 7-8A shows a cross section through one cell. The length dimension of the inner hair cell is almost constant throughout the cochlea. The cell is supported at its apex by the tops of the inner pillar cells and the border cells of the inner sulcus.

The top surface of the hair cell is oval, with its long axis parallel to the cochlear length. The *cuticular plate* is 1 to 2 μm thick and supports approximately 60 sensory hairs. The scanning micrograph of Figure 7-8B shows the arrangement and size of the stereocilia on the cuticular surface. These stereocilia extend to various lengths depending on their position on each cell and on the cochlear location. In general, stereociliar diameter varies up to 0.3 μm. The stereocilia (of all hair cell types) contain a number of structural proteins, including actin, that cross-link to form stiff filaments (Flock, Bretscher, and Weber, 1982). During embryonic development the inner hair cell has a kinocilium, which later degenerates and is not usually evident in adults.

The base of each inner hair cell has contact with about 20 afferent nerve endings of inner radial fibers. The afferent nerve endings contain some microtubule structures and large mitochondria. Their synapses with the hair cells are evident by thickenings of the postsynaptic membrane with less obvious thickening of the presynaptic membrane. Associated with the presynaptic membrane (hair cell) are synaptic vesicles. Most efferents (i.e., fibers of the descending system) synapse with the afferent dendrites rather than directly on the inner hair

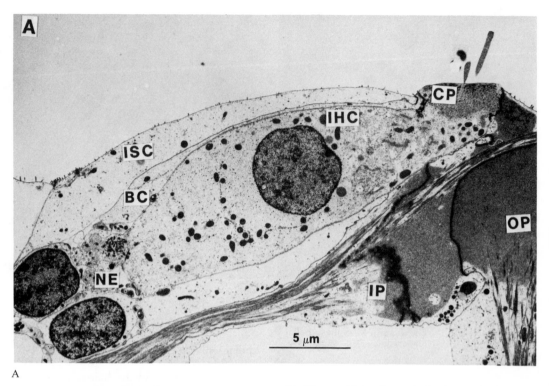

A

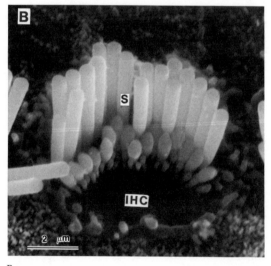

B

Fig. 7-8. A. Cross-sectional view of an inner hair cell and supporting structures as seen by transmission electron microscopy. B. Scanning electron micrograph of the stereociliar bundle of an inner hair cell. BC = border cell; CP = cuticular plate; IHC = inner hair cell; IP = inner pillar cell; ISC = inner sulcus cell; NE = nerve endings; OP = outer pillar cell; S = stereocilia.

cell. Thus within the spiral plexus, below the inner sensory cells, there are thin efferent inner spiral fibers that make contact with the radial afferent dendrites. Figure 7-9 summarizes the afferent and efferent innervation patterns.

The outer hair cells are of cylindrical form and are obliquely orientated (see, for example, Figures 7-10 and 7-11). The cell body length depends on its position in the cochlea. It is much longer at the apex than at the base. The sensory cells are supported at their cuticular (apical) region by the *reticular lamina*, and at their base they rest on supporting Deiters' cells. The outer hair cells are almost entirely surrounded by extracellular (Nuel's) space. A dense cuticular plate holds 50 to 150 stereocilia arranged in rows that assume a W or V shape, as can be seen clearly in Figures 7-4 and 7-12. The stereocilia are largest in the outermost row (away from the modiolus), their size tapering off medially. The average length of the stereocilia depends on cochlear position; thus at the apex the largest stereocilia measure more than 6 μm and at the base less than 2 μm. The number of stereocilia on the hair cell decreases from cochlear base to apex. For example, in the squirrel monkey each cell has about 135 stereocilia in the basal turn, which reduces to 80 in the third

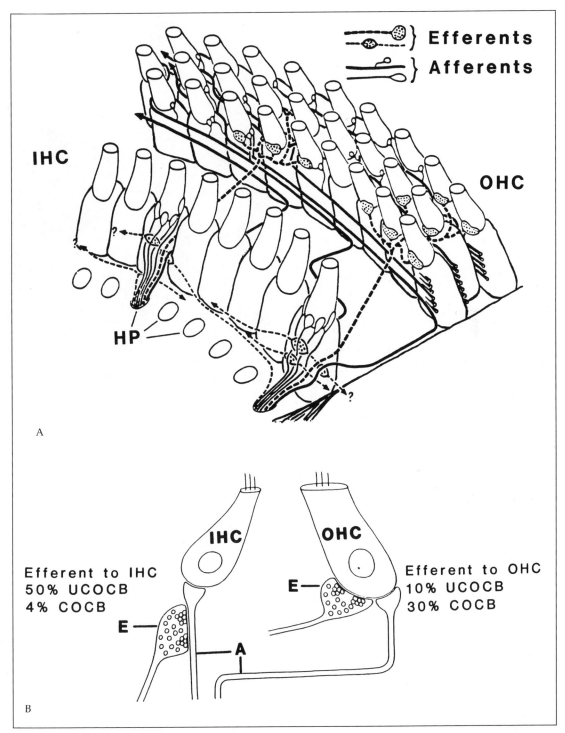

Fig. 7-9. A. Pattern of afferent and efferent innervation of the cochlea. B. Pattern of efferent innervation of the cochlear inner and outer hair cells. HP = habenula perforata; IHC = inner hair cells; OHC = outer hair cells; E = efferent terminal; A = afferent terminal; COCB = crossed olivocochlear bundle; UCOCB = uncrossed olivocochlear bundle. (A. Adapted from Spoendlin, H. The organization of the cochlear receptor. In: *Advances in Otolaryngology,* Vol. 13. Basel: Karger, 1966.)

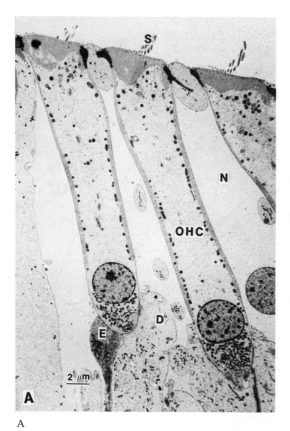

A

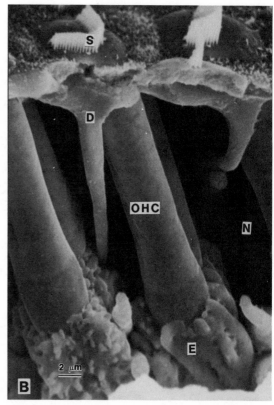

B

Fig. 7-10. Transmission (A) and scanning (B) electron micrographs of outer hair cells (OHC). D = Deiters' cell; E = efferent nerve terminals; N = Nuel's space; S = stereocilia.

turn. Each stereocilium is club-shaped, being narrow near the cuticular plate (130 nm) and wider near the tip (320 nm). A large number of horizontal cross-links join stereocilia of different rows together laterally. Also, the tip of each shorter stereocilium gives rise to a fine extension that joins the taller stereocilium of the next row (Pickles, Comis, and Osborne, 1984). Vestigial remains of a kinocilium can be found in some primate species, although in general no kinocilia persist in the adult animal.

The stereocilia are covered by a thin plasma membrane. Each has a cylindrical core and a dense tube-like rootlet that extends from the central core. The protoplasm contains long macromolecular fibers running the length of the hair with a similar fibrillar structure in the cone and rootlet. The cuticular plate is of a dense fibrillar material with a highly organized struc-

ture in the zone surrounding the stereociliar rootlets. Actin and other proteins have been identified in the inner hair cells that have a structural and possibly a contractile role.

The outer hair cells are in contact with efferent and afferent nerve endings (see Fig. 7-9). The efferent endings are those of the outer radial fibers. Their terminals are about 3 μm in diameter and thus larger than those of the afferents. In the basal turn of the cochlea they are numerous in all rows of outer hair cells, but toward apical regions they progressively disappear from the peripheral rows of outer hair cells. Efferent endings may occur anywhere from the bottom of the hair cell to the level of the nucleus (Fig. 7-10). The endings are rich in mitochondria and contain many synaptic vesicles (Fig. 7-13).

The afferent nerve endings of the outer hair cells are those of the *outer spiral fibers* that constitute only approximately 10 percent of the afferent neurons in the spiral ganglion. These fibers enter the cochlea at the habenula perforata

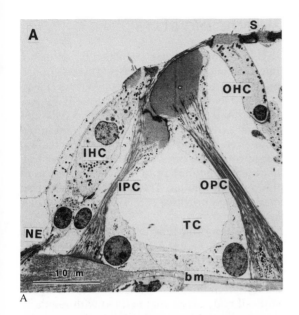

(the openings in the bony, inner spiral lamina) and cross the tunnel close to the basilar membrane, turn at right angles at the Deiters' cell region, and course some distance before contacting outer hair cells (Fig. 7-9). The afferent synapse is small and bouton-like. At the site of the synapse, both plasma membrane and postsynaptic membranes are thickened and have a synaptic gap of about 15 nm (see Fig. 7-13). There is no subsynaptic cistern associated with the afferent synapse, although there is often a synaptic bar or ring surrounded by small vesicles.

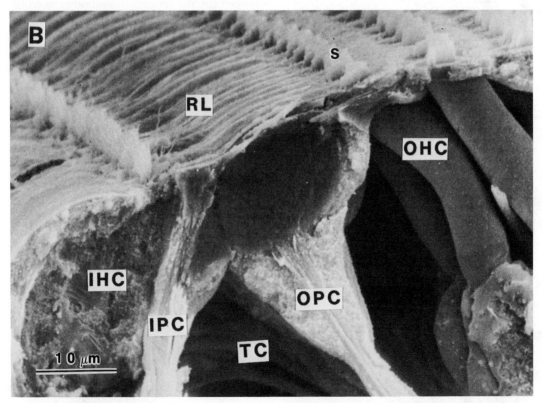

Fig. 7-11. Pillar cells of the organ of Corti as seen by transmission (A) and scanning (B) electron microscopy. bm = basilar membrane; IHC = inner hair cell; IPC = inner pillar cell; NE = nerve endings; OHC = outer hair cell; OPC = outer pillar cell; RL = reticular lamina; S = stereocilia; TC = tunnel of Corti.

Fig. 7-12. Scanning electron micrographs of the surface of the organ of Corti (A) and of an individual outer hair cell (B). d = Deiters' cell; h = Hensen cell; IHC = inner hair cell; mv = microvilli; OHC = outer hair cell; pc = pillar cell.

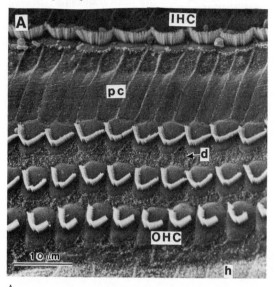

A

SUPPORTING CELLS

The sensory cells are stabilized by an elaborate system of supporting cells. These supporting cells were described fully by Retzius (1884), later by Held (1926), and more recently by Angelborg and Engström (1972). Pillar cells and Deiters' cells contain a number of rigid structural proteins and provide a firm mechanical framework that seems well suited to couple basilar membrane motion to the sensory region of the reticular lamina. The supporting cells also may serve a nutritive role for the sensory hair cells.

The supporting function of the pillar cells is illustrated in Figure 7-11. The footplate of the inner pillar cell is anchored to the basilar membrane by an electron-dense cement-like substance. From this base, a slender (1 to 2 μm) but stiff cell body arises that is filled with regularly arranged tubular tonofibrils and other microfilaments. At the surface of the organ of Corti, the pillar head makes contact with and supports the inner hair cells.

B

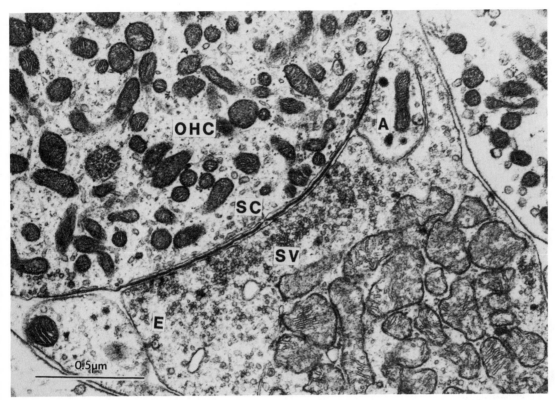

Fig. 7-13. Electron micrograph of the basal region of an outer hair cell showing afferent and efferent nerve terminals. A = afferent terminal; E = efferent terminal; OHC = outer hair cell; SC = subsynaptic cisterns; SV = synaptic vesicles.

The outer pillar cells have a structure similar to that of the inner pillar cells: They have a footplate that gives rise to a supporting shaft (see Fig. 7-11). At the surface of the organ of Corti, the pillar heads form the cuticular lamina around the second row of outer hair cells.

The supporting role of Deiters' cells is clearly illustrated in Figure 7-14. These cells are attached to the basilar membrane below the outer hair cell region and are equal in number to them. Each has a slender process containing tubular filaments and microfilaments similar to those found in the pillar cells. At the surface of the organ of Corti, each cell has a phalangeal process that forms part of the reticular lamina and supports the second and third rows of outer hair cells. At the reticular surface, Deiters' cells have abundant microvilli, especially at their cell borders. This feature contrasts with the pillar cells, which have relatively few microvilli (as is evident in Figure 7-12A).

Hensen cells are columnar cells positioned next to the Deiters' cells on the basilar membrane. They extend to the surface of the organ of Corti, where they also have many microvilli. Toward the apical turns, Hensen cells are packed with large (5 to 10 μm) lipid granules. There is some evidence that both Deiters' and Hensen cells can absorb small particles, suggesting that these cells may be involved in clearing cochlea debris.

The organ of Corti is bounded on the strial side by the Claudius cells, which form a layer over the basilar membrane. These cells are not highly differentiated and have few mitochondria and microvilli. Toward the base of the cochlea the Claudius cell area contains a group of Boettcher cells, forming a single cuboidal layer. These cells have invaginations and otherwise irregular contact with each other and with the basilar membrane, indicating a possible secretory or resorptive function.

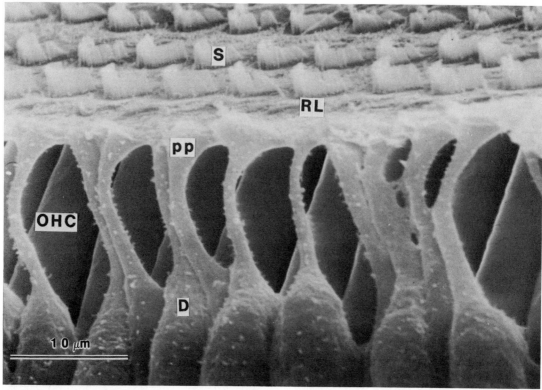

Fig. 7-14. Role of Deiters' cells in the support of outer hair cells (OHC). D = Deiters' cell; pp = phalangeal process; RL = reticular lamina; S = stereocilia.

SPIRAL LIGAMENT AND STRIA VASCULARIS

The spiral ligament forms the point of attachment of the basilar membrane with the cochlear wall and also supports the stria vascularis. The major portion of the ligament is made up of loosely arranged fibrous bundles, blood vessels, and connective tissue cells (fibrocytes) (Takahasi and Kimura, 1970). The spiral ligament is separated from the endolymphatic space by a surface epithelial cell layer.

The stria is the major vascular area of the cochlea. It has three main layers: marginal dark cell layer, intermediate light cell layer, and basal cell layer. A network of arterioles runs within these layers. The superficial stria is composed exclusively of large marginal cells that have numerous small microvilli at their endolymphatic surface. These marginal cells constitute the major part of the stria. The cells have finger-like processes that make intimate contact with the smaller intermediate cells. Cytoplasmic processes invade the marginal cells. Pinocytotic vesicles and melanin granules (melanocytes) are common. The basal cells are adjacent to the spiral ligament and are flat, with long extensions into the intermediate and marginal cell layers. Throughout these layers is an extensive network of blood vessels (Hinojosa and Rodriguez-Echandia, 1966; Kimura and Schuknect, 1970; Smith, 1957).

Blood supply to the stria is from the spiral modiolar artery via vessels passing over scala vestibuli to the lateral cochlear wall. Collecting venules in the wall of scala tympani return blood to the spiral modiolar vein. For further details on cochlear vasculature see Axelsson (1968).

INNERVATION OF THE COCHLEA

Innervation of the cochlea consists of (1) the afferent system—neurons transmitting information from the cochlea to the central auditory system; (2) efferent neurons of central origin exerting descending control on the cochlea; and (3) autonomic nerve fibers.

Afferent neurons have their cell bodies in the spiral ganglion. They are bipolar, have a peripheral portion extending into the organ of Corti, and innervate the sensory hair cells and a central axon that comprises the cochlear nerve and terminates in the cochlear nucleus of the brainstem. The central axon of the ganglion cell and its peripheral process are myelinated (as far as the openings of the habenula perforata). Within the organ of Corti all neurons are unmyelinated.

The innervation scheme for the mammalian cochlea is summarized in Figure 7-9 (Spoendlin, 1966). There are two main types of afferent neurons: the inner radial fibers, which innervate only the inner hair cells and make up most of the afferents, and the outer spiral fibers, which innervate the outer hair cells. The latter comprise approximately 10 percent of afferent neurons (Morrison, Schindler, and Wersall, 1975; Spoendlin, 1970). Approximately 20 inner radial fibers pass through each habenulum perforatum with one of perhaps two fibers destined for the outer hair cells. Inner radial fibers terminate directly on adjacent inner hair cells, whereas outer spiral fibers cross the tunnel of Corti and take a spiral course basalward, typically for approximately 0.5 to 0.7 mm, before terminating on about ten outer hair cells. For all animal species investigated there is considerable variation in the length (0.2 to 0.7 mm) and number (6 to 20) of outer hair cells innervated (Perkins and Morest, 1975). The afferent nerve endings occupy a very small portion of the outer hair cell base. Here, efferent endings dominate, especially in lower cochlear turns.

Within the spiral ganglion there are two types of cell body that are easily distinguishable. Type I gives rise to inner radial fibers, and type II belongs to the outer spiral fibers. The latter are smaller and have fewer cytoplasmic organelles than type I. Central to the spiral ganglion, the axons congregate in the modiolus and run together to the cochlear nucleus of the brainstem, maintaining their cochleotopic arrangement (Lorente de Nó, 1933; Sando, 1965). In cochleotopic organization adjacent cochlear neurons originate from adjacent parts of the cochlea, and thus a representation of cochlear position (and therefore place coded frequency) is maintained at the level of the cochlear nucleus and beyond. Because the cochlea codes stimulus frequency in terms of place along the cochlea, cochleotopic organization also implies tonotopicity. There is no histologic evidence to suggest that, from their origin at the hair cell(s) to their termination at the cochlear nucleus, the afferent neurons synapse with each other or with any other type of neuron.

The size of the cochlear nerve varies with the species. In humans and rhesus monkey there are approximately 30,000 axons, compared with 50,000 in the cat and 24,000 in the chinchilla and guinea pig (Harrison and Howe, 1974a).

Fig. 7-15. Major descending auditory pathways. AVCN = anteroventral cochlear nucleus; CN = central nucleus of inferior colliculus; COCB = crossed olivocochlear bundle; DCN = dorsal cochlear nucleus; DN = dorsal nucleus of medial geniculate body; DLPO = dorsolateral periolivary nucleus; DMPO = dorsomedial periolivary nucleus; EN = external nucleus of inferior colliculus; LSO = lateral superior olivary nucleus; MN = medial nucleus of medial geniculate body; MSO = medial superior olivary nucleus; MTB = medial nucleus of trapezoid body; PN = pericentral nucleus of inferior colliculus; PVCN = posteroventral cochlear nucleus; UOCB = uncrossed olivocochlear bundle; VN = ventral nucleus of medial geniculate body.

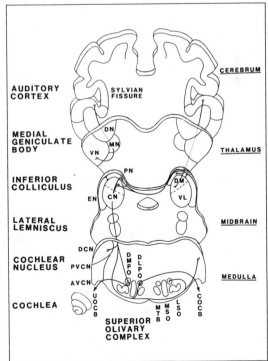

The efferents have their main origin in the brainstem (Iurato, 1974; Rasmussen, 1960; Smith, 1967; Spoendlin, 1966). The ipsilateral superior olivary complex gives rise to the so-called uncrossed olivocochlear bundle, and the contralateral olive is the origin of the crossed olivocochlear bundle (Fig. 7-15). The crossed bundle accommodates about three-fourths of all the efferent fibers (approximately 500 total).

Centrifugally the olivocochlear bundle runs initially with the vestibular nerve as far as the internal auditory meatus and then joins the cochlear nerve via a bony connecting channel called the anastomosis of Oort. Within the modiolus the efferents form the intraganglionic spiral bundle from where they branch out and send regular projections to the habenula perforata. The overall pattern of afferent and efferent innervation is summarized in Figure 7-9A (Spoendlin, 1966), and the relation between afferent and efferent nerve endings is illustrated in Figure 7-9B.

Within the spiral ganglion and osseus spiral lamina is a plexus of nonmyelinated fibers that originate in the superior cervical ganglion (Spoendlin and Lichtensteiger, 1966). This adrenergic (liberating norepinephrine at a synapse), sympathetic nerve supply is mainly associated with vasomotor control in the spiral ganglion area. However, some endings have been observed to end directly on nonmyelinated afferent neurons near the habenula perforata (Densert and Flock, 1974). This sympathetic innervation is not found within the organ of Corti or in the stria vascularis.

CENTRAL AUDITORY PATHWAYS

The principal afferent auditory pathways are shown in Figure 7-16. Here the neural connections relate to input from one ear only. In overview, the cell bodies of neurons that make up the pathways are contained in six major areas: cochlear nucleus, superior olivary complex, nuclei of the lateral lemniscus, inferior colliculus, medial geniculate body, and auditory cortex. Each of these areas contains many distinct regions or subdivisions identifiable on neuroanatomic grounds.

Primary afferent neurons separately innervate three subdivisions of the cochlear nucleus: a dorsal area and two ventral areas (anterior and posterior). There are separate output pathways from each of these areas. Axons from the ventral areas pass to the superior olivary complexes ipsilaterally and contralaterally. In the other areas, the main output from the dorsal cochlear nucleus connects directly with the central nucleus of the contralateral inferior colliculus.

The superior olivary complex, as its name suggests, is a collection of nine areas of cell bodies. For the afferent auditory pathway, only three are of major importance: the lateral and medial superior olivary nuclei and the medial nucleus of the trapezoid body. These nuclei are the first to receive input from both ears and have an important role in binaural processing, and thus sound localization. From the superior olivary complex, ascending axons pass anteriorly via the tracts of the lateral lemniscus to the central nucleus of the inferior colliculus in the midbrain region.

At the lemniscal and collicular levels there are connections across the brain midline: the commissures of Probst and of the inferior colliculus, respectively (see Fig. 7-16). The ventral nucleus of the medial geniculate body is purely auditory. It receives input from the inferior colliculus and projects to the primary auditory cortex. The dorsal and medial nuclei of the medial geniculate are multisensory and project to all auditory cortical areas. There are no commissural connections at the level of the medial geniculate. At the cortical level the connection between auditory areas is mediated via the corpus callosum, the massive fiber tract that connects left and right cerebral areas (cerebral hemispheres in humans).

Throughout the auditory pathways an important "mainline" structural feature, that of cochleotopic or tonotopic organization, is maintained from the periphery to the cortical level. Thus each nucleus in the afferent pathways has an organized representation of the length of the cochlear sensory epithelium.

COCHLEAR NUCLEI

The cochlear nuclei are the first aggregates of nerve cell bodies in the brainstem auditory pathway. These primary acoustic nuclei were

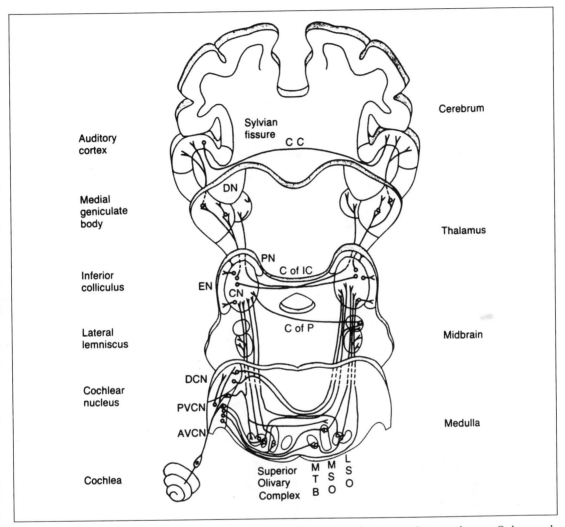

Auditory
cortex

Medial
geniculate
body

Inferior
colliculus

Lateral
lemniscus

Cochlear
nucleus

Cochlea

Sylvian
fissure

C C

DN

PN
C of IC
EN   CN

C of P

DCN

PVCN

AVCN

Superior
Olivary
Complex

M
T
B

M
S
O

L
S
O

Cerebrum

Thalamus

Midbrain

Medulla

Fig. 7-16. Ascending auditory pathways. Only neural connections relating to input from one ear are shown. The cochlear nucleus includes the dorsal cochlear nucleus (DCN), posteroventral cochlear nucleus (PVCN), and anteroventral cochlear nucleus (AVCN). The nuclei of the superior olivary complex associated with the ascending pathways are the medial nucleus of the trapezoid body (MTB), medial superior olivary nucleus (MSO), and lateral superior olivary nucleus (LSO). The inferior colliculus consists of the central nucleus (CN), pericentral nucleus (PN), and external nucleus (EN). The medial geniculate body consists of a ventral nucleus (VN), dorsal nucleus (DN), and medial nucleus (MN). Cross connections between auditory areas are made at the corpus callosum (CC), commissure of the inferior colliculi (C of IC), and commissure of Probst (C of P), as well as at midline crossing tracts in the brainstem.

originally described in full by Lorente de Nó (1933). More recent studies have been reported by Harrison and Warr (1962), Osen (1969), and Brawer, Morest, and Kane (1974). The cochlear nucleus can be divided into dorsal (DCN) and ventral (VCN) areas, the latter being further subdivided into an anterior part (AVCN) and a posterior part (PVCN).

Lorente de Nó (1933) used a Golgi staining technique to impregnate individual neurons with silver throughout their length, allowing them to be traced. Some of these input axonal pathways are shown in Figure 7-17A. In can be seen clearly that axons of the cochlear nerve bifurcate and send branches to AVCN and PVCN areas. Axons to the PVCN further innervate the dorsal area.

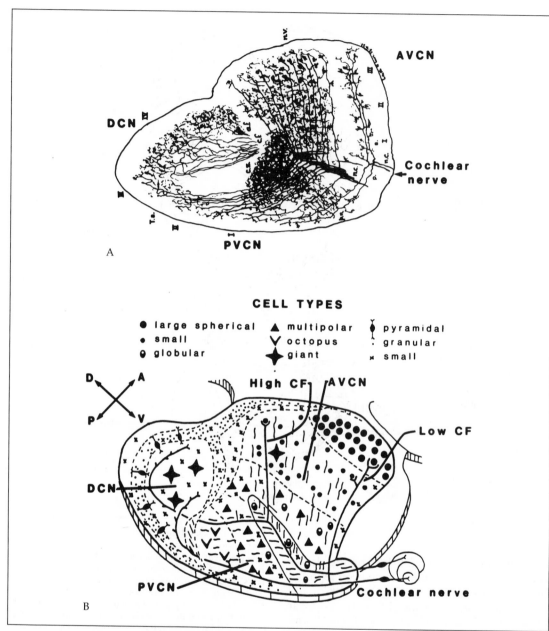

Fig. 7-17. A. Sagittal section of the cochlear nucleus showing Golgi-impregnated neurons. B. Cytoarchitectural map of the cochlear nucleus (sagittal section) showing the distribution of predominant cell types as defined after Nissl staining. AVCN = anteroventral cochlear nucleus; DCN = dorsal cochlear nucleus; PVCN = posteroventral cochlear nucleus. (A. From Lorente de Nó, R. Anatomy of the eighth nerve. I. The central projection of the nerve endings of the internal ear. *Laryngoscope* 43:1, 1933. B. Adapted from Osen K. K. Projection of the cochlear nuclei on the inferior colliculus in the cat. *J. Comp. Neurol.* 144:355, 1972.)

The ascending branches end in the AVCN, with many large synaptic endings called *end bulbs of Held*. The descending branch gives rise to a plexus in the PVCN and to diffuse ramifying terminals in the central region of the DCN.

Osen (1972) classified neuron cell bodies into nine types according to their light microscopic appearance after Nissl staining (Fig. 7-17B). In contrast to the homogeneity of the cochlear nerve, the cochlear nucleus contains a large variety of cell bodies.

There are a number of schemes for describing areas of the nucleus based on cytoarchitecture. In the classification used by Osen (1969), they are classified according to the cell types that dominate that region. Some cell types, for example large spherical cells, small spherical cells, and octopus cells, appear in well defined areas. Other cell types such as globular, pyramidal, and giant and small cells, are less confined to specific areas. Although useful, this scheme must be used with some caution because the cell types are determined specifically by their appearance with Nissl staining methods, which reveal mainly the cell body. Using Golgi techniques, a rather different and more detailed picture is seen because axon and dendrites become silver-impregnated (Brawer et al., 1974; Brawer and Morest, 1962; Lorente de Nó, 1933, 1981). The appearance of cells, and therefore their classification, is different from that derived with Nissl staining.

The input axons from the auditory nerve are organized in the AVCN in a systematic fashion such that there is cochleotopic arrangement of neurons. Thus neurons from the apex of the cochlea (responding best to low frequencies of sound stimulation) innervate the anteroventral areas of the AVCN, whereas cells more posterodorsal within the AVCN respond best to high frequencies (Evans and Nelson, 1973; Rose, Greenwood, Goldberg, and Hind, 1963). The PVCN and DCN are also cochleotopically organized. Thus neurons at the dorsal margin of the DCN receive input from high-frequency neurons from the cochlear base. More ventrally, neurons respond best to low frequencies. These organizations are shown in Figure 7-17B.

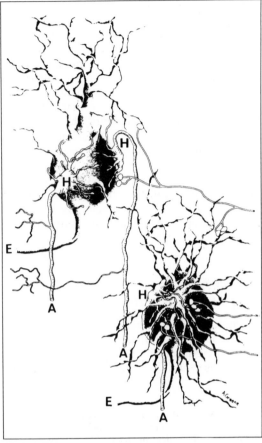

Fig. 7-18. Reconstruction of bushy neurons (spherical cells) from the anteroventral cochlear nucleus. Input axons (A) from the cochlear nerve synapse on the cell bodies with large end-bulbs of Held (H). The cells send their output axons (E) to the ipsilateral and contralateral superior olivary complex. (From Morest D. K., Kiang, N. Y. S., Kane, E. C., Guinan, J. J., Jr., and Godfrey, D. A. Stimulus coding at caudal levels of the cat's auditory nervous system. II. Patterns of synaptic organization. In A. R. Moller (ed.), *Basic Mechanisms in Hearing.* New York: Academic Press, 1973. Pp. 479–504.)

ANTEROVENTRAL COCHLEAR NUCLEUS

The most anterior area of the AVCN contains closely packed neurons, defined (using Nissl stain) as large spherical cells. More posteriorly, Nissl staining shows a small-cell region that also contains multipolar and giant cells. With Golgi staining the AVCN is characterized by two principal cell types: the stellate cell and the bushy or brush cell (Brawer et al., 1974). It is probable that the bushy/brush cells correspond to the large spherical cells seen in Nissl preparations (Lorente de Nó, 1981). The small cells in Nissl preparations found throughout the AVCN area are, in Golgi preparations, small stellate cells. The giant cells of Nissl preparations are probably larger stellate cells.

Two bushy (spherical) cells from the AVCN are shown in Figure 7-18 (Morest, Kiang, Kane, Guinan, and Godfrey, 1973). Relatively thick axons from the ascending branch of the auditory nerve form synapses with large end-bulbs of

Held. Each bushy cell receives one to three such synapses. The synaptic area is large, and as a consequence almost all activity in the input axon causes depolarization of the bushy cell. As a result of this *secure synapse*, the cell has response properties that are almost identical to those of the cochlear nerve. Of paramount importance, as discussed below, is that there is little or no degradation of timing information at this synapse. Indeed, these AVCN neurons can be considered to be simple relays. The output axons from these bushy cells as well as axons from stellate cells leave the AVCN via the ventral stria (band of fibers) and innervate the superior olivary complex on both the ipsilateral and contralateral sides of the brainstem (see Figs. 7-16 and 7-19).

POSTEROVENTRAL
COCHLEAR NUCLEUS

Classic anatomic studies (e.g., Lorente de Nó, 1933) have subdivided the PVCN into as many as eight regions. For the purpose of this review it is useful to consider only the major cell

types and their distributions. As always, the appearance and therefore the classification of cells depends on the histologic technique used to reveal them.

"Octopus cells" (Fig. 7-20) are found exclusively in the central area of the PVCN, where they are accompanied by a few smaller types of neuron. The octopus cell body is covered with somatic spicules, which effectively increase the surface area of the neuron to allow maximal area for synaptic endings, which cover about 70 percent of the cell body. Axons from the descending branches of the auditory nerve end with relatively large synapses (e.g., S1) as well as with smaller collaterals (S2). The input synapses to the octopus cell can be on the cell body or on the peripheral or distal dendrites. Electrophysiologic recordings from octopus cells show *onset* responses; that is, they initiate action potential spikes in coincidence with the onset of sounds. It is possible that these small collaterals are inhibitory, and that this inhibitory activity via the small diameter fibers is delayed with respect to the main afferent input to allow only an initial excitation response to sound (Morest et al., 1973).

In areas anterior to the central area of the PVCN, Osen (1969) distinguished multipolar cells and small cells based on Nissl staining. With Golgi techniques, stellate cells and small elongate neurons are found. Dorsal areas con-

Fig. 7-19. Main output pathways from the cochlear nucleus. AVCN = anteroventral cochlear nucleus; DCN = dorsal cochlear nucleus; LSO = lateral nucleus of superior olive; MTB = medial nucleus of trapezoid body; MSO = medial nucleus of superior olive; RB = restiform body.

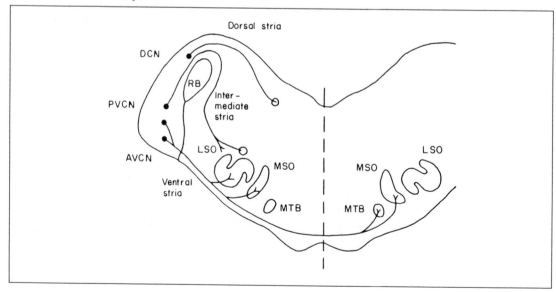

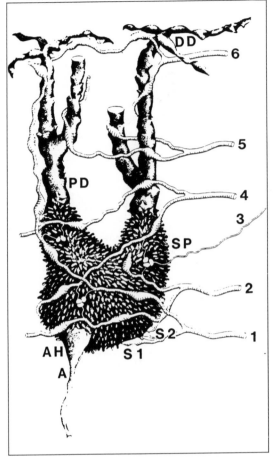

Fig. 7-20. Reconstruction of an octopus cell from the posteroventral cochlear nucleus. The cell body is covered with somatic spicules (SP). Input neurons are labeled 1 through 6. A = output axon of cell; AH = axon hillock; DD = distal dendrite; PD = proximal dendrite. (From Morest D. K., Kiang, N. Y. S., Kane, E. C., Guinan, J. J., Jr., and Godfrey, D. A. Stimulus coding at caudal levels of the cat's auditory nervous system. II. Patterns of synaptic organization. In A. R. Moller (ed.), *Basic Mechanisms in Hearing*. New York: Academic Press, 1973. Pp. 479–504.)

tain predominantly large elongate neurons and bushy multipolar and stellate cells.

It is not clear which Golgi-stained cell types correspond to the Nissl classification of Osen as shown in Figure 7-17B. The large elongate and stellate cells are probably the multipolar cells; the bushy cells may correspond with the globular cells or the small cells described by Osen.

Most of the output axons of neurons in the PVCN pass via the ventral stria to the superior

olivary complex, forming the trapezoid body. As shown in Figure 7-19, a small number of fibers pass from the PVCN dorsally over the restiform body and then through the intermediate acoustic stria to the superior olivary complex. This fiber tract may include axons from the onset-type octopus cells, transmitting onset timing information to the superior olivary complex.

DORSAL COCHLEAR NUCLEUS

The DCN has a laminar structure, and some authors, notably Lorente de Nó (1933) used the term cortex to describe the outer layers of the DCN. Figure 7-21 shows the cell types in the "cortex" based on Golgi-stained specimens (Lorente de Nó, 1981). The DCN can be classified into four layers: Layer I (molecular layer) contains small neurons with short axons (parallel to the surface) that make connections within the neuropil, the network of nerve fibers (e.g., cell types 6 and 7, see also the small cell region in Figure 7-17B). Layer II is termed the fusiform layer and contains small granule cells and larger *fusiform* cells. The granule cells have smooth cell bodies 6 to 8 μm in diameter and highly irregular dendrites (see cells 8, 10, 11, and 16 in Figure 7-21). They appear to surround the DCN (see also Osen's distribution of cell types in Figure 7-17B). The fusiform cells have smooth cell bodies, which taper into thick dendritic trunks that span the DCN cortex (cell 1 in Figure 17-21). These cells are labeled pyramidal cells in the Nissl-based classification of Figure 7-17B.

The deepest layer of the DCN, the polymorphic layer, is characterized by a variety of giant cells with cell bodies 30 to 40 μm in diameter (e.g., cells 3 and 4 in Figure 17-21) interspersed with smaller neurons. Three types of giant cell have been distinguished—radial, horizontal, and vertical—according to the orientation of the cell dendrites. The polymorphic area corresponds to layers III and IV in Figure 7-21, where some of the large variety of cell types are depicted.

In general, the DCN receives ascending input from the cochlear nerve via the PVCN. Some cell types within the DCN, notably the fusiform (pyramidal) and giant cells, give rise to axons that leave the DCN via the *stria of von Monokow* (dorsal acoustic stria of Figure 7-19). These out-

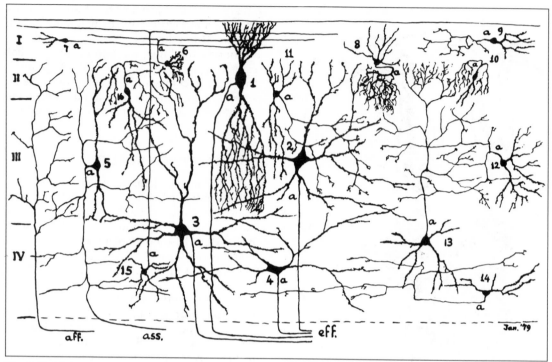

Fig. 7-21. Major neuron types in the cortex of the dorsal cochlear nucleus (DCN). Input fibers (afferent) terminate primarily in layers II and III. Four neuron types (1 to 4) give rise to ascending axons (efferent), which eventually project to the inferior colliculus. Cell types 6 to 16 are interneurons with short axons that remain within the DCN. ass. = association fiber; a = axon. (From Lorente de Nó, R. *The Primary Acoustic Nuclei.* New York: Raven Press, 1981.)

put axons project anteriorly toward both the ipsilateral and contralateral inferior colliculus.

Within the DCN cortex there are many neurons with short axons (e.g., 6 to 16 in Figure 7-21) that probably mediate activity within the DCN. There are also interneurons that arise in the DCN and connect with other areas of the cochlear nucleus. One such association fiber is depicted in Figure 7-21.

The main efferent (descending) pathways to the cochlear nucleus are as follows. From the olivocochlear bundle there are collaterals of the cochlear efferents (which terminate on the cochlear hair cells) that end in the cochlear nucleus, predominantly in the superficial layers of the AVCN. Substantial efferent connections exist between the lateral nucleus of the superior olive and the AVCN (Lorente de Nó, 1933; Rasmus-

sen, 1960). The cochlear nucleus also receives considerable descending input from the inferior colliculus (Fig. 7-15).

SUPERIOR OLIVARY COMPLEX

The superior olivary complex consists of a group of at least nine closely packed nuclei in the brainstem medulla. Three of these nuclei are important for the ascending auditory system, i.e., the lateral superior olivary (LSO) nucleus, the medial superior olivary (MSO) nucleus and the medial nucleus of the trapezoid body (MTB nucleus) (see Figs. 7-16 and 7-19). In nonprimate species both LSO and MSO nuclei are prominent. In humans the MSO nucleus is relatively large compared with the LSO nucleus. The superior olivary complex is the first site in the auditory pathway to receive innervation from both ears. Therefore it has an important role when comparing the input to the two ears (binaural processes)—and thus in sound localization.

The ascending input pathways to the main nuclei of the superior olivary complex are illustrated in Figure 7-19. Most input originates from the AVCN. These axons pass via the ventral stria (often termed the trapezoid body) and innervate the ipsilateral LSO and MSO nuclei as well as the contralateral MTB and MSO nuclei. The MTB nucleus acts as a relay for input to the contralateral LSO nucleus. In addition to this major input, neurons in the PVCN and DCN also send some axons to the ipsilateral and contralateral LSO nuclei, respectively (Harrison and Warr, 1962).

MEDIAL NUCLEUS OF THE TRAPEZOID BODY

Three major types of neuron are found in the MTB nucleus and have been termed principal cells, stellate cells, and elongate cells (Morest 1968, 1973). The principal cell is innervated from some of the largest axons in the trapezoid body by the large *calyces of Held* (Fig. 7-22). The calyx of Held is a *secure synapse* that can faithfully relay incoming neural activity directly to the LSO nucleus. The input and output axons are large in diameter and facilitate rapid information transfer from the AVCN to the (contralateral) LSO nucleus. In addition to the large calyx of Held, there are other, smaller synaptic contacts onto the cell body and dendrites. The main input axons also form some collaterals that innervate nearby principal cells (Fig. 7-22). The stellate cells and elongate cells are characterized by long dendritic fields that contact input fibers, often at some distance from their cell bodies (Lenn and Rees, 1966). The major ascending output from the MTB nucleus is to the ipsilateral LSO nucleus (Fig. 7-16).

MEDIAL SUPERIOR OLIVARY NUCLEUS

The MSO nucleus receives input from both cochlear nuclei, primarily the AVCN. The axonal endings line up in an ordered fashion along a dorsal to ventral axis that reflects the tonotopic organization of the AVCN (Goldberg and Brown, 1968). Thus neurons carrying high-frequency information are represented ventrally in the MSO nucleus, and lower frequencies are represented in more dorsal neurons. In general, there is a greater representation of low-frequency neurons in the MSO nucleus than high-frequency neurons.

Ascending axons from the ipsilateral cochlear

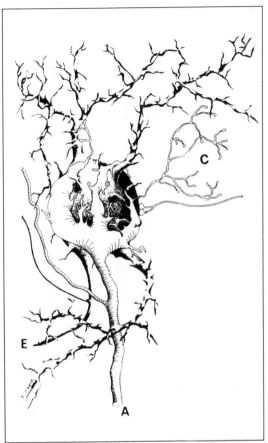

Fig. 7-22. Reconstruction of a principal neuron of the medial nucleus of the trapezoid body. The input axon (A) forms a large synaptic calyx on the cell body. The output axon (E) goes to the ipsilateral lateral nucleus of the superior olive. Thin collaterals (C) from the synaptic calyx innervate nearby principal cells. (From Morest, D. K., Kiang, N. Y. S., Kane, E. C., Guinan, J. J., Jr., and Godfrey, D. A. Stimulus coding at caudal levels of the cat's auditory nervous system. II. Patterns of synaptic organization. In A. R. Moller (ed.), *Basic Mechanisms in Hearing.* New York: Academic Press, 1973. Pp. 479–504.)

nucleus end in the lateral part of the MSO nucleus, whereas axons from the contralateral cochlear nucleus end in the medial half of the MSO nucleus. Between those extremes the main neurons of the MSO nucleus have elongated dendritic fields that are flattened in the horizontal plane and span 300 to 500 µm. The incoming axons branch within horizontal layers on either side of the MSO neurons. Incoming axons from both cochlear nuclei come from cells with secure synapses (end bulbs of Held) in the

AVCN. Thus the MSO cells appear well suited for comparing temporally accurate information from the two ears. Indeed, many cells appear to respond best to stimuli with a certain interaural time delay, so-called characteristic delay cells (Crow, Rupert, and Moushegian, 1978).

Animals with large heads, and therefore a relatively large distance between the ears, can more effectively use interaural timing cues for sound localization. Consequently, the MSO nucleus in those animals (e.g., humans) is large (Masterton and Diamond, 1967).

LATERAL SUPERIOR OLIVARY NUCLEUS

The LSO nucleus is tonotopically organized (Tsuchitani and Boudreau, 1966). However, in contrast to the MSO nucleus, most neurons in the LSO nucleus are sensitive to high-frequency stimuli. The ipsilateral input to the LSO nucleus arises mainly in the AVCN. The contralateral input originates in the AVCN and from rostral areas of the PVCN. These input pathways are interrupted by the synaptic relay of the MTB nucleus, described above. Most of the neurons in the LSO nucleus receive input from both ears. For some cells the response to stimulation of either ear is excitatory (EE cells). However, most neurons are excitatory to ipsilateral stimuli and inhibited by contralateral stimuli (EI cells) (Brownell, Manis, and Ritz, 1979; Goldberg and Brown, 1969). The main cells in the LSO are multipolar with flattened dendritic fields that spread considerably in an anteroposterior direction, perhaps as much as 1 mm (Scheibel and Scheibel, 1974).

Most cells in the LSO nucleus, particulary EI cells, appear to have a role in detecting interaural intensity differences. Animals with small heads tend to rely on these cues more than interaural time delays; and indeed in these species the LSO nucleus is relatively large. It is also important to note that the interaural intensity difference is greater for high frequencies of sound because they are more effectively attenuated or shadowed by the head. For this reason (probably) the LSO nucleus contains mainly neurons that respond best to high-frequency stimuli.

The ascending projections from the superior olivary complex are summarized in Figure 7-16. The MSO nucleus has strictly ipsilateral projections to the inferior colliculus via the fiber tracts

of the lateral lemniscus. The LSO nucleus projects to both ipsilateral and contralateral lateral lemnisci, ending in the ventrolateral part of the central nucleus of the inferior colliculus (Elverland, 1978; Rasmussen, 1946).

LATERAL LEMNISCUS

The lateral lemniscus (LL) consists of axons originating from a number of sources including the DCN, superior olivary complex, nuclei of the LL, and short fibers linking parts of the latter nuclei (Rasmussen, 1946). The cell groups that make up the nuclei of the LL fall into two distinct areas: the dorsal nucleus and the ventral nucleus. Axons from the DCN innervate a medial position in the LL, and some terminate in the ventral nucleus of the LL. Others, en route to the inferior colliculus, give off collaterals to the dorsal nucleus of the LL. In general, the ventral nucleus of the LL receives a binaural input and projects to both ipsilateral and contralateral inferior colliculi via the commissure of Probst (Aitkin, Anderson, and Brugge, 1970) (see Fig. 7-16).

Axons to the LL originating from the superior olivary complex do so from both MSO and LSO nuclei. The LL contains fibers from the ipsilateral and contralateral LSO nuclei but only from the MSO nucleus on the same side (Elverland, 1978). The tonotopic organizations of neurons from the DCN and the nuclei of the superior olivary complex are maintained in the fiber tracts and in both major nuclei of the LL (Aitkin et al., 1970).

Most ascending lemniscal fibers terminate in the central nucleus of the inferior colliculus. Only a small proportion of fibers enter or end in the external nucleus of the inferior colliculus (Goldberg and Moore, 1967).

INFERIOR COLLICULUS

The inferior colliculus forms a part of the midbrain tectum, which makes up the posterior pair of the four lobes on the dorsal surface of the midbrain. Pioneering studies by Ramon y Cajal distinguished three major regions: central nucleus, internuclear cortex, and lateral cortex. Later authors have used different terminology, preferring "external nucleus" to "lateral cortex," and "pericentral nucleus" to "internuclear cortex" (Rockel and Jones, 1973a). In the present text the latter terminology is used. Figure 7-16 indicates the main areas of the inferior colliculus. It receives input from the superior olivary complex and directly from the DCN. Because of this convergence of pathways, it is reasonable to suppose that the inferior colliculus integrates information from both sources.

CENTRAL NUCLEUS

There has been a number of detailed studies of the cytoarchitecture of the central nucleus (Geniec and Morest, 1971; Morest, 1964; Rockel, 1971; Rockel and Jones, 1973a). The central nucleus can be subdivided into dorsomedial and ventrolateral divisions. The former is dominated by large multipolar cells and receives descending fibers from the auditory cortex and ascending input from the LL and the contralateral inferior colliculus. The ventrolateral division receives input predominantly from the LL and is characterized by bitufted and fusiform cells with disc-shaped dendritic fields that are oriented so as to give a laminar appearance to Golgi-stained specimens (Fig. 7-23). This orientation of dendritic fields is paralleled by the incoming fibers of the LL (Fig. 7-24) (Rockel and Jones, 1973a). It appears that entering lemniscal fibers run for most of the length of each lamina and have multiple synaptic knobs throughout their extent that make contact with the dendrites of the principal cells. This structural organization maintains a strict tonotopic organization in that each lamina contains neurons tuned to the same frequency. These isofrequency sheets can be compared to the skin of an onion. In dorsal areas the sheets form complete spheres that contain neurons responding to low frequencies. More ventrally, the (higher) isofrequency layers become flatter. With regard to the tonotopic organization, Osen (1972) described a strict point-to-point projection from the cochlear nucleus to the central nucleus of the inferior colliculus.

In addition to, but less common than, the bitufted and fusiform neurons are stellate cells. The dendrites of these cells lie parallel or sometimes perpendicular to the main dendritic laminae. They receive small synaptic terminals from ascending afferents, and their axons send collaterals to many laminae and clearly form the basis for interaction between different frequency areas of the inferior colliculus.

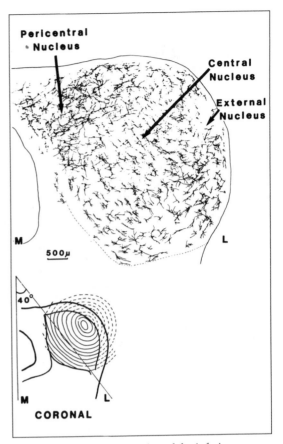

Fig. 7-23. Coronal cross section of the inferior colliculus showing a sample of neurons impregnated using Golgi techniques. Note the laminated arrangements of the dendritic fields of cells in the central nucleus. Inset. Lamina. L = lateral; M = medial. (Adapted from Rockel, A. J., and Jones, E. G. The neuronal organization of the inferior colliculus of the adult cat. I. The central nucleus. *J. Comp. Neurol.* 147:11, 1973a.)

There are four types of axon found in the central nucleus (Rockel and Jones, 1973a,b). Those from the LL, as described above, run along laminae. Also along the laminae but in the opposite direction are descending corticofugal axons. Another group of axons are widely ramifying and may arise with the central nucleus. Finally, there are the output axons of inferior colliculus neurons, which eventually project to the medial geniculate body or to the contralateral inferior colliculus.

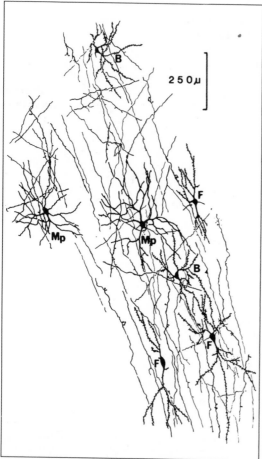

Fig. 7-24. Major cell types in the central nucleus of the inferior colliculus. The small parallel fibers are incoming axons that follow the orientation of the dendritic field of the neurons. B = bitufted cell; F = fusiform cell; Mp = multipolar cell. (From Rockel, A. J., and Jones, E. G. The neuronal organization of the inferior colliculus of the adult cat. I. The central nucleus. *J. Comp. Neurol.* 147:11, 1973a.)

PERICENTRAL AND EXTERNAL NUCLEI

Surrounding the central nucleus of the inferior colliculus are two main areas: the pericentral nucleus and the external nucleus. The pericentral nucleus has a laminar structure and receives a descending projection of fibers from the auditory cortex and an ascending projection from the dorsal nucleus of the LL (Geniec and Morest, 1971). The nucleus is composed of spiny and nonspiny cells (Rockel and Jones, 1973b). The former have numerous dendritic spines, large or small. Those cells with small dendrites are likely to be interneurons (i.e.,

communicating within the nucleus). The nonspiny cell types are large and multipolar or fusiform in shape. The dendrites of the multipolar cells extend through the thickness of the pericentral nucleus, and these cells are thought to give rise to efferent fibers. There is little evidence for direct projection from the central nucleus of the inferior colliculus to the pericentral nucleus.

The external nucleus is a caudal and dorsal extension from the central nucleus of the inferior colliculus and is described as a true cortex having different layers that may receive different inputs. These layers are crossed by dendrites whose cell bodies lie in other layers and appear to facilitate integration of the different inputs. Indeed, this nucleus does receive a significant somatosensory input as well as direct auditory projection from the central nucleus of the inferior colliculus, and it probably serves as an integrative area for these senses (Aitkin, Dickhaus, Shult, and Zimmerman, 1978; Robarts, 1979). There is some electrophysiologic evidence of tonotopic organization (Aitkin et al., 1978).

There are two major ascending output pathways from the inferior colliculus: the commissure of the inferior colliculus and the ipsilateral brachium connecting the inferior colliculus with the medial geniculate body (Fig. 7-16). Most commissural fibers arise in the dorsal area of the central nucleus of the inferior colliculus and terminate in the equivalent area of the opposite inferior colliculus; others, however, continue in the contralateral brachium to the medial geniculate body.

MEDIAL GENICULATE BODY

The medial geniculate body (MGB) is a "knee-shaped" region of the thalamus and can be roughly divided into three main areas: ventral, dorsal and medial divisions (Morest, 1964). The transverse section through the MGB of the cat (Fig. 7-25) shows the major subdivisions and some of the obvious cell types. A description of each major division of the MGB is given below. Most data are obtained from the cat or other nonhuman species. However, Winer (1984) has studied the human MGB and found similar anatomy except that the neuropil is much more elaborate. He described single or groups of neurons surrounded by expanses of fibers, clusters of glial cells, and associated dendrites and

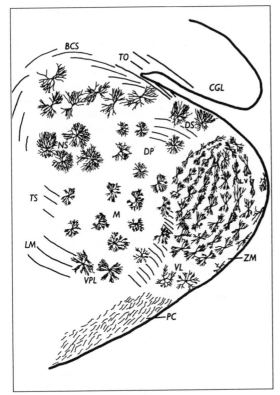

Fig. 7-25. Medial geniculate body (transverse section from cat) showing the major subdivisions and typical cell types. BCS = brachium colliculi superioris; CGL = corpus geniculatum laterale; DP = nucleus dorsalis profundus; DS = nucleus dorsalis superficialis; LM = lemniscus medialis; LV = nucleus ventrolateralis; M = medial division; NS = nucleus suprageniculatis; PC = pedunculus cerebri; TO = tractus opticus; TS = tracti spirothalamici; VL = nucleus ventrolateralis; VPL = nucleus ventralis posterolateralis thalami; ZM = zona marginalis. (Adapted from Morest, D. K. The neuronal architecture of the medial geniculate body of the cat. *J. Anat.* 98:611, 1964.)

intrinsic axons. Such observations suggest a higher level of development than in infrahuman species.

VENTRAL DIVISION

The ventral division of the MGB receives major input from the ascending axons originating in the inferior colliculus. It can be divided into an anterolateral "pars lateralis" and a ventromedial "pars ovoidea." The principal neurons of the pars lateralis are organized in parallel curved sheets and typically have six to eight dendrites and about 40 branching points; they are often described as "tufted" (see Fig. 7-25).

The dendritic fields are discoid with a long axis of about 200 μm. Their structure in the pars ovoidea is essentially the same as that in the pars lateral. These principal cells receive input from the inferior colliculus, with most ascending axons terminating in "synaptic nests" composed of the axonal endings and dendritic processes of the principal cells partially surrounded by lamellae of glial cells. The cells also receive input from the inferior colliculus via short axons of Golgi type II neurons. The latter have small flask-shaped soma and a thin axon ramifying in short unmyelinated collaterals (Morest, 1975).

The principal cells have a tonotopic organization (Aitkin and Webster, 1971) and project directly to the primary auditory cortex (geniculocortical neurons). There is a reciprocal, point-to-point descending (corticogeniculate) pathway, axons of which terminate on the distal dendrites of the principal cells or on the soma of the Golgi type II cells. Figure 7-26 illustrates a principal cell and a Golgi type II cell with their synaptic organization.

Winer (1984) has described a third neuron type in the ventral division of the MGB that has small cell bodies and a local and a distantly projecting axon. These cells receive much less ascending input than the principal tufted cells, and clearly they can act both locally and at a distance. The nature of the information they pass to the auditory cortex is unknown, but they probably have a role different from that of the principal cells.

DORSAL AND MEDIAL DIVISIONS

The neurons of the dorsal division receive few direct connections from the collicular region. Their main input is from the midbrain tegmentum, and their projections are largely to nonprimary auditory cortex. The dorsal division does, like the ventral area, receive descending corticogeniculate input. It is supposed that the dorsal division has input from a number of sensory modalities (Morest, 1964; Winer and Morest, 1983a).

The medial division receives a large ascending input from the inferior colliculus as well as other thalamic areas (Winer and Morest, 1983b). Some cells in the medial division are excited by somatosensory vibratory and vestibular stimuli (Poggio and Mountcastle, 1960). In posterior areas of the medial division there are numerous "radiate" neurons that have irregularly spaced

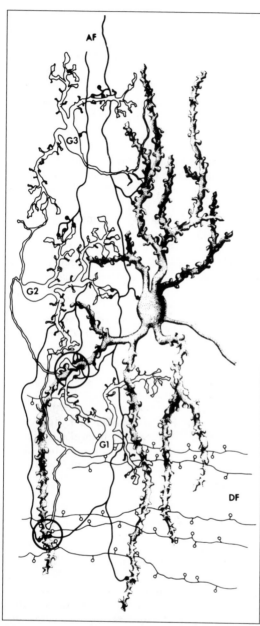

Fig. 7-26. Principal cell of the ventral nucleus of medial geniculate body (cat) showing its synaptic organization with ascending and descending fibers. The principal cell sends its axon to the auditory cortex. It receives input from ascending fibers (AF) from the inferior colliculus. These fibers also synapse with Golgi type II cells (G1, G2, G3), which in turn synapse onto the principal cell. Descending fibers (DF) from the cortex end mainly on the distal dendrites of the principal cells as well as the Golgi type II cells. (Adapted from Morest, D. K. Synaptic relationships of Golgi type II cells in the medial geniculate of the cat. *J. Comp. Neurol.* 162:157, 1975.)

dendritic branches and form oval dendritic fields (Fig. 7-25). The axons of these radiate neurons project to adjacent areas, particularly dorsal, suprageniculate, and ventral areas, and to the tufted neuron area of the dorsal region of the medial division. The axons from the tufted neurons project anteriorly to areas surrounding primary auditory cortex. The medial division also receives a descending input from several cortical regions, including insular and ectosylvian areas (Winer, Diamond, and Raczkowski, 1977).

AUDITORY CORTEX

The auditory cortex has been studied most extensively in subprimate species, notably the cat, in which it is largely exposed on the surface of the cortex. In humans and some other primates the main auditory area is within the sylvian fissure (Fig. 7-27B). It is assumed that the general principles of organization are similar for all mammalian species.

The auditory cortex has been defined using a variety of morphologic and electrophysiologic criteria. In general, the primary auditory cortex is surrounded by secondary auditory areas. The divisions of the (cat) auditory cortex are shown in Figure 7-27A (Woolsey, 1961). The neural architecture of the primary auditory cortex is similar to that of other primary sensory areas in the cortex, having six well defined layers (Fig. 7-28). In layers II, III, and IV there is a high density of pyramidal and granule cells, which give this region of cortex a "dust-like" appearance after Nissl staining. Indeed the term *koniocortex* (dust cortex) was originally used to define the primary auditory cortex (Rose, 1949).

Surrounding the primary auditory cortex are the secondary auditory cortex and the posterior ectosylvian gyrus, which were also defined by Rose (1949) on cytoarchitectural grounds. Other cortical areas were shown later to be responsive to auditory stimulation, notably the secondary somatosensory area and the insulotemporal region (Rose and Woolsey, 1958).

PRIMARY AUDITORY CORTEX

In general, the organization and cell types of auditory cortex are similar to those of other sensory cortical areas. Figure 7-28 depicts this general organization as realized with different staining procedures. Auditory cortex contains

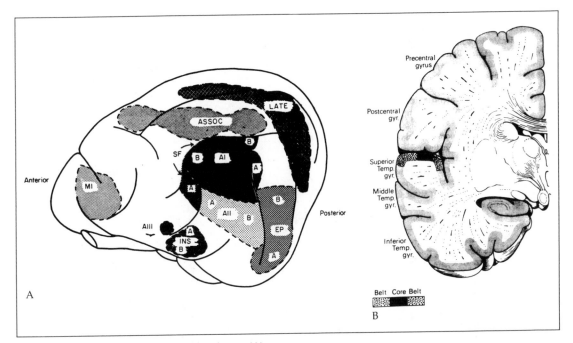

Fig. 7-27. Auditory areas of the cortex in the cat (A) and the human (B). A. Primary auditory area (AI) is surrounded by secondary and associated auditory cortices. AII = secondary auditory cortex; ASSOC = association area; EP = posterior ectosylvian gyrus; MI = precentral motor area; INS = insular area. Cochleotopic organization, if present, is indicated. Area A responds best to low-frequency stimuli to cochlear apex; area B is where basal cochlear stimulation (high frequency) is most effective. B. Cross section of one human cerebral hemisphere, showing the position of the auditory cortex in the sylvian fissure. (A. From Woolsey, C. N. Organization of cortical auditory system: a review and a synthesis. In G. L. Rasmussen and W. F. Windle, eds., *Neural Mechanisms of the Auditory and Vestibular Systems.* Springfield, IL: Charles C Thomas, 1960. Pp. 105–180.)

large pyramidal cells that have a vertical span of up to 500 μm through many cortical layers (Sousa-Pinto, 1973; Wong, 1967). These cells, with fusiform and stellate neurons, also have extensive dendritic fields in a horizontal plane, perhaps more so than in other types of sensory cortex (Wong, 1967). The major projections to the primary auditory cortex originate in the laminated portion of the central division of the MGB. This mainline connection is sometimes referred to as a *core system.* These afferent fibers terminate mainly in layer IV with some endings in layer III (Winer et al., 1977).

The cells in auditory cortex, particularly those in layers III to V, appear to be organized in vertical columns (Sousa-Pinto, 1973). This pattern is a general characteristic of cortical organization, as can be judged from Figure 7-28. There is electrophysiologic evidence of columnar organization in that vertical electrode penetrations through the primary auditory cortex yield responses from single cells that have nearly identical *characteristic frequencies* (sound frequency to which the neuron is most sensitive) (Merzenich, Kaas, and Roth, 1976).

Evoked potential and single unit studies (Merzenich, Knight, and Roth, 1975; Woolsey, 1960) have shown a tonotopic organization of neurons in the primary auditory cortex such that high frequencies (base of cochlea) are represented anteriorly and neurons more sensitive to low frequencies are located posteriorly. This organization appears to be common in many mammalian species including humans, where it has been confirmed by positron emission tomography (Lauter, Herscovitch, Formby, and Raichle, 1985) and magnetoencephalography (Elberling, Bak, Kofoed, Lebech, and Saermark, 1982). It should be noted that the absolute location of the primary auditory field and its tonotopic organization varies significantly among animals including humans (Merzenich et al., 1976; Penfield and Perot, 1963; Rose, 1949).

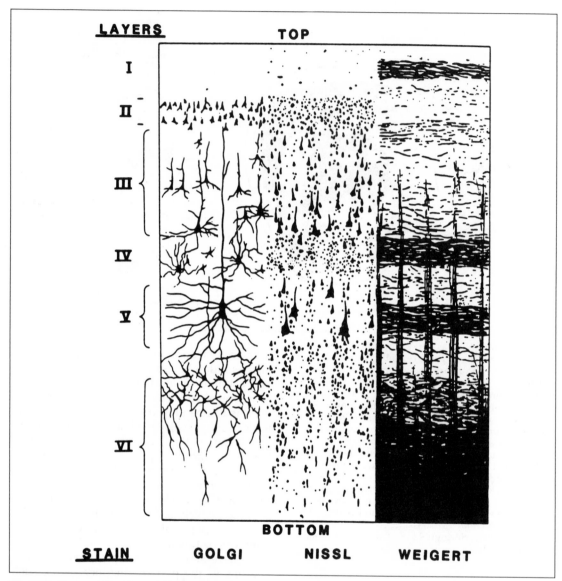

Fig. 7-28. Cross section through the sensory cortex, indicating its six layers. To the left are neurons as seen after Golgi impregnation. The center section shows the cell bodies (after Nissl staining). To the right are the main fiber tracts running across and along cortical layers (after Weigert staining). (Adapted from Ranson, S. W., and Clark, S. L. *Anatomy of the Nervous System*, 9th ed. Philadelphia: Saunders, 1953.)

OTHER AUDITORY CORTICAL AREAS

The medial division of the MGB projects to all areas of the auditory cortex, whereas the dorsal division sends axons to the insulotemporal region and posterior ectosylvian gyrus, and some projections to the secondary auditory cortex. The latter projections from the thalamus to secondary auditory cortical areas are sometimes called the *belt system*. Because the dorsal division of the medial geniculate body is multisensory and responds to somatosensory and visual modalities, cortical areas receiving input from this area, e.g., insulotemporal areas, also show multisensory properties. This situation is also the case with the secondary somatosensory area. Within the secondary auditory cortex and the posterior ectosylvian gyrus there is some tonotopic organization, but it is less obvious than in the primary auditory cortex. Many of the neurons in these *belt areas* do not have a single clearly definable best frequency.

For each ascending pathway from the thalamus to the cortex there is a substantial descending system (Harrison and Howe, 1974b). In addition, there are considerable corticocortical connections. Thus small lesions in the primary auditory cortex (AI) cause transneuronal degeneration into other (ipsilateral) areas of the AI, the posterior ectosylvian gyrus, the secondary auditory cortex (AII) and, to a lesser extent, the insular region. Contralaterally, the degeneration is found in AI over a region corresponding to the original lesion site. There is also some degeneration in the contralateral AII. Lesions of the AII also cause degeneration in the ipsilateral AI, AII, posterior ectosylvian gyrus, and insular and temporal regions, as well as the contralateral AII. The data suggest extensive interconnections of AI with other auditory areas ipsilaterally, as well as contralateral connections to corresponding auditory areas via the corpus callosum (the main fiber tracts between the cerebral hemispheres).

AUDITORY CORTEX IN HUMANS

In humans electrical stimulation of some auditory cortical areas outside the AI gives rise to "auditory hallucinations" (Penfield and Perot, 1963). Such auditory images may be complex, for example, voices or music. On the other hand, stimulation of AI gives rise to much more simple sensations.

Humans, of course, have a specialization of auditory function in the use of speech communication. In the cortex, an area primarily involved in speech analysis is Wernicke's area, an auditory association area on the posterior region of the temporal lobe of the dominant (usually left) hemisphere. Figure 7-29 shows evidence of increased blood flow in this area of the dominant hemisphere when a subject passively listens to speech. Broca's area, normally associated with speech production, also shows increased blood flow (Lassen, Ingvar, and Skin-

Fig. 7-29. Areas of greatest blood flow in the dominant cerebral hemisphere when a subject passively listens to speech. Blood flow is determined by detection of radioactive xenon 133 injected systematically. (Adapted from Lassen, N. A., Ingvar, D. H., and Skinhoj, E. Brain function and blood flow. *Sci. Am.* 239:50, 1978.)

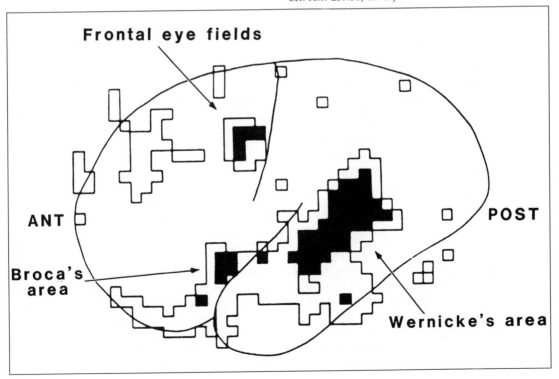

hoj, 1978). As with the absolute position of primary and secondary auditory areas, the exact position of these specialized speech areas appears to vary among subjects.

DESCENDING AUDITORY PATHWAYS

In mammalian studies it has been demonstrated that the auditory cortex gives rise to two possibly separate descending systems (Fig. 7-15). The first is a corticogeniculate pathway, where neurons originate in the primary auditory cortex and innervate the ventral division of the MGB. The pathway is ipsilateral and may end in the MGB. It is not clear if there are other descending pathways from the MGB (Harrison and Howe, 1974b).

The second system arises in the primary auditory cortex and descends to the dorsomedial area of the central nucleus of the inferior colliculus as well as its pericentral nucleus. In the central nucleus, these corticofugal fibers run along the laminations of the inferior colliculus in a direction opposite to that of the ascending fibers. Colliculi of both sides are thus innervated.

From the inferior colliculus, descending axons innervate the periolivary cell masses (principally dorsomedial and dorsolateral nuclei) and dorsal cochlear nucleus both ipsilaterally and contralaterally (Fig. 7-15). From the periolivary nuclei, both the cochlear nucleus and the cochlea receive descending fibers from several sources, the largest being the periolivary nuclei, but there are also inputs from the lateral lemniscus, inferior colliculus, and reticular formation (Adams and Warr, 1976). All divisions of the cochlear nucleus appear to receive some descending input. The descending efferent system to the cochlea was described at the beginning of this chapter. In brief, fibers arise in the contralateral dorsomedial periolivary nucleus and cross over the dorsal brainstem midline just below the floor of the fourth ventricle to form the crossed olivocochlear bundle (COCB). Ipsilaterally, cochlear efferents arise in the dorsolateral periolivary nucleus (uncrossed olivocochlear bundle, UOCB) and join the crossed olivocochlear bundle. In the cochlea the mode of innervation of inner and outer hair cells is as illustrated in Figure 7-9.

SUMMARY

The neural substrate of hearing, i.e., the hardware of the auditory system, has been reviewed. Starting at the periphery, the hair cells and their supporting and accessory structures provide the interface between the acoustic environment and the brain. At this peripheral level the system analyzes and converts sounds into neural codes. From this point on, "sound" is represented as voltage variations across neuronal membranes.

Among other functions, the cochlea performs a spectral analysis of sounds in which frequency components are represented by activity at certain places along the cochlear length. In all the auditory centers of the brain, this tonotopic or cochleotopic arrangement is maintained and can be considered a "mainline" organizational feature of the system.

At the first brainstem nuclei (cochlear nucleus), one set of neural inputs from the cochlea is relayed to the superior olivary complex, where comparisons between inputs from both ears provide cues for sound localization. From these centers fibers project to the inferior colliculus. Other neural input to the cochlear nucleus, particularly to the DCN, undergoes some processing (e.g., spatial or spectral, sharpening, and feature extraction, as implied from electrophysiologic response properties of neurons in the DCN). Outputs from the processors project to the inferior colliculus. At the level of the inferior colliculus the convergence of the two major pathways implies that information on the location of a sound in space and the features of the sound itself are superimposed or correlated.

From the collicular level to the cortex, at least two important features are evident from neuroanatomic considerations. First, there are many areas of sensory integration, where cells receive inputs originating from more than one sensory modality. For example, the superior colliculus integrates auditory, visual, and vestibular inputs. The medial division of the MGB receives somatosensory and vestibular input, and of course most nonprimary cortical areas are multimodal. Second, there is much evidence of highly organized, descending pathways that gate and otherwise modify auditory information reaching higher auditory areas, particularly the cortex.

Up to the collicular level, the auditory system in humans is essentially homologous with that of nonhuman mammals. At higher levels, more complex organization is evident in higher primates including humans, e.g., the more elaborate neuropil in the MGB and of course in humans in the specialization of some cortical areas for speech.

REFERENCES

Adams, J. C., and Warr, W. B. Origin of axons in the cat's acoustic striae determined by injection of horseradish peroxidase into severed tracts. *J. Comp. Neurol.* 170:107, 1976.

Aitkin, L. M., Anderson, D. J., and Brugge, J. F. Tonotopic organization and discharge characteristics of single neurons in the nuclei of the lateral lemniscus of the cat. *J. Neurophysiol.* 33:421, 1970.

Aitkin, L. M., and Webster, W. R. Tonotopic organization in the medial geniculate body of the cat. *Brain Res.* 26:402, 1971.

Aitkin, L. M., Dickhaus, H., Schult, W., and Zimmerman, M. External nucleus of inferior colliculus: auditory and spinal somatosensory afferents and their interactions. *J. Neurophysiol.* 41:837, 1978.

Angelborg, C., and Engström, H. Supporting elements of the organ of Corti. *Acta Otolaryngol. [Suppl] (Stockh)* 301:49, 1972.

Axelsson, A. The vascular anatomy of the cochlea in the guinea pig and in man. *Acta Otolaryngol. [Suppl] (Stockh)* 243:1, 1968.

Brawer, J. R., and Morest, D. K. Relations between auditory nerve endings and cell types in the cat's anteroventral cochlear nucleus seen with the Golgi method and Nomarski optics. *J. Comp. Neurol.* 199:341, 1962.

Brawer, J. R., Morest, D., and Kane, E. C. The neuronal architecture of the cochlear nucleus of the cat. *J. Comp. Neurol.* 155:251, 1974.

Bredberg, G. Cellular pattern and nerve supply of the human organ of Corti. *Acta Otolaryngol. [Suppl] (Stockh)* 236:1, 1968.

Bredberg, G., Ades, H. W., and Engström, H. Scanning electron microscopy of the normal and pathologically altered organ of Corti. *Acta Otolaryngol. [Suppl] (Stockh)* 301:1, 1972.

Brownell, W. E., Manis, P. B., and Ritz, L. A. Ipsilateral inhibitory responses in the cat's lateral superior olive. *Brain Res.* 177:189, 1979.

Crow, G., Rupert, A. L., and Moushegian, G. Phase locking in monaural and binaural medullary neurones: implications for binaural phenomena. *J. Acoust. Soc. Am.* 64:493, 1978.

Densert, Q., and Flock, A. An electron microscopic study of adrenergic innervation in the cochlea. *Acta Otolaryngol. (Stockh)* 77:185, 1974.

Elberling, C., Bak, C., Kofoed, B., Lebech, J., and Saermark, K. Auditory magnetic fields. *Scand. Audiol.* 11:61, 1982.

Elverland, H. H. Ascending and intrinsic projections of the superior olivary complex in the cat. *Exp. Brain Res.* 32:117, 1978.

Engström, H., Wersäll, J. The ultrastructural organization of the organ of Corti and of the vestibular sensory epithelia. *Exp. Cell Res.* 5:460, 1958.

Engström, H., Ades, H. W., and Anderson, A. *Structural Pattern of the Organ of Corti.* Stockholm: Almquist & Wiksell, 1966.

Evans, E. F., and Nelson, P. G. The responses of single neurones in the cochlear nucleus of the cat as a function of their location and the anaesthetic state. *Exp. Brain Res.* 17:402, 1973.

Flock, A., Bretscher, A., and Weber, K. Immunohistochemical localization of several cytoskeletal proteins in inner ear sensory and supporting cells. *Hear. Res.* 7:75, 1982.

Geniec, P., and Morest, D. K. The neuronal architecture of the human posterior colliculus: a study with the Golgi method. *Acta Otolaryngol. [Suppl] (Stockh)* 295:1, 1971.

Goldberg, J. M., and Moore, R. Y. Ascending projections of the lateral lemniscus. *J. Comp. Neurol.* 129:143, 1967.

Goldberg, J. M., and Brown, P. B. Functional organization of dog superior olivary complex: an anatomical and electrophysiological study. *J. Neurophysiol.* 31:639, 1968.

Goldberg, J. M., and Brown, P. B. Response of binaural neurones of dog superior olivary complex to dichotic tonal stimuli: some physiological mechanisms of sound localization. *J. Neurophysiol.* 32:613, 1969.

Harada, Y. *Atlas of the Ear by Scanning Electron Microscopy.* Lancaster: MTP Press, 1983.

Harrison, J. M., and Warr, B. A study of the cochlear nuclei and ascending pathways of the medulla. *J. Comp. Neurol.* 199:341, 1962.

Harrison, J. M., and Howe, M. E. Anatomy of the afferent auditory nervous system of mammals. In W. D. Keidel and W. D. Neff (eds.), *Handbook of Sensory Physiology* (Vol. 5/1). Berlin: Springer, 1974a. Pp. 283–336.

Harrison, J. M., and Howe, M.E. Anatomy of the descending auditory system (mammalian). In W. D. Keidel and W. D. Neff (eds.), *Handbook of Sensory Physiology* (Vol. 5/1). Berlin: 1974b. Pp. 363–388.

Held, H. Die cochlea der Säuger und der Vögel, ihre entwicklund und ihr Bau. In A. Bethe (ed.), *Handbuch der Normalen und Pathologischen Physiologie II.* Berlin: Springer, 1926. P. 467.

Hinojosa, R., and Rodriguez-Echandia, E. L. The fine structure of the stria vascularis of the cat inner ear. *Am. J. Anat.* 118:631, 1966.

Hoshino, T. Contact between the tectorial membrane and the cochlear sensory hairs in the human and the monkey. *Arth. Otorhinolaryngol.* 217:53, 1977.

Hunter-Duvar, I. M. Morphology of the normal and the acoustically damaged cochlea. *Scan. Electron Mi-*

crosc. 2:421, 1977.

Hunter-Duvar, I. M. Electron microscopic assessment of the cochlea. *Acta Otolaryngol. [Suppl] (Stockh)* 351:1, 1978a.

Hunter-Duvar, I. M. Reissner's membrane and endocytosis of cell debris. *Acta Otolaryngol. [Suppl] (Stockh)* 231:24, 1978b.

Hunter-Duvar, I. M. Anatomy of the inner ear. In J. E. Gerber and G. T. Mencher (eds.), *The Development of Auditory Behaviour.* New York: Grune & Stratton, 1983. Pp. 37–76.

Iurato, S. Submicroscopic structure of the membranous labyrinth. I. The tectorial membrane. *Z. Zellforsch.* 51:105, 1960.

Iurato, S. *Submicroscopic Structure of the Inner Ear.* New York: Pergamon Press, 1967.

Iurato. S. Efferent innervation of the cochlea. In W. D. Keidel and W. D. Neff (eds.), *Handbook of Sensory Physiology* (Vol. 5/I). Berlin: Springer, 1974. Pp. 261–282.

Kimura, R., and Schuknecht, H. The ultrastructure of the human stria vascularis. Part I. *Acta Otolaryngol. (Stockh)* 69:415, 1970.

Kimura, R. The ultrastructure of the organ of Corti. *Int. Rev. Cycol.* 42:1975.

Kronester-Frei, A. Ultrastructure of the different zones of the tectorial membrane. *Cell Tissue Res.* 193:11, 1978.

Lassen, N. A. Ingvar, D. H., and Skinhoj, E. Brain function and blood flow. *Sci. Am.* 239:50, 1978.

Lauter, J. L., Herscovitch, P., Formby, C., and Raichle, M. E. Tonotopic organization in human auditory cortex revealed by positron emission tomography. *Hear. Res.* 20:199, 1985.

Lenn, N. J., and Reese, T. S. The fine structure of nerve endings in the nucleus of the trapezoid body and the ventral cochlear nucleus. *Am. J. Anat.* 118:375, 1966.

Lim, D. J. Three dimensional observations of the inner ear with the scanning electron microscope. *Acta Otolaryngol. [Suppl] (Stockh)* 255:1, 1969.

Lim, D. J. Fine morphology of the tectorial membrane: its relationship to the organ of Corti. *Arch. Otolaryngol.* 96:199, 1972.

Lim, D. J. Fine morphology of the tectorial membrane: fresh and developmental. In M. Portmann and J-M. Aran (eds.), *Inner Ear Biology.* INSERM Colloque 68. Paris: INSERM, 1977. Pp. 47–60.

Lorente de Nó, R. Anatomy of the eighth nerve. I. The central projection of the nerve endings of the internal ear. *Laryngoscope (St. Louis)* 43:1, 1933.

Lorente de Nó, R. *The Primary Acoustic Nuclei.* New York: Raven Press, 1981.

Masterton, B., and Diamond, I. T. The medial superior olive and sound localization. *Science* 155:1096, 1967.

Merzenich, M. M., Knight, P. L., and Roth, G. L. Representation of the cochlea within the primary auditory cortex in the cat. *J. Neurophysiol.* 38:231, 1975.

Merzenich, M. M., Kaas, J. H., and Roth, G. L. Auditory cortex in the grey squirrel: tonotopic organization and architectonic fields. *J. Comp. Neurol.* 166:387, 1976.

Morest, D. K. The neuronal architecture of the medial geniculate body of the cat. *J. Anat.* 98:611, 1964.

Morest, D. K. The collateral system of the medial nucleus of the trapezoid body of the cat, its neuronal architecture and relation to the olivo-cochlear bundle. *Brain Res.* 9:288, 1968.

Morest, D. K. Auditory neurons of the brainstem. *Adv. Otol. Rhinol. Laryngol.* 20:337, 1973.

Morest, D. K., Kiang, N. Y. S., Kane, E. C., Guinan, J. J., Jr., and Godfrey, D. A. Stimulus coding at caudal levels of the cat's auditory nervous system. II. Patterns of synaptic organization. In A. R. Moller (ed.), *Basic Mechanisms in Hearing.* New York: Academic Press, 1973. Pp. 479–504.

Morest, D. K. Synaptic relationships of Golgi type II cells in the medial geniculate of the cat. *J. Comp. Neurol.* 162:157, 1975.

Morrison, D., Schindler, R. A., and Wersall, J. A quantitative analysis of the afferent innervation of the organ of Corti in the guinea pig. *Acta Otolaryngol. (Stockh)* 79:11, 1975.

Osen, K. K. Cytoarchitecture of the cochlear nuclei in the cat. *J. Comp. Neurol.* 136:453, 1969.

Osen, K. K. Projection of the cochlear nuclei on the inferior colliculus in the cat. *J. Comp. Neurol.* 144:355, 1972.

Penfield, W., and Perot, P. The brain's record of auditory and visual experience—a final summary and discussion. *Brain* 86:595, 1963.

Perkins, R. E., and Morest, D. K. A study of cochlear innervation in cats and rats with Golgi methods and Nomarski optics. *J. Comp. Neurol.* 168:129, 1975.

Pickles, J. O., Comis, S. D., and Osborne, M. P. Crosslinks between stereocilia in the guinea pig organ of Corti and their possible relation to sensory transduction. *Hear. Res.* 15:103, 1984.

Poggio, G. F., and Mountcastle, V. B. A study of the functional contributions of the lemniscal and spinothalamic systems to somatic sensibility. *Bull. Johns Hopkins Hosp.* 106:266, 1960.

Ranson, S. W., and Clark, S. L. *Anatomy of the Nervous System* (9th ed.). Philadelphia: Saunders, 1953.

Rasmussen, G. L. The olivary peduncle and other fibre projections of the superior olivary complex. *J. Comp. Neurol.* 84:141, 1946.

Rasmussen, G. L. Efferent fibres of the cochlear nerve and cochlear nucleus. In G. L. Rasmussen and W. F. Windle (eds.), *Neural Mechanisms of the Auditory and Vestibular Systems.* Springfield, IL: Charles C. Thomas, 1960. Pp. 105–115.

Retzius, G. *Das Gehörorgan der Reptilien, der Vögel und der Säugethiere.* Stockholm: Samson & Wallin, 1884.

Robarts, M. J. Somatic neurons in the brainstem and neocortex projecting to the external nucleus of the inferior colliculus: an anatomical study in the opossum. *J. Comp. Neurol.* 184:547, 1979.

Rockel, A. J. Observations on the inferior colliculus of the adult cat, stained by the Golgi technique. *Brain Res.* 30:407, 1971.

Rockel, A. J., and Jones, E. G. The neuronal organization of the inferior colliculus of the adult cat. I. The central nucleus. *J. Comp. Neurol.* 147:11, 1973a.

Rockel, A. J., Jones, E. G. The neuronal organization of the inferior colliculus of the adult cat. II. The pericentral nucleus. *J. Comp. Neurol.* 149:301, 1973b.

Rose, J. E. The cellular structure of the auditory region of the cat. *J. Comp. Neurol.* 91:409, 1949.

Rose, J. E., and Woolsey, C. N. Cortical connections and functional organization of the thalamic auditory system of the cat. In H. F. Harlow and C. N. Woolsey (eds.), *Biological and Biochemical Bases of Behaviour.* Madison: University of Wisconsin Press, 1958. Pp. 127–150.

Rose, J. E., Greenwood, D. D., Goldberg, J. M., and Hind, J. E. Some discharge characteristics of single neurones in the inferior colliculus of the cat. *J. Neurophysiol.* 26:294, 1963.

Sando, I. The anatomical interrelationship of cochlear nerve fibres. *Acta Otolaryngol. (Stockh)* 59:417, 1965.

Scheibel, M. E., and Scheibel, A. B. Neuropil organization in the superior olive of the cat. *Exp. Neurol.* 43:339, 1974.

Schuknecht, H. F. *Pathology of the Ear.* Cambridge, MA: Harvard University Press, 1974.

Smith, C. A. Structure of the stria vascularis and spiral prominence. *Ann. Otol. Rhinol. Laryngol.* 66:521, 1957.

Smith, C. A. Innervation of the organ of Corti. In I. Iurato (ed.), *Submicroscopic Structure of the Inner Ear.* London: Pergamon, 1967.

Smith, C. A. Innervation of the cochlea of guinea pig by use of the Golgi stain. *Ann. Otol. Rhinol. Laryngol.* 84:442, 1975.

Smith, C. A. Structure of the cochlear duct. In R. F. Nauton and C. Fernandez (eds.), *Evoked Electrical Activity in the Auditory Nervous System.* New York: Academic Press, 1978. Pp. 3–19.

Sousa-Pinto, A. The structure of the first auditory cortex in the cat. I. Light microscopic observations on its organization. *Arch. Ital. Biol.* 111:112, 1973.

Spoendlin, H. The organization of the cochlear receptor. In: *Advances in Otolaryngology* (Vol. 13). Basel: Karger, 1966.

Spoendlin, H., and Lichtensteiger, W. The adrenergic innervation of the labyrinth. *Acta Otolaryngol. (Stockh)* 61:423,1966.

Spoendlin, H. The structural basis of peripheral frequency analysis. In R. Plomp and G. F. Smoorenburg (eds.), *Frequency Analysis and Periodicity Detection in Hearing.* Leiden: Sijthoff, 1970. Pp. 2–36.

Steel, K. P. The tectorial membrane of mammals. *Hear. Res.* 9:327, 1983.

Takahashi, T., and Kimura, R. S. The ultrastructure of the spiral ligament in the rhesus monkey. *Acta Otolaryngol. (Stockh)* 69:46, 1970.

Tsuchitani, C., and Boudreau, J. C. Single unit analysis of cat superior olivary complex. *J. Neurophysiol.* 40:296, 1966.

Warr, W. B., and Guinan, J. J. Efferent innervation of the organ of Corti: two separate systems. *Brain Res.* 173:152, 1979.

Winer, J. A., Diamond, I. T., and Raczkowski, D. Subdivisions of the auditory cortex in cat: the retrograde transport of horseradish peroxidase to the medial geniculate body and posterior thalamic nuclei. *J. Comp. Neurol.* 176:387, 1977.

Winer, J. A., and Morest, D. K. The neuronal architecture of the dorsal division of the medial geniculate body of the cat: a study with the rapid Golgi method. *J. Comp. Neurol.* 221:1, 1983a.

Winer, J. A., and Morest, D. K. The medial division of the medial geniculate body of the cat: implications for thalamic organization. *J. Neurosci.* 3:26, 1983b.

Winer, J. A. The human medial geniculate body. *Hear. Res.* 15:225, 1984.

Wong, W. C. The tangential organization of dendrites and axons in three auditory areas of the cat's cerebral cortex. *J. Anat.* 101:419, 1967.

Woolsey, C. N. Organization of cortical auditory system: a review and a synthesis. In G. L. Rasmussen and W. F. Windle (eds.), *Neural Mechanisms of the Auditory and Vestibular Systems.* Springfield, IL: Charles C. Thomas, 1960. Pp. 105–180.

CHAPTER 8

Neurophysiology of Hearing

Ben M. Clopton

- ❏ Transformations of Auditory Information: Stimulus Information and Linearity

- ❏ Cochlear Transduction

- ❏ Codes for Spike Activity

- ❏ Coding Properties of Primary Afferents

- ❏ Information at the Cochlear Nuclei

- ❏ Implications for Auditory Perception

Preparation of this chapter was partially supported by NIH grants NS21769 and NS05785.

This chapter concerns acoustic information and its representation in the electrochemical activity of the auditory pathways of the brain. It is intended as an introductory overview, although the concepts treated are central to current understanding of how speech and other biologically important sounds are represented and processed in the brain. A wealth of anatomic and functional observations are available for those interested in going beyond this introduction (Brugge and Geisler, 1978; Cant and Morest, 1984; Young, 1984).

Auditory information is, in essence, a resolution of alternative acoustic stimuli, a difference in sounds that can provide a basis for choice. These choices may be as basic as deciding if a sound has occurred or as subtle as distinguishing between passages in speech or music. Neural activity representing auditory information must differentiate between sounds if it is to carry the information underlying choice behaviors. Therefore the most elementary definition of information in sounds and the neural activity they evoke is a difference on which discrimination is based.

Discrimination between two sounds implies that two patterns of activity exist in neural structures of the auditory system in association with these sounds. These patterns must differ along dimensions that are discriminable, so it is accurate to say that brain states are distinguished as surely as sounds. These two patterns of activity may differ in many respects. This chapter examines the dimensions and measures of differences in the electrophysiologic activity of hair cells of the cochlea and neurons of the auditory pathways that can carry information about simple and complex sounds.

Stimulus information is related to neural information by *encoding,* a physiologic sequence that transforms a pressure waveform into a spike code in the thousands of afferent axons of the auditory nerve. The process of encoding is equivalent to the mechanical and transduction events of the basilar membrane and hair cells. *Processing* of the encoded information might then occur to *enhance differences* between alternative neural states, to change the manner in which information is represented through *recod-*

ing, or to produce *selective responses* to specific patterns of neural activity and presumably aspects of the stimuli they represent. In the end, sensory brain states must be associated with responses through a *decision process* if the information is to be utilized.

In reality, these concepts of information—representation, processing, and utilization—find substance in the operation of membranes and synapses of hair cells and neurons. Intracellular communication is by means of graded electrical current flow and voltage differences. Intercellular communication is believed to involve primarily electrochemical mechanisms at synapses driven by discrete spike-impulse codes that carry the information between individual neurons in a nucleus or between nuclei of the auditory system. A complete understanding of the overall phenomena of information flow is not possible by considering spike behavior alone. Synaptic morphologies, graded electrical changes, membrane biophysics, and chemical events underlie the generation of these spike patterns. Information processing may occur within individual neurons or within individual networks of neurons as a result of specific dendritic, membrane, or synaptic activities. Spike activity is all that is usually observed in the output of a single neuron. If the spike activities of two or more neurons are observed simultaneously, members of a functional network may be sampled. A network would be a group of neurons whose outputs depend on incoming stimuli and the interactions of members of the network. A spike train from a single neuron provides information about the result of a neuron's internal processing, but it need not give much insight into how that processing occurs.

This chapter first examines the representation and evaluation of auditory information in sounds. Important questions about information processing in the auditory system are raised. Second, the influence of the cochlear transduction process on this information is examined, followed by the representation of this information in the spike activity of fibers of the auditory nerve. Finally, more central sites, especially the cochlear nuclei, are discussed.

TRANSFORMATIONS OF AUDITORY INFORMATION: STIMULUS INFORMATION AND LINEARITY

The pressure waveform of a sound completely represents its information content, that is, its potential contribution to a decision, assuming that binaural localization is not involved. Sound waveforms can be summarized as a sequence of pressure values over time, and many interesting manipulations can be made on these numbers. Mathematic operations vary in their utility for extracting information from or for distorting information in sounds. Insofar as numerical manipulations resemble encoding, processing, or decision events in the auditory system, one can gain insight into the flow of information in central pathways by considering some of their properties.

Two major classes of mathematic operations are relevant to sensory signals in general and auditory signals in particular. *Linear operations* consist of manipulations such as adding a constant to all of the values of a waveform (e.g., a change in the atmospheric pressure on which sound-induced variations occur) or multiplying all of the values by a constant (amplifying or attenuating a sound). A more involved linear operation is the Fourier transform, which translates a time waveform into spectral values. Linear operations can be reversed through a corresponding inverse linear operation. In the examples given, reversing the manipulation consists in subtracting or dividing by the original constant or performing an inverse Fourier transform. If the effects of a manipulation can be reversed, it is an indication that no informa-

Fig. 8-1. Cochlear mechanisms produce narrow-band filtering which, for wide-band, complex sounds such as the noise shown at the top, respond with a carrier waveform whose amplitude envelope varies slowly, as shown in the bottom waveform. Variations of the carrier and envelope in these filtered waveforms that occur over time approximate the information available in the forces that drive hair cells.

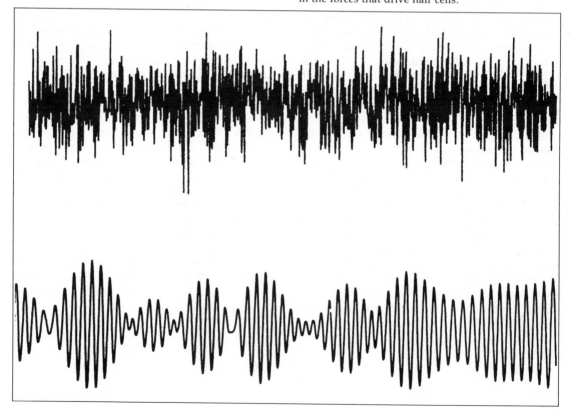

tion in the signal has been lost because it can be reconstituted from the result.

Nonlinear operations consist in such mathematic procedures as power transforms (e.g., squaring) or multiplying or dividing by a value that varies with time or with the magnitude of the signal value. A common nonlinear process is one that has a threshold so that no information about the signal is transmitted unless the signal magnitude exceeds the threshold value. Neurons have thresholds for spike generation, so threshold processes affect auditory information. Generally, nonlinear operations are difficult or impossible to reverse, suggesting that information is to some extent lost in the process. Even squaring, which at first appears reversible by taking the square root, produces an ambiguously reconstituted signal if both positive and negative values of the signal were originally squared. Thresholds clearly exclude reversal because nothing is left of the subthreshold stimulus information. It becomes apparent that nonlinear aspects of auditory processing are perhaps the most interesting, owing as much to the selection of information to be retained as to the loss of information.

A sound waveform can be represented as a sum of sinusoids, the familiar Fourier representation. It can also be considered as a sinusoidal carrier whose amplitude is determined by the waveform's envelope. The latter is especially descriptive of narrowband waveforms, as shown in Figure 8-1. Because of cochlear filtering, narrow-band waveforms derived from more complex sounds supply the mechanical stimulation to hair cells. Therefore the features of the carrier and envelope for the many component waveforms into which speech and other important sounds are analyzed carry almost all of the information available from the original wide-band sound. The representation of these features is the primary measure of information in the following discussion.

COCHLEAR TRANSDUCTION

Much is known about the *macromechanics* of the basilar membrane, the displacements of this partition related to the traveling wave (Bekesy, 1960). The details of the local mechanical events that underlie the stimulation of hair cells, the *micromechanics* of the cochlea, are still uncertain and under intense study. It is generally thought that the inner hair cells (IHCs) provide the ultimate output of cochlear processing, as they make contact with most of the dendrites of neurons of the spiral ganglion. Intracellular voltage records from IHCs provide a view of sound information at this stage.

Intracellular voltage records from an IHC responding to tone bursts of different frequencies are shown in Figure 8-2. Tone bursts have a carrier at the frequency of the tone and an envelope determined by the gate used to turn it on and off. It is apparent that both carrier and envelope components appear in the intracellular voltage, the carrier being predominant at lower frequencies and the envelope at higher frequencies. In essence, carrier fluctuations are followed well up to about 1 kHz but progressively decrease and become insignificant above 4 kHz. The envelope appears as an offset in the response at approximately 500 Hz and grows to dominate the response above 1 kHz. The envelope does not produce independent frequencies in the spectrum of the original stimulus. The appearance of the envelope as a separate feature raises questions about processes in the cochlea that extract it and the information it carries. Offsets in the cochlear microphonic related to the envelope, the summating potential, have long been observed in the extracellular potentials recorded near the inner ear.

To extract the envelope waveform, one must perform a nonlinear operation. *Rectification* is one such commonly encountered process. In hair cells rectification is likely to occur at the level of the stereocilia, where mechanical displacement is transduced into variation of ionic current, which in turn causes the intracellular voltage of the hair cell to vary (Brownell, 1982). This ionic flow, probably carried by positive potassium ions, would push the intracellular voltage more positive (depolarization). Stereocilia appear to bend more easily in one direction than the other and thereby cause a greater change in the intracellular voltage (Strelioff and Flock, 1984). The result is enhancement of that polarity of the waveform, i.e., rectification. The envelope appears as a displacement of the baseline; and because this baseline is proportional to the amplitude of the waveform, it signals the amount of energy present, although the fine time structure of the carrier is reduced. The membrane of the hair cell, which acts as an electrical capacitor, is likely to further reduce the rapid carrier fluctuations of the intracellular voltage through its filtering action.

The intracellular voltage of the IHC referenced to the surrounding extracellular voltage, that is the voltage difference across its cellular membrane, is probably the main determinant of transmitter release on dendrites of the primary afferents. Spike generation occurs through the influence of transmitter substance released in packets from the hair cell and its subsequent depolarization of the dendrites of the spiral ganglion (SG) neurons. The precise dynamics of this process are not known, but both packet release and spike occurrence are discrete, unitary events described primarily by their rate of occurrence (Ishii, Matsura, and Furukawa, 1971). The greater the depolarization of the IHC, the more rapid is the release of transmitter packets from presynaptic vesicles in the IHCs and the more rapid is the spike generation in the afferent fibers.

Large currents have been observed to flow in

the cochlea near the basilar membrane (Brownell, Manis, Zidanic, and Spirou, 1983; Garcia and Clopton, 1987). These currents probably represent the movement of potassium ions, which is regulated by hair cells (Brownell, 1982). What role they might play in transduction is uncertain, but their influence on hair cell contributions to transduction cannot be discounted.

The distribution of information from a single IHC to afferent fibers of the auditory nerve is not on a one-to-one basis. One to twenty dendrites of SG cells innervate a single IHC in the cat, suggesting that numerous parallel lines are available for carrying information (Liberman and Simmons, 1985). Important questions remain about the independence of the spike activity in axons activated by a single IHC (Johnson

Fig. 8-2. Intracellular voltage changes in the inner hair cells of a guinea pig for tone bursts of different frequencies. As the frequency of the carrier of the tone burst increases, phase locking decreases and the envelope dominates voltage fluctuations in the hair cell above 2 to 3 kHz. (From Russell, I. J., and Sellick, P. M. Low frequency characteristics of intracellularly recorded receptor potentials in guinea pig cochlear hair cells. *J. of Physiol.* (Lond.), 338:179, 1983.)

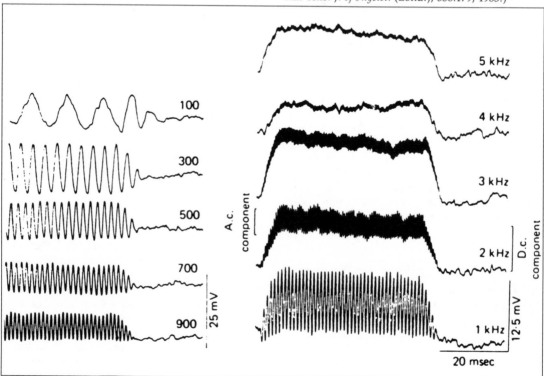

and Kiang, 1976), but numerous studies bear on the representation of stimulus information in single fibers and neurons.

CODES FOR SPIKE ACTIVITY

SPIKE TRAINS

A voltage waveform recorded extracellularly from a microelectrode in the cochlear nucleus is shown in Figure 8-3. A recurrent pattern is seen in this record that is attributable to spike generation in a single neuron near the electrode tip. The only significant information given by a

Fig. 8-3. Extracellular voltage waveform from a microelectrode whose tip is near a spike-generating neuron in the cochlear nuclei is shown in the upper trace. Unitary spike events suggested from the recording are conceptually represented as the lower "point process" with event times indicated by vertical marks. It is generally assumed that the intracellular transmission of large collections of point-process information between auditory nuclei underlies central processing of sound information.

spike is its time of occurrence because it does not vary in any meaningful way from spike to spike. The usual procedure is to represent the spike train as a sequence of spike times, as shown in Figure 8-3 by representing the spike with a marker when the spike waveform exceeds a certain threshold value. All of the ways in which information in neural activity is discussed here are based on the timing of spikes, as each spike is of equal importance informationally except for its place in time relative to others. Such a representation is called a *point process*.

Stimuli such as tone bursts or, more recently, more complex sounds such as short speech-like sounds (Reale and Geisler, 1980; Sachs and Young, 1979, 1980; Young and Sachs, 1979) are usually presented repeatedly to evoke patterns of spike activity. It is necessary because spike generation in auditory neurons is a *stochastic process*; that is, it is predictable only within limits for repeated presentations of a sound. Repeated, identical sound stimuli evoke spike patterns that differ from presentation to presentation (Johnson and Swami, 1983; Seibert, 1965). Much of what follows here deals with ways in which sound information is represented and processed by neurons whose spike

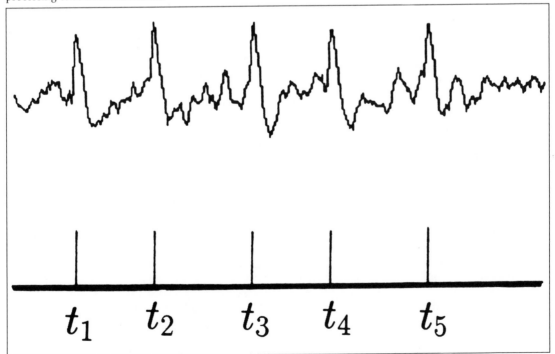

activity incorporates stimulus-controlled randomness.

CODES

A spike code is a feature of a spike train that carries information about a sound. This definition is not restrictive, and there is an infinite number of codes for using spikes to signal auditory information; however, discovering codes used by the auditory system presents a challenge. For a start, one must be able to measure or control the sound properties that are under investigation and to observe the candidate spike activity present in neurons. If experimental variation in the sound (e.g., intensity) is observed to be reliably associated with a change in the spike-train measurement (e.g., rate of firing), a code may have been at least partially revealed, but the full extent of the sound parameters signaled by the code generally requires extended observations. It is possible, indeed likely, that the same sound property is represented by another measure of spike activity (e.g., synchronization, as discussed below). The question then becomes one of deciding on the code that conveys information upon which decisions are based, and it is not unlikely that both are functional simultaneously or under different listening conditions. Identification of "the code" thus may be elusive and a concept of codes somewhat misleading. The caveat is that an understanding of sound encoding does not rest on a single measure of neural activity.

TEMPORAL AND PLACE CODES

Single axons in the cochlear portion of the vestibulocochlear (VIII) nerve signal different stimulus events by changes in spike activity over time. In this sense, all stimulus coding is temporal in nature. In a stricter sense, correspondence between the temporal structure of a stimulus, such as the individual cycles of a sinusoid or fluctuations in the envelope, and the temporal pattern of spike occurrence is the accepted criterion for a temporal code. The spike patterns that correspond to some extent to a temporal pattern in the stimulus waveform are called time-pattern or *temporal codes*. The best known time-pattern code involves spikes occur-

ring at a specific phase of the cycles of a tonal stimulus, a *phase code* representing carrier information. For lower stimulus frequencies, the spike pattern tends to be synchronized to cycles of sinusoids because fibers in the vestibulocochlear (VIII) nerve follow carrier detail that survives the processes of hair cell transduction and transmitter release. As expected from the hair cell observations, in most mammals phase codes signal frequencies up to 4 to 5 kHz. Envelope fluctuations are represented as a temporal code as well. This area has been studied using amplitude-modulated (AM) tones consisting of a high-frequency carrier whose amplitude is varied sinusoidally. In the auditory nerve and cochlear nuclei, sinusoidal variations in the envelope as rapid as 100 to 500 Hz are followed (Javel, 1980; Miller, 1972; Palmer, 1982).

The interpretation of temporal codes depends on the comparison of times of spike occurrence in order to detect patterns they might contain. If a 1-kHz tone was presented, spikes would signal the presence of the carrier frequency if adjacent spikes in a presentation were separated by an interspike interval of 1 millisecond (ms). This code allows accurate reconstruction of the stimulus if only tones are used, and the task is to decide the frequency of the tone; however, it requires that the neurons spike rapidly for higher frequencies. In the case of the 1-kHz tone, an *instantaneous rate* of 1,000 spikes per second, the inverse of the interspike interval between two spikes, would be implied by a pair of spikes separated by 1 ms.

Tonotopic organization is apparent in central auditory pathways as maps of stimulus frequency within a nucleus or over a cortical surface. These maps underlie the concept of *place coding* for the frequency spectra of sounds. The cochlea encodes sound as a spatial pattern of neural acitivity across a number of afferent fibers, each acting as a frequency-specific channel. The pattern varies over time as the energy present in these different frequency channels changes depending on the analysis of the sound pressure waveform into bands of frequency components. They, in turn, activate specific afferent fibers in the auditory nerve. Because fibers originate from different points on the basilar membrane, they can be considered to be "labeled" as to frequency, which implies that a comparison of the relative rates of spike activity in two fibers signals the relative energy content of a stimulus for their two frequency bands. Utilization of this code requires only that the relative activity of neurons representing different spectral regions be compared; thus it is called a *rate-place* code.

Spike rates are usually estimated over an interval of time, such as the duration of a tone burst, instead of as an instantaneous rate. This value, the *average rate*, is obtained by summing spikes over the duration of the stimulus and dividing by the interval length. Average rates rarely exceed a few hundred spikes per second in the auditory nerve. If two afferent fibers tuned to different frequencies responded with different average rates, the code would indicate that the energy at one frequency exceeded that at the other on that presentation. Three questions arise about the relations between temporal and rate-place codes in the auditory system. Are they incompatible? Do they appear in neural activity? Does the brain use them to discriminate sounds? The first question is examined now and the others later.

PHASE VERSUS RATE-PLACE CODES

If two ways of encoding information are compatible, they may be used simultaneously. If they are truly independent codes, each could signal changes in the stimulus without influencing changes signaled by the other. For a neuron spiking continuously with approximately equal interspike intervals during a stimulus presentation, it is apparent that an instantaneous spike rate tells us something about the average spike rate. Temporal and rate-place codes may conflict because they depend on related measures of neural activity.

Average and instantaneous spike rates may be dissociated for some response patterns. If a neuron responds with bursts of spikes, the average instantaneous rate can exceed the average rate by a great amount. A neuron responding with only two spikes 1 ms apart during a 1-second presentation has an instantaneous rate of 1,000 spikes per second but an average rate of 2 spikes per second. Such a neuron would retain the capacity to increase its average spike rate (perhaps to signal increased energy at the frequency to which it was tuned) without giving up the possibility of representing temporal fea-

tures of the sound with bursts of spikes. Of course such a combination of temporal and rate-place codes would be incompatible with continuously signaling stimulus frequency with a phase code.

CODING PROPERTIES OF PRIMARY AFFERENTS

To this point in the chapter, possible codes of spike-train data have been introduced. Brief summaries of experimentally observed properties of the auditory system follow.

SPONTANEOUS ACTIVITY

The primary auditory afferents, axons in the auditory portion of the vestibulocochlear (VIII) nerve, spike spontaneously even in quiet environments. In the cat, where primary afferents in the nerve have been most studied, spontaneous rates range from 25 to 100 spikes per second for most axons (high-spontaneous fibers), but a smaller and distinct group fires at 10 spikes per second or less (low-spontaneous fibers). The time pattern of this spiking is that expected if the probability of an axon's spiking was the same from moment to moment except for an absolute refractory period within about 1 ms after a spike when another spike cannot occur and a brief relative refractory period when another spike is less likely to occur.

The interspike-interval histogram (ISIH) is the graphic display commonly used to summarize information about spontaneous activity. It shows the number of intervals of a given length between pairs of spikes. The period over which these interval data are taken usually covers a time when no changes in the stimulus occur. The goal is to have the ISIH be representative of a neuron's responses for constant conditions. It is common to collect ISIHs for spontaneous activity because they are often of a characteristic shape, especially for primary afferents (Kiang, 1965).

An ISIH for spontaneous activity in a fiber of the auditory nerve of the guinea pig is shown in Figure 8-4. Other than for very short intervals

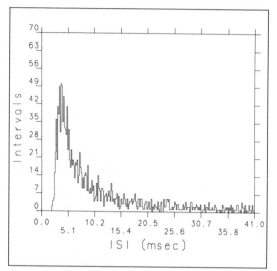

Fig. 8-4. A single fiber in the auditory nerve of a guinea pig, spontaneously active in the absence of sound stimulation, had interspike intervals described by this ISIH. The form of this ISIH agrees with the distribution of intervals expected from a Poisson process with a brief refractory period that prevents the occurrence of very short intervals.

influenced by these refractory processes, the ISIH for the spontaneous activity of an axon is well described by a *Poisson distribution*. This stochastic process is analogous to drawing a marble from a container of many white ones and a few black ones at each instant in time and responding only when a black one is drawn. The ratio of black to white marbles, always small, is kept constant by replacing the marble each time. The presentation of a stimulus causes a change in the probability of a response, that is, a stimulus briefly increases or decreases the number of black marbles. This type of probabilistic coding for a single axon is exactly what one would expect if time and spatial independence of spike patterns were needed to overcome the limitations of individual neural elements (Johnson and Swami, 1983). Spontaneous activity is assumed to be due to the release of transmitter substance from hair cells, primarily the inner ones, in the absence of overt sound stimulation.

EVOKED RESPONSES

Characterizing the manner in which sounds evoke spike activity in auditory neurons deter-

mines the information one is able to detect in that activity. The peristimulus–time histogram (PSTH) is the most common representation of evoked spike activity. It shows spike count as a function of time after the onset of a stimulus for a number of stimulus presentations. At any point in this peristimulus time, the spike count is the total of the spikes that occurred at that time after the start of the stimulus over all of the stimulus presentations. The abscissa, or time axis, is divided into bins representing small time intervals. The PSTH, originally expressed in terms of spike counts, can be transformed to the probability of a spike occurring during the bin interval, or it can be expressed as the instantaneous rate of spike occurrence during the interval. This measure of spike rate can be great because it does not hold for any one presentation, only for the composite where spikes may have occurred with precise timing.

SINUSOIDS

THRESHOLD

Changes in the afferent spike activity that signal the presence of a tone at threshold clearly illustrate frequency tuning in afferents. A PSTH for a repeated tone burst that is below threshold tends to be flat, except for stochastic variation, in agreement with the concept of a Poisson process with equal probability of spiking in each bin. Examples of PSTHs are given in Figure 8-5, one for a unit responding to a low-frequency tone and the other for a unit responding to a tone of higher frequency. Phase locking to cycles of the low-frequency tone burst can be seen, but the higher-frequency tone burst is signaled only by an increase in firing probability.

Figure 8-6 shows a threshold tuning curve for an auditory nerve fiber based on an increase of one spike or more over the spontaneous rate for combinations of tone-burst frequency and in-

Fig. 8-5. Peristimulus–time histograms (PSTHs) for spike responses to tone bursts of 40 ms. The upper PSTH is for a fiber of the auditory nerve responding to a tone burst of 1260 Hz, whereas the lower one is for a fiber responding to a burst of 11 kHz. Phase locking to individual cycles of the tone burst appears in the first, but only the envelope of the tone burst with a brief period of reduced firing after tone onset, are evident in the second.

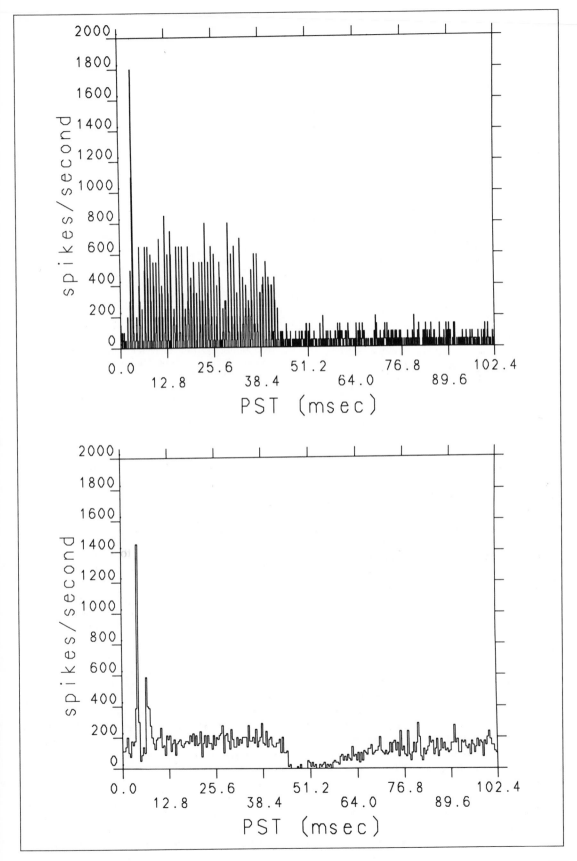

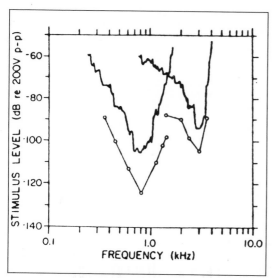

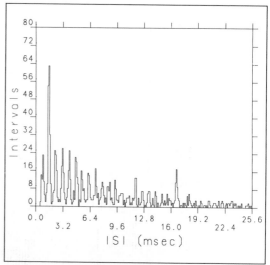

Fig. 8-6. Threshold tuning curves for two primary afferent fibers responding to tone bursts. Two criteria for threshold were used, the upper, solid curves represent a rate criterion (one spike over the spontaneous rate), and the lower circles indicate the intensities at which a significant increase in synchronization occurred. (From Johnson, D. H. The relationship between spike rate and synchrony in responses of auditory fibers to single tones. *J. Acoust. Soc. Am.* 68:1115, 1980.)

Fig. 8-7. An ISIH for an auditory nerve fiber responding to a tone of 1270 Hz shows preferred intervals for responding. The shortest interval is at 0.787 ms, which is 1/1270 sec, and the other peaks are at multiples of 0.787 ms. Some intervals thus represent the period of the sinusoidal stimulus while most are only stochastically related to it. The PSTH for this fiber is shown in Figure 8-5 (upper).

tensity. This *rate–threshold tuning curve* has a minimum at the best or "characteristic" frequency of the fiber, and it responds to an increasingly wide range of frequencies at higher intensities. Another criterion for establishing a threshold curve as a function of the frequency and intensity of a tone is synchrony.

SYNCHRONIZATION

Phase locking, as shown in Figure 8-5, is detectable in mammalian vestibulocochlear (VIII) nerve axons for tones below 4 to 5 kHz. The ISIH is useful for its ability to reveal repeating time patterns in spike trains. If a phase code exists for a sinusoid, an ISIH obtained while a tone is present has intervals related to the period of the sinusoid. An ISIH for auditory nerve responses to a 1.270-kHz sinusoid is shown in Figure 8-7. The largest peak corresponds to the interval that is the period of the sinusoid. Later peaks are produced by spikes "skipping" a period so that multiples of the original interval occur. A neuron locking to a

1-kHz tone responds with multiples of 1 ms so that instantaneous spike "frequencies" in the progression 1,000, 500, 333, 250, 200, 167, . . . Hz are signaled.

The cycle histogram is a display related to the PSTH and is often used to summarize spike synchronization to a sinusoid. The time axis is the duration of the cycle period for a sinusoid, e.g., 2 ms for a 500-Hz tone. Responses to all of the cycles of a continuous tone stimulus for which spikes are collected are "folded" in time so that cycles are superimposed. This situation is illustrated in Figure 8-8 for a neuron responding at specific phases of a 1-kHz tone, as in the previous example. The cycle histogram clearly reveals if more spikes are associated with one portion of the stimulus cycle. A flat cycle histogram indicates a lack of phase locking to the sinusoid. A single number is often calculated to summarize the degree of phase locking represented in a cycle histogram, the synchronization coefficient. It ranges from zero for a flat histogram, indicating no relation between spike generation and the phase of the stimulus, to 1.0 for a histogram with all of its counts in one bin due to perfect phase locking. A number of pro-

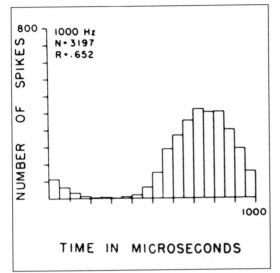

TIME IN MICROSECONDS

Fig. 8-8. A cycle histogram for a neuron phase locked to a 1000 Hz tone. Counts of spike occurrence are selectively high for portions of the period of the tone, 1000 μs, shown on the abscissa. A synchronization coefficient of 0.652 (based on 3197 spikes) indicates a moderate degree of phase locking in this case in contrast to a coefficient of zero for a flat histogram. (From Brugge, J. F., Javel, E., and Kitzes, L. M. Finds of functional maturation of peripheral auditory systems in discharge patterns of neurons of anteroventral cochlear nucleus of kitten. *J. of Neurophysiol.*, 41:1557, 1978.)

cedures exist for its calculation from PSTHs and cycle histograms (Johnson, 1980).

The synchronization coefficient for fibers of the cat auditory nerve that respond to different frequencies is shown in Figure 8-9. Synchronization coefficients tend to decline above 1 kHz. As stimulus frequency increases, the cycle histograms become progressively flatter until spikes no longer occur at preferred phases of the tone. This lack of synchronization is greater for some species than others (Palmer, Winter, and Darwin, 1986).

If a minimal increase in the synchronization coefficient to the tone is taken as the threshold criterion, a *synchrony–threshold tuning curve* is obtained; and as shown in Figure 8-6, it can be as much as 20 dB more sensitive than the rate curve (Johnson, 1980). This rule holds only for tones of low enough frequency to allow phase locking. As a subthreshold tone burst is increased in intensity, it begins to impose a phase-locked temporal pattern on afferent spike trains before it causes an increase in the average rate of firing.

DYNAMIC RANGE

An afferent's dynamic range is the stimulus-intensity range over which useful information about the stimulus is represented in neural activity. It depends on the neural-response variable representing it. If a rate code represents a change in stimulus intensity, the dynamic range of an afferent is the intensity range over which a change in rate occurs for a change in intensity. It is the intensity range from a threshold increase in activity over spontaneous to the level at which no further increase in rate is seen (Viemeister, 1987). This upper plateau on the intensity–rate curve is due to rate saturation. The dynamic range has been shown to be in the range of 20 to 50 dB for most fibers in the vestibulo-cochlear (VIII) nerve (Sachs and Abbas, 1974). On the other hand, a temporal code for frequency generally has a much larger dynamic range because phase locking is present from below rate threshold to intensities well above rate saturation (Johnson, 1980; Sachs and Young, 1980).

ADAPTATION

When a suprathreshold tone is turned on, the probability of a spike occurring is high; however, the auditory nerve fibers adapt, and spike probability declines with time. This decline in spike rate seems to be governed by more than one mechanism (Smith, Brachman, and Goodman, 1983). Adaptation establishes a new baseline against which changes in stimulus intensity act to produce increments or decrements in rate.

TWO-TONE INTERACTION

If two tones of different frequency are presented simultaneously, the response they evoke is usually not the sum of the responses to each separately. This statement is one definition of a nonlinear interaction, so two-tone experiments allow investigation of nonlinear processes in the auditory system. Both rate and temporal response measures point to nonadditive effects of stimulus pairs (Abbas and Sachs, 1976; Javel, 1981). If the response to an original tone has a given rate and synchronization, the presence of a second tone, which may not cause a response itself, can decrease both the increment in rate and phase locking caused by the first one. These effects are termed *rate suppression* and

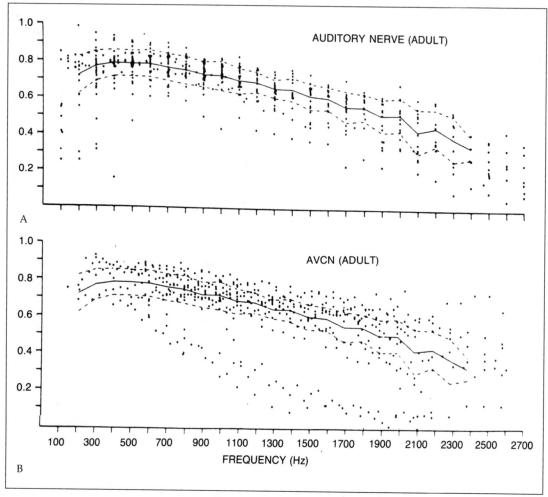

Fig. 8-9. Synchronization coefficients for fibers in the auditory nerve and neurons in the anteroventral cochlear nucleus (AVCN) of a cat for tones of different frequencies. The auditory nerve data of graph A are reproduced in the upper part of graph B. Note that synchronization for a set of neurons in the AVCN (lower part of graph B) is distinctly lower than fibers of the nerve. (From Brugge, J. F., Javel, E., and Kitzes, L. M. Finds of functional maturation of peripheral auditory systems in discharge patterns of neurons of anteroventral cochlear nucleus of kitten. *J. of Neurophysiol.*, 41:1557, 1978.)

synchrony suppression, and they arise from cochlear mechanisms that are poorly understood. They have important implications for the processing of sounds with many spectral components, such as speech, because the components are likely to interact.

COMPLEX SOUNDS

Tones are considered "simple" because they have a single frequency component, and they activate a small number of fibers in the auditory nerve. In contrast, it is appropriate to consider sounds "complex" if they have a rich spectrum, that is, many frequency components. Various classifications of complex sounds can be made,

the elementary dichotomy of artificial versus biologic being a possible but not entirely exclusive one. Artificial complex waveforms designed to explore specific encoding questions include clicks, amplitude- and frequency-modulated sinusoids, and noise. Some examples of complex sounds used experimentally are shown in Figure 8-10. Biologic sounds used ex-

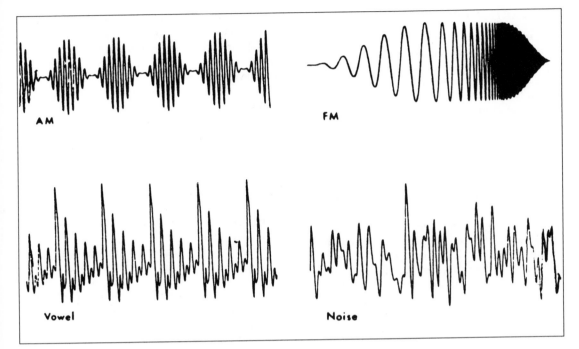

AM

FM

Vowel

Noise

Fig. 8-10. Examples of complex sounds that have important experimental usage including amplitude modulation (AM), frequency modulation (FM), speech sounds (vowel), and synthesized noise.

perimentally include human speech and animal vocalizations. It is becoming increasingly common for nonhuman–primate vocalizations, bird song, and bat biologic sounds to be approximated using digital synthesis techniques.

Another distinction to be made for complex sounds is that of having an unchanging or stationary spectrum for the time of presentation, in contrast to frequency components, which vary in amplitude over time. A continuous tone has a stationary spectrum, whereas a tone swept in frequency has a nonstationary spectrum. Most biologic signals, such as speech, have nonstationary spectra that allow encoding of more alternatives, and thereby more information, in terms of sequences of changing spectral features. In this sense, nonstationary spectra can carry more information than stationary spectra for given frequency limits.

TRANSIENTS

Clicks have been the most commonly presented complex stimuli. They are useful be-cause they have a rich frequency spectrum and provide a precise time reference. PSTHs to clicks from the vestibulocochlear (VIII) nerve have an initial latency that reflects travel time along the basilar membrane to the point of maximal excitation for the fiber observed and a neural delay. High-frequency fibers have minimal latencies, whereas those responding to low frequencies have latencies of 3 to 5 ms (Greenwood, 1961). If the characteristic frequency of the fiber is not too great, regularly spaced peaks appear in the PSTH with a separation at the period of the characteristic frequency (Horst, Javel, and Farley, 1986; Kiang, 1965). This pattern is due to mechanical ringing at that frequency produced by the transient. It illustrates the separation of spectral components in the click by the basilar membrane, which acts as an underdamped filter, i.e., a filter that tends to "ring" for a while after excited.

If two clicks are presented together with a small time separation, they interact in a nonlinear manner (Goblick and Pfeiffer, 1969); that is, the sum of the PSTHs to each alone does not completely predict the PSTH to the clicks presented together. This situation is an example of two-tone interaction in time instead of frequency.

MODULATED SIGNALS

If the amplitude or the frequency of a tone is changed with time, spectral components are added. Amplitude-modulated (AM) sinusoids have spectral sidebands around the original or carrier frequency, and this spectrum is stationary. If the modulating waveform is sinusoidal, as is commonly the case, the two sideband components are symmetric about the carrier frequency at a distance equal to the modulation frequency (Fig. 8-11). A tone at a fiber's characteristic frequency is usually amplitude-modulated with a low-frequency sinusoid, the modulator. Afferents in the auditory nerve represent the modulation waveform with a temporal code if it is not too high or too low in frequency (Javel, 1980; Miller, 1972). It appears as a synchronization to the modulating waveform; and by varying the frequency of sinusoidal modulation, a *modulation-transfer function* (MTF) can be obtained. The MTF shows the degree to which the modulation appears in the response of the unit, that is, the gain for the modulator as a function of its frequency. Primary afferents

Fig. 8-11. A comparison of the time waveform (upper) and frequency components (lower) of an amplitude-modulated sound. A carrier of higher frequency is modulated (multiplied) by a lower frequency sinusoid that is offset so that it does not go negative. The filled circles illustrate the actual amplitudes of the frequency components in the sound, while the open circles at DC and the value of low-frequency modulation indicate frequency components that exist in the modulator and that appear after the sound undergoes rectification and other processes known to occur in transduction.

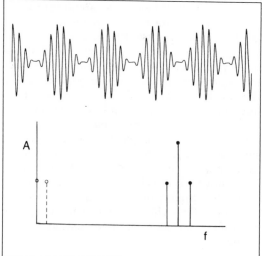

follow rapid modulations, some at 500 Hz or above, which suggests that single fibers encode AM information using a temporal code when all three spectral components fall within their frequency range, whereas adjacent afferent channels respond separately to the outer spectral components or sidebands. As the intensity of an AM signal is raised from threshold, the gain of the MTF increases followed by a decrease at high intensities due to rate saturation. However, the gain of the MTF is greater than one would predict from responses to the different stimulus intensities without modulation for much of the intensity range, suggesting enhancement of the modulation waveform (Smith and Brachman, 1980).

Frequency-modulated (FM) signals are common parts of biologic sounds that have nonstationary spectra. Many species of bats detect prey and the range of objects using FM cries that they emit (Simmons, Fenton, and O'Farrell, 1979). Primary afferents respond as the FM signal passes through their frequency range, and their responses do not differ greatly if the frequency transition is from low-to-high or high-to-low. Such symmetry indicates that direction and rate of sweep are encoded spatially in the nerve without processing, which might favor a sweep direction.

NOISE

White noise has a wide-band, flat-amplitude spectrum, but the phases of the components are random. This produces a gaussian distribution of amplitude for the time waveform, often called gaussian noise. Noise obtained from certain electronic devices is truly stochastic; that is, it is predictable only within the limits of its gaussian distribution. Deterministic noise can be digitally produced with an inverse-Fourier transform from a flat-amplitude, random-phase spectrum. It is gaussian but entirely known in its time and frequency structure. The use of noise to mask other signals has been its most common use (e.g., Miller, Barta, and Sachs, 1987), but both stochastic and deterministic noises have been used to study fiber responses in the nerve (de Boer and de Jongh, 1978; Ruggero, 1973; Wickesberg, Dickson, Gibson, and Geisler, 1984), as it is a "rich" complex signal that excites all of the afferents. To some extent the spike patterns evoked by noise are predictable from the filtering actions of the basilar membrane, nonlinearities of hair cell transduction, and stochastic spike generation.

SPEECH

Speech sounds have seen increasing usage as stimuli for neurophysiologic studies (Delgutte, 1984; Delgutte and Kiang, 1984a,b,c; Palmer, et al., 1986; Reale and Geisler, 1980; Sachs and Young, 1979; Sinex and Geisler, 1984; Young and Sachs, 1979). Vowels are well approximated as periodic, wide-band stimuli with characteristic spectral peaks or formants. Sachs and Young observed afferent responses in the cat to synthesized vowels over various intensity levels (Fig. 8-12). At lower levels the spectral shapes that allow discrimination of vowels based on their formants were obvious in both rate and synchrony codes across fibers covering the frequency range of the stimuli. At higher levels, where rate–intensity functions saturate, the rate code no longer signaled formants. The afferents were firing maximally so that rate no longer reflected differential frequency excitation from the stimulus. Of course the synchrony code, which is not limited by saturation, continued to carry information about the spectral peaks in the vowels. Units having characteristic frequencies near these spectral peaks had responses that were synchronized to them so that patches of formant-synchronized responses appeared in the neuronal population. Because we can still distinguish vowels at high intensities, this evidence supported the temporal over the rate code on the basis of its dynamic range agreeing with behavior, specifically pointing to a *synchrony–place code.*

Using two harmonically related tones that approximated the lowest formants of a group of vowels, Reale and Geisler (1980) observed that significant nonlinearities were present in the temporal coding of the waveforms. If one of the tones was near the characteristic frequency of an afferent, it dominated the time pattern of firing, and complicated suppressive interactions between the components occurred when they bracketed the characteristic frequency. Sachs and Young observed similar effects. It appears that spectral peaks are accentuated in responses because they suppress responses to surrounding components.

The addition of noise to speech signals tends to reduce synchrony to much of the fine temporal structure, i.e., carrier information for speech. However, for the spectral peaks in the speech stimuli, fibers with characteristic frequencies near these peaks tend to remain synchronized to these frequency bands. Masking noise reduces synchronization to tones and speech components, more in fibers not tuned to the tone or formant than for others (Miller, et al., 1987; Sachs, Voigt, and Young, 1983). This finding suggests that a synchrony–place code is

Fig. 8-12. Over a number of auditory nerve fibers with different CFs, it is observed that synchronization reveals the presence of characteristic frequency peaks in the energy of vowels. Synchronization, shown here in terms of a rate measure, is higher for fibers in the region where a vowel has more energy, and this pattern holds over a wide range of vowel intensities. (From Sachs, M. B., and Young, E. D. Encoding of steady-state vowels in the auditory nerve: representation in terms of discharge rate. *J. Acoust. Soc. Am.* 66:470, 1979.)

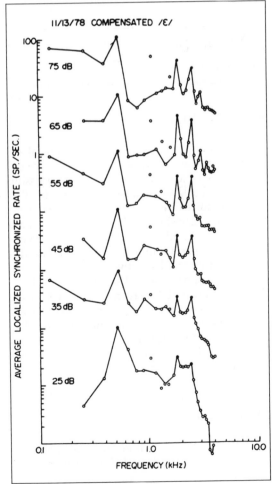

operating even under conditions where noise partially masks some of the speech information.

MULTIPLE SPIKE TRAINS

In an attempt to determine the degree of relation between information carried in afferent fibers of the auditory nerve, Johnson and Kiang (1976) inserted two microelectrodes that were independently maneuverable. Recording from fibers with nearly the same characteristic frequency, they looked for a correlation in activity beyond that expected from the stochastic processes discussed. They did not find such evidence, thus supporting the assumption of independent encoding processes. No evidence is available bearing on the independence of spike trains in fibers from the same inner hair cell.

INFORMATION AT THE COCHLEAR NUCLEI

STRUCTURE

The first obligatory synapse in the central auditory pathway is at the cochlear nucleus. Discussion of central coding and processing concerns this level because the most detailed neurophysiologic investigations are focused here. The primary divisions of the cochlear nuclei are ventral (VCN) and dorsal (DCN), and the ventral division has a number of subdivisions with cell types that are distinctive anatomically and, apparently, functionally. The DCN is not divisible regionally, but it is layered in many species. Responses have been studied most extensively in the VCN (Rhode and Smith, 1986). Responses in the dorsal nucleus are more complicated and often involve inhibitory inputs (Young and Voigt, 1982).

SINUSOIDS

Distinctive PSTHs to tone bursts at characteristic frequency have provided the primary basis for partitioning spike patterns in the cochlear nuclei into functional subgroups. These PSTH patterns fall into the major classes of primary-like, chopper, and onset (Rhode and Smith, 1986) with variations on these classes, including the pause and buildup (Fig. 8-13). The primary-like response type is identified with bushy cells of the ventral division, choppers with stellate cells (which tend to occur throughout the cochlear nuclei), and onset responses with many anatomic types but especially the octopus cells of the posteroventral subdivision (Young, 1984). The change from primary-like responses in the nerve to the other response types in the cochlear nuclei appear to imply that recoding or processing occurs there in some of the subpopulations of neurons. Although they have been useful for classifying neurons into functional classes that seem to have some correspondence with anatomic classes, the informational significance of the response types is intuitive and largely unknown. Primary-like units clearly retain much of the information present in afferents whether related to rate or synchrony, and it has been suggested that onset units provide precise timing information (Rhode and Smith, 1986). Many neurons in the DCN have large inhibitory areas where tones reduce spontaneous activity or suppress responses to excitatory tones, suggesting that their most effective stimuli are more complicated than for the VCN. Beyond this explanation, little insight into the relevance of the patterns is available.

MODULATED SIGNALS

Both AM and FM sounds evoke responses in some neurons of the cochlear nuclei that are significantly different from those in the auditory nerve (Møller, 1972; Shore, Clopton, and Au, 1987). Such changes suggest that information processing occurs at this level. For example, greater responses to one direction of frequency sweep can underlie FM discrimination and enhance the effect of many biologic sounds that contain frequency translation. The MTF of some neurons in the cochlear nuclei for AM tones shows a broad maximum from 50 to 200 Hz (Møller, 1972), and there is evidence that lower AM frequencies are most effective at higher centers (Schreiner and Urbas, 1986).

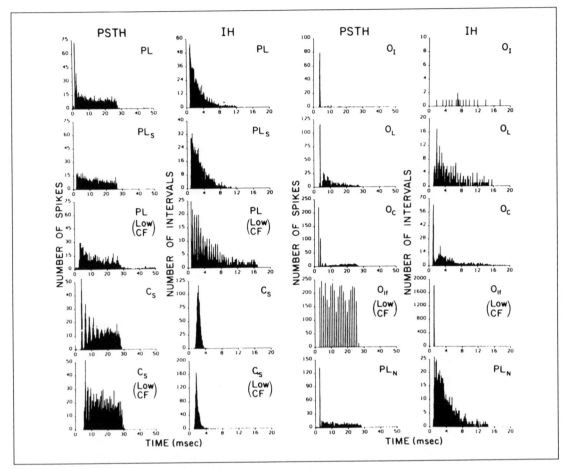

Fig. 8-13. Examples of PSTHs and ISIHs (IH) for neurons in the VCN of a cat responding to tone bursts. These response measures suggest categories of responses that underlie functional classifications. For this nucleus these categories are PL (primary-like), C (chopper), and O (onset) with variations on these patterns providing more detailed categorization. (From Rhode, W. S., and Smith, P.H. Encoding timing and intensity in the ventral nucleus of the cat. *J. Neurophysiol.* 56:261, 1986.)

NOISE

Wide-band noise has been used to excite neurons of the cochlear nuclei, and most neurons of the VCN are excited by this stimulus. In contrast, many cells of the DCN respond poorly or not at all to wide-band noise, at least as measured by changes in the rate of firing. Deterministic noise may or may not change spike rate, but it does tend to impose time structure on the spike train. Continuous noise stimulation keeps many units near threshold for firing so that their latency of response to a peak in the noise energy is less than would be expected from their latency of response to a click or tone burst (Møller, 1981). Other information about unit response characteristics can be obtained from responses to noise, but a description of such information is beyond the scope of this chapter (de Boer and de Jongh, 1978; Harrison and Evans, 1982; Møller, 1981; Ruggero, 1973; Wickesberg et al., 1984).

SPEECH

The transformations that speech and speech-like stimuli undergo in the cochlear nuclei have been the subject of only a few studies (Palmer et al., 1986). Primary-like units in the AVCN retain much of the temporal detail present in the nerve, although the glottal pulse period in vowels is emphasized at some expense to finer temporal detail. It is reasonable to expect that fine temporal detail is not retained as sound information ascends the central auditory pathways because of the demands on synaptic transmission.

MULTIPLE SPIKE TRAINS

Pairs or larger groups of neurons in the cochlear nuclei can respond in a coordinated manner for two major reasons: They are driven by the same stimulus, and they are interconnected in a network. Both are important to the representation and processing of complex sounds. Other influences, such as strong regional electrical current flow or biochemical conditions, might induce relations in the spike activity of neuronal groups, but their effects are probably secondary. For these reasons, it is important that neural spikes be observed simultaneously in two or more neurons. It has been technically difficult, but new electrode fabrication and signal processing techniques have made it possible to separate spike waveforms from different neurons and to put more contacts on an electrode so that more points in the cochlear nuclei can be sampled.

An example of neuronal interaction in the DCN is the decrease in firing rate in type IV neurons (broad response areas that are largely inhibitory) following a spike in a type II/III neuron (excitatory central response area flanked by inhibition) observed by Voigt and Young (1980). Of 17 pairs of type II/III and IV neurons recorded from the same electrode, 12 showed this type of relation in their spike trains. The excitatory region of the type II/III neurons generally coincided with the inhibitory region of the type IV neuron, suggesting that the type II/III neurons act as inhibitory interneurons influencing the type IV neurons.

INTRACELLULAR RECORDING

Intracellular recording in the cochlear nuclei is difficult owing to brain pulsation and the small size of neurons. Brain slice techniques have been applied to this problem. Oertel (1983) maintained slices of cochlear nuclei from mice about 0.25 mm thick, entered cells with a glass micropipette, and activated units in the tissue by electrically stimulating the stump of the vestibulocochlear (VIII) nerve. It was also possible to investigate the reaction of the cell membrane to currents introduced by the electrode. Two types of membrane response were found, one resulting from a linear relation between membrane current and voltage and the other from a nonlinear relation. These two responses in different types of neuron (probably stellate and bushy cells, respectively) indicate that membrane properties partially account for their different PSTHs to tone bursts.

ANESTHETIC EFFECTS

General anesthetics are normally used for animal preparations where single units are observed, and there is some concern about the influence of these chemical agents on the neural activity under study. Some investigators have used decerebration and other procedures to prevent the experience of pain without the continued need of a general anesthetic. They have often found significant differences in details of response types, especially features that may depend on inhibitory influences such as the DCN (Evans and Nelson, 1973; Ritz and Brownell, 1982). One must be conservative when drawing conclusions about information processing in central auditory pathways of the anesthetized preparation even at the level of the cochlear nuclei.

IMPLICATIONS FOR AUDITORY PERCEPTION

As discussed in this chapter, spike patterns in fibers of the auditory nerve evoked by speech and other complex stimuli are largely predictable owing to the extensive study they have undergone. These patterns are influenced primarily by the bandpass tuning properties of the basilar membrane, some nonlinear processes in hair cells that tend to produce saturation of the response at high intensities, hair-cell filtering of high-frequency components, and the stochastic nature of spike generation. Despite some distortions in this sequence, spike trains in the nerve represent a great amount of information about sounds. Single fibers do not carry a complete representation of such stimuli, suggesting that much work on the interdependence of spike codes between afferent fibers is necessary. Overall, however, there is good understanding of the details of the representation of complex sounds in the nerve.

Disagreement concerning the use of spike codes exists, (i.e., the extraction of information from neural activity in the nerve) (Javel and Mott, 1987; Viemeister, 1987). Study of neural mechanisms in the cochlear nuclei and higher centers may resolve some of the controversy, but a complete resolution lies only in a full translation between spike activity in the nerve and behavioral decision. In addition, it is assumed that data from the central auditory pathways of nonhuman animal models represent accurately the information available to humans.

The neural processes that affect the neural representation of sounds will be the major focus of future research in auditory neurophysiology. In effect, this work will determine codes and their use in neural mechanisms. As this work progresses, the controversies of resolving neural codes will give way to specific questions about how neural membranes and groups of interacting neurons act on differences of incoming spike patterns to produce pattern differences that ultimately underlie the discrimination of speech and other sounds of importance.

REFERENCES

Abbas, J., and Sachs, M. B. Two-tone suppression in auditory-nerve fibers: extension of a stimulus-response relationship. *J. Acoust. Soc. Am.* 59:112, 1976.

Bekesy, G. von. *Experiments in Hearing.* New York: McGraw-Hill, 1960.

Brownell, W. E. Cochlear transduction: an integrative model and review. *Hear. Res.* 6:335, 1982.

Brownell, W. E., Manis, P. B., Zidanic, M., and Spirou, G. A. Acoustically evoked radial current densities in scala tympani. *J. Acoust. Soc. Am.* 74:792, 1983.

Brugge, J. F., and Geilser, C. D. Auditory mechanisms of the lower brainstem. *Annu. Rev. Neurosci.* 1:363, 1978.

Cant, N. B., and Morest, D. K. The structural basis for stimulus coding in the cochlear nucleus of the cat. In C. I. Berlin (ed.), *Hearing Science.* San Diego: College-Hill Press, 1984. Pp. 372–421.

De Boer, E., and de Jongh, H. R. On cochlear encoding: potentialities and limitations of the reverse correlation technique. *J. Acoust. Soc. Am.* 63:115, 1978.

Delgutte, B. Speech coding in the auditory nerve. II. Processing schemes for vowel-like sounds. *J. Acoust. Soc. Am.* 75:879, 1984.

Delgutte, B., and Kiang, N. Y. S. Speech coding in the auditory nerve. I. Vowel-like sounds. *J. Acoust. Soc. Am.* 75:866, 1984a.

Delgutte, B., and Kiang, N. Y. S. Speech coding in the auditory nerve. III. Voiceless fricative consonants. *J. Acoust. Soc. Am.* 75:887, 1984b.

Delgutte, B., and Kiang, N. Y. S. Speech coding in the auditory nerve. V. Vowels in background noise. *J. Acoust. Soc. Am.* 75:908, 1984c.

Evans, E. F., and Nelson, P. G. The responses of single neurons in the cochlear nucleus of the cat as a function of their location and the anesthetic state. *Exp. Brain Res.* 17:402, 1973.

Garcia, P., and Clopton, B. M. Radial current flow and source density in the basal scala tympani. *Hear. Res.* 31:55, 1987.

Goblick, T. J., Jr., and Pfieffer, R. R. Time domain measurements of cochlear nonlinearities using combinations of click stimuli. *J. Acoust. Soc. Am.* 46:924, 1969.

Greenwood, D. D. Critical bandwidth and the frequency coordinates of the basilar membrane. *J. Acoust. Soc. Am.* 33:1344, 1961.

Harrison, R. V., and Evans, E. F. Reverse correlation study of cochlear filtering in normal and pathological guinea pig ears. *Hear. Res.* 6:303, 1982.

Horst, J. W., Javel, E., and Farley, G. R. Coding of fine structure in the auditory nerve. I. Fourier analysis of period and interspike internal histograms. *J. Acoust. Soc. Am.* 79:398, 1986.

Ishii, Y., Matsura, S., and Furukawa, T. Quantal nature of transmission at the synapse between hair cells and eight nerve fibers. *Jpn. J. Physiol.* 21:91, 1971.

Javel, E. Coding of AM tones in chinchilla auditory nerve: implications for the pitch of complex tones. *J. Acoust. Soc. Am.* 68:133, 1980.

Javel, E. Suppression of auditory nerve responses. I. Temporal analysis, intensity effects and suppression contours. *J. Acoust. Soc. Am.* 69:1735, 1981.

Javel, E. and Mott, J. B. Physiological and psychophysical correlates of temporal processes in hearing. *Hear. Res.* 34:275, 1988.

Johnson, D. H., and Kiang, N. Y. S. Analysis of discharges recorded simultaneously from pairs of auditory nerve fibers. *Biophys. J.* 16:719, 1976.

Johnson, D. H. The relationship between spike rate and synchrony in responses of auditory-nerve fibers to single tones. *J. Acoust. Soc. Am.* 68:1115, 1980.

Johnson, D. H., and Swami, A. The transmission of signals by auditory-nerve fiber discharge patterns. *J. Acoust. Soc. Am.* 74:493, 1983.

Kiang, N. Y. S. *Discharge Patterns of Single Fibers in the Cat's Auditory Nerve.* Cambridge, MA: MIT Press, 1965.

Liberman, M. C., and Simmons, D. D. Applications of neuronal labeling techniques to the study of the peripheral auditory system. *J. Acoust. Soc. Am.* 78:312, 1985.

Miller, M. I., Barta, P. E., and Sachs, M. B. Strategies for the representation of a tone in background noise in the temporal aspects of the discharge patterns of auditory-nerve fibers. *J. Acoust. Soc. Am.* 81:665, 1987.

Møller, A. R. Coding of amplitude and frequency modulated sounds in the cochlear nucleus of the rat. *Acta Physiol. Scand.* 86:223, 1972.

Møller, A. R. Neural delay in the ascending auditory pathway. *Exp. Brain Res.* 43:93, 1981.

Oertel, D. Synaptic responses and electrical properties of cells in brain slices of the mouse anteroventral cochlear nucleus. *J. Neurosci.* 3:2043, 1983.

Palmer, A. R. Encoding rapid amplitude fluctuations by cochlear-nerve fibres in the guinea pig. *Arch. Otorhinolaryngol.* 236:197, 1982.

Palmer, A. R., Winter, I. M., and Darwin, C. J. The representation of steady-state vowel sounds in the temporal discharge patterns of the guinea pig cochlear nerve and primary-like cochlear nucleus neurons. *J. Acoust. Soc. Am.* 79:100, 1986.

Reale, R. A., and Geisler, C. D. Auditory-nerve fiber encoding of two-tone approximations to steady-state vowels. *J. Acoust. Soc. Am.* 67:891, 1980.

Rhode, W. S., and Smith, P. H. Encoding timing and intensity in the ventral nucleus of the cat. *J. Neurophysiol.* 56:261, 1986.

Ritz, L. A., and Brownell, W. E. Single unit analysis of the posteroventral cochlear nucleus of the decerebrate cat. *Neuroscience.* 7:1995, 1982.

Ruggero, M. A. Response to noise of auditory fibers in the squirrel monkey. *J. Neurophysiol.* 36:569, 1973.

Sachs, M. B., and Abbas, P. J. Rate versus level functions for auditory-nerve fibers in cats: tone-burst stimuli. *J. Acoust. Soc. Am.* 56:1835, 1974.

Sachs, M. B., and Young, E. D. Encoding of steady-state vowels in the auditory nerve: representation in terms of discharge rate. *J. Acoust. Soc. Am.* 66:470, 1979.

Sachs, M. B., and Young, E. D. Effects of nonlinearities on speech encoding in the auditory nerve. *J. Acoust. Soc. Am.* 68:858, 1980.

Sachs, M. B., Voigt, H. F., and Young, E. D. Auditory nerve representation of vowels in background noise. *J. Neurophysiol.* 50:27, 1983.

Schreiner, C. E., and Urbas, J. V. Representation of amplitude modulation in the auditory cortex of the cat. I. The anterior auditory field (AAF). *Hear. Res.* 21:227, 1986.

Seibert, W. M. Some implications of the stochastic behavior of primary auditory neurons. *Kybernetik* 2:206, 1965.

Shore, S. E., Clopton, B. M., and Au, Y. N. Unit responses in ventral cochlear nucleus reflect cochlear coding of rapid frequency sweeps. *J. Acoust. Soc. Am.* 82:471, 1987.

Simmons, J. A., Fenton, M. B., and O'Farrell, M. J. Echo location and pursuit of prey by bats. *Science*, 203:16, 1979.

Sinex, D. G., and Geisler, C. D. Comparison of the responses of auditory nerve fibers to consonant-vowel syllables with predictions from linear models. *J. Acoust. Soc. Am.* 76:116, 1984.

Smith, R. L., and Brachman, M. L. Response modulation of auditory-nerve fibers by AM stimuli: Effects of average intensity. *Hear. Res.* 2:123, 1980.

Smith, R. L., Brachman, M. L., and Goodman, D. A. Adaptation in the auditory periphery. *Ann. N.Y. Acad. Sci.* 405:79, 1983.

Strelioff, D., and Flock, A. Stiffness of sensory-cell hair bundles in the isolated guinea pig cochlea. *Hear. Res.* 15:19, 1984.

Viemeister, N. F. Intensity coding and the dynamic range problem. *Hear. Res.* 34:267, 1988.

Voigt, H. F., and Young, E. D. Evidence of inhibitory interactions between neurons in dorsal cochlear nucleus. *J. Neurophysiol.* 44:76, 1980.

Wickesberg, R. E., Dickson, J. W., Gibson, M. M., and Geisler, C. D. Wiener kernel analysis of responses from antero-ventral cochlear nucleus neurons. *Hear. Res.* 14:155, 1984.

Young, E. D., and Sachs, M. B. Representation of steady-state vowels in the temporal aspects of the discharge patterns of populations of auditory-nerve fibers. *J. Acoust. Soc. Am.* 66:1381, 1979.

Young, E. D., and Voigt, H. F. Response properties of type II and type III units in dorsal cochlear nucleus. *Hear. Res.* 6:153, 1982.

Young, E. D. Response characteristics of neurons of the cochlear nuclei. In C. I. Berlin (ed.), *Hearing Science.* San Diego: College-Hill Press, 1984. Pp. 423–460.

CHAPTER 9

Neural Correlates of Language Function

Catherine A. Mateer

❑ Historic Perspective of the
Biologic Bases of Language

❑ Asymmetry and
Lateralization of Function in
the Human Brain

❑ Intrahemispheric
Localization of Language

❑ Contributions of the Right
Hemisphere to Language

❑ Biologic Bases for
Language Development

Grateful acknowledgment is given to Julie Barber, M.A., for her substantial contribution to this chapter's form and content and to Dr. Margaret Naeser for use of her CT scan research.

Although the representational, cognitive, and communicative aspects of language most often determine how it is conceived, language is fundamentally like any other behavior. It depends on input from sensory receptors, decoding of signals, analysis of information, and organization of motor systems for language output. This chapter summarizes *what* is known about the nervous system substrates for these various functions and *how* it is known. It conveys basic information about the brain structures and physiologic mechanisms that appear to be important for language function.

HISTORIC PERSPECTIVE OF THE BIOLOGIC BASES OF LANGUAGE

Historically, the notion that complex mental processes have biologic bases has ancient antecedents. Plato acknowledged the brain as an organ dedicated to rational processes, whereas Aristotle located these processes in the heart. During succeeding centuries proponents for each of these hypotheses argued their cases. Slowly, through careful argumentation and experimentation, the brain's role in human behavior became more clearly recognized. During the seventeenth century Rene Descartes, in his statement of the mind/body problem, set the course for modern thinking. Descartes believed that the mind was located in the pineal body surrounded by protected cortex. He also viewed the mind as unified and therefore set the stage for the debate between theories of localization of function and those of unitary function.

The concept of cerebral localization of function has a colorful history. It arose from the phrenologic theory proposed by Franz Joseph Gall and Johann Casper Spurzheim. These anatomists recognized that the cerebral cortex was composed of cells that were connected with subcortical structures. They also recognized that the symmetric halves or hemispheres of the brain were connected by commissures. Gall concluded that the external structure of the skull might reflect specific areas of cortical de-

velopment, and that these specific areas were correlated with certain behaviors. A bump on a particular part of the skull was believed to reflect a well-developed area of underlying cortical gyri, whereas a depression reflected lack of development. Behaviors such as benevolence, veneration, self-esteem, and hope were ascribed to specific cranial areas, and insights into the personality of an individual were gained by feeling the bumps on his skull. Gall and Spurzheim were so convinced of the veracity of this theory that they failed to recognize objective evidence concerning relations between the shape of the outer skull and the surface features of the neocortex.

Phrenologic analysis also invited superficial personality analysis and quackery by its adherents. As a result, all of Gall and Spurzheim's work quickly fell into disrepute, including objective descriptions of aphasia following a penetrating wound of the frontal lobe of the left cerebral hemisphere. It was a classic case of "throwing the baby out with the bath water."

Pierre Flourens delivered the final blow to phrenology through his experimental work with animals. By developing the technique of lesioning specific areas of the brain and observing changes in animal behavior, he demonstrated objectively that a specific behavioral consequence might result from a lesion at any one of a number of sites. On this basis he concluded that there was no localization of function in the cerebrum. This antilocalization concept supported the unified mind theories of Descartes and had its major proponents during the nineteenth and twentieth centuries. Chief among the proponents was Carl Lashley, who doubted that psychological functions could be localized successfully, and others who argued that the nonspecific potential of the cerebral cortex provides for recovery of function after injury.

Despite the disastrous results of the phrenologic movement, evidence for the localization of language function began to mount during the early part of the nineteenth century. Jean Baptiste Bouillaud presented a paper, based on clinical studies, before the Royal Academy of Medicine in France, arguing that speech was localized in the frontal lobes just as Gall had suggested. Bouillaud also focused attention on the notion of handedness and the contralateral relations of motor movement to cerebral func-

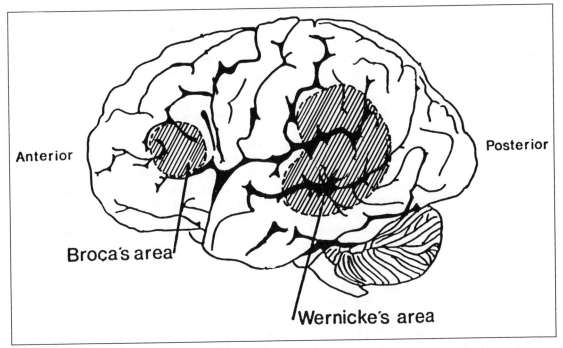

Fig. 9-1. Classic localization of Broca's and Wernicke's areas in the left lateral cortex.

tioning. Marc Dax in 1836 documented a series of clinical cases demonstrating that disorders of speech were associated with lesions of the left hemisphere. Neither Bouillaud's nor Dax's work, however, generated much attention.

It was not until 1861, when the French neurologist Paul Broca presented the celebrated case of Tan to the Anthropological Society of Paris that localization theories were taken seriously. Broca provided postmortem evidence that Tan's speech disorder, a severe aphasia characterized by repeated production of a single syllable ("tan") was related to a frontal lesion. By 1863 Broca had presented evidence involving eight cases similar to Tan's and stated, "Here are eight instances in which the lesion was in the posterior third of the third frontal convolution . . . and the most remarkable thing is that in all the patients the lesion was on the left side. I do not dare draw conclusions from this." Broca described in detail a syndrome that consisted of an inability to speak despite an intact vocal mechanism and normal comprehension. He called this syndrome "aphemia" and correlated it with a specific anatomic site. The term aphemia was criticized by Trousseau, who ar-

gued that it had roots in the Greek word for "infamous" and therefore was not appropriate as a clinical designation. Trousseau offered the word aphasia—"the state of a man who had run out of arguments"—and the term was taken up by others.

Although Broca's work seemed to mount evidence for proponents of the strict localization of language function, Carl Wernicke soon presented findings that language also could be disrupted when lesions occurred in the temporal lobe of the cerebral cortex. He suggested a relation between hearing and speech and described aphasic patients with lesions in the auditory projection area. Wernicke's descriptions differed from those of Broca. In his patients, damage was located in the first temporal gyrus, and the individuals who suffered this damage could speek fluently. Their speech, however, was confused and made little sense. They could hear but could not understand or repeat what they had heard. Wernicke hypothesized that this kind of aphasia was the result of a disconnection of fibers connecting two speech areas (Fig. 9-1), one involving speech movements (Broca's area) and the other involving comprehension of speech (Wernicke's area) (Wernicke, 1977).

Despite the accumulated evidence for localization of function, antilocalizationists continued to argue their position. Henry Head attacked the "diagram makers" on the basis of their oversimplification of the deficits that followed brain damage. Ann Golts, in a series of experiments that involved ablation (removal) of specific portions of neocortex in dogs, demonstrated that the size of a cortical lesion was more important than its specific location. Golts' experiments demonstrated that cortical removal did not abolish movement in animals; instead, decortication appeared to reduce all functions to some extent. These experiments seemed to support those previously done by Flourens and the conclusions of the twentieth century antilocalizationists such as Lashley.

John Hughlings-Jackson, the English neurologist (a major figure in the founding of modern neuropsychology), resolved the fundamental difference between Golts and the localizationists. Hughlings-Jackson conceived of the nervous system as being organized in terms of a functional hierarchy. This concept views the nervous system in terms of levels: spinal cord, midbrain, diencephalon, basal ganglia and cortex. Each level controls more complex aspects of behavior. Neural function at the level of the spinal cord supports a number of simple reflexive motor responses linked to stimulation of the somatosensory system. Neural function at the level of the brainstem provides postural support, mediates righting reflexes, and regulates the sleep/wake cycles. At a higher level, midbrain function adds at least three new components to behavior. First, it supports response to simple features of auditory and visual stimulation. Second, these sensory systems appear to be linked with voluntary motor systems that allow response to distant stimuli by producing voluntary movement (e.g., walking, turning) toward or away from them. Third, the midbrain appears to contain programs that allow automatic, stereotypic behaviors such as chewing and sucking. The hypothalamus, thalamus, and basal ganglia can support well integrated but poorly directed or modulated affective behavior, such as rage and fight/flight reactions. This level adds the dimension of increased energy and coordinated voluntary movement to behavior. Finally, the cortex constructs sequences or

patterns of voluntary movements in response to external and internal cues and discriminates patterns of sensory input.

In Hughlings-Jackson's view, disorders at the highest levels would produce dissolution of behavior (the reverse of evolution). The organism would retain a repertoire of behaviors, but these behaviors would be simpler, more like an organism that had not yet evolved a higher level brain structure. In light of this concept, ablation experiments with animals might be explained in hierarchic terms. According to Hughlings-Jackson's model, removal of cortical areas does not disrupt elementary functions; rather, it reduces these functions to more primitive levels. In a similar manner, damage to specific cortical sites in humans does not totally disrupt complex systems of behavior; rather, specific elements associated with specific cortical sites were reduced in complexity. For example, if damage occurred to an area of the brain that was not associated with language function, language might be impoverished because functions associated with that area could no longer be mediated through the language system. In other words, this information would no longer be available. Hughlings-Jackson's ideas are particularly contemporary and are receiving much more serious consideration at this time than they did during his lifetime.

Alexander Luria, the renowned Russian professor of psychology and "father of modern neuropsychology," proposed a similar hierarchic organization. Luria's conception of the cortex is as follows: sensory input enters the primary sensory zones, is elaborated in the secondary zones, and is integrated in the tertiary zones of the posterior brain. For an action to be executed, activity from the posterior tertiary sensory zones is sent to the tertiary zones of the frontal brain, then to its secondary zone, and finally to the primary frontal motor zone where execution is initiated.

The work of Norman Geschwind also explored the relation between structure and function—between the anatomy of the brain and the higher behavior of humans. As a clinical neurologist, Geschwind was led to these studies particularly by his interest in those pathologies having to do with human perception and language. His research addressed the anatomic substrates of specific disorders, including the aphasias. Geschwind was also interested in defining those features that most distinctly set off humans in the animal kingdom. His approach concentrated on the anatomic organization of the brain, the evolutionary changes of which have determined the special biologic adaptiveness of humans. The study of relations between brain function and behavior has a long and colorful history. Careful observation, systematic investigation, and serendipitous occurrences have played a role. Language, by virtue of its tremendous development in the human species, has always enjoyed a central place in debates about the nature of functional brain organization. A set of historical references pertaining to the development of aphasiology and neurolinguistics is provided in the Bibliography.

ASYMMETRY AND LATERALIZATION OF FUNCTION IN THE HUMAN BRAIN

It is now common knowledge, even among educated laypersons, that the cerebral hemispheres are functionally asymmetric. The evidence for hemispheric specialization of function is overwhelming. Studies of brain-damaged individuals have shown that damage to the left hemisphere selectively impairs some aspects of cognition (e.g., language) while sparing others (e.g., face recognition), whereas damage to the opposite hemisphere has opposite effects (Beaumont and Dimond, 1973; Milner, 1974; Springer and Deutsch, 1985).

The functional asymmetry of the hemispheres is also reflected in the performance of non-brain-damaged individuals. Because sensory projections have privileged access to the contralateral hemisphere, individuals without neurologic impairment have a perceptual bias in favor of information presented to the sensory field contralateral to the hemisphere that specializes in processing that information. Asymmetries are also evident in electrophysiologic recordings and other neurodiagnostic procedures that target hemispheric processes. A review of the an-

atomic, behavioral, and physiologic indices of hemispheric specialization in both patients and control subjects follows.

INVESTIGATIONS OF CEREBRAL ASYMMETRY IN PATIENT POPULATIONS

LESION STUDIES

Behavioral data that have been collected from patients with spontaneous unilateral brain lesions have probably yielded the greatest amount of information about the neurologic bases of language. In general, studies have indicated that lesions of the left hemisphere often result in language dysfunction, commonly termed *aphasia*, whereas lesions of the right hemisphere do not. Also associated with left hemisphere dysfunction are disorders of motor planning and motor sequencing for volitional actions including limb and orofacial structures. Disorders of this kind are termed *apraxia* and have been taken to indicate a greater left hemisphere role in complex voluntary movement.

In contrast, lesions of the right hemisphere, which usually spare basic expressive and receptive speech and language capabilities, often disrupt performance on tasks requiring spatial judgments and perception. Thus right-hemisphere-damaged patients often demonstrate disordered drawing, copying, and constructional capabilities, as well as impairments in face and form perception.

A dissociation of hemispheric functioning based on processing of verbal versus spatial information is the most commonly cited difference, but many investigators have broadened these distinctions to reflect perhaps more fundamental differences in information processing style between the two hemispheres. The left hemisphere has been conceptualized as more logical, analytic, or sequential in its processing and the right hemisphere as more holistic or gestalt-oriented in its processing (Springer and Deutsch, 1985). Under such schemes, it is not so much the kind of information that is under analysis that determines which hemisphere is more involved but the kind of processing the information demands. Language can be conceived of as a logical, sequential, rule-based system in which small features (specific sounds, words, or word orders) are crucial in its analysis. Speech depends at some level on rapid, precise, sequenced movement. Given these aspects of basic speech and language production and perception, it is most parsimonious that this system would depend primarily on the hemisphere with greater analytic or sequential processing capability, presumably the left.

SPLIT-BRAIN STUDIES

Split-brain surgery, or commissurotomy, involves surgically separating some of the nerve fibers that connect the two cerebral hemispheres. The operation usually involves splitting major portions of the corpus callosum, the huge band of fibers that crosses between the hemispheres providing direct connections primarily between homologous areas in each hemisphere. The first such operations were performed during the early 1940s on approximately two dozen patients with intractable epilepsy. It was hypothesized that limiting interhemispheric communication would reduce or prevent the spread of seizure activity. These patients gave scientists their first opportunity to study systematically the role of the corpus callosum in humans, a role that has been debated for decades.

The corpus callosum was a puzzle for researchers who expected to find functions commensurate with its large size, strategic location, and apparently important communication function within the brain. Animal research, however, had shown the consequences of split-brain surgery on healthy organisms to be minimal. The behavior of split-brain monkeys, for example, appeared indistinguishable from what it was before the operation.

Based on casual observation and standard psychological tests, individuals who underwent this operation appeared to function normally. Striking differences in abilities were revealed, however, by a variety of experimental tasks that selectively allowed access to information by only one cerebral hemisphere. For example, visual images presented in one visual field are projected to the contralateral hemisphere in persons whose callosal connections are intact. Split-brain patients, however, because their hemispheres cannot communicate normally, do not receive visual information at both hemispheres. When images were presented tachistoscopically in the right visual field and projected to the left hemisphere in split-brain patients, they were readily named. In contrast, images presented tachistoscopically to the left visual field and thus largely restricted to right hemisphere processing could not be named and, in fact, were denied to have been seen when an individual was queried. However, when the individual was presented with an array of objects including the object presented visually, he was able to point to the correct object . . . but only with his left hand.

The results of these and similar tasks seemed to demonstrate clearly not only functional lateralization of the two hemispheres but also that the hemispheres could, in many respects, function independently. Roger Sperry, the chief investigator of these studies, received a Nobel Prize in Medicine in 1966 for his contribution to the understanding of hemispheric function.

AMYTAL SODIUM STUDIES

In some patients with epilepsy, it is possible to surgically remove the epileptic focus in the brain. It usually involves resecting portions of the temporal lobes, a common site of seizure foci. Before operations, however, the surgeon needs to know if language or memory are critically dependent on the side of the brain to be operated on.

Amobarbital sodium (Amytal Sodium) is a fast-acting barbiturate that, when injected directly into the carotid artery of each hemisphere, effectively blocks the function of most of that hemisphere for a few minutes. Such injections are used to determine hemispheric laterality of speech in patients prior to brain surgery (Wada and Rasmussen, 1960). Lateralization of speech and memory functions are determined by having the patient count, name the days of the week, name objects, and remember information presented after the injection. If the drug has inactivated the hemisphere responsible for speech, the patient's production is halted or seriously disrupted. When the nondominant hemisphere is inactivated, neither the ability to count nor to name objects is interrupted for more than a few seconds.

The Amytal Sodium test, or Wada test as it has come to be known, has been useful for determining the hemisphere that controls speech in a large number of patients. Table 9-1 shows

TABLE 9-1. SPEECH LATERALIZATION AS RELATED TO HANDEDNESS

Handedness	No. of cases	Speech representation (%)		
		Left	Bilateral	Right
Right	140	96	0	4
Left	122	70	15	15

Adapted from Rasmussen, T., and Milner, B. The role of early left brain injury in determining lateralization of cerebral speech functions. *Ann. N.Y. Acad. Sci.* 299:355, 1977.

the relation between hand preference and the lateralization of cerebral speech processes in a sample of patients studied by Rasmussen and Milner (1977). There was a strong preponderance for left hemisphere speech representation; 96 percent of right-handers and 70 percent of left-handers showed speech disturbance after Amytal Sodium injection into the left hemisphere and not after injection into the right. Only 4 percent of right-handers had right hemisphere speech representation. In contrast, 15 percent of left-handers had speech on the right and 15 percent had bilateral speech representation. More recent investigations of atypical speech representation (Mateer and Dodrill, 1983) have shown that in cases of bilateral speech representation there is not a duplication of function, i.e., "two left hemispheres," but relative separation of different speech/language functions between the two hemispheres. Analysis of errors made during Amytal Sodium injections suggested that in cases with bilateral language, articulatory and grammatic functions still depended predominantly on the left hemisphere, whereas more semantic, meaning-based aspects of language were often shared.

ANATOMIC ASYMMETRIES

Right–left asymmetries on the lateral surface of the human brain in the region surrounding the sylvian (lateral) fissure were beginning to be documented before the turn of the century. Several authors noted right–left differences in the length and angulation of the sylvian fissure, with the left being longer and more horizontal in direction than the right (Geschwind, 1974; Witelson, 1977b). In addition to this external asymmetry, it was noted early that within

the sylvian fissure the transverse gyrus, also called Heschl's gyrus or the planum temporale, showed marked variation in gross morphology, with the left planum often being larger.

It was not until 1968, however, that Geschwind and Levitsky measured the exposed planum temporale in a large number of specimens. The primary asymmetry they found was in the length of the planum temporale. As can be seen in Figure 9-2, this area comprises the posterior region of the superior surface of the temporal lobe. In their study of 100 brains measured postmortem, 65 percent were found to have a longer planum temporale in the left hemisphere than the right, 11 percent had a longer temporal plane on the right, and the remaining 24 percent showed no difference. On average, the temporal plane was one-third longer on the left than on the right.

Subsequent studies replicated the findings of Geschwind and Levitsky, demonstrating a larger planum in about 70 percent of both infant and adult brains overall (Witelson, 1977a). All studies found the left planum temporale larger by about one-third to almost twice the size of the right planum, differences easily observed on gross visual inspection.

The planum temporale, the superior part of the first temporal gyrus, is continuous with the supramarginal and the angular gyrus, regions known to be relevant for language and praxis (coordinated movement sequence). The planum temporale is clearly part of Wernicke's posterior language region. Its functional specificity, coupled with its greater expanse on the left side, readily lends credence to the hypothesis that this anatomic feature represents a substrate of cerebral dominance.

There is, however, reason for some skepticism. It is not known, for example, if a larger region is necessarily associated with dominant

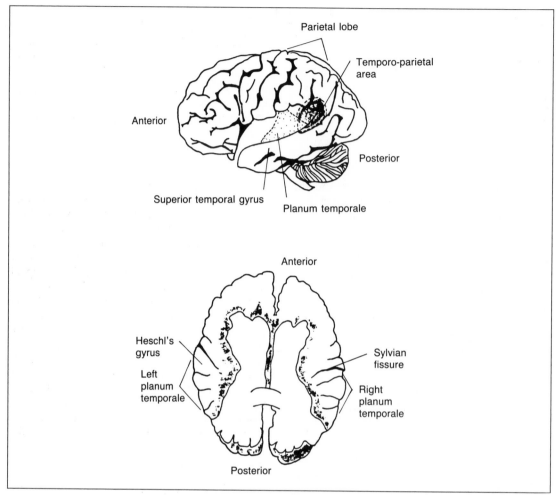

Fig. 9-2. Anatomic asymmetry. Top. View of the left lateral cortex with the temporal lobe pulled out and down to reveal the upper posterior surface of the temporal cortex, or planum temporale. Bottom. Horizontal brain section exposing the planum temporale. It illustrates the typically larger area of the planum temporale in the left versus the right. It also identifies Heschl's gyrus, the cortical focus of the primary auditory projections. This anatomic asymmetry has been postulated to underlie, at least in part, some of the functional asymmetry between the cerebral hemispheres.

function. Also, the distribution of dominance in the population estimated by the morphologic asymmetries and by behavioral studies is different. On average, only 70 percent of brain studies are characterized by a larger left planum, but estimates of left hemisphere dominance based on Amytal Sodium studies and incidence studies of aphasia suggest that more than 90 percent of the total population have speech function lateralized to the left hemisphere.

Other neuroanatomic asymmetries have been observed but with less documentation. Asymmetries exist in the ventricular system, in the vascular pattern, and in the breadth and alignment of the frontal and posterior regions of the hemispheres. In general, these asymmetries have not proved as reliable and are more diffi-

cult to interpret in terms of function because they do not include regions as clearly associated with behavior as the planum temporale. Undoubtedly, studies of gross and fine morphologic asymmetries will continue and will hopefully contribute to the understanding of brain–behavior relations and the nature of hemispheric specialization.

FUNCTIONAL ASYMMETRIES IN THE NORMAL BRAIN

Lateralization of function in normal populations has been explored and detailed using a variety of behavioral and electrophysiologic techniques, some of which are ingenious. The behavioral techniques involve experimental paradigms in which one looks at responses to stimuli that have preferential access to one hemisphere. Included are studies of dichotic listening (auditory stimuli), tachistoscopic presentation (visual stimuli), dichaptic presentation (tactile stimuli), and competition paradigms. Electrophysiologic studies, which directly measure electrical brain activity, include electroencephalographic and event-related potential procedures.

BEHAVIORAL STUDIES

Several procedures take advantage of the contralateral connections that characterize the major visual, auditory, and tactile input channels. Sensory stimuli are presented simultaneously to each hemisphere, and a behavioral response is required. Assumptions regarding the predominant function of each hemisphere are made on the basis of which of the stimuli are better, more fully, or more quickly perceived.

Dichotic Listening Studies

Dichotic listening studies involve indirect comparisons between left and right temporal lobe regions (primary and secondary auditory projections). With this procedure, two stimuli are presented simultaneously, one to each ear. Although both hemispheres receive projections from each ear, there is a preponderance of the contralateral connections, which are better developed and may actually inhibit ipsilateral pathways; thus information presented to the left ear has preferred access to the right hemisphere (Fig. 9-3). Access of this information to the left hemisphere is then possible but only via interhemispheric corpus callosum connections. In the same way, information presented to the right ear has preferential access to left hemisphere processing.

Following the simultaneous bilateral presentation of the two auditory stimuli, the subject is asked to report what is heard. Kimura, who was working at the Montreal Neurological Institute with patients who had temporal lobe

lesions, was the first to report using this technique for the evaluation of hemispheric asymmetry. She reported that when brief verbal stimuli such as digits were presented, all subjects, regardless of lesion focus, reported hearing the digit presented to the right ear more often than the digit presented to the left ear. This right ear advantage (REA) was also found in normal control subjects and was taken to indicate dominance of the left hemisphere for language processing (Kimura, 1961).

Since that early study, several hundreds of dichotic listening studies have been reported. Although there are many conflicting results, there have been a number of consistent findings. In general, REAs are found for verbal or language-based stimuli (e.g., words, nonsense syllables, backward speech, and stop consonants). Left ear advantages (LEAs), suggesting greater right hemisphere processing, have been shown for stimuli such as melodic patterns and nonspeech sounds (e.g., cough, laugh). Vowels have typically failed to yield a strong ear advantage in

Fig. 9-3. Dichotic listening. Note the bilateral projections from each ear to each hemisphere. The contralateral projections are, however, preponderant. Note also the capacity for information to cross from one hemisphere to the other via the corpus callosum. In dichotic listening studies an advantage of perceiving stimuli presented to one ear suggests primary processing of that stimuli by the contralateral hemisphere. A right ear advantage for simultaneously presented words thus suggests better left hemisphere processing of verbal stimuli.

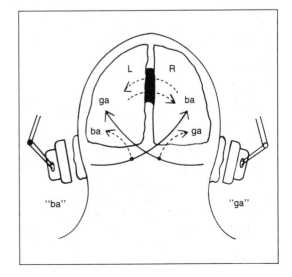

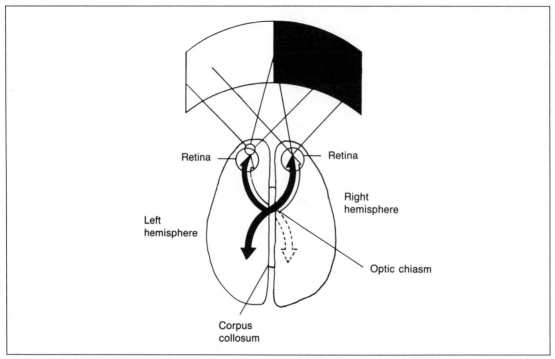

Fig. 9-4. Visual projections. Information presented in the right visual field stimulates receptors in each eye, but because of the crossed and uncrossed pathways (from the right and left retinas respectively) it is projected only to the left cerebral cortex. This anatomic and functional organization is exploited in tachistoscopic studies of hemispheric specialization. Field advantages for different kinds of stimuli thus reflect hemispheric processing asymmetries.

either direction. Although the verbal/nonverbal distinction is most often discussed in this regard, studies by Efron (1963) have suggested that an REA is seen whenever rapid or sequential processing is required. The acoustic nature of most speech sequences involves rapidly sequenced transitions (the exception is isolated vowels), and this processing capacity may underlie the left hemisphere's role in speech perception. Indeed, Tallal has demonstrated that impaired rate of auditory processing may underlie comprehension problems in both developmental and acquired aphasia (Tallal and Newcome, 1978; Tallal and Piercy, 1974).

Researchers have used the dichotic listening studies to develop theories about the nature of hemispheric specialization, but limitations of the technique should be noted: Not all subjects show the expected ear advantages in dichotic studies; the ear differences are often small when they occur; and dichotic results are significantly affected by various contextual and practice effects. Nevertheless, dichotic listening will undoubtedly continue to be used as a technique for exploring hemispheric asymmetry in the normal brain.

Tachistoscopic Studies

Tachistoscopic studies, which utilize another technique for investigating functional asymmetries in the human brain, take advantage of the natural split in the human visual pathways. This split neatly divides our visual worlds into two fields, each of which projects to one hemisphere. Information perceived in the right visual field stimulates visual receptors in the back left portion of each eye. It then is transmitted back via the visual pathways to the left occipital lobe (Fig. 9-4). Eye movements to rapid visual stimuli are not under voluntary control, and bringing a stimulus into central fixation stimulates both visual field receptor areas. For this reason, the one-sided presentations must last only a fraction of a second. Even brief exposures, however, are sufficient to allow investigators to compare the processing abilities of one hemisphere with those of the other. In tachistoscopic studies, visual stimuli are presented briefly (less than 50 ms) to the left or right of a central point where a subject is visually fixating. In this way, the visual stimuli have preferential access to one hemisphere only.

As with dichotic studies, there have been numerous tachistoscopic studies that have addressed functional hemispheric asymmetries. The strongest evidence that visual field differences in tachistoscopic studies are measuring functional asymmetries in the brain is that the visual field asymmetries in tachistoscopic tasks are the same as those demonstrated in neurologic patients. A right visual field advantage is found with normal subjects in a variety of tasks using verbal material such as words and letters. A left visual field advantage is often found for nonverbal stimuli thought to be processed by the right hemisphere, including faces, two-dimensional point localization, matching of slanted lines, and stereoscopic depth perception (Kolb and Whishaw, 1985).

Dichaptic Studies

In dichaptic stimulation studies, the subject simultaneously feels two objects held out of view, one in each hand. In one study, subjects held *meaningless* shapes for 10 seconds, then chose the two shapes from a field of six objects that were displayed visually (Witelson, 1975). The number of objects correctly selected by each hand was tabulated. The results showed a left hand (right hemisphere) superiority in the tactile recognition of objects. In another study (Gibson and Bryden, 1983), cutouts of irregular shapes or letters of sandpaper were slowly moved across the fingertips of subjects. The authors reported a right-hand (left hemisphere) superiority for identifying letters and a left-hand (right hemisphere) superiority for identifying nonsense shapes (Varney, 1986).

Competition Paradigms

Competition paradigms provide another method for exploring functional lateralization. With this paradigm the time required to complete simultaneous activities, e.g., moving blocks one at a time from one container to another while reciting the alphabet or balancing a dowel while reciting nursery rhymes, is compared to the same tasks produced in silence (Lomas and Kimura, 1976). Theoretically, if these tasks involve a common brain region (one, for example, involved in processing sequential information or controlling sequential motor activity), a longer time to accomplish the manual motor task would be expected for the silent task condition than for the condition that involved simultaneous verbalization. Such differences in sequential motor control have in fact been observed. More interestingly, differential task performance during silent trials and trials with verbalization has not been seen when nonmotor tasks (e.g., recognizing faces or complex geometric patterns) were used. On the basis of such studies, it has been concluded that certain cognitive processes share functional brain systems, whereas others do not. Such experiments yield further information concerning the lateralization and localization of separate functions.

ELECTROPHYSIOLOGIC ASYMMETRIES

Patterns of electrical activity from the brain recorded from electrodes placed at various points on the scalps of humans were discovered by Austrian psychiatrist Hans Burger during the late 1920s. These patterns were called the electroencephalogram (EEG), literally meaning "electrical brain writing." An EEG has characteristic rhythms that reflect the overall activity of the brain; it is useful for detecting a variety of neurologic diseases and disorders. By recording EEG activity from symmetric positions on either side of the head while subjects perform verbal tasks such as writing a letter and spatial tasks such as constructing geometric figures, investigators have been able to demonstrate task-related differences between right and left hemisphere electrical activity.

In addition, EEG studies in patients who have had damage to one hemisphere of the brain have provided some insight into mechanisms of recovery. In patients with left hemisphere damage and aphasia, investigators have demonstrated increased EEG activity in the right hemisphere during language-processing tasks, suggesting that the right hemisphere may play a role in language recovery.

Event-related potentials (ERPs), also called evoked potentials, as discussed in Chapter 1, are refinements of EEG measurement in that they represent more discrete, localizable electrophysiologic responses that are time-locked to specific behaviors, sensory perceptions, or as-

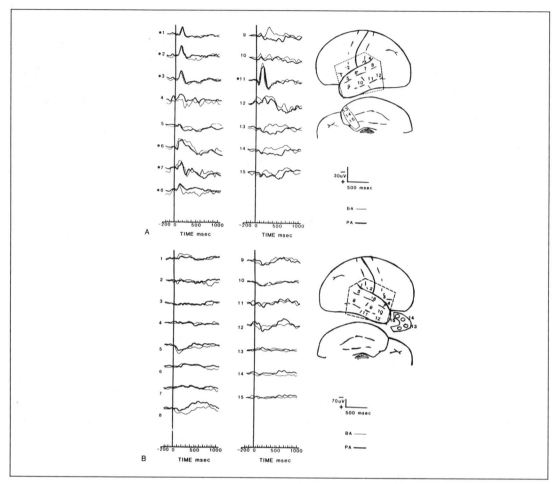

Fig. 9-5. Electrophysiologic asymmetries. Note the evoked potential correlates of speech sound perception from electrodes placed directly on the cortical surface during neurosurgical procedures. Sites in the perisylvian region of the left cortex (frontal, temporal, and parietal) are associated with clear responses to presentations of the speech sounds /ba/ and /pa/ (top), whereas sites on the right cortical surface are not (bottom).

sumed cognitive processes. The ERP is derived from computerized analysis of the complex continuous electrical activity of the brain. It is based on the assumption that if a stimulus has a consistent specific effect on cerebral activity, over many stimulus presentations this effect can be summated by a computer (all irrelevant activity is averaged out). The reflection of specific cortical activity appears on a recording as a visible peak representing the averaged evoked potential. Using this procedure, left-right asymmetries have been observed: a greater left-hemisphere ERP to verbal stimuli and greater right-hemisphere ERP to nonverbal stimuli (Kutas and Van Patten, in press; Molfese, 1983; Neville, 1980; Wood, Goff, and Day, 1971).

More recently, increasingly detailed study of the shape and location of the waveform has been made possible through the use of elec-

trode strips laid directly on the cortex during neurologic evaluations. Such direct cortical recording avoids the dispersion and reduction of power in the electrical signal that occurs with scalp recording. One such study investigated ERP responses to specific speech sounds. Evoked potential responses to both /ba/ and /pa/ syllables were clearly seen from the left but not the right temporal lobe (Mateer, Cameron, Polly, and Thompson, 1986) (Fig. 9-5). These procedures will become increasingly sophisticated and should shed important new light on the electrophysiologic aspects of speech and language processing.

In view of the wide spectrum of information presented in this section, it is not surprising that the functional asymmetry between the two hemispheres of the human brain has fascinated not only neuroscientists but also philosophers. The study of differences in hemispheric functioning has prompted the development of a variety of innovative and creative techniques for gleaning information about brain organization. The development of functional asymmetries not only in phylogeny but also in ontogeny has been argued. Is it a phenomenon restricted to *Homo sapiens*? What selective advantages has it granted in evolution? How and when does it develop in individuals and in response to what biologic influences? Hereditary, hormonal, gender, and experimental factors have all come under the scrutiny of researchers involved in this area. Whereas traditional theories have focused on verbal/nonverbal differences, the accumulating evidence for right hemisphere involvement in some aspects of linguistic processing and for left hemisphere involvement in some visuospatial operations has resulted in attempts by researchers to define processing or operational styles that might allow more basic conceptualizations of differences in hemispheric functioning. Such dichotomies as analytic versus holistic, sequential versus gestalt, focal versus diffuse, serial versus parallel, and rapid versus slow have been proposed to characterize left and right hemisphere functioning, respectively. There is little doubt research in this area will continue to further the understanding and conceptualization of functional brain organization.

INTRAHEMISPHERIC LOCALIZATION OF LANGUAGE

APHASIC SYNDROMES AND THEIR NEURAL CORRELATES

The relation between area of brain damage and aphasic deficit has been a major focus of study in the search for neurologic underpinnings of language. Damage to the left perisyl-

vian region commonly gives rise to aphasic symptoms in right-handed individuals. Symptoms tend to cluster into syndromes, and the probability of a particular syndrome varies with the location of the lesion. The correlation between anatomy and functional deficit becomes less clear, however, when one considers the exact boundaries of lesions responsible for aphasic deficits and the relative contribution of different structures within lesion boundaries. Whereas some studies have reported "clean" findings between locus of lesion and aphasic syndromes, others have reported more variability or exceptions to classic results. Finally, clinical experiences indicate that the symptom profile of many aphasic patients does not allow the patient to be classified clearly as having one of the aphasic syndromes. Given this caveat, however, it is valuable to understand the behavioral features and lesion localization for a set of classically recognized aphasia syndromes.

BROCA'S APHASIA

One of the major reported aphasic syndromes is Broca's aphasia. The symptoms associated with Broca's aphasia are (1) effortful, poorly articulated speech; (2) expressive language reduced in phrase length and grammatic complexity; (3) better use of content words than function words or grammatic markers; (4) impaired repetition skills; (5) impaired writing; (6) variable but relatively intact reading comprehension; and (7) relatively intact auditory comprehension (Goodglass and Kaplan, 1972). Although sensitive tests of auditory comprehension frequently reveal deficits in phonemic and syntactic processing (Caramazza, Gordon, Zurif, and DeLuca, 1976; Heilman and Scholes, 1976), patients with Broca's aphasia demonstrate a general discrepancy between severely limited expressive skills (often characterized as nonfluent because of articulatory struggle and short phrase length) and good functional comprehension skills.

The classic localization theory has designated Broca's area, the posterior portion of the third frontal convolution (F3), as responsible for Broca's aphasia (Fig. 9-6). Work by Mohr and his colleagues (Mohr, 1976) challenged that assumption. By reviewing previously published reports that had localizing information, evaluating longitudinal data, and presenting new cases, Mohr concluded that the lesion giving

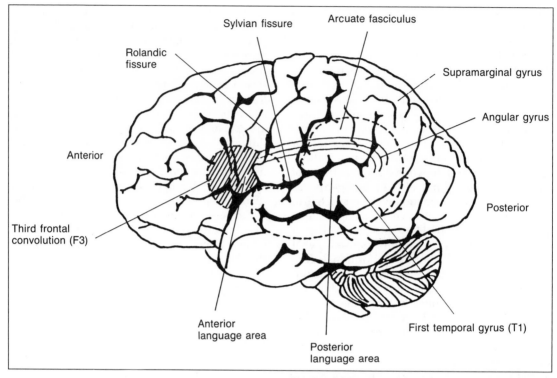

Rolandic
fissure
Sylvian fissure   Arcuate fasciculus

Supramarginal gyrus

Angular gyrus

Anterior

Posterior

Third frontal
convolution (F3)

Anterior
language area

Posterior
language area

First temporal gyrus (T1)

Fig. 9-6. Major cortical landmarks in reference to which the damage underlying aphasic syndromes has been localized.

rise to Broca's aphasia was much larger than F3: It included the frontal and parietal operculum, with some extension into the supramarginal gyrus, the white matter deep to Broca's area, and the insula. In general, it was the region supplied by the upper division of the middle cerebral artery (Fig. 9-7). Lesions in F3 alone gave rise only to transient mutism, which evolved rapidly into normal language with some residual articulatory defects.

Numerous studies have confirmed and extended Mohr's findings. All of the patients with Broca's aphasia studied by Naeser and Hayward (1978) and by Kertesz, Harlock, and Coates (1979) had broad lesions comparable to those outlined by Mohr. Figure 9-8 exemplifies such lesions. Although there was variability in the extent of lesions, the insula was damaged in all cases. Results also indicated that the severity of aphasia was increased with involvement of other subcortical structures, including the basal ganglia.

Thus there is general agreement that isolated lesions in Broca's area (F3) result in transient aphasia and that large fronto-temporal-parietal lesions, sometimes extending into Wernicke's

area and often including the insula and deep white matter, are likely to result in long-standing aphasia. The chronic aphasia is likely to be Broca's aphasia, but there is a possibility of global aphasia as well.

WERNICKE'S APHASIA

Whereas Broca's aphasia is considered a nonfluent aphasia, Wernicke's aphasia and conduction aphasia are fluent types. Wernicke's aphasia is characterized by (1) spontaneous, fluently articulated speech; (2) expressive language of normal phrase length but reduced content; (3) superficially acceptable syntactic structure; (4) the presence of paraphasias (word or letter substitutions) or neologisms in expressive language; (5) poor repetition skills; and (6) impaired comprehension. Reading and writing also are impaired. The lesion site commonly associated with Wernicke's aphasia, Wernicke's area, includes the posterior portion of the first temporal gyrus (T1) (Fig. 9-6). The degree to which the supramarginal gyrus and lower tem-

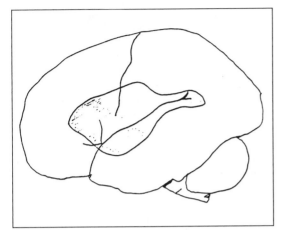

Fig. 9-7. Topography of the infarct found in Broca's case Leborgne. Note that Broca's aphasia results from large perisylvian lesions (including insula and sometimes subcortical structures). Isolated lesions of Broca's area (F3) result in only transient aphasic symptoms. (From Mohr, J. Broca's area and Broca's aphasia. In H. Whitaker and H. A. Whitaker (eds.), *Studies in Neurolinguistics*, Vol. 1. New York: Academic Press, 1976. Pp. 201–236.)

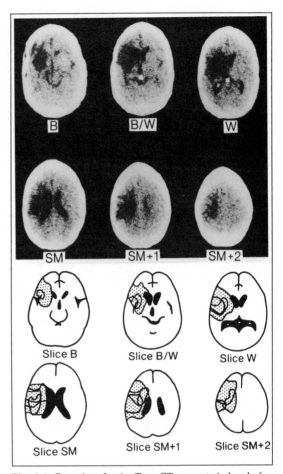

Fig. 9-8. Broca's aphasia. Top. CT scan at six levels for a 51-year-old patient 7 years after a stroke. Bottom. CT scan lesion sites; each slice (level) is a composite of four cases. Large lesions were located in Broca's area on slices B and/or B/W, and the peak amount of tissue damage was high in the frontoparietal areas at slices SM and SM +1. B = Broca's area slice; B/W = Broca's/Wernicke's area slice; W = Wernicke's area slice; SM = supramarginal gyrus slice; SM +1 = one slice above supramarginal gyrus; SM +2 = two slices above supramarginal gyrus. (From Naeser, M. A., CT scan lesion and lesion locus in cortical and subcortical aphasias. In A. Kertesz (ed.) *Localization in Neuropsychology*. New York: Academic Press, 1983.)

poral gyri are included in Wernicke's area varies considerably with descriptions (Bogen and Bogen, 1976; Goodglass and Kaplan, 1972).

Almost all studies confirm the importance of at least posterior T1. This area was involved in patients with Wernicke's aphasia in computed tomography studies by Naeser and Hayward (1978) and Kertesz (1979). Acute, recent, and chronic cases with posterior T1 lesions (Mazzochi and Vignolo, 1979) had deficits associated with fluent aphasia, although there was some variability in whether the syndrome was classified as Wernicke's or conduction aphasia. In the various studies, considerable variation in the extent of temporal and parietal lesions has been observed, so it is possible that in some patients additional critical areas may be involved (Fig. 9-9).

GLOBAL APHASIA

With large lesions involving both anterior and posterior language areas and subcortical regions deep to each (Fig. 9-10), a more pervasive and complete aphasia may result. Global aphasia is characterized by a severe depression of all aspects of receptive and expressive language function. Because anterior areas are affected, speech is typically nonfluent. The severity of impairment of communication skills in all modalities is such that patients with global aphasia often express feelings and simple wishes through facial, vocal, and manual gestures. Speech is usually limited to the nonpropositional level, with verbal stereotypes commonly produced. Comprehension is severely impaired.

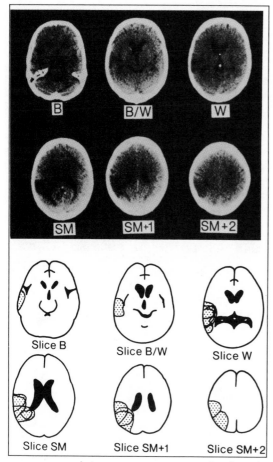

Fig. 9-9. Wernicke's aphasia. CT scan of a 55-year-old patient 4 months after a stroke (top) and composite CT scan lesion sites for four cases (bottom). Lesions were located in Wernicke's area at slice W and in the supramarginal gyrus area at slice SM. (From Naeser, M. A., CT scan lesion and lesion locus in cortical and subcortical aphasias. In A. Kertesz (ed.) *Localization in Neuropsychology.* New York: Academic Press, 1983.)

CONDUCTION APHASIA

With conduction aphasia: (1) comprehension is good, although syntactic deficits similar to those exhibited by patients with Broca's aphasia can often be identified (Goodglass and Kaplan, 1972; Heilman and Scholes, 1976; Rothi, Mc-Farling, and Heilman, 1982); (2) spontaneous speech is fluent but may contain phonemic paraphasia (sound substitutions); and (3) repetition is seriously impaired. The relatively preserved comprehension distinguishes the patient with conduction aphasia from the patient with Wer-

nicke's aphasia. The classic lesion associated with conduction aphasia is in the supramarginal gyrus and the arcuate fasciculus, a band of cortical fibers connecting anterior and posterior speech areas (Fig. 9-11). Such a lesion originally was hypothesized to result in a disconnection between Wernicke's and Broca's areas (Geschwind, 1965) (Fig. 9-6). Sparing of Wernicke's area would allow comprehension of language, and sparing of Broca's area would allow internally generated expression, but a severing of connections between the two would not allow the patient to repeat what he heard.

TRANSCORTICAL MOTOR AND TRANSCORTICAL SENSORY APHASIA

Two additional, though rare, aphasic syndromes are transcortical motor aphasia (TMA) and transcortical sensory aphasia (TSA). Although they each bear a strong resemblance to Broca's aphasia and Wernicke's aphasia, respectively, the ability to repeat is strikingly preserved in both TMA and TSA. There has been speculation that spared repetition reflects intact connection between cortical areas. TMA has been associated with frontal lobe lesions either low (anterior to Broca's area) or high (above Broca's area) on the lateral surface or from mesial frontal lobe lesions involving the supplementary motor area. TSA has been associated with damage to the border-zone region of the parietotemporal junction (Benson and Geschwind, 1985). Other investigators have suggested, alternatively, that the lesions involve subcortical structures—basal ganglia in the case of TMA and thalamus in the case of TSA. These subcortical areas are known to be directly connected to Broca's and Wernicke's areas, respectively. Despite the controversy over lesion sites responsible for TMA and TSA, it is almost universally accepted that the immediate perisylvian structures in frontal, temporal, and parietal lobes are intact. The spared connection between the primary language comprehension area (T1) and language expression (F3) thus supports the ability to repeat.

To better comprehend the relations among classic aphasia syndromes, the major clinical characteristics of each are included in Table 9-2. The probability of motor signs and the integrity of the perisylvian cortex for each syndrome are also noted.

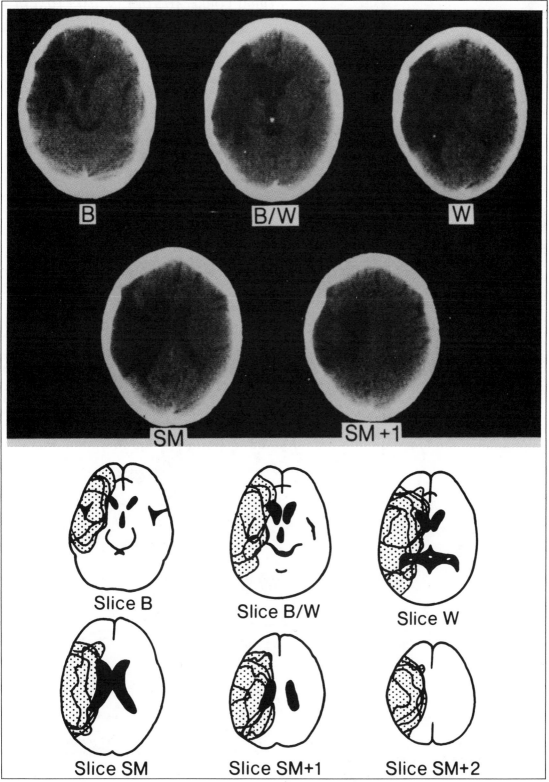

Fig. 9-10. Global aphasia. CT scan of a 61-year-old patient 7 months after a stroke (top) and composite CT scan lesion sites for five cases (bottom). Large lesions were present in every language area (Broca's slices B and B/W), (Wernicke's slices B/W and W), and the supramarginal gyrus and arcuate fasciculus (slices SM and SM + 1). (From Naeser, M. A., CT scan lesion and lesion locus in cortical and subcortical aphasias. In A. Kertesz (ed.) *Localization in Neuropsychology.* New York: Academic Press, 1983.)

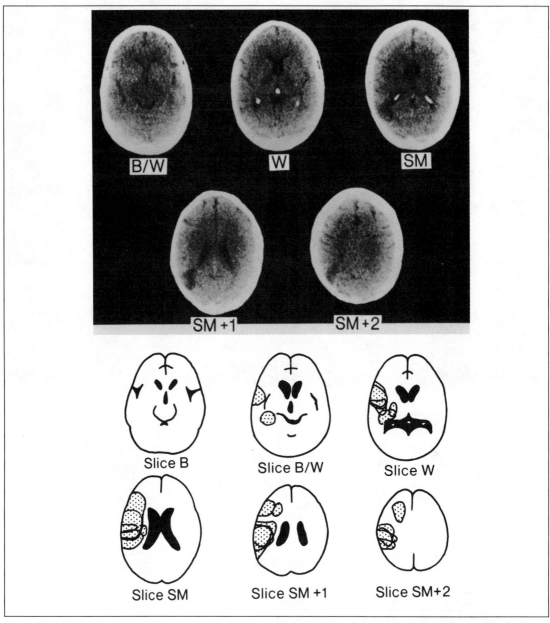

Fig. 9-11. Conduction aphasia. CT scan of a 53-year-old patient 4 months after a stroke (top) and composite CT scan lesion sites for six cases (bottom). Small lesions were primarily deep to Wernicke's area (slice W) or in the supramarginal gyrus (slices SM and SM + 1). (From Naeser, M. A., CT scan lesion and lesion locus in cortical and subcortical aphasias. In A. Kertesz (ed.) *Localization in Neuropsychology.* New York: Academic Press, 1983.)

SUBCORTICAL APHASIA

The studies reported thus far have related primarily to cortical lesions. Increasing numbers of studies indicate that subcortical mechanisms must be considered when one evaluates the effect of cortical lesions and that subcortical lesions may themselves produce aphasic symptoms.

TABLE 9-2. CLINICAL FEATURES OF THE APHASIA SYNDROMES

Syndrome	Spontaneous speech	Auditory comprehension	Repetition	Naming	General motor
Global	Nonfluent	−	−	−	Hemiparesis
Broca's	Nonfluent	+	−	∓	Hemiparesis
Transcortical motor	Nonfluent	+	+	−	∓ Hemiparesis
Wernicke's	Fluent	−	−	−	Normal
Transcortical sensory	Fluent	−	+	−	± Hemiparesis
Conduction	Fluent	+	−	∓	Normal

(+) relatively spared function; (∓) often but not always impairment; (−) almost always impaired; (±) occasionally impaired.
Adapted from the Boston Classification System. After Goodglass, H., and Kaplan, E. *The Assessment of Aphasia and Related Disorders.*
Philadelphia: Lea & Febiger, 1983; and Benson, D. F. *Aphasia, Alexia, and Agraphia.* New York: Churchill Livingstone, 1979.

Penfield and Roberts (1959), in their classic *Speech and Brain Mechanisms*, were among the first to articulate that subcortical integration was of great and probably greater importance to speech and language function than the transcortical association tracts. Functional areas of human cortex have important connections with one or more subcortical structures. These subcortical areas of gray matter, by means of their projection fibers, coordinate and utilize the functional activities of the more recently evolved cortical areas and integrate that activity with the rest of the brain. The posterior speech areas have projection connections with the pulvinar and lateral posterior nuclei of the thalamus. The anterior speech area has connections with the centrum median and dorsomedial nuclei of the thalamus. The importance of these connections has only recently been appreciated.

Aphasic symptoms following isolated basal ganglia lesions have been reported. Although the specific lesions are so variable that it is not yet possible to attribute symptoms to specific nuclei, the putamen and caudate head appear to be frequently involved. Given that the symptoms are so variable from case to case, there is not yet justification for suggesting a specific behavioral syndrome. Damasio, Damasio, Rizzo, Varney, and Gersh's (1982) subjects with basal ganglia lesions had symptoms varying widely in type and severity, with the common element being long-lasting aphasic symptoms. Patients with comparable-sized lesions in adjacent white matter showed dysarthria (motor speech problems) but no aphasia. Basal ganglia lesions also may be contributing to the severity of Broca's aphasia syndromes, as the Broca's lesion is frequently described as involving the insula and basal ganglia. Symptoms reported with lesions that involve both cortical structures and the basal ganglia are stereotypic and automatic utterances, although Damasio and his colleagues reported perseverative and repetitive utterances in individuals with isolated subcortical lesions.

Some of the patients reported in studies on the basal ganglia have had lesions extending to the thalamus (Fig. 9-12). There are many additional studies reporting thalamus-specific lesions with ensuing aphasic deficits (Fisher, 1959, earliest report; see Mateer and Ojemann, 1983, for review). There are both cognitive and linguistic deficits reported after thalamic lesions, with the former more consistent across studies than the latter. Fluctuations in alertness have been reported repeatedly and have been related to the role of the thalamus in alerting and vigilance mechanisms (Laitinen and Vilkki, 1977; Riklan and Levita, 1969) and to the general cognitive role of the thalamus in attention and memory. Brown (1976, 1979) has suggested that linguistic deficits are secondary to cognitive deficits. Luria described the thalamic syndrome as quasiaphasic (1977).

The linguistic deficits reported for thalamic lesions include paraphasias, neologisms, and anomia, often with perseveration. Repetition is typically spared and speech is fluent (Mateer and Ojemann, 1983; Reynolds, Turner, Harris, Ojemann, and Davis, 1979). Although there appear to be differences between thalamic and purely basal ganglia lesions in the areas of alertness and cognition, too many patients in the studies reported have had overlapping lesions. Specific language symptoms cannot yet be attributed to thalamic versus basal ganglia le-

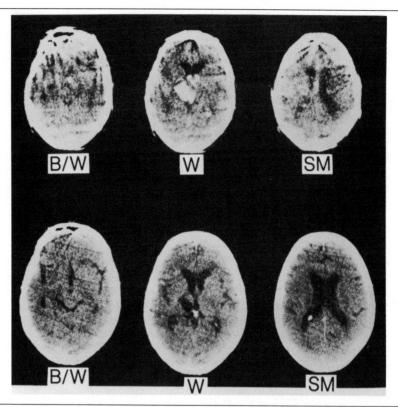

Fig. 9-12. Subcortical aphasia with thalamic lesion site. CT scan of a 69-year-old patient: acute (hemorrhage, top row) and at 4 months after stroke (bottom row). The small lesion was located primarily in the pulvinar and posterior limb, internal capsule (slice W, bottom row). (From Naeser, M. A., CT scan lesion and lesion locus in cortical and subcortical aphasias. In A. Kertesz (ed.) *Localization in Neuropsychology*. New York: Academic Press, 1983.)

sions. Further studies and longitudinal data are needed to distinguish linguistic and nonlinguistic components of thalamic disturbance.

APRAXIA

The term *apraxia* refers to impairment of selecting and executing voluntary movement in the absence of significant paralysis. Following lesions of the left hemisphere, limb apraxia may manifest as an inability to (1) imitate a hand or limb posture, (2) copy a series of meaningless hand or limb movements, or (3) demonstrate the movements necessary to carry out a functional activity. Left hemisphere lesions affect the contralateral right limb and usually the ipsilateral left limb (Kimura, 1976). Kimura has interpreted these results to reflect an underlying superiority of the left hemisphere for selecting and sequencing movement.

Oral apraxia refers to the similar inability to produce or mimic nonverbal orofacial movements of a meaningful nature (kiss, blow) or nonmeaningful nature (stick out tongue, purse lips). Mateer and Kimura (1977) reported that nonfluent aphasic patients often had difficulty with such simple nonverbal oral movements. Aphasics with fluent speech, although usually able to produce such isolated movements, had difficulty producing a sequence of such movements. Errors on nonverbal oral movement tasks paralleled errors on expressive speech tasks involving phonemic selection and sequencing in terms of error frequency and type (e.g., perseveration, substitution) (Mateer and Kimura, 1977). These results were taken to suggest that underlying speech production is a motor-based capacity involving selection and ordering of articulatory postures and movements.

In some patients it appears that the major difficulty is one of selecting and sequencing the movements to produce speech sounds. Non-phonetically based aspects of language expression and comprehension may be relatively spared in these patients. The problems can occur in the context of either nonfluent or fluent expression. Errors usually consist of speech sound substitutions or omissions rather than distortions (i.e., tork/folk). More difficulty is seen with consonant blends, which are more challenging motor productions. Errors are usually inconsistent from one production to another even for the same target word. Commonly, the individual is acutely aware of when an error is made and attempts a series of self-corrections until the desired target is achieved.

When this phenomenon occurs in the context of relative sparing of other linguistic deficits (e.g., naming, comprehension, reading, grammatic usage), it has been termed a primary *speech apraxia*, as distinguished from an aphasia. Apraxia, then, is seen as a motor-based disorder and aphasia as a language-based disorder. This distinction has been most frequently made by speech/language pathologists (in contrast to neuropsychologists or neurologists), probably because the underlying basis of the disorder has such important treatment implications. Some, however, choose to view the breakdown as aphasia or an aspect of a larger aphasic syndrome that happens to involve the phonemic or phonetic level of language. The errors are then assigned such labels as literal or phonemic paraphasias rather than apraxic errors.

Semantics aside, it is important to recognize the existence of this descriptive distinction. The areas of brain underlying praxic function, and thus giving rise to "apraxic" errors, are somewhat variable depending on the range of symptoms included. Some reserve the term "apraxia" for expressive problems characterized by struggle at the level of single phoneme production associated with Broca's type nonfluent aphasia. Others include the fluently articulated phoneme substitutions of the Wernicke or conduction-type aphasic. Isolated speech sound production appears to parallel isolated oral movement production, and speech sound sequencing appears to parallel oral movement sequencing. These functions appear to depend on anterior and posterior perisylvian cortex, respectively. The greatest theoretical significance of the aphasic/apraxic distinction may be that it points out the tremendous dependence of "higher level" cognitive and linguistic function on basic sensorimotor systems of the brain that undoubtedly developed to meet other evolutionary needs, pressures, and opportunities.

LOCALIZATION OF LANGUAGE VIA STUDIES OF APHASIA

Several characteristics of spontaneous lesions make studying their behavioral effects difficult. Lesions in the cerebral cortex are rarely discrete. Those unilateral lesions resulting from cerebral vascular bleeds or infarcts sufficient to affect function most often involve damage to several cortical areas. They also often result in damage not only to the cerebral cortex but also to subcortical structures including thalamus, basal ganglia, and white matter tracts. Thus conclusions about functional localization are difficult. Additionally, unusual organization of functions related to the central nervous system's attempt to compensate for the disruption of function must be considered. At some point in recovery, the lesion site may provide more information about capacity for recovery or reorganization of function than it does about its role in normal language functioning.

Even a cursory review of the neurologic literature reveals considerable inconsistency and overlap in the localization of lesions that result in different aphasic syndromes. A major variable giving rise to these inconsistencies appears to be the time after lesion onset. Mazzochi and Vignolo (1979), for example, found that in acute cases a Wernicke's area lesion was associated only with Wernicke's aphasia but that in some chronic cases a similar lesion was associated with conduction aphasia. The authors suggested that Wernicke's aphasia may resolve into conduction aphasia as comprehension skills improve. These same researchers also reported that global aphasia may occur even when Wernicke's area is spared. Similarly, large anterior lesions involving Broca's area may produce global aphasia during the acute stage but evolve to Broca's aphasia over time. These examples clearly demonstrate that there is not a perfect correspondence between a lesion site and its classically associated aphasia symptoms. Given this phenomenon, it is imperative that clinical approaches and interventions rely on systematic and comprehensive evaluation of the actual speech/language behaviors of individuals with aphasia.

Despite the need to focus on behavioral manifestation, however, more precise localization of lesions via current radiologic techniques may have the potential to provide valuable prognostic information. A study by Selnes, Knopman, Niccum, Rubens, and Larson (1983) evaluated recovery of language comprehension from acute to stable stages (1 to 6 months after onset). Recovery was then correlated with lesion localization based on CT scans. Nearly all the patients with good comprehension skills at 1 month had lesions that spared posterior T1 and the supramarginal gyrus. Of the patients with impaired comprehension at 1 month, lack of recovery was strongly related to the presence of T1/supramarginal gyrus lesions. Better prediction of long-term outcomes of aphasia would assist in making clinical decisions and recommendations.

Improvements in both linguistic and anatomic analyses are needed in future study of the brain bases of language behavior. Localization data for any given patient may fit with predictions about probable syndrome and vice versa. However, the exceptions, variability, and total surprises continue to emerge. Perhaps as the subcortical contributions and the cortical–subcortical interactions are better understood, there will be fewer unclassifiable cases and a greater understanding of the dynamics of brain/behavior relations for language.

TOOLS FOR STUDYING LANGUAGE ORGANIZATION IN THE BRAIN

Aphasic symptomatology as it relates to brain structure and function has been studied mainly by techniques that focus on how specific language deficits are related to specific lesion sites. The enormous developments in imaging techniques have contributed substantially to this effort and will continue to do so in the future. Following is a brief review of several techniques used to measure brain structure and function that, when coupled with behavioral studies, help to study the complexities of neurolinguistic function. The techniques themselves are described and discussed in Chapter 1.

COMPUTED TOMOGRAPHY

The computed tomographic (CT) scan provides an x-ray image of what are essentially "slices" through the living brain. This technique has allowed good identification of the site and extent of lesions resulting in aphasia. It has been particularly helpful for delineating small lesions and lesions in subcortical structures. A CT image of a left thalamic lesion associated with aphasia is shown in Figure 9-12.

However, CT scanning does have its limitations. Timing considerations are particularly important for any anatomic correlation with aphasic behavior. Soon after onset, language deficits may be more severe than lesion size would predict because of diffuse dysfunction caused by a lesion. Later, because of compensation, speech and language performance may be better than one would predict from the CT image. It is important to bear in mind that the CT scan indicates only structural integrity or abnormality; it says nothing about which brain areas are functional or what behavioral/cognitive functions can be supported.

POSITRON EMISSION TOMOGRAPHY

Positron emission tomography (PET) is used to study brain metabolism. Metabolic activity in the brain is primarily attributed to neuronal demands, with changes in neuronal function corresponding to changes that occur in local cerebral metabolic rates for glucose. Thus metabolic rate reflects not only structural brain integrity but brain activity. In PET studies of aphasic patients with cortical lesions, the most striking finding has been consistent metabolic abnormality in subcortical structures. In one study of a 57-year-old man with a left cerebrovascular accident and Wernicke's aphasia, the CT scan showed only a left temporal and parietal lesion with damage to Wernicke's area. The PET scan indicated a 67 percent reduction in glucose metabolism in the area of structural damage. In addition, however, metabolic depression was noted throughout the left temporal lobe and posterior frontal lobe above Broca's area as well as in the thalamus and basal ganglia (Metter, Wasterlain, Kuhl, Hansan, and Phelps, 1981).

Findings with PET have thus focused attention on the distant effects of a structural lesion. A focal lesion may produce secondary metabolic changes in regions distant from the structural damage. When the size and extent of structural and metabolic lesions are similar, traditional anatomic classifications of aphasia may suffice. When substantial mismatches occur in structural and metabolic effects, however, a new taxonomy based on consideration of both local and distal lesion effects may be required.

MAGNETIC RESONANCE IMAGING

The magnetic resonance imaging (MRI) technique represents a new generation of neuroimaging. This technique is better able to (1) detect white matter lesions, edema, atrophy, and hematomas; (2) identify the extent of demyelinating disease; and (3) measure metabolism and blood flow. MRI will undoubtedly be used for anatomic correlation studies of aphasia, apraxia, and dysarthria with the potential for significant gains in knowledge about the anatomy and time course of these disorders.

CEREBRAL BLOOD FLOW STUDIES

The close link between functional activity and metabolic activity in brain regions is also reflected in the blood supply to these areas. In cerebral blood flow (CBF) studies the rate and amount of blood flow to brain areas are measured. This technique has been used to identify lateralization and localization of cerebral functioning for language. When subjects listen to speech, both hemispheres show regional changes in cerebral activation especially within the auditory cortex, but the left hemisphere also shows activation in Broca's and Wernicke's areas. When speaking, subjects show activation of the motor representation of the face, mouth, and supplementary motor cortex of the left hemisphere (Ingvar and Risberg, 1967). The powerful advantage of this technique for cerebral localization is that it is currently the only one that provides specific information about what parts of the brain are active during the course of ongoing speech/language behavior.

CORTICAL STIMULATION MAPPING

Focal application of a small electrical current has been known to alter cortical function in animals and humans (Cushing, 1909). Focal electrical stimulation in humans was first introduced by Penfield and his colleagues at the Montreal Neurological Institute in association with surgical methods for cortical resection of epileptic foci under local anesthesia. Stimulation mapping was used to identify functional areas of the cortex, including cortical areas important to language and other cognitive processes (Penfield and Jasper, 1954; Penfield and Perot, 1963; Penfield and Roberts, 1959). Performance on such tasks as naming and counting is commonly disrupted in association with stimulation at discrete cortical sites on the dominant, usually left, cortex. Identification of sensorimotor cortex and of cortex important to language by the stimulation-mapping procedure allows these areas to be spared during resection, greatly increasing the margin of safety associated with the operation.

The effects of stimulation at a particular site on behavior are often both repeatable and different from the repeated effects of stimulation at sites only a few millimeters away (Ojemann and Whitaker, 1978). Stimulation effects thus are modeled as temporary lesions localized in both space and time. One major advantage of cortical stimulation studies over spontaneous lesion studies is the small size of the involved cortical area disrupted during stimulation. This situation provides a much greater degree of spatial resolution for evaluating functional cortical localization. A second advantage is the sudden onset and immediate reversibility of the effect. It is unlikely that observations obtained in stimulation-mapping studies are as affected by recovery of function and compensatory reorganization as are observations made in studies based on spontaneous brain lesions. A third advantage of the stimulation-mapping technique is that stimulation effects on multiple behaviors can be assessed at multiple cortical sites in an individual patient. The resultant pattern of changes not only provides evidence for the involvement of particular areas in aspects of language function but can provide valuable insights into the relative dependence and/or independence of different language-related functions. Spontaneous lesions involving a much broader area usually result in a wider variety of symptoms and are thus far more likely to mask these important interrelations.

The specific data discussed in this section were derived from cortical stimulation studies carried out in the Department of Neurological Surgery at the University of Washington in Se-

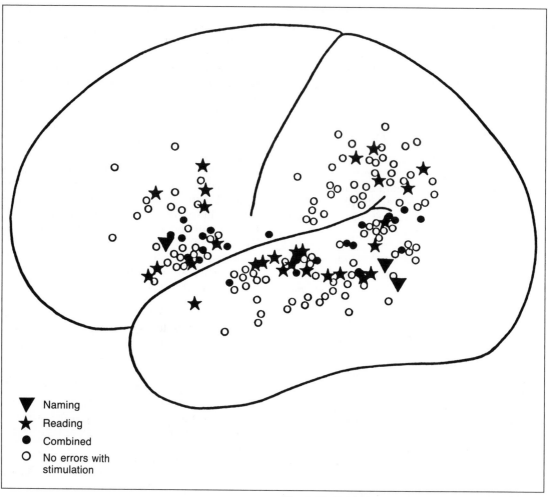

Naming

Reading

Combined

No errors with stimulation

Fig. 9-13. Cortical sites involved in naming and reading. Cortical sites that were stimulated during surgery in conjunction with language tasks are shown (14 subjects). Sites associated with naming and/or reading errors are indicated. (From Mateer, C. Localization of language and visuospatial function by electrical stimulation. In A. Kertesz, (ed.) *Localization in Neuropsychology.* New York: Academic Press, 1983.)

attle. All the studies were conducted during awake craniotomies for the resection of medically intractable epileptic foci, carried out under local anesthesia. In most cases the epileptic focus was in the anterior temporal lobe, and the surgical exposure included superior portions of the lateral temporal lobe, inferior-posterior portions of the frontal lobe, and the inferior parietal lobe adjacent to the sylvian fissure.

Five language functions measured during these stimulation-mapping studies are discussed here: naming, reading, short-term verbal memory, mimicry of single and sequential orofacial movements, and phonemic identification.

Naming Sites

Naming errors have been demonstrated with stimulation of a broad area of the lateral dominant cortex (Ojemann, 1979; Ojemann and Mateer, 1979a,b; Ojemann and Whitaker, 1978). Some of the individual sites where naming changes have been evoked are located well outside the traditional limits of the lateral cortical language areas, but most are located in the immediate perisylvian cortex. Figure 9-13 depicts the sites associated with naming or reading disruption in 14 patients (Mateer, 1983).

There have been a few studies involving cortical stimulation with mapping and naming in multiple languages (Mateer, Rapport, and Ketrick, 1984; Ojemann and Whitaker, 1978). In all cases, there have been some dissociated sites implicated in each language, that is, cortical sites where stimulation altered naming in one language but not in the other. This dissociation of cortical sites involving different languages is consistent with the differential rate and degree of recovery of different languages seen in cases of aphasia in bilingual individuals (Paradis, 1977).

Reading Sites

Most sites associated with naming errors were also associated with reading errors. Stimulation at many sites, however, is associated only with errors on the more sensitive reading task. Two of the three sites involved with naming only were located in the posterior portion of the middle temporal gyrus. These findings are strikingly consistent with the lesion data. Although naming deficits are ubiquitous with almost all aphasic types and usually overlap to some extent with other kinds of linguistic disruption, anomic patients in whom the naming deficit is prominent and often isolated have been reported to have restricted lesions in this region involving the posterior midtemporal gyrus (Mazzochi and Vignolo, 1979).

Reading tasks provide for much more varied language performance than a naming task, and stimulation of the dominant cortex during the reading of simple sentences has demonstrated unexpected patterns of linguistic alteration. The major error categories associated with stimulation-related alteration include speech arrest (an inability to produce any speech), articulatory (phonetic or phonemic) errors, grammatic errors, and semantic errors.

Articulatory errors were divided into literal paraphasias (productions that had 50 percent or more of the target word; i.e., tencil/pencil) and neologisms (productions that displayed acceptable phonological form but contained less than 50 percent of the phones of the target word; i.e., "If next *winzer* is worth and sucks. . . . "). Sites associated with articulatory/phonological errors were distributed broadly but always within the perisylvian cortex.

Grammatic errors associated with stimulation were widely distributed throughout superior temporal, parietal, and frontal regions of the lateral cortex. Disruptions of grammar with stimulation of sites in the mid-superior temporal lobe and parietotemporal region were similar to the paragrammatic deficit seen in aphasic patients with posterior lesions. These aphasic patients often misuse function words and demonstrate errors in verb forms, though all parts of grammar are represented. An example of a grammatic error made during electrical stimulation of the posterior temporal lobe is "She *will be visit* the mountain."

Semantic errors were, like grammatic errors, distributed widely in frontal, temporal, and parietal regions. Semantic errors include productions marked by inappropriate meaning (e.g., "Should the soap be too salty, you can add in salt water"), as well as productions marked by categorical substitutions (soldier/sailor, mother/sister).

Overlap of Evoked Linguistic Errors During Reading

One of the unique capabilities of the stimulation mapping technique is the focal, restricted nature of the cortical disruption. It thus provides a unique way of assessing the detailed organization of functional language sites. Detailed functional analysis of other cortical systems for vision, audition, and sensorimotor control have revealed exquisitely fine "mosaics," or "columns," of functional capacity in tightly structured cortical neuron systems. A study by Ojemann and Mateer (1979a,b) looked in this way at the relative independence and interdependence of language function at different cortical sites. Only those sites at which a single error type was observed are illustrated in Figure 9-14, which shows eight sites associated with only phonological (articulatory) errors. These sites were in all cases located within one gyrus of the perisylvian fissure. Five sites were associated only with semantic errors; four of these sites were located at the farthest "corners" of the sample area, outside the perisylvian region. Grammatic errors were seen in isolation at only three sites, and these sites were again located more than one gyrus distal to the perisylvian core.

Overall the pattern of cortical organization revealed in this analysis suggested that the mo-

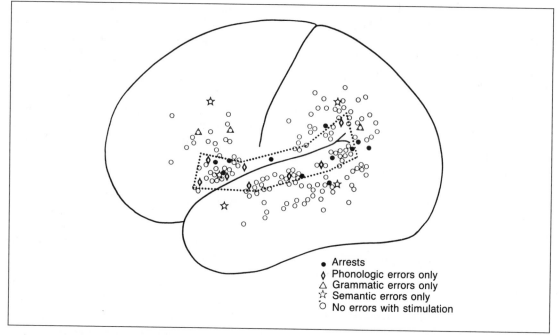

● Arrests
◊ Phonologic errors only
△ Grammatic errors only
☆ Semantic errors only
○ No errors with stimulation

toric execution of speech as reflected in speech sound selection and production (articulatory/ phonological errors) was highly dependent on the perisylvian core. Both the traditional anterior "motor" area and the posterior perisylvian areas were critically involved. Aspects of reading relating to more linguistically based aspects of language, including grammatic and semantic selection, occupy more distal sites. The concentric "ring-like" appearance of the distributions (Fig. 9-14) is highly reminiscent of the concentric field features associated with the primary, secondary, and tertiary association fields of other major cortical motor and sensory systems.

Fig. 9-14. Linguistic alterations during reading associated with cortical stimulation. Sites statistically associated with a single type of linguistic change when stimulation was applied during a reading task are shown. Sites marked by diamonds were associated only with articulatory/phonological errors and cluster in the perisylvian core. Sites marked by triangles and stars mark sites associated with grammatic and semantic errors, respectively. They tend to be broadly distributed but are generally located at least one gyrus distal to the sylvian fissure. (From Mateer, C. A., and Cameron, P. A. Electrophysiological correlates of language: Stimulation mapping and evoked potential studies. In F. Boller and J. Grafman, eds., *Handbook of Neuropsychology.* Amsterdam: Elsevier, in press.)

Oral Movement Sequencing and Phonemic Identification

Insight into motor mechanisms supporting speech/language function was obtained by mapping the effects of cortical stimulation on the ability to mimic repeated single and sequential orofacial movements (Mateer, 1983; Ojemann and Mateer, 1979a,b). The results of such studies are shown in Figure 9-15. These studies were prompted by the observations of Mateer and Kimura (1977) that the ability to mimic sequential facial movements is altered in both fluent and nonfluent aphasic patients compared to either normal subjects or those with brain damage not associated with aphasia.

Repetition of the same movement was disrupted with stimulation of sites only in face premotor cortex. This region corresponds roughly to, but is smaller than, the traditional motor speech area. In all cases, these sites were also associated with arrests on naming and reading, suggesting that these sites represent part of the cortical pathway for orofacial movement that is critical for speech. It is not part of the face motor cortex per se, as no oral or facial movements were evoked. Sequences of oral movements were disrupted over a broader area from sites throughout the extent of perisylvian cortex and well outside the classic sensorimotor cortex.

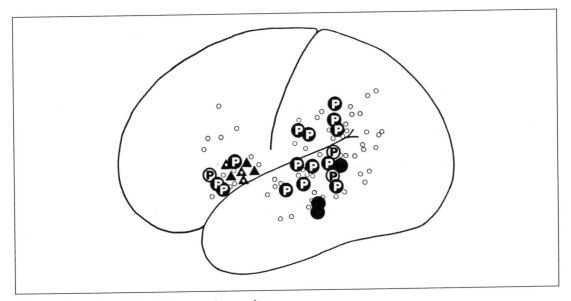

Fig. 9-15. Composite of stimulation mapping results on the mimicry of nonverbal orofacial postures and identification of phonemes in eight patients. All sampled sites are indicated by a circle or a triangle. The triangles indicate sites where repeated production of the same movement was altered. Sites where repeated production of a single movement was intact but production of sequences of three movements was impaired are indicated by solid black circles. Evoked alterations in phoneme identification are indicated by a black triangle with a white center at repeated movement sites and by a large P at all other sites. The overlap between sites where oral movement production and phonemic identification were altered is significant at the $p<0.01$ level. (From Mateer, C. A., and Ojemann, G. O. Thalamic mechanisms in language and memory. In S. J. Segalowitz (ed.), *Language Functions and Brain Organization.* New York: Academic Press, 1983.)

Disruption of consonant identification was also evoked from a broad range of perisylvian cortex. Of interest was the high degree of overlap between sites associated with disrupted phoneme identification and disrupted sequencing of oral movements. These changes localized a region in language cortex important for oral motor sequencing and phonemic identification, functions critically involved in speech production and comprehension. It was hypothesized that these areas of perisylvian cortex that are involved in both the production of oral movement sequences and the perception of phonemes provide the neural bases for much of the basic production and perception of speech. This perisylvian region is clearly implicated when one looks at sites that alter articulatory/phonological aspects in the reading task. The extent of lesions that give rise to a permanent motor aphasia as identified by Mohr (1976) also encompasses this same perisylvian region. This area is crucial for the generation of langauge, and damage to it is hypothesized to account for phonemically based production and comprehension deficits associated with most aphasias. Many of these production errors may include those errors sometimes incorporated under the term *verbal apraxia.*

This section has reviewed important ideas regarding the localization of language in the human brain. Knowledge, however, is growing at an exponential rate. Although certain basic principles of language organization in the brain are likely to hold true, the nature of forthcoming information promised by the new techniques for studying brain function should add immeasurably to current models. Greater understanding of language organization, as always, depends critically on the interaction of speech/language pathologists, neuropsychologists, neurologists, neuroscientists, and linguists, each bringing a body of skills and knowledge. Although localization of a lesion per se may not immediately help the individual suffering from a language disorder, it may have an impact on clinical practice in terms of supporting clearer diagnoses of clinical symptoms, suggesting prognostic implications, and providing information that suggests an extension of medical problems and thus the need for referral.

CONTRIBUTIONS OF THE RIGHT HEMISPHERE TO LANGUAGE

There have been a few reported cases of what is termed *crossed aphasia*—aphasia following right hemisphere lesions in right-handed individuals. Generally, however, basic aspects of speech and language, including articulation, syntax, and semantics, are not disrupted following right hemisphere lesions. The possible contributions of the right hemisphere to communicative function, however, have been of considerable interest particularly because of a number of observations that right-hemisphere-damaged patients often have somewhat socially inappropriate behavior or their communicative behavior is unusual.

Initial assessment of the right hemisphere of the split-brain patients (Gazzaniga, 1970; Gazzaniga and Hillyard, 1971; Gazzaniga and Sperry, 1967) suggested that the right hemisphere was mute but that it had an extensive receptive vocabulary with complex associations among the items in its lexicon. Some phrases and simple commands could be understood by the isolated right hemisphere, but its knowledge of syntax was primitive, being restricted to understanding simple active and negative sentences. It could comprehend written nouns but not verbs or nouns derived from verbs. Subsequent investigations by Zaidel (1978) indicated that the range of linguistic tasks at which the right hemisphere could succeed was larger than was previously suspected. Two split-brain patients were tested by Zaidel using a unique contact lens system (Z lens) that blocked one visual field and allowed longer segments of stimuli than had previously been used in language studies with split-brain patients. He found that the right hemisphere could comprehend not only abstract words but also a variety of simple syntactic structures.

Although there is little evidence to suggest that the right hemisphere contributes substan-

tially to normal performance on traditional linguistic tasks, studies have demonstrated that it plays an important role in processing paralinguistic aspects of language. Such attributes of speech as intonation, emotional tone, context, inference, and connotation are often impaired in patients with right hemisphere lesions. Those aspects of language are considered part of pragmatics or the discourse function of language (Blumstein and Cooper, 1974; Schlanger, Schlanger and Gerstmann, 1976; Weintraub, Mesulum, and Kramer, 1981). Inappropriate reactions to humor, misinterpretation of metaphors, poor appreciation of antonymic contrasts and connotative aspects of pictures and speech, and difficulty producing and perceiving emotional tone of linguistic utterances may be seen in patients with right hemisphere damage (Buck and Duffy, 1980; Tompkins and Mateer, 1985; Wapner, Hamby, and Garner, 1981).

The term *pragmatics* refers to a system of rules that clarifies the use of language in terms of situational or social context. For example, language may be used to command, placate, query, impress, threaten, or establish rapport with the listener. Cues conveyed through tone of voice may be important for perceiving communicative intent and interpreting indirect expressions of affect. These abilities are typically ascribed to the right hemisphere. *Prosody* refers to the distribution of stress and melodic contour in speech. Modulation of prosody can be used to impart affective tone, introduce subtle grades of meaning, and vary emphasis in spoken language. Normal speech is always subject to the modulation of prosody. These modulations may be minimal, signaling subtle connotation, or, more significant, changing the same sentence from a statement to a question. Studies have demonstrated that right hemisphere lesions may selectively disrupt a patient's ability to interpret and express the affective component of prosody (Ross, 1983). Some of these patients were unable to discriminate or identify the emotional tone of a sentence, whereas others could not impart affective tone to their speech. Prosody appears to contribute a great deal to the overall effectiveness and appropriateness of oral communication. Thus the social inappropriateness often described as symptomatic of right hemisphere damage may be due to impairment of the appreciation and production of these features.

The communicative function of speech is thus not confined to the transmission of grammatic and lexical information. There are additional messages in speech more appropriately labeled *pragmatic* or *sociolinguistic* that are frequently conveyed by prosodic modulation as well as by other speech devices. It appears that right hemisphere damage may interfere with the pragmatic aspects of communication and that the loss of prosody may be just one component of this more general impairment. There is now accumulating evidence that recognition of faces and both the production and appreciation of facial expression are more dependent on the right hemisphere than on the left. Recognition of faces has been proposed to have an important role in species-specific communication in complex social networks, wherein recognition of relation, rank, and age would accompany facial recognition. Facial expressions convey the mood and emotional state of an individual and thus set the stage for important dynamics of a communication setting (Ekman, Hager, and Friesen, 1981; Strauss and Moscovitch, 1981).

In summary, the right hemisphere appears to play an important role in the integration of verbal and situational context. Its relative specialization in the reception and expression of verbal and facial affect gives it an integral function in social communication. Although it has negative effects on communication when it is damaged, the right hemisphere also appears to be helpful in some compensatory functions when there is damage to the left hemisphere. Melodic intonation therapy, for example, is a form of aphasia therapy that in theory utilizes the preserved intonational capacities of the right hemisphere to assist in the redevelopment of expressive speech and language capabilities (Sparks, 1981; Sparks and Holland, 1976).

BIOLOGIC BASES FOR LANGUAGE DEVELOPMENT

Thus far the discussion has focused on language organization in the brain and breakdown of language function with acquired brain damage in the adult. The focus now is on the neurologic bases for language during infancy and childhood.

A wide variety of prelinguistic capacities suggest a powerful biologic predisposition for speech and language development. All normal infants coo and babble during the first 6 months of life. Even infants who are deaf demonstrate this behavior, though they are unlikely spontaneously to develop expressive speech. Also, infants demonstrate the capacity to categorically perceive speech sounds or phonemes (e.g., /ba/ versus /pa/) within the first few weeks of life, well before any formal speech or language learning has occurred. This capacity for auditory perception of commonly utilized phonemic boundaries is also seen in a variety of primate and other mammalian species, suggesting that the phonemic structure of language itself may be based in such innate biologic capacities (Kuhl, 1987).

There is also considerable evidence suggesting that brain asymmetry and the predeterminants of hemispheric specializations are present at least by the time of birth. As previously discussed in the section on anatomic asymmetry, fetal and infant brains studied between 10 and 48 weeks of gestation featured a planum temporale that was larger on the left in approximately 70 percent of cases (Wada, Clark, and Hamm, 1975). In addition, anatomists have shown that parts of the right hemisphere develop more rapidly than corresponding parts of the left hemisphere during the fetal stage of human life. The folding of the right cortex into the brain's characteristic convoluted shape occurs as much as 2 weeks ahead of folding on the left. Although the left hemisphere language regions may develop more slowly, they ultimately reach a greater size and complexity of organization (Galaburda, Lemay, Kemper, and Geschwind, 1978).

There also have been behavioral studies of hemispheric asymmetry in infants and children. Standard dichotic listening studies have been used with children as young as age 3, and a right ear superiority (REA) for words has been found. Studies based on the dichotic listening concept using newborn infants have been reported, but results are as yet somewhat equivocal. Similarly, studies that have attempted to determine if the magnitude of ear advantage changes with time have met with mixed results. In some studies the left/right ear difference changed over time, whereas in others it appeared stable from an early age.

Electrophysiologic recording techniques do not require deliberate responses and so are ideal for the study of asymmetries in the infant. Molfese (1983) reported the results of electrical recordings from the left and right brain to speech and nonspeech sounds in infants from 1 week to 10 months of age. In nine of ten infants he found responses of greater amplitude, presumably reflecting greater involvement in the processing of the sounds, on the left-side recordings. With nonspeech sounds, such as a noise burst or a piano chord, all ten infants showed evoked potentials of greater amplitude in the right hemisphere.

Another approach to the investigation of support for language in the developing brain is to study the effects of brain pathology. Woods and Teuber (1978) reported on 65 cases of children up to about 5 years of age with unilateral hemispheric injury occurring after speech onset; 73 percent of children with left hemisphere lesions (including two left-handers) were aphasic. Considered as a whole, these data suggested that the pattern of language functions seen in adults is essentially complete soon after birth and certainly by early childhood. There is, however, a substantial body of evidence suggesting that the right hemisphere can take over many language functions if a left hemisphere lesion occurs early in life. There are dramatic differences in recovery from aphasia in children and adults. Although the right hemisphere may not play an active role in speech production in normal children, it appears that it has the capacity to do so.

In some rare cases, it becomes medically necessary to remove most of one cerebral hemisphere during early childhood. Initially, reports noted that hemispherectomy, if performed early enough, resulted in no permanent signs of lateralized deficits in higher mental functions. This finding suggested that the remaining hemisphere, whether right or left, is able to take over those functions that would ordinarily be lateralized to the other half of the brain. Upon further in-depth study of early left hemispherectomized patients, however, subtle signs of language dysfunction have been found (Dennis and Whitaker, 1976). Ten-year-old children who had sustained an early left hemispherectomy had difficulty dealing with complex syntax, the rules for combining words into grammatically correct sentences, and other organizational and analytic aspects of language.

This finding suggested some limit to the plasticity of the young brain and confirmed that hemispheric asymmetries in linguistic capacity are present very early in life.

Plasticity effects also depend on having uninjured brain as a resource. Amytal Sodium studies in adults suggested that language shifts to the right hemisphere during early childhood only when central left hemisphere "speech areas" are removed or severely damaged. When damage is bilateral or diffuse, language in some cases appears to develop bilaterally but is significantly impaired in almost all such cases (Mateer and Dodrill, 1983).

A variety of developmental disorders of speech and language often are not associated with any clear-cut neurologic injury or pathology. They include developmental aphasia (severe receptive and expressive language disorders), developmental dyspraxia (severe articulatory disorder), and developmental dyslexia (severe impairments in the acquisition of reading skill). Detailed microscopic investigations of postmortem brains in several individuals with dyslexia have demonstrated abnormal assemblies of cells in subcortical layers (Galaburda, 1985), which should normally have migrated to more surface cortical layers. These abnormalities were seen only on the left side of the brain and in areas associated with speech/language function. Other developmental language-based disorders may have similar neuropathologic substrates indicating abnormalities in fetal brain development. Neural bases of language in the developing brain are in many respects more difficult to study, but this area represents a challenging and rewarding frontier.

CONCLUSION

Some of the interrelations between brain function and language behavior have been reviewed. The discussion of hemispheric specialization should be convincing in its support of the phenomena but leaves one asking questions about the underlying nature of that specialization.

Discussion of the intrahemispheric localization of language focused on two primary sources of information: lesion studies of aphasia and cortical stimulation studies. The evidence from stimulation mapping suggests that language may be concentrically organized around the sylvian fissure in the left dominant cortex. A small inferior frontal region appears to be critical to voluntary orofacial motor functions, including basic speech production. Surrounding this area in the perisylvian cortex of the frontal, temporal, and parietal lobes is a broad region that appears to subserve the selection and sequencing of orofacial movements and speech. This perisylvian region also appears to be involved in the phonemic decoding of speech sounds. At both the frontal and parietotemporal sites surrounding this perisylvian region are sites related to specialized language functions: naming, reading, grammar, and semantics. The data for the organization of language functions derived from electrical stimulation mapping indicate discrete functional localization. These data predict that the effects of brain damage depend on the location of the injury, with increasing lesion size related to greater impairment primarily because of the greater likelihood of damage to multiple, yet discrete, functional areas.

Several of the aphasias (agrammatic aphasia, anomic aphasia, semantic jargon aphasia) are characterized predominantly by one kind of linguistic disruption. These syndromes usually involve not only small lesions but also lesions that do not involve the immediate perisylvian cortex (Mazzochi and Vignolo, 1979). In the context of results from stimulation mapping, they might be seen as disrupting aspects of language function that are more separately represented outside of perisylvian cortex. In contrast, most patients with persisting aphasia present with a broad array of expressive and receptive deficits involving multiple linguistic, memory, and motoric deficits. Lesions underlying these more common aphasias typically involve large portions of the perisylvian cortex or underlying connections and subcortical structures. The role of these subcortical lesions in language function—both when they are the primary lesion site and when their function is disrupted by lesions of areas to which they connect—is just beginning to be recognized.

Much additional work is needed before we can fully understand this complex neurolinguistic system, but phenomenal advances have been made over the last quarter-century. The hope for increased understanding of brain organization for language and the search for new treatments following brain injury has never been greater. Exciting new neuroimaging techniques, a greater appreciation of the right hemisphere contribution to language, and dramatic revelations about anatomic abnormalities in developmental dyslexia have emerged. New tools, new insights, and the intrigue of what is certainly one of the most complicated human behaviors will serve as the impetus for continued investigation of brain and language functions for decades to come.

REFERENCES

Beaumont, G., and Dimond, S. Brain disconnection and schizophrenia. *Br. J. Psychiatry* 123:661, 1973.

Benson, D. F., and Geschwind, N. Aphasia and related disorders: a clinical approach. In M. M. Mesulum (ed.), *Principles of Behavioral Neurology.* Philadelphia: Davis, 1985.

Blumstein, S., and Cooper, W. Hemispheric processing of intonation contours. *Cortex* 10:146, 1974.

Bogen, J. E., and Bogen, G. M. Wernicke's region—where is it? *Ann. N.Y. Acad. Sci.* 280:834, 1976.

Brown, J. The neural organization of language: aphasia and lateralization. *Brain Lang.* 3:482, 1976.

Brown, J. W. Language representation in the brain. In H. E. Steklis (ed.), *Neurobiology of Social Communication in Primates: An Evolutionary Perspective.* New York: Academic Press, 1979.

Buck, R., and Duffy, R. Nonverbal communication of affect in brain damaged patients. *Cortex* 16:351, 1980.

Caramazza, A., Gordon, J., Zurif, E., and DeLuca, D. Right hemisphere damage and verbal problem solving behavior. *Brain Lang.* 3:41, 1976.

Cushing, H. A note upon the faradic stimulation of the postcentral gyrus in conscious patients. *Brain* 32:44, 1909.

Damasio, A., Damasio, H., Rizzo, M., Varney, N., and Gersh, F. Aphasia with nonhemorrhagic lesions in the basal ganglia and internal capsule. *Arch. Neurol.* 39:15, 1982.

Dennis, M., and Whitaker, H. Language acquisition following hemidecortication: linguistic superiority of the left over the right hemisphere. *Brain Lang.* 3:404, 1976.

Efron, R. Temporal perception, aphasia and deja vu. *Brain* 86:403, 1963.

Ekman, P., Hager, J., and Friesen, W. The symmetry of emotional and deliberate facial expression. *Psychophysiology* 18:101, 1981.

Fisher, C. M. The pathologic and clinical aspects of thalamic hemorrhage. *Trans. Am. Neurol. Assoc.* 84:56, 1959.

Galaburda, A. M., Lemay, M., Kemper, T., and Geschwind, N. Right-left asymmetries in the brain. *Science* 199:852, 1978.

Galaburda, A. M. Developmental dyslexia: a review of

biological interactions. *Ann. Dyslexia* 35:21, 1985.

Gazzaniga, M. S., and Sperry, R. W. Language after section of the cerebral commissures. *Brain* 90:131, 1967.

Gazzaniga, M. S. *The Bisected Brain.* New York: Appleton-Century-Crofts, 1970.

Gazzaniga, M. S., and Hillyard, S. A. Language and speech capacity of the right hemisphere. *Neuropsychologia* 9:273, 1971.

Geschwind, N. Disconnexion syndromes in animals and man. *Brain* 88:237, 1965.

Geschwind, N., and Levitsky, W. Human brain: left-right asymmetries in temporal speech region. *Science* 161:186, 1968.

Geschwind, N. Late changes in the nervous system: an overview. In D. G. Stein, J. J. Rose, and N. Butters (eds.), *Plasticity and Recovery of Function in the Central Nervous System.* New York: Academic Press, 1974.

Gibson, C., and Bryden, M. P. Dichaptic recognition of shapes and letters in children. *Can. J. Psychol.* 37:132, 1983.

Goodglass, H., and Kaplan, E. *The Assessment of Aphasia and Related Disorders.* Philadelphia: Lea & Febiger, 1972.

Heilman, K. M., and Scholes, R. J. The nature of comprehension errors in Broca's, conduction and Wernicke's aphasics. *Cortex* 12:258, 1976.

Ingvar, D.H., and Risberg, J. Influence of mental activity upon regional blood flow during mental effort in normals and in patients with focal brain disorders. *Exp. Brain Res.* 3:195, 1967.

Kertesz, A. *Aphasia and Associated Disorders: Taxonomy, Localization, and Recovery.* New York: Grune & Stratton, 1979.

Kertesz, A., Harlock, W., and Coates, R., Computer tomographic localization, lesion size, and prognosis in aphasia and nonverbal impairment. *Brain Lang.* 8:34, 1979.

Kimura, D. Cerebral dominance and the perception of verbal stimuli. *Can. J. Psychol.* 15:166, 1961.

Kimura, D. The neural basis of language qua gesture. In H. Whitaker and H. A. Whitaker (eds.), *Studies in Neurolinguistics* (Vol. 2). New York: Academic Press, 1976.

Kolb, B., and Whishaw, I. Q. *Fundamentals of Human Neuropsychology.* San Francisco: W. H. Freeman, 1985.

Kuhl, P. A. Perception of speech and sound in early infancy. In: *Handbook of Infant Perception* (Vol. 2). New York: Academic Press, 1987.

Kutas, M., and Van Patten, C. Event-related brain potential studies of language. In P. K. Ackles, J. R. Jennings, and M. G. H. Coles (eds.), *Advances in Psychophysiology* (Vol. 3). Connecticut: JAI Press (in press).

Laitinen, L. V., and Vilkki, J. Observations of physiological and psychological functions of ventral and internal nucleus of human thalamus. *Acta Neurol. Scand.* 55:198, 1977.

Lomas, J., and Kimura, D. Intrahemispheric interaction between speaking and sequential mammal activity. *Neuropsychologia* 14:23, 1976.

Luria, A. R. On quasi-aphasic speech disturbance in lesions of the deep structures in the brain. *Brain Lang.* 4:359, 1977.

Mateer, C. A., and Kimura, D. Impairment of nonverbal oral movements in aphasia. *Brain Lang.* 4:262, 1977.

Mateer, C. A. Functional organization of the right nondominant cortex: evidence from electrical stimulation. *Can. J. Psychol.* 1:36, 1983.

Mateer, C. A., and Dodrill, C. B. Neuropsychological and linguistic correlates of atypical language lateralization: evidence from Sodium Amytal studies. *Hum. Neurobiol.* 2:135, 1983.

Mateer, C. A., and Ojemann, G. O. Thalamic mechanisms in language and memory. In S. J. Segalowitz (ed.), *Language Functions and Brain Organization.* New York: Academic Press, 1983.

Mateer, C. A., Rapport, R. R., and Kettrick, C. Cerebral organization of oral and signed language responses: case study evidence from Amytal and cortical stimulation studies. *Brain Lang.* 21:123, 1984.

Mateer, C. A., Cameron, P. A., Polly, D., and Thompson, P. Intracranial evoked potentials of voice-onset-time: two case studies. Presented at the VIII International Conference on Event Related Potentials of the Brain, EPIC, 1986.

Mazzochi, F., and Vignolo, L. A. Localization of lesions in aphasia: clinical CT scan correlations in stroke patients. *Cortex* 15:627, 1979.

Metter, J., Wasterlain, C., Kuhl, D., Hansan, W., and Phelps, M. ^{18}FDG positron emission computed tomography in a study of aphasia. *Ann. Neurol.* 10:173, 1981.

Milner, B. Hemispheric specialization: scope and limits. In F. D. Schmitt, F. G. Wordon (eds.), *The Neurosciences: Third Study Program.* Cambridge: MIT Press, 1974.

Mohr, J. Broca's area and Broca's aphasia. *Stud. Neurolinguist.* 1:201, 1976.

Molfese, D. Event related potentials and language processes. In A. W. K. Gailland and W. Lotter (eds.), *Tutorials in ERP Research: Endogenous Components.* Amsterdam: North Holland, 1983. Pp. 345–367.

Naeser, M. A., and Hayward, R. W. Lesion localization in aphasia with cranial-computed tomography and Boston diagnostic aphasia exam. *Neurology* 28:545, 1978.

Neville, H. J. Event-related potentials in neuropsychological studies of language. *Brain Lang.* 11:300, 1980.

Ojemann, G. A., and Whitaker, H. Language localization and variability. *Brain Lang.* 6:239, 1978.

Ojemann, G. A. Individual variability in cortical localization of language. *J. Neurosurg.* 50:164, 1979.

Ojemann, G. A., and Mateer, C. Cortical and subcortical organization of human communication: evidence from stimulation studies. In H. D. Steklis and M. J. Raleigh (eds.), *Neurobiology of Social Communication in Primates: An Evolutionary Perspective.* New York: Academic Press, 1979a.

Ojemann, G. A., and Mateer, C. Human language cortex: localization of memory, syntax and sequential motor-phoneme identification systems. *Science* 205:1401, 1979b.

Paradis, M. Bilingualism and aphasia. *Stud. Neurolinguist.* 3:65, 1977.

Penfield, W., and Jasper, H. *Epilepsy and the Functional Anatomy of the Human Brain.* Boston: Little, Brown, 1954.

Penfield, W., and Roberts, L. *Speech and Brain Mechanisms.* Princeton: Princeton University Press, 1959.

Penfield, W., and Perot, P. The brain's record of auditory and visual experience—a final summary and discussion. *Brain* 86:595, 1963.

Rasmussen, T., and Milner, B. The role of early left brain injury in determining lateralization of cerebral speech functions. *Ann. N.Y. Acad. Sci.* 299:355, 1977.

Reynolds, A. F., Turner, P., Harris, A. B., Ojemann, G. A., and Davis, L. E. Left thalamic hemorrhage with dysphasia: a report of five cases. *Brain Lang.* 7:62, 1979.

Riklan, M., and Levita, E. *Subcortical Correlates of Human Behavior.* Baltimore: Williams & Wilkins, 1969.

Ross, E. D. Right-hemisphere lesion in disorders of affective language. In A. Kertesz (ed.), *Localization in Neuropsychology.* New York: Academic Press, 1983.

Rothi, L. J., McFarling, D., and Heilman, K. M. Conduction aphasia, syntactic alexia and the anatomy of syntactic comprehension. *Arch. of Neurol.*, 39:272, 1982.

Schlanger, B., Schlanger, P., and Gerstmann, L. The perception of emotionally toned sentences by right hemispheric-damaged and aphasic subjects. *Brain Lang.* 3:396, 1976.

Selnes, O. A., Knopman, D. S., Niccum, N., Rubens, A. B., and Larson, D. Computed tomographic scan correlates of auditory comprehension deficits in aphasia: a prospective recovery study. *Ann. Neurol.* 13:558, 1983.

Sparks, R., and Holland, A. L. Method: melodic intonation therapy for aphasia. *J. Speech Hear. Disord.* 41:287, 1976.

Sparks, R. W. Melodic intonation therapy. In R. Chapez (ed.), *Language Intervention Strategies in Adult Aphasia.* Baltimore: Williams & Wilkins, 1981.

Springer, S., and Deutsch, G. *Left Brain, Right Brain.* San Francisco: W. H. Freeman, 1985.

Strauss, E., and Moscovich, M. Perception of facial expression. *Brain Lang.* 13:308, 1981.

Tallal, P., and Piercy, M. Developmental aphasia: the perception of brief vowels and extended stop consonants. *Neuropsychologia* 13:67, 1974.

Tallal, P., and Newcombe, F. Impairment of auditory perception and language comprehension in dysphasia. *Brain Lang.* 5:13, 1978.

Tompkins, C., and Mateer, C. The affect of context on appreciation of implicit attitude in patients with unilateral temporal lobe seizure foci. In R. H. Brookshire (ed.), *Clinical Aphasiology Clinical Conference Proceedings,* Minneapolis: BRK, 1985.

Varney, N. R. Somesthesis. In H. J. Hannay (ed.), *Experimental Techniques in Human Neuropsychology.* New York: Oxford University Press, 1986.

Wada, J. A., and Rasmussen, T. Intracarotid injection of Sodium Amytal for the lateralization of cerebral speech dominance: experimental and clinical observations. *J. Neurosurg.* 17:266, 1960.

Wada, J. A., Clark, R., and Hamm, A. Cerebral hemispheric asymmetry in humans. *Arch. Neurol.* 32:239, 1975.

Wapner, W., Hamby, S., and Garner, H. The role of the right hemisphere in the apprehension of complex linguistic materials. *Brain Lang.* 14:15, 1981.

Weintraub, S., Mesulum, M., and Kramer, L. Disturbances in prosody, a right hemisphere contribution to language. *Arch. Neurol.* 38:742, 1981.

Wernicke, C. The aphasia symptom complex: a psychological study on an anatomic basis. In G. H. Eggert (translator), *Wernicke's Works on Aphasia: A Sourcebook and Review.* The Hague: Mouton, 1977.

Witelson, S. F. Sex and the single hemisphere: specialization of the right hemisphere for spatial processing. *Science* 193:425, 1975.

Witelson, S. F. Developmental dyslexia: two right hemispheres and none left. *Science* 195:309, 1977a.

Witelson, S. F. Early hemisphere specialization and interhemispheric plasticity: an empirical and theoretical review. In S. J. Segalowitz and F. A. Gruber (eds.), *Language Development and Neurological Theory.* New York: Academic Press, 1977b.

Wood, C. C., Goff, W. R., and Day, R. S. Auditory evoked potentials during speech perception. *Science* 173:1248, 1971.

Woods, B. T., and Teuber, H. L. Changing patterns of childhood aphasia. *Ann. Neurol.* 3:273, 1978.

Zaidel, E. Auditory language comprehension in the right hemisphere following cerebral commissurotomy and hemispherectomy: a comparison with child language and aphasia. In A. Caramazza and E. Zurif (eds.), *Language Acquisition and Language Breakdown.* Baltimore: Johns Hopkins University Press, 1978.

BIBLIOGRAPHY

Davis, A. G. *A Survey of Adult Aphasia.* Englewood Cliffs, N.J.: Prentice-Hall, 1983.

Gardner, H. *The Shattered Mind.* New York: Vintage Books, 1974.

Geschwind, N. Language and the brain. *Sci. Am.* 226:76, 1972.

Goodglass, H., and Kaplan, E. *The Assessment of Aphasia and Related Disorders.* Philadelphia: Lea & Febiger, 1972.

Head, H. *Aphasia and Kindred Disorders of Speech.* London: Cambridge University Press, 1926. Reprinted by Hafner, New York, 1963.

Hecaen, H., and Albert, M. L. *Human Neuropsychology.* New York: Wiley, 1978.

Heilman, K. M., and Valenstein, E. *Clinical Neuropsychology.* New York: Oxford University Press, 1985.

Hughlings-Jackson, J. Notes on the physiology and pathology of learning. In J. Taylor (ed.), *Selected Writings of John Hughlings-Jackson.* London: Hodder, 1932.

Kolb, B., and Whishaw, I. Q. *Fundamentals of Human Neuropsychology.* San Francisco: W. H. Freeman, 1985.

Lashley, K. S. *Brain Mechanisms and Intelligence.* Chicago: University of Chicago Press, 1929.

Lenneberg, E. H. *Biological Foundations of Language.* New York: Wiley, 1967.

Luria, A. R. *Higher Cortical Functions in Man.* New York: Basic Books, 1966.

Mesulum, M. M. *Principles of Behavioral Neurology.* Philadelphia: Davis, 1985.

Schuell, H. M., Jenkins, J. J., and Jimenez-Pabon, E. *Aphasia in Adults.* New York: Harper & Row, 1964.

CHAPTER 10

Neurolinguistics

David Caplan • Howard Chertkow

The work reported in this chapter was partially supported by the Medical Research Council of Canada (grants MA 8602 and 9671) and the Fonds de Recherche en Sante du Quebec through a Chercheur Boursier Senior Award to David Caplan and a postdoctoral award to Howard Chertkow.

The work that has been done regarding theories of how language is represented and processed in the human brain, and the relation of these theories to descriptions of language disorders, are dealt with in this chapter. Historically, theories of the neural bases for language have used syndromes and specific features of lesions in the brain as their primary data-based correlations of clinically recognized disordered language. In recent years this database has been supplemented by studies of electrical and chemical activity in the brain that occurs while a normal subject is processing language (Desmedt and Robertson, 1977; Metter, Sepulueda, Jackson, Mazziotta, Benson, Hanson, Roege, and Phelps, 1985) and by experimental electrical stimulation of points in the brain during neurosurgical procedures (Ojemann, 1983). These sources of data regarding brain activities related to language have enormous promise and potentially can illuminate aspects of the neural bases for language that might not otherwise be ascertained by clinical neurology and radiology.

These techniques, however, are only just beginning to be applied to the study of carefully specified details of language structure and language processing. There is a need for studies that take into account specific detailed subcomponents of language structure. Such a source of data can be found in linguistic and psycholinguistic analyses of deficits that affect the representation of the language code and processing of language. These studies have progressed rapidly and now have begun to be related more specifically to parameters of lesions in the brain. This chapter focuses on this new work and sets it in the broader context of previous studies. The work that merges careful analysis of specific language parameters with neurologic concepts and procedures is called *neurolinguistics*.

LANGUAGE AREAS OF THE BRAIN

It is well established that portions of the telencephalic cortex are essential for the exercise of human linguistic functions. Though many other areas of the brain are necessary for normal perception and production of language, these areas are involved uniquely in a more specific aspect of overall language function—that of storage and processing of the abstract representations that constitute the language code. As reviewed in Chapter 9, these areas primarily involve cortical structures surrounding the sylvian fissure and are lateralized to one dominant hemisphere in many humans. Neurolinguistics is largely concerned with the functional localization of language subcomponents within the area of the sylvian fissure based on the nature of the impairments of language function that occur after brain lesions to this area. Before focusing on these issues, the roles that other telencephalic structures may play in language functioning are considered.

NONPERISYLVIAN LESIONS

Observations of the language abilities of patients with nonperisylvian lesions in the dominant hemisphere, such as lesions of the thalamic nuclei (Mohr, Pessin, Finkelstein, Funkenstein, Duncan, and Davis, 1978), caudate nucleus (Damasio, Damasio, Rizzo, Yarney, and Gersch, 1982), white matter structures surrounding these subcortical gray matter areas (Naeser and Hayword, 1982), and supplementary motor cortex (Masdeu, Schoene, and Funkenstein, 1978), have documented language deficits. These findings suggest that structures outside the dominant perisylvian cortex are involved in normal language functioning in the intact brain. Despite these discoveries, it is possible that what may be termed *core* language processing is carried out exclusively in the dominant perisylvian cortex. Roughly speaking, one might consider these processes that recognize the form of the words and sentences of an utterance and assign a literal meaning to these elements as core language processing functions. In contrast, core expressive language functions are those that select, structure, and produce the formal codes of these lexical, morphologic, and sentential elements. It is reasonable to divide language structures into these core elements, which constitute the essential forms and semantic values conveyed by the language code. Other aspects of language (e.g., discourse structure, inferences) interact with these core aspects. This division roughly corresponds to distinctions made in current linguistic theory, which is mainly restricted to what is being called core aspects of language. It may be that this division is incorrect, but currently it is a viable system, given the present state of knowledge (Chomsky, 1981; Fodor, 1982).

The possibility that core aspects of language are managed by the dominant perisylvian cortex alone is supported in that some of the language functions that are impaired following nonperisylvian dominant hemisphere injuries do not fall into these core areas of language processing. They include, for example, the ability to initiate speech. Such ability is impaired following dominant supplementary motor area lesions (Masdeu et al., 1978). In other instances, injuries in other areas may yield physiologic rather than direct anatomic impairment in the dominant perisylvian cortex. As has been described elsewhere in this text, lesions in locations deep within the dominant hemisphere that are found on computed tomography (CT) scans may be accompanied by physiologic impairments in the overlying cortex (Metter et al., 1985), especially in vascular cases. They constitute most of such lesions in which an aphasia has been documented, perhaps because the middle cerebral artery and its branches supply all these structures. Aphasic symptoms found following injury to any nonperisylvian structure in the dominant hemisphere are transient, which weakens the argument that these areas are normally involved in language processing. At the least, it indicates that their functions (if any) are rapidly taken over by other brain areas. It is not unreasonable to maintain the hypothesis that only the perisylvian cortex is involved in core language processes in the oral-auditory modalities. Various models have been suggested to elaborate on this point.

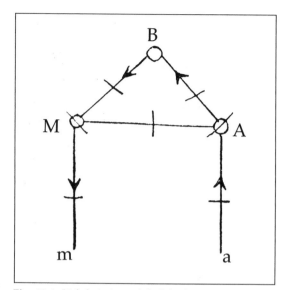

Fig. 10-1. Lichtheim's model of the language processing system. *A* represents the auditory word form center; *B* the concept center; *M* the center for speech planning. In speech, the concept center (*B*) simultaneously activates the auditory word form (*A*) and the center for speech planning (*M*). Representations in the auditory word form center (*A*) are passed on to the center for speech planning (*M*). The center for speech planning (*M*) sends signals to the articulatory musculature (*m*). In comprehension, peripheral auditory stimuli in the auditory pathways (*a*) activate the auditory word form center (*A*) which, in turn, activates the concept center (*B*). See the text for more complete description of the sequence of activation of these centers in tasks of language use and the alleged consequences of breakdown in these centers and pathways.

TRADITIONAL (LICHTHEIM'S) NEUROLINGUISTIC MODEL

The traditional neurolinguistic model pertaining to the functional neuroanatomy of the perisylvian association cortex for language is based on observations of aphasic patients and the interpretation of those observations, which were first made more than a century ago (Broca, 1861; Lichtheim, 1885; Wernicke, 1874). Figure 10-1 represents the basic "connectionist" model of language processing and its relation to areas within the dominant perisylvian cortex. According to this model, the permanent representations for the sounds of words are stored in Wernicke's area. They are accessed following auditory presentation of language stimuli. These auditory representations of the sounds of words in turn evoke the concepts associated with words in the concept center. According to Lichtheim (1885), the concept center is diffusely represented in the association cortex of the dominant hemisphere and may even involve both hemispheres and hence to some degree the nondominant side. Gaining access to the phonological representations of words and the subsequent concepts associated with these representations constitutes the function of comprehension of auditory language in Lichtheim's model. In spoken language production, concepts are translated into the phonological representations of words in Wernicke's area and then transmitted to the motor programming areas for speech in Broca's area. Accurate execution of the speech act depends on Broca's area receiving input from both the auditory center and the concept center, each conveying different types of linguistically relevant representations.

The principal evidence in favor of this model is said to be the occurrence of specific syndromes of language disorders that can be accounted for by lesions of these centers and the connections between them (Table 10-1). A disturbance in Broca's area leads to *Broca's aphasia*, the severe expressive language disturbance without concomitant disturbances of auditory comprehension noted by Broca (1861). A disturbance of Wernicke's area leads to the combination of fluent speech with erroneous choices of the sounds of words (*phonemic paraphasias*) and the auditory comprehension disturbances described by Wernicke (1874). A lesion of the input pathway to Wernicke's area leads to *pure word deafness*, in which spontaneous speech is normal but comprehension and repetition are disturbed. A lesion in the outflow pathway from Broca's area leads to *pure anarthria* or *dysarthria*, in which both repetition and spontaneous speech are misarticulated but comprehension is preserved. Broca's area is thought also to be involved in the planning stages for written language, and therefore Broca's aphasia is accompanied by an agraphia whereas dysarthria is not. A lesion between the concept center and Broca's area leads to *transcortical motor aphasia*, in which spontaneous speech is reduced because of the failure of the concept center to provide its input to Broca's area but repetition is intact. A lesion of the pathway between the concept center and Wernicke's area leads to *transcortical sensory aphasia*, a comprehension disturbance without a disturbance of repetition. Finally, a lesion of the pathway connecting Wernicke's and Broca's areas leads to a disturbance in spontaneous speech and repetition without a disturbance in auditory comprehension, termed *conduction aphasia*. All of these syndromes were alleged to have been discovered in relatively pure form by Lichtheim (1885) and to have resulted from lesions in the appro-

TABLE 10-1. CLINICAL VARIETIES OF APHASIA

Aphasia with repetition disturbance
  Broca's aphasia
  Wernicke's aphasia
  Conduction aphasia
Aphasia without repetition disturbance
  Isolation of speech area
  Transcortical motor aphasia
  Transcortical sensory aphasia
  Anomic aphasia
Disturbance primarily affecting reading and writing
  Alexia with agraphia
Total aphasia
  Global aphasia
Syndromes with disturbance of a single language
    modality
  Alexia without agraphia
  Aphemia
  Pure word deafness
Nonaphasic misnaming

From Benson, F. D., and Geschwind, N. Aphasia and related disturbances. In A. Baker and L. Baker (eds.), *Clinical Neurology*. New York: Harper & Row, 1971. P. 5.

priate cortical and subcortical areas of the brain.

The Wernicke-Lichtheim analysis has been subject to considerable criticism from both internal and external sources. Internal criticism consists in arguments that the proposed account of language functions or their neural bases is either incomplete or inaccurate. For instance, Freud (1891) pointed out that the occurrence of an alexia with Broca's aphasia was common and could not be accounted for by any natural extension of the Wernicke-Lichtheim model. The documentation of anomias without disturbances of single word auditory comprehension demonstrated that the pathway from the concept center to Wernicke's area must be separate from that in the opposite direction. A similar conclusion can be reached from the presence of transcortical sensory aphasia without anomia. Patients with transcortical sensory aphasia have disturbances of auditory word comprehension due to a lesion affecting the pathway connecting the concept center and Wernicke's area but need not have either anomia or a disturbance of the sound pattern of words in speech production. In general, the relation between the concept center and Wernicke's area in the Lichtheim model was poorly understood at the level of the psycholinguistic mechanisms involved and in terms of neurologic location. The latter is not surprising given the fact that the concept center itself never received a clear anatomic locus.

REVIVED (GESCHWIND'S) NEUROLINGUISTIC MODEL

Despite the criticisms discussed above and other, similar criticisms, the model of language as connections between language representation and processing in the brain was revived by Geschwind (1965) and his colleagues. Geschwind's model has achieved considerable popularity in North America. Geschwind and his colleagues' basic model of the representation of language in dominant perisylvian cortex differs little from that proposed by Wernicke, Lichtheim, and the other nineteenth century connectionists and is consistent with them in many ways. The major innovation proposed by Geschwind is the location of one aspect of the concept center. Geschwind proposed that the inferior parietal lobule, specifically the supramarginal and angular gyri, is the location at which the fibers projecting from somesthetic, visual, and auditory association cortices converge. According to the model, associations between word sounds and the sensory properties of objects can be established in this area as a consequence of this convergence. Geschwind argued that the establishment of these associations is a prerequisite for the ability to name objects. Aside from this innovation, the revised modern version of the connectionist model does not substantially change the earlier theory.

The modern revision of connectionism therefore is subject to the same criticisms as the earlier versions. Although some of the internal criticisms have been addressed as described above, external criticisms are of a different sort. They hold that details of the descriptions of the phenomena presented in connectionist modeling are inadequate or that the phenomena described are not the principal language-related functions that should be modeled, for either normalcy or pathologic states. Classic objections of this external sort were levied by Head (1926), Marie (1906), Goldstein (1948), and others. Many of these critics argued that features such as motivational state and level of arousal influence language performance and so must be incorporated into models of both psycholinguistic function and the neural bases for language.

More recent external objections are dealt with here. They are concerned with the level of empiric descriptions of core processes of language found in the literature.

OBJECTIONS TO THE CLASSIC APHASIC SYNDROMES

The first problem raised in the modern literature is that each of the classic aphasic syndromes consists of a variety of symptoms. For instance, the severe expressive speech disorder seen in Broca's aphasia consists of various combinations of disorders, including dysarthria, apraxia of speech, and agrammatism. Similarly, Wernicke's aphasia has numerous forms, including paragrammatism (frequent substitutions of inflections and function words), phonologically based phonemic paraphasias, morphologic errors, anomia, and others. The disturbances in repetition found in conduction aphasia have been shown to have at least two sources, one in disturbances of short-term memory and one in disturbances of single-word production. Thus it can be seen that the multiplicity of deficits within a given syndrome points to the need for much more detailed analyses of aphasic performance than the classic theory provides. The number of deficits found within a syndrome also leads to serious questions about the homogeneity of patients who are considered to have a single syndrome. Schwartz (1984) called it the problem of the "polytypicality" of clinical syndromes. In the extreme, a patient said to have Broca's aphasia may have no symptoms in common with another patient with the same diagnosis. This situation is a serious problem because the location of lesions underlying these classic syndromes therefore cannot lead to specific linguistic-anatomic correlations, and the isolation of such specific correlates (anatomic-functional) is of primary concern to the neurolinguist.

A second problem with classic symptoms is that many linguistic disturbances occur in more than one syndrome. As with the first problem, it leads to difficulty classifying patients. Patients who show only given language disturbances, such as anomia and the production of phonemic paraphasias in spontaneous speech, cannot be unequivocally classified into a single aphasic syndrome. In fact, more studies attempting to classify patients into the traditional clinical groups on the basis of clinical observations have failed to classify a significant number of patients unequivocally. Again, clinicopathologic correlations based on these cases are of limited use for establishing the neural bases of isolated components of the language system and as such are of limited use for advancing neurolinguistic theory.

These problems with the classic aphasic syndromes point to a fundamental limitation in aphasiology. This limitation is a consequence of the inadequate level of description of aphasic syndromes and symptoms found in both classic work and its contemporary revival. As increasing attention has been paid to linguistic structures and their abnormalities, and attempts have been made to incorporate these observations into descriptions of aphasic patients and model construction, the problems of fractionating the syndromes into smaller functional components and of the overlap of functional disturbances across the classic syndromes have become increasingly apparent. These problems have lead to serious questioning of the connectionist neurolinguistic model.

AGRAMMATISM: EXAMPLE OF PSYCHOLINGUISTIC ANALYSIS OF AN APHASIC SYMPTOM

To illustrate how modern neurolinguistic work on aphasia has developed, the symptom of expressive agrammatism is considered. Agrammatism classically constitutes part of the syndrome of Broca's aphasia. The most noticeable deficit in agrammatism is the widespread omission of "function words" and morphologic affixes compared to "content words" in spontaneous speech. Contemporary work deals with the exact delineation of the items that are affected in agrammatism, the abnormalities of

processing that give rise to agrammatism, and the symptoms associated with agrammatism.

The class of words that are affected in agrammatism has been described in two frameworks. The first is a psychological framework, and the second is linguistic. According to the psychological account, the words that are affected in agrammatism are those that belong to a closed set of vocabulary elements. This set consists of all the vocabulary elements of a given language other than nouns, verbs, and adjectives. The distinguishing feature of these vocabulary elements is that their number is fixed in the language at any given point in time, whereas the number of nouns, verbs, and adjectives may be increased in a person's vocabulary once it has been acquired in a language. According to this psychological account, certain vocabulary elements belong to this "closed class," which sets them apart and is related to their impairment in this syndrome.

A somewhat different approach to the characterization of agrammatism has been taken by several linguists. Kean (1977) first used linguistic theory to enunciate a theory of the vocabulary elements affected in agrammatism. Kean proposed that the key characteristic of the class of elements affected in this syndrome is their sound pattern. He argued that the vocabulary elements affected in agrammatism do not bear main stress in normal intonation (though they may bear main stress when they are emphasized). The rules for assignment of stress to words, phrases, and sentences in English ignore these elements and assign stress to stems and roots of nouns, adjectives, and verbs. One of the principal pieces of evidence supporting this analysis is that agrammatism affects both free-standing function words (e.g., prepositions, articles, pronouns) and "bound-morphemes" (which signal verb agreement, adjectival agreement, and certain noun- and verb-forming suffixes). These different elements accomplish different syntactic and semantic functions but have in common the feature that they are all "phonological clitics"; that is, they are elements that do not affect stress placement in English. Other linguistic descriptions have been suggested, mainly in reaction to Kean's theory. Lapointe (1983) argued that the class of elements affected in agrammatism can be described morphologically in a linguistic theory that distinguishes a level of morphologic structure in addition to levels of syntactic structure, semantic structure, and phonological structure. Grodinsky (1984) argued, on the basis of data in Hebrew, that the basic abnormality in agrammatism is not omission but, rather, substitution of elements that are not phonologically represented at a certain abstract level of linguistic structure.

Despite the fact that these accounts of the elements affected in agrammatism are difficult to compare and evaluate at present, the linguistic analyses serve an important function. For instance, they provide a formal basis for the description of agrammatism (Caplan, 1986). They also suggest a number of directions for further research. For instance, there are some differences in the vocabulary elements specified by each of these linguistic theories of agrammatism, and it may be possible to devise experimental tests that can choose between these theories.

Linguistic analyses also have led to an appreciation that agrammatism varies from patient to patient (Goodglass, 1973; Luria, 1971; Tissot, Mounin, and Lhermite, 1973). Patients with agrammatism can show different patterns of retention of morphologic inflectional, derivational, and free-standing function word vocabulary (Miceli, Mazzuchi, Menn, and Goodglass, 1983; Tissot et al., 1973). Moreover, these patients vary considerably in their ability to produce certain open class vocabulary items, notably verbs (Miceli, Silveri, Villa, and Caramazza, 1984).

In addition, investigators have emphasized the fact that agrammatism is not easily distinguishable from "paragrammatism," in which substitutions of morphologic elements and free-standing function word vocabulary items predominate in expressive speech. Obler, Menn, and Goodglass (1984) reported the results of a large cross-linguistic study of agrammatic patients and noted that all of the patients studied showed both omission and substitutions of vocabulary elements. These linguistic descriptions indicate that the symptom of agrammatism itself includes a variety of disturbances of speech production and is not easily distinguished from other abnormalities affecting the same vocabulary elements. More work is needed to characterize all the variants of agrammatism and the relation of agrammatism to other similar speech disorders (Badecker and Caramazza, 1985; Caplan, 1986).

It is possible to relate linguistic descriptions

of agrammatism to processing models. A question that has been raised since the early twentieth century (Pick, 1913) is if the omission of function of words is related to other abnormalities in sentence structure. Garrett (1980), on the basis of the occurrence of normal speech errors, suggested that much of the syntactic structure is constructed at the same stage of sentence planning at which function words and inflections are accessed. Though the results of this process remain to be understood, it suggests that a disorder affecting function words and inflections might lead to simplification of syntactic structure in speech (Caplan, 1985; 1986; Kean, 1980).

Traditional and modern investigations show such simplification in syntactic structure. Goodglass (1973) documented the syntactic constructions produced by one agrammatic patient and found virtually no syntactically well formed utterances. Based on these results, Caplan (1985) suggested that agrammatic patients do not construct *phrasal* nodes (noun phrase, verb phrase) in their utterances but, rather, encode semantic values only through linear sequences of *category* nodes (noun, verb, adjective). This characterization is now known to be too strong, but all agrammatic patients studied so far show some impoverishment of syntactic structure. For instance, all fail to produce embedded verbs with normal frequency (Nespoulous, Dordain, Perron, Caplan, Bub, Mehler, and Lecours, 1984; Obler, 1984). These observations suggest that agrammatic patients have an impairment in the construction of normal syntactic structures. On the other hand, agrammatic patients can express thematic roles using simple structures (Caplan, 1985; Farrell and Caplan, 1985; Kolk and Van Grunsven, 1985), which suggests that their problem does not affect basic concepts such as agent or theme. This finding is consistent with the predictions of Kean (1980).

EXPRESSIVE VERSUS RECEPTIVE DISTURBANCES

Another consequence of the linguistic and psycholinguistic approach to agrammatism is that it led to hypotheses regarding abnormalities in language function other than speech production. Zurif, Caramazza, and Myerson (1972) discovered that agrammatic aphasics performed abnormally on a task of judging the degree of relatedness of words in sentences. Given a series of sets of three words from a particular sentence and asked to say which two words were most closely related, normal subjects indicated that words that were syntactically grouped together in the sentence were most closely related. Agrammatics, in contrast, grouped together the major lexical items on a semantic basis and totally omitted the function words from these relatedness judgments. This result suggested that agrammatics may have a central disturbance in the processing of the function word vocabulary. The most obvious manifestation of this abnormality is in sentence production, but it could be demonstrated in other tasks as well.

Caramazza and Zurif (1976) directly tested the hypothesis that agrammatics have a central processing disturbance by a series of experiments dealing with sentence comprehension. These authors showed that agrammatic patients were unable to interpret certain sentences whose meaning required syntactic analysis. For instance, agrammatic patients were unable to interpret sentence 1, below, but were able to correctly understand sentence 2, in which meaning can be inferred once individual words are understood.

1. The boy that the girl was chasing is tall.
2. The apple that the boy was eating was red.

Somewhat similar results were obtained by Heilman and Scholes (1976) and Schwartz, Saffron, and Marin (1980). Heilman and Scholes found that agrammatic patients could not appreciate a difference in meaning between sentences 3 and 4, below. Schwartz et al. found that agrammatic patients assigned thematic roles randomly in sentences, e.g., as in sentence 5, below, and sometimes in sentences such as 6.

3. Can you show her the baby pictures?
4. Can you show her baby the pictures?
5. The boy pushed by the girl.
6. The boy pushed the girl.

These results suggested that the disturbance in agrammatism is not limited to expression but

may also affect the ability of the patient to recognize function words and morphologic vocabulary and to utilize them syntactically regardless of the tasks. On the other hand, some agrammatic patients do not have these associated disturbances. For instance, Nespoulous et al. (1984) described an agrammatic patient without syntactic comprehension deficits. The relation between "expressive" and "receptive" agrammatism thus is in need of further study.

UNDERLYING DYNAMICS OF AGRAMMATISM

Why do agrammatic patients have difficulty producing function words and certain affixes, and sometimes comprehending certain syntactic structures? One study of agrammatic aphasics' language processing abilities attempted to answer this question by investigating how agrammatic patients access vocabulary items. Bradley, Garrett, and Zurif (1980) reported that the recognition of function words was abnormal in agrammatic aphasics. Bradley and her coworkers gave agrammatic patients and normal controls a number of lexical decision tasks in which a string of letters was presented on a screen and the subject was required to indicate as quickly as possible if the letter string was a word. Under these conditions, normal subjects' reactions times are proportional to a word's frequency in the language, with faster reaction times for more frequent words. Bradley and colleagues discovered that this linear relation between frequency and reaction time was true only for open class vocabulary words such as nouns, verbs, and adjectives. Closed class vocabulary words did not show any effect of frequency on reaction time in the experiments conducted with normal subjects. Agrammatic aphasic patients continued to show the normal relation between reaction time and word frequency for open class items but also showed this same proportional relation between reaction time and frequency for closed class words.

In a second set of experiments, Bradley et al. (1980) investigated the way in which the presence of a substring of letters that actually constitutes a word interferes with the ability to reject a longer string of letters that is not a word. These authors found that if a non-word-string began with an actual word, there was an interference effect on the rejection of the nonword. This nonword interference effect was observed only when an open class word occurred at the beginning of a non-word letter string. Words occurring later in the letter string did not produce an interference effect, nor did the closed class words. On the other hand, agrammatic aphasic patients did show interference effects for open class and closed class words when these words occurred at the beginning of a nonword letter string.

Bradley and her colleagues concluded that the basic process of recognizing closed class words was abnormal in agrammatic patients. They argued that closed class words are normally recognized by a specialized recognition routine that is not frequency-sensitive and does not operate in a left-to-right manner. Open class words normally are recognized by a routine that *is* frequency-sensitive and *does* operate in a left-to-right manner. The authors concluded that agrammatics are forced to use this open class routine for the recognition of closed class items. They further suggested that this reliance on an inefficient and inappropriate recognition routine characterizes not only the perceptual and recognition abilities of agrammatic patients but also the way they access closed class items in general. Bradley et al. suggested that a disturbance in lexical access underlies the inability of the agrammatics to use closed class vocabulary elements, leading to omission of these elements in spontaneous speech, disturbances in syntactic expression and comprehension, and other disturbances found in agrammatic patients.

The work of Bradley and her colleagues and the formulations they put forth have been questioned. Gordon and Caramazza (1982) reanalyzed the Bradley et al. results using a different statistical procedure. Gordon and Caramazza argued that when nonlinear regression analyses were applied to Bradley's data closed class and open class words behaved similarly with respect to the relation between word frequency and recognition reaction time. Replicating the studies of Bradley et al., Gordon and Caramazza also found no differences between agrammatic patients and normal controls, other than a generally increased reaction time on the part of agrammatic patients. Therefore they concluded that a disturbance in lexical access for the closed class vocabulary did not underlie the abnormality seen in agrammatic patients. The Gordon and Caramazza results are, at best, consistent with the possibility that agrammatic patients have a disturbance in recognition that affects their ability to access the most frequent words of the language as quickly as normally. Because the most frequent words in the language are primarily closed class items, this disturbance primarily affects these elements.

CONCLUSION

Some of the directions and implications of contemporary neurolinguistic work on the aphasic syndromes are touched on in this chapter. When more linguistic detail is considered, it is apparent that the classic aphasic syndromes are very broad categories indeed. Not only are syndromes that are thought to consist of disturbances in such general functions as speech production very broad, but even symptoms within these syndromes, such as agrammatism, are made up of many individual types of impairments. One consequence of the fractionation of symptoms and syndromes is that investigators now rely heavily on individual case studies to study language disturbances (Caramazza, 1986), because a series of patients with identical symptoms is difficult (or impossible) to obtain. In many ways, this development is not surprising. The language code consists of an extremely complex and abstract set of representations, and the processes whereby these representations are accessed and interconverted are equally complex. If disturbances in language functions are related to isolated aspects of the structure and processing of language, the number of different aphasic impairments that can be identified is bound to be very large. Modern neurologic and linguistic work points to some of the abnormal language features and detailed characterizations of aphasic symptoms that some patients may have. A review of this work also shows how difficult it is to characterize even a single aphasic symptom as the result of a specific deficit. Despite this difficulty, linguistic aphasiology has vastly increased understanding of aphasic impairments. It has provided a much greater degree of detail in the description of aphasic symptoms and syndromes. It has begun the task of linking aphasic symptoms and syndromes to disturbances in normal language processing mechanisms and in detailing compensatory strategies.

Linguistic studies of aphasia have implications for concepts of the neural bases for language. Clearly, it will be necessary to characterize neural structures and processes in more detail than is presently conducted to describe the neural mechanisms responsible for each of the components of processing and aspects of linguistic structure that are found disturbed in aphasia. One implication of contemporary investigations of aphasia is that the localization of neurologic lesions that are correlated with deficits in language functioning is just a first step in developing neurolinguistic theory.

A second implication of more detailed studies of aphasia is that the classic model of language localization is incorrect. This model links disturbances in language function to sensory and motor regions of the brain. However, the data that have just been reviewed clearly show that a disturbance in sentence comprehension can occur with lesions in and around Broca's area. In such cases it appears that this area supports an abstract aspect of language structure and associated psycholinguistic processes, not tasks and functions strictly related to motor planning. Expressive agrammatism is also apt to follow lesions of many sizes in many areas of the perisylvian association cortex (Vanier and Caplan, in press). In general, studies have shown that many parts of the perisylvian cortex support central processes related to abstract components of the language code (Caplan, 1987; Caplan, Baker, and Dehaut, 1985).

Contemporary investigations of the aphasias have produced many questions about the detailed nature of deficits that underlie aphasic symptoms and the relation between language and the brain. The complexity of the language code and the processes involved in its utilization are substantial. When considered in detail, disturbances of linguistic structure and their processing appear to be due to any of a large number of deficits. Despite the many unanswered questions regarding these deficits and their relation to overt symptoms, the achievements of contemporary linguistic aphasiology are impressive in the areas of description of aphasic symptoms and in the generation of hypotheses regarding the mechanisms that produce these syndromes and symptoms. This work presents enormous challenges for workers involved in research into the nature of aphasic disturbances. It provides even greater challenges for researchers interested in the neural bases for language and the neuropathologic determinants of aphasic impairments.

REFERENCES

Badecker, B., and Caramazza, A. On considerations of method and theory governing the use of clinical categories in neurolinguistics and cognitive neuropsychology: the case against agrammatism. *Cognition* 20:97, 1985.

Bradley, D. C., Garrett, M. F., and Zurif, E. B. Syntactic deficits in Broca's aphasia. In D. Caplan (ed.), *Biological Studies of Mental Processes*. Cambridge: MIT Press, 1980.

Broca, P. Remarques sur le siège de la faculté de la parole articulée, suivies d'une observation d'aphémie (perte de parole). *Bull. Soc. Anat. (Paris)* 36:330, 1961.

Caplan, D. Syntactic and semantic structures in agrammatism. In M. L. Kean (ed.), *Agrammatism*. New York: Academic Press, 1985.

Caplan, D., Baker, C., and Dehaut, F. Syntactic determinants of sentence comprehension in aphasia. *Cognition* 21:117, 1985.

Caplan, D. In defense of agrammatism. *Cognition* 24:263, 1986.

Caplan, D. *Neurolinguistics and Linguistic Aphasiology*. Cambridge: Cambridge University Press, 1987.

Caramazza, A., and Zurif, E. B. Dissociation of algorithmic and heuristic processes in language comprehension: evidence from aphasia. *Brain Lang.* 3:572, 1976.

Caramazza, A. On drawing inferences about the structure of normal cognitive systems from the analysis of patterns of impaired performance: the case for single-patient studies. *Brain Cogn.* 5:41, 1986.

Chomsky, N. *Lectures on Government Binding*. Dordrecht: Foris, 1981.

Damasio, A., Damasio, H., Rizzo, M., Yarney, N., and Gersch, F. Aphasia with nonhemorrhagic lesions in the basal ganglia and internal capsule. *Arch. Neurol.* 39:15, 1982.

Desmedt, J. E., and Robertson, D. Search for right hemisphere asymmetries in event-related potentials to somatosensory cueing signals. In J. E. Desmedt (ed.), *Language and Hemispheric Specialization in Man: Cerebral Event-Related Potentials*. Basel: Karger, 1977.

Farrell, G., and Caplan, D. The use of word order to encode thematic roles by agrammatic aphasics. Presented at the Canadian Learned Societies, Montreal, 1985.

Fodor, J. A. *The Modularity of Mind*. Cambridge, Bradford Books, MIT Press, 1982.

Freud, S. *On Aphasia*. Leipzig: Deuticke, 1891. Reprinted in translation by International Universities Press, New York, 1953.

Garrett, M. F. Levels of processing in sentence production. In B. Butterworth (ed.), *Sentence Production*. London: Academic Press, 1980.

Geschwind, N. Disconnection syndromes in animals and man. *Brain* 88:237, 585, 1965.

Goldstein, K. *Language and Language Disturbances*. New York: Grune & Stratton, 1948.

Goodglass, H. Studies on the grammar of aphasics. In H. Goodglass and S. Blumstein (eds.), *Psycholinguistics and Aphasia*. Baltimore: John Hopkins University Press, 1973.

Gordon, B., and Caramazza, A. Lexical decision for open- and closed-class words: failure to replicate differential frequency sensitivity. *Brain Lang.* 15:143, 1982.

Grodinsky, Y. The syntactic characterization of agrammatism. *Cognition* 16:99, 1984.

Head, H. *Aphasia and Kindred Disorders of Speech*. Cambridge: Cambridge University Press, 1926.

Heilman, K. M., and Scholes, R. J. The nature of comprehension errors in Broca's, conduction, and Wernicke's aphasics. *Cortex* 12:258, 1976.

Kean, M. L. The linguistic interpretation of aphasic syndromes: agrammatism in Broca's aphasia, example. *Cognition* 5:9, 1977.

Kean, M. L. Linguistic representations and the description of language processing. In D. Caplan (ed.), *Biological Studies of Mental Processes*. Cambridge, MA: MIT Press, 1980.

Kolk, H. H., and van Grunsven, M. Agrammatism as a variable phenomenon. *Cogn. Neuropsychol.* 2:347, 1985.

Lapointe, S. Some issues in the linguistic description of agrammatism. *Cognition* 14:1, 1983.

Lichtheim, L. On aphasia. *Brain* 7:433, 1885.

Luria, A. R. *Traumatic Aphasia*. Reprinted in translation by Mouton, The Hague, 1971.

Marie, P. Révision de la question de l'aphasie: la troisième circonvolution frontal gauche ne joue aucun rôle spécial dans la fonction du language. *Sem. Med. (Paris)* 26:241, 1906.

Masdeu, J. C., Schoene, W. C., and Funkenstein, H. Aphasia following infarction of the left supplementary motor area: a clinicopathologic study. *Neurology* 28:1220, 1978.

Metter, E. J., Sepulueda, C. A., Jackson, C. A., Mazziotta, J. C., Benson, D. F., Hanson, W. R., Roege, W. J., and Phelps, M. E. Relationships of temporal-parietal lesions and distant glucose metabolism changes in the head of the caudate nucleus in aphasic patients. *Neurology* 35(suppl.):120, 1985 (abstract).

Miceli, G., Mazzuchi, A., Menn, L., and Goodglass, H. Contrasting cases of Italian agrammatic aphasia without comprehension disorder. *Brain Lang.* 19:65, 1983.

Miceli, H., Silveri, M., Villa, G., and Caramazza, A. On the basis for agrammatic's difficulty in producing main verbs. *Cortex* 20:207, 1984.

Mohr, J. P., Pessin, M. S., Finkelstein, S., Funkenstein, H. H., Duncan, G. W., and Davis, K. R. Broca's aphasia: pathologic and clinical. *Neurology* 28:311, 1978.

Naeser, M. A., and Hayward, R. W. Lesion localization in aphasia with cranial computed tomography and the Boston diagnostic aphasia examination. *Neurology* 28:545, 1978.

Nespoulous, J. L., Dordain, M., Perron, C., Caplan, D., Bub, D., Mehler, J., and Lecours, A. R. Agrammatism in sentence production without comprehension deficits. *Brain and Lang.* 33:273, 1988.

Obler, L. The neuropsychology of bilingualism. In D. Caplan, A. R. Lecours, and A. Smith (eds.), *Biological Perspectives on Language*. Cambridge, MA: M.I.T. Press, 1984.

Obler, L., Menn, L., and Goodglass, H. Cross-linguistic studies of agrammatism. Presented at the Academy of Aphasia, Minneapolis, 1984.

Ojemann, G. A. Brain organization for language from the perspective of electrical stimulation mapping. *Behav. Brain Sci.* 6:180, 1983.

Pick, A. *Die Agrammatisch Sprachstorungen*. Berlin: Springer, 1913.

Schwartz, M., Saffran, E., and Marin, O. S. M. The word order problem in agrammatism. I. Comprehension. *Brain Lang.* 10:249, 1980.

Schwartz, M. What the classical aphasia categories can't do for us, and why. *Brain Lang.* 31:3, 1984.

Tissot, R. J., Mounin, G., and Lhermite, F. *L'Agrammatisme*. Brussels: Dessart, 1973.

Vanier, M., and Caplan, D. CT scan correlates of agrammatism and their implications for the neural basis of sentence planning processes. In L. Menn, L. Obler, and H. Goodglass (eds.), *A Cross-Language Study of Agrammatism*. New York: J. Benjamin Press. In press.

Wernicke, C. The aphasic symptom complex: a psychological study on a neurological basis. Breslau: Kohn & Weigert, 1874. Reprinted in R. S. Cohen and M. W. Wartofsky (eds.), *Boston Studies in the Philosophy of Science* (Vol. 4). Boston: Reidel, 1964.

Zurif, E. B., Caramazza, A., and Myerson, R. Grammatical judgments of agrammatic aphasics. *Neuropsychologia* 10:405, 1972.

INDEX